JEWISH CULTURAL STUDIES

VOLUME FOUR

The Jewish Cultural Studies series is sponsored by the Jewish Folklore and Ethnology Section of the American Folklore Society in co-operation with the Council on the Anthropology of Jews and Judaism of the American Anthropological Association.

Members of the Section receive volumes as a privilege of membership. For more information see <http://www.afsnet.org/?page=JewishFLE>.

The Section is also the sponsor of the international Raphael Patai Prize, given to an outstanding student essay in English on Jewish folklore and ethnology. The chapters in this volume by Magdalena Luszczynska and Amy Milligan were winners of the prize in 2011. For more information, see the website listed above or visit <http://littman.co.uk/jcs/>.

D1707551

THE LITTMAN LIBRARY OF JEWISH CIVILIZATION

Dedicated to the memory of
LOUIS THOMAS SIDNEY LITTMAN
*who founded the Littman Library for the love of God
and as an act of charity in memory of his father*
JOSEPH AARON LITTMAN
יהא זכרם ברוך

'*Get wisdom, get understanding:
Forsake her not and she shall preserve thee*'
PROV. 4:5

Jewish Cultural Studies

VOLUME FOUR

Framing Jewish Culture
Boundaries and Representations

Edited by
SIMON J. BRONNER

Oxford · Portland, Oregon
The Littman Library of Jewish Civilization
2014

The Littman Library of Jewish Civilization

Chief Executive Officer: Ludo Craddock
Managing Editor: Connie Webber

PO Box 645, Oxford OX2 OUJ, UK
www.littman.co.uk

———

Published in the United States and Canada by
The Littman Library of Jewish Civilization
c/o ISBS, 920 NE 58th Avenue, Suite 300
Portland, Oregon 97213-3786

A catalogue record for this book is available from the British Library

Library of Congress Cataloging-in-Publication Data

Framing Jewish culture : boundaries and representations / edited by Simon J. Bronner.
p. cm.—(Jewish cultural studies : volume 4)
Includes bibliographical references and index.
1. Jews—Identity. 2. Jews—Identity—History. 3. Jews—Social life and customs.
4. Judaism and culture. 5. Jews—Cultural assimilation. 6. Jews—Civilization.
I. Bronner, Simon J., editor.
DS143.F73 2013   305.892´4–dc23   2013007934
ISBN 978–1–906764–08–1

Publishing co-ordinator: Janet Moth
Copy-editing: Agnes Erdos
Index: Caroline Diepeveen
Design, production, and typesetting by Pete Russell, Faringdon, Oxon.
Printed in Great Britain on acid-free paper by
TJ International Ltd., Padstow, Cornwall

The editor dedicates this volume to

D O V   N O Y
(1920–2013)

founder of the Haifa Ethnological Museum and Folklore Archives, including the Israel Folktale Archives at Haifa University, and the Hebrew University Folklore Research Center. Author and editor of numerous important works, and professor at dozens of universities around the world, Noy's reach was truly global, and his impact on Jewish cultural studies extraordinary

Editor and Advisers

Acknowledgements

THIS VOLUME has its genesis in discussions with a remarkable group of scholars from around the globe gathered at the Fifth Wrocław International Conference on Jewish Studies entitled 'Modern Jewish Culture: Diversities and Unities', held at the University of Wrocław, Poland, in 2008. The Department of Jewish Studies, University of Wrocław, and the Littman Library of Jewish Civilization, Oxford, UK, organized the meeting with support from the Rothschild Foundation, the University of Wrocław, and the Pennsylvania State University, Harrisburg. I am grateful for the herculean organizational efforts of Connie Webber, Jonathan Webber, Marcin Wodziński, and Agnieszka Jagodzinska for creating a stimulating environment for intellectual exchange. I can recount many 'ah-ha' moments, but I want to recognize Jonathan Webber's particularly inspiring talk entitled 'Representing Jewish Culture: The Problem of Boundaries' for setting gears of thought whirling for all the participants, many of whom contributed to this volume. We continued the conversations at subsequent meetings, including Association for Jewish Studies and American Folklore Society conferences. Jewish Cultural Studies editorial board members who attended the meetings are worth naming for their contributions: Dan Ben-Amos, Haya Bar-Itzhak, Mikhail Chlenov, Sander Gilman, Harvey E. Goldberg, Ruth Ellen Gruber, Barbara Kirshenblatt-Gimblett, Mikel Koven, Suzanne Rutland, Joachim Schlör, and Steve Siporin. Let me also recognize other figures whose ideas further fuelled this volume, including Batsheva Ben-Amos, Gabrielle Berlinger, Richard I. Cohen, Konstanty Gebert, Galit Hasan-Rokem, András Kovács, Erica Lehrer, Andrea Lieber, Jay Mechling, Wolfgang Mieder, Amy K. Milligan, William Pencak, Moshe Rosman, Shalom Sabar, Karen Sarhon, and Michael Steinlauf.

I want to acknowledge academic evaluators Haya Bar-Itzhak and Steve Siporin, who served on the Raphael Patai Prize committee and had the difficult task of selecting the cream of a hearty crop of papers. Other colleagues who provided professional service by reading manuscripts were Michael Barton, Sergio Della-Pergola, Jillian Gould, Kamini Grahame, Scott Kline, Charles Kupfer, Neil Leifert, Carolyn Lipson-Walker, Elliott Oring, Natasha Pravaz, Ilana Rosen, Faydra Shapiro, Matthew Singer, Elly Teman, and Seth Ward.

On the organizational front, Matti Bunzl and Marcy Brink-Danan deserve credit for their leadership of the Council on the Anthropology of Jews and Judaism and their contributions to the Jewish Folklore and Ethnology listserv. My appreciation also goes out to Timothy Lloyd, executive director, and Lorraine Cashman, associate director, of the American Folklore Society, for working so well with the Society's Jewish Folklore and Ethnology section.

I would be remiss if I did not recognize the contribution of my wife Sally Jo Bronner, who shared experiences with me the last few years as this volume was percolating in Israel, Europe, and North America and offered deep insights on the framing of Jewish culture. My children, Shulamit and Eitan, also contributed by constantly questioning boundaries.

Contents

Note on Transliteration

THE transliteration of Hebrew in this book reflects consideration of the type of book it is, in terms of its content, purpose, and readership. The system adopted therefore reflects a broad approach to transcription, rather than the narrower approaches found in the *Encyclopaedia Judaica* or other systems developed for text-based or linguistic studies. The aim has been to reflect the pronunciation prescribed for modern Hebrew, rather than the spelling or Hebrew word structure, and to do so using conventions that are generally familiar to the English-speaking reader.

In accordance with this approach, no attempt is made to indicate the distinctions between *alef* and *ayin*, *tet* and *taf*, *kaf* and *kuf*, *sin* and *samekh*, since these are not relevant to pronunciation; likewise, the *dagesh* is not indicated except where it affects pronunciation. Following the principle of using conventions familiar to the majority of readers, however, transcriptions that are well established have been retained even when they are not fully consistent with the transliteration system adopted. On similar grounds, the *tsadi* is rendered by 'tz' in such familiar words as barmitzvah.

The distinction between *ḥet* and *khaf* has been retained, using *ḥ* for the former and *kh* for the latter; the associated forms are generally familiar to readers, even if the distinction is not actually borne out in pronunciation, and for the same reason the final *heh* is indicated too. As in Hebrew, no capital letters are used, except that an initial capital has been retained in transliterating titles of published works (for example, *Shulḥan arukh*).

Since no distinction is made between *alef* and *ayin*, they are indicated by an apostrophe only in intervocalic positions where a failure to do so could lead an English-speaking reader to pronounce the vowel-cluster as a diphthong—as, for example, in *ha'ir*—or otherwise mispronounce the word.

The *sheva na* is indicated by an *e*—*perikat ol, reshut*—except, again, when established convention dictates otherwise. The *yod* is represented by *i* when it occurs as a vowel (*bereshit*), by *y* when it occurs as a consonant (*yesodot*), and by *yi* when it occurs as both (*yisra'el*).

Names have generally been left in their familiar forms, even when this is inconsistent with the overall system.

Framing Jewish Culture

SIMON J. BRONNER

THE PURPOSE OF THIS VOLUME is to analyse the ways Jews in complex, heterogeneous societies identify themselves as a cultural group to non-Jews, and equally the means by which non-Jews separate themselves from Jews, or even recognize Jews, in material or social space. The awareness by Jews of a history of non-Jewish differentiation, and indeed discrimination, has resulted in a tendency to view identity as a binary of either being Jewish or non-Jewish. This view also presumes a total identity rather than the kind of behaviour that could be called Jewish in selected situations or settings or the desire by participants to present themselves in a variety of ways, one of which might be Jewish. Sociologist Erving Goffman (1974) is often given credit for the view of identities being selected for presentation according to the social context, and he referred to the study of such situations as 'frame analysis'. Although Goffman meant this view to apply to people generally, the question arose in response to his groundbreaking work about how individuals with ties to ethnic and religious groups negotiate the myriad situations of modern life differently. This volume extends his consideration of cultural framing in different social contexts and asks about the special issues confronted by Jews in communicating their identities to one another and to non-Jews. Further, it turns an interpretative lens on the analysts of Jewish presentation of self to enquire about how their backgrounds and perspectives inform their generalizations about the complexities of Jewish identity.

One added layer to Goffman's approach to identity shaped by the moment is the idea of 'double consciousness' suggested by sociologist W. E. B. Du Bois (2008: 12). He wrote that African Americans distinctively identify as a group not only as one affiliates socially with others but also by taking into account how outsiders view the group, and called this perceptual process double consciousness to bring out the paradoxes of an identity that is shaped from without as well as within. Du Bois editorialized that 'It is a peculiar sensation, this double-consciousness, this sense of always looking at one's self through the eyes of others, of measuring one's soul by the tape of a world that looks on in amused contempt and pity' (2008: 12). Part of the peculiarity to which Du Bois refers is that this gaze can also be complimentary, apparently elevating artistry or emotion of one's otherness as poignant, authentic, or exotic. Although applied to Jewish identity by later scholars, the idea of double consciousness is complicated by contributors to this volume by their consideration of, first, the differentiation of

Jews among themselves; second, the ensuing problem of presenting a Jewish identity to outsiders in light of the outsiders' perception of Jewish characteristics; third, incorporation or rejection of the surrounding culture by a mobile Jewish population, and fourth, consideration of explanatory theories of ethnicity generally that derive from Jewish experience. Contributors' analyses of shifting strategies employed by Jews and non-Jews in relation to one another take a different turn from the prevalent scholarly approach that presumes a continuous Jewish history in which Jews live out an inheritance from, and indeed are defined by, the distant past—usually the biblical era. Contributors to this volume are primarily concerned with Jewish agency acted out in frames or 'situations' in mostly modern contexts. They analyse the negotiation of identities through processes of boundary maintenance, public presentation of self, and representation of cultural distinction through ritual enactments and public exhibitions. The ancient historical background of the group's origin can certainly be significant but not always determinative or even operative in the social frames in which Jews operate or reveal themselves.

The term 'framing' refers to this agency, which responds to the situation or context in which Jews find themselves. Instead of generalizing the perception of non-Jews, and strata of Jews, authors in this volume are careful to identify the outlooks of participants with different affiliations within various cultures. As with the selection of a frame around a painting representing a border complementing a symbolic image, Jews in various settings described in the essays below make decisions about where and how they will be displayed both materially and socially. Analysts note symbolic messages about what is inside and outside the frame. The framing is material in the sense that images and their messages are contained in outward signs such as dress, food, and customs and set the group apart from others like the boundaries of a picture. It is also social because the process of selecting appropriate behaviour for a situation invites people to engage one another, whether informally or in organizations, and Jewishness becomes a form of communication. In other words, the frame might be perceived by Jews in interaction with one another to allow some kinds of behaviour that would not be understood or tolerated outside the margins of the group.

To introduce the perspectives on framing Jewish culture in this volume, largely drawn from anthropology, sociology, history, and folkloristics, I offer examples that epitomize this turn towards Jewish agency in identity formation and then discuss the terms of framing, representation, and boundaries with reference to individual contributions to this volume.

Frames

Goffman underscored the often latent negotiation of socially constructed frames by participants in a cultural 'situation' when he wrote, 'I assume that definitions of a situation are built up in accordance with principles of organization which govern events—at least social ones—and our subjective involvement in them' (1974: 10–11). By 'subjective involvement' Goffman meant the way that individuals in a social situation fit their actions and speech to what they perceive others expect of them. Participants might have different ideas of those expectations and work in their actions and speech to steer the organization of the encounters to their own needs. Goffman found that the discourse of people could be read for its literal content at a surface level, but beneath this, speech and body language were intended to engage other people in a common understanding of the event. He suggested that frames, that is, the constructed contexts, of these situated encounters created social meaning.

Although credited with promoting frame analysis, undoubtedly influenced by his experience in a family of Ukrainian Jews migrating to Canada in the late nineteenth century, he did not include many Jewish situations in his scholarship (Burns 1992: 8; Cuddihy 1974: 68; Fernandez 2003: 206–7; Goffman 1963: 60, 114). Nonetheless the problem of socially constructed frames, according to those who knew him, was raised by issues of Jewish identity and his negotiation of social interactions far from his Manitoba home. Classmate Saul Mendlovitz, who shared a Jewish background with Goffman, remarked of their graduate school experience together at the University of Chicago, for instance, 'Erving was a Jew, acting like a Canadian, acting like a Britisher . . . he felt that he was Jewish yet didn't want to be Jewish. He wanted to be something else. He really wanted to be an English gentleman [in line with] the picture of him that he had in his head' (Shalin 2009). A central problem in Goffman's paradigm-changing approach to social interaction was how identity could be appropriated and related through expressive acts of gesture and talk in selected settings, often outside the awareness of the participants.

Goffman never wrote about his childhood but he was quoted as asserting that 'being a Jew and a Russian Jew at that, explained a lot about me', which biographer Ronald Fernandez took to mean that 'he was a perennial outsider, caught between his ancestry and the prejudices of the larger society' (2007: 206–7). Taking the analytical role of observer looking in on someone else's culture, Goffman sought to be an insider looking out, and developed theatrical metaphors for cultural behaviour of stages and performances to describe variable social roles, much like those of touring actors who adapted to different physical settings and audiences. Mendlovitz indicates that Goffman 'was very much into that observational stuff very early on', owing to his concern to fit as a Jew and Canadian into different social groups on campus. Mendlovitz, who also had an impression of himself as an outsider in Chicago, recalls that, as Jews,

Erving and I used to go to [ethnically mixed] parties and agree that we would exchange [thoughts on] what we had seen. He especially was interested in what we had seen and then he would take copious notes on that . . . And we would then go over very carefully what the girl said to him, who was going off into another room, what was the content, how come there were no paintings on the wall, but it was a full range of ethnography and that kind of stuff. (Shalin 2009)

In these settings often populated by strangers, Goffman noticed that a standard part of dialogue would be the extraction of information such as birthplace, occupation, and ethnicity from one another to figure out another person's identity and gauge what to expect socially from that person. Goffman was apparently concerned about what the label 'Jew' meant to others and how that identity matched his own self-awareness. If Goffman was aware of his Jewish background as a basis for frame analysis, as a professor he encouraged ethnographers, including his Jewish students, to avoid studying their own families or cultural groups so as to maintain an objective distance from the observed scenes.[1]

One can discern attention to interaction between individuals who have an ethnic self-awareness in Goffman's reference to 'stereotype' in his groundbreaking study, *The Presentation of Self in Everyday Life* (1959):

If unacquainted with the individual, observers can glean clues from his conduct and appearance which allow them to apply their previous experience with individuals roughly similar to the one before them or, more important, to apply untested stereotypes to him. They can also assume from past experience that only individuals of a particular kind are likely to be found in a given social setting. (1959: 1)

Although 'stereotype' has been read by sociological scholars to mean a general social 'image', Goffman's Jewish background and awareness of Du Bois's 'double consciousness' concept probably had an influence on his choice of the word 'stereotype' to represent outsiders' ethnic portrayal that has a bearing on a person's awareness of him or herself (Saville-Torike 2003: 172).

Before Goffman applied the terminology of the frame drawn from the work of anthropologist Gregory Bateson, he used the looser terminology of 'situation' to refer to a recognizable context, or at least recognizable by participants, that drives the distinctive forms of expression, and impression, whereby people communicate to one another. Goffman was interested in the attempts of participants to manage situations, often through symbolic communication in talk and action, to advance their own interests. A proposition of his that drew consideration in scholarly circles is that in these situations boundaries as well as connections are established through the use of proverbs, slang, and body language, reminiscent of artistic performances. Participants in a social situation do more than relay information to one another, he hypothesized; they transform space into stages with different functions (backstage for informal, intimate communication and front stage for more formal, official presentation) upon which to perform to reinforce the kind of identity they want others to recognize in them. Social encounters thus often become a negotiation between performer and audience, and analysis can turn to the simultaneous roles played by participants as actor and viewer.

Goffman's microsociological approach attracted wide notice because of the implication that participants have agency in the formation of their social life rather than blindly following the precedents of tradition or repeating fixed texts of lore in their expressive talk (Scheff 2006). He outlined the ethnographic goal of determining, through close observation, whether the expressive and often ethnically inflected communication that occurs within a situation is dictated by the setting, or is strategically guided by one or more figures in the frame. Setting up a frame socially is an attempt by interacting participants to gain social order by emphasizing connections among them and by moving potential conflicts to the edges of the frame. Goffman declared that this constant negotiation of different social settings is a function of modern everyday life, in which identities are open to alteration in response to conditions of high mobility, social diversity, and extreme individualism. He conceptualized modern society as one in which people are strangers to one another and consequently create social frames constantly to establish familiarity and construct an identity appropriate to the situation (see Kim 2002; Packard 1972; Sennett 1977). Identities are, therefore, not shaped by family line or locality alone but are flexible and overlapping. Modernity offers individuals choices for who they want to be or how they appear to other strangers, but with those choices comes the often difficult cultural work of formulating and managing their identities in various social relations on a daily basis. Forced into this role of presenting themselves, individuals become actors to one another and learn from culture the dimensions of acts they can adapt variously to communicate and to impress others. To this sociological premise, scholars today have added historical and psychological enquiries into the experiences and drives that shape socially framed behaviour, particularly in Jewish contexts, where issues of stereotype, migration, boundary, and difference abound (Boustan, Kosansky, and Rustow 2011; Boyarin and Boyarin 1997; Bronner 2012; Bush 2011: 57–67; Heilman 2006; Prell 1989; Sklare 1993).

Some scholars prefer 'scenes' or 'stages' to frames so as to emphasize the performative, presentational, and emergent nature of socially contextualized expressions in modern everyday life, but many analysts have found that these theatrical terms do not fully denote the repetitive patterns of cultural impressions that arise from daily and ceremonial encounters. For many visual ethnographers, the frame used as a tool of ethnography draws on the documentary operations of framing, centring, and focusing in photography, and on the interpretation provided by sequentially arranging images in a gallery or exhibition (Bateson 1956: 175–6, 2000: 186; Bateson and Mead 1942; Mechling 2004, 2009). In this view, the observer looks through a lens and identifies boundaries that will not be apparent to the subjects. The observer as analyst is able to variously focus on, or bring into relief, different activities in the shot. The analytical act of framing scenes and arranging them in a sequence of communicative acts captures a narrative as well as actions that have a bearing on the perception of the event by the participants and assorted viewers. Consequently, frames refer to the ways insiders and outsiders comprehend activity in their heads before they act. They suggest that in modern heterogeneous societies, people make sense of their social environment by dividing it into various scenes and situations in the course of daily life. People therefore adjust their behaviour according to their ideas about ways to communicate in these various scenes and the symbols or inferences of the communication in them. The use of frame does not imply a singleness of mind or of society among participants, because as a culturally derived construct based on precedent that has been adapted to new situations, the elastic social frame is open to negotiation and contention (Abrahams 2005; Bronner 2010; Fine 1983; Mechling 1980; Raspa 1991; Sherzer 1993).

The social negotiation of frames is apparent in this volume, for example, in Steve Siporin's study of Pitigliano, Italy, known in the region as 'the Little Jerusalem'. Siporin finds this moniker significant for its reference to the area not only as historically having a large Jewish population but also for supposedly possessing interreligious harmony. He describes a contemporary situation in which town leaders celebrate the local Jewish experience and actively contribute to the development of tourism around Jewish sites, although the town is almost completely devoid of Jews. Among the settings for social interaction between tourists and townspeople is the Ghetto Wine Bar and Caffè. Siporin notes that visiting Americans find the use of 'ghetto' in bad taste as an allusion to a history of forced exclusion, but for many locals the shop's name and setting present an occasion to recount narratives about the rescue of Jews during the Second World War and about the good relations between Jews and non-Jews. Siporin interprets the fact that tourists feel compelled to experience Pitigliano first-hand even if the historical representations are inaccurate as a sign of deeper messages at work about local social relations. Within the setting, locals and tourists negotiate the meaning of the experience as one that bespeaks Italian or Jewish heritage or a combination of both in symbolic acts involving consumption of Jewish foods to gain a sense of authenticity and hearing stories about the town's Jews to confirm affinity for Jews. Photographing themselves against staged Jewish backdrops as in a theatre and participation in festivities that relate in this 'frame' a subtext about post-Holocaust Italian experience add other dimensions to communicating Italian and Jewish identity. Siporin asserts that 'From an early time the Jews of Italy brought the host (Italian) culture into their own Jewish frame to a degree probably unsurpassed elsewhere in western Europe.' This observation leads him to ask, 'To what extent might non-Jewish Italians today be incorporating Jewish culture into their understanding of Italianness?' His answer is that Italians have promoted a Jewish cultural revival as a frame in which the narratives and nostalgic behaviour they enact can salvage Italian identity.

In Amy Milligan's case study the participants all identify as Jewish but in a small-town setting, Jews ranging from Conservative to strictly Orthodox come together in a single synagogue and negotiate the kinds of practices that can bind them together not just in a building, but socially into a single cultural frame. The congregants are forced to reconcile different levels of observance among them, and in so doing dance around the very definition of 'Orthodox' and its connection to historical Jewish tradition. Part of the negotiation in this particular context is the creative adoption of some practices, such as the use of head coverings that connect the women in the congregation and signal their commitment to Orthodoxy even if their numbers are small. The surrounding cultural context of Amish and Mennonites, known as 'plain groups' in the area, is significant because the Jewish women have created a link with the head coverings worn as a sign of pietism by non-Jews. Hair-covering, more so than other familiar markers of Jewish observance, materializes their joint identity, but also allows for variability, from using a snood to wearing a *sheitl* (wig). Through their hair-covering choices the women in the congregation situate themselves on the scale of Orthodoxy and feel empowered to take responsibility for the continuity of the group and its maintenance of traditions.

Throughout the various locations covered in this volume, authors frequently refer to the cognition of the frame in terms of action (or act) and interaction. Using the frame as a key to the distinction between reality and fantasy, everyday and ceremonial, and play and work, ethnographic observers and historical chroniclers focus their analytical lenses on the way that ordinary activities—such as watching, lighting, sitting, and standing—become culturally significant symbols (the kind of symbols that elicit responses in the form of gestures and ideas from others), with props, names, or narratives brought into the situation to support different meanings held by organizers and participants (see Blumer 2004; Duncan 2002: 92–106; Mead 1967: 61–81; Musolf 2003: 72–93). A historical example is provided by Marcin Wodziński, who examines the disputes in nineteenth-century Poland over whether the hasidim constituted a sect. Besides noting this widespread classificatory act by non-hasidim whereby they differentiated the hasidim from Judaism in an attempt to curtail their influence in Polish civic affairs, Wodziński analyses the significant symbolism in the ritual of *shiva* enacted by many Jewish parents when their children left home to join hasidic courts. The message of these staged mourning periods was that taking up hasidism amounted to conversion to a non-Jewish religion, implying that hasidism was not part of Judaism. Of significance in Wodziński's historical study is his innovative use of court records, diaries, and narratives to provide insight not only into the sequence of events but also into the frames of social interaction that changed over time.

Wodziński places the loaded terms of 'sect' and 'cult' in the historical context of the relationship of Jews and non-Jews in Polish public policy and of the Jews' attempt to criminalize hasidic religious practice. In analytical terminology the frame and context may appear similar. Anthropologist Gregory Bateson, who inspired Goffman's frame analysis, distinguishes the frame as the perception of a setting in which interaction occurs from the context, or surrounding condition, of an event. Bateson muses that

we assume that the psychological frame has some degree of real existence. In many instances, the frame is consciously recognized and even represented in vocabulary ('play,' 'movie,' 'interview,' 'job,' 'language,' etc.). In other cases, there may be no explicit verbal reference to the frame, and the subject may have no consciousness of it. The analyst, however, finds that his own thinking is simplified if he uses the notion of an unconscious frame as an explanatory principle; usually he goes further than this and infers its existence in the subject's unconscious. (2000: 186–7)

One can read in this statement a call for understanding the cognitive process that produces the frame, as well as the social, historical, and cultural forces apparent in communication that affect the comprehension of the frame. Following Bateson, social theorist Jay Mechling proposes that the use of frame signals a scholarly turn away from 'positivist and formalist epistemologies to an epistemology that sees reality as created, mediated, and sustained by human narratives' (1991: 43). This emphasis on the process of narration and action (often in reference to gesture, play, and festivity) is especially discernible in Jewish cultural studies, which depart from the conventions of literal readings of Judaic texts to assessments of expressions, inferences, and impressions communicated in everyday life (Boyarin and Boyarin 1997; Bronner 2008).

Frame analysis takes into account the role of the observer or analyst in the perception of the function of the frame. Much as I have discerned the effect of Erving Goffman's Jewish background on the development of his microsociological approach (and one could expand this analysis to other notable Jewish contributors to Goffman-inspired approaches including Roger Abrahams, Richard Bauman, Dan Ben-Amos, Alan Dundes, Gary Alan Fine, Kenneth Goldstein, Barbara Kirshenblatt-Gimblett, and Elliott Oring[2]), an important aspect of the enquiry into framing is those historiographical studies that question the impact of personalities and movements on the discourse of impressions that the public or scholarly community has about groups and their interactions. Jonathan Boyarin, in this volume, for example, examines the relationship between anthropologists Paul Radin (1883–1959) and Stanley Diamond (1922–91) and their conceptualization of otherness based upon their own experiences in Jewish culture even though most of their studies were about other groups. He uses this enquiry to address the broader question of the 'avoidance' of Jewish culture in the social sciences by Jews who were formulating concepts of ethnic difference based on social interaction to replace the racial classifications that were based on a natural history model. He finds paradoxes in the ways that these scholars framed the social problems that could be resolved by ethnography of non-Jewish groups. For example, German Jewish immigrant Franz Boas (1858–1942), often called the 'father of American anthropology', used studies of Native American diversity to decry racial models of culture that ostracized Jews as a unified 'backward race'. He called for a particularism by which a tradition-centred group would be studied in the context of distinctive historical and cultural conditions rather than being relegated to a lower global level of culture (see Baker 2004; Bronner 1998: 129–38; Diner 1977; Frank 1997; Glick 1982; Messer 1986; Morris-Reich 2008: 4–17). One problem that Boyarin ponders is that the arguments Boas and Radin advanced for the artistry of so-called primitive groups rooted in a locality to demonstrate that Jews did not constitute a race were also used to show that Jews were artless or placeless. Other chapters in this volume also take up the question of how scholars connect Jews to a broader concept of ethnicity rather than arguing for the specialness of their situation. This is particularly evident in Sophie Wagenhofer's and David Clark's discussions of the messages of Jewish museums, such as the Museum of Moroccan Judaism in Morocco and Jewish exhibitions in Italy, in relation to their surrounding cultural and geographical contexts.

Material Frames—Exhibitions

This volume's theme of 'framing' Jewish culture as a rhetorical and material action related to the representation of ethnic difference is exemplified by a signature event in the annals of Jewish display—the Anglo-Jewish Historical Exhibition of 1887. The popular press hailed the exhibition installed in the majestic Royal Albert Hall in London as a momentous achievement which triggered, according to the *Jewish Encyclopedia*, 'a distinct revival of interest in the history of the Jews in England' and apparently elsewhere (Adler 1906: 509; Cohen 1888: 295). The idea of the grand event came from English-born engineer and art aficionado Isidore Spielmann, who, at the age of 33 in 1886, proposed to journalist and Jewish civic leader Lucien Wolf, also of his generation, that a large exposition of historical and artistic relics could have a profound salutary effect on the state of Jews in England. Spielmann argued that placing Jewish documents in cases for public viewing and displaying artefacts on pedestals would serve to highlight, especially to non-Jews, the breadth and depth of the contributions of Jews to English civilization as participants rather than outsiders, and would also freeze these items in time to encourage their analysis as art, particularly by Jews.

Recollecting the impetus for Spielmann's brainstorm, Ephraim Levine pointed to an obvious identity conflict within the young rising star that the act of literally framing and displaying Jewish cultural materials might resolve. Levine referred to Spielmann's 'double allegiance' to both national and ethnic society with the assumption that the national devotion meant a Christian as well as political affiliation (Levine 1924–7: 234). Yet Levine observed that Spielmann, in all his

public appearances, came across as a genuine Englishman. He described Spielmann as 'completely identified with England and all that English culture con-
noted'. Levine was surprised, then, when in the face of a wave of Jewish refugees
fleeing from persecution in eastern Europe washing over English shores,
Spielmann loudly called for 'a well-organised community', publicly promoting
Jewish identity to accommodate the new arrivals (Levine 1924–7: 234). According
to Levine, at a time when differences could be visibly discerned between native
and immigrant Jews, Spielmann viewed working on the exhibition as an
opportunity to show a long-standing tradition of Jewish integration with English
society while at the same time maintaining ethnic variance, whether imposed
from outside or within the community. Levine summarized Spielmann's paradoxical psychological profile as one of simultaneously 'anglicizing [i.e. assimil-
ating] the foreign Jew in this country [England] and . . . protecting [or separating]
him in other countries' (1924–7: 235).

Often mentioning the 'peculiar' situation of Jews in host countries, curators
guided by Spielmann contextualized sections of the popular exhibition for the
primarily non-Jewish attendees. In the introduction to the section of Jewish
ecclesiastical art, Wolf and folklorist Joseph Jacobs wrote,

like the jargons of the Hebrew people, their manners and customs, their superstitions
and other phenomena of their social life, their art is little more than a composite deposit
of the contrastful impressions of a wide geographical dispersion, and of a varied and
chequered history . . . whatever the normal artistic capacities of the Hebrew people, they
must have been strongly affected, if not altogether transformed, by the stupendous
catastrophe of the Dispersion, and the career of ceaseless wandering and misery which
subjected them to the perplexing influences of ever-changing surroundings. (Jacobs
and Wolf 1888: 83)

By this account, Jews sought a home in which they could thrive as citizens of the
realm. Their cultural legacy need not separate them; it provided ingredients that
could be mixed with those from the local environment into a joint identity. At the
same time, Wolf and Jacobs recognized that differences existed between Jew and
non-Jew in England—particularly in terms of how they worshipped rather than
in their essential character. They pronounced that Judaism, with its distinctiveness, should be respected and even praised as one of many constituent faiths in
the nation. Exposing the historically 'anomalous' position of Jews in England, the
curators arranged objects in a progressive order from medieval exclusion to
modern inclusion. The exhibition was on the one hand a call for preservation,
especially as the organizers bemoaned the loss of physical remains of the Jewish
'element' in England, and, on the other, a rhetorical act of framing Jews socially as
worthy constituents within a larger British culture. This act served to present
Jews as one group among others within the host society and delineate the kinds of
scenes or boundaries within which Jews could establish their differences. More
than providing a historical record of Jews in England, the exhibition was, in the

words of the organizing group's president F. D. Mocatta, 'designed to alter this state of things', by which he meant that the emphasis on artistic ability in the frames of the exhibition suggested that Jews had a vibrant living culture, as well as a long historical legacy, which formed the basis of their ethnic distinction (Mocatta 1887: 290).

Assessing the impact of the exhibition, Barbara Kirshenblatt-Gimblett in 1998 underscored the significance of the display in launching the 'Jewish plan' of organizing Judaica, which would become standard in world fairs and museums through the twentieth century. Moreover, Kirshenblatt-Gimblett asserts, this plan was a strategy of presenting a distinctive Jewish identity for Jews to embrace in everyday life outside the exhibition. The arrangement followed the ritual settings of synagogue, home, and person (life-cycle events), thus suggesting physically and socially bounded spaces in which Jews could express their difference. She interpreted the strategy as conveying a double consciousness of showing the discreteness of Jewish practices in confined instances on the one hand, while on the other assuring Victorian visitors that Jews shared with non-Jews a national value system of fidelity to home, family, and faith (1998: 85–6). Lest visitors imagine Jews felt unaffiliated to the host country, Jacobs and Wolf included in the exhibition a framed written copy of the 'Prayer for the Royal Family', placed, they emphasized, near the Tablets of the Law so that it could be read by the congregation (Jacobs and Wolf 1887: 96). Although pointing out the distinctively Jewish lavish ornamentation of Torah scrolls, the curators observed further connections of Jews to non-Jewish faiths in England by noting, of Jewish betrothal rings, 'except that they bore a Hebrew inscriptions signifying "Good Luck", they rarely differed from the similar rings in vogue among the Gentiles' (1887: 83). Presenting a memorial for fallen Jewish soldiers serving in British regiments, Spielmann told his audience,

This memorial stands here in eloquent testimony to the fact that British Jews are inspired by a love of King and country no less enthusiastic and no less devoted than that which animates their fellow-subjects. It testifies that in vindicating their claim to the same liberties and rights, they share an equal privilege of defending and of dying for the country which confers them. (1902–5: 58)

The design of the tablets drew attention to the difference of these soldiers, as the words in memoriam stated, 'of the Jewish race and faith', by having one tablet with their names in English and another in Hebrew surrounded by an elaborate Sephardi design.

More than a hundred years after the exhibition, museums acknowledged the inspiration of Spielmann's pioneering plan to display the evolving status of Jewish expressiveness. For example, London's Jewish Museum, established in 1932, proclaimed in 2006, with the publication of *Treasures of Jewish Heritage*, a need, first expressed in the Anglo-Jewish Historical Exhibition, to showcase the cultural worthiness of Jews with a demonstration of their artistry. It also continued the theme of dispersion among Jews that raised the question whether a unified Jewish identity exists, let alone an anglicized one. Even more conspicuous in the twenty-first-century catalogue than the Anglo-Jewish exhibition's reference in the nineteenth century to the plight of Jews from eastern Europe is the challenge of creating a Jewish community and identity out of the variety of Jews that included immigrants from Asia, South America, and Africa in the United Kingdom. The curators declared that 'the clothes, religious artefacts, photographs and other objects are characteristic of the widely divergent societies where Jewish people have lived over the centuries, ranging across Europe, Asia and North Africa. These objects embody the diversity of the community whose stories the Jewish Museum seeks to tell' (Burman, Marin, and Steadman 2006: 187). The London museum's exhibition questioned whether a single Jewish cultural frame existed or whether, in multiplicity, Jewish identity depended on the geographical background of the Jews involved in myriad cultural scenes.

The lesson that frame analysts draw from these exhibitions is not so much about museum techniques as it is about the agency behind the acts of framing, bounding, representing, and exhibiting Jewish difference by Jews and non-Jews in both formal institutional and informal social contexts. Manifested materially in a public exhibition, ritual objects presented as communal possessions lead viewers to comprehend the cultural traits that compose an identity in everyday life in the bounded physical settings of the home and synagogue. Rhetorical acts of circumscribing, exhibiting, and representing identity can also be discerned in various social encounters between Jews and non-Jews and of Jews with one another in which intangible 'frames' referring to Jewish difference are enacted by participants. The question that arises is whether these frames are intentionally constructed or are enacted outside the awareness of participants, especially when the boundaries of the frame emerge from an unselfconscious change in behavioural action and mode of communication. In the absence of material walls separating Jews into ethnic zones or of dress demarcating Jewish religious pietism, participants signal to one another a Jewish consciousness by employing language and gesture meant to be esoteric. Physical context still comes into play because of the perception of where such encounters are appropriate—on the street, at work, in the market, at the theatre, in the restaurant, in the synagogue, or at home—and with whom.

Representations and Boundaries

The idea of strategically framing communication in selected situations, whether as an analyst or a participant, to demarcate social boundaries is common to the experience of many ethnic groups, who by definition operate with a double consciousness of a national association and a subcultural identity based upon a supposedly foreign ancestry. The Jewish challenge to this classical theory of ethnicity is the combination of diversity in global Jewish experience that comes out of a mobile diasporic rather than national ancestry and the intersection of religion and race with locality. A statistical reflection of this mobility relative to other religions is the 2012 study by the Pew Forum on Religion and Public Life, which found that Jews have by far the highest level of migration among all faiths. It concludes that one-quarter of Jews alive today have left their birth country and now live somewhere else. In contrast, just 5 per cent of Christians, 4 per cent of Muslims, and less than 3 per cent of other religious groups have migrated across international borders, according to the Pew survey.[3] Often there is an assumption that Jews reside in community with one another as ethnic groups are expected to do, and yet they defy easy categorization because they mix and move in a socially heterogeneous workaday world but are, at the same time, capable of living in isolation as religious Jews. Whereas social difference may frequently be tabulated by governments as well as neighbours by residents' consistency of appearance, language, and habits, Jews have not been easily separated by racial characteristics, despite antisemitic efforts to scientifically categorize them as a race (Gilman 1991; Goldstein 2006; Patai and Patai 1989).

The issue of boundaries is prominent in Jewish studies because the mobility of Jews has led to the presumption that they always have neighbours whose animosity or friendliness to the idea of Jewishness, as well as relations with Jews, are constantly in question. Against this contextual backdrop, boundaries for Jews are frequently points of interface rather than separation (Bush 2011: 60–1). Although mobility and its associations with personal freedom and socio-economic enhancement are highly valued in modernism generally, Jews have especially embraced mobility as a test of their status because of historical associations with restrictions on their movement or with being forced into slavery.

Other social factors of boundary join with mobility in the highly publicized matter of marital choice and family formation, because of general demographic patterns in Europe and the Americas of relatively high intermarriage and late marriage rates. Surveying Jewish mobility in the United States, for example, Sidney and Alice Goldstein comment that 'If Jews marry at later ages, if more Jews choose not to marry at all, if marital disruption increases and if fertility remains low, conditions conducive to locational stability may continue to weaken so that even higher levels of longer-distance movement may result' (1996: 2). The question this view has raised is whether the demographic decentring of Jewish communities means the loss of Jewish identity. The Goldsteins are convinced that it does (1996: 317–31). Moving away from statistics to social observations, other scholars are not so sure. Carole Fink, Ruth Gruber, and Diana Pinto, for example, ponder the meaning of phenomena constituting a twenty-first-century renaissance of Jewish culture and renewal of Jewish identity in Europe (Fink 2010: 226–8; Gruber 2002: 68–9; Pinto 2006). This revival implies, however, a challenge to, or replacement of, the model of assimilation leading to white ethnicity, with one of Jewish intensity enacted at pivotal moments and in designated or constructed spaces—physical and social—that suggests a social interactional perspective on frames as permeable limits, always under construction (Brauch, Lipphardt, and Nocke 2008; Cohen 1999: 1–5; Pinto 2006). Occasions when Jewishness rises to the surface and needs enactment take on more significance in such a social interactional model. Along these lines, Holly Pearse, in this volume, notes the ways in which identity at points of interface, related to the question of consequences of Jewish mobility and interfaith romance, is expressed on movie screens by encoding filmmakers and for decoding audiences. She views a historical change in screened representations from the assimilationist message of harmonious ethnic mixing in couples in an open democratic society to patterns of stress and strain in interfaith relationships.

Another occasion that brings out questions of boundary in the representations, or symbolized expressions, of culture occurs in December every year in many countries because of the symbolism of Christian Christmas as a national cultural holiday. The 'December dilemma', as it has been called by Jewish communal leaders in Europe and North America, concerns choices of Jews to become involved in non-religious aspects of Christmas, even displaying festive trees and lights, or reject and prohibit Christmas participation as a force working against Jewish identity, or elevate Hanukah as a gift-giving festivity to join Christmas in the 'holiday season'. If Hanukah is not elevated, then another alternative has been to ritualize Jewish activities on Christmas Day: eating Chinese food, watching movies, volunteering at hospitals and charitable agencies, and attending concerts and comedy performances. A famous incident bringing out this ritualization of difference is when a southern Christian US senator asked candidate for the Supreme Court Elena Kagan at her confirmation hearing where she had been on Christmas Day 2009. She drew a laugh when she answered, 'You know, like all Jews, I was probably at a Chinese restaurant' (Plaut 2012: 65; see also Li 2011). The serious side of this humour born out of the tension of Jews exhibiting their difference from the majority culture is the effect of decisions to incorporate or reject Christmas celebrations, especially for impressionable youth. Joshua Eli Plaut, in *A Kosher Christmas* (2012), claims that, since the late twentieth century in North America, Jews have lessened the anxiety of Christmastime by redrawing the boundaries of the festival along national rather than religious lines. Or boundaries are dissolved, especially by Jews, judging from media representations, by inventing hybrid celebrations such as Chrismukkah popularized by the television show *The O.C.* (2003–7) and Festivus featured on *Seinfeld* (1989–98). By redefining a blended 'holiday season', even if it means recasting the meaning of Hanukah from a religious to a cultural celebration (sometimes referred to colloquially as 'the Jewish Christmas'), Jews, according to Plaut, have transformed Christmas into an inclusive festival that broadcasts a message of hope and diversity (Plaut 2012: 153). 'In responding to Christmas in a myriad of ways', Plaut writes, 'Jews across the country have not only satisfied their respective holiday needs but have also opened the way for other minority groups to bring to national attention the importance of their own December holidays festivities' (2012: 173). For Plaut, who observes more social tension and cultural divisions historically over pressure to observe Christmas in other countries, particularly in eastern Europe, this transformation is a uniquely American story. Undoubtedly there are various narratives of 'December dilemma' strategies globally, but what is demonstrated in Plaut's critical example is the negotiation of boundaries between identities of minority and majority, ethnicity and nationality, and foreign and native in the negotiation over public cultural expressions observed by Jew and Christian.

Ethnic theory often presumes minority status for the group in question (Sollors 1996), although the modern challenge has been the ethnographic and historical understanding of Israel as a Jewish majority state whose residents nonetheless have perceptions of localized difference based upon national and cultural origins, level of religious piety, institutional affiliation to a kibbutz or moshav, and even political orientation. A key to this modern diversity that links Jews in other national settings is the concept of situated identity, particularly as set against cultural landscapes in urban and suburban spaces, forming 'Jewish topographies' or 'traditions of place' (Brauch, Lipphardt, and Nocke 2008). Sociologist Herbert Gans was influential on such approaches in developing a definition of situated identity out of his studies of an urban Italian neighbourhood after taking on suburban Judaism (Gans 1957, 1962; see also Sklare and Greenblum 1979). He defined identity simply as 'the sociopsychological elements that accompany role behavior' (1996: 434). His observation in a post-immigrant society in the 1970s was that the

ethnic role is today less of an ascriptive than a voluntary role that people assume alongside other roles. To be sure, ethnics are still identified as such by others, particularly on the basis of name, but the behavioral expectations that once went with identification by others have declined sharply, so that ethnics have some choice about when and how to play ethnic roles. Moreover, as ethnic cultures and organizations decline further, fewer ethnic roles are prescribed, thus increasing the degree to which people have freedom of role definition. (Gans 1996: 434)

Ethnic identity is expressed as action or feeling, or a combination of these, often in social situations or cultural spaces in which the various kinds of expression of identity may be unconsciously perceived or overtly organized. This kind of identity is not an objective, historical category but subjective and modern in the sense that individuals claim an identity and work to reinforce it with participation in social events or expressive performances in selected cultural scenes or frames.

Not all scholars agree with Gans that the influence of ethnic organizations has evaporated; that the options for creating identity are quite as limitless as he implies, or that assimilation is inevitable. For instance, writing generally on the 'enigma of ethnicity', Wilbur Zelinsky has noted the 'virtually worldwide resurgence of fundamentalism', which suggests a total and often exclusive immersion in formal institutions and social structures (2001: 175). Within Jewish studies, Samuel Heilman, David Landau, and Jerome Mintz all observed in the 1990s the growth of ultra-Orthodoxy (whose adherents are known collectively by the Hebrew term 'haredim') as a separatist movement bucking the creative ethnicity trend (Heilman 1992; Landau 1993; Mintz 1992). Landau editorialized that 'the haredim, regarded only a few decades ago as a dying breed, have confounded forecasts of their demise. In their resurgence, they have proved that the dismissal of haredism as anachronistic may itself be an anachronism in the modern world' (1993: 334). In addition to fundamentalism, religious renewal and cultural revival projects revolving around new Jewish priorities placed upon the environment, spiritualism, or feminism have spawned intentional framing of group differences—from the larger secular society as well as between various stripes of Jews. Again it appeared that Jewish diversity complicated the understanding of ethnicity as boundary maintenance in relation to religion and culture.

Zelinsky has speculated that rekindled religiosity was a side effect of globalization and a response to the shortcomings of modernization (2001: 175). Jews as a diasporic group are especially aware of varieties of tradition that demarcate the difference between Jews and host societies in a wide number of communities around the world. Before every Jewish festival, popular press reports broadcast recipes and customs not only in a descriptive sense of affirming Jewish diversity but also to suggest that traditions far from the original source or from one's background can be adapted to one's observance (see Nathan 1994, 2004; Rose 1992; Uvezian 1999). Even representations of foods and holiday observances focused on Israel typically emphasize the many cultural communities with distinctive traditions (see Nathan 2001). Whether as a form of cross-cultural bonding or a response to assimilation, such diversifying practices lead past religiosity back to the concept of ethnicity and to the questions raised by Spielmann concerning the consciousness of identity.

In material space one can consider the controversies related to the separation (*hafradah*) fence erected by Israel in 2002 mainly in the West Bank. Supporters viewed it as a security measure to prevent Arab terrorism but opponents protested that it was an illegal barrier that did not follow recognized borderlines. Commenting on the heightened global controversy regarding the fence, geographer Shaul Cohen notes that 'the construction of walls has long been a tool in regulating—or attempting to regulate—human passage and the defense of territory' (2006: 12). Yet for many Jews this structure was a wall that raised images of ghetto enclosures of Jews limiting mobility or the political divide between East and West represented by the Berlin Wall. At issue is the claim of territory signified by a wall that suggests a border designating the separation of national as well as ethnic groups. The heated response is also partly owing to the perception of unhindered mobility as a given in modernity. More than serving as a security barrier, the material 'fence' raised different inferences depending on the cultural context of groups observing it.

Ethnic theory based upon the exclusion of often racialized groups whose identities are assigned or involuntary shifted at the dawn of the twenty-first century in light of political developments of 'border-crossing' and 'border-erasure' that represented a break with twentieth-century patterns of immigration and assimilation to nation-states. In a supposedly new postmodern age of extreme individualism and transnationalism that challenge the hegemony of the nation-state, there has been a notable re-examination of the alignment of Jewish identity with a dynamic concept of voluntary, temporary, or creative ethnicity. Introducing a Dutch conference in 2011 on borders and boundaries among Jews in the Netherlands, Judith Frishman and Ido de Haan signalled a break with past assumptions of binaries between Jew and non-Jew when they pronounced, 'If identity is no longer to be regarded as something set but rather something that is subject to change and negotiation, then logically attention should be paid to the "continuous construction, maintenance, or transgression of boundaries between ethnic and other collective identities"' (2011: 7–8). They sought to re-examine history in light of the view that 'postmodernist historians have been turning their gaze to a wide range of identities once taken for granted, identities located on the borderlines between Jews and non-Jews as well as on those between one group of Jews and another' (2011: 8). A year earlier, a symposium entitled 'Boundaries of Jewish Identity' sought to depart from the definition of Jews dictated by their enemies or within the discourse of surrounding majorities. Similarly disputing the idea that Jewish identity is set or static, organizers Susan A. Glenn and Naomi Sokoloff called for an understanding of identity based upon the 'different social, intellectual, and political locations of those who are asking' (2010: 4). Much as Ephraim Levine speculated on Isidore Spielmann's motives for creating an exhibition of Jewish history and artistry that would affirm the place of Jews in England, so the 'reflexive' analysis suggested by Glenn and Sokoloff looks to find the agents for the forging of Jewish identity in varied circumstances, especially by and for groups outside the mainstreams of Jewish life such as the Lemba of southern Africa, the Subbotniks of Ukraine, the Kuki-Chin-Mizo of India, and crypto-Jews of the American Southwest. Yet another conference, this one sponsored by the American Jewish Historical Society in 2012 and bearing the title Beyond Boundaries, urged the reinterpretation of disciplinary divisions between scholars studying Jews as well as of the difference between Jews and non-Jews in a post-modern ethnicity.[4] *Framing Jewish Culture* extends this discourse on a global scale, with Jewish cultural studies as an exemplary guiding structure for a problem-centred enquiry into the thinking behind the rhetoric of boundaries as well as the manifestation of difference in social life.

The reference in the above works to boundaries and borders suggests that much of the effort to define Jewish culture has been focused at the centre of groups rather than out at their boundaries with other communities. The rhetoric of boundaries is meant to show that the lines of demarcation between Jews and non-Jews, and between different groupings of Jews, are varied, negotiated, and mutable. Several contributors to this volume, including Samuel Gruber, who looks at the interaction between Jews and non-Jews in medieval Italy, and Magdalena Luszczynska, who examines family relationships in German-speaking regions during the same period, find that it is the tenuous ethnic boundary that defines the group, not the cultural forms that the boundary encloses. This concept builds on Gregory Bateson's suggestion that the social construction of a cultural frame in the absence of a physical boundary is a way for the group to handle paradox and tension in their situation, especially in the communication of play, which gives licence for transgressive behaviours or messages that subvert the society outside the frame (2000: 184–92).

Related to the idea that boundaries are constantly reconstituted in interethnic interactions is anthropologist Fredrik Barth's famous observation in *Ethnic Groups and Boundaries* that 'cultural differences can persist despite inter-ethnic contact and interdependence', which he explained by pointing to the social construction of boundaries in societies where there is constant interethnic contact (1969: 10). In this view, identities in a modern context are not inherited but rather composed anew in the sense of being enacted strategically in different social situations. The danger of this presentist perspective is that it does not take into account processes of heritage transmission through generations in daily life and the impact of historical events such as the exodus from Egypt, the destruction of the Second Temple, the erection of the Venetian ghetto walls, the expulsion of Jews from Spain and the Spanish Inquisition, the establishment of the Russian Pale of Settlement, the influx of east European immigrants to the United States between 1880 and 1920, or the Nazi institution of the Final Solution and the Holocaust on present-day thinking and collective memory. Several contributors to this volume take up this challenge of assessing the influence of historical narrative and memory on the awareness, and reinterpretation, of contemporary boundary maintenance and construction. Rella Kushelevsky, for instance, analyses the realignment of narratives about the historic Prague ghetto in Zionist and post-Zionist Israel. Magdalena Waligórska explores the mixed messages of Jewish heritage revival in twenty-first-century Poland against the background of historical Polish–Jewish relations. Steve Siporin examines the lingering effects of Holocaust and Italian nationalist memories in narrative performances about Jews in Pitigliano.

These enquiries have as their context an abundant number of references to awareness of boundaries in Jewish custom and sacred texts. The earliest biblical materialization of Jewish difference is the reference to an exclusive covenant with

God through the circumcision of every male (Gen. 17: 9–14). Although not a publicly visible marker of Jewish identity like the later-evolving customs of head-covering for men and women, circumcision became emblematic of a communally imposed celebration of difference in the *berit milah* (Cohen 2005; Glick 2005; Silverman 2006). Further into the Tanakh, one can hardly overestimate the impact of the Exodus story, to the present day, on holiday observances of Passover, politics, art, and, ultimately, on world-view (Sarna 1996; Waskow and Berman 2011). Self-reflection on boundaries and identity is also evident every Purim when the memorable narrative of Esther involves a realization that the first figure to be named a Jew in the Tanakh is Mordecai, who, in his family line, recounts an experience of exile and presumably diverse relations between Jews and non-Jews in different localities: 'In the fortress Shushan *lived a Jew* by the name of Mordecai, son of Jair son of Shimei son of Kish, a Benjaminite. Kish had been exiled from Jerusalem in the group that was carried into exile along with King Jeconiah of Judah, which had been driven into exile by King Nebuchadnessar of Babylon' (Esther 2: 5–6; emphasis added). Mordecai admonishes his adopted daughter Esther not to reveal her Jewish roots to King Ahasuerus and to blend in with the other maidens in the king's palace. Esther becomes queen, and when Haman issues a decree to exterminate Jews, she aligns herself with her 'people' and implores the king to countermand Haman's plan (Esther 7: 3–4). Although Esther espouses what could be described as ethnic feeling, there is evidence in the narrative of boundary markers of language. The book of Esther relates that the king's scribes send letters 'to the Jews in *their own script and language*' (Esther 8: 9; emphasis added). Additionally, the weekly performed Jewish custom of the Havdalah (or 'distinction') ritual emphasizes the division between the sabbath and the ordinary weekday. The Mishnah contains guidance about business dealings with non-Jews during the week that assumes an awareness of boundaries. In tractate *Avodah zarah* Jews are prohibited from doing business with non-Jews for three days before and three days after the 'festivals of gentiles' (Mishnah, *AZ*: 1–3), and there follow long lists of restrictions often based upon a binary between Jewish maintenance of cleanliness or purity and unclean or impure. Although such business constraints appear anachronistic in the modern era, divisions between pure and unclean states are evident in the laws of *kashrut*, which also serve to identify boundaries between Jew and non-Jew (Douglas 1966: 30–41; Dundes 2002: 75–88; Fabre-Vassas 1997: 138–60).

Judaism is replete with reminders of differences between men and women, and certain practices revolving around these distinctions—such as women reading from the Torah and mixed seating in the synagogue—often serve as a basis for the erection of religious boundaries between Reform, Conservative, and Orthodox wings. The extent of the *meḥitsah*, literally a partition in Hebrew, dividing men and women in synagogue, is often negotiated and conceptualized as a representation of observance. In some Orthodox synagogues women sit in balconies or galleries, whereas in many congregations calling themselves 'modern' the partition is symbolic, with men and women sitting on opposite sides of the same floor. Conservative and Reform congregations usually forgo the division altogether. The inclusion of the *meḥitsah* in synagogue architecture derives from mishnaic references to men and women being allotted separate space at festivities (*Suk.* 5: 2; *Mid.* 2: 5). There is a symbolic connection between the *meḥitsah* and identity formation because many liberal Jews view the abolishment of the partition as an embrace of egalitarian or Enlightenment ethics associated with the emergence of modern mass society. According to Meir Ydit, however, 'Orthodox Jewry has come to regard the retention of the *mehizah* as a cardinal principle and as a mark of the preservation of the Orthodox character of the synagogue' (1972: 1235). This Orthodox character implies the visible announcement of a primary Jewish identity and a continuity with historic practices based on the maintenance of boundaries (Sztokman 2011: 167–70; see also Heilman 2006).

Physical boundaries carry messages of exclusion that launch a discourse about the importance for Jews of ethnic distinction that is imposed by their enemies or initiated by themselves for a sense of inclusion. Following on the renewed attention to sources of border-crossing in antiquity (see Cohen 1999), Samuel Gruber discusses in this volume Jewish strategic uses of physical boundaries in medieval Italy and the points of tension in spaces at the boundaries between Jews and non-Jews, especially in performative festivities such as parades and holidays through public streets. He finds evidence of much more border-crossing than had been thought to exist in medieval times and suggests that, in the attention to spaces in identifying Jewish and Christian sectors, the dynamic processes of cultural confrontation and negotiation between Jews and Christians in civic spaces are often overlooked. He finds evidence in art and documents of Jews symbolizing these supposedly publicly accessible spaces as social frames in which their place, literally and figuratively, in society was constantly tested. He shows the way that the expected behaviour in these public spaces, such as market centres, took on religious associations as a result of these confrontations and negotiations, because while Jews were resented, and sometimes attacked, by Christians, they were also needed, and praised, in the political economy of medieval Italy. Such is a 'liminal' status that becomes heightened in mixed settings such as public civic space or on the peripheries of areas viewed as boundaries.

Moving into the modern period, scholars have argued about the persistence of outlooks by Jews as they move about or the persistence of historical boundaries, real or imagined, between Sephardi and Ashkenazi, west and east European, and American and Israeli heritages. Charles Liebman and Steven M. Cohen, for example, open their study of the Israeli and American experience by noting the disparity between the rhetoric of Jewish fund-raising appeals declaring 'we are one' and the perception, expressed in social encounters, of a deep divide between

American and Israeli Judaism (1990: 1–12). Zvi Gitelman (1998) has posited that the national difference is not just between brands of Judaism but also in relations with the surrounding society. He observes that, in Israel, Jews are easily defined by both cultural and political boundaries, but outside the Jewish state the boundaries that once demarcated Jews are fading and the visible content that defined them is disappearing. Yet Eliezer Ben Rafael, in *Contemporary Jewries: Convergence and Divergence* (2003), argues that, both in Israel and the diaspora, Jews share multiple, localized 'imagined communities', which leads to awareness of various sub-identities under the broad heading of Jewishness.

Sander Gilman suggests that the modern metaphor of the frontier, where forces of change, confrontation, and accommodation dominate, ought to displace the model of centre–periphery in Jewish history (2003; see also Gilman and Shain 1999). This metaphor is in line with the emphasis on social dynamics in the concept of the variable cultural frame, where identity is formed and reconstituted through expressive acts. A border is usually construed as a demarcated line that is enforced politically or culturally (Johnson and Michaelsen 1997: 1–5). Boundaries are not always manifest and they imply differences existing on either side of them, even if the boundary areas are fuzzy. To Gilman, the frontier is a broader concept, highlighting the significance of mobility and social interaction in the definition of identity. In his view emphasizing the social dynamics of identities, the frontier 'is the conceptual and physical space where groups in motion meet, confront, alter, destroy, and build. It is the place of the "migrant culture of the in-between" as both a transitional and translational phenomenon, one that "dramatizes the activity of culture's untranslatability," according to Homi Bhabha' (2003: 15).[5] This idea also follows from anthropologist Victor Turner's seminal idea of liminality, or a 'betwixt-and-between frame' that sets off from reality and fantasy a position to evaluate the meaning of society through symbolic practices (Turner 1977, 1979, 1995). In a Jewish cultural context, Jews often take on liminal roles between insider and outsider and create impressions on festivals and in public civic spaces (such as the museums and festivals described in this volume) that in their edginess inevitably raise questions of the dimensions of identity (Biale, Galchinsky, and Heschel 1998). An example following the earlier discussion of the ritualization of Jewish activities at Christmastime is the growing attention in the twenty-first century to comedic performances by Jews during the festival. Plaut describes the Kung Pao Kosher Comedy in San Francisco, which uses the liminal frame of play to provide 'an extended commentary on the status of Jews at Christmas time and their quest to find relief from a Christmas-dominated holiday season' (2012: 81). The skits and songs frequently draw laughter from the frustration with 'being different and marginalized during the holiday season' (Plaut 2012: 82). There is also often criticism of the Jewish acceptance of Christmas commercialism to fit in. Comedian Scott Blakeman is known at Kung Pao Kosher Comedy for his biting humour: 'Did you ever notice that on television they say "We want to wish a Happy Chanukah to our Jewish friends" and a week later they say "Merry Christmas to all" and there are lots of Christmas sales but never a Chanukah sale? We bought enough merchandise to last one day and it's lasted eight days—it's a miracle' (Plaut 2012: 81). The stage, or often the community centre, allows for comedic commentaries that reframe Christmas with a Jewish context. Symbolic inversion occurs in these liminal spaces with Santa wearing a prayer shawl and having a counterpart of Hanukah Harry or Rudolph the reindeer becoming Reuben and sporting menorah lights. Plaut observes that Jews, in particular, 'whose minority status prevented them from embracing Christmas, developed humorous formats for reducing, if not redefining, its significance' (2012: 114). In the twenty-first century such parodic performances have migrated from the stage to social media, but still serve the function, as Turner has suggested, of using the betwixt-and-between frame to evaluate the meaning of a society's values.

The divide between actual settlements on the landscape and communities that are imagined or formed temporarily in social encounters bears out Jonathan Webber's point that Jewishness that is not circumscribed physically is often an 'illusion' created by participants and viewers to anticipate behaviour. Even if it is an 'illusion' or 'fleeting', the exchanges in social encounters are consequential for answering the question of what difference being Jewish implies for the impression of a person or of the community of which they are a part. In *Presentation of Self in Everyday Life* Goffman observes that 'Information about the individual helps to define the situation, enabling others to know in advance what he will expect of them and what they may expect of him. Informed in these ways, the others will know how best to act in order to call forth a desired response from him' (1959: 1). A number of contributors to this volume explore the attributes that expressing Jewishness or having Jewish identity ascribed to a person implies for expectations or perceptions of difference. Webber writes, for example, of blurred margins of social boundaries because there are people at the edge of any culture who have, or think they have, dual membership, dual citizenship, ties of all kinds with people on both sides of the boundary. Such people may nevertheless present themselves, perfectly reasonably, as authentic members of the culture, even if they in fact live on the brim—just as there are people whose active membership of a given culture may have lapsed, even for several generations, but who, for whatever reason, subsequently return to the group and similarly present themselves as fully authentic members, producers, and consumers of the culture. The other possibility in this re-examination of boundaries is that people who navigate frequently at the brim, whether identified as Jewish or non-Jewish, develop a hybridized 'border culture' that is an amalgamation of several identities (Kaplan 1997: 105–16; Paredes 2002; Weiner and Richards 2008: 112–15). At issue in the lively forum in Part IV of this volume, for example, is how Jewish Polish culture might be construed in the light of Polish 'allosemitism' (an ambivalent communication of both philo- and antisemitism) even in the absence of self-identified Jewish residents after the Holocaust (Bauman 1998). Another example of this collapse of borders is the contemporary cultural label in global media representations and in American stereotyping of the 'New Yorker', which implies Jewish sensibilities and cultural traits without differentiating them as such. Even the nineteenth-century Anglo-Jewish Historical Exhibition could be interpreted as an attempt to show that English culture indeed incorporates rather than excludes a Jewish 'ingredient', as the curators put it.

Whereas the question of Jewish difference within host societies was primarily stated in the twentieth century as a choice between ethnic isolation and integrated assimilation, this volume expands the twenty-first-century discourse on the social dynamics of Jewish identity. In this approach Jewish culture is not necessarily gained or lost but is used as a resource in the negotiation of identity. Contributors locate texts and contexts that reveal the variety of human agency in boundary work as part of everyday life. The volume begins with four essays dealing with the construction and maintenance of boundaries either by scholars who, in their classificatory acts, map divisions on an ethnic landscape or by participants on the ground who, in their spaces, question and adjust distinctions among neighbours. Of the first type, Jonathan Webber and Jonathan Boyarin examine scholarship through much of the twentieth century that laid the foundation for maintaining ethnic difference. Samuel Gruber and Marcin Wodziński round out the section with historical analyses of interaction between Jews and non-Jews in medieval Italy and intra-Jewish squabbles over the place of hasidism in eighteenth- and nineteenth-century Poland.

The second section focuses on the expressive means of conveying identity and memory. The first two essays, by Magdalena Luszczynska and Rella Kushelevsky, deal with different regions of Jewish settlement, but both analyse the significance of narrating the past to understanding the present in everyday life. Amy Milligan's study of hair covering is an ethnographic foray into a contemporary 'frontier' situation—as Gilman might conceptualize the construction of Jewish space in a small town—in which congregants with different levels of observance negotiate an Orthodox identity that can include the small group. Holly Pearse closes the section by interpreting the representation of interfaith romances in popular American movies.

Museum exhibition and festive performance are also linked as representations in the third part of this volume. Steve Siporin opens the section with an exploration of the distinctions between Jewish and Italian identities in the presentation of tourist narratives and spaces in Pitigliano, Italy. David Clark, in his chapter, understands exhibitions of Jewish presence in Italian museums as performances of identity. Sophie Wagenhofer complicates this enquiry further, examining the perceptions of curators and viewers of exhibitions in Morocco's only Jewish museum. Magdalena Waligórska unravels the paradoxes of Jewish heritage revival in Poland manifested through art, literature, and festival. Ruth Gruber picks up this thread in her thoughts raised by her participation in a memorial contest in Lvov, Poland. Gruber, who has gained notice for her label 'virtually Jewish' to describe the growing Jewish presence in eastern Europe without the conspicuous habitation of Jews, presents factors for the phenomenon and its impact on Jews as well as non-Jews in eastern Europe. Others in the forum look for cognate situations in which Jewish culture is symbolized and framed in often surprising ways. Francesco Spagnolo interprets Jewish responses to Jewish cultural revival across Europe, while Annamaria Orla-Bukowska takes the perspective of Poles in the allosemitic embrace of Jewish culture. Erica Lehrer, who has studied some of the same turf in Poland, offers an alternative view to Gruber's labels and interpretations.

Overall, the present volume expands the study of Jewish identity to the physical and rhetorical processes of framing culture that establish often dynamic, if not paradoxical, social relations among Jews and their various publics. Such processes typically include actions of boundary construction and maintenance between groups, representing and symbolizing meaning in cultural expression, and exhibiting artefacts and behaviour in an institutional as well as a social context. Scholars in this volume uncover historical, psychological, and ethnographic aspects of this process to find explanations for the various cultural manifestations of being Jewish. In so doing, they open dialogue on the strategic act and art of framing Jewish culture.

Notes

1   Renowned ethnographer Gary Alan Fine, who has a Jewish background, recalled that Goffman emphatically told him with a Jewish inflection when he proposed to study a Jewish wedding that 'anyone who studies their own family is a schmuck'. He told this anecdote as part of his delivery of the Francis Lee Utley Memorial Lecture, 'The Folklore of Small Things: Tiny Publics and Realms of Local Knowledge', at the American Folklore Society annual meeting, October 2010.

2   Most of these figures were participants in the path-breaking volumes *Toward New Perspectives in Folklore* (Paredes and Bauman 1972) and *Folklore: Performance and Communication* (Ben-Amos and Goldstein 1975), advocating a social-interactional approach to culture. Of these figures, Alan Dundes, Barbara Kirshenblatt-Gimblett, and Elliott Oring have been the most involved in applying attention to Jewish 'frames', although Roger Abrahams, known primarily for studies of the African American experience (another outsider group) contributed the lead essay on the definition of ethnicity from a Jewish perspective to *Studies in Jewish Folklore* (Talmage 1980), and Richard Bauman wrote on his grandmother's rendering of Yiddish folk song in 'Y. L. Cahan's Instructions on the Collecting of Folklore' (1962).

3   *Faith on the Move: The Religious Affiliation of International Migrants* (Philadelphia, 2012). <http://features.pewforum.org/religious-migration/Faithonthemove.pdf>.

4   See 'Call for Papers: 2012 Biennial Scholars' Conference on American Jewish History'. H-Judaic Discussion Log, 9 Sept. 2011. <http://www.h-ne.org/~judaic>.

5   Gilman cites Bhabha's *The Location of Culture* (1994), 224, as the source of his quotation. Bhabha's challenge of boundaries is apparent in his post-colonial ideas on hybridization and the emergence of new cultural forms from multiculturalism. See Bhabha 2006; Huddart 2006.

References

ABRAHAMS, ROGER D. 1980. 'Folklore in the Definition of Ethnicity: An American and Jewish Perspective'. In Frank Talmage, ed., *Studies in Jewish Folklore*, 13–20. Cambridge, Mass.

—— 2005. *Everyday Life: A Poetics of Vernacular Practices*. Philadelphia.

ADLER, CYRUS. 1906. 'Sir Isidore Spielmann'. In Cyrus Adler, ed., *Jewish Encyclopedia*, xi. 509–10. New York.

BAKER, LEE D. 2004. 'Franz Boas Out of the Ivory Tower'. *Anthropological Theory* 4: 29–51.

BARTH, FREDRIK. 1998. *Ethnic Groups and Boundaries: The Social Organization of Culture Difference*. Long Grove, Ill.

BATESON, GREGORY. 1956. 'The Message "This is Play"'. In Bertram Schaffner, ed., *Group Processes: Transactions of the Second Conference*, 145–242. New York.

—— 2000. *Steps to an Ecology of Mind*. Chicago.

—— and MARGARET MEAD. 1942. *Balinese Character: A Photographic Analysis*. New York.

BAUMAN, RICHARD. 1962. 'Y.L. Cahan's Instructions on the Collecting of Folklore'. *New York Folklore Quarterly*, 18: 284–9.

BAUMAN, ZYGMUNT. 1998. 'Allosemitism: Premodern, Modern, Postmodern'. In Bryan Cheyette and Laura Marcus, eds., *Modernity, Culture and 'the Jew'*, 143–56. Stanford, Calif.

BEN-AMOS, DAN, and KENNETH S. GOLDSTEIN, eds. 1975. *Folklore: Performance and Communication*. The Hague.

BEN RAFAEL, ELIEZER. 2003. *Contemporary Jewries: Convergence and Divergence*. Leiden, The Netherlands.

BHABHA, HOMI K. 1994. *The Location of Culture*. London.

—— 2006. 'Another Country'. In Fereshteh Daftari, *Without Boundary: Seventeen Ways of Looking*, 30–5. New York.

BIALE, DAVID, MICHAEL GALCHINSKY, and SUSANNAH HESCHEL, eds. 1998. *Insider/Outsider: American Jews and Multiculturalism*. Berkeley, Calif.

BLUMER, HERBERT. 2004. *George Herbert Mead and Human Conduct*, ed. Thomas J. Morrione. Walnut Creek, Calif.

BOUSTAN, RA'ANAN, OREN KOSANSKY, and MARINA RUSTOW, eds. 2011. *Jewish Studies at the Crossroads of Anthropology and History: Authority, Diaspora, Tradition*. Philadelphia.

BOYARIN, JONATHAN, and DANIEL BOYARIN, eds. 1997. *Jews and Other Differences: The New Cultural Studies*. Minneapolis.

BRAUCH, JULIA, ANNA LIPPHARDT, and ALEXANDRA NOCKE, eds. 2008. *Jewish Topographies: Visions of Space, Traditions of Place*. Aldershot.

BRONNER, SIMON J. 1998. *Following Tradition: Folklore in the Discourse of American Culture*. Logan, Utah.

—— 2008. 'The Chutzpah of Jewish Cultural Studies'. In Simon J. Bronner, ed., *Jewishness: Expression, Identity, and Representation*, 1–26. Oxford.

—— 2010. 'Framing Folklore: An Introduction'. *Western Folklore*, 69: 5–27.

—— 2012. 'Jewish Naming Ceremonies for Girls: A Study in the Discourse of Tradition'. In Nathaniel Riemer, ed., *Jewish Lifeworlds and Jewish Thought*, 211–20. Wiesbaden.

BURMAN, RICKIE, JENNIFER MARIN, and LILY STEADMAN. 2006. *Treasures of Jewish Heritage: The Jewish Museum London*. London.

BURNS, TOM. 1992. *Erving Goffman*. New York.

BUSH, ANDREW. 2011. *Jewish Studies: A Theoretical Introduction*. New Brunswick, NJ.

COHEN, MAX. 1888. 'Maimonides' Library'. *Menorah*, 4: 293–7.

COHEN, SHAUL. 2006. 'Israel's West Bank Barrier: An Impediment to Peace?' *Geographical Review*, 96: 682–95.

COHEN, SHAYE J. D. 1999. *The Beginnings of Jewishness: Boundaries, Varieties, Uncertainties*. Berkeley, Calif.

—— 2005. *Why Aren't Jewish Women Circumcised? Gender and Covenant in Judaism*. Berkeley, Calif.

CUDDIHY, JOHN MURRAY. 1974. *The Ordeal of Civility: Freud, Marx, Lévi-Strauss and the Jewish Struggle with Modernity*. New York.

DEFLEM, MATHIEU. 1991. 'Ritual, Anti-Structure, and Religion: A Discussion of Victor Turner's Processual Symbolic Analysis'. *Journal for the Scientific Study of Religion*, 30: 1–25.

DINER, HASIA. 1977. *In the Almost Promised Land: American Jews and Blacks, 1915–1935*. Westport, Conn.

DOUGLAS, MARY. 1966. *Purity and Danger: An Analysis of Concepts of Pollution and Taboo*. London.

DU BOIS, W. E. B. 2008 [1903]. *The Souls of Black Folk*. Rockville, Md.

DUNCAN, HUGH DALZIEL. 2002. *Communication and Social Order*. New Brunswick, NJ.

DUNDES, ALAN. 2002. *The Shabbat Elevator and Other Sabbath Subterfuges*. Lanham, Md.

FABRE-VASSAS, CLAUDINE. 1997. *The Singular Beast: Jews, Christians, and the Pig*, trans. Carol Volk. New York.

FERNANDEZ, RONALD. 2003. *Mappers of Society: The Lives, Times, and Legacies of Great Sociologists*. Westport, Conn.

FINE, GARY ALAN. 1983. *Shared Fantasy: Role-Playing Games as Social Worlds*. Chicago.

FINK, CAROLE. 2010. 'Jews in Contemporary Europe'. In Roland Hsu, ed., *Ethnic Europe: Mobility, Identity, and Conflict in a Globalized World*, 212–40. Stanford, Calif.

FRANK, GELYA. 1997. 'Jews, Multiculturalism, and Boasian Anthropology'. *American Anthropologist*, 99: 731–45.

FRISHMAN, JUDITH, and IDO DE HAAN. 2011. Introduction. In Judith Frishman, David J. Wertheim, Ido de Haan, and Joël J. Cahen, eds., *Borders and Boundaries in and around Dutch Jewish History*, 7–18. Amsterdam.

GANS, HERBERT. 1957. 'Progress of a Suburban Jewish Community'. *Commentary*, February, 120–5.

—— 1962. *The Urban Villagers: Group and Class in the Life of Italian-Americans*. New York.

—— 1996. 'Symbolic Ethnicity: The Future of Ethnic Groups and Cultures in America'. In Werner Sollors, ed., *Theories of Ethnicity: A Classical Reader*, 429–59. New York.

GILMAN, SANDER. 1991. *The Jew's Body*. New York.

—— 2003. *Jewish Frontiers: Essays on Bodies, Histories, and Identities*. New York.

—— and MILTON SHAIN, eds. 1999. *Jewries at the Frontier*. Urbana, Ill.

GITELMAN, ZVI. 1998. 'The Decline of the Diaspora Jewish Nation: Boundaries, Content, and Jewish Identity', *Jewish Social Studies*. NS, 4: 112–32.

GLENN, SUSAN A., and NAOMI B. SOKOLOFF. 2010. 'Introduction: Who and What is Jewish?' In Susan A. Glenn and Naomi B. Sokoloff, eds., *Boundaries of Jewish Identity*, 3–11. Seattle.

GLICK, LEONARD. 1982. 'Types Distinct from Our Own: Franz Boas on Jewish Identity and Assimilation'. *American Anthropologist*, 84: 545–65.

—— 2005. *Marked in Your Flesh: Circumcision from Ancient Judea to Modern America*. Oxford.

GOFFMAN, ERVING. 1959. *The Presentation of Self in Everyday Life*. New York.

—— 1963. *Stigma: Notes on the Management of Spoiled Identity*. New York.

—— 1974. *Frame Analysis: An Essay on the Organization of Experience*. New York.

GOLDSTEIN, ERIC. L. 2006. *The Price of Whiteness: Jews, Race, and American Identity*. Princeton, NJ.

GOLDSTEIN, SIDNEY, and ALICE GOLDSTEIN. 1996. *Jews on the Move: Implications for Jewish Identity*. Albany, NY.

GRUBER, RUTH ELLEN. 2002. *Virtually Jewish: Reinventing Jewish Culture in Europe*. Berkeley, Calif.

HEILMAN, SAMUEL. 1992. *Defenders of the Faith: Inside Ultra-Orthodox Jewry*. New York.

—— 2006. *Sliding to the Right: The Contest for the Future of American Jewish Orthodoxy*. Berkeley, Calif.

HUDDART, DAVID. 2006. *Homi K. Bhabha*. New York.

JACOBS, JOSEPH, and LUCIEN WOLF. 1887. *Catalogue of the Anglo-Jewish Historical Exhibition, 1887*. London.

JOHNSON, DAVID E., and SCOTT MICHAELSON. 1997. 'Border Secrets: An Intro-duction'. In David E. Johnson and Scott Michaelsen, eds., *Border Theory: The Limits of Cultural Politics*, 1–42. Minneapolis.

KAPLAN, LOUIS. 1997. 'On the Border with *The Pilgrim*: Zigzags across a Chapl(a)in's Signature'. In David E. Johnson and Scott Michaelson, eds., *Border Theory: The Limits of Cultural Politics*, 97–128. Minneapolis.

KIM, KWANG-KI. 2002. *Order and Agency in Modernity: Talcott Parsons, Erving Goffman, and Harold Garfinkel*. Albany, NY.

KIRSHENBLATT-GIMBLETT, BARBARA. 1998. *Destination Culture: Tourism, Museums, and Heritage*. Berkeley, Calif.

LANDAU, DAVID. 1993. *Piety and Power: The World of Jewish Fundamentalism*. New York.

LEVINE, EPHRAIM. 1924–7. 'Sir Isidore Spielmann, 1854–1925'. *Transactions of the Jewish Historical Society of England*, 11: 233–7.

LI, MU. 2011. 'Jewish Activities on Christmas: An Online Case Study'. *Voices: The Journal of New York Folklore* 37(3–4): 27–33.

LIEBMAN, CHARLES S., and STEVEN M. COHEN. 1990. *The Two Worlds of Judaism: The Israeli and American Experiences*. New Haven, Conn.

LIPPHARDT, ANNA, JULIA BRAUCH, and ALEXANDRA NOCKE. 2008. 'Exploring Jewish Space: An Approach'. In Julia Brauch, Anna Lipphardt, and Alexandra Nocke, eds., *Jewish Topographies: Visions of Space, Traditions of Place*, 1–26. Aldershot.

MEAD, GEORGE HERBERT. 1967. *Mind, Self, Society from the Standpoint of a Social Behaviorist*, ed. Charles W. Morris. Chicago.

MECHLING, JAY. 1980. 'The Magic of the Boy Scout Campfire'. *Journal of American Folklore*, 93: 35–56.

—— 1991. '*Homo Narrans* Across the Disciplines'. *Western Folklore*, 50: 41–51.

—— 2004. 'Picturing Hunting'. *Western Folklore*, 63: 51–78.

—— 2009. 'Is Hazing Play?' In Cindy Dell Clark, ed., *Transactions at Play*, Play & Culture Studies 9, 45–62. Lanham, Md.

MESSER, ELLEN. 1986. 'Franz Boas and Kaufmann Kohler: Anthropology and Reform Judaism'. *Jewish Social Studies*, 2: 127–40.

MINTZ, JEROME R. 1992. *Hasidic People: A Place in the New World*. Cambridge, Mass.

MOCATTA, F. D. 1887. 'Report to the Members of the General Committee of the Anglo-Jewish Historical Exhibition'. In *Papers Read at the Anglo-Jewish Historical Exhibition, Royal Albert Hall, London, 1887*, 289–300. London.

MORRIS-REICH, AMOS. 2008. *The Quest for Jewish Assimilation in Modern Social Science*. New York.

MUSOLF, GIL RICHARD. 2003. *Structure and Agency in Everyday Life: An Introduction to Social Psychology*. Lanham, Md.

NATHAN, JOAN. 1994. *Jewish Cooking in America*. New York.

—— 2001. *The Foods of Israel Today*. New York.

—— 2004. *Joan Nathan's Jewish Holiday Cookbook*. New York.

PACKARD, VANCE. 1972. *A Nation of Strangers*. New York.

PAREDES, AMÉRICO. 2002. 'Border Identity: Culture, Conflict, and Convergence along the Lower Rio Grande'. In Simon J. Bronner, ed., *Folk Nation: Folklore in the Creation of American Tradition*, 199–214. Wilmington, Del.

—— and RICHARD BAUMAN, eds. 1972. *Toward New Perspectives in Folklore*. Austin, Tex.

PATAI, RAPHAEL, and JENNIFER PATAI. 1989. *The Myth of the Jewish Race*. Detroit.

PINTO, DIANA. 2006. 'The Jewish Space in Europe'. In Sandra Lustig and Ian Leveson, eds., *Turning the Kaleidoscope: Perspectives on European Jewry*, 179–86. Oxford.

PLAUT, JOSHUA ELI. 2012. *A Kosher Christmas: 'Tis the Season to Be Jewish*. New Brunswick, NJ.

PRELL, RIV-ELLEN. 1989. *Prayer and Community: The Havurah in American Judaism*. Detroit.

RASPA, DICK. 1991. 'A Short History of Giglio's: Occupational Role as Play Frames'. *Western Folklore*, 50: 201–8.

ROSE, EVELYN. 1992. *The Complete International Jewish Cookbook*. New York.

SARNA, NAHUM M. 1996. *Exploring Exodus: The Origins of Biblical Israel*. New York.

SAVILLE-TROIKE, MURIEL. 2003. *The Ethnography of Communication: An Introduction*, 3rd edn. Malden, Mass.

SCHEFF, THOMAS J. 2006. *Goffman Unbound: A New Paradigm for Social Science*. Boulder, Colo.

SENNETT, RICHARD. 1977. *The Fall of Public Man*. New York.

SHALIN, DMITRI. 2009. 'Saul Mendlovitz: Erving Was a Jew Acting Like a Canadian

Acting Like a Britisher'. *Remembering Erving Goffman* website. <http://cdclv.unlv.edu//archives/interactionism/goffman/mendlovitz_08.html>, accessed 24 Jan. 2013.

SHERZER, JOEL. 1993. 'On Puns, Comebacks, Verbal Dueling, and Play Languages: Speech Play in Balinese Verbal Life'. *Language in Society*, 22: 217–33.

SILVERMAN, ERIC KLINE. 2006. *From Abraham to America: A History of Jewish Circumcision*. Lanham, Md.

SKLARE, MARSHALL. 1993. *Observing America's Jews*. Hanover, NH.

—— and JOSEPH GREENBLUM. 1979. *Jewish Identity on the Suburban Frontier: A Study of Group Survival in the Open Society*, 2nd edn. Chicago.

SOLLORS, WERNER. 1996. 'Theories of American Ethnicity'. In Werner Sollors, ed., *Theories of Ethnicity: A Classical Reader*, pp. x–xliv. New York.

SPIELMANN, ISIDORE. 1902–5. 'South African War Memorial: Unveiling at the Central Synagogue'. *Transactions of the Jewish Historical Society of England*, 5: 58.

SZTOKMAN, ELANA MARYLES. 2011. *The Men's Section: Orthodox Jewish Men in an Egalitarian World*. Waltham, Mass.

TURNER, VICTOR W. 1977. 'Process, System, and Symbol: A New Anthropological Synthesis'. *Daedalus*, 106: 61–80.

—— 1979. 'Frame, Flow and Reflection: Ritual and Drama as Public Liminality'. *Japanese Journal of Religious Studies*, 6: 465–99.

—— 1995. *The Ritual Process: Structure and Anti-Structure*. New York.

UVEZIAN, SONIA. 1999. *Recipes and Remembrances from an Eastern Mediterranean Kitchen: A Culinary Journey through Syria, Lebanon, and Jordan*. Austin, Tex.

WASKOW, ARTHUR O., and PHYLLIS O. BERMAN. 2011. *Freedom Journeys: The Tale of Exodus and Wilderness Across Millennia*. Woodstock, Vt.

WEINER, MELISSA F., and BEDELIA NICOLA RICHARDS. 2008. 'Bridging the Theoretical Gap: The Diasporized Hybrid in Sociological Theory'. In Keri E. Iyall Smith and Patricia Leavy, eds., *Hybrid Identities: Theoretical and Empirical Examinations*, 101–16. Leiden.

WOLF, LUCIEN. 1911–14. 'Origin of the Jewish Historical Society of England', *Transactions of the Jewish Historical Society of England*, 7: 206–15.

YDIT, MEIR. 1972. 'Mehizah'. *Encyclopedia Judaica*, xi. 1234–5. Jerusalem.

ZELINSKY, WILBUR. 2001. *The Enigma of Ethnicity: Another American Dilemma*. Iowa City.

PART I

Boundary Construction and Maintenance

Representing Jewish Culture: The Problem of Boundaries

J O N A T H A N W E B B E R

Introduction: Some Basic Paradigms

In attempting to make a contribution to Jewish cultural studies, it has to be said at the beginning that the word 'culture' is very difficult to work with.[1] What do we mean by this word? In the classic anthropological definition it refers to something abstract, namely, the totality of the social heritage or socially acquired lifestyle of a group of people—in other words, a rather complex whole which includes all the knowledge, beliefs, art, law, morals, and customs residing among a particular group of people. Culture in this sense is like the grammar of a language: everyone possesses it in their head but would find it difficult to specify comprehensively and in detail just what it actually consists of. Outside the field of anthropology, however, the notion of culture was originally not used to refer to an entire society but rather to a superior class—it came to have a strongly elitist meaning, referring to supposedly 'advanced' Western societies and their 'cultured' classes who believed they possessed refined manners, a civilized sense of taste, and a wide range of learning. But in recent years this elitist tradition has been almost completely reversed, and 'culture' seems, at least in the public mind, to have gone back to its original anthropological meaning, referring to any cluster of common ideas, emotions, and practices of any group of people who regularly interact. Thus we speak today of 'immigrant culture', for example, or 'women's culture' or 'business culture'—in short, the word 'culture' seems to mark the attribution or celebration of significant difference, not only for its own sake but often with reference to important public concerns such as ethnicity, social change, or political issues. The problem is that the actual content and scope of these different cultures or subcultures is not really as comprehensive, detailed, or predictable as in the original meaning of the word. It can be used in a narrow and elitist sense, if it refers to a group or class of people who are learned and refined; or alternatively it can even refer to a state of mind, a form of consciousness, covering a wide group of people, such as that which underpins the outlook and identity of an entire ethnic group.

So what is Jewish culture? The short answer, it seems to me, is that the concept of Jewish culture ranges across all these things—a comprehensive coverage of religion, law, art, folklore, music, dance, food, dress, language, cinema, theatre, and many other things besides. It also could refer to a selection, perhaps an arbitrary selection, of just some of these things, and thereby provide scope for identity formation or identity attachments for Jews seeking to express themselves as Jews but who, for whatever reason, may not desire the full range. This might be particularly true of non-Jews who wish to partake of Jewish culture, or who have a stereotype of it, but for their own reasons do not desire a total immersion in it. The point is that it is possible to enjoy Jewish culture, either from the inside or from the outside, without feeling the need to know it all, but on the other hand to be perfectly tolerant of other people with other special interests as being equally valid participants, members, or consumers. So if the concept of Jewish culture possesses such a wide range of meanings and applications, the consequence is that the *representation* of Jewish culture—whether, for example, in books, films, theatre, or in museums or the works of scholars—is similarly open to very wide interpretation.

The purpose of this essay is to draw attention to one rather fundamental aspect of all this, namely what I am calling the problem of boundaries. What kinds of boundaries are there that define Jewish culture? It is a very elaborate subject, ideally requiring detailed attention to all the constituent components of culture that I have mentioned. What I wish to do here, beyond suggesting some basic paradigms, is to focus on the relationship between establishment Judaism and everyday Jewish life, and in subsequent sections of this essay to present several extended case studies in order to address various angles of the problem.

Perhaps the best way to open up a discussion of the complexity of this subject is to suggest the existence of two extreme positions, at opposite ends of a spectrum. At one end, it can be argued that there may be boundaries, but that they are not watertight. The edges are blurred—for example, there are people on the periphery of any culture who have, or think they have, dual membership, dual citizenship, ties of all kinds with people on both sides of the boundary. Such people may nevertheless present themselves, perfectly reasonably, as authentic members of the culture, even if they in fact live on the margin—just as there are people whose active membership of a given culture may have lapsed, even for several generations, but who for whatever reason subsequently 'return' to the group and similarly present themselves as fully authentic members, producers, and consumers of the culture. So both these two cases suggest (at this one end of the spectrum) that the existence of the boundary is in some important sense an illusion. It can be crossed, and very often is crossed, without any obvious harm to the integrity of the culture. The other curious thing about any culture, and indeed any language, is that it is constantly changing, often even from one generation to the next, and without its members even being aware of the changes—or, if they are aware, not necessarily feeling that their culture has in some real sense been damaged. On the contrary, change is seen as natural and organic—I would have great difficulty understanding the English spoken in London 500 or 600 years ago, but we still call that language 'English', just because of the organic continuities that connect present-day Londoners with those Londoners so many centuries ago. All culture, and all social identities—certainly including Jewish culture and Jewish identities—are similarly fluid, and susceptible—indeed often hospitable—to outside influences, and thus not fixed.

But on the other hand, all that is only part of the picture. The extreme position at the other end of the spectrum is the common belief held by many people that there are tight, indeed watertight, boundaries around their culture and tradition —that the existence of a boundary is perfectly real, and not at all an illusion. Even if the English language borrows loanwords from French, we still think of our language as English. This attitude to boundaries is also particularly clear in the Jewish tradition. Jews have historically defined themselves as a people biologically and spiritually descended from a common ancestor (the biblical patriarch Abraham), even if converts from other biological and spiritual origins are accepted. What has characterized Jewish law is precisely its assertion of preserving the distinctiveness, chosenness, and otherness that separate the Jewish culture from other cultures (for the *locus classicus* in the Torah, see Num. 23: 9, which refers to 'a nation that dwells in solitude, not reckoned among the nations').

A few details may be helpful to clarify this latter point. The way the notion of otherness is followed through in the Torah is at least twofold: (*a*) by emphasizing the essentialist character of boundaries as a cosmic principle reflecting an order and structure that are understood to govern the very nature of the world itself. Hence, for example, whereas the universe had begun as a disordered chaos (*tohu vavohu*) dominated by darkness (Gen. 1: 2), the creation narrative in the first chapter of Genesis describes light as something 'divided' from darkness (verse 4), rainwater as 'divided' from rivers and seas (verse 6), the division between day and night (verse 14), or the seventh day of rest as 'sacred', something totally different from the other days of the week (2: 1–3). If the nature of the world is predicated in this way on the existence of an ordered reality resting on such divisions and boundaries, then (*b*) when the Torah gets to specify the nature of an enclosed Jewish religion and culture, what one can find in the text is (once again) the assertion of a cosmic dividing line surrounding the Jewish people—hence, for example, the dietary laws, which 'divide' animals and their meat into food that is permitted and food that is forbidden (Lev. 11: 47), thereby making it possible for the people to be 'holy' (set apart from others), 'because I [says God] divided you off [or 'set you apart'] from other peoples' (Lev. 20: 26). No other explanation is given for those dietary laws: boundary-making is treated as self-evident, a central feature of the nature of reality. As for other cultures and religions, they belong to an outside world that is fundamentally dangerous, characterized collectively as *avodah zarah* ('foreign' or 'strange' worship). *Avodah zarah* was seen as a denial and rejection of the one God who created the world and continues to sustain it. The principal referent of *avodah zarah* for the Torah was both polytheism (worship of more than one god) and idol worship: idols are not gods at all, they are false gods, and the religions they represent are false religions (for a concise statement see Deut. 4: 15–20). Yes, the Torah does mention that during the departure from Egypt—the foundational event when the Israelites became a people—there was an *erev rav*, a group of riff-raff from other social origins that somehow attached themselves (Exod. 12: 38); and in fact this riff-raff was in some interpretations blamed for some of the troubles the Israelites experienced later on in their history.[2] But the awareness of the presence of non-Israelite riff-raff serves only to confirm the general point that Hebrew life, and the later Jewish tradition, were in principle understood to be fully coherent, stable, and well fashioned. In post-biblical Jewish culture, as elaborated in the Talmud and its commentaries, the job of the rabbis, as they saw it, was indeed to erect a boundary surrounding the Jewish people and its traditions—the principle of *seyag latorah* (a fence around the Torah), mentioned, for example, in *Avot* (Ethics of the Fathers) 1: 1. The purpose of such a boundary (as with the erection of any physical boundary) was to assert ownership and prevent free access from the outside. In this context (exile and diaspora following the destruction of Jewish sovereignty in the Land of Israel in the first century CE) it was intended by the rabbis to legitimate their exclusive authority to interpret the Torah and, thereby, to govern the people, including the right to amplify the laws of the Torah by introducing additional rules and regulations. Among such new rules of this protective 'fence around the Torah' were provisions for consolidating the boundaries around the Jewish people itself—in particular, resisting alien influences—known in general terms as *ḥukot hagoy*, that might corrupt it (Lev. 18: 3). Maybe some such influences did manage to creep in (folk superstitions, for example), but so what? The important thing was to protect the integrity of the group by preserving its boundaries, by basing Jewish identity on a belief in the importance of the differences that (at least notionally) separate Jews from other groups—or at the very least on the sense of the existence and importance of boundaries. As the Norwegian anthropologist Fredrik Barth famously remarked forty years ago, although in quite a different context, it is the ethnic boundary that defines the group, not the cultural stuff it encloses (Barth 1969: 15).

So there is a problem with the concept of boundaries: are they important or not? The short answer is that both things are true. Jewish culture contains both of these extreme positions, which are obviously in tension with each other and permitting considerable scope for intermediate positions. At any rate, there is a strong case for considering the importance of boundaries and boundary-making in the history of Jewish culture, and this is the subject of the present essay. Efforts at boundary-making, successful or unsuccessful, partial or thoroughgoing, contested or uncontested, can be found everywhere, on a very large range of topics. A comprehensive review is well beyond the scope of this essay, and so I shall limit myself here merely to some illustrative examples of their use and functioning.

For example, it is very likely that the Jewish rule to separate meat foods from dairy foods, which is only very briefly mentioned three times in the text of the Torah (e.g. at Exod. 23: 19, instructing simply 'not to boil a kid [i.e. a young goat] in its mother's milk') but given no further details or explanation, derived from a desire to avoid a culinary practice which was common among the idolatrous ancient Canaanites[3]—even if the Torah did accept the practice of animal sacrifices, which was also common among the surrounding pagan societies of the time (Eilberg-Schwartz 1990: 46). The boundary, in other words, was thus not total, and perhaps could not be. Strictly Orthodox Jews today, to take an example from our own times, tend to stress visible boundaries that mark a conspicuous Jewish distinctiveness through their use of specific forms of dress, head covering, and hair styles. They do so precisely so as to confirm their sense of Jewish apartness and special mission, alongside the sense of sanctity and spiritual otherness induced by a strict sexual ethic and ritual duties such as the observance of the dietary laws and of the weekly sabbath—which incidentally is concluded by a 'division' ceremony (Havdalah) that liturgically restates the cosmic boundary separating the sacred and the profane, in this case the onset of the working week.[4] Non-Orthodox Jews find other ways to assert their Jewish identities (as will be discussed later on), but a strong and thoroughgoing reliance on boundary-making—distinguishing Jews from the rest of the world and closely following the emphasis on boundaries found in the Torah—is crucial to the world-view of the strictly Orthodox Jewish tradition (now generally called haredi, today adhered to by a substantial, growing, and increasingly visible minority of the world Jewish population).[5] Other nations and peoples, in the haredi view, are characterized precisely in terms of their lack of any comparable divine purpose or mission: Jews and non-Jews are seen simply as two opposites, analogous to the distinction between the sacred and the profane, which (in this view) cannot, by definition, coexist. Modern Jews (even modern Orthodox Jews) with a university education would position the boundary differently, acknowledging Jewish ideas about the sacred as being embedded in their ordinary daily (profane) life. But in the haredi world secular profane knowledge has to be kept out, or at least cannot normally be combined with the study of the Torah (Heilman 1992: 19). In the traditional haredi educational system, especially that of the yeshiva (Talmud seminary), of course the students need at the very least to learn arithmetic, or how to read and write the national language of the country where they live, but (also because of the fear of modernism) there has historically been strong opposition to including such subjects into the curriculum, although—once again—the boundary is not total, and compromises were eventually introduced (on the attitude to this issue of the leaders of Volozhin and the other great Lithuanian yeshivas of the nineteenth century, see Stampfer 2012, esp. 164–5, 199–209). Traditional rabbinic theology largely preached a distinctly oppositional, antagonistic Judaism, even (in the eyes of some) a bigoted, supremacist Judaism. To put the point more mildly, Jewish theology is understood in the tradition as a private Jewish matter concerning the relationship between the Jewish people and the God of Israel, in which other religions and other societies cannot, by definition, intrude or have a say. The boundary, in other words, is very clear: the sabbath, for example, is private Jewish testimony to this relationship (thus Exod. 31: 17), and non-Jews are simply not allowed in to sabbath observance (BT *San.* 58*b*).[6]

The creation and maintenance of boundaries should also, by definition, be seen as a two-way process: they can be imposed and regulated from the outside, not merely from the inside. For many Jews today, especially those who are acculturated into wider society, this is a central issue. The non-Jewish world has repeatedly demonstrated its willingness and its capacity to mark out Jews for sinister purposes, unequivocally identifying them as a defined target of discrimination and violence. As is well known, there is a long history to this; and there are long Jewish memories of ghettoization, persecution, forced conversions, inquisitions, pogroms, martyrdom, the antisemitic labelling of the Jews as a distinct race, and of course the Holocaust. Nowadays the constantly invoked refrain of a resurgent antisemitism, suggesting indeed a genuine fear of the potential of the other to demonize the Jews and stage violence against them, seems to be a clear strategy of Jewish leaders used in order to mobilize Jewish loyalties and increase their Jewish self-awareness. In other words, even if the great majority of present-day diaspora Jews do not share the insider attitudes to otherness as specified in the Torah, they are told they essentially cannot hide; they are definable from the outside as Jews, and antisemitism will catch up with them sooner or later. Seen in that perspective, the boundary separating Jews from non-Jews is clear, particularly of course during the Holocaust. But the boundary was not total even then: there were marginal cases, such as Jews who had converted to Christianity before the war. They had, in effect, become outsiders, and were viewed with hostility by most Jews; but they were nevertheless regarded as Jews by the Nazis. In Warsaw they were incarcerated in the ghetto, where there were in fact two active churches (Paulsson 2002: 31–2).

Boundary-making is also in wide use *within* the Jewish world, whether with reference to sub-communities relating to clusters of diasporic traditions deriving from purported geographical origins—such as the Ashkenazim (notionally from Germany) or Sephardim (notionally from Spain), and indeed those groups may also be subdivided, such as the common distinction in the nineteenth century between Litvaks (Ashkenazim from Lithuania) and Galitzianers (Ashkenazim from Austrian Galicia)—or with reference to institutional denominations, such as Reconstructionist, Reform, Conservative, Orthodox, and haredi. All these boundaries may be reinforced by an array of folk stereotypes offering attributed characteristics to members of the group (often to make fun of one another, and hence to supply material for popular Jewish jokes),[7] with the result that crossing boundaries can be difficult. Border-crossing between the denominations can sometimes be a daunting task, highly charged with emotion and rhetorical language, and even simply rendered impossible, as for instance the routine refusal of Orthodox authorities to recognize conversions to Judaism undertaken by non-Orthodox rabbis, or the common stereotyping of Orthodox Jews by non-Orthodox Jews as insular, self-obsessed, and preoccupied with small legal technicalities. Probably the single most important (and divisive) issue in the modern Jewish world is that of gender equality, first introduced as a matter of ideological principle by Reform Judaism about 200 years ago. Its near-total absence (that is, despite some marginal exceptions and compromises) firmly characterizes the boundary around Orthodox Judaism, much to the dismay of modernists fully accustomed in their daily lives to an egalitarian ethic.

Boundaries in general are of course a universal feature of human society—imposing order, eliminating or at least minimizing ambiguity, or offering rigid signposts that enable people to structure their experience of the social world according to a seemingly limitless range of possible criteria, which are, furthermore, constantly changing. As a transnational society, Jews have a wealth of possibilities and cultural experiences to choose from in shaping and reshaping such signposting. After the establishment of the State of Israel in 1948, of course there developed a new boundary between Israeli and diaspora Jews, once again maintained through folk stereotypes (in addition to formal issues of citizenship). That boundary can be traversed, although not entirely without difficulty—it is not clear whether culturally or sociologically the large numbers of Israeli Jews who have left Israel in order to live in London or New York have thereby become diaspora Jews in any meaningful sense,[8] or for that matter how long it takes diaspora Jews who have gone on *aliyah* to become Israeli in cultural terms and to be accepted as such (on which see e.g. Tabory and Lazerwitz 1995). But once again the negative stereotyping reinforces the boundary: the common Israeli reference to the *golah* (diaspora) mentality, alongside other negative perceptions of diaspora Jewish history and culture, suggest the continuing entrenchment of a substantive boundary that characterizes ordinary Israeli Jewish thinking on the subject.

Boundary-Making in Jewish Culture and Society: Prescriptive Rules versus Everyday Realities

But the most interesting boundary of all, to which the rest of this essay is dedicated, is the more abstract one between religion and culture. It is a complex subject at many levels, lying as it does at the heart of the whole problem of the representation of Jewish culture. To illustrate this I shall be taking up some more extended examples, beginning with some general points here and then elaborating on three specific issues in the following sections of this essay—Jewish secularism, Jewish self-definitions in the context of attitudes to other faiths, and, lastly, the shifting boundaries of Jewish community life.

The key question to start the discussion is whether the cultural history of the Jewish people is to be defined theologically, that is, in terms of its supposedly eternal, totally changeless spiritual mission, or whether, on the contrary, it is to be understood as a succession of constantly changing cultural adaptations as the Jews continually renegotiated their sense of distinctiveness in the context of the different languages and cultures of their diasporic environments over the past two thousand years. Is Jewish identity something fixed and permanent, or should we rather emphasize its composite, malleable nature and its ability to constantly reinvigorate itself by changing as the cultural context changes? It is not at all an easy question to answer because in truth it is not a fair choice on a level playing field. Until quite recently, Jews knew far more about the theology than they did about the social and cultural history. Jewish religious practice is still routinely described in normative terms, not at all in terms of what an anthropologist would call the actual ethnography. For example, consider the sentence 'On Passover, Jews eat matzah.' It is the sort of sentence one is likely to hear nowadays at an interfaith gathering, or in the lectures of schoolteachers when describing Jewish religious practice. Note the use of the timeless present tense, 'Jews eat', which comes straight out of the rabbinical law books. The point is that there is no tradition of an ethnographic discourse that would distinguish between 'what Jews eat on Passover' and what Jews *actually* eat on Passover. Even though of course one could say that 'practising Jews eat matzah on Passover', or perhaps 'some Jews eat matzah on Passover some of the time', there has not been a reliable discourse to describe the habits of the broad masses of assimilated and secularized Jews who do not necessarily eat matzah on Passover at all. Instead what passes as a description of the Jewish world is the broad generalization that 'on Passover, Jews eat matzah'.

The reason for this situation is not far to seek. Until modern times, Jewish identity was framed by the rabbis more or less exclusively in normative theological terms. Cultural history was simply not relevant (it was secular knowledge, and in that sense profane) and was simply not transmitted. Even today, Jewish children are still not taught in school about their own diaspora history, except for the great catastrophes;[9] they barely know even the place-names where Jewish communities exist, let alone where they used to exist. In other words, there has been no normative transmission of the love of the Jews for their local food, local landscape, or local music, even though all of these things unquestionably influenced their behaviour and most probably their sense of local identity also. It was largely written out of the script. Pre-modern Jewish identity, in the singular, was preordained, and (normatively) unrelated to everyday, local realities. Yes, there certainly were exceptions to this, and more of them are being researched nowadays, for instance, the love of Spanish Jews for their country, or the world inhabited by Jewish women. The promotion in the modern Jewish world of the academic study of Jewish social and cultural history, together with both popular and scholarly literature on present-day Jewish life (including of course the contribution of the Jewish Cultural Studies series), have so completely revolutionized our understanding of Jewish society that the point needs to be made that until a few generations ago things looked very different. The pre-modern Jewish world rested on this most basic boundary, which is what enabled it to function—shutting out the social realities of Jewish cultural adaptations in favour of the imagined, the normative, and the sense of spiritual, eternal mission.

Where we have got to today, in the study of the present-day Jewish world, is this: we can now problematize that very boundary, and indeed problematize all the boundaries that I have been speaking about. Let me state my conclusions first. I do not think we have to choose between an essentialist view of Judaism, closed, rounded, perfect, unchangeable, on the one hand, and an ethnographic view on the other that would emphasize the hybrid quality of Jewish life in its interactions with, and cultural borrowings from, the non-Jewish environments over so many centuries. The two ran in parallel anyway, and our job is to learn how to read both of them together, to understand that what really characterizes Jewish life is the simultaneity of perspectives. This is what I mean by referring to the *problem* of boundaries: they are there but they can be, and must be, transcended.

Indeed, it is precisely by confronting the contradictions and insisting on the simultaneities that new possibilities can emerge. This is, as I have said, not at all to deny the existence of boundaries and boundary mechanisms but rather to become ever more inclusive—to try to see over the wall or through a gap in the wall and thereby bring the different sides together in some way. This is, after all, the current mode in a number of circles. The late Shlomo Carlebach, an outstanding Jewish religious songwriter, constantly stressed Judaism's fundamental concern with universal love, and he was fond of pointing out that the very first prayer mentioned in the Torah was that of Abraham trying to intercede with God to save the people of Sodom from destruction (Gen. 18: 23–33). Certainly it is not difficult to find references in the classical sources, both biblical and talmudic, to demonstrate Jewish ethical and moral concern with the world at large—not just, therefore, the antagonistic and oppositional attitude that I mentioned earlier. The following sections of this essay are devoted to some extended examples; but the general point I want to make here is that the Jewish theological tradition contains both hospitable and hostile approaches to other religions.

In taking such texts together, rather than just one type at the expense of the other, one may be sacrificing the coherence and stable narratives that come with the aesthetic satisfaction of a perfect, enclosed, and intelligible world-view. Social life does include such realities, and we need to be aware of them. But in representing Jewish culture both to outsiders and to insiders we also need to be aware of *in*coherence, that in making sense of the world people do struggle with contradictions, that they do doubt, hesitate, and theorize—and they do cross borders, or at least they cross over what in other contexts may have been seen as borders.[10] In our postmodern age the latter is becoming increasingly common, as both scholars and practitioners recognize the cultural debts that Jewish life owes to majority societies. Nowadays there is no shame if klezmer music, for example, is presented in Jewish cultural festivals as being a jazz form—a music that is both Jewish and non-Jewish at the same time, appreciated at concerts moreover by audiences that are both Jewish and non-Jewish (for an important discussion of this complex topic see Gruber 2002: 183–234, esp. ch. 11, 'Whose Music?'). The specifics of such public scenes may be altogether new in terms of the Jewish historical experience, but they draw attention to a reality which has long existed— the simultaneity of both an independent, authentic Jewish tradition based on the law codes and also a local Jewish culture that is fashioned out of hybrid elements including large-scale borrowings from the outside, whether in music, dress, folklore, synagogue architecture, or food. Jewish museums do the same: they tend to show both the classical Jewish religion and also the local Jewish cultural history and traditions. There is no one grand narrative that seamlessly integrates the histories of all the individual Jewish communities that have existed in the diaspora. That is why it is better to speak of Jewish identities, in the plural (thus Webber 1994), and of Jewish cultures, also in the plural (thus Biale 2002), as well as of Jewish histories, once again in the plural (thus Rosman 2007: 53–4). Over at least these past twenty years, the growth in popularity of seeing Jewish identity, culture, and history all in the plural has been unmistakable, and it is rapidly becoming conventional wisdom. But at the same time it is necessary to sound an important note of caution. Diversity there certainly is (and was), and yet the diversity also coexists with the belief, which Jews have always retained about themselves, that they indeed possess a common culture. There is thus both singularity and plurality, both particularism and universalism, both the desire to assimilate and the desire to retain a distinctive identity. It is precisely in the context of these multiple, contradictory realities that Jewish life has functioned and continues to function.

What this all means is that in celebrating and analysing a vigorous and reinvigorated Jewish culture today we can take pleasure in the fact that the horizons are expanding, Jews are finally becoming more and more inclusive in their gaze, and that they recognize the old boundaries but begin to bring together into view what lies on either side of the wall.

Renegotiating the Boundaries

Jewish Religious Claustrophobia

But what about the boundary between religion and culture? It may, similarly, turn out on closer inspection to be an epistemological illusion. After all, the distinguished American anthropologist Clifford Geertz proposed long ago that religion is just one part of culture anyway—a part of culture that is more interested in the use of symbols than other parts of culture (Geertz 1966). Thus the concept of Jewish culture cannot exclude religion, which in any case is deeply embedded across the full range of Jewish social life. It is not only hard, it is probably also counter-productive to assert the analytical importance of a boundary separating religion and culture in the Jewish case.

An insistence on this particular boundary, however, has a long and important pedigree among the Jews in modern times. Religious claustrophobia—a phrase I would put forward that is intended to express the passionate longings of those who see themselves locked in to a tradition, a belief system, and a set of ritual practices from which they want to escape—summarizes a very large swathe of Jewish social history during the twentieth century. In the middle of the nineteenth century, just about 90 per cent of the world's Jews lived in Europe (Della-Pergola 1994: 62), and when they finally began to obtain social and political emancipation (over a period of about a hundred years, beginning with the French Revolution in 1789)—to live where they liked, to study at whatever university they liked and enter whatever profession they liked, and indeed voluntarily to continue considering themselves Jewish if they liked—what happened was little short of a stampede. It was a profound *Kulturkampf*, a clash of civilizations between the traditional norms of Jewish life and those of the wider world the Jews could now enter. Vast numbers of Jews steadily began to ease themselves out of the imposed Jewish identity—and the communal autonomy—that they had inherited during the two thousand years of exile and diaspora. Even though they were no longer obliged to live in ghettos, such Jews started to perceive their own Jewish world as a self-imposed, virtual ghetto, with its own 'ghetto mentality', and they developed a self-induced claustrophobia in order to persuade themselves of the urgency of leaving. Their ideological destinations were many and varied—first and foremost secularism and assimilationism, but also humanism, socialism, communism, sexual liberation, and nationalism. Some of this was driven by a sense of conflict that Jews may have had with their own Jewishness; there were even conversions to Christianity (on Heinrich Heine, for example, see Abramson 1989: 325–7). And so there began the fierce controversies within families, within neighbourhoods, within Jewish society. The Jewish world became fractured, with new energies being devoted to internal Jewish boundaries. But it became united once again, most suddenly and most violently from the outside, when the Nazi Holocaust was unleashed onto the totality of this fragmenting society. All Jews, without exception, were to be deported and murdered, and they all met each other, as one people, in the gas chambers of Auschwitz. And then, after Auschwitz, the Jewish state was reborn, and the old divisions came to the fore once again. In the State of Israel today, the strong sense of a boundary, if not indeed a straight binary divide, between secularism and religious traditionalism has become probably the single most significant area of domestic political conflict—especially including the right to speak for the aims and purposes of the entire Zionist project. Zionism began, very specifically, as an expression of religious claustrophobia, the desire physically to break out of diasporic Jewish identity and to find a new life, in a new country, free of what was seen as the oppressive and culturally suffocating control of everyday behaviour by the religious establishment, and free of what is now commonly called 'religious coercion'. It was only after the large-scale immigration of Jews after the establishment of the Israeli state that religious Zionists could form enough of a critical mass to be able to pose a challenge to this secularist project. And today the emotions run high, on both sides of the boundary, as to the overall direction the state should be taking as well as its policies on many specific issues.

There can be little doubt that an overt sense of antagonism towards establishment religion was one of the key features of the Jewish world in the twentieth century; its most important project, to build a modern Jewish nation-state, derived from this source, and succeeded in confirming secularism as a perfectly legitimate and indeed authentic form of Jewish identity.[11] Revolutionary Jewish opposition to the inherited traditions first came out into the open towards the end of the eighteenth century, in the context of a European movement for Jewish social and educational reform that later came to be known as the Haskalah ('enlightenment'). Emerging first in Germany, the ideas of the Haskalah spread eastwards to the main centres of Jewish population in Austrian Galicia and then to Russia. Its supporters ('maskilim') wanted to see Jewish society modernize itself and become integrated into the wider world, best achieved in the first instance through the introduction into Jewish schools of secular education, especially European languages and science. Interestingly, language was an important plank in their programme, doubtless influenced here by parallel revival movements of national languages elsewhere in Europe at that time: they saw Yiddish (the near-universal mother tongue of Jews in eastern Europe) as a corrupt 'jargon' which had to be swept away; and its writers and intellectuals, focusing on the production of a modern Hebrew literature (particularly poetry and novels), promoted a new, quasi-biblical style of Hebrew, which they deemed more aesthetic and more pure than the rabbinic Hebrew of the traditionalists. But these were not just academic efforts at redefining boundaries confined to the classroom or at the publishing house: there were issues of political control at stake here, and there were fierce and bitter controversies between the maskilim and the traditionalists (who at this point were largely hasidim) over issues affecting representation, taxation, and loyalty to the government. Most probably there was a strong class element to the Haskalah in its creation of a new boundary within the Jewish world —the maskilim tended to favour capitalist ideology (wealth as a natural reward for economic initiative, energy, and education) and so their movement generally attracted the new rising Jewish bourgeoisie of nineteenth-century Europe (wealthy merchants, teachers, doctors, etc.), as opposed to the largely impoverished, lumpenproletarian masses of the pre-capitalist hasidim (on which see Mahler 1985: ch. 2). Although of course that line should not be too sharply drawn (there certainly were impoverished maskilim and wealthy hasidim), the point is worth recalling these days, given that much seems to have changed since then: particularly in the United States, hasidim have succumbed to the temptations of a creeping embourgeoisement, as noted by observers familiar with their society (Heilman 1992: 248–52; Soloveitchik 1994: 116 n. 35).

Present-day opposition to establishment religion is found among a number of different Jewish groups and movements. Secular Jewish humanists are an interesting case, particularly as they stress the central role of 'Jewish culture', which is understood in a consciously pluralist mode—that is, as having historically consisted of different groups and different approaches. For example, the celebration of Jewish religious festivals is to be marked (by those who still continue to mark them, that is) by thinking about them in terms of their historical origins and evolution, so as to be free of the rigidity and exclusivity of religious interpretation and the focus on the traditional rituals (for a clear insider exposition see Malkin 1998). The argument is that being Jewish today means, first and foremost, an identification with 'Jewish culture'—for example, Jewish food, Jewish music, Jewish literature, Jewish humour, Jewish folklore, dance, film, theatre, painting, sculpture, philosophy, and scholarship in the humanities—all of which have become freshly available to Jews in the modern world and so have come to replace the monopoly of activity formerly located in the synagogue or talmudic yeshiva under the authority of the rabbis. But there is little conceptual clarity about the boundary that identifies the 'Jewish culture' of such contexts: on the contrary, Abramson's major, encyclopaedic *Companion to Jewish Culture* admits in the preface that 'there is no artistic means that exclusively expresses Jewish experience' (Abramson 1989: x). How to define 'Jewish' art, 'Jewish' literature, or 'Jewish' cultural creativity generally? Her own answer to such questions is to include artists, writers, and scholars in her *Companion* whose concerns may not be 'overtly Judaic but which have come to be . . . closely associated with Judaism or Jewishness—among them ideas concerning liberalism, oppression, nationalism, alienation, self-criticism, survival, and morality' (1989: x). Jewishness, she continues, does not necessarily rest on obvious iconography or imagery, but rather in certain patterns of thinking and seeing—which may indeed include the aggressive absence of acknowledgement of Jewishness; it is a code, a 'semiotics of

Jewishness', which incorporates internal Jewish attitudes to non-Jewish society, to non-Jews, to religion, and to Jews themselves, attitudes which are rarely articulated but are displaced into other themes and ideologies. It is a useful and important statement. It should only be added (as noted above) that the entrepreneurs who have committed themselves to staging 'Jewish cultural events', including Jewish cultural festivals (now rather widespread in many European countries), may themselves not even be Jewish at all (Gruber 2002: 45–7).

Jews certainly possess the cultural resources—whether through their traditional music, art, cuisine, and so on, or through devoting new creative energies to recasting, if not reinventing, such traditions—to provide an alternative style of operationalizing an ethnic identity which does not have to lean strongly on religious styles, narrowly defined. But at the same time there is no need to insist on the reification of a boundary between religion and culture. Even if what I have been calling religious claustrophobia has encouraged many notable new features of Jewish social life in recent generations (in particular, the rise of avowedly secular political parties, including those within the diaspora Zionist movement and thereafter in Israel), nevertheless, both analytically and ethnographically the picture is more complex and does allow room for the simultaneity of perspectives and the presence of contradictions that I have mentioned above.

For example, there is certainly evidence that Jewish 'cultural' events can be motivated both by an antagonism to religion and also by a willingness to be inclusive of religion. The annual Jewish Culture Festival in Kraków (Poland) consistently includes performances held in local synagogues by *haredi* cantors from American or Israeli hasidic communities, even if these are marketed on the programme simply as 'Jewish music'. The boundary separating off religion, in other words, is not always clear-cut, even if the 'Jewish music' may be represented in new transformations according to contemporary aesthetic idioms. A secular interest in 'Jewish architecture' certainly includes visits to aesthetically interesting synagogues, regardless of whether such synagogues are actually functioning as synagogues or whether, having become derelict, they have been restored and turned into museums or converted for some other use. The 'Jewish culture' phenomenon of recent years thus includes carefully constructed, conscious reinventions which indeed draw on resources from within the tradition, even if this has been reshaped for the purpose. In fact it is not a straightforward matter to provide a truly secular Jewish discourse altogether free of religious associations. The Jewish festivals that Jewish humanists have rewritten are still the same Jewish festivals that derive from the Bible.

Another important example is the case of modern Hebrew, a language that was central to the Zionist project (which in any case needed a common and authentically Jewish language for use among the returnees to the Land of Israel, coming from many different lands of the Jewish diaspora, with many different mother tongues). The astonishing success of the pioneers in creating a new spoken language (or recreating a previously dead vernacular language) is probably without parallel elsewhere in the world, certainly in modern times. However, there has been a difficulty with the literary language: numerous layers of biblical, mishnaic, and medieval Hebrew (and Aramaic) were profoundly embedded in diaspora Jewish literary culture, but for many novelists or poets writing in modern Hebrew there was a strong awareness (as part of their Zionist outlook) of the need for a boundary so as to set off their use of language against those forms of the older Hebrew which were now seen not merely as linguistically archaic but as culturally inappropriate. Such authors, deeply conscious of this boundary, have wanted a style of language that is context-free. The 'pure', quasi-biblical Hebrew of the Haskalah (along with much else in its ideology) was not at all a Zionist objective. Hebrew expressions from the world of biblical religion and the Talmud, as well as loan translations of Yiddish proverbs and idioms, were rejected when their origins were recognized, even if Yiddish ways of expression did penetrate everyday modern Hebrew speech, especially in slang. The Hebrew Bible is most certainly venerated in Israel (and taught in schools), but its language is not Israeli Hebrew; using a biblical phrase is as if one were quoting from another language (on this subject see Harshav 1993: ch. 25). For example, Avraham Shlonski (1900–73), the first prominent Hebrew poet to be educated in the first Hebrew secondary school in Palestine (as it then was), who went on to become a prominent and influential member of the literary avant-garde there in the 1920s, specifically demanded a language that was free of biblical associations and of the burden of classical texts—the burden of history and the constraints of tradition. Of course there was controversy, notably in Shlonski's iconoclasm against the great Hebrew writer Hayim Nahman Bialik, who heavily relied on a biblical style; but through Shlonski we can see clearly how the Zionist ideal wanted to create something perfectly new, and through language provide a cultural autonomy free of allusions leading people straight back to the Abraham of the Bible (see Harshav 1993: 130; Abramson 1989: 702–3).

But this sense of religious claustrophobia, implying that a religious culture has clear, fixed boundaries setting it off from other faith traditions or indeed other, secular cultures, is itself problematic. There may be a strong awareness of the boundaries, but this awareness has existed alongside ethnographic facts on the ground in which a good deal of cultural 'cross-over' has been taking place, even if not normally registered in the idealized writings of the religious authorities.[12] As noted above, everyday Jewish culture has in practice always been the product of the intense interactions with the cultures of the non-Jewish majority in which the Jews found themselves; and it constantly underwent change. New wine was constantly being poured into old bottles. It was precisely in their engagement with the cultures of their environment that Jews constructed their own distinctive identities, conditioned by how the majority society saw them (defining them as a religion, for example) and also by how the Jews both adopted and at the same time resisted the majority culture's definition of them. As is normal for any minority group, Jewish identity was constantly being negotiated and renegotiated, in somewhat syncretistic fashion, place by place, generation by generation. But this process also means, by definition, that Jewish identity was neither fixed nor immutable; it changed as the cultural context changed. Theology provided the sense of continuity (in the Jewish imagination, the biblical land of Israel has remained the Jewish homeland, even for many Jews who consider themselves perfectly secular): nothing had changed at all, or to put it another way, cultural change may be merely an illusion. In any case, it has no formal theological status in rabbinic Judaism, let alone normative status. It may be new wine, but because the bottles are old bottles, the new wine is not necessarily perceived as new after all. In Orthodox Judaism, changes in the detailed specifications of Jewish law (which certainly do happen, as briefly noted below in the Conclusion) may not be readily perceived as genuine change, following the principle of the impermissibility of *lehotsi la'az al ha'avot* (slandering or finding fault with [the practices of] previous generations), that is, of implying that Orthodox Jewish life in the past was somehow different, less scrupulous perhaps, than in the present (Friedman 1987: 236–7, 250–1 nn. 4–5). What all this means is that it is possible to innovate in religion, even fairly substantially, while also retaining a strong sense of continuity, as well as a lack of awareness of cultural borrowing or cultural hybridity— even if in fact there is a strong interdependence between religious and other cultural systems.

What I have collectively termed here 'religious claustrophobia' does indeed provide important ethnographic evidence from inside the Jewish world about perceptions of religion having clear, fixed boundaries. But wider considerations of all kinds suggest that in analytical perspective this is unsatisfactory, if only because estrangement from Jewish religious culture is in any case never total or treated as total—in an important sense, secular Jewish cultural creativity is often in dialogue with it, not to mention the possibility of returning to it in some form (even in some subsequent generation, as is well attested nowadays; for a particularly interesting ethnography of how such return is actually navigated, see Benor 2012). In practice, religions—like all cultural systems—are multidimensional, containing within themselves differences of opinion and differences of emphasis of many kinds. To treat a particular religion as hermetically sealed, constituting a single fixed position, may be (at least in some contexts) to miss the point. The structure and content of the Talmud reflect the basic idea that the biblical text contains multiple truths, that there is no one correct reading of any biblical text. Or, as the anthropologist Clifford Geertz was fond of saying, culture is not a finished text but rather a space, a podium perhaps, from which a person addresses the world (for a key discussion of this approach see Fuchs 2002). The idea that a religion, or indeed any culture, is an enclosed, bounded, finished system is not at all what the anthropologist sees when describing life as it is actually lived.

There is a spectrum of possibilities that inheres in any given situation. In this sense there is no a priori need for a feeling of suffocation; within the system itself there is plenty of room for manoeuvre, plenty of varieties and strands of religious ideas and practices within what is notionally regarded as a single faith tradition. All this is now taken for granted amongst anthropologists, and especially those working on post-colonialism (including the colonial legacy of reified boundaries): the old European idea that a civilization could be defined by the combination of a piece of territory together with its dominant religion and its literary language is not taken seriously any more. We are all aware now of the interdependence of cultural systems, whether through trade, migration, or globalization—or simply the physical proximity of any one culture to another.

Jewish Attitudes to Other Faiths

There are important implications of all this for interfaith dialogue, very much a growing phenomenon these days. Interfaith dialogue by definition sets out from the awareness of boundaries, with the specific aim of transcending them—and in that sense it is surely a key issue that needs to be considered here. One very common way in which the boundaries are transcended is through emphasizing the idea that all the great world religions are in fact fundamentally saying the same thing, or at least that there is major common ground between Judaism and Buddhism, Christianity, Islam, Hinduism, Sikhism, and the others. All these religions preach the need for social justice, charity to the poor, comforting the lonely, the elderly, and the sick; and they all have deep traditions of spiritual wisdom, as well as a robust commitment to ethical principles concerning humanity in general—just the sort of vision that is needed nowadays for the universal moral imperative to address many of today's problems, for example the desperate situation regarding climate change. And so in this sense the boundaries between the religions are an illusion. On the other hand, at an interfaith meeting when the session is over and they go off and have lunch, the Jewish participant may well ask for a kosher meal. This in turn may give rise at such gatherings to an interest in just those things in which Judaism differs from the other faiths, and what may then be seen as characterizing Judaism are precisely those exotic aspects of its tradition, like eating matzah on Passover, about which people feel they need to know more because they appear to constitute significant boundary-markers, despite the universalist rhetoric articulated by the Jewish participant during the session. So when a Jew meets a Sikh, does she start with an account of Jewish exotica, for example, the dance music of the hasidim or some details about the kosher food laws, or does she explain that most Western Jews now live in suburbia and watch the same TV programmes and shop at the same supermarkets as everyone else, while at the same time being heirs to a tradition of universal spirituality and the common brotherhood and sisterhood of all humanity? What is, or should be, stressed here? Similarity or difference? Boundaries or their absence? My answer to this is that we are now in a position to do both, and that to do our scholarly job properly we *must* do both.

It is important to be sensitive to all the contradictions. I am not convinced that the monothematic platitudes that one sometimes hears being put forward by delegates at interfaith meetings, each ostensibly representing a specific faith tradition, are particularly helpful. After all, it is not difficult to summon up universalist statements of good intent—even those of the type 'we accept all religions as true' or 'bigoted narrow-mindedness towards other traditions is ugly and unworthy of a spiritual attitude towards humanity'. Nor is it difficult to take care to repress the negative evidence—of the type 'we are superior to other faiths', or 'if there is something in common between my religion and yours, then it must be that you got it from us'. But what really needs to be said is to confess that it is indeed a struggle, that a given faith tradition does contain a good deal of internal contradiction as regards its universalist intent. The truth is that there are competing visions; the reality is both multi-vocal and multidimensional. Certainly the temptation is there to present a stable narrative, smoothing out the inconsistencies between a religion's historical legacy that contains both universalism and particularism, ignoring the experience of religious claustrophobia, masking out those uncertainties, and altogether presenting a sense of theological coherence and a robust commitment to a general concept of humanity. Or shouldn't the strategy be to be open and honest about the contradictions, to acknowledge incoherence, to be inclusive of those who experience religious claustrophobia of some kind, to struggle with the doubts and hesitations within one's own tradition? Most of the time, I suspect, people in a dialogue situation prefer the soft option and claim that their tradition has all along emphasized nothing else but a love of humanity; and they pull out a carefully crafted selection of scriptural quotations to prove it. My reading of Judaism, however, is that one should start from the multivocality. After all, as the Talmud laboriously makes clear, spiritual meanings are often hidden within the text and can sometimes be brought to light only when compared and contrasted with other passages in the text. The very awareness of this intertextual multivocality within the Torah, through the close contemplation of the divine word, is treated as spiritually fruitful. The system retains the contradictions; the Talmud has not ironed out the inconsistencies and differences of opinion; on the contrary, they are built into the whole structure of the enterprise.

The multivocality starts from the very beginning of the Torah. God says to Abraham: 'Leave your country, leave your family, leave your father's house, and go and live in a land which I will show you. I will make of you a great nation, and I will bless you. I will bless those people who bless you, I will curse those people who curse you, but through you all the nations of the world will be blessed' (Gen. 12: 1–3). The paradox could not be more clear: on the one hand, the Jewish people, as the descendants of Abraham, are supposed to be different and remain distinct from others ('leave your family and your father's house'—Abraham's father was clearly a pagan, as described at Joshua 24: 2), but at the same time they are supposed to remain deeply aware of a universal spiritual vision for the rest of humanity. Jews are to be unique and universal at the same time. They must be spiritually and culturally isolated, and ready to endure spiritual and cultural isolation in order to protect themselves from idolatrous cultures which promote false gods and false religions. Hence the need for boundaries—but the underlying theological purpose is for the greater good of humanity. The Jewish dream here, expressed repeatedly in the traditional liturgy, is that all the world will eventually come to accept its fundamental unity, with a single God as its creator and ruler. In that cosmic sense the boundaries are (once again) an illusion, merely something necessary in this world to maintain ordinary mortal vision. They have a reality and a purpose, but at the same time the vision remains that they will be transcended. King Solomon, for example, is described as seeing the Temple he built in Jerusalem as the religious centre for all humanity, not just the Jewish people (1 Kgs 8: 43, 60). 'My house shall be a house of prayer for all peoples', as the prophet Isaiah put it (56: 7).

Post-biblical, rabbinic Judaism of the Talmud built very consciously on these foundations. Jewish ethical and moral concern for the world at large was given substantial attention through the detailed elaboration of seven principles by which the world ought to live—the so-called 'seven duties of the descendants of Noah' (i.e. the whole of humanity): the need to establish courts of justice, and to forbid idolatry, blasphemy, murder, sexual immorality, theft, and cruelty to animals (Novak 2011). Accompanying this vision of universal social justice was the clearly expressed sentiment that the righteous people of all nations and faiths have what was called a 'share in the world to come', that is, God's blessings in the heavenly sphere. The ongoing concern with idolatrous religions, to which Judaism indeed remained profoundly antagonistic, is well represented in talmudic literature, but beyond that there is nothing at all in rabbinic Judaism equivalent to the Christian idea that outside the Church there is no salvation. On the contrary, it became perfectly normal, certainly by medieval times, for Jewish teachers to respect the intrinsic value of other religions—even if the rabbis also declared the objective truth of the Torah as superior to other faiths. For example, Moses Maimonides (twelfth century) wrote that the religions of Christianity and Islam were preparing the whole world for the worship of the one God, were thus in fulfilment of biblical prophecy, and so were making major contributions towards messianic times, when the world would be at peace and in harmony (cited in Korn 2012: 209). Another influential scholar, Rabbi Menahem Me'iri (thirteenth-century Provence) was similarly positive about Christianity and made it very clear in his writings that the European world had manifestly moved on since ancient times, when the Jews had been surrounded by peoples who were idol-worshipping pagans, practitioners of *avodah zarah*, regarding whom the Torah was emphatic about the need for Jews to keep their distance. That theology of rejectionism (including a host of rules forbidding numerous areas of social and economic relations with pagans), as described in the Bible and then given substantial elaboration in the Talmud, was now no longer relevant. Members of other faiths could certainly know God, even if what they believed in was not absolutely true in Jewish terms.[13] It was not an issue of truth claims at all; what was important was correct behaviour—social justice, kindness, the dignity of man, and humility—these were the things that God wanted from humanity, as the prophet Micah had written (6: 8). If followers of other religions did not engage in crime or immorality, and in effect promoted the universal laws for the descendants of Noah, then of course they could be respected for who they were. Christianity and Islam were thus entirely acceptable as faiths for non-Jews, because they emphasized holiness and good moral behaviour. In short, the protective boundary around Jewish identity and the Jewish tradition was still certainly required; but through a focus on upright ethical behaviour there was just a glimpse of the monotheistic world beyond, with which Jews could indeed be in sympathy. From this perspective, Jews could see their own place in the world as being genuinely based on a mission—to be a 'light unto the nations' (Isa. 49: 6, 42: 6), to teach the world about God and his moral law (see Korn 2012: 211 for a listing of the influential rabbinic authorities who have stressed this). God had put the Jews into the world in order to make their own distinctive contribution to humanity in general, through three key principles: *tikun olam* (helping to repair the world of its defects), *darkhei shalom* (promoting peace in the world), and *kidush hashem* (setting standards of moral behaviour in Jewish dealings with non-Jews in order to proclaim the greatness of the monotheistic ideal) (for the talmudic references and a concise survey, see Solomon 1991: 209–44). But seen in a wider perspective, it has to be said that the classical Jewish theological tradition contained and sustained two competing approaches towards the outside world: one which is hostile to other faiths and not really interested in them, and one which is hospitable to other faiths and concerned with their welfare. I would prefer to characterize this as a simultaneity—a struggle between the sense of mission and the sense of rejectionism, a struggle between universalism and particularism, a struggle between those who search for an interfaith discussion and those who see little value or purpose in such ventures at all.

In that case, then, how have Jews actually constructed an interfaith strategy in the real world? How have they chosen between these different points of view? After all, their image of non-Jews would profoundly influence the way they interact with them, as well as shaping their understanding of their own identity, determining what distinguishes them from the non-Jews around them. In practice, the sense of the importance of boundaries here has rested on the social context—sometimes the emphasis is on one approach, sometimes on another.

For example, during biblical times there was a strongly hostile attitude to idolatry. During medieval times, the Jews were struggling to preserve their identity as Jews and survive in a context dominated by the missionary activities of Christianity and Islam. During modern times, the Jewish religion has had to compete with the rise of secularism, with the result that there is a new interest in making alliances with other faiths so that Jews can participate in a wider interfaith dialogue to present the case for religion and spirituality alongside them, and thereby play a full part in the improvement of humanity. Religion, as it would now be said, contributes to harmony, tranquillity, human dignity, social justice, and ethical behaviour, and in this sense it is perfectly consistent with the fundamental Jewish ideals of peace and reconciliation. Recent examples would include the substantial participation of Jews in the American civil rights movement in the 1960s, or the wealth of Jewish agencies and philanthropic foundations which (often under the self-proclaimed banner of Tikkun Olam) nowadays offer humanitarian pro-grammes for famine relief, disaster relief, or Jewish voluntary service in Third World countries. A somewhat different but notable contemporary context that nevertheless promotes similar messages about a common humanity and the importance of hope and 'new beginnings' regarding the need for healing, peace, and reconciliation can often be found in public events commemorating the Holo-caust, especially the lectures given by survivors to non-Jewish audiences, illus-trated by recounting their personal experience of negative stereotypes, betrayal, intimidation, humiliation, violence, and loss. All such discourses can include warm memories of a golden age when Jews lived peacefully and productively with their neighbours. On the other hand, at a time of war or interfaith tension, or in situations when governments repress and persecute the Jews, this type of dis-course is of course of not much relevance. On the contrary, if Jews are suffering from state-sponsored antisemitism, then what they are most likely to feel is that there is no common ground that they share with others, and their leaders will remind them of a long history of discrimination against Jews—for example, how the Church started out by rejecting their religion and then continued over many centuries to persecute them through massacres, expulsions, blood libels, and pogroms. Theologically, this could be explained (and often is explained by rabbis) through pointing to the antisemitism believed to be endemic to non-Jewish culture—the congenital 'hatred of Esau' against the Jewish people, as it is put in haredi circles (Heilman 2006: 51), a symbolism alluding originally to the sib-ling rivalry between Esau and Jacob, but (following Gen. 27: 41) understood as a resolve by the descendants of Esau to kill the descendants of Jacob at any time, whenever the opportunity arose. Exceptions are made for those non-Jewish individuals who can demonstrate a sense of their true humanity, as, for instance, if they risked their lives to rescue Jews during the Holocaust (they are known in modern Hebrew as *ḥasidei umot ha'olam*, 'the righteous people of the nations of the world', a phrase borrowed from BT *San.* 105a); but the exception here confirms the rule.[14] Secular Jewish historiography (especially when written from a Zionist perspective) has often supported the idea that Jew-hatred is omnipresent in the wider society, and negative evidence of such a stereotype (i.e. if there were historical periods of apparent peace when there was no anti-Jewish violence) is usually dismissed on the grounds that the hatred has remained 'just under the surface' and could reappear at any time.[15] In such a context both religious and secular Jews are more likely to feel that they have much more in common with each other than with a holy person from another religion.

What all this means is that boundaries between religions can be manipulated according to the circumstances—sometimes essentialized and reified (in defence of Jewish self-interest), sometimes transcended (also in defence of Jewish self-interest, albeit of another kind). In the Jewish cultural reservoir, both kinds of attitude are available, both kinds of memory, each with its own set of justifications and historical and literary/scriptural reference points. As I have been arguing, these diverse approaches and cultural strategies constitute a simultaneity, an entanglement of ideas, and multiple styles of reading, all complete with the ambivalences, the ambiguous options, and the paradoxes, the dreams, the memories, and the fantasies. Looking at all this from a distance, it becomes clear that there is no need to insist on one fixed model of Jewish religion and culture to the exclusion of all others, any more than it is necessary to take up a religiously claustrophobic, secularist battle against all forms of religious expression. If we can see the Jewish world as a podium, and not as an enclosed, bounded, finished system, then it becomes possible to understand how all these (apparently) contradictory styles of self-expression come to be articulated. The old boundaries are both there and not there, at the same time—lurking in the wings, so to speak, waiting to be summoned up. As far as interfaith dialogue is concerned, reconciliation with the other does not have to be based on the restatement of closed sets of meanings and other fixed positions, and then finding some point of common reference for the discussion; of course it can be, and it often is. But—to cite the visionary approach of the leading Jewish theologian Abraham Joshua Heschel (1907–72)—just looking for simple common ground between the faiths, such as shared moral values, is not really important enough as an objective. What Heschel believed to be essential was to develop the feeling that religions do share a sense of God's eternity—and if the members of different faiths could comprehend that, then there would really be peace between them. What separates people are all those outer rituals and dogmas, the externalities of faith. What can bring people together is a state of mind in which religious pluralism is not seen as a barrier to unity, and if that could be achieved it would bring about a sense of transcendence and renewal. Religious Jews and religious non-Jews should not be isolated from each other. They should not hope and pray for each other's failure, but rather pray for each other's health and indeed set about helping one another in preserving a common spiritual legacy, and the common fight against nihilism (on these striking ideas of Heschel see Korn 2012: 211–12; Coward 2000: ch. 1). Or, to put that another way, what is important is the attempt to sense the open horizon, to be aware of the wide spectrum of possibilities, to transcend what seems fixed.

There is considerable urgency to this task in today's world—to reconsider the boundaries and stimulate a new approach to humanity in an era of globalization, an approach which would encompass all civilizations while at the same time emphasizing their particularism and diversity. It is surely one of the most pressing issues of our times. Certainly all religions have universalist concepts, valid for all people, to which those suffering from particularist claustrophobia try to reach out. But these universalisms are still usually very culture-specific, such as the talmudic agenda of the seven laws of Noah, which is all that there is of substance as regards a detailed Jewish blueprint for world society (on which, for a classical exposition, see Lichtenstein 1981). Unfortunately, as Alon Goshen-Gottstein has argued in an important essay on the need for new Jewish conversations with other faiths (2012), those seven laws lack at least one major dimension of the religious life that can be found in certain other religions, namely, the development of a personal relationship with God, including prayer, spiritual sensitivity, humility, and the fulfilment of emotional needs. A full religious life implies much more than upright ethics and morals, as Jewish teachers know very well. These should therefore be the criteria with which Jews can encounter other faiths, understand them, and develop a sensitivity and respect for them, in particular the ability of religions and their saintly leaders to have an impact on the spiritual lives of their followers. If the Jewish role is indeed to be a 'light unto the nations', there is an enormous amount that can be achieved through interfaith encounters—if only the boundaries can be perceived as opportunities rather than as buffers. It is a tall order: such new ways of viewing the other may be rather difficult to achieve, let alone incorporate into mainstream thinking, and, as in any constructed relationship, may remain very fragile. As for a new universalism, all that there currently is, in effect, are competing sets of universalist ideas, rather than a culturally neutral universalism with which all religions could identify, while acknowledging the boundaries of religious difference. But reality ultimately depends on the imagination: all social identities are composite and malleable, multiple, and fluid; we become who we are. Could there ever in fact be a general concept of human dignity with shared norms of dialogue, in which the boundaries demarcating religious differences are seen only as internal differentiations?[16]

Shifting Boundaries of Belonging

Reconsideration of the boundaries between diaspora Jewish society and its non-Jewish neighbours is in fact a process which has been under way for several generations, as is well known to those social scientists who have specialized in the sociology of the contemporary Jewish world, particularly in the USA. Learning new ways of how to belong is one of the key features of present-day Jewish life, and, for example, in a recently edited volume under the title *Boundaries of Jewish Identity* (Glenn and Sokoloff 2010) the editors note early on the 'shifting boundaries of belonging' and indeed the 'porous' nature of ethnic boundaries, especially given the struggle for ownership of Jewishness as different constituencies negotiate with one another over where the border lies between Jews and non-Jews (2010: 5, 9, 11). Once again, the focus in understanding the socio-cultural situation of the present-day diaspora Jewish world seems to hinge on problematizing the nature of the boundaries. In this section my approach will be an ethnographic one, to illustrate at a micro-level how an obsession with rigid boundaries and the need for introducing suitable mechanisms for boundary maintenance— so often used by community leaders concerned with rising intermarriage rates and falling affiliation rates—is only one part of the picture. In the real world, Jews renegotiate the boundaries. That is, they may have moved them in one area of their social life but have retained and respecified them in another. Renegotiating the boundaries is something Jews have always done, even if, as we have seen, the continuing process of renegotiation does strengthen the presence of contradictions of all kinds.

Mention has been made above of the simultaneity of contradictory Jewish cultural goals during this process of high assimilation to majority culture in recent generations—to retain some form of Jewish group identity on the one hand, but on the other to find ways of allowing it to disappear. To put that another way, it would seem that the category of 'assimilation' is uneven, or at least not adequately descriptive of the totality of Jewish life, in which identity is formed and developed in contexts that are notionally on both sides of the boundary—hence the shifting boundaries. One of the key issues here is the long-term effect of Jewish political emancipation that steadily came about during the nineteenth century in Europe: in political terms, Jewishness became a voluntary matter, a voluntary performance of self-presentation or act of self-identification, whereas national citizenship, or loyalty to the nation-state, is the direct opposite—it is a given, imposed (at least in a Jewish perspective) from the outside. In pre-modern times the situation was more or less exactly the reverse: when Jews then possessed their own socio-political autonomy (usually inside a ghetto of some kind), it was Jewish identity which was the given, while a feeling of political or cultural loyalty to the state was a voluntary act of self-identification by those Jews who, for whatever reason, felt they wanted to be associated with the country and national culture where they lived. Modern times can, in this context, therefore be defined as a period in which Jews have been gradually moving from one system of self-identification to the other, with a considerable degree of cultural uncertainty and cultural incoherence along the way. There is not much uniformity characterizing the transition: some

Jews are moving along the road faster than others; some Jews (perhaps because of the Holocaust) are slowing down or even going into reverse. This, essentially, is the background to why the steady process of Jewish 'assimilation' to the majority culture in the old nineteenth-century sense is highly uneven, especially among the different generations of the mass migrations to the New World, and why it may, for example, affect men and women differently.

It is this cultural incoherence which provides the opportunity, in a voluntaristic Jewish society, both for the shifting of boundaries and for new areas of cultural creativity of all kinds—especially as regards the shifting boundaries between competing Jewish denominations (Reform, Conservative, Orthodox, and their respective sub-denominations) and new 'post-denominational' identities. If, in addition, traditional Jewish education is weak, and leadership is weak, the boundaries are likely to be weak: under such circumstances it is hardly surprising if people thinking about their Jewish identity make it up as they go along. Or at least this is the sociological context in which one might expect to find the simultaneous use of contradictory attitudes to boundaries. A classic study by the anthropologist Jack Kugelmass of a dying community in the South Bronx illustrates this well (Kugelmass 1987). His object of study was a poor neighbourhood which once had a thriving Jewish community but from which virtually all the Jews had moved out into the middle-class suburbs of New Jersey and elsewhere, leaving behind just one remaining synagogue, frequented by those Jews who were either too poor to move or stayed behind for other reasons. Kugelmass's ethnography is reminiscent of what has been happening in many places in continental Europe after the Holocaust, where a small surviving Jewish community remains, often called 'nominally Orthodox'—ostensibly committed to Orthodox norms but in fact imposing no such code of conduct on its members outside the synagogue itself. But how does this play out *inside* the synagogue?

In answering this question let me pick out just a few features. The congregation is led not by a rabbi but by a lay person who is Orthodox (whatever that means, but certainly Jewishly well educated). Kugelmass quotes him as saying '*halachah* [Jewish law] is like a rubber band: you can stretch it and bend it, just so long as you don't break it' (1987: 50). So he manages to conduct a full sabbath service on Saturday mornings even if there is no *minyan* (ten Jewish males, the required quorum for an Orthodox prayer service). His 'unorthodox' strategies to make up the *minyan* include opening the holy ark, which contains the Torah scrolls, so as notionally to count in the Shekhinah (the 'divine presence') as the tenth male, or simply not enquiring too closely into the Jewish identity of the street bums and other unattached types who wander in to the services and then partake of the kiddush (refreshments) afterwards. It is an inclusive view of group boundaries: 'anyone who calls himself a Jew is welcome', as he puts it (1987: 53). Inclusiveness is of course relative and in this case would not seem to allow for the possibility of, for example, counting in women to the *minyan*.

Because of his charismatic personality he manages to hold his own, especially against the more exclusivist views of some of his congregants who murmur darkly such things as 'to be a Jew you have to act like a Jew' (1987: 78). In these and in numerous other ways he stretches the religious law and invents his own traditions—tolerant of a certain amount of deviation and extending the boundaries, in other words, but creatively so.

What is particularly interesting about this invention of traditions is what happened with the seating arrangements in the synagogue. Whereas, following traditional Jewish law, Orthodox congregations formally divide the available architectural space into separate seating sections for men and women, using for the purpose either an upstairs gallery for women or a *meḥitsah* (a physical partition, such as a piece of wooden lattice-work), Reform Judaism has insisted on gender equality throughout the ritual system and so its synagogues contain only 'family pews', where men and women sit together without the use of a *meḥitsah* at all. Conservative synagogues either do the same or rely on a compromise solution—for example, by providing separate seating sections for men and women, but separated by a gangway rather than a physical partition as such. The abandonment of the *meḥitsah* (which of course has significant consequences at many levels, including architectural aesthetics) was seen by Orthodox Jews not merely as an untraditional innovation but as an unwarranted external influence on synagogue practice, probably Christian in origin—something, in other words, from the other side of the boundary (or in this case perhaps an illusory or imagined boundary, given that it is far from true that all boundaries are mutually agreed by people on both sides of it). But in the middle-class suburbia of North America, to which Jews steadily migrated from the inner cities during the twentieth century, pressure to follow the Reform and Conservative lead in this matter heavily influenced newly founded congregations that otherwise considered themselves Orthodox. In the immediate post-war period there were huge debates within many Orthodox-affiliated congregations over proposals by congregants to remove the *meḥitsah*, and a number of these disputes came before the civil courts in the 1950s (see e.g. Diamond 2000: 73–4). For the sake of unity, Orthodox rabbis were permitted at the time to serve such 'non-*meḥitsah*' Orthodox congregations for a limited period (up to five years, for example), on the understanding that they would use their influence during their tenure to persuade the membership to restore the previous status quo (2000: 74). Such permissiveness, albeit pragmatic and temporary, is a good example of the presence of contradictions at the boundaries.

But to return to that small community in the South Bronx. What Kugelmass noted in his ethnography was that the synagogue space there was invisibly divided into three. At the front of the synagogue, between the *bimah* (the centrally positioned desk from where the Torah is read to the congregation) and the holy ark at the eastern end, the synagogue displays its ideal Orthodox self. Ritual practice strictly conforms to Orthodox norms, and this front section is where the community leader has his regular seat, together with his Orthodox fellow-congregants. Then there is what Kugelmass calls the 'back-stage', which is at the rear of the synagogue space, between the *bimah* and the hallway. This back-stage occupies a full three-quarters of the total floor space, though the people who usually sit there, who in fact constitute most of the congregation, are often quite out of step with the actual service that is taking place in the front section. They treat the place casually and informally—for instance, sitting when one should be standing, or chatting with each other when they should be praying. Interestingly enough, the back-stage is itself divided into two, once again invisibly: at the very back, what Kugelmass calls 'off-stage', is where women or complete strangers wander in and sit down (1987: 71–3).

In this particular setting (which, however, can be observed in many 'nominally Orthodox' synagogues elsewhere), deviant or at least ambiguous behaviour is permissible, but only in certain parts of the synagogue space, and in that sense it is a good example of how cultural incoherence functions at the micro-level. But on closer inspection it turns out that things are not quite as incoherent as they might appear at first sight; there are, in fact, social conventions which govern how the incoherence is managed and related in practice to the stated ideals of the congregation. The ethnography of this tiny synagogue is thus potentially of considerable interest as a microcosm of something much more general in today's Jewish world: a simultaneous toleration and non-toleration of failures in boundary maintenance. The back-stage is tolerated by the front-stage, and the back-stage in turn tolerates the off-stage; but at the same time the front-stage does not tolerate any intervention by the back-stage in running its affairs. The back-stage people simply opt out of any control of the total social space, while the approach of the front-stage is simply to turn a blind eye to the behaviour of those on the back-stage and not apply any sanctions—or, to use the Yiddish phrase that is commonly cited in such contexts, *makhen zikh nishvisndik* (to look the other way, not to get involved) (Kugelmass 1987: 71–3). *Makhen zikh nishvisndik* is not at all a formal category of Jewish law, let alone a guiding principle for how rabbis are supposed to act; on the contrary, the law says that lack of social concern is wrong in principle, and that Jews must always ensure that their fellow Jews behave correctly. From a study of the rabbinic law one would never have been able to infer the Jewish folk sociological principle of *makhen zikh nishvisndik*. But it may turn out to be a critical element in the whole functioning of boundary maintenance within the Jewish world—even if (and this is critical) those who operate this principle also subscribe to the importance of upholding the boundaries. The contradictory positions are held simultaneously.

Although it is conventionally imagined that the natural condition of societies is that they are essentially characterized by unity, stable relations, social harmony, and the avoidance of conflict, there is in fact nothing bizarre about finding contradictory positions within a single society simultaneously. One will nearly always find different dialects within a single language, whether these are distinguished by different accents, different words, or different grammatical rules; and the existence of linguistic variation within a single language may turn out to be an important marker for how a given language changes from one generation to the next (such as the adoption by mainstream speakers of previously regional, class-based, or occupation-specific usages). Social life similarly. The point is that there is a fluid quality to social life, which is why it constantly changes. What people actually believe, or at least purport to believe, is in any case complex to determine, because beliefs and attitudes are rarely fully systematized. Hence under normal conditions contradictory attitudes can be held without posing a threat to the system, just as people are tolerant of different accents in ordinary speech. But of course there does come a point at which dialects of language A come to be thought of as dialects of a neighbouring language B—for instance, the local vernaculars across that swathe of northern European countries where Flemish, Dutch, German, and Danish are spoken, and where the presence of political boundaries in effect determines how a particular local dialect is to be classified (which language it is deemed to 'belong to'). A 'non-*meḥitsah*' Orthodox synagogue—theoretically a contradiction in terms, straddling the boundaries—may survive for an extended period, doubtless characterized by the principle of *makhen zikh nishvisndik*. Or, alternatively, there may be tensions between community members. If at some point such tensions, or disparate ideological positions, begin to coincide with a critical mass of other kinds of division (for example, differences in social class or age-groups, pressure from institutional sources or from the rabbi's peer group, disputes over a particular scandal, or arguments over political orientation or political control), the boundaries become manifest, and conflict breaks out. That is the interesting moment. Either peace is restored or, if the pre-existing divisions are strong enough, the community could split or its dissenting membership (or its rabbi) leaves—perhaps, if there is a critical mass, to found a new synagogue, whether defined denominationally or (as is increasingly common nowadays) post-denominationally. Some would say that the existence of conflict is in fact a sign of life, marking the absence of indifference. Too much emphasis on harmony (and an apathetic, perfunctory maintenance of stable boundaries) may miss other key features of Jewish life in the modern world. After all, argumentativeness, even major disagreements with the leadership, are recurring themes in Jewish social history, not only in modern Jewish history. The Torah itself characterizes the forty years spent in the desert as dominated to a considerable extent by such events as the disturbances associated with Korah (Num. 16), the disastrous episode of the spies (Num. 13–14), the colossal plague following the enticement of the people into sexual debauchery and idolatry at Shittim (Num. 25), and the sin of the golden calf (Exod. 32 f.); and when Moses gives his narrative of Israelite history, as set out in the book of Deuteronomy, he does not tell them they are a great people but instead—right from the beginning of the book—focuses on how sinful and rebellious they have been. Maybe the indifference of Kugelmass's back-stage people is where the social harmony could be ethnographically located; but there were differences of outlook among the front-stage people, and these deserve attention.

This idea has been explored at some length by the outstanding ethnographer Barbara Myerhoff in her landmark book *Number Our Days* (1980), which describes a Jewish old-age home in Venice, California. What Myerhoff couldn't help noting was how the old people there constantly hurt each other—for example, by disrupting ceremonies, making each other agitated, irritated, and enraged, either by a small gesture (such as a frown, or placing a glass of water in front of someone who is too excited), or more directly by actually cursing each other ('you don't look well today'), or even naming, shaming, gossiping, and generally aggravating each other and wishing each other harm. How she accounted for this culture of anger and fury is interesting. Let me just make two points here. The expression of grievance and an atmosphere of dissension allow people to express their personal identities and give them a sense of autonomy with regard to their circumstances. But at the same time, by the very fact of demonstrating a responsiveness to each other and thus restating the shared membership of the group, this culture of aggressiveness is one of the things which keep the group together. It enables its members to redirect their energies towards the commonalities, stable norms, and symbols that they in fact share, including the ordinary human need for poise and dignity. The old people cannot escape from each other; they are thus both tolerant and intolerant of each other at the same time. Of course it is a paradox. But every society has to allow space for outbursts of passion expressing resentment, envy, and fear that people may feel vis-à-vis those who are too powerful and who are deemed to harbour hostile feelings towards the rest: such people are part of the society but not part of it at the same time. The deviance in this sense has to be controlled, and what Myerhoff saw in the old people's home in Venice, California, were mechanisms to achieve that.

Secondly, Myerhoff points to people's historical consciousness to justify this behaviour—rooted, in this case, not in the Torah, but in the sense that 'that's how it always was, back in the *heim*, in the old country in Poland'. These old people in California are first- or perhaps second-generation incomers from Poland. Myerhoff quotes one of them telling her that 'Sholem Aleichem said: we fight in order to keep warm, and that's how we survive' (1980: 188). It doesn't matter if the Yiddish writer Sholem Aleichem (1859–1916) actually said that; the important thing is that there is clearly here a statement of the belief that Jewish in-fighting is understood as normal (and thus socially acceptable) because it is an inheritance from the remembered past. The boundaries are both important and unimportant at the same time. Especially in the nineteenth and twentieth centuries, intense in-group struggling in the shtetl appears to have been common and indeed accepted as a way of life. 'We fight in order to keep warm, and that's how we survive.'

The ability to renegotiate boundaries, including the ability (when it suits the circumstances) to turn a blind eye to areas of cultural incoherence, is probably a key feature of Jewish life today, and probably always has been. It may be impor-tant in accounting historically for Jewish cultural survival amidst pressures of all kinds to disappear as a defined group. Of course it doesn't always work: there have been enough cases when Jewish sub-communities (not to mention people on the margins of Jewish society) have assimilated into the wider world and then vanished. But internal aggressiveness, and other forms of moral disequilibrium, do not necessarily lead to that result, as Myerhoff's micro-level evidence suggests. It very nearly did, two thousand years ago—the destruction of Jerusalem and its Second Temple was attributed in the rabbinic literature to *sinat ḥinam*, the collapse of social justice and good moral relations. But thereafter, diaspora Jewish life proved durable, perhaps just because the boundaries were drawn and re-drawn so as to accommodate what could be seen as limited inner conflict, in the interest of maintaining solidarity and a sense of continuing identity alongside the syncretistic interactions of Jews with others.

Conclusion

The material I have presented in this essay suggests that the simple binary distinction with which I started—the official 'theology', with its strong sense of boundaries coherently separating Jews from the outside world, versus the every-day 'ethnography' (the sociological realities), with blurred edges at its bound-aries—has to a considerable extent broken down in today's Jewish world. The rise of quite new forms of Jewish identity and Jewish commitment over the past two hundred years, and even quite recently, can be characterized as a succession of attempts to institutionalize different styles of everyday Judaism, attempts that have drawn their strength from various kinds of ideological conversation with the wider transnational environment, whether with regard to reform and renewal, secularism, nationalism, interfaith dialogue, or concern with antisemitism. Present-day globalization and the use of the internet offer particularly important new opportunities for this, including scope for virtual communities, complete with their own leadership. On the other hand, the historical evidence also sug-gests that the binary distinction between establishment and everyday Judaism was in any case too rigid—what is characteristic about Jewish life in all ages has been a simultaneity of coherence and incoherence, a belief in some sort of unified bounded culture *alongside* the strong awareness of other realities (especially local realities) where the boundary around Jewish society and culture is blurred. What has changed today is the rise not only of specific new challenges (such as the question of how Judaism in the Western world can make room for Hinduism, Buddhism, and other eastern religions encountered now, for the first time in Jewish history, partly through backpacker holiday travel, partly through New Age influences) but also of new discourses in the Jewish world more generally which challenge the idea of a unified, bounded culture and appear to accept fragmentation and hybridizing as normative. One of the main issues here is likely to involve the legitimacy of the new Jewish identities, with the result (already visible in certain circles) of uncertainty over questions relating to authenticity. My argument is that, analytically speaking, at the heart of all these uncertainties lies the vexed problem of boundaries: just how real are the boundaries, how real should they be, where can they or should they be drawn, and how far does present-day Jewish life need to be understood (anachronistically?) in terms of the historical legacy of where the boundaries used to be drawn? The ambiguous phrase 'shifting boundaries'—ambiguous as it can both refer to an unnamed agent doing the shifting, or suggest that the boundaries have somehow got a life of their own—nicely hints at the need to problematize the concept. For example, it is one thing to be blurred at the edges that are adjacent to the boundaries, but surely quite another if there is blurring at the centre. For many people today, the centre *is* at the 'periphery' adjacent to the boundary (see especially Aviv and Shneer 2005 for the drawing of 'a new Jewish map' of the world, or, for quite a different reading of the centre–periphery model, where Jewish life altogether sits permanently on a symbolic frontier, a space of both contestation and accommodation, see Gilman 1999). Do we know how to identify where precisely is the centre of the collective Jewish world and where is its periphery? For if not, we shall remain with the uncertainty about its boundaries.

The blurring of the shifting boundaries within the Jewish world is plain now for all to see—for example, in the conscious attempts at inclusiveness in new post-denominational identities, known variously also as 'cross-denominational' or 'trans-denominational', such as 'Conservadox' (Kaplan 2009, esp. chs. 4 and 6). Further instances include major new arenas of feminist social change, the path-breaking worldwide Limmud phenomenon (continually expanding, and building new worlds), the considerable growth of Jewish museums, or substantial new developments in the sphere of public Jewish culture, which is today a rather fast-growing, multi-dimensional movement, including large-scale festivals, specialized magazines, and community programming of Jewish cultural events more generally. Jewish 'cultural' identity is particularly fluid and inclusive, even hybrid (attracting both Jews and non-Jews as members, performers, and consumers), and it seems to be steadily consolidating itself as a significant alternative option to previous styles of ethnic or religious affiliation. One of the major consequences for the individual here is the scope for multiple allegiances (i.e. to several communities simultaneously), and a genuine feel for the existence of diversity—for example, this is a feature of queer (LGBT) Jews, seeking both to integrate into established communities and to maintain separate spaces for themselves (Aviv and Shneer 2005: ch. 4). To some extent this can also be noted in the political sphere, in the context of attitudes towards Israel (new boundaries identifying liberally minded, 'self-hating' Jews active in circles deeply critical of Israel and its policies with regard to the Palestinians). Reconstructionist Judaism, following the work of Mordecai Kaplan (1881–1983) and his view of Judaism as a religious civilization, has been saying much of this all along: it sees boundaries as essential in principle, but recognizes that they are unsubtle and uncomfortable (hence the need for a flexible attitude to the dietary laws in order to enable Jews to eat in non-Jewish homes, or for finding ways of being inclusive and welcoming towards non-Jewish marriage partners). If anything, shifting boundaries is an important part of the institutional, denominational identity of the Reconstructionist movement, and it consciously draws attention to the fact that definitions of what is Jewish have changed over time and will continue to change (Levine 1994). Another interesting example is the rise of an 'Ashkefardi' liturgical pronunciation of Hebrew, a fusion of traditional Ashkenazi and modern Hebrew (Sephardi) pronunciations—a very recent phenomenon but rather common nowadays in synagogues in the English-speaking world, indeed almost normatively so among Jews young enough to have received their Jewish education in the past three or four decades.[17]

Shifting boundaries have also been observed in haredi society. From the outside it may appear solidly traditionalist, but in fact it has experienced profound changes in modern times—due to a number of reasons, including the consequences of migration in the nineteenth century from the villages and small towns of eastern Europe to the large cities, and then onward migration (especially by Holocaust survivors) to Australia, Belgium, Israel, the UK, the USA, and elsewhere. The new haredi communities in such places are enclaves, free of geographically defined local communities as in the old country, which are now seen in retrospect as having been too inclusive (relatively speaking), too 'modern', too entrenched in local politics, too tolerant of deviation in the interests of minimizing local conflicts (Friedman 1987: 239–45). Yes, the real-world fluidity of the boundary as it functioned in the past is implicitly acknowledged.[18] One particular feature of contemporary haredi society is its rejection of the authenticity of a culture based on inherited, mimetic, oral traditions, which had always relied on the continuance of an Orthodox way of life imbibed informally from parents and friends, and patterned on conduct regularly observed in home and street, synagogue and school, in favour of a new text-based culture that consciously sets out to define correct religious performance (Soloveitchik 1994: 66 ff.). The habits of a lifetime no longer suffice; parents can no longer be trusted to know the law accurately ('ask my daughter', one can hear a mother saying in response to a technical query; 'she's just been learning that at the sem [seminary for girls]'). Authority has passed to the heads of the yeshivas, and the new haredi 'enclave identity' is governed by an elite of learned specialists (1994: 94–8). To protect these shifting boundaries the elite has introduced new stringencies (*humrot*) in the interpretation of Jewish law—for example, announcing a new, increased size for the wine goblet used for sabbath domestic rituals and declaring the old, traditional goblets not fit for purpose (Friedman 1987: 235–8). Such 'maximum compliance' stringencies, highly popular among graduates of the haredi yeshivas (which were deliberately established so as to be independent of a local community and away from the students' home environment (Stampfer 2012: 3, 35)), have become a mark of membership in the haredi enclaves. However, some of these new patterns of ritual behaviour have also spread beyond the haredi world, causing new areas of uncertainty for mainstream Orthodox Jews over the boundaries that used to define their own world and their sense of continuity with the past. In an important study of fragmentation, divisions, and other uncertainties within Jewish society, and particularly among Orthodox Jews, the British chief rabbi writes that 'Orthodoxy itself is no longer a single entity, but a congeries of communities often denying one another's religious credentials' (Sacks 1993: 40).

Boundaries, then, continue to have vitality but at the same time are distinctly permeable and constantly shifting. In assessing the norms of Jewish society one needs to assume that there may well be deeply contradictory beliefs and values which may or may not surface in actuality. Jewish identity is a constantly expanding category nowadays, including not only 'non-halakhic Jews' but also non-Jews who by virtue of family ties to Jews are eligible for Israeli citizenship. The situation of these people, once they get to Israel, is profoundly ambiguous (eligibility for service in the Israeli army, but lack of eligibility for burial in a Jewish cemetery, for instance)—another good example of shifting boundaries. 'Nominally Orthodox' synagogues may offer ritual honours to Jews who publicly desecrate the sabbath by driving their cars there; but this does not mean to say that all such Jews are fully accepted by members—on the contrary, they may well not be sought after for taking on communal office or, in extreme cases, as marriage partners for their children. Such Jews may be both tolerated and not tolerated at the same time, depending on context. It is this kind of simultaneity that I have been emphasizing in this essay.[19] Today's Jewish world is clearly plural in character, but that does not necessarily imply that it is unequivocally plural*ist*, in the sense of an ideological commitment to its plural character. 'Shifting boundaries' will always need careful scrutiny, to bring out both the coherence and the incoherence. It is precisely by juxtaposing the contradictions that the sociological analysis of the Jewish world can be sharpened.

Notes

1   The main ideas for an essay on this topic were originally presented at a conference on 'Modern Jewish Culture: Diversities and Unities', held at the University of Wrocław in June 2008, but here considerably expanded. I am very grateful to Professors Simon Bronner, Moshe Rosman, and Marcin Wodziński for their intellectual support and helpful comments at that conference, and to Simon Bronner both for the encouragement to write up the paper for publication here and for some very useful editorial suggestions. I would also like to thank Agi Erdos for copy-editing the text with enormous skill and attention to detail.

2   Notably the sin of the golden calf (see Rashi's commentary on Exod. 32: 4). Given both the semantic and phonetic similarity, it would be pleasing to think that the word 'riff-raff' (members of a society who are disreputable, undesirable rabble) is cognate with *erev rav*, but the *Oxford English Dictionary* derives it etymologically from Old or Middle French—a language which Rashi would have been familiar with, but unfortunately he makes no such etymological suggestion to confirm the point.

3   This is the opinion of Maimonides, conjecturing (on the basis of the fact that the instruction collocates in the text with laws about the celebration of the Jewish festivals) that the practice might have been part of the ritual of certain pagan festivals—and that that was the reason for the ban. Ancient inscriptions unearthed at Ras Shamra-Ugarit by modern archaeologists seem to confirm his conjecture, and it is a view found also in the key relevant work of the founding father of modern anthropology, Sir James Frazer, in his *Folklore in the Old Testament* (cited in *Encyclopaedia Judaica* (1971) vi. 43–4). The Talmud substantially extended the ban, to include the cooking together of any meat and any dairy foods, eating such a mixture, and deriving any commercial or other benefit from such a mixture; and yet further development of Jewish law led to the requirement to have two sets of cooking utensils, dishes, cutlery, and even dishcloths and tablecloths—one set for meat foods and another for dairy. It should be noted that the original law of the Torah here did attract alternative explanations in the classical commentaries—for example, that milk represents life, and that since the Torah opposes the mixing of opposites, a dead goat should not be cooked in the milk of its own mother. Contemporary anthropologists, who would argue that ritual practices might encode more than one set of distinctions (thereby endowing rituals with diverse ways in which they reflect other elements of the cultural system), would propose additional explanations—for example, that to the extent that food and eating may often serve as metaphors for sexual activity (as widely reported cross-culturally), this rule about goats and milk echoes an incest prohibition, that of a male having sexual intercourse with his mother (thus Eilberg-Schwartz 1990: 128–34, 248 n. 19).

4   Jewish law regarding sabbath observance is the context for a number of precise regulations reflecting a territorial approach to divisions and boundaries governing the nature of the Jewish world in physical space—most notably in the context of the prohibition on carrying objects outside one's personal domain, but mitigated through a legal fiction known as an *eruv*. Through the use of physical fixtures (such as wires strung from poles) the *eruv* is deemed to cordon off and thus in a sense to domesticate an urban enclave (even in a large metropolis), within which it is permitted to carry objects from one place to another on the sabbath—perhaps a somewhat literalist application of a 'fence around the Torah'. For two interesting studies of the *eruv* in a contemporary British socio-cultural setting, see Cousineau 2010 and Cooper 2002. Jewish law similarly specifies the boundary around a

town or village (approximately three-quarters of a mile beyond the last house) outside which it is not permitted to walk on the sabbath (the *teḥum shabat*; for details see *Shulḥan arukh*, 'Oraḥ ḥayim', 396–407).

5   The blurred boundaries of Jewish society can perhaps be nowhere better grasped than in the difficult work of the Jewish demographer, whose job it is to measure Jewish populations. Does the demographer count only those Jews who have a Jewish mother (the formal definition according to Jewish law)—and if so, how is such data collected? The Israeli repatriation law, offering citizenship to Jews worldwide, is mindful of the Nazi persecutions and so defines 'Jewish' for this purpose as someone who may have just one Jewish grandparent (and who is entitled to emigrate to Israel with all his or her offspring and their spouses). The local consequence of this is that 'Jewish' status in some diaspora countries, particularly in eastern Europe, follows this definition even for membership of the local Jewish community. There are thus also non-Jewish members of Jewish households as well as other people who imagine they are Jewish, or have some Jewish origins, but may not know for sure. Conversions to Judaism are yet another difficulty—recognized by some rabbinical authorities but not by others. These uncertainties have given rise to a new category of 'non-halakhic Jews'—people who regard themselves as Jewish, in whatever sense, and may be regarded as Jewish by others, but not so by Orthodox rabbis guided by halakhah (Jewish law), for whom the phrase 'non-halakhic Jew' is a contradiction in terms, despite its sociological reality. For all these reasons, Jewish population figures need to be treated with some circumspection (for an overview of the subject by the leading specialist see DellaPergola 2002). As far as haredim (haredi Jews) are concerned, recent figures for the New York area (today the largest diaspora Jewish community, with the largest diaspora concentration of haredim) suggest that they constitute 10 per cent of all Jewish households, although in absolute numbers they are possibly as many as 22 per cent of all Jews living in the area (336,000 out of a total of 1.54 million); they demonstrate an 'explosive population growth', especially when compared with the declining numbers of those identifying with Conservative and Reform Judaism (UJA Federation of New York 2011: 212, 215). A similar pattern of substantial growth among haredim and significant decline among non-haredi Jews has been reported elsewhere. In the UK, for example, figures put out by the Board of Deputies of British Jews say that in 2007 haredim numbered about 10 per cent of the British Jewish population of 300,000, with an estimated growth rate of about 4 per cent per annum; but in the younger age cohorts the percentage is markedly higher—about 33 per cent of British Jews under the age of 18 are haredim (Vulkan and Graham 2008: 15–16). However, these British figures are accompanied by the noteworthy disclaimer that in fact there is no 'haredi community' as such, and that the boundaries between this group and the rest of the Jewish population are far from clear-cut (2008: 4).

6   Another important example of the boundary enclosing the group, and indeed defining membership of it, is male circumcision. Its absence is how the Torah defines the non-Jewish male resident alien (*arel*). The *arel* is excluded from the annual Passover celebrations—the rituals surrounding the community memory of the departure from Egypt, the key historical moment when the Jews became a people—but male conversion to Judaism through the act of circumcision reverses this exclusion, as indicated in the text (Exod. 12: 48–9). However, as should be evident, my purpose here is merely to offer a schematic approach to what is obviously highly complex material, in some cases hinted at in these notes. Biblical and rabbinic law governing the consequences of the clear boundary between Jews and non-Jews (not only in matters of ritual but also as regards a very wide

range of issues in civil and criminal law, as well as conversion procedures) is the subject of at least one talmudic tractate, in addition to incidental treatment in many other tractates, not to mention the evolution of rabbinic law in medieval times as found in numerous commentaries and the rabbinic responsa literature. For a convenient overview of this topic see Hirsch and Eisenstein 1903.

7   For example, Zvi Gitelman (University of Michigan) has described the stereotypes underlying the Litvak–Galitzianer boundary, popular in North America in the early 20th century, in the following terms: Litvaks were considered rational, unemotional, reserved, sardonic, and very well versed in Talmud. They were proud of being from small towns, where the great yeshivas were located. They made their *gefilte fish* (stuffed fish, at that time an extremely common, well-nigh universal dish served in Jewish homes on the sabbath) with sugar and pronounced Yiddish differently. Galitzianers, on the other hand, were regarded as not being very bright, as crafty and cunning, excelling at business, not very educated, but very pious. They were ashamed of being from small towns. They made their *gefilte fish* with pepper and salt, and pronounced Yiddish differently (see Gitelman, as reported by Clingan 2010). Of course it should be noted that whereas Galicia was a formal province of the Austro-Hungarian empire from 1772 to 1918, with its own political autonomy from 1873 (and in this sense a real place with precise borders), 'Lithuania' was in this context a construct of Jewish geography, referring to a territory that had long since been defunct as a political unit (it was, at least notionally, the Lithuanian part of the old Polish–Lithuanian Commonwealth, including not only Lithuania but also parts of what are today southern Latvia, Belarus, and northern Ukraine). This lack of linkage to empirical reality does seem to lend substance to the mythologized nature of the stereotypes; they have largely faded away, along with the Litvak–Galitzianer boundary, as North American Jews have today quite different preoccupations. In this sense the boundary, and the stereotypes to maintain the boundary, can be seen functionally as very context-bound, enabling that particular generation of Jewish immigrants to navigate their social world. Interestingly, a further lack of linkage to reality can be noted as regards the two *gefilte fish* recipes: they do indeed differ, but Clingan (or perhaps Gitelman) have reported them the wrong way round. In Galicia the fish was sweet, and no pepper was used (for the actual two recipes, see Sternberg 1993: 38–9). Enough said: there is no need to comment further on the supposed accuracy of these two sets of stereotypes: their existence is all that is important here.

8   See Shokeid 1988 for a classic anthropological study of this largely invisible 'symbolic community', whose members are often unsympathetically stigmatized by American Jews as *yoredim* ('those who have moved down' by voluntarily leaving their homeland) but who, for their part, look down on diaspora Jewish life. The pattern is repeated elsewhere. For example, in a fine ethnographic study Frankental (1999: 162) describes how secular Israeli Jewish migrants to South Africa 'are conspicuously absent from almost all organized [Jewish] communal activities'. Local South African Jews tend to see them as Jewish 'others' and so stereotype them negatively, a view that is reciprocated by the Israelis' negative attitude towards the '*golah* [diaspora] mentality' they encounter there (1999: 167, 171). The shared Jewishness, in other words, conceals completely different value-systems and cultural orientations—for example, those of Israeli 'cosmopolitans', unaccustomed to dealing with their Jewish identity and who see little need to build their own sub-community or contribute to diaspora Jewish society, versus locals.

9   The Holocaust certainly (except to some extent in the haredi world). But other great catastrophes, such as the Chmielnicki massacres of 1648–9, were not specifically institutionalized in the rabbinic historical memory and so their details are largely forgotten (Yerushalmi 1982: 48–52). The Jewish liturgy (for example, for the fast day of the Ninth of Av) certainly preserves elegies written in the aftermath of a number of massacres and public humiliations (for example, those perpetrated during the Crusades)—but such elegies focus on the pan-chronic significance of these events and so do not include historical narratives that would mention the dates or places when and where they occurred (Webber 2000: 116).

10   The ethnographic realities cannot be read off from the prescriptive rules alone. For example, in early modern Poland (during the 16th and 17th centuries), there were mutually constructed boundaries between Jews and Christians, i.e. rules for separation that came both from the Polish side and from the Jewish side—on such matters as enforcing distinct dress, fear of the pollution of wine touched by the other, discouraging eating and drinking with the other, attending each other's weddings or religious celebrations, or anxiety over women who (for example, as midwives, nurses, or domestic servants) came in contact with males of the other religion. The invention of printing, towards the end of the 15th century, encouraged the widespread dissemination of Jewish legal codes, which contributed to new, more sophisticated tools to enforce the boundaries in such areas (the groundbreaking work in this field is Katz 1962, esp. ch. 4 ('Social and Religious Segregation'); for a more recent review see Teter 2010). But there is good evidence (from rabbinic responsa to questions asked, or from *pinkasim*, books containing the minutes of community meetings) that in practice many of those detailed requirements and ideals, of both canon law and Jewish law, were either ignored or at least interpreted by the religious authorities with some flexibility (Fram 1997: ch. 1)—for example, that Jews drank non-kosher wine (1997: 99–105), that women and also travellers wore non-Jewish clothes (1997: 30; Teter 2010: 259–65), that there were sexual relations between Jewish employers and their female Christian servants (2010: 267 n. 98), or that non-Jews would be relied on to enter a Jewish home on the sabbath to light the fire in winter (the so-called *shabbes goy*, on which, for a detailed study, see Katz 1989). Total segregation notionally remained the ideal as expressed in the law codes but was in practice unattainable, and heavily influenced by pragmatic compromises of all kinds, as Teter concludes (2010: 269–70).

11   The results can be seen in many contexts, such as secularist Jewish opposition to the recent construction of an *eruv* in London (for an interesting ethnography on this, see Cooper 2002; on the *eruv*, see n. 4 above). A cogent and somewhat unexpected example can be found at the site of Auschwitz, where to this day there is no religious Jewish monument. Indeed, in the 1990s, secular Jewish leaders succeeded in convincing religious Christian leaders that there should be no religious symbols whatever at the site of Auschwitz. Jewish religious claustrophobia is sufficiently legitimate that the Jewish president of the international committee of Auschwitz survivors (himself a former communist) managed at the time to block a proposal for a particular inscription on the main monument there simply because it was a quotation from the Hebrew Bible (not even one that mentioned the word 'God'). The text to which he finally agreed includes the words 'For ever let this place be a cry of despair'—where 'despair', probably understood by some as pointing to the failure of human society, could also function as a codeword for the collapse of religious faith that, for many Jews and others, Auschwitz is deemed to represent

(for further details on the contested status of religion at the present-day Auschwitz site, see e.g. Webber 2006).

12   For example, Polish Jewry is usually held up as one of the most 'Jewish' of Jewries, only minimally affected by its surroundings (Rosman 2002: 523). Indeed, there is certainly plenty of evidence to support the view that (at least until the end of the 18th century) Jews were alienated from Poland culturally—including the absence of a Judaeo-Polish language (in contrast with Judaeo-German (Yiddish) or Judaeo-Arabic) and indeed the widespread absence of full literacy in Polish, or the double standards in Jewish capitalist practices, which were regulated within the Jewish community but with non-Jews they were more commercially aggressive and did not follow local Polish commercial conventions. There was certainly an underlying perception of insecurity and powerlessness. However, 'to say that Jews in Poland felt and acted alienated to a significant degree is not . . . the same as saying that they did not share in Polish culture' (2002: 524–5), and among the numerous examples Rosman cites is the case of synagogue architecture (not only the urban masonry synagogues that followed Polish architecture but also wooden synagogues, whose style was clearly borrowed from local wooden churches and manor houses). In these and many other areas of everyday life (such as food and music, even ritual objects), 'for Polish Jews, the aesthetic standard was Polish' (2002: 530). Rosman has argued strongly elsewhere for the fluidity of cultural interrelations and what he calls the polysystemic quality of Jewish life in Poland (2007: 93 ff.).

13   For this reason it should be mentioned that the position of Maimonides was more complicated—even though he recognized (along with many other rabbis after him) the major contribution of Christianity to the spiritual history of the world, he nevertheless considered Christianity as *avodah zarah*, because of its use of statues in its churches, its reliance on saints, and its doctrine of the Trinity. For these reasons he believed that Jews should not live in a town where there was a church. But unlike R. Me'iri (who did not consider Christianity *avodah zarah*), he did not live among Christians and did not seem to know much about them at first hand (see Korn 2012: 195 ff.)—in short, he had a strong sense of the boundary with Christianity, but in philosophical terms it was ambiguous given his support in theory for that religion. However, many later rabbinical authorities living in a European Christian environment followed the view of R. Me'iri in clearly stating that Christianity is not to be seen by Jews as *avodah zarah* but, on the contrary, that it is a perfectly valid religion for non-Jews—including such figures as R. Moses Isserles (Rema) (16th-cent. Poland), R. Jacob Emden (18th-cent. Germany), and R. Samson Raphael Hirsch (19th-cent. Germany) (2012: 197 ff.). Their technical reasoning for this was clear: as far as belief in the one God was concerned, there was one standard for Jews (a pure monotheism) and another standard for non-Jews (for whom, in addition to monotheism, it is theologically acceptable to hold supplementary ideas such as the Trinity). The latter was based on an exegetical reading of the second of the Ten Commandments, which says, 'There shall not be *for you* any other gods before me' (Exod. 20: 3; emphasis added)—'for you' (Jews, but not for others) (2012: 198). In this sense Judaism does not view itself as 'the religion for all peoples of the world; it is the religion of the Jews alone.

14   The 'hatred of Esau' surfaces even during the domestic liturgy of the Passover festival, still recited to this day. Quoting from the books of Psalms and Lamentations, the liturgy says: 'Pour out your wrath on the nations that do not know you, and upon the kingdoms that have not called upon your name. For they have devoured Jacob and laid waste his habita-

tion . . . Pour out your anger over them, and let the fire of your anger overtake them. Pursue them with anger and destroy them from under the heavens of the Lord.'

15   A clear, well-known example of this habit of thought can be found among popular Jewish attitudes towards Poland—a country which until the 1920s had for several centuries contained far and away the largest and most important centre of diaspora Jewish life in the world, and where six major German death camps were located during the Holocaust. Such negatively stereotyped attitudes towards Poland, Polish culture, the antisemitic Pole, and Polish co-responsibility for the Holocaust are usually so extreme (and uninformed) that not unreasonably they could be described as demonization. The subject has been discussed at length by both Polish and Jewish scholars; for a useful recent survey see Biskupski and Polonsky 2007, especially the introduction and the chapters by Engel, Polonsky, and Pawlikowski.

16   In his discussion of the particular problems posed by Hinduism (and its apparent worship of images) for a contemporary Orthodox Jewish theology that recognizes and makes room for other religions, Goshen-Gottstein (2012: 283–90) draws attention to the exceptional, open-minded work of the distinguished talmudic scholar Adin Steinsaltz. Writing in 2005, Steinsaltz points out that the Jewish dream of a messianic era, which will bring an ultimate vindication of truth as Judaism understands it (a time when the God of the patriarchs Abraham, Isaac, and Jacob will assert his dominion over all the world), does not presuppose that the nations of the world will become Jewish or follow Jewish law. Maimonides has said this clearly: messianic times mean a time of peace, not a time of uniformity. When the prophet Isaiah (11: 6) speaks about the wolf and the lamb, and the lion and the calf, all lying down together, what he envisions is not a change in the nature of creation—wolves will still be wolves, and lambs will still be lambs. What will change is the relationship between them. The different peoples of the world will not become less different; they will not share one religion, but rather they will introduce a radically new and harmonious vision of their relationships, and in particular people will everywhere abandon violence against each other. In short, different standards apply to different groups; the Jewish view of other faiths is that they should be faithful to their own religious traditions (within the bounds, of course, of the seven rules for the descendants of Noah).

17   This new pronunciation of liturgical Hebrew in the Ashkenazi synagogue is usually referred to by its members as 'Sephardi', since it is deemed to approximate Israeli modern Hebrew, which uses a Sephardi style of pronunciation. It was introduced (probably no earlier than the 1960s) notionally as a gesture to the modern Hebrew linguistic realities in Israel, although by definition it also clearly implies, following Zionist ideology, a rejection of diaspora Ashkenazi linguistic traditions—contrary to the rabbinic principle of *minhag avoteihem* (to follow ancestral custom), and indeed this change of pronunciation has not been followed at all among haredim (even those living in Israel itself), who resist Zionist innovations in this as in other areas of Jewish culture and encourage the old Galitzianer accent (Heilman 2006: 192). But this switch of Hebrew pronunciation has not been done well. Purists would immediately recognize it as a 'fusion' pronunciation, not really authentically Sephardi in its details (hence the term 'Ashkefardi'): for example, Ashkenazi word stress (usually on the penultimate syllable, as opposed to Sephardi word stress, usually on the last syllable) has often survived in the new pronunciation, combined with modern Hebrew consonantal qualities (such as Sephardi [t] for Ashkenazi [s] in pronouncing the letter *tav/sav*). Ashkefardi in fact retains both [s] and [t] indiscriminately, as, for example, in the phrase *es hashabat* (for Sephardi *et hashabat*); and there are other dissonances,

especially the widespread Ashkefardi ignorance of Sephardi traditions over the use of the *kamets katan* vowel, or simply combining Ashkenazi and Sephardi vowels indiscriminately (e.g. Ashkefardi *borukh atah* or *barukh atoh* for Ashkenazi *borukh atoh* or Sephardi *barukh atah*). It is not clear if Ashkefardi is deliberately intended to be inclusivist in these ways—it could be simply the result of ignorance, language interference among diaspora Ashkenazim who have been to Israel, or sociologically due to a cultural inconsistency between a mimetically received Ashkenazi pronunciation among immigrants to the USA, the UK, and elsewhere, and that of hired Israeli teachers of Hebrew in Jewish schools in these countries. Interestingly enough, the US-based ArtScroll publishers of the Torah, prayer books, and talmudic works, in very wide use among both Orthodox and haredi congregations, rely in their bilingual Hebrew–English editions on a similar Ashkefardi fusion transliteration of Hebrew, consciously using a somewhat bizarre combination of Sephardi vowels and Ashkenazi consonants (thus *akeidas yitschak*, rather than *akeidat izhak* or *akeidas yitzchok*): 'True,' as it is stated in the preface to the standard ArtScroll bilingual edition of the Torah after citing those examples, 'this blend may require some adjustment on the part of many readers, but it has proven successful' (whatever that means) (Scherman 1997: xiv). I am not aware of any in-depth academic studies of this subject, although the term 'Ashkefardi' is occasionally encountered in fusion cookery contexts or to describe Jews of mixed parentage, now increasingly common.

18   It is doubtful, for example, if the common haredi Yiddish term *klal yisroel* ('the Jewish people'), ostensibly fully inclusive, actually would in practice include Reform or non-practising Jews. Other established categories similarly need questioning as regards their fluidity—for example, how 'Ashkenazi' identity came about in the 16th century. This was principally the result of a major codification of Jewish law by the Rema which came to be accepted as binding for central and east European Jews. But it was not so simple: rabbinic law contains two important principles determining religious practice and authority, that of *minhag hamakom* (local custom) versus *minhag avoteihem* (ancestral custom). They would normally coincide in their application—but what was the law for Jews who migrated from one country to another? Should they follow their own laws and way of life from home, or should they adopt the laws and way of life of the new place? Whose religious authority should they follow? Where were the boundaries of Polish Ashkenazi authority—did this include Germany and Hungary, for example? Was an Ashkenazi family moving, say, from Poland to a Sephardi environment in Salonika (in the Ottoman empire) supposed to remain Ashkenazi—or, on the contrary, become in some sense Sephardi Jews? In other words, was Ashkenazi identity portable and transmissible, regardless of the social milieu? Was it acceptable for Ashkenazim to form their own community in Salonika—and if so, could others join it? The rabbis of the time had different opinions. Such debates have largely been forgotten (the category 'Ashkenazi' has been taken for granted), but of course there was substantial fluidity in resolving such issues, as detailed in a fascinating paper by Davis (2002).

19   A useful illustrative example is the complex situation in present-day Poland (which is where I currently live). Although there are certainly adult Jews in Poland who have identified as Jews from their childhood (especially those who see their Jewishness in terms of an ethnic self-identification rather than a religious one), Polish Jewish communal life in general is dominated by people of mixed Jewish–Christian socialist or atheist backgrounds whose Jewish identity is thus best characterized as fluid, provisional, and exploratory. There are numerous inconsistencies of all kinds. The notion of a Jewish 'com-

munity', or *gmina*, is a formal one (it is a corporate body recognized by the state), as opposed to Jewish 'society', or *społeczność*, which includes relatively small-scale groups using a wide range of criteria for affiliation, depending on context. For example, people who are in the lengthy process of undergoing religious conversion to Judaism may in some circumstances be socially accepted as Jewish (although usually not among those who define Jewishness ethnically), but would not be eligible for membership of the *gmina*. In practice, 'potential converts' would also be in this category, i.e. people who have shown an interest in the Jewish heritage over a period of time but may not have reached the decision that they would actually like to embark on a conversion course. People who are eligible for Israeli citizenship because they have a Jewish grandparent (see note 5 above) but who may also attend church on a regular basis, or are involved in the Jews for Jesus movement, would be accepted as Jews in some organizations but not others. In other words, attendance at a Jewish school, Jewish summer camp, Jewish student society, or Limmud conference does not presuppose a consistent or exclusive definition of Jewish identity—even if the question may simply be asked on the application form 'Are you Jewish?' The question is deemed to be non-controversial, inasmuch as it would appear to rely just on self-definition (although documentation may sometimes be requested, or there may be other follow-up enquiries). It is by no means uncommon in Poland to find tombstones in the Jewish cemetery where all that the inscription has to say about the deceased is that she was a 'former Auschwitz prisoner'; and there is the continuing post-Holocaust awareness here that Jewish identity, however defined, may be totally real for individuals whom others might dismiss as non-halakhic Jews or 'non-Jewish Jews'—although that is far from saying that all such individuals acknowledge their Jewish ancestry. Incoherence thrives alongside attempts to impose clarity, structure, and order (I am grateful to Rabbi Tyson Herberger of the Warsaw Jewish community for helpful comments in our discussions of this subject).

References

ABRAMSON, GLENDA, ed. 1989. *The Blackwell Companion to Jewish Culture: From the Eighteenth Century to the Present*. Oxford.

AVIV, CARYN, and DAVID SHNEER. 2005. *New Jews: The End of the Jewish Diaspora*. New York.

BARTH, FREDRIK. 1969. 'Introduction'. In Fredrik Barth, ed., *Ethnic Groups and Boundaries*, 9–38. Boston.

BENOR, SARAH BUNIN. 2012. *Becoming* Frum: *How Newcomers Learn the Language and Culture of Orthodox Judaism*. New Brunswick, NJ.

BIALE, DAVID, ed. 2002. *Cultures of the Jews: A New History*. New York.

BISKUPSKI, MIECZYSŁAW, and ANTONY POLONSKY, eds. 2007. *Polish–Jewish Relations in North America*. Polin: Studies in Polish Jewry 19. Oxford.

CLINGAN, CAROL. 2010. 'Programme Report: Zvi Gitelman, "Culture Wars: Litvaks vs. Galitzianers in Eastern Europe"'. *Mass-Pocha: Journal of the Jewish Genealogical Society of Greater Boston*, 24(1) (issue 64): 5–7. <http://www.jgsh.org/Newsletters/File0086.pdf>, accessed 14 Aug. 2012.

COOPER, DAVINA. 2002. 'Out of Place: Symbolic Domains, Religious Rights and the Cultural Contract'. In Michael Saltman, ed., *Land and Territoriality*, 93–111. Oxford.

COUSINEAU, JENNIFER. 2010. 'The Domestication of Urban Jewish Space and the North-West London Eruv'. In Simon J. Bronner, ed., *Jews at Home: The Domestication of Identity*. Jewish Cultural Studies 2, 43–74. Oxford.

COWARD, HAROLD. 2000. *Pluralism in the World's Religions: A Short Introduction*. Oxford.

DAVIS, JOSEPH. 2002. 'The Reception of the *Shulhan 'Arukh* and the Formation of Ashkenazic Jewish Identity'. *AJS Review*, 26(2): 251–76.

DELLAPERGOLA, SERGIO. 1994. 'An Overview of the Demographic Trends of European Jewry'. In Jonathan Webber, ed., *Jewish Identities in the New Europe*, 57–73. London.

—— 2002. 'Demography'. In Martin Goodman, ed., *The Oxford Handbook of Jewish Studies*, 797–823. Oxford.

EILBERG-SCHWARTZ, HOWARD. 1990. *The Savage in Judaism: An Anthropology of Israelite Religion and Ancient Judaism*. Bloomington and Indianapolis.

FRAM, EDWARD. 1997. *Ideals Face Reality: Jewish Law and Life in Poland, 1550–1655*. Cincinnati.

FRANKENTAL, SALLY. 1999, 'A Frontier Experience: Israeli Jews Encounter Diaspora in Cape Town, South Africa'. In Sander L. Gilman and Milton Shain, eds., *Jewries at the Frontier: Accommodation, Identity, Conflict*, 155–84. Urbana, Ill.

FRIEDMAN, MENACHEM. 1987. 'Life Tradition and Book Tradition in the Development of Ultraorthodox Judaism'. In Harvey E. Goldberg, ed., *Judaism Viewed from Within and from Without: Anthropological Studies*, 235–55. Albany, NY.

FUCHS, MARTIN. 2002. 'The Praxis of Cognition and the Representation of Difference'. In Heidrun Friese, ed., *Identities: Time, Difference, and Boundaries*, 109–32. New York.

GEERTZ, CLIFFORD. 1966. 'Religion as a Cultural System'. In Michael Banton, ed., *Anthropological Approaches to the Study of Religion*, 1–46. London.

GILMAN, SANDER L. 1999. 'Introduction: The Frontier as a Model for Jewish History'. In Sander L. Gilman and Milton Shain, eds., *Jewries at the Frontier: Accommodation, Identity, Conflict*, 1–25. Urbana, Ill.

GLENN, SUSAN A., and NAOMI B. SOKOLOFF, eds. 2010. *Boundaries of Jewish Identity*. Seattle and London.

GOSHEN-GOTTSTEIN, ALON. 2012. 'Encountering Hinduism: Thinking Through *Avodah Zarah*'. In Alon Goshen-Gottstein and Eugene Korn, eds., *Jewish Theology and World Religions*, 263–98. Oxford.

GRUBER, RUTH ELLEN. 2002. *Virtually Jewish: Reinventing Jewish Culture in Europe*. Berkeley.

HARSHAV, BENJAMIN. 1993. *Language in Time of Revolution*. Stanford.

HEILMAN, SAMUEL. 1992. *Defenders of the Faith: Inside Ultra-Orthodox Jewry*. New York.

—— 2006. *Sliding to the Right: The Contest for the Future of American Jewish Orthodoxy*. Berkeley.

HIRSCH, EMIL G., and J. D. EISENSTEIN. 1903. 'Gentile'. *Jewish Encyclopedia*, v. 614–26. New York and London.

KAPLAN, DANA EVAN. 2009. *Contemporary American Judaism: Transformation and Renewal*. New York.

KATZ, JACOB. 1962 [1961]. *Exclusiveness and Tolerance: Jewish–Gentile Relations in Medieval and Modern Times*. New York.

——1989. *The 'Shabbes Goy': A Study in Halakhic Flexibility*. Philadelphia.

KORN, EUGENE. 2012. 'Rethinking Christianity: Rabbinic Positions and Possibilities'. In Alon Goshen-Gottstein and Eugene Korn, eds., *Jewish Theology and World Religions*, 189–215. Oxford.

KUGELMASS, JACK. 1987 [1986]. *The Miracle of Intervale Avenue: The Story of a Jewish Congregation in the South Bronx*. New York.

LEVINE, HERB, ed. 1994. 'Negotiating Boundaries'. *The Reconstructionist*, 59: 2.

LICHTENSTEIN, AARON. 1981. *The Seven Laws of Noah*. New York.

MAHLER, RAPHAEL. 1985. *Hasidism and the Jewish Enlightenment: Their Confrontation in Galicia and Poland in the First Half of the Nineteenth Century*, trans. Eugene Orenstein. Philadelphia.

MALKIN, YAAKOV. 1998. *What Do Secular Jews Believe*, trans. Batya Stein. Jerusalem.

MYERHOFF, BARBARA. 1980 [1978]. *Number Our Days*. New York.

NOVAK, DAVID. 2011. *The Image of the Non-Jew in Judaism: The Idea of Noahide Law*, 2nd edn. Oxford.

PAULSSON, GUNNAR S. 2002. *Secret City: The Hidden Jews of Warsaw, 1940–1945*. New Haven.

ROSMAN, MOSHE. 2002. 'Innovative Tradition: Jewish Culture in the Polish–Lithuanian Commonwealth'. In David Biale, ed., *Cultures of the Jews: A New History*, 519–70.

——2007. *How Jewish Is Jewish History?* Oxford.

SACKS, JONATHAN. 1993. *One People? Tradition, Modernity, and Jewish Unity*. Oxford.

SCHERMAN, NOSSON, ed. 1997 [1993]. *The Chumash* (ArtScroll Series, Stone edition), 8th edn. Brooklyn.

SHOKEID, MOSHE. 1988. *Children of Circumstances: Israeli Emigrants in New York*. Ithaca, NY.

SOLOMON, NORMAN. 1991. *Judaism and World Religion*. Basingstoke.

SOLOVEITCHIK, HAYM. 1994. 'Rupture and Reconstruction: The Transformation of Contemporary Orthodoxy'. *Tradition*, 28(4): 64–130.

STAMPFER, SHAUL. 2012. *Lithuanian Yeshivas of the Nineteenth Century: Creating a Tradition of Learning*, trans. Lindsey Taylor-Gutharz. Oxford.

STERNBERG, ROBERT. 1993. *Yiddish Cuisine: A Gourmet's Approach to Jewish Cooking*. Northvale, NJ.

TABORY, EPHRAIM, and BERNARD LAZERWITZ. 1995. 'Americans in the Israeli Reform and Conservative Denominations'. In Shlomo Deshen, Charles S. Liebman, and Moshe Shokeid, eds., *Israeli Judaism: The Sociology of Religion in Israel*. Studies of Israeli Society 7, 335–45. New Brunswick.

TETER, MAGDA. 2010. '"There should be no love between us and them": Social Life and the Bounds of Jewish and Canon Law in Early Modern Poland'. In Adam Teller, Magda Teter, and Antony Polonsky, eds., *Social and Cultural Boundaries in Pre-Modern Poland*. Polin: Studies in Polish Jewry 22, 249–70. Oxford.

UJA Federation of New York. 2011. *Jewish Community Study of New York*. Available at <http://www.ujafedny.org/jewish-community-study-of-new-york-2011/>, accessed 22 Aug. 2012.

VULKAN, DANIEL, and DAVID GRAHAM. 2008. *Population Trends among Britain's Strictly Orthodox Jews*. London. Available at <http://www.bod.org.uk/content/StrictlyOrthodox.pdf>, accessed 22 Aug. 2012.

WEBBER, JONATHAN ed. 1994. *Jewish Identities in the New Europe*. London.

——2000. 'Lest We Forget! The Holocaust in Jewish Historical Consciousness and Modern Jewish Identities'. in Glenda Abramson, ed., *Modern Jewish Mythologies*, 107–35. Cincinnati.

——2006. 'Memory, Religion, and Conflict at Auschwitz: A Manifesto'. In Oren Baruch Stier and J. Shawn Landres, eds., *Religion, Violence, Memory, and Place*, 51–70. Bloomington.

YERUSHALMI, YOSEF HAYIM. 1982. *Zakhor: Jewish History and Jewish Memory*. Seattle and London.

Trickster's Children: Genealogies of Jewishness in Anthropology

JONATHAN BOYARIN

CHRIS BRACKEN'S 1997 volume *The Potlatch Papers*—a rich study of Euro-Canadian efforts to control the 'wasteful' social practices of native peoples—opens with a remarkable vignette. The time is the late 1880s. Franz Boas, having emigrated from Germany to the United States in 1884, has arrived at what Bracken convincingly describes as what was then thought to be the north-west extremity of Europe—namely, Vancouver Island—in search of unspoiled native Americans. Bracken quotes Boas's explicit description of the native individuals in the city of Victoria as having been overtly Europeanized, and thus having lost much, if not most, of their proper, 'native' character. We can guess why Boas did not deem these city natives worthy of ethnographic attention: aboriginal peoples were of primary value when their distinctive cultures were intact and when, therefore, those cultures could serve as 'a kind of Archimedean leverage point for the criticism of [Boas's own European] civilization' (Stocking 1979: 47). It was precisely those individuals who maintained cultural forms as different from European civilized patterns as possible that were useful for this purpose, rather than those 'dress[ing] mostly in European fashion' (quoted in Bracken 1997: 8).

But why, Bracken wonders, did Boas never express a concern that the Europeanization of the natives might in turn have made Boas *less European*—that is, that their acquisition of European dress and the like might have diminished his own identity? The question is certainly a perspicacious one, from the perspective of current critical enquiry into the politics and rhetorics of collective identity: if the Other can so easily become like me, how distinctive, how secure, how unitary is my identity really?

Bracken's question is almost certainly rhetorical, for Boas was hardly unusual in failing to reflect the colonial gaze upon himself. It was a rare European ethnographer who reacted to the permeability of identity markers by wondering about the contingency of his own identity. Or, we should say, who left the traces of any such self-reflection in his own texts. We do not know, of course, what unrecorded thoughts passed through Boas's mind on the streets of Victoria. But it is hardly beyond the range of plausibility to suppose that Boas, seeing the apparent anomie of so-called 'Europeanized' native people in Victoria, was led to wonder about the relation between this particular colonial encounter and the continuing process, back in Old Europe, whose result is best described not as the Europeanization of the Jews, but rather as the progressive obviation of Jewish difference as a possible constituent element of European identity itself.

This question—the relation between the problematic Jewishness of certain, indeed many, European or Euro-American ethnographers and the identity of those whom they studied and about whom they wrote—is a complex and delicate one. To be sure, their objects of study have been in the main precisely *not* Jews: until recently, Jewish ethnographers' attention to the ethnography of Jews was quite exceptional. The argument that I suggest, but cannot fully develop here, is that on a broader scale the Jewishness of these ethnographers shaped their scholarly practice and their world-view in ways that continue to shape, in turn, the disciplines within which Jewish culture is studied. In this sense, the 'framing' effect pertinent here must be understood (doubtless in overly schematic fashion) as at least a twofold process: Jewishness frames the scholars and their scholarship, and they in turn help mould the epistemological frames through which Jewish culture is subjected to processes of rescue, secularization, valorization, denigration, transformation, and the like.

Moreover, the question of the relation between the Jewishness of (some) ethnographers and the identity of their research subjects is, at best, only partially resolved today, more than a century after Boas walked the streets of young Victoria. Jewish ethnographers of my generation have inherited this question and, for the most part unlike our scholarly forebears, we have highlighted and sometimes even celebrated our own Jewishness. In this essay I hope to contribute to documenting this process of inheritance and transformation, in part by frankly situating myself within a genealogy that stretches back to Boas himself. As anthropologists know full well, this form of genealogical insertion is a form of self-authorization, but I trust nevertheless that readers will find the exercise more illuminating than mystifying.

In fact, perhaps the most awkward aspect of this kind of exploration is that it requires us to treat our own intellectual ancestors as subjects of ethnography. We place ourselves, if we want to do more than just tally up what they did and did not say (and of what we do or do not have a record), in the position of knowing about them more or differently than they knew themselves—routine in our relationship to the 'subjects' of ethnography but less so in our relationship to peers. Moreover, since the Jewishness of Jewish ethnographers, especially in the foregoing generations, seems to be as much a story of absence (to say 'suppression' might really be to presume too much here) as of expression, we are forced to tease out intimations concerning abstract matters of personal identity from the kind of fragmentary evidence archaeologists might confront in attempting to reconstruct ancient mentalities.

Nevertheless, I will try to hold myself here to a slightly higher standard than that of mere plausibility. Indeed, although Boas's name will come up more than once in my essay, this is not a study of Boas's own Jewishness, even less of his European identity (see Glick 1982; Frank 1997). Rather, I wish merely to borrow from Bracken the image of Boas walking down the street in Victoria, 'at the rim of Western thinking' (Bracken 1997: 7), ready to defend and fight for the ideals of universalist, rational, liberal Europe, equally ready to defend the human equality and, indeed, human value of integral non-European cultures, but not especially interested in or sympathetic to those in between, who no longer represent a valid version of human *Kultur* but have not achieved autonomous individuality. For Boas and for many of his successors, this scheme for framing or categorizing types of humans largely excluded their Jewish contemporaries, and their Jewishness, from the purview of the newly developing cultural anthropology. Most Jews were European (or white) but not quite yet, and—as we shall see—they seemingly had no culture of their own to speak of. Whether, in regard to Jewishness, Boas and his Jewish successors were more like colonizers or more like colonized is perhaps not the best way to frame this discussion, and in any case certainly cannot be answered here.

My story more properly begins a few decades after the 1880s, and a few thousand miles east of British Columbia, with a figure who was a younger associate of Boas's, and with whom Boas had a rather troubled relationship. I speak now of Paul Radin. As will become clear below, of the many Jewish immigrant students of Boas, I focus here on Radin because he has remained, until now, a kind of shadow ancestor ('intellectual', as if there was any such thing as a non-intellectual ancestor!) of my own.

Radin in England

The cultural anthropologist Paul Radin was born in Łódź, Poland, the son of a Reform rabbi. Raised and educated in the United States, he became a student of Franz Boas at Columbia University, and, by this time already a veteran and well-respected ethnographer and writer especially on Native American cultures, he went to London in 1924 to address the Jewish Historical Society of England on the topic of 'Monotheism Among Primitive Peoples'. Cultural anthropologist Jonathan Boyarin was born and raised in a family of New Jersey chicken farmers whose ideological heritages included both the Lithuanian Orthodox yeshiva world and Yiddishist socialism. He was a student of Stanley Diamond at the New School for Social Research, and, after two decades without an academic home is now professor of—of all things, for an anthropologist!—modern Jewish thought. He first conceived of these reflections in response to an invitation, some eighty-odd years after Boas's London visit, to address the Anthropology Department colloquium at the London School of Economics.[1] Now Radin and Diamond were

Jews, as I am a Jew; something of a physical, transgressive thrill still goes through me as I write and as I say these rather old-fashioned words. Neither Radin nor Diamond hid his Jewishness, but certainly neither chose, as I have, to make it the leitmotif of his life and career.

Tracing out a genealogy of Jewishness and professional anthropology through Diamond and Radin, then, I confront two linked areas of suppressed discourse in the historical and current relations between identity and difference in anthropology, both admittedly far less generally suppressed than they were even twenty years ago. One is talking about Jewishness; the other is talking about the ethnographer's self. We are reminded, for example, of a categorical assertion by Robert J. Smith that 'The subjects of ethnographies, it should never be forgotten, are always more interesting than their authors' (quoted in Tweed 1997: 10). We may even agree that, as a general rule, this remains a salutary caution; but at the very least it reinforces the assumption that a clear distinction may be drawn between those who are properly authors of ethnography and those who are properly its subjects. It also erases from consideration the problematic but viable subgenre known as autoethnography: problematic because the phrase itself risks reification of the ethnographer's self; viable because the frames of one's own identity are more often than not a major shaping source of anthropological analysis and probably better brought to the surface than left unstated (see Orlove 1997).

In any case, when we open the slim volume in which Radin's 1924 lecture was published, such a clear distinction between 'the subjects of ethnography' and the 'authors' of ethnographies becomes impossible to maintain. Radin had, I surmise, been invited to cross the Atlantic and address the Jewish Historical Society not only because of his scholarly reputation but because of his Jewishness; moreover, from the text of his talk, as I will discuss in a moment, one gets the impression that his listeners' interest in primitive monotheism was largely motivated by a desire to understand where they, as Jews, stood in relation to so-called 'primitive peoples'. More prosaically, the press of events then current is strikingly evident in Israel Zangwill's foreword to Radin's lecture, which points to the racist atmosphere of the United States, and not only of Europe, in the 1920s. This is not surprising, since Zangwill is best remembered now as the author of the play *The Melting Pot,* and since the United States drastically limited immigration, largely on racial grounds, first in 1921 and then more firmly in May 1924, just weeks after Radin's lecture in London. In his foreword, Zangwill casts doubt on the notion of a progressive ethicizing and universalization of the notion of the one God, and suggests that, instead, precisely the opposite has taken place. In modern times, he claims, the trend is rather for national groups to claim a privileged and exclusive relation to the divinity: 'America, in speaking of herself as "God's own country", and in now further narrowing her land-Lord to an exclusive interest in "Nordics", gives us the clearest modern illustration of the universal tendency'

(Radin 1924: 13). Zangwill continues:

Fortunately Dr Radin is not an armchair anthropologist. Though he has been a Professor, he is by no means of the type that evolves camels from inner consciousness. It is from the life that he has drawn his deduction. For five years on behalf of the Government he studied the Red Indians of the United States, and for four years those of Canada. Both these surviving minorities nourish burning political grievances against the white man, who does not seem even to have observed the terms under which they were dispossessed and secluded. It will be interesting to hear from our lecturer how far their mentality is inferior to that of their contemptuous conquerors. One remembers the Indian Chief in Dickens's 'American Notes', whose impression of Congress was that 'it lacked dignity'. (Radin 1924: 13–14)

Radin, in his lecture on that occasion, is at pains to point out how different a stance he is taking from the evolutionism of the ethnologists. He writes, 'to have admitted among primitive peoples the existence of monotheism in any form would have been equivalent to abandoning the [professional ethnologists'] whole doctrine of evolutionary stages' (1924: 20). Instead, regarding the question of monotheism, Radin posits a universal presence, in varying degrees, of 'two concepts': that of a 'Supreme Deity . . . unapproachable directly and taking but little interest in the world after he has created it; and the Transformer, the establisher of the present order of things, utterly non-ethical' (1924: 22). These are held, respectively, in every society by individuals of two differing 'temperaments': 'that of the permanently devout man and the idealist, and that of the intermittently devout, the practical man, the realist' (1924: 37). In any case, Radin firmly concludes that 'the possibility of interpreting monotheism as part of a general intellectual and ethical progress must be abandoned' (1924: 55). So much, though Radin does not here spell out this implication, for any transhistorical Jewish chauvinism concerning any possible claim to being the advance guard of monotheistic humanity. Indeed, he *does* take some pains to refute the view of one Dr Buchanan Gray that Hebrew monotheism itself had only appeared as late as the sixth century, and as the result of a gradual evolution (Radin 1924: 60–2; Gray 1922–3). Denying the uniqueness of the mental capacities of ancient Jews, he describes the peculiar process by which 'monotheism . . . became the prevailing and exclusive official religion of a particular people' as 'something in the nature of an historical accident' (1924: 65). There is no concession to cultural evolution here, not even in the sense of turning the doctrine on its head by claiming pride of place for the ancient Hebrews as having been at the forefront of any such evolution.

Before moving on from this moment in 1924, it is certainly worthwhile to point again to the historical situation—one in which Euro-American nativism and scientific racism had limited the possibilities of European Jewish emigration in what turned out, in retrospect, to be a fatal way; and to the social situation, where the anthropologist Paul Radin was addressing an audience at once *Jewish* and *civilized*. By suggesting that the apperception of a single and universal God was, in various times and places, the accomplishment of randomly distributed, yet extraordinary, intellects, Radin certainly seems to have endorsed that idea as one worth treasuring. But at the same time he seems to have wished to assure his audience that they were, on the whole, neither more nor less advanced members of the species than their own 'ancestors' the ancient Hebrews, or than the so-called primitives or, indeed, the other European peoples of their day.

More on Radin

There is more that bears saying about Paul Radin and Jewishness here, though this is not the place for a full biographical sketch. First, while it is hardly the case that Radin had nothing to say about Jews or Jewishness—for example, he translated from German to English two volumes of Louis Ginzberg's *Legends of the Jews*, while his brother Max, a prominent Berkeley legal scholar, published extensively on ancient Judaism—nevertheless, as far as I have been able to determine, he published nothing or next to nothing on contemporary or even recent Jewish culture. In this he followed his mentor Boas (Glick 1982: 557; Frank 1997: 734). Second, the premises of his 1924 lecture—opposing the idea of evolutionary stages from primitive to civilized intellect, stressing the distribution of the same intellectual appetites and capacities in primitive as well as civilized individuals—appear to have been fundamental to his intellectual, ethical, and scholarly outlook. They are already evident in a letter he wrote, as early as 1905, to Robert Lowie, where he stated that he intended to study 'neither history nor ethnology but both, to see, just exactly and to what degree historical development still shows distinct signs of primitive mind, to what degree each one of us past and present still has undercurrents of primitive weltanschauung'.[2] Third, I have mentioned that Radin was a student of Boas's. It is clear that there was later antagonism between the two, and it may well have had to do, as some have suggested, with Radin's emphasis on the individual or with Boas's continued emphasis on diffusionism.

It may also, it seems, have been linked in a more prosaic way to tensions that both men experienced surrounding their position as Jews in the institutions of American scholarship. In a draft paper for an unfinished manuscript that would have been the only full-length biography of Radin, a graduate student at Berkeley named Mary Sacharoff-Fast Wolf describes the following incident from 1911: Radin, then employed by the Bureau of American Ethnology to study the Winnebago, was unable to account for certain funds, thus possibly offending Frederick Webb Hodge, ethnologist in charge at the Bureau, on whom Boas was in turn dependent for publication of his own *Handbook of American Indian Languages*. Sacharoff-Fast Wolf notes, without further documentation or comment, that

Hodge was 'well known to be an anti-Semite'.[3] The intimation is clearly that Boas feared that Radin's indiscretion, whatever it may have been, would bring the wrath of the antisemite down on his head as well. Now Herb Lewis, of the University of Wisconsin, writes in his response to an earlier draft of my paper: 'Given Boas' record for speaking out—even at the cost of his own interests and position . . . I think it more likely that he *believed Hodge's* accusations than that he backed down for fear of retribution.'[4] In any case, it appears that among the circle of Boas's students concerns circulated about the possible antisemitism of fellow anthropologists (see also Bronner 1998: 132–7).

The archival records of Mary Sacharoff-Fast Wolf's research on Radin's life and work include her attempt at some précis of Radin's legacy. That attempt bears quotation, with the caveats that Sacharoff never passed the student phase of her own career, that these materials were never published, and that she is now deceased. In a draft entitled 'Paul Radin: In Search of the Man', she wrote:

What I have gathered to date from my network of informants, and particularly from those who were very close to him in his lifetime, was a quality in Radin which is certainly to be desired in an anthropologist; a quality which is not always found. This is the ability to divest oneself of their own cultural yoke while remembering, nevertheless, what its restrictions were. Paul Radin, as I gather from interviews with various informants, was unhappy with some of the restrictions of life even within his liberal and intellectual family . . . This was certainly not a unique alienation. It was not uncommon among families immigrating from Europe and facing the abrupt transformation from the traditional patterns of their countries of origin to the 'American experience'. One positive result of Radin's growing up in this household, however, was that he was to be comfortable in two cultures, that of Europe and that of America. Stanley Diamond comments on this in *Totems and Teachers* and adds that in a sense he, Radin, links the two cultures. Nevertheless, he was fully aware of the restrictions of his own culture. These were chafing and binding upon him intellectually and he did manage to divest himself of them. In time he went forth unencumbered to do his work.[5]

I will say more anon about the Diamond essay Sacharoff refers to, but for now it is worth noting that this is a Bildungs plot, a story of evolution away from a childish or atavistic milieu (she refers elsewhere to the 'stagnant' character of traditional Talmud study) to a mature philosophical stance. Furthermore, since the work that Radin went forth to do was so much bound up with denying a categorical difference in capacity between primitive and civilized intellects, there is a kind of double and, it may be fair to say, almost tragically confused movement of time and progress here. On one hand Radin is said to have 'divest[ed] himself' of the restrictions of his own culture; on the other he is concerned to prove that we are still 'primitive' and that, indeed, our primitive ancestors were as smart as we are.

It seems fair at this point to pose a rhetorical question, to wit: if we still want to hold that the ethnographic subject is always more interesting than the ethnographer, who's the subject here—Radin? Sacharoff?—and who's the ethnographer? Radin, the professional ethnographer, is being identified in terms of his relation to and distance from something called 'his own culture', the kind of thing that the subjects of ethnography were once supposed to have, although that supposition has itself come under interrogation in recent criticism (see e.g. Michaels 1992; Boyarin and Boyarin 1993).

Stanley Diamond

Who, more prosaically, is Stanley Diamond, to whom I have now referred twice? Younger yet doubtless less well known than Radin, Diamond was born in New York City in 1922 into an intellectual and progressive Jewish family living on St Marks Place on the Lower East Side, a family that included a grandfather who was a founder of the Yiddish theatre. He early experienced a loss of rich and intimate daily kinship ties: 'This sensuous and exciting child world collapsed when the family gradually nucleated and he moved into the remote exile of the Bronx and Upper Manhattan' (Gailey 1991a: 2–3).

While still a graduate student at Columbia, Diamond 'presented two departmental seminars on the comparative and historical study of the Jews, dismantling on the way [Earnest] Hooton's racist portrayal of the Jews as a "people of genius"' (1991a: 5). This must have been in the late 1940s, in the years after Boas's death, and it does indeed suggest some continuation of the Boasian agenda for anthropological discourse pertinent to Jews—an agenda focused on, and for the most part limited to, combating racism (Glick 1982). In any case, Diamond's graduate work did not centre on any Jewish question, but was rather a seminal study of what he called the 'proto-state' of Dahomey, focusing, in his student Christine Gailey's words, 'on state formation as an historically inconclusive process that pits kin communities against civil authorities and priorities in all areas of cultural life' (Gailey 1991b: 105–6). Whether such concerns for this process of state formation, long ago and far away, might have been inspired by Diamond's childhood experience of the loss of precisely such a 'kin community' is a suggestion I will leave open for now; in my case, however, I think it did, and I have already speculated as much in print (Boyarin 1996: 8).

Over the course of his career Diamond produced several critical articulations involving the anthropology of Zionism, types from the Bible, or the figure of the Jew in the West. His 1957 article 'Kibbutz and Shtetl: The History of an Idea' (based on early fieldwork in Israel that appears not to have resulted in further publication but may have done much to shape Diamond's thinking about the politics of Jewish collectivity and identity) is perhaps his most sustained articulation regarding the fate of Jewish culture. In it he argues that the social organization of the pioneering kibbutzim was consciously structured by the effort to reject and overcome what the Zionist pioneers understood as the pathological family structure and abnormal class structure of the predominant Jewish settlement patterns in eastern Europe (Diamond 1957). To my mind this essay remains a profoundly acute analysis of the consequences of cultural rejection, and a harbinger of the more general crises of secular Zionist culture. At the same time, a careful reading of the essay leaves one often puzzled, since it is hard to tell where Diamond's description of the Zionist fantasy of shtetl pathology ends and his own description of shtetl culture, almost equally fantastic in my perspective, begins. This inattention to the historical specificity of the world of Jewish eastern Europe considerably blunts his critique of the *vatikim*, the Zionist pioneers, while suggesting the necessity of a larger critique of Ashkenazi-descendant cultural rejection. Some of Diamond's own statements about Jewish identity would serve as primary data for that cultural rejection.

Diamond, who had for a time been a younger colleague of Radin's in the anthropology department at Brandeis University, wrote a preface to Radin's classic study, *The Trickster* (Radin 1956). His preface later became an independent essay under the title 'Job and the Trickster' (Diamond 1974: 281–91). For Diamond, the biblical sufferer Job, undialectical, uncreative, civilized, was the very antithesis of the unpredictable and creative primitive Trickster. Diamond refers to the book of Job as exemplary of the 'Judeo-Christian tradition'.[6] Forty years on, it should be clear to us that even to utter that phrase, 'the Judeo-Christian tradition', is not only to invoke its necessary critique, but to point to so much of what has been the burden of Jewish studies for the past generation; that is, to undo that hyphen—to decouple the Jewish from the Christian—yet without once again reifying the dichotomy between the two.

Later Diamond wrote a brief essay entitled 'The State of Being Jewish', as the introduction to a 1983 special issue of the journal *Dialectical Anthropology*, which he had founded and edited. There he wrote:

Hence, the incessant and curious question—what is a Jew? Who am I? The answer: A people without a culture (a text is not a culture), without a society, haunted by archaic references, trying to live in abstractions, and, having been close to extinction on several occasions, nevertheless maintaining an indomitable passion for survival. (Diamond 1983: 1)[7]

Note (in addition to a certainly unwitting reiteration of the ancient Christian trope that accuses the Jews of attachment to superannuated doctrines, practices, and texts) the extraordinarily strident representation, the *speaking-for* here, in which Diamond assumes the subject position of 'the' Jew (if there is only one answer, then there can be only one Jew, and I, Stanley Diamond, as a marginal critical intellectual, hereby answer this question). Diamond adds:

This ambivalence [in non-Jewish projections about Jewishness] reveals the storied existence of the Jews as the *unresolved* primitive myth of Western civilization, a myth without a resolving ritual, a myth that is therefore acted out to the climax of self-destruction in the polities of the West. (1983: 2)

This, a complex statement in itself, is, so far as I know, the closest Diamond comes in any available utterance to an explicit association of Jewishness with the primitive that he so urgently values.

However, the overall sense of Diamond's 1983 article is that Jewishness was doomed to extinction as a substantive identity, *because it could not maintain a people's 'unity' any longer*. This very assumption of cultural holism, of culture as 'whole or nothing', is much less self-evident to students of culture today than it was in the world of American cultural anthropology in which Diamond was trained and where he worked. In any case, this observation seems to have led Diamond to assert that Jewishness could only authentically be maintained in something like Lyotard's later articulation of the identities of lower-case 'jews' (Lyotard 1990)—or, in Diamond's phrase, once again combining an extraordinary individualism with extraordinary masculinism, 'denying any history except that which must be morally willed' (Diamond 1983: 5), so that Jewishness is valid only insofar as it occupies a space of marginality, an assumed alienation.

Diamond and Me

The special issue of *Dialectical Anthropology* in which Diamond's essay was published grew out of a seminar he taught, together with Harold Bloom, at the New School in the academic year 1982/3. I was in Paris doing a year of doctoral fieldwork then, immensely relieved that I would be far away from New York and not have to face what I was certain would have been the exhausting task of arguing throughout the semester with both Bloom, may he live long, and Diamond—may his memory be a blessing.

My own engagement with Diamond, perhaps less profound by the world's criteria but certainly important in the shaping of my intellectual and political impulses, began with my senior undergraduate thesis—a comparison of Diamond's version of Marxist anthropology, based as it was on a humanist and, some would say, romanticized vision of the primitive prior to the class alienations of civilization, to the current state of French Marxist anthropology, out of Louis Althusser by way of figures such as Maurice Godelier and Emmanuel Terray. In that thesis I came out strongly in favour of Diamond's version. It is not mere coincidence that, during those same undergraduate years, I was also developing a conscious nostalgia for the world of Jewish eastern Europe that I had never known. Accordingly, as I was writing my thesis I was much tempted to tie Diamond's notion of the primitive to a retrospective account of what it pleased us then to call 'traditional' east European Jewish life.

Hence, this reflection on the subject of the Jewish ethnographer in relation to Jews as ethnographic subjects provides me, more than three decades later, with a chance to return to a hunch I had and which I suppressed at the time of writing my undergraduate thesis on Diamond's work, before I became his student. My sense was that somehow the dichotomy between the primitive and the civilized, and the discussion of the movement from one to the other and even the possibility of recuperating resources from the former to help heal the alienation and dehumanization of the latter, was in some way, perhaps coded or masked, mirrored in a transition in east European Jewish life 'out of the ghetto' (Katz 1973). I felt that, indeed, it was this very transition that sparked, at least in part, the creative meditation on European society identified in John Morrow Cuddihy's still classic, and still troubling, *Ordeal of Civility* (1974). I was dissuaded at the time by Katz's clearly showing that (unlike Diamond's primitive), the 'shtetl', whatever that was, was riven by class divisions, and soon enough by an awareness that Cuddihy only had access to a caricatured notion of 'premodern' east European Jewish culture as lacking 'civility'. I do not intend to reopen the investigation along these lines now, but I do hope to set you wondering as I continue inevitably to wonder, inspired most recently by the Jewish historian Haym Soloveitchik's suggestion that, like their fellows, today's Jews 'submit to rule rather than to custom' (Soloveitchik 1994), a phrase in itself strikingly reminiscent of Diamond's essay on 'The Rule of Law versus the Order of Custom'.

I may add, anecdotally, that while Diamond praised my senior thesis, and eventually accorded me the Ph.D. in anthropology, he was most sceptical about my voluntary public identification with Jewishness, probably especially as symbolized by the characteristic head covering, which I believe he saw as a chauvinistic gesture. My strongest memory in evidence of this suspicion was Diamond's unsolicited and unexpected phone call to me early on a weekend morning, sometime at the very beginning of the 1980s, in which he conveyed his fear lest I become part of a mainstream Jewish organizational framework, something I had no desire or intention to do, even had the mainstream Jewish organizations been interested in having me. My father urged me along those lines when it was clear that no university would take me for the time being; but it never happened.

I will never be sure to what extent my own subsequent work is an investigation of, or on the contrary, an avoidance of, this question of analogy or elective affinity between the primitive and the traditionally Jewish, which I identified and set aside as a tyro anthropologist. I do know that at one point I was powerfully motivated by a desire to see Trickster himself as a Jewish figure. I did so, at least indirectly, in an essay comparing Gerald Vizenor's *The Trickster of Liberty* to Patrick Modiano's *Place de l'Étoile* (Boyarin 1992: 9–31). And when I came to write up the life history of my teacher Dr Shlomo Noble (Boyarin 1994), it pleased me to imagine him as a trickster, and I even wanted to call that book 'Trickster's Education in Europe and America'. I was dissuaded from this, among other reasons, by the argument that it would have been disrespectful; and a quick glance at Radin's edition of the Winnebago Trickster cycle, presenting a figure of whom the least that might be said is that he is a figure of Bakhtinian excess, convinces me now that this may have been correct.[8] What I had in mind was perhaps something more like the figure Radin identifies, in the 1924 lecture, as the transcultural type of the Transformer, who reshapes worlds—and who gets himself out of intercultural perils—with his interlinguistic dexterity.

Diamond on Radin

We have returned to Paul Radin. If Stanley Diamond was an important figure for me, then Radin most certainly was an important figure, even a kind of hero, for Stanley Diamond. His profound engagement with Radin and his work is evident in his article on Radin in the 1964 edition of the *International Encyclopedia of the Social Sciences*; in his work as editor of *Culture in History*, the Radin Festschrift (1960); in the preface to Radin's book on the trickster figure, which I have already mentioned; in his reliance on Radin in his central essay, 'In Search of the Primitive' (1974: 116–75), and in his reflections on Radin's legacy in the 1991 volume *Totems and Teachers*, a collection of essays subtitled 'Key Figures in the History of Anthropology'. As the editor of that volume, Sydel Silverman, pointed out in the new 2004 edition, the original edition had been dedicated to 'our students', and 'Many of them are now teachers and researchers themselves [that would be me, for example], and another generation has succeeded them as students' (Silverman 2004: xi)—a caution to me, no doubt, that under the very best of hopeful scenarios I will someday be subject to the same pitiless retrospective gaze I am now casting on Diamond and his recollections of Radin. May my judgement be tempered, therefore, by the recognition that it has doubtless been considerably easier for me to be Jewish than it was for either of those men.

Certain moments in Diamond's essay on Radin stand out in the light of the retrospective gaze. Thus Diamond writes, 'The Old World solidarity of [Radin's] family of origin . . . had shattered under the impact of the American experience' (1991: 52). This suggests at least one source of the affinity between the two scholars, since Diamond might plausibly have said the same of his own lost Lower East Side childhood. Since Radin's father was an immigrant Reform rabbi, Diamond refers to 'The reaction against Orthodox Judaism in the Reform movement, which had among its objectives the replacement of Yiddish—the voice of the ghetto—by Hebrew as a literary and secular tongue' (1991: 53). At least three observations must be made here: first, that the highly conventionalized reference to Yiddish as 'the language of the ghetto' reflects anything but critical thinking or careful attention to the dynamics of diaspora Jewish culture; second, that the suggestion that Reform Judaism sought to promote literary and secular Hebrew indicates Diamond's inattention to any differences among various European Jewish responses to modernity, since Hebrew modernism is associated with the brief Jewish Enlightenment and with Zionism, but not particularly with the Reform movement; and third, that (as historians of Jewish culture now understand, admittedly better than they did in the early 1980s) the formulation of something called, by others and then by itself, 'Orthodox Judaism' was a response to the challenge of Reform, rather than some unchanging traditional pre-modern baseline.

What was 'distinctively Jewish' about Radin, in Diamond's view? His 'passion for scholarship, commitment to human ethics, cosmopolitanism, radicalism, conception of learning as a moral enterprise', and his unworldliness 'represent further elements that characterize the Jewish scholar en passage from the traditional milieu to the modern industrial and urban world' (1991: 53). It should be noted that this is both a Kantian and progressivist analysis, in that it identifies as characteristically Jewish both an undifferentiated concern for 'human ethics' and a 'radicalism' in the interest of human betterment. Moreover, this statement reinforces the impression I gradually obtained, over the years that I studied with Stanley Diamond, that for him the *only* value of Jewishness is the marginal stance it affords. Likewise, this thumbnail sketch of Radin as a characteristically 'Jewish scholar' repeats stereotypes and makes anodyne the same transition from 'traditional' to 'modern industrial and urban' that, when Diamond elsewhere describes it as a transition from 'primitive' to 'civilized', is by no means treated as an accomplishment but more as a tragic loss of human possibilities. Later, in the discussion after Diamond's talk that is also reproduced in the volume *Totems and Teachers*, he states: 'I was aware, sometimes painfully, of the results of the narrow socialization and cultural deprivation to which he was subject . . . In short, he was in many ways a victim' (1991: 71). Rather than praising Radin, as he might have, for letting the primitive grow within him, Diamond is suggesting here that Radin had failed to 'recognize [and hence to break] the shackles that tradition has laid upon us', an effort that Boas had called for in 1938 (quoted in Bronner 1998: 133).[9] And that is where the talk—Diamond's and then his discussants'—about Paul Radin ends. In sum, Jewishness acquires something of the bivalent figure of 'Greekness'—revered ancestors, degraded contemporaries—that Michael Herzfeld so acutely analyses in his *Anthropology through the Looking Glass* (1987). At the same time, Diamond's account of the cultural transformations inevitable upon immigration is remarkably anodyne, conducive to an implicit view of what was once called 'assimilation' to Americanism as a benign or even liberating process. By contrast, without engaging in any triumphalist or even overly nostalgic assertions about the particular resources of the central and east European Jewish cultures (and we may leave them as either 'part' or 'whole' cultures for now), it is safe enough to surmise for Radin a family history in which interactions among, acquisitions of, and losses of a range of idioms including Polish, Yiddish, German, Hebrew, and English would have been an apt training for his extraordinary (less so in his remarkable generation!) attention to Native American languages and the worlds they contained and created.

For Diamond, however, it is 'medieval education and the order of argument in Saint Augustine' (1991: 54) that represent Radin's 'own culture' or his 'culture of origin'. He writes that Radin had 'a thorough knowledge of his own civilization. He was at ease in German, French, Spanish, Latin, and Greek' (1991: 63). My claim is certainly not that these Christo-European humanities were not Radin's own, or that he properly possessed some 'other culture'. I am not saying that because his father was a rabbi we should think of the son in the first instance as a bearer of Jewish culture. On the other hand, Stanley Diamond *did* claim to describe the culture that was Radin's own, and the culture he described as properly Radin's was clearly marked as not Jewish (most notably here, of course, in the reference to Augustine).

At the same time, Diamond makes free to describe Radin as 'A contemporary transformation of an eighteenth-century Hasidic rabbi . . . [with his] colleagues and students . . . he would spontaneously set up a Hasidic court' (1991: 55–6). In Diamond's analogy, 'Boas . . . played the orthodox rabbi of the shul to Radin's rebellious Hasid' (1991: 60). Radin's Jewishness is not so much suppressed here, then, as occluded in a welter of mutually contradictory 'types' of modern Jewish intellectual. Nor, to present a fuller picture, did Diamond limit his analogies to Jewish types: further on in his Radin essay he writes that A. L. Kroeber was 'a sort of Confucius to Radin's Lao Tzu' (1991: 63). None of these analogies, whether with Jewish or with Chinese figures of the classical intellectual, seems to directly relate to what Diamond says of Radin's fundamental anthropological stance. It was a view that deeply informed Diamond's work as well, and with this I have no quarrel: 'His radicalism, then, was rooted in his respect for the aboriginal human potentiality, which he insisted was already formed even among the most primitive of those societies that he held to be the proper subject of ethnology' (1991: 60).

In the recorded discussion following Diamond's talk on Radin, Paul Rabinow remarked to Diamond, 'You painted Radin's picture as a traditional intellectual, a secularized Jew at the end of his tradition' (1991: 70). I can scarce begin to unpack the welter of tropes contained in this sentence: traditional, secularized, living at the end of one's own tradition . . . Diamond's reply to Rabinow invokes yet another stock figure from the schematized collective memory of east European Jewish immigrants (beyond the repressed Orthodox legalist and the rebellious hasidic free spirit): 'he was something of a *yeshiva bocher* . . . he was an Eastern European Jew, basically' (1991: 71).

It may be, however, that Diamond's various characterizations of Boas as

'Orthodox rabbi' and of Radin as 'Hasidic rabbi' and as 'yeshiva bocher' are not merely evidence of the contempt that familiarity breeds. They are also determined by the legacy of the search for, and consequently the rhetoric of, 'the invention of the authentic Jews' that Michael Brenner has traced back to German-speaking Jewry during the Weimar period (Brenner 1996: 129). If there is any validity to this, it must make us wonder once again at the caesura or the possibility of hidden affinities between, on the one hand, the German Jewish search for a Jewish authenticity in 'unmodernized' eastern Europe, and, on the other, the efforts by cultural anthropologists working in North America—so many of them of recent German or east European Jewish origin—to search for a human authenticity in non-Jewish, 'primitive' pasts. It may also be that this caesura provides some clues to the diagnosis of the crisis of a cultural anthropology based on the search for 'whole cultures', even in their fragments, rather than the kinds of hybrids, creoles, multicultures, and the like that were, I contend, early on explored in the work precisely of Yiddish sociolinguists such as Max Weinreich and his son Uriel—scholars trained in Germany and the United States, but still actively and assertively grounded in the Yiddish-Ashkenazi culture of eastern Europe. I would even venture that in the works of the Weinreichs—such as Max's short classic essay on 'the reality of Yiddish versus the ghetto myth' (1964) or his massive *History of the Yiddish Language* (2008), or the volume on *Languages in Contact* that Uriel, still in his twenties, edited as early as 1953 (U. Weinreich 1953) —we may see, alongside figures such as Roger Bastide (Bastide 1968), some seeds of the current openness towards processes of hybridization and fascination with the very margins of culture.

Anthropology's Jewish Problem, Again

Let me move towards some kind of ending. Part of my trepidation about this topic has to do with its evident narcissism; indeed there is a fine and not always obvious line between a responsible practice of reflexive anthropology and a closure against the demands to seek ways to know and describe otherness. More troubling, however, is the reductionism inherent in the attempt to relate individual intellectual genealogies to social structure and social change—here, in the attempt to relate what Radin and Diamond did or did not say about Jews to the assimilation or continued difference of American Jewry as a whole. Trying to reduce their scholarship in a way that lets us map them convincingly onto broader social processes is a reminder that what we write today may someday be subject to similar analysis and reduction.

We are left, at minimum, with a clearer statement of the question. That question is the putative pertinence of the Jewishness of scholars such as Radin and Diamond to their choice of research topics and what they chose to say about them. I mean, specifically, Diamond's critique of the state and his articulation of a broad concept of the primitive, and Radin's research on the American Indian and 'his' intellectual equality with 'us'. The latter, in particular, is of course not particular to Radin but then again, his Jewishness is hardly unusual among his generation of North American ethnographers. My hunch about the fascination for Diamond and Radin of the concept of the primitive as a kind of screen for a sense of loss of 'authentic' Jewishness, and moreover a sense that neither could acknowledge more explicitly, is of the same order as the speculation of the anthropologist Erika Bourguignon (in the 1940s) and of Melford Spiro (in 1999) that Melville Herskovits's 'interest in American blacks was in part a displacement for Jewish concerns' (Spiro, quoted in Frank 2001: 199).

A painful but as yet insufficiently understood corollary of the attributed Jewishness of so many American anthropologists in the first half of the twentieth century was, in turn, a propensity precisely *not* to focus on, let alone celebrate, any distinctive aspects of what might be termed Jewish culture or Jewish cultures. One key to understanding the negative correlation between the Jewishness of American anthropology and its avoidance of study of Jewish culture may well be, as Barbara Kirshenblatt-Gimblett pointed out over twenty years ago, the Boasian effort of 'erasing the [Jewish] subject' as part of his overall effort against racism. As Kirshenblatt-Gimblett wrote then, 'Virtually the same arguments used to demonstrate that Jews did not constitute a race were rallied to prove that they were also without a distinctive and/or distinguishable culture. If they did not exist—neither in racial nor in cultural terms—then they might cease to be a target of anti-Semitism' (Kirshenblatt-Gimblett 1987: 3). More broadly, as she notes, 'the battle in Boas's time was to be free of involuntary categorizations . . . Boas almost always defined identification in negative terms as the fate of outsiders who are consigned to despised groups by the in group, and criticized voluntary identification as "racial solidarity" or as bondage to the "shackles of tradition"' (1987: 9).

Yet the near-elimination of contemporary Jewish culture, especially east European Jewish culture, as a subject of ethnographic enquiry and comparison was neither universal nor inevitable among Radin's cohort. Thus, as Kirshenblatt-Gimblett has pointed out elsewhere, Edward Sapir had attended to Yiddish in his scholarship of the years around the First World War. Moreover, contact between Sapir and Max Weinreich at Yale in the 1920s was mutually inspiring for both scholars (Kirshenblatt-Gimblett 1996: 3). As Kirshenblatt-Gimblett drily points out, 'These were not fashionable subjects during a period when many anthropologists defined Jews as a race and even someone as distinguished as Sapir was excluded from the prestigious Yale Graduates Club' (1996: 4; Siskin 1986: 289). In 1931 Sapir suggested to Hortense Powdermaker that she make hasidic Jews in New York the subject of her fieldwork, a suggestion that she rejected due, as she wrote, to 'lack of interest, no knowledge of Hebrew or Yiddish, and a feeling that I lacked the necessary objectivity to study orthodox

Jews' (Powdermaker 1966: 131). Yet Sapir, too, had written in 1918 'of the petrifaction of the Jewish religion in medieval and modern times into the mechanical routine of prayer and dull ritual', what he called 'the burden of orthodoxy' (quoted in Kirshenblatt-Gimblett 1996: 40). It is most striking to see this trope of 'fossilized' Judaism—a millennial standard element of the Christian rhetoric for describing the superseded position of Jews in Christendom since Jews had been described as 'living letters of the Law', as Jeremy Cohen paraphrases the words of Bernard of Clairvaux (Cohen 1999: 2). Kirshenblatt-Gimblett wrote, just a few years ago, that 'Jews have remained a marginal subject in anthropology to this day. As Virginia Domínguez recently asked, "Does anthropology have a Jewish problem?" The answer is yes and the history of anthropology's Jewish problem is fraught with anxiety whose genealogy leads back to the body' (Kirschenblatt-Gimblett 2005: 457). While Kirshenblatt-Gimblett uses the term 'genealogy' here in the sense that we loosely think of as Foucauldian, it also seems clear that anthropology's Jewish problem is fraught with anxiety connected to genealogy in a more prosaic and common sense: that of kinship and ancestry.

In 2004 Jeffrey Feldman noted the significant new attention and legitimacy granted to the ethnography of Jewish communities, and asserted that 'What remains to be scrutinized of anthropology's "Jewish problem" is not the exclusion of Jews and Judaism from the list of viable ethnographic topics, but the absence of critical debate on exactly how anthropology treats the Jewishness in its own history' (Feldman 2004: 108). But this, again, draws too neat a distinction between ethnographers and the subjects of ethnography. I would suggest, rather, that—especially insofar as much of twentieth-century cultural anthropology was about the search for what we may call a usable ancestry—the place of Jews and Jewishness as proper 'subjects' of ethnography is inseparable from 'how anthropology treats the Jewishness in its own history'. To that extent, the genealogies of the discipline of anthropology—as of so many other areas in the humanities and social sciences—are matters at once both of kinship and what we call 'intellectual' descent, and far more than a footnote to something putatively 'outside' our proper subject.

Meanwhile, compared to the situation in Radin's heyday, and to Diamond's or even my own student years some three decades ago, the idea that Jews are not a fit subject for ethnography has been at least partially dispelled, along with the broader notion that somehow anthropologists should not study 'their own'. Older taboos against linking Jewishness to 'the primitive' have been productively transgressed (see Eilberg-Schwartz 1990). Erstwhile denials, such as Diamond's, that Jews 'have a culture' or that Jewishness 'is a culture' seem obviated by vigorous scholarship, teaching, and academic programmes in Jewish cultural studies. How much of a long-term advance in understanding this will turn out to be is not clear, since the culture concept itself has undergone sustained and cogent critique in recent years. The advent, for example, of a major university publisher's new series on 'Jewish Cultures of the World' seems accordingly at once a substantive milestone and conceptually somewhat flat.

In terms of institutional dynamics—to the extent that a greater place for the ethnographic study of Jews is part of an expansion of Jewish studies funded largely by outside donors rather than part of the university's own agenda—the place of Jewishness within global cultural studies remains perhaps somewhat tenuous. Moreover, the culture-framing role of cultural anthropology in general, as part of the academic humanities and social sciences, seems considerably more modest than it promised to be at the middle of the twentieth century.

Academics and others continue to experience ongoing pressures to confirm or deny 'their' Jewishness, though, for now at least, such pressures no longer need result in the suppression of recent and contemporary Jewish life as a fit subject of academic research. What forms of avoidance, denial, or (if I may coin a phrase) subject matter transference 'we' unwittingly enact today is of course difficult to discern. My critical remarks on the problem of Jewishness in the careers of Paul Radin and Stanley Diamond here are inspired by, and not meant to displace, my belief that their work constituted honest efforts to document and understand people in a way that promotes human continuity, freedom, and connection. It is enough to conclude with the hope that there will be future generations of scholars after us, that they will similarly value our work, and that they will struggle to understand us in ways that we ourselves could not.

Notes

1   A subsequent version was given as the Ruth Fredman Cernea Memorial Lecture, sponsored by the Washington Association of Professional Anthropologists (1 Nov. 2009). The late Ruth Fredman Cernea, whose books included *The Passover Seder* (1992), *Cosmopolitans at Home: The Sephardic Jews of Washington, D.C.* (1982), and a volume of contributions to 'The Great Latke Hamantash Debate' (2006) held annually at the University of Chicago, was one of the first cultural anthropologists in the United States to set the study of contemporary Jews squarely at the centre of her own research.

2   Quoted in Sacharoff, *Paul Radin: Early* [title erased], Marquette University Archives, Paul Radin Series (henceforth PR Series) 4, Box 3, Folder 18.

3   Sacharoff, *Radin and Boas: Conflict and Concurrence*. PR Series 4, Box 3, Folder 23.

4   Email communication from Herb Lewis, 19 Dec. 2009.

5   PR Series 4, Box 3, Folder 14.

6   In the second edition of *Totems and Teachers* (Silverman 2004 [1991]: 70).

7   In asserting the culturelessness of the Jews, Diamond was effectively echoing earlier writings of Melville Herskovits, who had stated in 1927 that 'The Jew has ever taken on the color of the culture in which he lives' (cited in Frank 2001: 183).

8   See, for example, pp. 25–7 of the 1972 edition of Radin's *The Trickster* (Trickster's uncontrollable defecation).

9   As Leonard Glick underscored in his 1982 article, George Stocking had already wondered 'just how far Boas was able to bring the shackles of his own tradition fully to consciousness' (Stocking 1979: 47).

References

BASTIDE, ROGER. 1968. *Les Amériques noires: Les Civilizations africaines dans le nouveau monde*. Paris.

BOYARIN, JONATHAN. 1992. *Storm from Paradise: The Politics of Jewish Memory*. Minneapolis.

——1994. *A Storyteller's Worlds: The Education of Shlomo Noble in Europe and America*. New York.

——1996. *Thinking in Jewish*. Chicago.

BOYARIN, DANIEL, and JONATHAN BOYARIN. 1993. 'Diaspora: Generation and the Ground of Jewish Identity'. *Critical Inquiry*, 19: 693–725.

BRACKEN, CHRISTOPHER. 1997. *The Potlatch Papers: A Colonial Case History*. Chicago.

BRENNER, MICHAEL. 1996. *The Renaissance of Jewish Culture in Weimar Germany*. New Haven.

BRONNER, SIMON. 1998. *Following Tradition: Folklore in the Discourse of American Culture*. Logan, Utah.

COHEN, JEREMY. 1999. *Living Letters of the Law: Ideas of the Jew in Medieval Christianity*. Berkeley, Calif.

CUDDIHY, JOHN MORROW. 1974. *The Ordeal of Civility: Freud, Marx, Lévi-Strauss, and the Jewish Struggle with Modernity*. New York.

DIAMOND, STANLEY. 1957. 'Kibbutz and Shtetl: The History of an Idea'. *Social Problems*, 5: 71–99.

——ed. 1960. *Culture in History: Essays in Honor of Paul Radin*. New York.

——1964. 'Radin, Paul'. *International Encyclopedia of the Social Sciences*, xiii. 300–3.

——1974. *In Search of the Primitive: A Critique of Civilization*. New Brunswick, NJ.

——1981. 'Paul Radin'. In Sydel Silverman, ed., *Totems and Teachers: Perspectives on the History of Anthropology*, 67–99. New York.

——1983. 'The State of Being Jewish'. *Dialectical Anthropology*, 8: 1–5.

——1991. 'Paul Radin'. In Sydel Silverman, ed., *Totems and Teachers: Key Figures in the History of Anthropology*. Walnut Creek.

EILBERG-SCHWARTZ, HOWARD. 1990. *The Savage in Judaism*. Bloomington, Ind.

FELDMAN, JEFFREY D. 2004. 'The Jewish Roots and Routes of Anthropology'. *Anthropological Quarterly*, 77: 107–25.

FRANK, GELYA. 1997. 'Jews, Multiculturalism, and Boasian Anthropology'. *American Anthropologist*, 99: 731–45.

——2001. 'Melville J. Herskovits on the African and Jewish Diasporas: Race, Culture and Modern Anthropology'. *Identities*, 8: 173–209.

GAILEY, CHRISTINE. 1991a. 'Introduction: Civilization and Culture in the Work of Stanley Diamond'. In Gailey, ed., *Dialectical Anthropology: Essays in Honor of Stanley Diamond*, i: *Civilization in Crisis: Anthropological Perspectives*, 1–27. Gainesville, Fla.

——1991b. 'Stanley Diamond: In Memoriam', *Dialectical Anthropology*, 16: 105–6.

GLICK, LEONARD. 1982. 'Types Distinct from Our Own: Franz Boas on Jewish Identity and Assimilation'. *American Anthropologist*, 84: 545–65.

GRAY, C. BUCHANAN. 1922–3. *Hebrew Monotheism*. Oxford.

HERZFELD, MICHAEL. 1987. *Anthropology through the Looking Glass: A Critical Ethnography in the Margins of Europe*. Cambridge.

KATZ, JACOB. 1973. *Out of the Ghetto: The Social Background of Jewish Emancipation, 1770–1870*. Cambridge, Mass.

KIRSHENBLATT-GIMBLETT, BARBARA. 1987. 'Erasing the Subject: Franz Boas and the Anthropological Study of Jews in the United States'. Paper presented to the annual meeting of the American Anthropological Association, Chicago, 20 Nov.

——1996. 'Coming of Age in the Thirties: Max Weinreich, Edward Sapir, and Jewish Social Science'. In Deborah Dash Moore, ed., *YIVO Annual*, 1–103. Detroit.

——2005. 'The Corporeal Turn'. *Jewish Quarterly Review*, 95: 447–61.

LYOTARD, JEAN-FRANÇOIS. 1990. *Heidegger and 'the jews'*. Minneapolis.

MICHAELS, WALTER BENN. 1992. 'Race into Culture: A Critical Genealogy of Cultural Identity'. *Critical Inquiry*, 18: 655–85.

ORLOVE, BENJAMIN. 1997. 'Surfacings: Thoughts on Memory and the Ethnographer's Self'. In Jonathan Boyarin and Daniel Boyarin, eds., *Jews and Other Differences: The New Jewish Cultural Studies*, 1–29. Minneapolis.

POWDERMAKER, HORTENSE. 1966. *Stranger and Friend: The Way of an Anthropologist*. New York.

RADIN, PAUL. 1924. *Monotheism among Primitive Peoples*. Foreword by Israel Zangwill. London.

——1956. *The Trickster: A Study in American Indian Mythology*. New York.

SILVERMAN, SYDEL, ed. 1981. *Totems and Teachers: Perspectives on the History of Anthropology*. New York.

——ed. 2004 [1991]. *Totems and Teachers: Key Figures in the History of Anthropology*. Walnut Creek.

SISKIN, EDGAR E. 1986. 'The Life and Times of Edward Sapir'. *Jewish Social Studies*, 48: 283–92.

SOLOVEITCHIK, HAYM. 1994. 'Rupture and Reconstruction: The Transformation of Contemporary Orthodoxy'. *Tradition*, 38: 64–130.

STOCKING, GEORGE. 1979. 'Anthropology as Kulturkampf: Science and Politics in the Career of Franz Boas'. In Walter Goldschmidt, ed., *The Uses of Anthropology*, 33–50. Special Publication of the American Anthropological Association 11. Washington, DC.

TWEED, THOMAS. 1997. *Our Lady of the Exile: Diasporic Religion at a Cuban Catholic Shrine in Miami*. New York.

WEINREICH, MAX. 1964. 'The Reality of Yiddish versus the Ghetto Myth: The Sociolinguistic Roots of Yiddish'. In *To Honor Roman Jakobson*, iii. 1199–1222. The Hague.

——2008. *History of the Yiddish Language*, trans. Shlomo Noble with the assistance of Joshua Fishman. New Haven.

WEINREICH, URIEL. 1953. *Languages in Contact*. The Hague.

THREE

Selective Inclusion: Integration and Isolation of Jews in Medieval Italy

SAMUEL D. GRUBER

THIS ESSAY PRESENTS episodes, mostly from the thirteenth to the fifteenth centuries, that demonstrate how Jews existed within the spatial framework of Rome and elsewhere in medieval Christian Italy, straddling social, economic, and spatial boundaries. Using a variety of sources to physically locate Jews in Italian urban culture allows a better understanding of the civic space available to them in Italian cities in the Middle Ages and the early Renaissance. Stretching from just before the promulgation of anti-Jewish decrees at the Fourth Lateran Council until the creation of the Venetian ghetto in 1516, this was a tumultuous but transformative period of Italian and Jewish history, in which Jewish communities settled and thrived throughout the entire peninsula.

Boundaries between Jews and Christians

Léon Poliakov has written that, before the Counter-Reformation, 'the social and judicial conditions of the Jews in Italy had not sunk anywhere near the level of degradation they reached elsewhere', and that 'the Jews' everyday relationships with Christians were often imbued with a cordiality' (Poliakov 1977). Many reasons have been put forward for the disparities between the fate of Italian Jewish communities and that of their co-religionists further north. These include the millennium-long presence of Jews in Italy, Italy's fragmented political structure, and the greater tradition of urban life and of acceptance of trade and a money economy. The presence of the pope, too, made a difference: politically and financially, Roman popes often worked closely with Jewish financiers, and the medieval papacy regarded the protection of its Jews as a religious responsibility.

In Rome, the oldest and strongest of Italian communities, Jews maintained their identity as a people with deep roots in the ancient past on the one hand and actively involved in contemporary events on the other. They were an ancient presence, carved in stone on the 'Arch of the Seven-Armed Candlestick' (Arch of Titus), but were also contemporary moneylenders and merchants, even in the atrium of St Peter's basilica, where in the fourteenth century at least one bookseller was a Jew (Krautheimer 1980: 266, 299). Granted 'absolute freedom of the city of Rome' (Poliakov 1977), Jews were, at the same time, frequently reminded of their distinctive 'otherness' through Christian laws, rituals, art, and sermons that insisted that Judaism's religious relevance and validity had been surpassed by the New Law and the Roman Church (Simonsohn 1991: 122).

Fortunately for Jews, pre-modern Italy was not a homogeneous society. Although their Judaism set them apart, Jews were just one of a large number of regional, linguistic, ethnic, social, occupational, and even religious groups that maintained their distinctive identity in medieval and early modern culture. Forced segregation of these groups was rarely required, but various forms of social and spatial self-segregation were not uncommon in medieval Italian (and Mediterranean) society. In Rome there were many such *scholae* of the Greeks, Frisians, Saxons, Longobards, and Franks going back to the eighth century (Krautheimer 1980: 78, 82).

Group separation of this type, often enforced, was common in Muslim and Christian trading centres in North Africa and the eastern Mediterranean (Colorni 1956: 55). In southern Italy throughout the thirteenth century populations were very diverse, with ancient communities of Greeks and Slavs, Muslims originally from North Africa and Sicily, and Christians from every part of Italy and many parts of Europe. Initially under Byzantine and Muslim rule and then under Norman and other western Christian rulers, these groups usually lived in 'fairly demarcated areas', but these were not ghettos (Abulafia 2002: 76). In Sicily, part of the Muslim legacy was towns where 'strong quarters, clans, gangs and other local groups remained basic to the urban social structure' (Lapidus 1984: xii). The Meschita quarter in Sicilian Palermo and the Giudecca of the Apulian port city of Trani, inhabited by important Jewish communities, are among the best preserved and documented of these areas (Figure 1). Later, when southern Italy came under Spanish rule, there were also distinct communities, including those of Jewish refugees from different parts of the Iberian peninsula—a distinction that would also be maintained by Jews in the Sephardi diaspora of the sixteenth century. There was a tradition of Jews owning property in parts of Italy. For the Byzantine period in southern Italy, Patricia Skinner cites the Jew Theophylact of Taranto, who is documented buying vineyards and other land in 1033 and 1039 (Skinner 2007: 5). Regulations and customs regarding Jews and property varied, however, over time and place in Italy, and these shifts still need to be further researched and established.

The medieval town or city was not unlike a modern one, where groups of immigrants from a particular place, whether a nearby village or a distant country, were likely to live in close proximity through choice or for convenience—as in modern Chinatowns or Little Italies. It was not until the late fifteenth century, however, that enforced separation of social groups became widespread in Italy (Calabi and Lanaro 1998).

Figure 1 Scolanova Synagogue, Trani. *Photograph by Giuseppe Calamita*

The separation of Jews was fully legislated as early as the Fourth Lateran Council in 1215, but such separation was rarely enforced in Italy and it began in earnest only with the expulsion of Jews from Sicily and various communities in southern Italy between 1492 and 1569, and with the creation of the Venetian ghetto in 1516 and the ghetto of Rome in 1555. These last moves were intended to make Jews and Jewish quarters marginal rather than integral parts of urban and Christian life.

The Fourth Lateran Council convened by Pope Innocent III has rightly been recognized as a turning point in the lives of Europe's Jews. The council passed sweeping regulations concerning almost all aspects of the lives of Jews and their communities, and especially those activities in which Jews might interact with Christians. The underlying motive of the decrees was to continually punish Jews for their alleged deicide. Although many of these regulations merely reiterated older laws that had either fallen into disuse or had been only intermittently enforced, the council for the first time articulated a vision of separate societies for Jews and Christians, and strove to strengthen all provisions to distinguish Jews from Christians when interaction was unavoidable.

The laws passed at the Fourth Lateran Council paved the way for a system of Jewish quarters that were almost entirely forced, rather than voluntary, neigh-bourhoods. Due to the fragmented political structure and historical prerogatives, however, the top-down effort at separation was slow to develop. Meanwhile, the 1230 law code of Emperor Frederick II offered legal protection for all of his subjects, whether foreign or native born, regardless of race or religion, probably reiterating existing legal practice. Some separation laws, however, remained in force, such as the requirement for Jewish and Muslim men to wear a beard. Frederick moved Jews from a condition of legal 'marginalization' to that of 'tolera-tion' (Miller et al. 2010: 62).

The security offered by Frederick was shattered at the end of the century: in 1290, under new Angevin rule, anti-Jewish riots throughout Apulia led large numbers of Jews to convert or to migrate northwards. Jews were forcibly expelled in 1291 from the Angevin capital of Naples, where they had lived since at least the sixth century and probably much earlier. A medieval synagogue in Naples was located near the Porta Nova as early as 984 (Capasso 1885: 243), and the city had a *vicus Judaeorum* that may refer to both a specific place and the particular jurisdiction over it.[1] After the expulsion the synagogue was consecrated as a church (now Santa Maria della Purità) and Jews did not return to the city until after 1444 (Sacerdoti 2003: 182). In 1312 King Frederick III of Sicily tried, unsuc-cessfully, to have the Jews of Palermo removed to a place outside the city walls. This period also saw the expulsion of Jews from England (1290) and from France (1306).

Only in the fifteenth century, when the widespread preaching of the mendi-cant orders led to the spread of anti-Jewish sentiment throughout all segments of Italian society, did economic restrictions on Jewish moneylending and the physical separation of Jews became more widely promoted as public policy. In 1427 Giovanna II forced the Jews of Lanciano in the Abruzzi to a single street. Similar, but unsuccessful, attempts were made in Piedmont in the 1430s, and proposals are also known to have been made in Bari, Cesena, and Ravenna throughout the fifteenth century.

In 1493 representatives of the Umbrian Commune of Spoleto went before the Apostolic Governor asking for Jews to be banned from living in streets in the city centre and to be confined to an outlying area far away from Christians, 'so that the latter shall not be obliged to witness their wicked customs'. The proposal was discussed several times in subsequent years but no decision was made until 1562, when, in a Renaissance version of a 'final solution', all Jews living outside the designated ghettos were expelled from the Papal State.

Shared Space in the Medieval City

Despite the decrees of the Lateran Council, throughout the thirteenth century Italian Jews were a legally and popularly recognized element of the social order and an integral part of the urban scene. This was the period when the Jewish quarter of Trani was most actively developed, including the erection of two synagogues of which the larger and more architecturally distinctive one stands on a public piazza. While this was a distinctly 'Jewish space' it was not closed to Christians, and the central location could hardly be avoided. Similarly, Jews and Christians (and Muslims) regularly interacted at the busy port, close to the cathedral and the Giudecca.

In 1384 in Siena Jews were forbidden by the city council to 'stay or live in any house or palace near the Campo' because they were 'scorners of the faith of Christ and of the most glorious Virgin Mary'.[2] This expulsion from the main square is an indication that Jews had been living there, and of the subsequent growing animosity towards them (Caferro 1998: 108). In northern Europe Jewish purchase of high-end properties led to resentment and even serious violence. In Italy there was no tradition of the physical destruction of Jewish houses and quarters —as was the case in the Rhineland (Haverkamp 1995: 24).

As with many medieval statutes that attempted unsuccessfully to regulate the behaviour of urban populations, the very fact of the frequent reiteration of restrictions on Jewish–Christian relations can be taken as evidence that those restrictions were often circumvented or entirely ignored.

In the 'Eternal City' of Rome, the seat of the pope's authority, Jews' age-old but sometimes tenuous place in the social and spatial order was expressed in many ways, including required civic ritual. As part of the recognition of papal sovereignty over the city and its Jews the Jewish community regularly joined the acclamation of the newly crowned pontiff as he travelled along the processional route, the Via Papalis. This Possesso, in which a newly crowned pope would take possession of his episcopal church, St John Lateran, was a recurring event, described in sources from at least 1119 and undertaken with the election of every new pontiff (Krautheimer 1980: 278), but the full medieval procession is most fully described in the late thirteenth century, when Pope Boniface VIII ascended to the Holy See.

After passing through a series of surviving ancient triumphal arches the pope and his lengthy procession stopped at the Tower of Stephen Peteri near Monte Giordano in the *rione* (district) of Parione (Ridolfini 1971: 8), where he was met by a delegation of Rome's Jews, led by a rabbi who carried a covered Torah scroll and saluted the pontiff, hoping for continued tolerance of Jewish residence in the city.[3] According to oral tradition, the pope looked at the scroll and passed it back to the rabbi, reciting the words: 'We acknowledge the law, but we condemn the principles of Judaism; for the law has already been fulfilled through Christ.'[4]

Jews, as a resident population, and like the Mosaic Law itself, were acknowledged in fact but condemned in principle.

After the disgrace and death of Boniface, a similar public expression of allegiance was made in 1312, when Rome's Jews pledged loyalty to the new emperor, Henry VII. En route to the Lateran basilica (the ceremony avoided St Peter's church and was performed without papal approval) the procession moved from the Aventine Hill to the Circus Maximus, close to the Jewish quarter, where the new emperor, clad in white and mounted on a white horse, stopped at a bridge (or perhaps some Roman arches), where he swore to protect the Roman republic and its laws. Delegations of clergy welcomed him along the way, and the city's Jews (who were also taxed to help pay for the coronation) paid homage and handed him a Torah scroll ('Legem Mosaycam rotulo inscriptam': see Figure 2).[5]

Jews in other towns of Europe participated in similar rituals, especially in regard to popes and bishops—for example, in Saint-Denis, France, when Pope Innocent II entered the Jewish quarter upon solemnly passing through the town on 27 April 1131 (Coulet 1979). Jews' involvement in such processions—whether voluntary or coerced—demonstrates social integration as well as recognition of their physical presence as part of the urban fabric.

Jews could also be instigators of processions. In Sicily, at least, we know that they celebrated important life-cycle events with public displays, including processions, and that these events were tolerated and even expected by local non-Jewish communities. The travelling rabbi Obadiah of Bertinoro described a wedding procession in Messina and a funeral in Palermo:

At a wedding which took place near my residence I witnessed the following ceremony. After the seven blessings had been repeated, the bride was placed on a horse and rode through the town. The whole community went before her on foot, the bridegroom in the midst of the elders and before the bride, who was the only one on horseback; youths and children carried burning torches and made loud exclamations, so that the whole place resounded; they made the circuit of the streets and all the Jews' courts; the Christian inhabitants looked on with pleasure and no one disturbed the festivity. (Obadiah of Bertinoro 1965: 237)

In Palermo, where Obadiah had a lengthy stay, he noted the poverty of the Jews and the richness of the synagogue, and wrote of the funeral rituals and processions, again indicating that Jewish ceremonials traversed common space:

When anybody dies, his coffin is brought into the vestibule of the synagogue and the ministers hold the funeral service and recite lamentations over him. If the departed is a distinguished man especially learned in the law, the coffin is brought into the synagogue itself, a roll of the law is taken out and placed in the corner of the Ark, while the coffin is placed opposite to this corner, and then the funeral service commences and lamentations are recited; the same thing is done with all the four corners of the Ark. The coffin is then carried to the place of burial outside the town and upon arriving at the gate

Figure 2 Rome's Jews pay homage to Emperor Henry VII. *Codex Balduini Trevirensis. Koblenz, Landeshauptarchiv, fo. 24ʳ (MS mid-14th c.)*

of the town the reader begins to repeat aloud the forty-ninth and other psalms until they reach the burial ground. (Obadiah of Bertinoro 1965: 237)

Among the most destructive elements of the Lateran Council pronouncements of 1215 were the prohibitions on Jews owning land or living among Christians, and Jewish exclusion from guilds and public office. Jews were also required to wear identifying marks on their clothing, and while they were forced into the profession of moneylending, the new regulation controlled the amount of interest they could charge. Nonetheless, as we can see from the way Jews took part in the procession for Boniface in the late thirteenth century noted above, the Lateran decrees were only partially applied, dependent in large part on the preferences of local rulers. Still, from 1215 a legal basis was established for Jewish–Christian separation which zealous authorities could choose to enforce (Simonsohn 1991: 142).

In Italy especially, but also in the large Jewish centres of southern France and the German Rhineland, Jews and Christians were likely to speak the same language, wear similar clothes, eat similar foods, and live in similar houses within recognizable family units. While popular Christian imagery presented Jews as perpetually wandering, marked by sin in the manner of Cain, in actuality many Jewish communities lasted for decades and even for generations, more than enough time for Jewish families to put down roots and become integrated into local economies and communities (Chazan 2010: 185). It was for this reason that the Lateran Council resolved that Jews should wear a special badge to identify themselves—an attempt at urging separation. This helps explain the intermittent enforcement of the Lateran decrees: when Jews looked, sounded, and acted so much like their neighbours, that it was hard to demonize them.

About Rome, historian Robert Brentano wrote: 'it must be made equally clear that Jews did not live as outlaws or outcasts in thirteenth- and fourteenth-century Rome. Jews could be papal physicians, as Isaac ben Mordecai was to Nicholas IV. In the early fourteenth century Jews were rewarded with Roman citizenship' (Brentano 1974: 46–7). But there was also social and physical tension and even open conflict between Jews and Christians throughout the Middle Ages. Brentano went on to state:

The medieval Roman Jew would seem to have suffered a slight, prejudiced, informal inequality before the law when he was involved in processes not subject to his own law. The thirteenth century was not, to put it mildly, a century of unmixed benefit for the Jews of Western Europe . . . it is absurd to pretend that the position of the Jew in the thirteenth century was an ideal one, one free from persecution, and that bad things only came with the Renaissance. (Brentano 1974: 46)

The inclusion (albeit in a subservient role) of Jews in the papal Possesso demonstrates that Jews and Christians could occupy much of the same civic space throughout the Middle Ages, until this space became contested in the fifteenth century with the expansion of the Christian mendicant religious orders (Franciscans, Dominicans), with their anti-Jewish preaching and the establishment of new forms of moneylending, outside Jewish control. It was in this altered climate that, in 1484, Pope Innocent VIII heeded Jewish requests to allow the papal acclamation ceremony to be moved to a less publicly provocative location, within the walls of the Castel Sant'Angelo. Public space—even in Rome—was no longer easily shared. The last known such ceremony took place in 1513, after which Jews were required to provide costly decoration for the procession route but could not participate.

In general, unlike Jewish communities in England and northern Europe that suffered major persecutions, including massacres and expulsions, from the time of the First Crusade (1096) to the end of the fourteenth century, Italian Jewish communities remained mostly prosperous, physically unharmed, and legally protected until the fifteenth century (M. Cohen 1994: 168). The greatest harassment came from government taxes and increasing anti-Jewish preaching by friars, often despite specific government warnings to the contrary (Miller et al. 2010: 74–5).

It was not the Renaissance, however, but the Counter-Reformation that brought the institution of the ghetto and truly bad things to the Jews of Rome.

Figure 3 Rome ghetto as shown in a study for a bird's-eye view of the city by Antonio Tempesta, 1593. *After L. Finelli et al., Il Ghetto (Rome, 1986)*

Pope Paul IV's infamous pronouncement stated that on the 'holy day of lamentation for the destruction of the Temple of Jerusalem' (26 July 1555), all the city's Jews had to move to the area between Ponte Quattro Capi and the Portico d' Ottavia, the Piazza Giudea and the Tiber (Stow 1977: 291–8) (Figure 3).

The new ghetto area was in Sant'Angelo in the heart of Rome and had long been central to the life of the entire medieval city, not just to Jews. The Jewish quarter occupied a major crossroads where the route connecting the two sides of the Tiber over the Tiber Island—one of only two easy crossings in the city prior to the late sixteenth century—intersected the main river road that connected the northern and southern parts of the city. Merchants, pilgrims, and clerics daily passed this way.

Today's Trastevere, on the west side of the Tiber, was an area associated with Jews since antiquity, when Philo mentioned that 'the great section of Rome on the other side of the Tiber is occupied and inhabited by Jews, most of whom are emancipated Roman citizens' (Levine 2000: 264–5). On the east or city side of the river, as early as the year 1000 there is a reference to a prayer house named for a certain Joseph at Ponte Quattro Capi (Ponte Judaeorum), the bridge over the Tiber Island, and by 1337 a synagogue existed on the Piazza Giudea (Benocci and Guidoni 1993). As Alfred Haverkamp has noted for many German cities, the central location of Jewish quarters is often an indication of the early settlement of Jews in a town (Haverkamp 1995: 27). Jewish residences, however, were also scattered throughout the city and the move to the ghetto meant uprooting old families and the abandonment of synagogues.

Despite nineteenth-century descriptions of Sant'Angelo as a slum, before it became an enforced Jewish ghetto it was much like other older Roman neighbourhoods. In the early sixteenth century the average Jewish household consisted of five people, about the same as for Christians (Partner 1976: 101), and the medieval domestic architecture of Jews and non-Jews was indistinguishable. Some powerful Roman families also lived in the area and were often allied to local Jewish magnates. Several important Jewish families had converted to Christianity in this atmosphere of physical, and often symbiotic, coexistence, but continued to reside in the area. Notarial documents from the thirteenth to the sixteenth centuries show that Jews and Christians were often neighbours in the *rione*, occasionally sharing the same building. They sometimes competed for property and also entered into partnerships.

In Rome and throughout southern and central Italy, Jews and Jewish property are frequently mentioned by name without much further comment in contracts and other types of documents. In Rome, Brentano cites a 1363 notarial document that recorded how Luca de Beccariis, of a prominent Sant'Angelo family, rented a house he owned in the Jewish Street (Ruga Judeorum) for a year to the Jew Sagaczolo di Bonaventura, also of the *rione* Sant'Angelo. One of the witnesses was a priest, rector of the church of San Lorenzo in Piscinula, located at the edge of the Jewish quarter. Brentano thinks the rent may have been inordinately high, but this may have reflected the cost of living in a desirable district (Brentano 1974: 47). Obadiah of Bertinoro wrote that the Jews of Palermo, though clearly impoverished at the time of his visit in 1487, were 'all living on one street, which is situated in the best part of the town' (Obadiah of Bertinoro 1965: 234).

Because of the nature of the Roman documents we mostly know of Jewish–Christian interaction when disputes had to be adjudicated, but these conflicts indicate a relative normality in relations and in access to shared space. In 1238 a priest filed a complaint against four Jewish cloth-makers for throwing their dyes and dirty water out into the street in front of their house, which then ran down in front of the nearby church. The *magistri stratarum* (masters of the streets) ruled against the Jews, who were told that, if in the future they emptied such dyes into the street, they would have to build an underground covered conduit that would not obstruct the street and that would carry the waste to the main sewer (Brentano 1974: 47; Krautheimer 1980: 284). Though this case involved a priest and Jews it is otherwise a typical land use issue, and the judgment was very similar to those pronounced throughout Italy against those who dirtied or blocked public areas (see Gruber 1990).

In addition to the aforementioned Jewish bookseller and dyers, among the approximately 1,700 Roman Jews in the early 1500s there were thirty banking firms, doctors and musicians employed at the papal court, as well as tailors, clothiers, vendors of old clothes, furniture, and junk, a soap seller, tripe merchant, and small grocer (Partner 1976: 101).

This mix of professions represents only a small portion of the types of work in which Jews were engaged prior to the restrictions imposed in the sixteenth-century ghettos. According to documents, the most prominent Jews were moneylenders, doctors, or international merchants, but the majority in Italy and elsewhere had more prosaic jobs. Some worked within the Jewish community as religious functionaries and providing kosher food and other material goods. A large number of Jews were doubtless servants, workmen, and clerks within Jewish homes and businesses. Many were small merchants with market stalls and shops, as is indicated by complaints against Jewish shopkeepers in Retimo in 1412 (Lopez and Raymond 1968: 104). Others were craftsmen of fabric, metals, and books. Obadiah of Bertinoro writes of the 850 Jewish families of Palermo in 1487 that they are artisans, such as coppersmiths and ironsmiths, or porters and peasants, and are despised by the Christians because they wear tattered garments. As a mark of distinction they are obliged to wear a piece of red cloth, about the size of a gold coin, fastened on the breast. The royal tax falls heavily on them, for they are obliged to work for the king in any employment that they are given; they have to draw ships to the shore, to construct dykes, and so on. They are also employed in administering corporal punishment and in carrying out the death sentence (Obadiah of Bertinoro 1965: 234–5).

Throughout Europe some urban Jews, and especially rural Jews, maintained farms and vineyards. Some of these were no doubt held by tenant farmers, but some were also probably worked by Jews. The history of Jewish labour in the pre-modern period still needs to be written, but accepting the smaller size of their population, Jews in the fifteenth and sixteenth centuries probably engaged in as varied activities as their Christian neighbours (Roth 2003: 180–9).

Co-operation and Confrontation

Beginning in the thirteenth century Jews increasingly settled in central and northern Italy, where they were often invited by local governments that needed them to fill a financial role. At present we have documentation of Jewish presence for fewer than twenty northern Italian towns and cities before the late thirteenth century, but recently Michele Luzzati and others have put the number of places of Jewish settlement in central and northern Italy in the hundreds between the thirteenth and the mid-sixteenth centuries. These communities are thought to have numbered between 15,000 and 20,000 Jews altogether, or approximately 0.2 per cent of the population as a whole (Luzzati 1983: 191).[6]

The Jewish population in Italy continued to expand during the early Renaissance period. This was due in part to natural demographic growth—large families that suffered little violence—and also the increased immigration of Jewish refugees from other parts of Europe into Italy.[7] Native Italian Jews maintained ties to the Jewish community of Rome, where many banking families retained business connections and had family ties. Immigrant Jews tended to concentrate in fewer localities—usually trade centres. They formed their own communities and operated mostly independently of Roman Jewish supervision. Because immigrant Jews were often invited to reside in central and northern Italian towns, and because their numbers were relatively small, there were few real restrictions placed on their behaviour, including their choice of place of residence, until the fifteenth century. The 1384 case of Siena, mentioned above, is an exception, but a harbinger of changes to come.

Jews were often granted citizenship—at least temporarily—in a town, and Italian Jews developed attachments to particular towns and governments. Despite the decrees of the Lateran Council of 1215, they attained real legal, economic, and religious rights and privileges. In the thirteenth and fourteenth centuries, communal governments such as that of Umbrian Todi made special efforts to court and attract Jewish doctors and moneylenders, and their enticements could be quite generous. In Spoleto, Jewish occupations were more varied —Jews were both humble carters and more affluent cloth merchants. In Umbrian Cascia, they were dealers in valuable saffron who travelled the trade routes of central Italy and, like other merchants, leased space to store their goods and stable their horses. Favoured status could be granted by communal governments, and also by tyrants. In Lombardy, Gian Galeazzo Visconti invited Jews to open banks in Cremona, Pavia, Como, and Vigevano, and he appears to have favoured the Jews of Perugia, too (Toaff 1998: 41).

It was common for Jews to have shops on public streets and squares, and they would also set up booths and stands on market days in public places. However, these were often spaces which also had religious associations, particularly because of the placement of images or because they were on the route taken by religious processions. Any public space could, in fact, be defined in religious terms and Jewish presence could create a continuing tension—which sometimes simmered low but could also boil over into violence. The proximity of Jews to processions taking place during Holy Week, for example, was often the cause of anxiety and confrontation. They were expected—and sometimes forced—to close house and shop doors and windows, and even to vacate areas, when Christian religious processions passed their way. Since an important aspect of these processions was the active sacralization of everyday urban space, by their very existence they must be seen—in part, at least—as an aggressive affront to Jews.

At the end of the twelfth century Pope Alexander III had ordered Jews to close their doors and windows on Good Friday, and in 1205 Innocent III complained:

'on Good Friday Jews walk up and down the streets and public squares, without regard for the age-old custom, everywhere making mock of the Christians who adore the figure of Christ upon the cross, and seeking through their insults to have them desist from their worship'. In the decrees of 1215 there is a more comprehensive ban on Jews in public places during Holy Week: 'They shall not walk in public on the days of the Lamentation and Easter Sunday, for (as we have heard) some of them do not blush to go out on these days more than usually adorned, and are not afraid to make fun of Christians who exhibit signs of grief at the memory of the most holy Passion' (Simonsohn 1991: 132).

While we should treat these pronouncements with some scepticism we might also find some truth in them, if not exactly what the popes intended. In the substantial Jewish settlements through southern Italy and in Rome, one can easily imagine a lack of reverence for, or even acknowledgement of, Christian holidays in neighbourhoods filled with Jews. We have also seen that Jewish wedding and funeral processions took place within and without the Jewish neighbourhoods. Lent and Holy Week often coincided with the Jewish celebratory festivals of Purim and Passover (and, a little later in the calendar, Shavuot), which all celebrate God's intervention to save the Jews in a time of need. These were occasions when Jews dressed up, ate well, and could drink more wine than usually prescribed. At Purim and Passover non-Jewish oppressors (Pharaoh, Haman) are humiliated and ritually ridiculed. Perhaps Christians, especially clergy, viewed these celebrations with suspicion, and even as anti-Christian demonstrations.

Church councils continued to warn Jews to avoid encountering Christian processions carrying the cross or the sacrament, and this remained a constant concern in subsequent centuries. In Savoy in the early fifteenth century Jews were not allowed to appear in public at all during Holy Week, and had to keep their doors and windows shut (Segre 1986–90: 74–5). But Jewish leaders also urged their flock to remain apart from Christian religious rituals. While Christians feared contamination and blasphemy, rabbis, such as the twelfth-century Rabbi Eliezer of Metz (Germany), were concerned that Jews would be lured into Christian worship (J. Katz 1961: 45).

City authorities also made efforts to separate Jews on such occasions. As more and more Christian confraternities were formed in Italian cities, with more and more processions at all times of the day and night, it became nearly impossible for Jews to avoid them—even when, in the sixteenth century, they were confined behind ghetto walls. In Venice in the late sixteenth century the government expressed disapproval of balconies without bars in ghetto houses that faced the Cannaregio, providing a clear view of processions, and in 1625 there were complaints that Jews could look from ghetto windows and 'blaspheme when the sacraments were carried in processions along the Cannaregio promenade' (Ravid 1999: 257–9).

Jews, on their part, feared the frequent violence stirred up against them by

Holy Week preachers. They remained closeted at home as required by law and through the desire for self-preservation. Some Jews tried to leave town during this period. Still, there were regular confrontations. The most innocent of these was the *sassaiola*, a controlled stone-throwing attack that was common on many festive occasions, but sanctioned and ritualized as stoning of Jews' houses during Holy Week. Historian Ariel Toaff writes that 'the performance was therefore a game; it had its set script, its rules, which were scrupulously observed by the whole cast, and a rigid framework which left no leeway for spontaneous action' (Toaff 1998: 181).

As Natalie Zemon Davis has shown in her classic study of misrule, even ritualized performance could get out of hand (Davis 1975: 107), and this was a particular fear for Jews. Such violence was so clearly anticipated that protection from it was often a stated responsibility of the commune in the negotiated terms of Jewish settlement. In 1510 a Jew named Mosè, from Gualdo Tadino, was tried at Perugia for having, in the words of his accusers, 'the effrontery to stay at home with his family during the Easter triduum, keeping the windows open and standing at the balcony, making mock of the ecclesiastical ceremonies and performing other actions in contempt of the Christians' (Toaff 1998: 186). Contempt of Christianity was a common enough accusation made against Jews by Christian clerics, though often not upheld by the authorities. However, the Perugia court proceedings indicate that there was some truth in the charge against Mosè. Apparently he and others were watching the Good Friday procession of the Confraternità dei Disciplinati di San Bernardino when someone from the procession began to stone the onlookers. Mosè returned fire, hurling stones and invective against his assailants (Toaff 1998: 186).[8]

There is much that can be said about this incident and others, but for our purposes it suffices to say that even a Jew's private residence could become a public space in which he had to follow the rules of public (Christian) decorum. The incident is evidence, furthermore, to support my earlier claim that processions not only did not avoid the houses of Jews but passed right by them—quite possibly as a way of lecturing and humiliating the Jews, and at times provoking them. This was the same strategy that placed churches in proximity to Jewish neighbourhoods—for while it is true that Jews sometimes settled near churches, the reverse was also true, and Christian shrines were installed near Jews in order to confront and convert them.

As I have mentioned above, Jews also had to cope with Christian images in their midst, often upon their very houses. If Jews removed holy images from houses they rented or purchased without permission there could be dire consequences. In Mantua the Jewish banker Daniele da Norsa was accused of obliterating an image of the Virgin and Child on the wall of a house he purchased, and as a result he was forced to finance the building of a church dedicated to the Virgin, and its altarpiece by Andrea Mantegna, the *Madonna della Vittoria*.

An anonymous artist painted a second panel, the so-called Madonna of the Jews, in which Daniele and his family are depicted wearing their yellow badges (D. Katz 2008: 44).

A happier outcome was seen in 1449 in Ferrara, where the Jew Abramo obtained permission to cover with cloth some decorative frescoes of saints and prophets in an upstairs room in a rented house where they had been damaged by humidity. Abramo had the foresight to have notaries examine the house and the paintings in order to be relieved of any culpability (D. Katz 2008: 54). In Gubbio in 1471 Samuele di Consiglio bought a house in the San Pietro district on whose outer wall there was a painting of the Virgin and Child, St Anthony Abbot, and St Ubaldo. He wanted to remove the painting and so consulted the deputy of the local bishop. Permission was given for the image to be scraped off on the condition that Samuele commissioned a similar painting by the same painter— Jacopo Bedi—that would be placed in the oratory of the recently built Fraternità dei Bianchi, or some other suitable place (Toaff 1998). A similar episode occurred in Pisa in 1492 (Luzzati 1983: 137; D. Katz 2008: 54).

Jewish Spaces and Places

Documentary information, much of it compiled by Shlomo Simonsohn and Ariel Toaff, allows us to contemplate 'Jewish space' throughout medieval Italian cities, while topographical studies by local historians have begun to identify the locations of Jewish neighbourhoods in Italian towns.[9] Still, for the pre-ghetto period only a small number of medieval buildings have been positively identified as having served Jewish users. These are mostly synagogues, or houses which included spaces for worship, and are thus more fully described in communal documents. More generally, groups of houses in former Jewish quarters have been identified, but specific information about who might have lived in them and when is sketchy.

Many of these places are in southern Italy, where until the end of the fifteenth century the Jewish population was large and long-established, dating to antiquity. When Jews were expelled from Sicily in 1492, it is estimated that 35,000 people, or approximately 5 per cent of the population of the island, left. Jews had lived for centuries in at least fifty localities throughout southern Italy. Many Jewish toponyms can still be found in the region, particularly in rural areas such as Calabria (Vivacqua 1994), where we find Monte Giudei, Casale Giudeo, Acqua Judia, Judio Sottano, Judio Suprano, and other designations remembered long after the passing of the Jews.

Toaff has documented the surprisingly cordial relations between Christians and Jews in Umbria, a region which was the heart of both Franciscan Italy and Italian communal independence. The relative autonomy of cities and towns generally allowed more freedom for Jews, since towns acted first in their own interest and only acquiesced to larger policies, whether papal or imperial, when absolutely necessary. Assisi may have hosted a Jewish population of 80 to 100 Jews in the second half of the fourteenth century, and current research suggests that this was a substantial number of Jews for any community at the time (Toaff 1979: 27). Important Jewish banks were located in the Porta Santa Chiara district, and contracts are preserved for the construction in 1309 of houses for Mele di Maestro Salomone and Leone di Salomone. But Jews had the run of the town, including access to the great and growing friary of San Francesco. In general, the conventual Franciscans (*fratres minores*) had a tolerant attitude towards Jews; the Assisi friars were treated by a Jewish doctor and even purchased wine from him, and they employed a Jewish ironmonger to restore the roof of the church (we do not know if the Jew needed rabbinic dispensation to engage in the work). Friars of the Confraternity of San Stefano drank and ate at the Osteria del Campo, run by a Jew, and there are other references to Jews working for and with the Franciscan brothers (Toaff 1998: 166). This situation seems to have been relatively normal throughout Umbria, where religious institutions often rented and sold houses and land to Jews, and even provided land for Jewish cemeteries.

With the exception of Rome, Jewish populations were small, often no more than one or two banking families and their retainers. As Robert Chazan has pointed out in the case of northern Europe, the increased specialization of Jewish financial services limited the number of productive Jews within any small city or territory (Chazan 2010: 104). Sometimes—as already mentioned—there were Jewish doctors, though these could also be the same bankers filling an additional semi-civic role. A 'family' might easily consist of more than a dozen members, including blood relatives, servants, and employees. Thus, a community of two or more families might provide the *minyan* (quorum) of adult males required for the most important religious services, and the establishment of a synagogue (see below). There is still little evidence for the creation of other specifically Jewish spaces such as *mikvaot* (ritual baths), study houses, or advanced yeshivas, though such places probably existed in Rome, and there were no known monumental structures erected on the scale of the synagogue of Palermo in Sicily, or the thirteenth-century 'school of the Jews' discovered in Rouen, in northern France.

It does appear, however, that Jews clustered together. This may have been for practical reasons related to family connection and service, business partnership, and religious worship. Where there was a synagogue, it was natural for Jews to live in proximity for ease of access to prayer—since Judaism requires three prayer services daily—including the morning service likely to be held before sunrise, as well as attendance at the synagogue on the sabbath and numerous festivals. In Perugia many Jews lived in the district of Porta Sant'Angelo, along the via Vecchia (close to today's University for Foreigners). In Spoleto, Jewish families lived on the vaita Petrenga, which became commonly known as the 'street of the Jews', not far from the Piazza del Mercato (Toaff 1998: 189–90). This area was so associated with Jews that the nearby church was known as San Gregorio della Sinagoga.

Notarial documents give evidence of Jews renting or purchasing fine houses from Christians in the centres of Italian towns, though exactly which houses these were has not often been identified. In Perugia in the late thirteenth century, the rich banker Matassio da Roma owned a lavish palazzo in the Porta Sole district, on the street leading to the church of Santa Lucia. As late as 1475 the medical officer of Montone (Umbria) lived in a luxurious house owned by the monks of the abbey of San Bartolomeo da Camporeggio, near the palazzo of Count Carlo Fortebracci, lord of the town (Toaff 1998: 172). Other Jews were scattered throughout the city. Wealth, more than religion, seemed to determine one's area of residence.

Situations were not, however, uniform from decade to decade, and from place to place. They varied depending upon papal policies, changing political and economic fortunes of individual towns and regions, and the rise of minorite orders and their itinerant preachers.

Restrictions on Jewish use of public space were applied, though many seem to be rooted in local circumstance or tradition. A statute of Narni (Umbria) from 1371 states that 'no Jew, whether man or woman, may live near the fountains and aqueduct of Narni, that is, at a distance of less than twenty-five feet from the same'. Toaff suggests that this restriction, which dates from a period affected by plague, may have been a precaution against Jews contaminating or otherwise compromising the city's drinking water (Toaff 1998: 124). Overall, given the Jewish ritual need for clean water, it is likely that numerous misconceptions and superstitions arose around Jews and water. In contrast to the Rhineland, where we have been fortunate to discover several substantial *mikvaot*, such structures are virtually unknown in mainland Italy. One or possibly two *mikvaot* have recently been found in Sicily, however, where the Jewish population was once very substantial, but overall, little is known of how Italian Jews maintained ritual purity through the creation of their own spaces, or the adaptation of others.

Cemeteries

Public displays of Jewish autonomy in actions or in space were discouraged and often forbidden, especially from the fifteenth century on. While Jews were permitted access to Christian areas, there were few specifically Jewish spaces, and even these could be compromised. The establishment of cemeteries, for example, posed numerous problems. A cemetery was one of the first requirements in any new Jewish community, and negotiating a site for burial was often a delicate matter. Choice of town in which to settle might be determined by access to a cemetery. It was often difficult for Jews to obtain a plot to bury their dead, and when they did it was always outside a town's walls, often quite distant from where they lived. Though we are certain that there were many Jewish cemeteries in Italy, we only know the exact location of a small number.

Surprisingly, Jews were often allocated burial sites by the Church. For example, we have a notice from Norman Sicily, where in 1187–8 Guido of Anagni, bishop of Cefalu, ceded to the Jews of Syracuse a tract of land for the extension of their cemetery. This was apparently a lease of sorts, not a sale, requiring an annual payment of olive oil at harvest time (Simonsohn 1997: i. xxxix). Leasing land for cemeteries could cause difficulties, since the land could presumably be reclaimed—putting Jewish burials at risk. We do not know of cases of this happening, however, until the complete expulsion of Jews from a territory, at which time it is presumed the cemeteries were neglected and, in many cases— but at unknown times—plundered for stone (the example of Spain is better documented, where the Crown assumed ownership of cemeteries and sold the stones, while leaving burials untouched and the land open for pasture).

Jews and Christians had very different ideas concerning death and burial.[10] Except for the special case of Prague, pre-modern Jewish cemeteries were not near synagogues. Christians, on the other hand, strove to display holy relics— including body parts of saints—in their churches, and the faithful sought to be buried nearby, either within the church walls or just outside. For Jews, the perceived impurity of churches was one more compelling reason to avoid them. According to historian Robert Bonfil,

In the eyes of the Jews, Christians seemed in fact to idealize the image of the dead god, and therefore not to take a negative attitude toward death; indeed they went so far as to attribute sanctity to the relics of the dead. For the Jews, however, the exact contrary was true—in part because they adhered to the biblical ideal of the impurity of death . . . in part precisely as a result of their programmatic opposition in principle to what seemed to them the cardinal idea of Christianity. (Bonfil 1994: 280–1)

Jews sought to establish cemeteries away from inhabited areas to avoid contamination, but still close enough to allow prompt burial and regular protection of, as well as care for, the graves. Jews, like Christians, visited graves for a variety of personal and communal reasons; proximity was therefore an important factor, but they were also concerned that Jewish funeral rites should not be easily witnessed by Christians. While Obadiah of Bertinoro does not mention Christian interference with the Jewish funerals he describes, Christians did regularly disrupt and mock Jewish funerals, parodying them in popular theatrical productions.

Even with assurance from communal authorities, it was often difficult to transport the dead for burial in cemeteries outside the city walls. This often had to be done—sometimes by legal requirement—in the dead of night in order to reduce confrontation. Nonetheless, there is a substantial number of documented incidents throughout Italy where Jewish funerals turned bloody when processions were attacked en route to the cemetery, as was the case in Perugia in 1446 at the funeral of Elya the Jew (Toaff 1998: 54). Such incidents occurred in Italy even into the nineteenth century (Toaff 1998: 55 n. 66). In the same way that Jews were restricted in the types of everyday clothing they could wear, so too, they were often forbidden from wearing mourning clothes during funeral processions, since this was a privilege not afforded to non-Christians, though exceptions were often made for respected Jewish doctors and bankers.

Synagogues

Only the synagogue could offer Jews a secure place—but even these holy places could be invaded by aggressive preachers and angry mobs. In southern Italy physical and documentary evidence indicates that synagogues were often notable works of architecture and were prominently sited, at least within predominantly Jewish neighbourhoods. A few examples survive. There are two fine masonry synagogues in the Apulian port city of Trani (Miller et al. 2010: 63–9). They were turned into churches, but one of them, the Scolanova, has been returned to a reconstituted Jewish community for use as a synagogue.

Obadiah of Bertinoro described how the synagogue in Palermo which he visited in 1488—in all probability the famous Meschita after which the Jewish quarter was named—was 'surrounded by numerous buildings, such as the hospital, where beds are provided for sick people and for strangers who come there from a distant land and have no place to spend the night. There is a ritual bath there, and also a large and magnificent chamber where the representatives sit in judgment and regulate the affairs of the community' (Marcus 1972: 395). Like all the Jewish institutions in Sicily, the synagogue was closed when the Jews were expelled from the Kingdom of the Two Sicilies. In Rome, only a small building surviving in Trastevere is likely to have been a synagogue, but there would have been many others (Figure 4). The surviving structure is similar in size and form to Roman houses of the twelfth and thirteenth centuries (Gruber 2010).

Synagogues in central and northern Italy outside Rome were mostly established in private houses, which either continued to serve as residences or were in a few cases converted entirely to worship and community spaces. Synagogues were often located within the house of the community's wealthiest Jew, or in another house purchased by an individual Jew, and established for community use. These houses were typical of Italy's medieval urban centres, and there was no formal distinction between a house used by a Christian and one used by a Jew. Building exteriors were probably indistinguishable from neighbouring houses.

The synagogue of Perugia existed from the mid-fifteenth century until the Jews were expelled from that Umbrian Italian city in 1570. The synagogue (or *scola*) was located in the fine house (*palazzo*) in the district of Porta Sant'Angelo,

Figure 4 Rome: purported former synagogue (twelfth century), Via dell'Atleta 14, Trastevere. *Photograph by Samuel D. Gruber*

for which a rent of 7 florins a year was paid to a local nobleman. In 1448 the community also began to rent an adjacent building. Then both buildings were purchased by two wealthy Jewish brothers for 200 florins, and the Jewish community was allowed to continue use of part of the buildings as a synagogue, but ownership remained with the brothers, who restored and enlarged them for their own residence (Toaff 1998: 91–3).

In Assisi, the community rented a house for a synagogue until the mid-fifteenth century. This was probably located close to the Piazza del Comune (*versus plateam*), near the present Chiesa Nuova, behind the Palazzo dei Priori, on the site of the so-called birthplace of St Francis (Toaff 1979: 81).

Many Jewish communities were also located in Lazio, within the general vicinity of Rome. Though we have considerable documentary evidence of their settlement, few physical traces survive. In Sermoneta (Tetro 1977: 9–26) and in Campagnolo (Pavoncello 1990: 49) certain houses have been traditionally identified as synagogues, but without authentication.[11]

Figure 5 Sermoneta: purported former synagogue. *Photograph by Cal Greenbaum, International Survey of Jewish Monuments*

An example of such a house-synagogue is probably illustrated in a miniature from a fifteenth-century manuscript in the Biblioteca Palatina in Parma (Metzger 1982: fig. 121). We see the house of a wealthy Jew. The ground floor is articulated with a wide high arch, typical of the ground floor shops and work spaces of such houses. Two small windows surmount this arch, probably indicating a mezzanine. Above is the *piano nobile* illuminated by three Gothic windows. One can imagine a prayer room possibly set up behind these windows.

No medieval synagogue interiors have survived in Italy, and the description of the Palermo synagogue is the only contemporary detailed written account. An inventory of 1503 from Bologna, published by R. Rinaldi, of the private house of Abramo Sforno, where a synagogue functioned, provides some information: 'a chapel, or room for prayer with cloth of gold and silk brocade and silver lamps and chains, and lampshades and books left by various persons to the said chapel for the salvation of their souls' (Toaff 1998: 93). It has long been a custom for Jews to leave gifts to their synagogues upon leaving a community or upon their death, and this practice is recorded in a few fourteenth- and fifteenth-century wills. As with churches, precious silver and fabrics in synagogues could attract thieves. Such a theft was reported and solved in Perugia (Toaff 1998: 93–4), and should not be seen as a specifically anti-Jewish act as there was no desecration involved and the items were returned—only to be later stolen by Jews!

An even better idea of what the interior arrangement of an Italian house-synagogue might have looked like can be gleaned from a late fifteenth-century Italian manuscript illustration from Emilia. The illustration shows an open room with a tall wooden ark set against one wall and a lower reader's table before it. To either side of the room is a series of chests or desks at which the worshippers sit, facing the centre of the room. A prayer book (*siddur*) and a candle burning in a candlestick are placed on each desk. This is a night service—or perhaps early morning. It is dark outside the four Romanesque-style double-light windows. The room is elegant, with a wood-coffered ceiling and a large decorated arch supported on Corinthian columns that create more space than ordinary. Each ceiling coffer is decorated with a painted star. The floor is covered with red ceramic tiles.[12]

Such synagogues appear, and typically must have served (despite the theft mentioned above), as the most secure and easily identifiable Jewish spaces. Just as Jews were not expected to enter churches under normal circumstances, so too most Christians would not enter synagogues. But there are no Jewish laws prohibiting Christian presence in synagogues—whether during worship or not. At the same time, Christian authorities regularly placed restrictions on Jews employing Christians as servants and on Jews speaking to Christians about religious matters. This did not, however, stop clerics from entering synagogues. In good times they would occasionally attend learned Jewish sermons; at other times they forced themselves upon Jews, preaching conversionary sermons about the truths of Christianity and the falsehoods of Judaism.

Ultimately, for Jews, no place, even the synagogue, was an entirely Jewish space and under Jewish control. With the rise of the Christian preaching orders the synagogue became a contested space between Christians and Jews (J. Cohen 1978; Myers and McMichael 2004). Pope Nicholas III's papal bull *Vineam Sorec* of 1278 was addressed to the orders of friars and encouraged preaching to the Jews (Simonsohn 1991: 257–8). We do not hear of such efforts in Italy, but in Spain, where the Jewish population was much larger, Christian preachers were given permission and even urged to preach conversion sermons to Jews, including in the synagogue. King James I of Aragon promulgated an edict in 1242 ordering royal officials to force Muslims and Jews to attend conversionary sermons. A Hebrew source from around 1250 records the Jewish communal response to such a sermon delivered by a Dominican preacher in the synagogue of Narbonne (Chazan 1980: 255–63).

Incursions into the synagogue were especially promoted by the Aragonese

Benedict XIII, one of several competing papal claimants of the early fifteenth century, and his confessor Vincent Ferrer, the most active of Spain's advocates of forceful conversion of Jews. Ferrer is said to have forced his way with upraised cross into synagogues in Valencia (1391), Santiago (1408), and Alcañiz (1413) and dedicated them as churches. These policies, however, were in marked contrast to Jewish–Christian relations in Italy, where, after the renunciation of Benedict XIII and the reunification of the papacy at the Council of Constance, Pope Martin V repealed Benedict's oppressive laws. Nonetheless, Benedict had emboldened mendicant orders across Europe, which increased their anti-Jewish activities.

The Ghetto: A New Kind of Jewish Space

The three centuries between the Fourth Lateran Council and the creation of the Venetian ghetto were a period of remarkable political, religious, social, and economic change throughout what is today Italy, but what was in the Middle Ages a patchwork of often independent and rival cities, states, and kingdoms. While the status of Jews varied from time to time and from place to place, overall this was, as the historian Salo Baron first pointed out in 1928, a period or relative security and prosperity for Jews (Baron 1928; Biale 1994: 9). There were, of course, instances of real acts of violence, but these, while long remembered, were not indicative of the experience of most Jews most of the time.

The consensus among scholars, however, is that tensions over Jewish religious, social, and economic activities as well as public presence increased dramatically in Italy throughout the fifteenth century as a consequence of the anti-Jewish polemics of Dominican and Franciscan friars. This led, in the first half of the fifteenth century, to increased demands that Jews wear a distinctive yellow badge—something required by the Fourth Lateran Council but apparently seldom enforced. It is clear from the calls for the badge that Jews had long been in the habit of frequenting public places without restriction.

Within a short time the definition for Italian Jews of what constituted public space and civic space changed dramatically. Throughout the fifteenth century deliberate and aggressive strategies of confrontation upset the delicate but workable balance of coexistence that had mostly prevailed in Italy for centuries. In some ways this helped strengthen Jewish communities internally, but it marked a very different era in Jewish–Christian relations.

The age of the ghettos began when anti-Jewish rhetoric became action. At first, with the founding of the ghetto in Venice in 1516, a compromise was reached. For Jews to be able to remain permanent residents of Venice, not far from the commercial centre of the Rialto, could be seen as a privilege, not too different from the way Jews had lived in trading cities such as Trani. This arrangement was advantageous to Jews and to many Venetians. Already used to controlling and enclosing different social groups, Venetian authorities found no problem with confining Jews at night to a recently constructed housing development—the ghetto. For decades Venetian policies towards Jews vacillated between restriction and permissiveness, especially when, after 1541, Sephardi Jews from Portugal and the Ottoman empire could offer expanded trade opportunities.

Pope Paul IV, however, did not understand or accept Venice's nuanced approach, and he created much tighter legal, social, economic, and physical enclosures around the Jews in Rome and Ancona in 1555. It was this model that spread throughout Italy in the second half of the sixteenth century.

The blurred boundaries often crossed by Jews and Christians in the medieval period became the hard walls and locked gates of the ghetto; in most of Italy these remained intact and oppressive until the mid-nineteenth century.

Notes

This essay was originally presented in the session 'Civic Spaces in the Renaissance City' organized by the Italian Art Society at the International Congress on Medieval Studies, Kalamazoo (10–13 May 2007). I am grateful to Barbara Deimling for inviting me to participate. My essay is part of a larger study of Jewish spaces in Italy in the 16th century, when the first ghettos were created in Venice (1516), Rome (1555), Florence (1571), and elsewhere. I thank Max Grossman for his constructive comments.

1   On the use of this term e.g. in London, see Blair et al. 2002: 15.

2   Archivio di Stato di Siena, Consiglio Generale 194 45^r [13 May 1384]: 'cosa che Judei dispregiatori della fede di Christo e dispregiatori della glorissima Vergine Maria . . . provido che nemmeno Judeo possa stare ne abitare in nessuna casa overo palagio el quale confini col Campo della Città di Siena' (cited in Caferro 1998: 214 n. 24).

3   The antiquity of such supplication ceremonies and suspicions about the intentions and expectations of Jewish participants is evident in the 6th-century writings of Gregory, bishop of Tours. In his *History of the Franks* Gregory relates how Jews were among those who participated in welcoming King Gunthram, shouting 'May all the nations honor you and bend the knee and be subject to you.' Gunthram (according to Gregory) would have none of it, declaring, 'Woe to the Jewish tribe, wicked, treacherous, and always living by cunning. Here's what they were after when they cried out their flattering praises to me today, that all the nations were to honor me as master. [They wish me] to order their synagogue, long ago torn down by the Christians, to be built at the public cost; but by the lord's command I will never do it.' See Gregory 1969: 189.

4   The fullest account of the solemn possession is in Ordo XIV of Cardinal Jacopo Stefaneschi, published in L. A. Muraturi, *Rerum italicarum Scriptores ab anno aerae christianae 500 ad annum 1500* (Milan, 1723–51), III, *De Coronatione Bonif. VIII.* Cited in Gregorovius 1897: 11–12. The essential source on the processions remains Francesco Cancellieri's *Storia de' solenni possessi dei Sommi Pontefici da Leone III a Pio* (1802).

5   According to the *Gesta Balduini*, c. xiv, 'Legem Mosaycam rotulo inscriptam sibi porrigentibus reddidit Judaeis'. See Gregorovius 1898: 59–60. The scene was also illustrated in the *Codex Balduini*.

6   Luzzati distinguishes between Jewish settlement, where at least one Jewish family perma-

nently settled for a number of years, and Jewish presence, where Jews are recorded as owning property.

7   Two major routes of immigration have been traced—one from Rome leading north into central Italy and then to the Po Valley, and one from Germany southwards into northern Italy, and also to central Italy. Other Jews came to Italy from Spain, Provence, France, Savoy, and southern Italy, especially after the expulsions in 1492.

8   A possible provocation, or at least a misunderstanding, occurred in 1475 when the Jews of Savona were accused of hanging enormous animal entrails 'inflated and full of filth' at their windows while the Corpus Christi procession was passing by. See E. Motta, 'Ebrei in Como ed in alter città del ducato Milanese', *Periodico della Società Storica per la provincia e antica diocesi di Como*, 5 (1885), 7–44. Cited in Toaff 1979: 186 n. 65.

9   Simonsohn's Herculean work collecting and editing documentary source material on church policies regarding Jews and on Jewish life in Italy, especially in Sicily, provides an essential foundation for the study of Jews in medieval Italy. Toaff has done the same for Umbria, with detailed archival studies of Jews in Assisi and Perugia, but also elsewhere in the region. He has summarized many of his findings in the remarkable *Love, Work and Death: Jewish Life in Medieval Umbria* (1998), one of the very best books ever written on Jews in the Middle Ages, and a work of which I have made extensive use in preparing this essay.

10   On Jewish attitudes to death and burial see Ehl et al. 1991; Sáros et al. 1993; Goldberg 1996, and Jewish Theological Seminary of America 1999.

11   Among the various other towns in which Jews are known to have settled are Civitavecchia, Ariccia, Genzano, Velletri, Frascati, Grottaferrata, Marino, Segni, Palastrina, Genazzano, Tivoli, Campagnolo, Castelnuovo di Porto, and Sacrofano.

12   The scene is in a *maḥzor* in the G. Weill Collection, Jerusalem, illustrated in Metzger and Metzger 1982, fig. 96.

References

ABULAFIA, DAVID. 2002. 'The Jews in Sicily Under the Norman and Hohenstaufen Rulers'. In N. Bucaria, M. Luzzati, and A. Tarantino, eds., *Ebrei e Sicilia*. Palermo.

BARON, SALO. 1928. 'Ghetto and Emancipation'. *Menorah Journal*, 14: 515–26.

BENOCCI, CARLA, and ENRICO GUIDONI. 1993. *Il Ghetto*. Atlante Storico della Città di Roma 2. Rome.

BIALE, DAVID. 1994. 'Modern Jewish Ideologies and the Historiography of Jewish Politics'. In Jonathan Frankel, ed., *Reshaping the Past: Jewish History and the Historians*, 3–16. Oxford.

BLAIR, IAN, JOE HILLABY, ISCA HOWELL, RICHARD SERMON, and BRUCE WATSON. 2002. 'The Discovery of Two Medieval Mikva'ot in London and a Reinterpretation of the Bristol Mikveh'. *Jewish Historical Studies*, 37: 15–40.

BONFIL, ROBERT. 1994. *Jewish Life in Renaissance Italy*. Berkeley, Calif.

BRENTANO, ROBERT. 1974 *Rome before Avignon*. New York.

CAFERRO, WILLIAM. 1998 *Mercenary Companies and the Decline of Siena*. Baltimore.

CALABI, DONATELLA, and PAOLA LANARO, eds. 1998. *La città italiana e i luoghi degli stranieri, XIV–XVIII secolo*. Rome and Bari.

CANCELLIERI, FRANCESCO. 1802 *Storia de' solenni possessi dei Sommi Pontefici da Leone III a Pio*. Rome.

CAPASSO, BARTOLOMEO. 1885. *Regesta Neapolitana, Monumenta ad Neapolitani Ducatus Historiam Pertinentia*, vol. ii, pt. i. Naples.

CHAZAN, ROBERT, ed. 1980. *Church, State and Jew in the Middle Ages*. West Orange, NJ.

—— 2010. *Reassessing Jewish life in Medieval Europe*. New York.

COHEN, JEREMY. 1982. *The Friars and the Jews: The Evolution of Medieval Anti-Judaism*. Ithaca, NY.

COHEN, MARK R. 1994. *Under Crescent and Cross: The Jews in the Middles Ages*. Princeton, NJ.

COLORNI, V. 1956. *Gli ebrei nel sistema del diritto commune fino alla prima emancipazione*. Milan.

COULET, NOËL. 1979. 'De l'intégration à l'exclusion: La Place des juifs dans les cérémonies d'entrée solennelle au Moyen Age'. *Annales*, 34(4): 672–83.

DAVIS, NATALIE ZEMON. 1975. *Society and Culture in Early Medieval France*. Stanford, Calif.

EHL, PETER, ARNO PARIK, and JIRI EDLER. 1991. *Old Bohemian and Moravian Cemeteries*. Prague.

FERORELLI, N. 1990. *Gli Ebrei nell'Italia meridionale dall'eta romana al secolo XVIII*. Naples.

GOLDBERG, SYLVIE-ANNE. 1996. *Crossing the Jabbok: Illness and Death in Ashkenazi Judaism in Sixteenth- through Nineteenth-Century Prague*, trans. Carol Cosman. Berkeley, Calif.

GRANARA, WILLIAM. 2010. 'Fragments of the Past: Reconstructing the History of Palermo's Meschita Quarter'. In Susan Gilson Miller and Mauro Bertagnin, eds., *The Architecture and Memory of the Minority Quarter in the Muslim Mediterranean City*, 35–55. Cambridge, Mass.

GREGOROVIUS, F. 1897. *The History of the City of Rome in the Middle Ages*, trans. Annie Hamilton, vol. v, pt. i. London.

—— 1898. *The History of the City of Rome in the Middle Ages*, trans. Annie Hamilton, vol. vi, pt. i. London.

GREGORY OF TOURS. 1969. *History of the Franks*, trans. Ernest Brehaut. New York.

GRUBER, SAMUEL D. 1990. 'Ordering the Urban Environment: City Statutes and City Planning in Medieval Todi, Italy'. In Warren Ginsberg, ed., *Ideas of Order in the Middle Ages* (= *Acta*, 15 (1988, pub. 1990)): 121–35.

—— 2010. 'Medieval Synagogues in the Mediterranean Region'. In Aliza Cohen-Mushlin and Harmen H. Thies, eds., *Jewish Architecture in Europe*, 53–65. Schriftenreihe der Bet Tfila 6. Petersburg.

HAVERKAMP, ALFRED. 1995. 'The Jewish Quarters in German Towns during the Late Middle Ages'. In R. Po-Chia Hsia and Hartmut Lehmann, eds., *In and Out of the Ghetto: Jewish–Gentile Relations in Late Medieval and Early Modern Germany*, 13–28. Washington, DC.

Jewish Theological Seminary of America. 1999. *From this World to the Next: Jewish Approaches to Illness, Death and the Afterlife*. New York.

KATZ, DANA E. 2008. *The Jew in the Art of the Italian Renaissance*. Jewish Culture and Contexts. Philadelphia.

KATZ, JACOB. 1961. *Exclusiveness and Tolerance: Jewish–Gentile Relations in Medieval and Modern Times*. Oxford.

KRAUTHEIMER, RICHARD. 1980. *Rome: Profile of a City, 312–1308*. Princeton, NJ.

LAPIDUS, IRA M. 1984. *Muslim Cities in the Later Middle Ages*. New York.

LEVINE, LEE. 2000. *The Ancient Synagogue*. New Haven, Conn.

LOPEZ, ROBERT S., and IRVING W. RAYMOND. 1968. *Medieval Trade in the Mediterranean World*. New York.

LUZZATI, M. 1983. 'Ebrei, chiesa locale, principi e popolo: Due episodi di distruzione di immagini sacre alle fine del Quattrocento'. *Quaderni Storici*, 22(54): 847–77.

——2004. 'Northern and Central Italy: Assessment of Research and Further Prospects'. In C. Cluse, ed., *The Jews of Europe in the Middle Ages (Tenth to Fifteenth Centuries)*, Proceedings of the International Symposium held at Speyer, 20–25 Oct. 2002, 191–200. Turnhout.

MARCUS, JACOB R. 1972. *The Jew in the Medieval World, a Source Book: 315–1791*. New York.

METZGER, T., and M. METZGER. 1982. *Jewish Life in the Middle Ages: Illuminated Hebrew Manuscripts of the Thirteenth to the Sixteenth Centuries*. Secaucus, NJ.

MILLER, SUSAN GILSON, ILHAM KHURI-MAKDISI, and MAURO BERTAGNIN. 2010. 'The Giudecca of Trani: A Southern Italian Synthesis'. In Susan Gilson Miller and Mauro Bertagnin, eds., *The Architecture and Memory of the Minority Quarter in the Muslim Mediterranean City*, 57–79. Cambridge, Mass.

MYERS, SUSAN E., and STEVEN J. MCMICHAEL. 2004. *Friars and Jews in the Middle Ages and Renaissance*. The Medieval Franciscans V/2. Leiden.

OBADIAH YAREH OF BERTINORO. 1965. 'My Journey, from Beginning to End'. In Leo W. Schwarz, ed., *The Jewish Caravan*, 234–54. New York. Trans. first published in *The Miscellany of Hebrew Literature* (London, 1872).

PARTNER, PETER. 1976. *Renaissance Rome, 1500–1559*. Berkeley, Calif.

PAVONCELLO, NELLO. 1980. 'Le comunità ebraiche laziali prima del bando di Pio V'. *Lunario Romano*, 9: 47–77.

POLIAKOV, LÉON, 1977. *Jewish Bankers and the Holy See*, trans. Miriam Kochan. London.

RAVID, BENJAMIN. 1999. 'Curfew Time in the Ghetto'. In E. Kittell and T. Madden, eds., *Medieval and Renaissance Venice*, 237–75. Urbana, Ill., and Chicago.

RIDOLFINI, CECILIA PERICOLI, ed. 1971. *Guide rionale di Roma: Rione VI—parione*, pt. II. Rome.

ROTH, NORMAN. 2003. 'Commerce'. In Norman Roth, ed., *Medieval Jewish Civilization: An Encyclopedia*. New York and London.

SACERDOTI, ANNIE. 2003. *The Guide to Jewish Italy*. New York.

SÁROS, LÁSZLÓ, DEZSŐVÁLI, and TAMÁS RAJ. 1993. *Tanú ez a kőhalom / This Cairn is Witness Today* (bilingual edn.). Budapest.

SEGRE, RENATA, ed. 1986–90. *The Jews in Piedmont*, 3 vols. Jerusalem.

SIMONSOHN, SHLOMO, 1991. *The Apostolic See and the Jews: History*. Toronto.

——1997. *The Jews of Sicily*, i. Leiden.

——2002. 'Sicily: A Millennium of Convivenza (or almost)'. In C. Cluse, ed., *The Jews of Europe in the Middle Ages (Tenth to Fifteenth Centuries)*, 105–20. Proceedings of the International Symposium held at Speyer, 20–25 Oct. 2002. Turnhout.

SKINNER, PATRICIA, 2007. 'Conflicting Accounts: Negotiating a Jewish Space in Medieval Southern Italy, *c*.800–1150 CE'. In M. Frassetto, ed., *Christian Attitudes Toward the Jews in the Middles Ages: A Casebook*, 1–13. New York and London.

STOW, KENNETH R. 1977. *Catholic Thought and Papal Jewry Policy 1555–1593*. New York.

TETRO, F. 1977. 'Gli ebrei a Sermoneta XIII–XIV sec.'. *Economia Pontina*, 4: 9–26.

TOAFF, ARIEL. 1979. *The Jews in Medieval Assisi, 1305–1487*. Florence.

—— 1998. *Love, Work and Death: Jewish Life in Medieval Umbria*. London.

VIVAQUA, SONIA. 1994. 'Gli ebrei in Calabria'. In *Architettura Judaica in Italia: ebraismo, sito, memoria dei luoghi*, 257–68. Palermo.

FOUR

The Question of Hasidic Sectarianism

MARCIN WODZIŃSKI

AARON LEYZER KOTIK was a prosperous and influential Jewish resident of Kamieniec Litewski in what is now western Belarus, a small town located in Grodno province (*guberniya* in the Russian empire), 37 versts (*c.*39 km) from Brześć Litewski. Like his fellow residents of Kamieniec, Aaron Leyzer and his son Moshe were mitnagedim, fierce opponents of hasidism. Around 1846 Moshe, then 14 years old, married Sara, the daughter of rabbi and mitnaged Eliezer Halevi from Grodno (d. 1853). Thus both families were connected to the Lithuanian anti-hasidic tradition, and the bride came from a well-known rabbinic family. But nuptial harmony was shattered immediately after the wedding, when Moshe left home and abandoned his newly wed wife to join the hasidic court of Moshe of Kobryń (d. 1858), having been recruited by his teacher, a devoted follower of the rebbe. The father of young Moshe, Aaron Leyzer, was understandably outraged. He demanded the immediate return of his son and ordered the *tsadik* (hasidic leader) of Kobryń to promise not to lure away any more boys. Neither the *tsadik* nor Moshe, who had become his zealous follower, acceded to Aaron Leyzer's demands, and consequently Aaron announced his estrangement from his son.

Reflecting on these events, diarist Yekhezkiel Kotik (1847–1921), son of Moshe and grandson of Aaron Leyzer, notes that his grandfather's response was hardly excessive. He could have called for mourning as if Moshe had died: Kotik mentions that a local rabbi (his great-uncle), upon hearing the news that a young community member had become a hasid, did in fact order the family of the 'apostate' to sit *shiva* (the seven-day ritual period of mourning) (Kotik 1998: 171; English translation in Assaf 2002: 187). Taking this action carried symbolic significance because according to Jewish custom (but not halakhah—religious law) seven days of mourning are observed not only after the death of a relative but also after someone's conversion to Christianity or any other religion. An apostate was regarded as deceased and uttering his or her name was taboo. Sitting *shiva* in such an instance symbolized the exclusion of the convert from the community (on the origin of the custom see Malkiel 2007: 11–12, and 2009: 124–5). The fact that the rabbi from Kamieniec ordered mourning following the boy's adoption of a hasidic identity shows that he perceived it as every bit as serious as renouncing Judaism to become a Christian or the member of another religion. Unlike other, lesser, transgressions defined during this period by Polish Jews, embracing hasidism warranted expulsion from the Orthodox Jewish community.

This episode from nineteenth-century Kamieniec Litewski was not an isolated incident. It illustrates a broader trend of perceiving hasidism as a form of apostasy and of constructing strict social boundaries between mainstream Judaism and hasidism. In this essay I argue that this perception was relatively widespread among east European Jews in the eighteenth and nineteenth centuries, and trace its origins to an ascription of sectarianism to hasidism. Asking whether, and to what extent, the distinguishing features of a sect were actually shared by the hasidic movement, I explore the discourse on the question of hasidic sectarianism through time and examine the social consequences of this perspective.

Hasidic Conversions?

Several other accounts from nineteenth-century eastern Europe echo Leyzer's response to his son's choosing to become a hasid, suggesting that the phenomenon was more widespread. A similar incident occurred in Brześć Litewski when two Jewish boys ran away to the court of the *tsadik* of Niesuchojeże (Neskhiz), and their families observed *shiva* (see Puchaczewski 1954: 174–5 after Kotik 1998: 171; Assaf 2002: 439). Similarly, the father of *tsadik* Barukh of Czyżew (1787–1877) after hearing about his son's joining the hasidim, exclaimed: 'we should sit *shiva* for our son Barukh, who has taken up with bad company and become attracted to the hasidic sect' (Rubinstein 1961: 317–18).

A widely circulated narrative has been preserved in hasidic circles about the conflict between Israel Elbaum of Łuków and his son, hasidic leader Shimeon Merilus Elbaum of Jarosław (1758–1850). The story presents a scenario somewhat different from that of Brześć Litewski but it refers to the same belief that joining the hasidim constituted conversion. The account is recorded in a hasidic collection of hagiographic narratives, which suggests that the episode is either based on real events or that it carries a lesson for hasidim. Presumably hasidic readers treat the story, together with the message that becoming a hasid constitutes a conversion, as ingrained in hasidic tradition.[1] The background of the story is that Israel of Łuków, the father of Shimeon of Jarosław, was a strong opponent of hasidism all his life. When his own son became a hasid and a disciple of the famous *tsadik* Ya'akov Yitshak Horovitz (1745–1815), known as the Seer of Lublin, Israel brought a lawsuit against his son in a rabbinical court, accusing him of disobeying Jewish law, and in particular of violation of the fifth commandment, 'Honour your father and your mother'. An even more radical sign of estrangement from his son was his formal letter, or, more precisely, an instruction regarding religious practices to be followed after his own death. In this letter Israel forbade his son to say Kaddish (the prayer recited following the death of a close relative) for him after his death if he wanted to recite it in a hasidic version and not according to *nusaḥ* Ashkenaz, the non-hasidic prayer custom of eastern Europe.[2] It should be noted here that, according to traditional Jewish belief, saying Kaddish at a parent's grave during the first thirty days of mourning (known as *sheloshim* from the Hebrew for 'thirty'), and then once a month for a year and then once a year on the anniversary of the death (that is, *yortseyt*), is supposed to be the most effective way of elevating the soul of the deceased parent. Even the prayer recited by the most sinful descendant possessed this power.[3] Renouncing the privilege of Kaddish said by a son at his father's grave was thus clearly a sign of delegitimizing the son and an assertion of his exclusion from the Jewish religious community. When Israel of Łuków learned that Shimeon had pledged to say Kaddish in the Ashkenazi way, he rose from his deathbed and danced, saying: 'my son Shimeon is still alive', signalling that he had considered him dead, having regarded his earlier act of becoming a hasid as one of apostasy.

Possibly the most intriguing source presenting the adoption of hasidism as conversion is an autobiographical narrative of the twentieth-century hasidic leader Israel Ber Odesser (1888–1994), founder of the Na Nach subgroup of Breslov hasidism. In his astonishing account, Rabbi Odesser recalls a journey to Damascus during which he fell and lost his eyesight for three days. The temporary blindness became for him a turning point of his spiritual life.[4] The description, for all its differences, echoes one of the most famous narratives of conversion, the fall of Saul (who was to become St Paul) (Acts 9: 1–6) on the way to Damascus, which is also accompanied by a three-day bout of blindness.

Less sensational but nonetheless significant references to the embracement of hasidism being seen as a conversion appear in many other nineteenth- and twentieth-century sources, for example in memoir literature (see e.g. Leo Baeck Institute Archives, MM93, p. 87). The evidence suggests that the term 'conversion' was commonly—and often unreflectively—used as an impartial appellation for becoming a hasid.[5] For instance, during a conflict in Koniecpol in 1839, the non-hasidic board of the community testified that conflict had been averted when the hasidim began to attend synagogue again: 'hence one may regard them as converted'.[6] Josef Perl (1773–1839), a famous writer of the Galician Haskalah (Jewish Enlightenment), in his anti-hasidic novel *Revealer of Secrets* (*Megaleh temirin*), describes people who became hasidim under social pressure as *anusim*, or forced converts (Perl 1819: no. 77; Perl 1997: 141). *Anus* (plural *anusim*; literally 'raped') is the Hebrew equivalent of the term Marrano, which was used to describe people who had been forcibly baptized in Spain during anti-Jewish persecutions in the fourteenth and fifteenth centuries. The term *anusim* underscores the shift to hasidism as an act of conversion, and, further, implies a perception of coercion.

The rhetoric of conversion when speaking about identifying with a hasidic community remains; showing the persistence of the term, modern historiography and sociology of hasidism consistently apply the term 'convert' to new followers of the movement.[7] This rhetoric also implies the durability of the paradigm for interpreting hasidism as a sectarian phenomenon. The terminology created by the eighteenth- and nineteenth-century critics of hasidism is applied, often unreflectively, in the scientific and popular understanding of hasidism to this day.

Why Was Hasidism Called a Sect?

Was a Jew's adoption of hasidism really a conversion? The answer to this question depends to some degree on the historical and social context, but, regardless of how we define conversion, the presumption underlying the use of this term in this particular case has been that hasidism is substantially different from Judaism. The term 'conversion' in nineteenth-century Poland frames the adoption of hasidic customs as a split with normative Judaism and crossing a boundary to a different religious community. In popular usage conversion meant embracing a different religion or a shift to another denomination within a larger religious entity, such as conversion from the Orthodox Church to Catholicism.[8] Historical evidence of the discourse regarding the adoption of hasidism suggests a parallel with the latter model. Is this assumption, however, justified?

The accounts of Aaron Leyzer Kotik, Israel of Łuków, and Josef Perl, or descriptions of the Paul-like conversion that was experienced by hasidic leader Israel Ber Odesser, certainly do not provide a sound basis for explaining why these authors see a move to hasidism as conversion or for judging whether their outlook is objectively justified. Although hasidism clearly arises from, and remains loyal to, Jewish practice and thought, the accusation of conversion rhetorically signals the delegitimization of the movement, even assigning to it non-Jewish status.

Further underscoring the placement of hasidism outside the bounds of Judaism was its designation as a sect. This accusation was especially prominent among the first mitnagedim as well as many maskilic writers (proponents of the Haskalah). In both cases identifying hasidism as a sect was an act of delegitimization, which would exclude hasidism from the framework of Judaism and from the Jewish community. The designations *kat ḥasidim* (sect of hasidim) or *kat mitḥasdim* (sect of bigots) were the terms most frequently used by anti-hasidic polemicists from the circle of mitnagedim in the late eighteenth and early nineteenth centuries, especially Israel Löbel of Słuck and David of Maków (see Wilensky 1990; Israel Löbel of Słuck 1807). Israel Löbel wrote, for example, that 'despite all bans [hasidism] creates a sect' and thus places itself on the margins of Judaism by breaking the biblical law and the teachings of prophets, who unambiguously forbid establishing sects (1807: 321).

The polemicists criticized hasidic forms of behaviour which they deemed sectarian, such as loud shouting and spontaneous, excited action during prayer (exclamations, swaying, clapping, sudden interruptions, and repeating fragments of prayers), or disobedience to halakhah in disregarding the set hours of prayers.

Even though the leaders of hasidism defended themselves by pointing to biblical precedents for loud recitation and gesticulation during prayer, and argued that specific prayer times were impossible to follow because of the necessity of properly preparing for this significant religious act, all their arguments were dismissed by the polemicists. The opponents believed that the precedents cited by the hasidim, such as King David dancing in front of the ark (2 Sam. 6), were exceptional cases and did not justify introducing these innovations into the everyday prayer ritual. One of the most aggressive anti-hasidic polemicists, Israel Löbel, claimed that the hasidim did not begin synagogue services at the proper time because having gathered in the house of prayer they wasted time on idle chat and gossip (Israel Löbel in Wilensky 1990: ii. 273; see also 1991: 250). Non-hasidic Jews suspected that the atypical behaviour was motivated either by religious exhibitionism or by a desire to demonstrate superiority over their fellow Jews with a claim to a special level of piety. Jewish polemicists not only saw hasidic pietism as an expression of arrogance but also as a perfidious attempt to dupe masses of simple-minded fellow believers in order to recruit new followers. To emphasize the hypocrisy and falsehood of these practices, the early polemicists refused even to call them *ḥasidim* (pious), labelling them instead *mitḥasdim* (bigots), 'karlin-chiks' (derived from a residence of one of the hasidic leaders, Aaron of Karlin), or *kitajowcy*, derived from *kitaj* (a fine silk or cotton fabric used in hasidic clothing). Thus, according to the mitnagedim, hasidism was a dangerous sect outside the boundaries of normative Judaism.

The attempt at delegitimizing hasidism was even more evident in an alternative term applied by the mitnagedim to the hasidic movement, namely, 'new religion' (*dat ḥadashah* or *emunah ḥadashah*). The term appeared, among others, in *Sefer vikuaḥ* by Israel Löbel, where the author makes mention of an imperial decree banning new religions, implying its connection to the rise of hasidism (Wilensky 1990: ii. 269, 274), and in *Sefer ḥasidim*, an early anti-hasidic treatise by an anonymous author (Gellman 2005: 102). The fact that some of the authors, Israel Löbel among them, use both terms interchangeably indicates that the term 'sect' was not meant loosely as a kind of undefined religious grouping but had a clear exclusory function rooted in the classical understanding of a sect as a small breakaway band of disaffected zealots. By implication, if hasidism constituted a new religion, it did not belong to the 'old religion' of Judaism and was a new religious phenomenon *outside* normative Judaism.

Effects: *Kahal,* Maskilim, Government

Labelling hasidism as sectarian had practical effects on many levels of social and political relations. In the regulations of the confraternity Hevrat Mishnayot in Radoszkowice (Mińsk area, Belarus), issued in 1800, one of the important prohibitive regulations was that the confraternity could not accept into its ranks candidates who belonged to the 'sect of *Hasidim*, i.e. attend their prayer house for three days or every day for at least one prayer, or travel to any Rebbe of their sect' (Wilensky 1990: i. 320). Thus defining hasidism as a sect served an exclusionary function, denying its members the right to belong to communal organizations. In addition, through much of the nineteenth century, hasidism is commonly referred to as a sect in anti-hasidic letters of *kahal* boards and individual Jews sent to the government authorities. In these letters petitioners complain about the separatism of the hasidim and ask for help in forcing them to abandon their cult-like behaviour. Here, too, the term 'sect' is supposed to emphasize hasidic separatism, which, according to the petitioners, required legal action. For example, in 1820, community elders from Łask, a small town in central Poland, lodged a complaint to the provincial authorities against a newly formed 'sect' which had set up a separate prayer hall (i.e. hasidic *shtibl*) and did not attend the synagogue.[9] In their petition the community elders ask the government authorities to ban the separate service because: (1) Judaism forbids holding a service outside a synagogue; (2) by missing synagogue services the sect's members would not be aware of new government regulations that were announced there; (3) by missing prayers at the synagogue they would cause a decrease in communal income from collection boxes and from donations offered when being called to the Torah. The Provincial Committee asked a maskil, Ezechiel Hoge (1791–1860), to express his opinion on this matter. He produced the following statement: 'the conflicts between the Jews in this town originated with the followers of the so-called sect of hasidim, who wish to differ from common Jews, and who are known to be the most dangerous of the Jews in his country' (Wodziński 2005a: 83).

Sometimes in the anti-hasidic polemics the alleged contrast between the hasidic sect and normative Judaism is emphasized even more strongly and is used as a tool of social exclusion of hasidism in communal conflicts, as in the example of Icek Bendermacher from Piotrków Trybunalski, who in 1845 reported that some Jews of that town 'belong to various sects of so-called Hussites' and because of this hated 'the true religion of Moses'. Similarly, Yankiel Koning of Hrubieszów wrote in 1852, on behalf of 103 people, that 'the sect of Hussites that fights against us, the truthful followers of the religion of Moses, has nested in the town of Hrubieszów'.[10] Thus hasidism was set against the 'truthful followers' of Judaism and thereby delegitimized.

Similarly, maskilim quite consistently called hasidism a sect and excluded it from the circle of followers of 'true' Judaism. In the eighteenth century Jacques Calmanson, in his treatise entitled *Uwagi nad niniejszym stanem Żydów polskich y ich wydoskonaleniem* (Essay on the Current State of the Polish Jews and their Betterment), wrote 'About a sect called Choside, that is, zealot-pious people' (Calmanson 1797: 18). He included this chapter in the part devoted to 'Jewish sects which are dispersed in old Poland', placing hasidim alongside Karaites and Frankists. When characterizing hasidism, Calmanson consistently uses the term 'sect', listing in his description a number of classic separatist features of a sect. He claims, for instance, that the followers of hasidism 'consider the spreading of godless and horrible dogmas as their most important duty' (1797: 19). The most famous of the anti-hasidic maskilic authors, Josef Perl, entitled his best-known polemical work *Uiber das Wesen der Sekte Chassidim* (On the Nature of the Hasidic Sect) (Perl 1977), and this is also how he wrote about hasidism in many other works (Perl 1977; see also Mahler 1960: 399–401, 358–60). Later maskilim and post-maskilic integrationists used similar language (see e.g. Eisenbaum 1818; x. 1845; Paprocki 1850: 285–7, 297).

By the end of the nineteenth century it had become commonplace to label the hasidim a sect. Arguably, the term had lost much of its original pejorative connotation and exclusionary function. Sometimes it was used by the hasidim themselves to draw attention to their distinctive identity rather than to suggest a derogatory judgement. A representative example is *Shivḥei habesht*, the oldest collection of stories on the putative founder of hasidism, Israel Ba'al Shem Tov (1700–60), published for the first time in 1814 (*Shivḥei habesht* 1991: 51). Further instances are found in later hasidic literature (see e.g. Tsitron 1996: no. 32; Horowitz 1873: 'Mishpatim' 39a). This does not mean, however, that the negative associations of the term disappeared entirely; quite the contrary. One of the late maskilic writers, Edward Hering (1818–88), not only called hasidism a sect but consistently used the term in a dismissive manner. He refused to regard its followers as fellow believers, instead calling them 'almost-fellow believers'.[11] Persistent use of the term throughout the nineteenth century to convey anti-hasidic bias and to exclude hasidim from Judaism indicates a continuous process of reinforcing boundaries between normative Judaism and hasidism.

Christian authors borrowed the mitnagedic and maskilic tradition of describing hasidism as a sect; most notable in this respect are the writings of Henri Grégoire (1789: 337–8), a French priest and reformer at the time of the French Revolution. After Grégoire the idea recurs in the works of almost all authors who wrote about Jewish religious life, among them such luminaries of the Polish Enlightenment as Julian Ursyn Niemcewicz, Franciszek Karpiński, and Stanisław Staszic.[12] These intellectuals played a significant role in shaping the policies of eastern European countries towards the hasidim (and towards Jews in general); thus their perception of hasidism as a sect had a direct influence on the development of these policies. In 1788 in Galicia, for example, as a result of a police investigation in Rzeszów, local authorities identified hasidism as a sect, albeit a harmless one (Manekin, forthcoming; Mahler 1985: 73). All subsequent investigations in Galicia treated hasidism as a sect. In 1799 Holy Roman Emperor Francis II (1768–1835) made a decision that the 'hasidic sect cannot be tolerated', and the ultimate expression of this policy was the passing of a 'law concerning the hasidic sect' in 1824 (Manekin, forthcoming). The example from Galicia is significant because—as Rachel Manekin convincingly shows—once hasidism was considered a sect, the law of movements of 'religious fanaticism' (*Religions-schwärmerei*) would apply to it, at least according to anti-hasidic petitioners, and, as a consequence, it could be delegitimized. However, the decision carried more bark than bite for the hasidim: despite labelling them a sect, the provincial authorities in Galicia and the central authorities in Vienna quite consistently extended their policy of religious tolerance to the movement and rejected its proposed delegitimization (Manekin, forthcoming).

In other instances, however, the perception of hasidism as a sect had serious policy consequences. Such was the case in Olkusz in the Kingdom of Poland. In 1817 information about Jakub Brüll, who had accused Michał Friedman and his friends of assault, reached the court in Olkusz (see Wodziński 2013: 65–9; see also Majmon 1894: 329; Schiper 1992: 101; Dynner 2006: 75–8). According to Brüll, the aggressor supposedly belonged to the Michałki sect, and the brawl resulted from 'the forming of a new denomination in the Jewish religion called Michałki, and the split among the Olkusz residents of the Jewish faith'. But the court ruled that the case concerned not only an assault but also the constitutional principle of religious tolerance. The court then asked the Voivodeship Commission for help in determining the legality of the formation of a new 'sect' and whether its aggression toward members of the 'Jewish faith' (*starozakonnego wyznania mojżeszowego*) was subject to regulations of the penal code.[13] The definition of hasidism as a sect compelled the court to apply the legal restrictions against sects to the movement.

The following year, during an investigation in Płock (also in the Kingdom of Poland), the head of provincial government of that region, General Florian Koby-liński, decided that the private prayer services of hasidim should be forbidden because they led to the establishment of a sect. He informed the government accordingly but, while undoubtedly defining hasidism as a sect, he voiced his doubts concerning the status of the movement, questioning its separateness. Similar uncertainties are reflected in other administrative deliberations of the time, too. These contradictory perceptions could lead to two mutually exclusive conclusions. If hasidism was a sect and thus distinct from traditional Judaism, it could be persecuted as an illegal religious organization (the intention of anti-hasidic informers), and yet, at the same time, limiting its right to assembly would contravene the constitutional right of freedom of religion guaranteed to all religious groups in the kingdom (the main argument of the hasidic defendants). On the other hand, if the hasidim did not differ from other Jews then it could be concluded that they were not entitled to hold separate services, but were no more threatening than other Jews, so there would be no reason to limit their other activities. In effect, the same arguments were used to support opposite claims. Both competing interpretations had their supporters, some of whom would have no qualms about using both of them, depending on the context.

The same tendency to apply the law regulating sects to hasidism is visible in the Kingdom of Poland's biggest investigation of the movement in 1824. The main line of investigation focused on the question 'whether said sect of hasidim is new and whether it belongs to the number of sects that are not tolerated in the country'.[14] A well-known writer and a government official of high rank, Wawrzyniec Surowiecki (1769–1827), prepared a report in which he analysed the regulations that had been applied to hasidism to that date and he asked the question whether the movement was a sect. If it was a sect, it was subject to the law that imposed a punishment of imprisonment for up to three years on people who established sects.[15] In the same investigation another official and writer, Jan Alojzy Radomiński (1789–1864), suggested that action should be taken against hasidism, giving voice to his conviction that the movement was a sect subject to a charismatic and often despotic leader.[16]

After-Effects: Hasidism in Antisemitic Discourse

The most radical consequence of attributing to hasidism the features of a sect—astonishing and unpleasant even for anti-hasidic exponents—was that hasidism became a subject in the more general discourse of the European Enlightenment and post-Enlightenment in the nineteenth century. This discourse had xenophobic undertones. Eighteenth-century Europe saw a rapid increase of interest in secret societies, organizations, and sects that were accused of anti-social conspiratorial acts and of exerting a subversive influence on the fate of states. Secret organizations and sects, including supposedly clandestine Jewish movements such as the hasidim and Frankists, were accused of destructive beliefs and practices and even of plotting to conquer the world. These accusations were fostered by the fear, spreading among European monarchies, of a recurrence of the murderous upheavals of the French Revolution (including insinuations of the role of the Bavarian Illuminati secret society in bringing about the downfall of the *ancien régime*). Salomon Maimon, one of the first maskilic critics of hasidism, wrote about the alleged similarity of the hasidim to the Bavarian Illuminati as well as other sects, and concluded: 'in our times, when so much is said both *pro* and *contra* about secret societies, I believe that the history of a particular secret society . . . should not be passed over' (1954: 168), because, as he explained, 'this sect was . . . in regard to its end and its means, a sort of secret society, which had almost acquired dominion over the whole nation; and consequently a great revolution would have been expected' (1954: 179). At the beginning of the nineteenth century anti-hasidic accusations of sectarianism were linked to antisemitic hysteria, dating from the sixteenth century, concerning 'fanatical sects' in Judaism, which had allegedly committed the most horrid crimes, including so-called ritual murders (about this accusation in the eighteenth and nineteenth centuries see Wodziński 2009). In 1835, in a comment following the acquittal of the defendant in a ritual murder case in Velizh, Tsar Nicholas I (1796–1855) wrote:

Numerous examples of similar murders prove that it is likely that fanatics or sectarians exist among the Jews who require Christian blood for their rituals . . . In a word, I do not believe that this custom is widespread among all Jews, but I cannot exclude the possibility that fanatics as horrifying as those among Christians exist amongst them. (Dubnow 1918: 93)

Although Nicholas was probably one of the most xenophobic rulers of his time, similar opinions pervaded all levels of society. For example, Stanisław Wodzicki (1764–1843), an influential politician, former president of the Senate of the Free City of Kraków, and a representative of the Polish aristocracy, wrote in 1840 of a blood libel in Olkusz in 1787, 'I am deeply convinced that even though animal blood is prohibited to Jews by the law of Moses, a fact corroborated by the removal of blood vessels from kosher meat, there is one sect, namely hasidism, which, in spite of this law, requires the blood of Christian children for its rituals' (Wodzicki 1873: i. 203–4; see also Wodziński 2009). Antisemitic opinions expressed by a leading Russian antisemite Hipolit Lutostański (1835–1915), in addition to those of Tsar Nicholas I and Stanisław Wodzicki, were also echoed by supposedly liberal figures such as Polish ethnographer Oskar Kolberg (1814–90) and outstanding Polish writer Stefan Żeromski, as well as representatives of the west European intelligentsia, such as an anonymous journalist of the London *Times* or German anti-Christian writer Georg Friedrich Daumer (1800–75). Thus labelling hasidism a sect became a contributing factor in the nineteenth-century revival of the blood libel (and, more generally, antisemitic stereotypes), which directly affected hasidim and rippled out to other Jews, including the most liberal post-maskilic circles (Wodziński 2009). This found its most threatening expression during the Beilis trial in Kiev in 1911–13, when the public prosecutors endeavoured to prove that Beilis was a hasid, or, more specifically, a follower of the *tsadik* of Lubavitch, and thus belonged to a sect using Christian blood for its rituals (Leikin 1993: 77–9, 81–2, 211; Sokolow 1913a, 1913b).

In sum, 'sect' was a loaded term, and from its earliest use served an exclusionary function, not only in theory but also in very concrete, sometimes painful, social applications. It was commonly used by mitnagedim and maskilim, as well as by a large group of Christian writers and officials. Its effects were detrimental not only to the hasidim but to the Jewish community as a whole. It seems surprising, then, that the term has survived into the present day, and authors commenting on hasidic communities in the New World often still refer to the movement as a sect (see e.g. Berman 2000; Gries 1987; Yoder 2001: 144–6). Modern researchers, usually drawing on the Jewish historiographical tradition of the Haskalah, Wissenschaft des Judentums, and nationalists such as Simon Dubnow often assume or address the sectarian status of hasidism.[17]

Was Hasidism Really a Sect?

Treating the move from one denomination to a related religious community as a conversion might be justified in light of the sociological discourse surrounding the concept of sects (before the term was replaced by the expression 'new religious movements'). Following Ernst Troeltsch's and Max Weber's classic definitions, which dominated much of the scholarly and popular reflection on the church–sect distinction, the majority of widely accepted interpretations mention exclusiveness, a drive towards radical religious and social divisions, satisfying all basic social needs within the sect, and strengthening inner-group bonds at the cost of the relative isolation of members from the surrounding environment. A sect differs from a denomination not only in doctrine and liturgy but also, or perhaps above all, in the organization of the religious community and in its exclusive character, as well as in an often openly hostile attitude towards the norms and rules in force outside the sect.[18] Therefore the social division between members of a sect and believers of mainstream denominations is much deeper than that between the different factions of mainstream religions.

Is hasidism really a sect? Has it ever been one? If we consider the constituent features of a sect, as listed in classical definitions, to be strongly emphasized doctrinal, liturgical, and organizational distinction, exclusiveness, a highly developed and often authoritative power structure, a substantial discrepancy between declared and realized objectives, and secretly held collective norms and rules which regulate the life of members as well as of the community, then hasidism does not meet a number of the sociological criteria that define a sect.

First of all, contrary to what they were accused of by the mitnagedim and maskilim, hasidim consistently denied the existence of any doctrinal distinctiveness, and asserted that their liturgical differences from the mainstream derived from traditions which were present within normative Judaism (Wertheim 1992: 128–214; Jacobs 1972: 36–45). The most distinctive liturgical feature of hasidism, the Lurianic-Sephardi (instead of Ashkenazi) prayer tradition, also characterized earlier Jewish pietistic groups in eastern Europe, who were not criticized by the mainstream Jewish community (Reiner 1993). Similarly dubious is the accusation of antinomian and heretical practices during ritual slaughter, which is sometimes brought up in anti-hasidic literature. In reality, these charges were grounded in the suspicions of a rival group rather than in any halakhic arguments. Furthermore, the halakhic validity of hasidic slaughter was decisively accepted even by Eliyahu Gaon of Vilna (1720–97), the most famous and fiercest adversary of emergent hasidism.[19] The same can be said about the vast majority of hasidic innovations. The custom of making a financial donation known as *pidyon hanefesh*, submitting slips of paper with requests to a *tsadik* (*kvitel*), wearing two sets of *tefilin*, and other hasidic 'innovations' had, in fact, a long tradition in Judaism. Modern historians, Mendel Piekarz most prominently, even claim that there is no content in the teachings of hasidism that is not known in the legacy of Judaism (Piekarz 1978). What was new was a shift of emphasis (the role of the *tsadik*, for example, was given greater significance in hasidism) and some modified interpretations of religious practices (such as gesticulations in prayer). These shifts were of much socio-political as well as religious concern to numerous Jews in the nineteenth century, both the hasidim and their opponents, as well as to the largest group—those Jews who were indifferent to hasidism.

Of course the hasidim themselves as well as their leaders underscored the fact that they belonged to true Judaism and that they were not a sect, especially when being seen as such could lead to acts of repression. The founder of the Schneersohn dynasty (Habad hasidism), the *tsadik* Shneur Zalman of Liady (1745–1812), testified during an interrogation conducted by Russian government authorities in 1798 that hasidism was not a sect and that it differed from the rest of Judaism only in some interpretations of biblical texts.[20] The same testimony was given by the followers of Shneur Zalman who were interrogated with him. For example, Mayer Rafalovich, the owner of a *shtibl* in Vilno, asserted that 'Karolins [i.e. hasidim] . . . do not differ from the old Hebrew faith at all, except for this: that they pray loudly and have different ceremonies', and his relative, Nochim Ickovich, said that 'this sect—as I gather—was founded on old Hebrew laws and only the time of prayer and some ceremonies are different from . . . Judaism'.[21]

Similarly in 1818 in Płock, in their letter to the president of the provincial government general Florian Kobyliński, the hasidim defined themselves as 'committed more than others to prayer and spiritual learning', and when writing about the difference between them and the rest of the Jews they asserted that, in truth, the only significant difference was that 'they commit themselves to a longer service and more spiritual study than others'.[22] In 1820 in Częstochowa the hasidim asserted:

there is no difference of religious rites between us and traditional Jews, and only because we pray longer, we arrange our prayer services in a separate hall. Regarding the accusation that we are different in that we take baths, other Jews go to the ritual bath as well. And if there is a need to list the names, we are ready to do so. Finally, we are appealing to other towns where hasidim live together with traditional Jews, so they can testify that there is no religious difference between us.[23]

Similarly, Abraham Kohen, who made space available for a hasidic prayer hall in Siedlce, testified in 1823 that 'hasidim observe the same rituals and the same prayers as other Jews and that we are distinguished only by our greater piety and longer services. Usually we pray in a separate house selected for this purpose. But sometimes we recite our prayers in the synagogue together with other Jews.'[24]

In the same vein the anti-hasidic Jewish community board in Parczew asserted in 1823 that 'they [the hasidim] observe the very same religious principles as we do . . . apart from praying in a synagogue, as they pray in their homes, with dancing, jumping, and rejoicing. And this is their principle, that with rejoicing they ought to pray. We do not see any other difference from our common religion'.[25] In their response the hasidim of Parczew declared: 'Our religion is no different from the religion of other Jews in any way, except that we are more pious, pray more, and because of that [we pray] in a separate hall. Our rituals are the same as those of [other] Jews' (1871: 11–21). All the above comments—and this is only a small selection from a large number of similar, and in general unanimous, voices— show the only vital difference between the hasidim and non-hasidim to have been a deeper commitment of the former to prayer and the development of some distinctive forms of rites. This casts doubt over the contention that hasidic liturgical practices warrant labelling the movement sectarian.

Equally disputable are other criteria based on which both anti-hasidic polemicists and later historians tried to classify hasidism as a sect. While being evidently separate organizationally, hasidism in its classic period, that is, before the Holocaust, was never exclusive, at least in its dominant trends. Hasidim would pray in non-hasidic synagogues without any reservations, and they likewise allowed non-hasidim to study and pray in their hasidic *batei midrash* (study and prayer halls). The overlap between *batei midrash* and other prayer quorums is well illustrated by countless conflicts in which hasidim and non-hasidic Jews fought for domination in local *batei midrash* or synagogues. Although such incidents underscore the antagonisms between hasidim and non-hasidim, they also indicate a fundamental fact, namely, that these two groups often spent time together, studied, and prayed at the same *batei midrash* (see, for example, the conflict over smoking tobacco in the *beit hamidrash* in Międzyrzec Podlaski in Wodziński 2005a: 148, 276–8; Wodziński 2013: 273–6). Moreover, for a very long time praying and studying together did not arouse any controversy. The leaders of both factions emphasized praying together and indicated in unison that this was proof of the essential religious unity of hasidim and their adversaries. *Tsadik* Me'ir Rotenberg of Opatów (1760–1831), when interrogated by a Polish ministerial official, was asked: 'Is it necessary for you to have a separate rabbi and a separate synagogue?' He replied: 'No, it is not necessary. One can seek the advice of any rabbi whom one trusts.' Another hasidic leader who was examined at the same time, Hayim Fayvel Kamienicer Wollenberg (d. 1835), was asked, 'Are the rabbis of other Jews less superb than yours?' He answered that 'they might be equally superb; also, one can seek the advice of a rabbi regardless of whether he is a hasid or not, and one may go to a synagogue'.[26] A decade later, in 1834, a government Jewish committee stated the following in a report sent to the Committee of Internal and Religious Affairs and Public Enlightenment (i.e. the Ministry of Internal Affairs, Religions, and Education) on the size and character of the hasidic movement as well as on the distribution of its printed materials in the Kingdom of Poland:

The rules of the sect of hasidim are different from the rules of the sect of Rabbanites in that they are governed not only by the teachings of Talmud, which constitute the basis for the sect of Rabbanites, but also by commentaries on the Talmud, generally known as kabbalah. Hasidim, as the name itself suggests, . . . regard themselves as more pious than other Jews and believe that a man chosen from among them for his piety and virtue is able to work miracles, that is, whatever he says, God confirms. *Nonetheless, they agree with other Jews on the essence of the teachings of Moses and seek advice from their rabbis* [i.e. of the non-hasidim] *in matters of conscience, just as other Jews seek the advice of hasidic rabbis.*[27]

A report that was probably prepared by influential Warsaw maskilim Abraham Stern (1762–1842) and Jakub Tugendhold (1794–1871) mentions hasidic separatism and a sense of superiority, but at the same time it emphasizes that hasidim do not differ from other Jews with regard to studies and that together with the latter they use the services of community rabbis. This again confirms the ritual and existential proximity of the two groups and challenges the image of hasidism as a closed, hostile sect.

Another accusation made against hasidism was that it had hidden objectives and concealed its true norms and rules. Working against this claim were hasidic publications, widely distributed from 1780, that openly promoted the teachings of the movement. Although some of the rituals and principles of hasidism, as with any other religious organization, were restricted to 'insiders', the vast majority of their religious practices were widely known, especially in the period of strengthening of the movement's social influence in the nineteenth century.

From among the previously mentioned features of a sect, the only characteristic which actually applied to hasidism was a specially developed hierarchy, usually based on the charisma of the *tsadik* or leader of a hasidic court, with a communitarian social structure.[28] One should add here, however, that, unlike in a sect, religious power in hasidism was never centralized and held by a single charismatic leader. On the contrary, power was shared among numerous *tsadikim*, who created loosely linked, and sometimes even competing, groups. Thus even this characteristic of hasidism might be considered sectarian only in the most general sense. The only content of the classic sect definition that really applied to hasidism was, thus, the pejorative value judgement attributed to the term and to the group labelled with it. Instead of being descriptive, the appellation had a clear polemical and delegitimizing function.

The Historical Dispute over Labelling Hasidism a Sect

Even if it was dominant, the contention that hasidism was sectarian was not as common among professed adversaries of the movement as the previously cited examples might suggest. The best example is the statements of Salomon Maimon, who compared hasidism to secret organizations and the sect of Bavarian Illuminati, and at the same time expressed the view that hasidim were not a sect and did not differ from their adversaries, who saw themselves as the faithful followers of Judaism. As he wrote: 'These sects were not in fact sects of different religions; their difference consisted merely in their religious practices' (Maimon 1954: 167). Similarly, in Radoszkowice, where in 1801 it was forbidden to accept members of a 'hasidic sect' into the Confraternity for the Study of Mishnah: several years later this ban was withdrawn by the board of the same society, which asserted that hasidism was not a sect (Wilensky 1990: i. 320). By so doing the elders of the confraternity joined an expanding number of people and institutions that questioned the sectarianism of hasidism and insisted that it should be defined differently. For example, a well-known maskil and fierce critic of hasidism, inventor Abraham Stern, wrote in the government report of 1824:

Members of this sect, or rather society, do not differ in their principles from other followers of Judaism in any way, and they do not have separate regulations for managing their affairs; nor can they have. Those who regard Hussites, that is, hasidim, as a separate branch of the Jewish religion, similar to separate branches of Christianity which have different rules and laws, are mistaken.[29]

In the following part of the report Stern elaborates on the same idea, questioning the sectarianism of hasidism: 'The members of this society join and leave it as they wish, without any preceding religious ceremony. A father might belong to the society, whereas his children might not, and vice versa.'[30] Thus, fiercely anti-hasidic Abraham Stern clearly denies the sectarian character of this movement and comments on the lack of any kind of ritual of conversion, the identity of doctrinal rules between hasidism and normative Judaism, and the fluid social boundaries of the former.

At the same time in a small pamphlet a Galician maskilic writer, probably Isaac Mieses, rejected the anti-hasidic hysteria of some followers of the Haskalah in Galicia when he wrote, 'Hasidim are certainly not a kabbalistic sect, contrary to what German writers claim (except for Salomon Maimon, who was the only one to have a correct opinion of them)' (Mieses 1832: 8). The author's conclusion is identical, then, to the opinion of Salomon Maimon and Abraham Stern. A dozen or so years later another anonymous author from Galicia echoed the view that hasidim 'do not constitute any specific sect; they are an integral part of the community as a whole and belong to a very observant part of Galician Jewry'.[31] Such opinions were a continuation of the above-mentioned political line of the Galician authorities, who rejected suggestions of applying to hasidism the law of religious fanaticism (*Religionsschwärmerei*) and of banning hasidic prayer halls. In 1823, in response to the letter of Lwów (Lemberg) maskil and obsessive anti-hasidic critic Judah Leib Mieses (d. 1831), the Galician provincial authorities dismissed the proposal to apply the above law to the hasidim and stressed that the movement could not be regarded as a sect. To justify their decision the authorities referred to the conclusion of the Lwów police that hasidism was not a sect as defined by Austrian law (Manekin, forthcoming).

Similarly, Jakub Tugendhold, the most active and probably most influential of the maskilim in Warsaw, questioned the ascription of sectarianism to hasidism. In his *The Defence of Israelites* (1831) he comments on a mid-seventeenth-century treatise by Manasse ben Israel defending Jews against the blood libel. Focusing on the charges of modern, 'enlightened' antisemites—including Catholic priest, professor of Warsaw University, and antisemitic writer Luigi Chiarini (1789–1832)—who 'now state that the concept of the requirement of blood for *matsot* by traditional Jews is a secret known only to a small number of certain sects' (Tugendhold 1831: xxiii–xxiv; German translation in Tugendhold 1856: 14), Tugendhold refutes the accusation by asserting that contemporary Judaism has no sects. Developing this thesis, he mentions several Jewish sects: Pharisees, Sadducees, Essenes, Sabbatians, Karaites, and Frankists, and adds that all of these ceased to exist long ago, and that most of the Frankists have converted to Christianity. In relation to hasidim, Tugendhold writes:

The hasidim who exist today cannot be regarded as a *sect*, if one considers the true meaning of that term in relation to the essence of religion. For these hasidim do not deviate in any way from the essential laws and regulations of the Old Testament, the Talmud, or other subsequent works that are respected by the nation of Israel for their religious value. Indeed every hasid considers it his duty to obey all such laws and regulations much more scrupulously than their law requires. (Tugendhold 1831; for more see Wodziński 2001: 13–41)

The defence of hasidism mounted by Tugendhold is important for several reasons. First, this was one of the first public defences of the movement by a supporter of the Jewish Enlightenment. Second, the fact that Tugendhold deemed it necessary to stand up for hasidism is significant in and of itself, the implication being that he had considered the definition of hasidism as a sect misguided, and had concluded that the consequences of such an accusation could be detrimental to the entire Jewish community. This argument was later even more strongly articulated by, among others, David Yafe, a correspondent of the maskilic weekly *Hatsefirah*, who claimed that the anti-hasidic criticism of the maskilim fuelled the antisemitic phobias of Hipolit Lutostanski and others who believed in the existence of sects among the Jews and in their criminal behaviour (Yafe 1880). Third, in the wake of Tugendhold's publication representatives of the Haskalah increasingly questioned the sectarian character of hasidism. For example, in 1862 Jewish publicist and social activist Hilary Glattstern wrote in the Polish Jewish weekly *Jutrzenka*:

If the country's Israelites do not differ in their understanding of the fundamental rules of the Mosaic religion as explained by the Talmud, then we cannot unconditionally maintain that they are divided into sects in a literal sense. This [term] smacks of religious isolation and persistent social exclusion. Therefore, their differing views on the practical observance of numerous rabbinic religious laws, based on the Talmud, allow us to assert that they rather represent certain shades of religious difference. (Glattstern 1862: 3–6)

Glattstern is unable to find an appropriate and precise term for the religious divisions within eastern European Judaism, and hence he writes about 'shades of difference', which is not an accurate term and certainly does not specify the boundaries of these 'shades'. At the same time, despite the fact that he cannot find an adequate term, Glattstern rejects the application of the concept of sect to the various religious strands of Polish Jewry—including, of course, hasidism. In this he joins a fairly long list of hasidic, anti-hasidic, and non-hasidic authors denying the validity of identifying hasidism as a sect.

Comments of this sort were numerous enough to demonstrate that already in the early stage of hasidic expansion there was some doubt concerning whether the movement constituted a sect and that a more functional definition was needed.[32] The above-mentioned authors were aware that attributing sectarian features to hasidism would have political, and social, as well as psychological, implications which they did not want to encourage.

Conclusion

To sum up, talking and writing about becoming a hasid as a 'hasidic conversion' in the eighteenth and nineteenth centuries resulted from a perception of the hasidim as a sect based on the following criteria: doctrinal, liturgical, and organizational distinctiveness, exclusiveness and separatism, a strongly developed authoritarian power structure, a substantial discrepancy between declared and realized objectives, and concealment of the true norms and rules regulating the life of the community. Such strategies of equating hasidism with a sect developed from the earliest anti-hasidic polemics of the mitnagedim, and later of numerous representatives of the eastern European Haskalah. In the following decades this identification was quite unreflectively accepted by a large part of the public in eastern Europe, in both the Jewish and the non-Jewish community, including government authorities. The accusation of sectarianism levelled at the hasidim sometimes had an adverse effect on the entire Jewish community. This attitude turned out to be persistent throughout the nineteenth century, and is evident in the custom of mourning for those who had 'converted' to hasidism or in the exclusion of a son from the circle of mourners who can say Kaddish. Even if these strongly symbolic acts were not common, narratives about such responses circulated and reinforced the understanding of the relationship between hasidism and Judaism as one between a marginalized sect and the normative Jewish community.

This terminological equation of hasidism and sect has indeed been the reason for many scholarly misunderstandings in the historiography of the hasidic movement. The attribution of sectarianism to hasidism has induced researchers to interpret participation in hasidism as the adoption of an all-encompassing, uniform identity. In other words, a challenge for present-day research is to locate the beliefs and practices in the social contexts that result from hasidic elements in the identity of participants rather than presume that all their behaviour is hasidic. The construction of firm boundaries between the hasidim and the Jewish community resulted in problematic interpretations and a false perception of relations between hasidism and its surroundings in eighteenth-, nineteenth-, and early twentieth-century eastern Europe, and in the later twentieth century in new locales. As a consequence, historians have assumed the false dichotomy of a Jewish world torn between the hasidim and their adversaries. Even a casual glance at the complex social relations within the Jewish world shows that dividing lines did not necessarily run between hasidim and non-hasidim. Hasidic society is divided not only into different 'courts', but by a range of attitudes, much like its non-hasidic counterpart. Examined as a movement and a set of communities, the hasidim emerge as one of numerous 'shades of religious difference' in modern Jewish society.

Translated from the Polish by Isolda Wolski-Moskoff

Notes

I extend my gratitude to Uriel Gellman, Gadi Sagiv, Piotr Grącikowski, and Yehoshua Mondshine for providing sources for this study.

1   For the issue of credibility of hasidic hagiographic literature and for ways of using it in scholarly research, see Rapoport-Albert 1991; Rosman 2006: 143–58; Robinson 1991a, 1991b; Dynner 2009. Also see Etkes 2005: 203–48.

2   See Walden 1911: 16–17. For hasidic customs connected to the Kaddish see Wertheim 1992: 101. The story appears in other versions, where it is not related to Shimeon of Jarosław; see e.g. Lehrman 1967: 114.

3   For beliefs related to this custom among Polish Jews see Lilientalowa 1898–1900: 277, 280–1, 283, 318–19, 321, 640, 642; 1904–5: 106–12. A large collection of unpublished materials on this topic is located in the Public Library of the City of Warsaw, *Spuścizna Reginy Lilientalowej* collection, MS 2375.A.8: 'Wstęp do obrzędów pogrzebowych u Żydów'; *Spuścizna Reginy Lilientalowej*, MS 2377.1.1: Obrzędy pogrzebowe [1-3], 368 ff., 206 ff., 506 ff.

4   *Siḥot mitokh ḥayei hasaba yisra'el be'er odesser ba'al hapetek* (Jerusalem, 2000), 94. My thanks to Gadi Sagiv for pointing out this source

5   Yekhezkel Kotik, for example, wrote about an anti-hasidic flour supplier and his three sons, whom hasidim decided to force to 'convert' to hasidism; see Assaf 2002: 303–5.

6   Archiwum Państwowe w Łodzi, collection: Anteriora Piotrkowskiego Rządu Gubernialnego 2512, p. 307.

7   See Singer 1980: 170–85; Etkes 1994: 78–90. Etkes explains (pp. 86–7) that he used the term 'conversion' intentionally because joining hasidism was similar to the typical experience of religious conversion. Etkes's attitude is quite characteristic of a large number of researchers, especially American ones, into Jewish conversion, primarily applying in their description tools of behavioural analysis.

8   See the exemplary summary of definitions of conversion in Hałas 1992. One should add that nowadays the term 'conversion' is being used to signify other radical ideological swings, not only religious; thus one can hear, for example, about conversion to communism or Zionism. This metaphorical expansion of the term indicates a quasi-religious attitude towards the secular movements of which the late 19th- and 20th-century 'converts' became members.

9   See AGAD, CWW 1560, pp. 6–8; AGAD, Komisja Województwa Kaliskiego collection 702. See also Wodziński 2005a: 91–2; see also an analysis of Yekhezkel Hoge's report there.

10   AGAD, CWW 1560, pp. 191–4; AGAD, CWW 1602, pp. 262–3, 266–71.

11   Hering 1839: 279: 4. Almost the same description reappeared at the end of the 20th century during the controversy over the messianic aspirations of the followers of the *tsadik* Menahem Mendel Schneersohn (1902–94), a faction of hasidism known as Chabad. According to a well-known anecdote, an Orthodox rabbi, when asked which religion was theologically the closest to Judaism, answered 'Chabad'.

12   See Radomiński 1820: 63: 'The worst evil for the Jews and for society has been brought on by their various sects, one more perfidious than the other. And the most treacherous is the *Sect of zealots (hasidim)*.' See also Krasiński 1818: 31; Niemcewicz 1821; Karpiński 1898: 154; for Staszic see AGAD, CWW 1871, pp. 2, 58–9, 130.

13   Archiwum Państwowe w Kielcach, Rząd Gubernialny Radomski collection 4399, pp. 1–2.

14   AGAD, Komisja Rządowa Spraw Wewnętrznych collection 6634, fos. 231, 233–4; for more on the investigation see Wodziński 2013: 79–116.

15   AGAD, CWW 1871, pp. 80–3. For the relevant laws see *Dziennik Praw Królestwa Polskiego* (1817), v. 141.

16   AGAD, CWW 1871, pp. 131–64.

17   Dubnow distinguished between early and later hasidism, regarding the former as a sect but not the latter; see Dubnow 1931: i. 21–2. An insightful review of the historiography of hasidism can be found in Rosman 2009. For a broader analysis of the sectarian terminology in Jewish studies see Baumgarten 2011.

18   For classic sociological definitions of sects see especially Berger 1954; Swatos 1979, 1981; Troeltsch 1912; Weber 1973; Wilson 1959, 1982.

19   Controversies regarding hasidic *sheḥitah* (ritual slaughter) have generated great interest among scholars. So far the best work on the topic, convincingly explaining the nature of the conflict, has been Stampfer 1999: 197–210 (English version Stampfer 2010: 342–55). For more on the social aspect of the hasidic ritual slaughter, see Shmeruk 1955. For more on *sheḥitah* in anti-hasidic polemics see Wilensky 1991: 253–7; see also Gilman 2011; Wertheim 1992: 302–15.

20   'The two Tithes of our Rabbi of Old In the Light of New Evidence' (Heb.), *Kerem Habad* (1992), 4/1: 42.

21   This unpublished material was made available to me by courtesy of Yehoshua Mondshine, for which I am most grateful.

22   AGAD, CWW 1869, pp. 10–11.

23   AGAD, Komisja Województwa Kaliskiego collection 702, pp. 38–42, 67–72; also Wodziński 2005b: 290–1.

24   AGAD, CWW 1871, pp. 9–10.

25   Ibid. 11–21.

26   Ibid. 168–79, 181–6; see also Wodziński 1994: 235–9.

27   AGAD, CWW 1871, pp. 245–50 (emphasis added); see also Mahler 1960: 506–8.

28   Literature on the structure of hasidic communities is surprisingly modest, devoting somewhat more attention only to the position and function of the leader. For the most important works regarding the role of the *tsadik*, see Green 1977; Rapoport-Albert 1991; about the structure and economic circumstances of the hasidic court, see Assaf 1998.

29   AGAD, CWW 1871, pp. 41–2, 47.

30   Ibid.

31   See *Galizisch–Jüdische Zustände* (Leipzig, 1845).

32   What was hasidism, then? As I have already mentioned elsewhere (Wodziński: 2010), and as I try to show in a study which is currently in progress, in spite of the terminology of the day and the claims of earlier critics, hasidism was not a sect but, rather, resembled—if I may use an analogy to a well-known Jewish institution—a religious brotherhood, being similar to the many other *khevres* functioning in east European Jewish society. As in every brotherhood, there was an affiliation with a religious community that required from its members certain obligations and distinguished them from the rest of the community, sometimes creating a sense of elitism and superiority over other *proste yidn* (simple Jews). At the same time, the boundary between members of the brotherhood and those who did not belong to it was completely permeable, and the objectives and ideals of the brotherhood were open and did not contradict the rules and patterns of behaviour accepted by the larger society in any significant way.

References

Primary Sources

AGAD: Archiwum Główne Akt Dawnych
 CWW: Centralne Władze Wyznaniowe Królestwa Polskiego collection, ##1560, 1602, 1869, 1871.
 Komisja Rządowa Spraw Wewnętrznych collection, #6634
 Komisja Województwa Kaliskiego collection, #702
Archiwum Państwowe w Kielcach
 Rząd Gubernialny Radomski collection, #4399
Archiwum Państwowe w Łodzi
 Anteriora Piotrkowskiego Rządu Gubernialnego collection, #2512
Leo Baeck Institute Archives, MM93

Other Sources

ASSAF, DAVID. 1998. '"Money for Household Expenses": Economic Aspects of the Hasidic Courts'. *Scripta Hierosolimitana*, 38: 14–50.

——2002. *A Journey to a Nineteenth-Century Shtetl: The Memoirs of Yekheskel Kotik*, trans. Margaret Birnstein. Detroit.

BAUMGARTEN, ALBERT I. 2011. 'Prologue: How Do We Know When We Are On To Something?' In Sacha Stern, ed., *Sects and Sectarianism in Jewish History*, 3–19. Leiden and Boston.

BERGER, PETER L. 1954. 'The Sociological Study of Sectarianism'. *Social Research*, 21: 467–85.

BERMAN, ELI. 2000. 'Sect, Subsidy, and Sacrifice: An Economist's View of Ultra-Orthodox Jews'. *Quarterly Journal of Economics*, 115: 905–53.

[CALMANSON, JACQUES]. 1797. *Uwagi nad niniejszym stanem Żydów polskich y ich wydoskonaleniem. Z francuskiego przez J[uliana] C[zechowicza]*. Warsaw.

DUBNOW, SIMON. 1918. *History of the Jews in Russia and Poland from the Earliest Times until the Present Day*, ii: *From the Death of Alexander I until the Death of Alexander III (1825–1894)*. Philadelphia.

——1931. *Geschichte des Chassidismus*. Berlin.

DYNNER, GLENN. 2006. *'Men of Silk': The Hasidic Conquest of Polish Jewish Society*. Oxford and New York.

——2009. 'The Hasidic Tale as a Historical Source: Historiography and Methodology'. *Religion Compass*, 3(4): 655–75.

[EISENBAUM, ANTONI]. 1818. 'O rabinach'. *Rozmaitości*, 10: 37–40; 11: 41–4; 12: 45–6.

ETKES, IMMANUEL. 1994. 'R. Meshullam Feibush Heller and his Conversion to Hasidism'. *Studia Judaica*, 3: 78–90.

——2005. *The Besht: Magician, Mystic and Leader*, trans. Saadia Sternberg. Waltham, Mass.

GELLMAN, URIEL. 2005. *The Book of Hasidim: A Lost Anti-Hasidic Polemic and Its Place in the History of the Hasidic–Mitnagedic Conflict* [Sefer ḥasidim: ḥibur ganuz bigenutah shel haḥasidut umekomo betoledot hama'avak bein ḥasidim lemitnagedim]. Jerusalem.

GILMAN, SANDER L. 2011. 'Are You Just What You Eat? Ritual Slaughter and the Politics of National Identity'. In Simon J. Bronner, ed., *Revisioning Ritual: Jewish Traditions in Transition*, 341–59. Oxford.

GLATTSTERN, HILARY. 1862. 'Rzut oka na redakcyą Jutrzenki'. *Jutrzenka*, 2(1): 3–6.

GREEN, ARTHUR. 1977. 'The Zaddiq as Axis Mundi in Later Judaism'. *Journal of the American Academy of Religion*, 45: 328–47.

GRÉGOIRE, HENRI. 1789. *Essai sur la régénération physique, morale et politique des Juifs: Ouvrage couronné par la Société royale des sciences et des arts de Metz le 23 août 1788*. Metz.

GRIES, ZEEV. 1987. 'Hasidism: The Present State of Research and Some Desirable Priorities'. *Numen*, 34: 97–108.

HAŁAS, ELŻBIETA. 1992. *Konwersja: Perspektywa socjologiczna*. Lublin.

HERING, E[DWARD]. 1839. 'Rzut oka na stan oświaty Izraelitów w Polsce'. *Korespondent*, 279: 3–4; 281: 3–4.

HOROWITZ. ELI'EZER BEN YA'AKOV. 1873. *Sefer noam magidim vekavod hatorah.* Lemberg.

ISRAEL LÖBEL OF SŁUCK. 1807. 'Glaubwürdige Nachricht von der in Polen und Lithauen befindlichen Sekte: Chasidim genannt'. *Sulamith*, 1–2(5): 308–33.

JACOBS, LOUIS. 1972. *Hasidic Prayer.* London.

KARPIŃSKI, FRANCISZEK, 1898. *Pamiętniki,* introd. Piotr Chmielowski. Warsaw.

KOTIK, YEKHEZKEL. 1998. *Mah shera'iti: zikhronotav shel yeḥezkel kotik,* trans. and ed. David Assaf. Tel Aviv.

[KRASIŃSKI, WINCENTY]. 1818. 'O Żydach w Polsce: Tłumaczenie nowo wydanego w Warszawie w francuskim języku dziełka przez pewnego jenerała polskiego, posła na sejm'. *Rozmaitości,* 7: 25–8; 8: 29–33; 9: 37–40.

LEHRMAN, JOSEF. 1967. 'Hasidim, shtiblekh, minyanim'. In L. Losh, ed., *Memorial Volume for the Community of Radomsk and Its Surroundings* [Sefer yizkor likehilat radomsk vehasevivah]. Tel Aviv.

LEIKIN, EZEKIEL. 1993. *The Beilis Transcripts: The Anti-Semitic Trial that Shook the World.* Northvale, NJ, and London.

LILIENTALOWA, REGINA. 1898–1900. 'Przesądy Żydowskie'. *Wisła,* 12: 277–84; 14: 318–32, 634–44.

——1904–5. 'Wierzenia, przesądy i praktyki ludu żydowskiego'. *Wisła,* 18: 104–13; 19: 148–76.

MAHLER, RAPHAEL. 1961. *Hasidism and Haskalah in Galicia and Congress Poland in the First Half of the Nineteenth Century: Social and Political Background* [Haḥasidut veha-haskalah begalitsiyah uvefolin hakongresa'it bamaḥatsit harishonah shel hame'ah hatesha-esrei, hayesodot hasotsiyaliyim vehamediniyim]. Merhavia.

——1985. *Hasidism and the Jewish Enlightenment: Their Confrontation in Galicia and Poland in the First Half of the Nineteenth Century,* trans. E. Orenstein, A. Klein, and J. Machlowitz Klein. Philadelphia.

MAIMON, SALOMON. 1954. *The Autobiography of Solomon Maimon.* London.

MAJMON, SALEZY. 1894. 'Luźne kartki: Z dziejów rozkrzewienia się u nas chasydyzmu'. *Izraelita,* 29: 329.

——1913. *Autobiografia,* trans. Leo Belmont. Warsaw.

MALKIEL, DAVID. 2007. 'Jews and Apostates in Medieval Europe—Boundaries Real and Imagined'. *Past and Present,* 194(1): 3–34.

——2009. *Reconstructing Ashkenaz: The Human Face of Franco-German Jewry, 1000–1250.* Stanford, Calif.

MANEKIN, RACHEL. Forthcoming. 'Hasidism and the Habsburg Empire 1788–1867'. *Jewish History,* 25.

[MIESES, ISAAC]. 1832. *Schreiben eines Krakauer Israeliten an seinen Christlichen Freund auf dem Lande die Chassidim betrefend.* Breslau.

NIEMCEWICZ, JULIAN URSYN. 1821. *Lejbe i Sióra czyli Listy dwóch kochanków. Romans.* Warsaw.

PAPROCKI, A[BRAHAM]. 1850. *Krótki rys dziejów ludu izraelskiego od jego począ tku aż do naszych czasów (dla Izraelitów) ułożył.* Warsaw.

PERL, JOSEF. 1819. *Megaleh temirin.* Vienna.

——1977. *Uiber das Wesen der Sekte Chassidim,* ed. Avraham Rubinstein. Jerusalem.

——1997. *Joseph Perl's* Revealer of Secrets: *The First Hebrew Novel*, trans. Dov Taylor. Boulder, Colo.

PIEKARZ, MENDEL. 1978. *Biyemei tsemiḥat haḥasidut. Megamot re'ayoniyot besifrei derush umusar.* Jerusalem.

PUCHACZEWSKI, M. 1954. 'My Paternal Home in Brisk' (Heb.). In Eliezer Steinman, ed., *Entsiklopediyah shel galuyot*, ii. 174–5. Jerusalem.

[RADOMIŃSKI, JAN ALOJZY]. 1820. *Co wstrzymuje reformę Żydów w kraju naszym i co ją przyspieszyć powinno?* Warsaw.

RAPOPORT-ALBERT, ADA. 1991a. 'God and the Zaddik as the Two Focal Points of Hassidic Worship'. In Gershon D. Hundert, ed., *Essential Papers in Hasidism: Origins to Present*, 299–329. New York.

——1991b. 'Hagiography with Footnotes: Edifying Tales and the Writing of History in Hasidism'. In ead., ed., *Essays in Jewish Historiography*, 119–59. Ottawa.

REINER, ELCHANAN. 1993. 'Wealth, Social Standing, and Torah Study' (Heb.). *Zion*, 58: 287–328.

ROBINSON, IRA. 1991a. 'Literary Forgery and Hasidic Judaism: The Case of Rabbi Yudel Rosenberg'. *Judaism*, 40: 61–78.

——1991b. 'The Uses of the Hasidic Story: Rabbi Yudel Rosenberg and his Tales of the Greiditzer Rebbe'. *Journal of the American Association of Rabbis*, 1: 17–25.

ROSMAN, MOSHE. 1996. *Founder of Hasidism: A Quest for the Historical Ba'al Shem Tov.* Berkeley, Calif.

——2009. 'Israeli Historiography's Verdict over Hasidism' (Heb.). *Zion*, 74: 141–75.

RUBINSTEIN, AVRAHAM, ed. 1991. *Shivḥei habesht.* Jerusalem.

RUBINSTEIN, TANCHUM. 1961. 'Rabbi Barukh of Tshizhev' (Heb.). In Shimon Kants, ed., *Izker-bukh nokh der khorev-gevorener yidisher kehile tshizhev*, 317–22. Tel Aviv.

SCHIPER, IGNACY. 1992. *Przyczynki do dziejów chasydyzmu w Polsce*, ed. Zbigniew Targielski. Warsaw.

SHMERUK, CHONE. 1955. 'The Social Significance of Hasidic Slaughter' (Heb.). *Zion*, 20: 47–72.

SINGER, MERRILL. 1980. 'The Use of Folklore in Religious Conversion: The Chassidic Case'. *Review of Religious Research*, 22: 170–85.

[SOKOLOW, NAHUM]. 1913a. ''Al hatsadikim ve'al haḥasidim (al pi hastenogramah miyemei 1–2 oktober)'. *Hatsefirah*, 225: 4.

[SOKOLOW, NAHUM]. 1913b. 'Ḥasidim umitnagedim' (metokh hastenogramah miyom 4 oktober)'. *Hatsefirah*, 227: 3–4.

STAMPFER, SHAUL. 1999. 'Towards a History of the Controversy of the Sharpened Knives (Heb.)'. In Immanuel Etkes, David Assaf, and Josef Dan, eds., *Studies in Hasidism* [Meḥkerei ḥasidut], 197–210. Jerusalem.

——2010. *Families, Rabbis and Education: Traditional Jewish Society in Nineteenth-Century Eastern Europe.* Oxford.

SWATOS, WILLIAM H. JR. 1979. *Into Denominationalism.* Storrs, Conn.

——1981. 'Church-Sect and Cult'. *Sociological Analysis*, 42: 17–26.

TROELTSCH, ERNST. 1912. 'Kirche und Sekte'. In id., *Die Soziallehren der christlichen Kirchen und Gruppen.* Tübingen.

TSITRON, MENDEL. 1996. *Shivḥei tsadikim*, ed. Gedaliah Nigal. Jerusalem.

TUGENDHOLD, JAKUB. 1831. *Obrona Izraelitów, czyli odpowiedź dana przez Rabbi Manasse ben Izrael uczonemu i dostojnemu Anglikowi na kilka jego zapytań względem niektórych zarzutów Izraelitom czynionych*. Warsaw.

——1856. *Der alte Wahn vom Blutgebrauch der Israeliten am Osterfeste*. Berlin.

WALDEN, MOSHE MENAHEM. 1911. *Sefer nifle'ot harabi*. Warsaw.

WEBER, MAX. 1973. 'On Church, Sect, and Mysticism'. *Sociological Analysis*, 34: 140–9.

WERTHEIM, AARON. 1992. *Law and Custom in Hasidism*, trans. Shmuel Himelstein. Hoboken, NJ.

WILENSKY, MORDECAI. 1990. *Hasidim and Mitnagedim: Towards a History of the Controversy Between Them, 1772–1815* [Ḥasidim umitnagedim: letoledot hapulmus shebeineihem 1772–1815], 2 vols., 2nd edn. Jerusalem.

——1991. 'Hassidic Mitnaggedic Polemics in the Jewish Communities of Eastern Europe: The Hostile Phase'. In Gershon D. Hundert, ed., *Essential Papers on Hasidism: Origins to Present*. New York.

WILSON, BRYAN. 1959. 'An Analysis of Sect Development'. *American Sociological Review*, 24: 3–15.

——1982. *Religion in Sociological Perspective*. New York.

WODZICKI, STANISŁAW. 1873. *Wspomnienia z przeszłości od roku 1768 do roku 1840*. Kraków.

WODZIŃSKI, MARCIN. 1994. 'Sprawa chasydymów. Z materiałów do dziejów chasydyzmu w Królestwie Polskim'. In Krystyn Matwijowski, ed., *Z historii ludności żydowskiej w Polsce i na Śląsku*, 227–42. Wrocław.

——2001. 'Jakub Tugendhold and the First Maskilic Defence of Hasidism'. *Gal Ed*, 18: 13–41.

——2005a. *Haskalah and Hasidism in the Kingdom of Poland: A History of Conflict*, trans. Sarah Cozens. Oxford.

——2005b. 'Chasydzi w Częstochowie. Źródła do dziejów chasydyzmu w centralnej Polsce'. *Studia Judaica*, 8: 279–301.

——2009. 'Blood and the Hasidim: On the History of Ritual Murder Accusations in Nineteenth-Century Poland'. *Polin: Studies in Polish Jewry* 22: 273–90.

——2010. 'O bocianach z żabiej perspektywy, czyli Kobiety i chasydyzm'. In Joanna Lisek, ed., *Nieme dusze? Kobiety w kulturze jidysz*, 77–104. Wrocław.

——2013. *Hasidism and Politics: The Kingdom of Poland 1815–1864*. Oxford.

X. 1845. 'Aus ostgalizien'. *Allgemeine Zeitung des Judenthums*, 9(15): 223–4.

YAFE, DAVID. 1880. 'Disna [correspondence]', *Hatsefirah*, 7(4): 28–9.

YODER, DON. 2001. *Discovering American Folklife: Essays on Folk Culture and the Pennsylvania Dutch*. Mechanicsburg, Pa.

PART II

Narrating and Visualizing Jewish Relationships

Framing Father–Son Relationships in Medieval Ashkenaz: Folk Narratives as Markers of Cultural Difference

MAGDALENA LUSZCZYNSKA

HOW THE FATHER–SON BOND is imaginatively conceptualized, perceived, and represented by a given society forms a cultural frame of reference and becomes one of the ways in which that society defines itself. I propose an analysis of this aspect of social life in medieval Rhineland as it presents itself through Jewish folk stories, aetiological legends, and ethical parables in contemporary manuscripts. Narratives, given their descriptive rather than prescriptive character, may be used to interpret ethical and legal norms in a regional culture. A close reading of folk narratives, recorded in historical manuscripts circulating within a culture, for social patterns and functions reveals the world-view that framed the symbols, beliefs, and outlooks shared by the society in question (see Dundes 1971).

In this essay I examine German Ashkenazi texts as the backdrop of comparable Jewish cultures, namely, the French branch of Ashkenaz and the Sephardi traditions. The corpus of narratives I focus on comprises texts which were originally embedded in compositions belonging to various literary genres. A number of narratives come from prayer books, such as the German Ashkenazi *Sidur rabenu shelomoh* or the French *Maḥzor vitri*, which, besides outlining the order of prayers, provide numerous parables and exegeses together with vivid descriptions of local *minhagim* (Jewish customs; see Bronner 2011: 3–15). Another rich source of folk stories is *Sefer ḥasidim*, an ethical compendium composed in the circle of Hasidei Ashkenaz, a pietistic movement which flourished in the Rhineland in the twelfth and thirteenth centuries. The narrative of Rabenu Meshulam, which I discuss later, has come down to us in a sixteenth-century manuscript containing a collection of miscellaneous stories, preserved in the National Library in Jerusalem. Finally, the Sephardi version of Rabbi Akiva and the living dead narrative that I analyse comes from a version of *Midrash aseret hadiberot*, a commentary on the biblical Ten Commandments which circulated in medieval Europe in manifold versions (Shapira 1995: 204–5).

In addition to considering literary features of plot, characterization, and setting in my analysis, I rely on the structuralist concept that a narrative sequence and component actions reveal culturally distinct ways of thinking (Dundes 1976; Jason and Segal 1977; Propp 1968). Central to this approach is the identification and interpretation of motifemes, that is, invariable units of action in a narrative. Though dramatis personae may vary, the action does not. According to Russian formalist Vladimir Propp, 'an action cannot be defined apart from its place in the process of narration', and he called these minimal units of the narrative 'functions' to indicate their pivotal role in conveying the ideas of the story (1968: 19). Folklorist Alan Dundes (1962) suggested the designation of these minimal units as motifemes (a portmanteau of motif as the building block of a narrative and morphemes as the minimal grammatical unit of a language) to show their relative linguistic position in an expressive pattern that people recognize as a story, and scholars subsequently followed his analytical lead. To this analysis I add historical and religious context to interpret the rationale for choosing particular narrative patterns in different times and places.

Almost from the beginning of their presence in the Rhineland, Ashkenazi Jews saw themselves as different from other Jewish communities, and this worldview is reflected in their narratives. One of the distinctive features of this cultural milieu was the patrilineal transmission of a mystical tradition which determined methods of study and understanding of theological doctrines. Focusing on the father–son relationship as portrayed in folk narratives, I ask whether the theological significance of the father–son bond is reflected in the principles organizing everyday family life in medieval Ashkenaz and if so, whether it is plausible to call it a marker of the distinctive character of medieval German Jewry.

The Kaddish Yatom legend

The complex relations between fathers and children have often been addressed in the Jewish tradition, both in practical guides and in scholarly studies (Bronner 2010: 9–21; Grossman 1989; Kanarfogel 1992; Marcus 1996; Stow 1987). One example of how rabbinic notions of parental responsibility and the nature of the bond between fathers and sons came to be represented in a narrative form which in turn was used as the rationale for a particular religious practice is the history of the Kaddish Yatom (Orphan's Kaddish) legend.

The Orphan's Kaddish, a ritualized prayer said for the soul of the deceased by his or her son, is assumed by recent scholarship to be of medieval provenance (Freehof 1967: 27). The basis of the custom is the talmudic recognition of the expiatory power of the response *yehe shemeih raba mevorakh le'alam ule'almei almaya* ('May His great name be blessed for ever, and to all eternity', BT *Shabat* 119*b*) pronounced after the completion of study, which, however, does not mention the dead. Popular medieval aetiology links the custom with a legendary encounter between a certain sage (in most versions, Rabbi Akiva) and a living-dead man. The time and circumstances of the origin of this legend are a matter of scholarly debate; its earliest attestation is the appendix to the midrash *Seder eliyahu zuta*, which was composed in the late amoraic or early geonic period, but variations on the same motif appear in diverse sources spanning Persia, North Africa, and Christian Europe over several centuries (for a comprehensive list of sources containing the story, see Kushelevsky 2009: 288–90). Although rooted in the Babylonian milieu, the theme appears in different cultural contexts and acquires new meanings, adjusting each time to new cultural and geographical settings. This phenomenon is captured by the term oikotype, which refers to the capacity of folk motifs to adjust to different geosociological conditions. It was coined by the folklorist Carl von Sydow (Von Sydow 1977) and elaborated by Lauri Honko (Clements 1997; Honko 2002: 139–55).

In its west European version the tale became an aetiological legend explaining a custom, which acquired major importance in the Ashkenazi milieu. Rella Kushelevsky's folkloristic study of the narrative variations on the theme reconstructs its historical development and focuses on the structural variations and different social functions the story assumed (Kushelevsky 2010: 253–71). In her outline of the narrative contained in MS Parma 2295, 139b–140a, reconstructed on the basis of a contemporary version from *Maḥzor vitri*, Kushelevsky analyses in detail the French Ashkenazi version of the story, focusing specifically on the tension it reveals between internal Jewish elements, such as the figure of Rabbi Akiva or the introduction of the Kaddish prayer on the one hand, and, on the other, universal motifs, such as the encounter with one of the living dead who is being punished for his sins with eternal Sisyphean labour, or the liminal locality of the cemetery, which serves as the setting for a meeting between protagonists from different realms of existence, as well as symbols rooted in Christian imagery, such as the crown of thorns representing agonizing suffering. Kushelevsky's analysis thus combines a 'vertical' line of transmission, where certain elements are passed on from generation to generation, with 'horizontal' communication of contemporaneous texts originating in different cultures. In other words, the choice of motifs made by each author is determined by both a decision to preserve narrative tradition and the influence of foreign contemporary texts.

I propose to juxtapose the German version of the story, which represents the cultural milieu on which this study is focusing, with two other renderings of the same motif, one of Spanish provenance and the other originating in northern France (for a comprehensive list of all motifemes, i.e. structural functions or units of action in the narrative appearing in different variants of the story, see Kushelevsky 2009: 291–5).

The German variant of the motif comes from the circle of Hasidei Ashkenaz and is included in the *Sidur rabenu shelomoh* (*Sidur ḥasidei ashkenaz*) published by Moshe Hershel (1971: 129). The Sephardi example is a version of *Midrash aseret hadiberot*, one of the first collections of exegetical narratives arranged as a commentary on the Ten Commandments, and contained in the fourteenth-century Moscow Ginzburg manuscript (III–13, fos. 121b–122a), a critical edition of which was prepared by Anat Shapira (1995). The French adaptation of the motif is the version from *Maḥzor vitri*, a twelfth-century prayer compendium written by Rabbi Simhah ben Samuel of Vitry in northern France, which includes homiletical and exegetical insights as well as parables and the rationales for local customs (Simhah ben Samuel 1923).

The narrative of Rabbi Akiva and the living-dead man, as it appears in the *Maḥzor vitri*, is more elaborate than either the *Sidur rabenu shelomoh* version or its Sephardi counterpart. It provides a detailed description of the characters, changes the place of their meeting, and reorganizes the dialogue structure. Like its parallel versions, it offers an aetiological rationale for the custom of the Orphan's Kaddish, but this practical function does not obscure its literary qualities. The German Ashkenazi text, on the other hand, refers to the Orphan's Kaddish legend in no more than a few lines, and seems to mention only its most important, core elements in support of the argument regarding the wording of the prayer.

The story in its fullest and most popular version describes a meeting between the tannaitic sage Rabbi Akiva (in some earlier versions it is Rabbi Shimon bar Yohai) and one of the living dead who is condemned to carry out hard labour day after day as punishment for his sins. Akiva, who sympathizes with the miserable penitent, tries to find a way of ending his suffering. Indeed, as it turns out, absolution is possible, albeit contingent on a condition which is difficult to meet: if the sinner has a son who will stand up in the congregation and recite a particular blessing, the punishment will be annulled. Akiva takes upon himself the task of finding the son, if such a son exists, and teaching him the required prayer. Upon arriving in the dead man's home town he discovers that, although there is a son, he has been excluded from the community, as the name of his sinful father has been obliterated and even cursed. These difficulties notwithstanding, Akiva finds the boy, performs the ritual of circumcision on him and teaches him the prayer. In fact, most of the versions of the narrative provide a much longer list of what Akiva teaches the boy, for example, Torah and the Shema prayer. Once his education is complete, the dead man's son recites the Orphan's Kaddish in the synagogue, the community responds, and immediately the dead penitent father is released to heaven, his grateful soul appearing to Akiva in a nocturnal vision to thank him for his intervention.

A significant aspect of the narrative is the way it portrays the bond between father and son as represented in two configurations: as a relationship between the living-dead father and his still living son, and between Rabbi Akiva and the orphan. Understood in this way, the story reveals a number of characteristics of the father–son bond: it presents Rabbi Akiva as a model father figure, outlines the father's obligations to his son, and contributes to our understanding of the meta-physical element of the relationship, which remains valid even after the father's death. This narrative strategy used in the different versions shows how family roles were socially constructed in three distinct Jewish milieus, each telling the same story in its own way, projecting its ideal of the father–son relationship onto the relationship between the heroes.

The Sephardi version of the story begins as a journey narrative: Akiva is on the road when he encounters a mysterious stranger carrying a heavy bundle of wood. The opening of the Ashkenazi versions of the legend is somewhat different. As Kushelevsky has noted, the venue of the meeting in the *Maḥzor vitri* text is not the relatively neutral 'road' but rather the symbolically charged, liminal space of a cemetery, while the pietistic *Sidur rabenu shelomoh* variant is set in the woods—yet another example of a space situated outside the boundaries of human habita-tion (cf. Bar Levav 2004: 13–17). The different venue in each version signals which party initiates the encounter: while in the Sephardi *midrash* it is the living-dead father who makes his appearance in the human world, in the Ashkenazi versions it is Akiva who crosses the boundaries of the *ecumene*.

The interpretation of the opening scene in each version is closely connected to the role played by Akiva in the development of the plot. In *Maḥzor vitri* the *tana* has to stop his interlocutor from running away, and the more laconic *Sidur rabenu shelomoh* version reports that the sage 'found' (*matsa*) the living-dead man in the woods. Moreover, the Akiva of the latter versions commences the dialogue differ-ently. Once he has managed to stop the stranger from fleeing and engages him in conversation, he shows no interest in the man's name but enquires about the reason for his hard labour. The *Maḥzor vitri* goes even further: before hearing the stranger's response to his question, Akiva has already formulated alternative scenarios, planning how he will help the miserable sinner. The proactive attitude of the *tana* suggests that the Ashkenazi authors envisaged him as being primarily concerned with the fate of the wretched stranger. This might be interpreted as an attempt to draw the reader's attention to the function of Akiva, himself an ultimate father figure, as one who endeavours to put an end to the living-dead man's suffering and to repair his relationship with his son. Yet the two Ashkenazi versions differ from each other inasmuch as the *Maḥzor vitri* seems to stress Akiva's active role and the indispensable nature of his intervention, while *Sidur rabenu shelomoh* leaves much more room for the dead father's own action.

To illustrate this point let us analyse the way in which the figure of the son is introduced in each of the three texts. The Sephardi *midrash*, using the conditional *im hayah li ben* ('if I had a son'), calls into question the son's very existence; the *Maḥzor vitri* version ponders the question at length: 'I do not know whether the baby my wife bore is a male and if he is, whether he knows the Torah since there was no one to love him.' Here the living-dead man's redemption is predicated on two conditions: the existence of a male child and that child's religious education, which has a social dimension but is also linked to the emotional involvement of a loving father. The *Sidur rabenu shelomoh* version differs from the other two in that the living-dead man's uncertainty whether or not he has fathered a son—which will determine his chances of absolution—does not feature in the text. The *tana* does not take an active part in amending the relationship between family members. Instead he merely informs his interlocutor of the fact or, perhaps, he states what is obvious to them both, 'you have a son', and instructs the penitent about the exculpation procedure: 'tell him to say every day *yehe shemeh raba* and you shall rest'.

This subtle difference has a twofold impact on the message of the text. First, it raises the probability of the deceased father's successful penitence. While the two former variants present it as a multi-staged, almost Herculean task whose success is predicated on an unknown condition and requires a mediator, the German Ashkenazi version reduces the penitence to a relatively easy task, namely, to provide the son with religious education. Secondly, as hinted above, the Ashkenazi author, limiting the role of Akiva to uttering a piece of prophetic advice, suggests that, whether dead or alive, it is the father who bears responsibility for the relationship with his child. Finally, comparing the composition of each of the three versions reveals a shift of emphasis and, perhaps, a different moral lesson each variant was to convey. The Sephardi *midrash* comprises three dialogues involving Rabbi Akiva: the first is with the living-dead father, the second with the townspeople, and the third with the penitent father again, now rejoicing in paradise. The *Maḥzor vitri* text, which counts among the most elaborate renderings of the motif, adds a fourth dialogue, namely, one between Akiva and a voice from heaven. By doing so, it involves supernatural forces in the plot, turning the story into an arena for the interplay of hell (Gehenna), earth, and heaven. The structure of the version in *Sidur rabenu shelomoh* is strikingly different: while the first conversation between the *tana* and the living-dead man, albeit shortened, retains the form known from the Sephardi and French Ashkenazi texts, the other dialogues are virtually absent. The structural elements of Rabbi Akiva's engagement in the personal family story of the deceased, his undertaking the paternal responsibility of teaching the son the ancestral tradition and religious ritual, and, last but not least, his role in reintroducing the son (and, indeed, the penitent father) to the community are all missing from this version. Moreover, since in this version Akiva commands the father to talk to his son himself, the *tana*'s role as an agent is significantly reduced. The resolution of the core problem is brought about by the father's communication with his son rather than by any supernatural intervention.

Seemingly, the Ashkenazi narrative fulfils a variety of functions. It may be read as Rabbi Akiva's exemplar legend belonging to medieval Jewish hagiography (see Raspe 2004: 75–90; Yassif 1999: 321–42). Alternatively one can see it as the Jewish equivalent of *biblia pauperum*, a text the primary function of which is to introduce less sophisticated members of the public to a discussion of eschato-logical and ethical truths, or else as an aetiological narrative, a metaphor which had undergone a process of ritualization and been turned into the explanation of a religious rite (Marcus 1996: 6). Kushelevsky argues that one of the main functions of the narrative is to strengthen the sense of communal identity, constructed in response to Christian influence (hence the reworking of Christian imagery present in the *Maḥzor vitri* text). The comparison of two Ashkenazi variants—the Rhenish and the French—suggests that the former, *Sidur rabenu shelomoh*, by significantly shortening the narrative, concentrates on aspects con-sidered necessary for the parable to convey its intended message: that the absolu-tion of even the most abominable sin is possible,[1] and that it requires both a specific utterance (the core of the discussion in the *Sidur rabenu shelomoh*[2]) and a specific agent who will recite it, namely, the son of the penitent. Moreover, this version of the story alters the roles of R. Akiva and the living-dead man, and by doing so it reinstates the direct, unmediated relationship between father and son. This marks the *Sidur rabenu shelomoh* variant of the narrative as unique among its contemporary versions and raises the question whether the insistence on the father's direct involvement with his son, significant from the literary point of view, can be interpreted as an indication of the special importance attached in German Ashkenaz to the communication between father and son and perhaps to the nature of the bond between them.

The Blood Test Narrative: The (Meta)physical Aspect of the Bond

A poignant example of the supernatural character of the bond between father and son is to be found in *Sefer ḥasidim*, the main literary work produced by the leaders of the elitist group of Ashkenazi Pietists, conceived as a religious manual, and written in the form of ethical and exegetical teachings interwoven with parables and moralizing folk stories.

Section 291 contains a story about a merchant who, leaving his pregnant wife at home, takes his servant and goes abroad on business. When, having made a great fortune, he dies in a foreign land, his servant passes himself off as his son and takes his money. Soon afterwards, the sad news of the father's death reaches the legitimate son, who decides to set off to the foreign country where his father died and claim his inheritance by seeking out the local ruler. The king appoints a certain rabbi to deal with the case and the rabbi suggests the following test: the deceased father's bone should be dipped in the blood of both claimants on the assumption that, since father and son are one body, the immersion would reveal the authentic son. The test is carried out and, indeed, the bone absorbs the blood of the son and rejects that of the unfaithful servant.

Tamar Alexander has offered a comparative motif analysis of the son's identity trial as it appears in *Sefer ḥasidim* and two other sources: *Sefer sha'ashuim* (*Book of Delights*), a contemporary Sephardi text, and *Meshalim shel shelomoh*, a later text whose date of composition is debated (Alexander 1991: 39–57). Applying a folk-loristic methodology, Alexander discusses the variations in the motifemic structure of the three versions of the narrative. She also examines the paragraphs adjacent to the blood test story in *Sefer ḥasidim* in order to extract a more general message conveyed by this part of the pietistic work, namely, that the son's actions can ensure the peace of the deceased father's soul. She concludes that the originality of the pietistic narrative derives not from its literary qualities but from the practical purpose it serves.

In the *Sefer ḥasidim* variant of the motif the special bond between the father and the son is not based on emotional affinity, as might be inferred from the *Book of Delights* version, where the ordeal consists of testing the son's feelings towards the deceased father's corpse. In fact, among the three versions only *Sefer ḥasidim* states that the father and son have never met, as the former left home before the latter was born. The story thus seeks to remove any connection between father and son other than the biological, genetic match, testable by objective means. The fact that this particular narrative is used to support the existing social norm defining the obligations of the son towards the deceased father allows comparison with the Orphan's Kaddish legend in *Sidur rabenu shelomoh*, which served a similar purpose. In the Orphan's Kaddish story the special connection between the father and the son is indicated by the fact that only the son can redeem the father's soul. In the blood test narrative the connection is rationalized and explained scientifically: the father and the son are one body. Therefore, as Kushelevsky has perceptively pointed out, not only does the story promote, together with contiguous paragraphs, a particular moral lesson, but it also contributes to the reconstruction of the way in which the author and the readership conceptualized the father–son relationship.

The Barmitzvah Ritual: Change of Relationships?

From the moment of their birth, Jewish children—just like children in other cultures—were under their mother's care, and therefore they belonged to the female world, as the binary opposition between the private and the public spheres was gendered, more so than today: in Jewish society the world of women, evoking the mental image of nurses, cradles, and crying babies, was separated from the realm of the males, associated with intellectual speculation and the quest for spirituality or, in other words, with study and religious rituals. The separation of, and inherent incongruity between, the male and female spheres were evident in various aspects of social life. In terms of spatial arrangements, for example, they were marked by a separate entrance to the religious school, normally situated within the house that served as the rabbi's family residence. The separate entrance was designed to prevent merging of the (female) institution of the home with the (male) institution of the yeshiva. Similarly, scholars analysing the circumcision ceremony have argued that the exclusion of the mother from part of the ritual by replacing her with a male assistant called *sandak*, whose primary role was to hold the baby during the performance of the rite, was introduced in the Middle Ages as a symbolic expression of gendering the private and the public spheres (Baumgarten 2004: 55–92; cf. Grossman 2004: 185–6). The mother's role was reduced to preparing the child at home and escorting it through the neutral space of the town's streets, and she did not participate in the male-led public ritual of incorporating the infant boy into the androcentric religious community in the synagogue.[3]

The fact that children belonged to the female sphere accounts for the limited role ascribed to the father in traditional Jewish sources. His obligation towards his young son did not involve physical contact and was confined to providing spiritual care, which included prayers from the start of the pregnancy for the well-being of the baby and for the child to be a boy (Baumgarten, 2004: 53). When the child grew up the father would assume further duties such as ethical instruction and concern for his son's spiritual development. Baumgarten sees this division of roles as an expression of the medieval distinction between natural maternal affection and paternal spiritual love, which was a result of the father's conscious effort discernible in Jewish and Christian sources alike (2004: 161–3). Tending to the spiritual well-being of the son naturally included ensuring that he would receive a proper education, which encompassed at the time, just as much as it does today, instruction in the social norms and values adhered to by society. The pietistic exempla, despite their prescriptive rather than descriptive character, provide an insight into contemporary Jewish perceptions of parenthood and family life.

Arguing against Philippe Ariès' view that the medieval family was devoid of tender emotional attachment between parents and children, and indeed, that it valued babies much less than its modern counterpart, Israel Ta-Shma posits that Jewish society was founded on different principles: children were cared for and highly valued while the difference between them and adult members of society was not perceived as being of the essence (Ta-Shma 1991: 270). In other words, young Jewish boys were seen as 'adults to be' rather than belonging to a separate order of society. The question must therefore be asked whether there was a clear separation between childhood and adulthood, a moment at which the child became a fully fledged member of the community, or if the process of growing up was fluid and defied clear-cut demarcation.

The structure of the Jewish ritual life-cycle in the Ashkenazi tradition includes a number of ceremonies which can be defined as rites of passage, marking a boy's transition from the sphere of the private, associated with the female, to the 'male' sphere of the holy congregation. The ritual of barmitzvah, which introduces the boy to the public reading from the Torah scroll—considered a hallmark of integration into the religious life of the community—is, perhaps, the most poignant of these. It is of particular interest not only because it marks a boy's advancement to adulthood and thus to the status of member of a religious quorum (*minyan*) but also because it brings about a change in father–son relations.

Bourdieu, discussing the phenomenon of rites of passage, points to their social functions and argues that the primary importance of these incorporation ceremonies lies not in their impact on the individual psyche but in their function of reinstating and legitimizing social institutions. Despite the undeniable fact that the status of a community member before and after any rite of passage is totally different, in a phenomenological or biological sense the difference between 'before' and 'after' is hardly, if at all, discernible. The rite is an arbitrary social arrangement that establishes lines of demarcation and assigns specific roles to those who have crossed them, thereby creating an imaginary and yet almost tangible social order which it attempts to present as natural. By virtue of its tripartite structure the rite of passage forces both observers and participants to pay attention to the act of crossing a dividing line; its actual importance, however, lies in presenting that line as an objective boundary that must be crossed (Bourdieu 1991: 117–27; cf. Van Gennep 2004).[4]

Until the Jewish boy reaches ritual maturity it is incumbent on his father to educate him (the dire consequences of neglecting this duty are evident in the previous discussion of the Kaddish Yatom legend) and to prevent him from committing transgressions. This responsibility shifts to the boy himself at the barmitzvah ceremony. The ritual, which, as Marcus describes it, is in fact a communal religious experience (Marcus 2004: 84), takes place around the boy's thirteenth birthday and consists of three elements. Two of these are performed in public, in the presence of the community: the boy puts on his *tefilin* and is called up to read from the Torah scroll for the first time. But the third component is a special paternal blessing which can be recited anywhere (Marcus 2004: 98). As in the case of the Orphan's Kaddish, this ritual first emerged, took shape, and eventually became a universal religious obligation as an innovation of medieval German Jewry (Marcus 2004: 89–94; for a different view see Roth 1955: 15–22). Up until then, the boy's first Torah reading was not necessarily embedded in the public communal service celebrating his bar mitzvah, nor was it bound to a particular landmark age of maturity: male children who had not yet turned 13 but had already embarked on formal education were encouraged to participate fully in the synagogue ceremonies (Baumgarten 2004: 90). Most importantly, there was no formal, publicly acknowledged point at which the father renounced moral accountability for his son's actions.

This combination, marking the boy's attainment of a particular age and his assumption of full moral as well as legal responsibility with a publicly performed synagogue ritual in a single act is an example of Ashkenazi ceremonial creativity, to use Freehof's term (Freehof 1967), arguably as a result of 'inward accultura-tion' through adaptation of the Christian rite of confirmation (Marcus 1996: 8–13; 2004: 82–123).

The new barmitzvah ritual certainly redefined the relationship between father and son, which was now assumed to change with the latter reaching ritual maturity. Seen in the light of Bourdieu's thesis, the novelty of the ritual lay pre-cisely in this fact; Ashkenazi society made sure that the father's renunciation of moral responsibility for his son formed a part of the ritual performed in public when the boy reached a particular age, which suggests that there was a social need to distinguish between the quality of the father's relation to his son as a young boy, on the one hand, and as a mature adult, on the other (for other psychological interpretations see Bronner 2008–9: 7–34).

This distinction notwithstanding, the Ashkenazi social norms required that the son would remain living with his parents long into his adulthood (Kanarfogel 1985: 12). Moreover, if he travelled abroad, which happened frequently within the framework of international trade—a popular Jewish occupation in medieval Europe—he had to bear in mind his parents' concern for his well-being and return without delay (*Sefer ḥasidim*, paragraph 371). Therefore religious maturity, sealed with the bar mitzvah ritual, did not break the bond between father and son, nor did it render it any less intimate; the principle of family obligations, under-stood as a religious duty (Kanarfogel 1985: 14), remained but demanded that the son's role would now come to the fore.

The obligations to one's father, rooted in the biblical commandment 'honour your father and your mother' (Exod. 20: 12), were discussed at length by the talmudic sages (BT *Kid.* 31a), who declared it one of the four pillars on which the world rests. The rabbinic tradition obligates the son to provide for his father's physical needs, to ensure his parents' proper burial, and to obey his father's will. The matter was also of primary importance to medieval Jewish educators and it features in the narrative tradition of the period either explicitly, in the form of legal precepts, or implicitly, in morality tales.

The Legend of Rabbenu Meshulam and the Anger Management Parable: The Principle of the Son's Obedience

In this section I shall focus on the son's duty to obey his father as it is presented in two narratives. The first is an aetiological legend about Rabbi Meshulam of the Kalonymus family, which has come down to us in a sixteenth-century manuscript kept in the National Library in Jerusalem, and was published by Sara Zfatman (Zfatman 1993). The second narrative, expounding on the virtue of honouring one's father, is found in *Sefer ḥasidim*, paragraph 126. These two texts will serve as the basis for examining the principle of the son's obedience within the broader framework of father–son relations, and for tracing the sources of the notion of paternal authority.

The story of Rabbenu Meshulam belongs to the genre of foundation myths. On the one hand, it discharges its aetiological function by explaining the historical role and social status of the Kalonymus family. On the other hand, it provides a rationale and a legitimization for the establishment of the yeshiva in Magenza (Mainz), an institution that was, according to several scholars, independent of the influence of the Babylonian academies. Given the scarcity of contemporary historical evidence, the legend, which was most probably transmitted orally long before it was committed to writing, is a text of primary importance for reconstructing the history and character of the early Ashkenazi community in the Rhineland. It can be seen as proof of the Italian origin of German Jewry, and accounts for the links between the two communities (Grossman 1975: 154–85). Moreover, it hints at the conflict of loyalties that medieval Rhenish Jewry was facing. The Jewish world in the early Middle Ages was split between two major centres of rabbinic authority and cultural influence: northern Africa and those parts of Europe that were under Islamic rule deferred to the geonic academies in Baghdad, while the Jews of Byzantine Christendom maintained stronger bonds with the Palestinian tradition. The main protagonist of the Rabbenu Meshulam legend comes from the town of Lucca in southern Italy and therefore belongs to the Byzantine world, while the central plotline of the narrative conveys a sense of the superiority of Ashkenazi lore over the wisdom and authority of the Babylonian *nasi* (exilarch)—a sense which is discernible in both the narrative and the symbolic stratum of the legend (Ta-Shma 2006: 7–8).

At the same time the legend yields an insight into another feature of the Ashkenazi ethos. It describes an individual facing a dilemma of choosing between the acknowledged position of the Babylonian *nasi*'s son-in-law and fulfilling what he believes to have been his own father's will. I shall focus on this aspect of the narrative by analysing its literary features and reconstructing their philosophical underpinnings.

The story can be divided into four chapters. It opens with a scene in which the narrator introduces the 'causative agent' of the action to follow, the main protagonist's father, Rabbi Kalonymus. Despite the fact that the sudden reversal that lies at the heart of the story revolves around Rabbenu Meshulam, the opening line presents the narrative as the story of Rabbi Kalonymus the father, who has experienced a dream. It seems that the narrator consciously chose to mention the father before allowing the plot to unfold. As I have mentioned above, the explicit rationale for the legend is to account for the establishment of an independent yeshiva in Mainz, and to provide a prominent Rhenish family with an Italian genealogy. However, the author seems to have had an additional method of investing his early Ashkenazi protagonists with legitimacy: so long as they kept up the tradition of their forefathers they were entitled to claim independence, and therefore the character of Rabbi Kalonymus, the father, figures prominently in the very opening sentence of the narrative.

The second chapter can be summarized as the concealment of the hero's true identity: Rabbenu Meshulam, scion of a distinguished family, is captured and taken to a foreign land, where he becomes a servant of the Babylonian *nasi*; as such, he is not even admitted to the study room. In the third chapter the plot culminates in the revelation of his true identity, which denotes the symbolic triumph of Ashkenaz over Babylon. Having witnessed Meshulam's display of remarkable exegetical acumen, the *nasi* kneels in front of him, begs for forgiveness, and vacates his own chair for him, which symbolically represents granting him supreme authority. Following this the *nasi* offers his daughter in marriage to Rabbenu Meshulam, who, however, declines, explaining that he must obtain his father's permission first. Subsequently, in what can be called the fourth chapter, he returns to his homeland, marries a local girl (his relative, in fact) and establishes the first Ashkenazi yeshiva: an independent centre of Jewish studies. The content of the narrative, as well as its structure, seem therefore to be determined by the principle of the 'tradition of the forefathers' and the obedience of the son. It concludes in a triumph of Ashkenazi scholarship and of the authority of the father.

Zfatman juxtaposes this narrative with a Sephardi legend 'The Story of the Four Captives' as it appears in Abraham ibn Daud's *Sefer hakabalah* (Ibn Daud 1887: 47–82; cf. Cohen 1960–1: 55–6). The analysis of the literary structure of the two narratives, their prominent motifemes (sea travel between Babylon and Europe, the victory of a hero whose concealed identity as a local religious and communal leader is not recognized) as well as temporal proximity and, last but not least, the political implications of the events, lead her to the conclusion that the Ashkenazi counterpart of Ibn Daud's narrative may have originated as part of the same foundational text and Rabbenu Meshulam may have been one of the protagonists of the 'Story of the Four Captives'.[5]

Notwithstanding the similarities between them, both in content and in historical function, the two narratives differ in how they portray the relation with Babylonia. Despite the use of parallel narrative structures, they make different use of the leading motifeme: in the Sephardi version the main protagonist, who is to become the founding father of the Cordova yeshiva, 'imports' knowledge from overseas, since he himself is one of the great sages of Babylonia. As a result of his coming to Spain, Cordova becomes an independent centre of learning, but derives its legitimization from the Babylonian academies and remains a loyal branch of the geonic tradition. In other words, it is the local tradition that is conquered. In the Ashkenazi version, on the other hand, it is the head of the Babylonian yeshiva, who is proven to lack Meshulam's knowledge on his own turf. Victorious Meshulam comes back from Babylonia and establishes what is depicted almost as a European counterpart of the geonic academies.

Notably, the difference between the two legends is also evident in the presentation of the main protagonists as the ultimate halakhic authorities. In the Sephardi aetiological legend the protagonist is an adult whose knowledge is a personal attribute rather than being ascribed to another source, and it is clearly manifested as he speaks in front of the congregation. The Ashkenazi tradition, on the other hand, describes quite a different scenario: the main protagonist, a youth of 14, passes on merely what he had learned at his father's house. Zfatman focuses on this point to highlight the importance of ancestral tradition in the Ashkenazi milieu, which is virtually absent from the Sephardi world (Zfatman 1993: 147–52 n. 187).

The tendency to prioritize *minhag*—custom or way of life passed on through generations—is indeed believed by some to be a distinctive feature of the Ashkenazi world and has been the subject of extensive research (see Bronner 2011: 3–14). Tradition has it that the founding fathers of the Rhenish Ashkenazi community received esoteric teachings (*torat hasod*) while still in Italy from a mythical figure known as Abu Aharon, who had brought them to Italy from Baghdad (Bonfil 2009: 53–8). The mystical teachings are believed to have consisted of the art of composing liturgical poems, exegetical tradition based on esoteric mystical doctrines, and particular customs.

It is conceivable that, as Zfatman sees it, the Meshulam narrative, which presents the father, Kalonymus, as the ultimate source of knowledge, hints at the importance of the Ashkenazi tradition, tracing itself back to Italian Kalonimide origins, while at the same time transmitting an important moral teaching that promotes compliance with one's father's will and adherence to his instructions, which is a keystone of the Ashkenazi ethos. Meshulam's return lays the foundation for a new and evidently successful community: his son Todros is referred to as *rosh yeshivah*, which suggests that he was able to maintain his father's prominent status and to establish talmudic learning in the community on a permanent basis. One can infer, then, that a desired quality in a successful leader was first and foremost his adherence to the duty of obeying his father.

In his typology of authority in rabbinic tradition, Avi Sagi applies a theoretical model developed by sociologist Richard T. De George to distinguish between two types of authority: epistemic and deontic (Sagi 1995: 1–24). The source of legitimacy in the former model is knowledge; epistemic authority is supported by, and dependent on, a broader system of social relations and requires epistemological consensus: the expertise of a person acknowledged as a leader has to be recognized and appreciated by the society. The deontic type, on the other hand, derives from public consent, which grants certain individuals or positions unlimited and unconditional authority, and it can therefore be attached to a charismatic individual or an institution. The legitimization of deontic authority can either be a matter of social agreement or rest on the belief in its divine sanction (God can either command people to obey a person holding a given position or inspire particular individuals who, as a result, present themselves as worthy leaders). Each of the models is contingent on a different religious ethos and prioritizes, or even symbolizes, one of the different values constitutive of Jewish social organization: either the centrality of the written tradition, to which all individuals have equal access (and its best exponents become figures of authority) or the leadership of sages, who embody traditional wisdom. Since the two elements coexist in the Jewish tradition and are both indispensable for Jewish communal identity, they are but ideal types. The actual realization of leadership is situated somewhere between the two poles.

In the light of this typology, the Rabbenu Meshulam story may be read as the promotion of the ancestral tradition as a source of epistemic authority, but also of the figure of the father as a deontic authority.[6] Rabbi Kalonymus is presented as an expert in biblical exegesis, but he is also a father figure whose opinion should be taken into account because of his position (which is why Rabbenu Meshulam refuses to decide about his own marriage without resorting to his father's advice). Moreover, the son's obedience is viewed almost as an ethical test which, if passed, would result in both personal and, by implication, communal prosperity (the establishment of an independent and successful yeshiva).

A parable in *Sefer ḥasidim*, paragraph 126, provides another example of the benefit of compliance with one's father's will: not only can it bring about personal deliverance, this time in the form of spiritual or perhaps psychological enhancement, but it can also save the family from disaster. The parable speaks of a man who respects his father and is ready to obey all his wishes. On his deathbed, the father summons his son and commands him as follows: 'Just as you have respected my will during my lifetime, do so also when I am no longer here', and he goes on to instruct him to control his anger, especially on 'one particular night'. Following the father's death, the son sets off on a journey to a foreign country leaving his wife at home, not aware that she is pregnant. Having spent a number of years abroad, he returns and reaches his home town late at night. Entering his house, he overhears a stranger kissing his wife. Outraged, he takes out his sword and is ready to kill his wife and her lover, when he suddenly remembers his father's last words. This recollection calms him down, at which point he hears his wife speak tenderly, not to a lover but to her son: 'so many years have passed since your father left me. If only he knew that a son has been born to him and that it is now time for us to marry you off!' Realizing that his suspicion and rage were the result of a mere misunderstanding, the man enters the room praising God and his father, whose wisdom has saved the family.

The story employs a traditional sequence of motifemes, or functions, as Vladimir Propp calls them (Propp 1963: 206–31), which are ubiquitous in folk narratives: the main hero receives an order from his father (Propp categorizes it as an 'interdiction'), leaves his homeland and travels abroad ('absention'), returns but does not yet enter his home ('unrecognized arrival'). He discovers what he interprets as his wife's betrayal ('villainy') and, incited by fury ('violation of the interdiction'), plans to kill the apparent lovers. However, reminded of the commandment of his deceased father ('mediation'), he manages to subdue his evil inclination ('counteraction', 'struggle', 'victory', 'transformation') and is reconciled with his wife ('wedding'). While Propp's scheme extrapolates the essential pattern of functions and characters that make up any story, names them, and employs them in the comparative analysis of different tales, the structuralist approach advocated by Claude Lévi-Strauss (1963: 206–31) sets it as its objective to unearth the paradigmatic structure of a given narrative and, through it, to arrive at the particular character of the particular culture that originated it (Dundes 1997: 39–50). Structural analysis rests on the following set of principles: economy of explanation, unity of solution, and the ability to reconstruct the whole from its fragment. Lévi-Strauss invites the cultural critic to see the text (understood in its broad sense, that is, not necessarily as a written piece of work but as a cultural message) as bundles of binary oppositions whose combination and permutation (rather than their linear syntagmatic order) yield the meaning and can be reduced to an algebraic formula. Although the primary interest of structural analysis is myth, seen by Lévi-Strauss as the purest form of symbolic language, the method also proves informative and fruitful when applied to more 'conscious' creations, i.e. texts which, like *Sefer ḥasidim*, have an author, a practical purpose, and an intended moral.[7]

Read in the light of Lévi-Strauss's analytical method, the story presents itself as an interplay between two sets of oppositions: the tension between death and salvation on the one hand and, on the other, between two opposing qualities: uncompromised reverence for one's father and the tendency to give way to overwhelming rage. At the outset, the reader is assured of the son's respect for his father, yet no evidence is furnished for this claim. At the same time, the story employs the motifeme of the father's death, which it presents as an unquestionable fact. The relation of actual (the father's death) and potential (the son's obedience to his father) is reversed in the second part of the narrative. Now it is the possibility of the man killing his son that may or may not be actualized, while obedience, which has now become the dominant quality of the protagonist's character, is realized and functions as the active factor determining the trajectory of events. The replacement of anger with obedience translates metaphorically into substituting unavoidable death from the first part of the narrative with last-minute salvation in the second. Importantly, all four elements—death, salvation, anger, and obedience—are situated within the network of father–son relations.

The intended moral of the narrative—the benefits of controlling negative emotions—is indisputable and readily apparent, especially in the context of the adjacent paragraphs in *Sefer ḥasidim*. Paragraph 126, the morality tale that concerns us here, is preceded by a short exegetical exposition (para. 125) which high-lights the positive aspect of anger, when experienced by a righteous one, who is appalled by the sin of others, his anger resulting in the expiation of the sin of the entire ungodly community. Paragraph 127, which follows our morality tale, and similarly focuses on the issue of anger management, refers to a 'certain righteous man' (*tsadik eḥad*), while our exemplum introduces the main character as 'a son'. Arguably, given that in the course of the narrative the hero appears as a son, a husband, and a father, the designation 'a man', or 'a righteous one' would have been more appropriate. The label 'son', adopted by *Sefer ḥasidim* in the opening line of paragraph 126, seems, therefore, to emphasize even further the bond between the father and the son. Notably, the Rabbenu Meshulam story achieves a similar effect by drawing the reader's attention to Kalonymus, the hero's father, in the short introduction to the tale. The two narratives share another feature, namely, the unusual abilities ascribed to the leading protagonist's father. Both Kalonymus and the anonymous parent from *Sefer ḥasidim* (para. 126) seem to have a supernatural insight into the future and, especially in the latter case, to play the role of guardian angels of their sons.

These similarities notwithstanding, a significant difference must be noted, which suggests that the two narratives belong in separate literary genres. The Rabbenu Meshulam narrative speaks of a particular individual, indeed, a venerated founding father of Ashkenazi Jewry, and as such can be considered an example of Jewish hagiography (Raspe 2004: 75). The narrative from *Sefer ḥasidim*, on the other hand, speaks of an 'everyman' and presents itself as a paradigmatic case of intergenerational relations described here as conventional, if ideal. While including the Rabbenu Meshulam narrative in the corpus of Ashkenazi hagiographical literature may raise questions about the extent to which the father–son relationship can be seen as universal and not moulded by the fact that we are dealing with a particular prominent authority (a Jewish 'saint') and his son, the moral anecdote from *Sefer ḥasidim* is intended to be applicable everywhere and at any time. Allowing for some degree of interpretative freedom, one could argue that the Meshulam narrative, which features heroes belonging to the mythical generation of the founding fathers, promotes the ideal type of the father–son relationship and establishes the father as a deontic authority figure, while the pietistic exemplum aims to reinforce and actualize the pattern in the daily praxis of members of the community.

Conclusion

In this essay I have analysed the relationship between fathers and sons in medieval Ashkenazi Jewish culture as it is represented specifically in narrative form, and the ritualized behaviours prescribed and recorded in these narratives. Scholars who have made the medieval Ashkenazi family the subject of their research have asked different questions and studied various types of sources. Avraham Grossman, for instance, has examined the patriarchal system rooted in mystical theology as an organizing principle of the community's social and political structure, while Ephraim Kanarfogel has studied the attitude towards children in pietistic Ashkenazi families based on prescriptive dicta from *Sefer ḥasidim*. The analysis of memorial lists has enabled Kenneth Stow to present an impressive demographic and economic profile of the medieval Ashkenazi family. Elisheva Baumgarten has revisited the sources to shift the focus of scholarly investigation to the role of women in the Jewish community, as juxtaposed with the neighbouring Christian society.

I have aimed at further broadening the scope of sources used to investigate specifically the father–son relationship by focusing primarily on folk literature. This choice of textual material derives from my conviction of its importance for the study of a past culture. Its significance as historical evidence does not necessarily lie in its accuracy, and I do not attempt to uncover the historical kernel, which the narratives may or may not contain. Rather, I subscribe to the view that the differences between versions of the same story or similar stories can help establish the particularity of the discourse which gave birth to them. This can be defined either as the distinctive agenda which a given author had when adapting a universal motifeme, or as the reflection of a specific set of ethical values held in high esteem in the society for which he wrote, leading him to emphasize certain elements and omit others.

The examination of a variety of texts has shown how reference to the father–son relationship could fulfil a number of functions in the narrative tradition. In the texts I have studied, it served as the basis for establishing a new religious ritual (the bar mitzvah); as a means of legitimization of a novel communal institution (an independent yeshiva); as support for deontic authority (Rabbi Meshulam and the father), and as an explanation or rationale for a normative ethic (obedience to one's father).

The multifaceted analysis I have undertaken has enabled me to conclude that the importance of intergenerational relations in the Ashkenazi milieu, which scholars have hitherto placed in the context of the Ashkenazi attachment to ancestral tradition, esoteric knowledge, and customs passed on through the generations, is detectable also on the personal plane. The narratives I have examined suggest that not only did these relations play out in the organization of the society and in the normative framework of communal life, but they were also regarded as essential for personal reasons: the father should care for his son in order to ensure the eternal peace of his soul, while the son should be motivated by the prospect of personal accomplishment resulting from respect towards his father and compliance with his commandments.

This conclusion invites further analysis of family relations in Ashkenazi culture and of *minhag ashkenaz* more generally. The question arises whether later texts also attest to the importance of the father–son bond, thus allowing it to be seen as a general feature of Ashkenazi Jewry rather than an exclusively medieval phenomenon. Another possible direction further studies could take would be to review other relations within the medieval Ashkenazi family. One could ask whether the father–son bond may be considered a paradigm for intergenerational relations in the community at large, or, for instance, for the mother–daughter relationship. The point here, however, is that folk narratives serve to frame complex social relations and are vitally pertinent to studies of medieval Ashkenazi culture.

Notes

1   Sexual offences were used in pietistic parables to illustrate extreme cases, for example, the story of the three penitents, paras. 52–3.

2   The French Ashkenazi tradition, as recorded in *Maḥzor vitri*, does not see the recitation of the prayer as an obligation of every orphan, nor does it attach importance to the wording of the prayer: at the end of the sabbath one who has lost his father or mother says 'Kaddish or Barekhu'.

3   There was a female-led ceremony, the ritual of Holle, which may be seen as a counterpart of the official ceremony (Hammer 2005: 62–87). However, it was also confined to the private sphere of a household.

4   Rites of passage are seen as comprising three stages: exclusion from the society and abrogation of one's status; a transitional or liminal phase, and finally reincorporation into the society with the assumption of a new role.

5   Ibn Daud mentions that, although among the captives there were four rabbis, he only knows the names and the whereabouts of three of them. Gerson Cohen, who analysed the legend focusing on its factual plausibility, sees in this statement the author's wish to boost his trustworthiness as a historian. This reading is not far-fetched, as verisimilitude is known to be a common feature of historical novels. He asserts that the number of the captives—four, not three as in the *midrash* on which he claims the narrative is based—is symbolically charged and as such adds to the authority of the text (Cohen 1960–1: 86–94). Zfatman (1993: 133–8) proposes a different reading of this detail, maintaining that Rabbenu Meshulam may have been the nameless protagonist in Ibn Daud's story. In other words, the author might have known who the fourth captive was but decided to conceal his identity. Such a selective attitude towards facts is not an uncommon feature of pre-modern historiography. History-writing was intended to create collective knowledge and assert communal identity. Accordingly, the author decided which facts were worthy of remembering and omitted what would not fit, or would even collide with, the picture he thought should be passed on.

6   Sagi acknowledges that charisma might provide epistemological authority with additional reinforcement: 'Since charisma assures the sage he is in possession of the truth, the charismatic argument could be perceived as lending support to the epistemic model, although the two are certainly far apart' (1995: 17).

7   Bonfil points out the validity of the application of structuralist analysis as a heuristic tool for understanding not only myths but also historical documents (2009: 131).

References

ALEXANDER-FRIZER, TAMAR. 1991. *The Pious Sinner: Ethics and Aesthetics in the Medieval Hasidic Narrative*. Tübingen.

BAR LEVAV, AVRIEL. 2004. 'A Different Place: The Cemetery in Jewish Culture' (Heb.). *Pa'amim*, 98–9: 13–17.

BAUMGARTEN, ELISHEVA. 2004. *Mothers and Children: Jewish Family Life in Medieval Europe*. Princeton, NJ.

BONFIL, ROBERT. 2009. *History and Folklore in a Medieval Jewish Chronicle: The Family Chronicle of Ahimaaz ben Paltiel*. Leiden.

BOURDIEU, PIERRE. 1991. 'of Institution'. In id., *Language and Symbolic Power*, 117–27. Cambridge.

BRONNER, SIMON J. 2008–9. 'Fathers and Sons: Rethinking the Bar Mitzvah as an American Rite of Passage'. *Children's Folklore Review*, 1: 7–34.

——2010. 'The Dualities of House and Home in Jewish Culture'. In Simon Bronner, ed., *Jews at Home: The Domestication of Identity*, 1–40. Oxford.

——2011. 'Ritualizing Jewishness'. In Simon Bronner, ed., *Revisioning Ritual: Jewish Traditions in Transition*, 1–44. Oxford.

CLEMENTS, WILLIAM M. 1997. 'Oikotype/Oicotype'. In Thomas A. Green, ed., *Folklore: An Encyclopedia of Beliefs, Customs, Tales, Music, and Art*, 604–5. Santa Barbara, Calif.

COHEN, GERSON D. 1960–1. 'The Story of the Four Captives'. *Proceedings of the American Academy for Jewish Research*, 29: 55–131.

DE SOLA POOL, DAVID. 1909. *The Old Jewish-Aramaic Prayer, the Kaddish*. New York.

DUNDES, ALAN. 1971. 'Folk Ideas as Units of Worldview'. *Journal of American Folklore*, 84: 93–103.

——1976. 'Structuralism and Folklore'. *Studia Fennica*, 20: 75–93.

——1997. 'Binary Opposition in Myth: The Propp/Lévi-Strauss Debate in Retrospect'. *Western Folklore*, 56: 39–50.

FREEHOF, SOLOMON B. 1967. 'Ceremonial Creativity among the Ashkenazim'. *Jewish Quarterly Review*, 57: 210–24.

GROSSMAN, AVRAHAM. 1975. 'The Migration of the Kalonymus Family from Italy to Germany' (Heb.). *Zion*, 40: 154–85.

——1989. 'From Father to Son: The Inheritance of Spiritual Leadership in Jewish Communities of the Middle Ages'. In David Kraemer, ed., *The Jewish Family: Metaphor and Memory*, 115–32 . New York.

——2004. *Pious and Rebellious: Jewish Women in Medieval Europe*. Waltham, Mass.

HAMMER, JILL. 2005. 'Holle's Cry Unearthing a Birth Goddess in a German Jewish Naming Ceremony'. *Nashim*, 9: 62–87.

HERSHEL, MOSHE, ed. 1971. *Sidur rabenu shelomoh meyuḥas lerabenu shelomoh bar shimon migermaiza*. Jerusalem.

HONKO, LAURI. 2002. 'Four Forms of Adaptation of Tradition' (Heb.). In Tamar Alexander and Galit Hazan-Rokem, eds., *Jerusalem Studies in Jewish Folklore* [Meḥkarei yerushalayim befolklor yehudi], 139–55. Jerusalem.

IBN DAUD, ABRAHAM. 1887. *Sefer hakabalah*. In *Texts, Documents, and Extracts Chiefly from Manuscripts in the Bodleian and Other Oxford Libraries*, i: *Medieval Jewish Chronicles and Chronological Notes*, ed. Adolf Neubauer. Oxford.

JASON, HEDA, and DMITRI SEGAL, eds. 1977. *Patterns in Oral Literature*. The Hague.

KANARFOGEL, EPHRAIM. 1985. 'Attitudes Toward Childhood and Children in Medieval Jewish Society'. In David R. Blumenthal, ed., *Approaches to Judaism in Medieval Times*, ii. Chico, Calif. 1–34.

—— 1992. *Jewish Education and Society in the High Middle Ages*. Detroit, Mich.

KUSHELEVSKY, RELLA. 2009. 'The *Tana* and the Wandering Dead Man' (Heb.). In Yo'av Elshtain, Avidav Lipsker, and Rella Kushelevsky, eds., *Story after Story: Encyclopedia of the Jewish Story* [Sipur okev sipur: entsiklopediyah shel hasipur hayehudi], 281–96. Ramat Gan.

——2010. *Self-Denial and Temptation* [Sigufim ufituyim]. Jerusalem.

LÉVI-STRAUSS, CLAUDE. 1963. 'Structural Study of Myth'. In *Structural Anthropology*, trans. Claire Jacobson and Brooke Grundfest Schoepf, ii. 206–31. New York.

MARCUS, IVAN. 1996. *Rituals of Childhood. Jewish Acculturation in Medieval Europe*. New Haven, Conn.

——2004. *The Jewish Life Cycle: Rites of Passage from Biblical to Modern Times*. Seattle.

PROPP, VLADIMIR. 1968. *Morphology of the Folktale*, trans. Laurence Scott. Austin, Tex.

RASPE, LUCIA. 2004. 'Jewish Saints in Medieval Ashkenaz: A Contradiction in Terms?' *Frankfurter Judaistische Beiträge*, 31: 75–90.

——2006. *Jüdische Hagiographie im mittelalterlichen Aschkenas*. Tübingen.

ROTH, CECIL. 1955. 'Bar Mitzvah: Its History and Its Associations'. In Abraham I. Katsh, ed., *Bar Mitzvah Illustrated*, 15–22. New York.

SAGI, AVI. 1995. 'Models of Authority and the Duty of Obedience in Halakhic Literature'. *AJS Review*, 20: 1–24.

SHAPIRA, ANAT, ed. 1995. *A Midrash on the Ten Commandments* [Midrash aseret hadiberot]. Jerusalem.

SIMHAH BEN SAMUEL OF VITRY. 1923. *Maḥzor vitri lerabenu simḥah eḥad mitalmidei rashi zal*, ed. Simon Hurwitz. Nuremberg.

STOW, KENNETH. 1987. 'The Jewish Family in the Rhineland in the High Middle Ages: Form and Function'. *American Historical Review*, 92: 1085–1110.

TA-SHMA, ISRAEL M. 1991. 'Children of Medieval German Jewry: A Perspective on Aries from Jewish Sources'. *Studies in Medieval and Renaissance History*, 12: 261–80.

——2006. *Creativity and Tradition: Studies in Medieval Rabbinic Scholarship, Literature and Thought*. Cambridge, Mass.

TELSNER, DAVID. 1995. *The Kaddish: Its History and Significance*. Jerusalem.

VAN GENNEP, ARNOLD. 2004. *The Rites of Passage*, trans. Monika B. Vizedom and Gabrielle L. Caffee. London.

VON SYDOW, CARL W. 1977. *Selected Papers on Folklore*. New York.

WIESELTIER, LEON. 1999. *Kaddish*. London.

YASSIF, ELI. 1999. *The Hebrew Folktale: History, Genre, Meaning*. Bloomington, Ind.

YEHUDA HEHASID. 1924. *Sefer ḥasidim* [al pi nusaḥ ketav yad asher befarma], ed. Yehuda Wistinetzki. Frankfurt am Main.

ZFATMAN, SARA. 1993. *Between Ashkenaz and Sefarad: Towards a History of the Medieval Jewish Story* [Bein ashkenaz lisefarad: letoledot hasipur hayehudi biyemei habeinayim]. Jerusalem.

Sites of Collective Memory in Narratives of the Prague Ghetto

RELLA KUSHELEVSKY

SINCE THE BEGINNING of the sixteenth century the term 'ghetto' has referred to an urban district serving as a compulsory residential quarter for Jews, generally surrounded by a wall separating it from the rest of the city and having gates that were bolted at night. The institution, however, antedates the word and can also refer to the voluntary gathering of Jews in a secluded quarter.[1] In Prague the presence of Jewish communities living in separate Jewish districts dated back to the mid-tenth century, and such districts existed until the late nineteenth and early twentieth centuries, when the ghetto was abolished for hygienic reasons. Over a period lasting ten centuries, Jewish communities in Prague knew both good times and, more frequently, bad times, which included pogroms, persecutions, segregation in the ghetto, and expulsions.[2]

Josefov, the Jewish quarter and former ghetto, a Prague district since 1852, is located between the northern border of the old city and the right bank of the Moldau River. Its important historical sites include ancient synagogues such as the Dusní Synagogue (formerly the Altschul), built in 1605 and reconstructed in 1866; the Altneuschul, founded in 1270 and still in use today; and the Pinkas Synagogue, founded in 1535. Other historical monuments include the Jewish town hall and a large part of the ancient cemetery where Rabbi Judah Loew (known as the Maharal), the illustrious rabbi of Prague, is buried.

In the collective memory of the Jewish people the Prague ghetto is not simply the actual geographical entity on the banks of the Moldau River along with its historic buildings, but is rather a *lieu de mémoire* (site of memory; Nora 1989), an experience that, although it has passed, is retained as a tangible and dynamic memory (cf. Ben Amos and Wiessberg 1999; Bar-Itzhak 2008: 161–76; Rosen 2009: 105–6; Kochavi 2006: 71–99). The encounter with the ghetto is mediated by oral and written collective narratives that embody the heritage of generations and preserve the ghetto in the collective memory as an authentic and still relevant experience. Their suggestive power is derived from their adaptation to the changing socio-historical circumstances of the narrators and informants. While focusing on figures and events of the past in the Prague ghetto, they respond to, and moreover give rise to, central concerns of the narrating society in various historical periods. The relationship between Jews and non-Jews in the diaspora, the view of Israel as the melting pot of Jewish immigrants, and the attitude to Jewish cultural heritage are all themes handled by the narrators as components of cultural and national identity.

The images of the ghetto and its cultural symbols shape its shifting meanings, born of the encounter between itself and the society returning to the past from its present. As a *lieu de mémoire*, a living and breathing entity, the Prague ghetto collects over the years new strata of asserted meaning that shape and reformulate Jewish collective identities. After its gates were opened and its walls torn down, and the ghetto had become a tourist attraction, its narrow alleyways, Gothic architecture, Judaica exhibits in the local museum, the Maharal's ancient synagogue, and the golem's attic associated with it became—by way of the legends of the Prague ghetto, as I demonstrate throughout this essay—an object of nostalgia. In focusing on the power of popular narratives to constitute ethnic and national identities I am following in the footsteps of other scholars (Bar-Itzhak 2001: 11–25, 159–62; Alexander-Frizer 1999: 193–206; Rosen 2008: 213–38). This identity-shaping power derives in large part from an acceptance of the narratives as authentic records of the past: they thus belong to the genre of legend. The legends of the Prague ghetto have the power to evoke and preserve cultural images, an essential function of legends within a given culture. Whether the belief factor, which is a salient one in every definition of legend, implies a debate about belief, as Dégh (2001: 97) puts it, or a concern with 'matters of truth', as Oring prefers, it produces a 'belief language', 'the language of tradition, a common fund of knowledge that forms the belief vocabulary from which communications are constructed' (Oring 2008: 128).

In this essay I examine a selection of legends about the Prague ghetto from various periods that, each in its own way, inform the Prague ghetto as a relevant site of memory that is important for the narrating society, and demonstrate the rhetoric that allowed these legends to be accepted as credible. I further trace the questions of identity they evoke, which represent the doubts, needs, and shortcomings of a society as it relates to the definition of ethnic, cultural, and national boundaries. Finally, I examine the changing images of the ghetto, in other words, the dynamic shaping of the ghetto as a site of memory to reflect the socio-cultural circumstances of a given period. By doing so I also shed light on the cultural function of the legends in framing the Jewish experience of the ghetto in time and place.

Two of the narrative selections share a common motif, that of blood libels in the Prague ghetto, and they will be discussed at length, particularly as they touch on issues of cultural boundaries and collective identities. Others will be dealt with only in general terms. I have used two main sources:

(*a*) *Sippurim*, a series of anthologies of stories first published by Pascheles, and after his death by his son-in-law Jacob Brandeis and others (Pascheles 1976).

Special attention will be paid to 'Jajin Kiddush oder Die Falsche Beschuldigung' ('Kiddush Wine or The False Accusation; Brandeis 1909: 75–122), by L. Wiesel, on the background of the gradual but radical process of emancipation and assimilation taking place among the Jews of eastern Europe during the nineteenth century. The story, first written in 1858, was reworked in 1926 (Schmitz and Wiener 1926: 62–114).

(*b*) IFA—the Israel Folktale Archive—in Haifa, especially IFA 3171: 'The Golem from Prague saves Jews from a blood-libel', and IFA 11363,[3] which were narrated, collected, and preserved during the 1960s and 1970s in Israel. These sources will be studied against the Zionist discourse in Israel in that period. The hagiographical legends about the Maharal, the famous sixteenth-century rabbi of the Prague ghetto (Rosenberg 1991), will not be explored in this essay, whose subject matter is the ghetto as a metonym for the diaspora in general.

Sippurim: Legends about the Prague Ghetto

Wolf Pascheles (1814–57) was a well-known Hebrew publisher and bookseller in Prague. In 1846 he began collecting and publishing Jewish folk sayings, biographies of medieval and modern personalities, tales from Prague's ghetto, and other materials, calling them *Sippurim: Eine Sammlung Jüdischer Volksagen*.[4] The first four collections were published during his lifetime, while the others, from 1858 on, by his sons and his son-in-law, Jacob B. Brandeis. Besides Prague, *Sippurim* was also extremely popular in eastern Europe and went through several editions. Pascheles' contributors had been German rabbis and other spiritual leaders, as well as collectors and authors of folk literature such as L. Weisel, Salomon Kohn—whose novel *Gabriel* was first published in *Sippurim*—I. M. Jost, R. Fürstenthal, and S. I. Kaempf. They embellished, expanded, and reworked the folk tales according to their own tastes and cultural or didactic purposes as they mediated between the folkloric materials and contemporary readers (Schmitz and Wiener 1926: 385–91).

The history of *Sippurim* during the nineteenth century, especially from the second half of the century onwards, developed in parallel to the socio-historical changes occurring in the Prague ghetto. Its narratives were circulated, collected for *Sippurim*, and, as noted, thoroughly revised at a time of changes in the status of the ghetto. Whereas the ghetto still existed when Pascheles published the first volumes of *Sippurim* (1846–7), the 1858 collection appeared in the Jewish quarter of Josefov after the ghetto had been abolished in 1852 and united with the other districts of Prague.

Along with the changing status of the ghetto as a whole, during the 1840s restrictions on Jews as individuals were gradually removed. In 1841 Jews were allowed to own land; in 1846 the Jewish tax was abolished; in 1848 Jews were granted equal rights. Finally, in 1867 the process of legal emancipation, which had begun with the *Toleranzpatent* issued by Joseph II in 1782, was completed.

These changes brought about a gradual process of secularization and assimilation. In the early decades of the century Prague Jewry still observed a traditional lifestyle, but in its second half the mainstream of Jewish life was no longer essentially religious. Jews welcomed the opportunities that opened up for them and adopted the German language and other cultural elements. Mixed marriages and conversion to Christianity became more widespread, reaching one of the highest rates in Europe by the early twentieth century.[5]

When viewing the outstanding success of *Sippurim* (to the surprise even of its publishers), the historical background of Prague should be borne in mind. Pascheles' *Sippurim*, like Tendlau's collection of stories a few years earlier (Tendlau 1842), was a product of its time. The Romantic trend was sweeping over western Europe, expressing the desire to return to national roots and favouring 'authentic' folklore, simplicity, naturalness, and spontaneity. Collections of local folklore and Jewish legends from the Talmud, Midrash, and medieval literature became popular as part of a general revival of stories, legends, and fairy tales (the stories of the Brothers Grimm, for example, were published in seven editions between 1812 and 1857).

The ghetto narratives go back to earlier days—to the first Jewish settlement in Bohemia in the Middle Ages (twelfth and thirteenth centuries) and to the time of the Maharal in the sixteenth century. In a period of gradual transition from a traditional to a secular lifestyle around the mid-nineteenth century, and later, when secularization became prevalent, *Sippurim* expressed a Romantic nostalgia for the 'authentic' walled ghetto, with its simplicity and thriving vitality—notwithstanding the pogroms and disasters—its festivals, traditions, customs, and beliefs, which the narrators saw as local folklore shaping their own Jewish identity. The narratives in the collection depict Jewish themes, present black-and-white characters from an idealized viewpoint (Kestenberg-Gladstein 1968: 56), and portray the ghetto to their audience as an enchanting and eventful place, one that is 'natural' and 'authentic', albeit not lacking in hardship or religious and social conflicts (cf. Kieval 1992: 271). Fantasy and magic, pathos, an overflow of emotions, and dramatic turns of plot recur time and time again, representing the viewpoint and poetic taste of the nineteenth-century narrators. This point is evident from the editors' comment on 'Kiddush Wine' in the introduction to their anthology (Schmitz and Weiner 1926). They express regret over their failure in their edition to remove all the 'additional' and redundant elements woven into the 'original' legends by Pascheles' narrators, since that would have damaged the plot itself. Their comment reflects the taste of their time, but, luckily for us, the 'pathetic', 'overly sweet', and didactic elements that they sought to eliminate are the very materials needed for studying the narratives of *Sippurim* in the socio-historical context of Prague in the second half of the nineteenth century.

Thus, fantasy and magic, as well as other representations of the narrators' poetic taste, are indicated in the various tales *of Sippurim*. In 'Die Pinchasgass' ('Pinchas Lane'; Pascheles 1976: 72–9) a treasure of golden coins is unexpectedly found in the carcass of a giant gorilla, bringing sudden fortune to a poor and wretched family. The gorilla was hurled into the poor Jewish family's house with the intention of mocking and frightening them, while the perpetrator was unaware of the treasure it carried in its belly. In 'Die Goldene Gasse' ('The Golden Lane'; Pascheles 1976: 52–5), which is an adaptation of the well-known medieval 'Ma'aseh yerushalmi' ('The Tale of the Jerusalemite'), a beautiful young girl, dazzled by her love for a non-Jew, enters into the kingdom of the demons under the Moldau River, where she discovers that her lover is a demon. She marries him, bears him a child and is permitted to visit the ghetto for a limited time disguised as a black cat. In the above-mentioned 'Kiddush Wine' (Brandeis 1909: 122–75) a forbidden love between a non-Jewish man and a Jewish girl is consummated when, in an unexpected twist, the 'gentile' identifies himself as a Jew (Brandeis 1909: 72–175). 'Die Belelesgass' ('Beleles Lane'; Pascheles 1976: 79–81; Thieberger 1955: 135–9) introduces the medieval motif of the *danse macabre*, which was further developed in the Romantic period in different artistic forms, first by Goethe in his *Totentanz* (1815) and later on in the nineteenth century by Franz Liszt, Henri Cazalis, and Saint-Saëns (see Kats 1993: ii. 114–18 and his reference to Kurtz 1975). At midnight, the dead ghetto children emerge from their tombs and start to dance. The Romanticism is also implied in the tendency to introduce simple and anonymous characters rather than famous rabbis. Such is the protagonist of 'Das Stille Jüdel' ('The Silent Jew'), who sacrifices himself for the sake of his community when it is threatened by a pogrom (Schmitz and Weiner 1926: 106–14). Even the Maharal, in the famous story 'The Golem', is presented simply as 'a certain Bezalel Loewe', who 'lived among the Jews of Prague' (Pascheles 1976: 51; Thieberger 1955: 134). Accordingly, the motif of the golem, which later became central in Rosenberg's hagiographical legends, fulfils only a minor function in Pascheles' narratives, actually featuring in only one of the stories, the one in which the Maharal fashions the creature (Pascheles 1976: 51–2).

In these and other narratives in *Sippurim*, it is the ghetto that is placed at the centre, with all the upheavals and woes of everyday life. We are told the names of ghetto residents, their nicknames and occupations; we learn about the common folk and community dignitaries, along with all their concerns, celebrations and tragedies, their loves and hates. The Moldau River, which borders on the ghetto, becomes a magical space, both promising and menacing, a metonym of the ghetto itself. Thus the ghetto, an alienated 'space', becomes an intimate 'place' through human experiences mediated by traditional narratives (cf. Tuan 1977: 136–48; Bar-Itzhak 1988: 165).

The focus on the ghetto as a source of traditional folklore and nostalgia is also apparent in the editorial strategy. A section of the legends in Pascheles' *Sippurim* deals with the ghetto's street names—Belelesgasse, Pinchasgasse, and Goldene Gasse—their origins in the Prague ghetto, and their 'historical' background. Other legends are centred around the ghetto's most important synagogues, the Altneuschul and the Altschul, and explain local customs: why in the Altneuschul Kaddish was recited before the 'Kol Nidrei' prayer on the eve of the Day of Atonement (Pascheles 1976: 82–102) and why, in the Altschul, they did not recite the Kiddush over wine on the sabbath (Brandeis 1955: 122–75).

Social relations among the residents of the ghetto, as well as between them and the surrounding non-Jews, are established along two horizontal axes of movement: (*a*) within the ghetto itself; (*b*) from the ghetto outwards and then back inwards.

Events within the ghetto take place inside the home, at family gatherings, such as a betrothal party ('Kiddush Wine'), or on Jewish festivals, such as Passover ('Pinchas Lane'). On very special occasions, such as during the king's procession through the ghetto ('The Silent Jew'), excitement also spills over into the crowded streets. The ghetto's cemetery is a world unto itself; although located in the ghetto, it has its own special rules ('Beleles Lane').

Beyond the ghetto walls reside the ruling authorities of Prague, the aristocrats—and the mob. Kings of Bohemia mentioned in *Sippurim* include Vaclav II (1283–1305) in 'Kiddush Wine' (Brandeis 1955: 73) and Rudolf II (1583–1612) in 'Beleles Lane' (Pascheles 1976: 79). There are several references or allusions to historical events that took place in Bohemia, especially in Prague. One of these references, an allusion in 'The Silent Jew' to the famous Defenestrations of Prague (in 1415 and 1618), is particularly interesting. In this tale a stone 'falling' from a house in Beleles Lane almost kills the king in the midst of his visit to the ghetto and has severe consequences. Years later the truth is revealed: it was the local governor who planned the incident, intending that the blame should fall on the Jews.

The Jews in Pascheles' *Sippurim* move in and out of the ghetto and maintain contact with the non-Jews outside. Salom in 'Kiddush Wine' pays regular charitable visits to a non-Jewish widow and her four children, one of whom will become, later on in the tale, the victim of a blood libel. His daughter Dina also exits the ghetto: like other Jews, she eagerly takes in the festivities held at the king's palace to celebrate the birth of the prince. At night, however, it is dangerous to leave the ghetto. One night on his way back Salom is accused of robbing the local church and savagely beaten.

Those residing outside the ghetto also move in and out of it. Non-Jews enter to meet with Jewish acquaintances; for example, the benevolent count in 'Pinchas

Lane', who supports Pinchas, a destitute ghetto Jew, and celebrates Passover with him. However, hostile characters also enter the ghetto to pursue blood libels. In 'Kiddush Wine' it is a Jew who instigates a blood libel as an act of revenge, moving in and out of the ghetto to carry out his plan.

The ghetto's proximity to the non-Jewish areas around it creates both continuity and contrast against the socio-cultural background of the second half of the nineteenth century and the process of emancipation and secularization that characterized the ghetto in its relations with its surroundings in Prague. Undermining the image of the Jew as the ultimate Other and eternal victim of pogroms, and seen from a Romantic perspective, the ghetto in Pascheles' anthologies is vibrant and enchanting, reflecting an atmosphere of intimacy, despite disasters and periods of crisis. In the mind of the narrators, during an era of emancipation and the loss of their unmediated connection with the ghetto, when questions of national identity have become paramount in a new reality of increased contact between Jews and non-Jews, the ghetto is the object of a memory that can still define their cultural identity as Jews who are connected to their ethnic heritage.

'Kiddush Wine': Rhetorical Strategies for Conveying Truth

On the basis of a repository of shared knowledge, the legends in *Sippurim* make a claim for the truth or the plausibility of the events that they relate. 'Kiddush Wine' will now be analysed as the point of departure for a discussion of the rhetorical techniques of persuasion. The belief factor is the key to understanding the power of *Sippurim* to imprint the Romantic images of the ghetto embedded in them on their audience and to establish it as a site of memory and of cultural heritage.

'Kiddush Wine', as noted above, explains the local custom at the Altschul of reciting the Kiddush blessing over the sabbath loaves rather than over wine. The background for this was the miraculous rescue of Prague's Jews from a blood libel brought against the community by a Jewish bully in revenge for the cancellation of his engagement to the daughter of one of the community's dignitaries. The disaster was averted at the last minute on the eve of Passover, thanks to a heavenly voice that guided the rabbi and his assistant to the Torah Ark in the Altschul. Behind the Ark they discovered that the usual bottle of Kiddush wine had been replaced by a bottle of blood. They then removed all traces of the blood and replaced the bottle with one containing wine. As a result, the truth came to light and the blood libel was thwarted.

This plot is interwoven with yet another plot about a secret, forbidden love between a Jewish girl and a Christian benefactor of the community, the man who exposed the villain responsible for the blood libel—none other than the girl's spurned former fiancé. The story ends with a complete resolution: the 'Christian' confesses that he is in fact Jewish, that he abandoned his family and community as a young man, taking on a Christian identity. He repents and marries the girl.

The narrator needs to convince his audience of the truth of the ghetto Jews' miraculous rescue from the blood libel. The main tension is between tradition as represented in motifs such as the custom of Kiddush at the Altschul and the heavenly voice, and the weakened tradition of the narrator's society. Accordingly, the narrator's efforts are directed at creating authenticity through a nostalgic return to the roots, without necessarily claiming absolute truth.

In his study of popular and folk legends, Oring applies Aristotle's three categories of rhetoric: (*a*) ethos, which is concerned with the credibility of the narrator and his source; (*b*) logos, which relates to the argument of the narrative; and (*c*) pathos, which focuses on the dispositions of the audience: the emotional, cognitive, and moral aspects of its response. Ethos, logos, and pathos are all employed in 'Kiddush Wine' to present tradition as the story's source and the basis for its authority.

Ethos

Leopold Wiesel, the author/informant of 'Kiddush Wine', was a doctor, ethnographer, and writer who lived in Prague while studying medicine. In the 1830s and 1840s he devoted most of his literary efforts to capturing, preserving, and disseminating the rich folk traditions of the Jews of Bohemia, and especially of the Prague ghetto, out of a deep consciousness of his status as a Jew who was losing contact with the world of traditional Jewish culture. 'Kiddush Wine' was written, as noted, in 1858, after he had converted to Catholicism and married the non-Jewish Ann Pavlovska. As we have seen above, the motif of mixed marriage figures prominently in 'Kiddush Wine' itself (Kieval and Polakovic 2008: ii. 2016–17).

The credibility of the story lies in its sources—the older residents of the Jewish quarter whom Wiesel interviewed to record their stories. The story takes on the authority of a narrative tradition which was accepted among the Jewish society of Prague as an aetiological explanation for the local custom in the Altschul, and passed down from one generation to the next.

The preface details the 'historical' background of the community of Portuguese Jews in Prague, within which the Kiddush custom developed, and the wider context of thirteenth-century Bohemia in the days of King Johann of Luxembourg. This kind of historical framing is typical of stories related as a tradition. In the specific socio-historical context the story's power of persuasion stems from its added value as a tradition emphasized through the historical setting and the multitude of detail. An emotional link is created to the ghetto's folklore, customs, and symbols, and to the Jewish roots of the contemporary audience. While the custom is apparently no longer current in large parts of Prague's Jewish society, it exists in its collective memory as an experience of tradition in a way that is conducive to accepting the story as reliable.

Logos

The story's reliability is further conveyed through its narrative strategy, the intersection of the two plotlines around the blood libel, and its resolution on two levels: the miraculous, by means of the heavenly voice, and the romantic-secular one, through the mediation of the 'Christian' benefactor on behalf of the community and the steps he takes to expose the man behind the plot.

In a structure where the miraculous plot is supported by the rational one, the legendary elements of the story become more readily acceptable. The resolution occurs on two levels: on the miraculous level the Jewish community is saved thanks to the rabbi's divine revelation. On the rational and romantic level Leon the 'Christian', who, it turns out, is really a Jew, manages to disprove the blood libel in his own way, and out of his love and concern for Dina and her family he manages to track down the villain who in reality abducted the Christian boy, reveals the identity of the Jew who enlisted him for the job—his beloved's former fiancé, who wished to avenge the cancellation of their engagement—and finds the boy safe and sound. The resolution on both levels occurs at a critical moment, when the bottle of 'blood' is discovered in the holy ark in the Altschul. The soldiers find a bottle of wine instead of the blood that they expect, and almost immediately afterwards, Leon enters the Altschul together with the widow and her son as irrefutable proof of the mendacity of the libel.

The role of the above-mentioned combination of the rational and the miraculous-nostalgic as a factor in the story's acceptance as truth, at least as legendary truth, by the contemporary narrating society is further emphasized when comparing 'Kiddush Wine' to 'The Dream of the Beadle and Elijah the Prophet' (IFA 3371),[6] which appears to be an adaptation of the printed version of the former. The dream leads to the discovery of a bottle of blood in the Holy Ark. Although this version of the narrative is clearly based on the story published in *Sippurim*—a well-known phenomenon in the dissemination of folk tales—the romantic-rational plotline is missing. It is further notable that the local characteristics of the story are also missing from this IFA version, which was reported without being related to any particular time or place.

Pathos

The melodramatic developments in the narrative and the romantic motif suit the aesthetic tastes of the narrator's society and its desire to hear a story that will move people to tears. The conclusion, with the foiling of the blood libel, also meets the audience's expectations for a satisfactory moral resolution. The pathetic mode of the story is salient in comparison to the oral adaptation preserved by the IFA, 'Tale of a pro-Jewish gentile' (7848), where the romantic line is implied, but without the pathos and melodrama of *Sippurim*. Here too, as in the above-mentioned 'Dream of the Beadle and Elijah the Prophet', local features are omitted; rather, the tale reports the plot as an event that occurred 'many years ago in one of the cities'.

Pascheles' *Sippurim* establishes a Romantic image of the Prague ghetto as a source of Jewish roots through its use of the 'belief language' of the Prague ghetto, its 'language of tradition' still prevalent among Prague Jews, who are already secular but yearn for memories of a collective past. These include, for example, the ghetto's history and its lifestyle, and the cycle of the Jewish year. While the ghetto becomes the repository of Jewish memory in Prague as the identity signifier of the collective, the boundaries between it and the non-Jewish expanse are blurred, and movement is bi-directional: both outwards and inwards. The blood libel narrative is adapted from the perspective of the narrators, who are already at the culmination of, or past, the process of emancipation. From their perspective the ghetto in 'Kiddush Wine' and in the other stories by Pascheles and Brandeis blurs the identity of the Jew as the Other, while at the same time it intensifies the Jewish folkloristic heritage of the Prague ghetto.

Through the above rhetorical devices, belonging to the categories of ethos, logos, and pathos, the narrator establishes his credibility and moves his readers to identify with the figures and symbols of the ghetto, appropriating its traditions as a reservoir of collective memory. In a period of emancipation and assimilation processes, the ghetto—as presented in *Sippurim*—produces a Jewish cultural identity born of a sentimental link to a romanticized past that was once but is no more, without having to return behind its walls. In these narratives the ghetto is preserved as an authentic and deep-rooted experience, significant for the narrating collective in Prague as a 'site of memory'.

The Israel Folktale Archive

Images of the ghetto change through history. In order to substantiate this claim I will now proceed to explore the tales of the Israel Folktale Archive (IFA) in Haifa University, comparing images of the ghetto in these stories to their parallels in *Sippurim*. Like Pascheles' and Brandeis's *Sippurim*, the IFA tales establish a strong link between the ghetto and definitions of identity, but here it is done against the background of the reality of the lives of the informants—Czech immigrants—in Israel.

The IFA was founded in the 1950s by Professor Dov Noy with the mission of documenting the wealth of folklores of the different Jewish communities. The massive wave of immigration to Israel in the 1950s provided a unique opportunity, and Noy's students readily volunteered for the task, going out into the field and documenting the immigrants' tales. These were catalogued and preserved in the IFA, which continues to add to and enrich its collection, employing modern and more sophisticated documentation methods that take into account modes of performance in addition to content.

The selection discussed here includes thirteen IFA tales centred around famous figures of the Prague ghetto: the Maharal and the golem that he created, R. Yehezkel Landau, and R. Jonathan Eybeschutz; the famous edifices of the Altschul and the Altneuschul, and blood libels against the Jewish community.[7] As mentioned above, these tales were often reported by Czechoslovakian immigrants to Israel, most notably Pinhas Gutterman and Ephraim Schechter.

The tales represent a dual perspective: that of the informants, who carry their ethnic traditions with them, and that of the Israeli collectors, either by means of the techniques and modes of documentation (comments on the tale; editing and 'improving') or through the internalization of Israeli self-images among the informants themselves. This double perspective must be taken into consideration when viewing the implied images of the ghetto in the IFA tales from Czechoslovakia and their significance and impact on their audience. The power of these tales, which, again, employ a variety of rhetorical devices, lies in their acceptance as a credible and relevant ethnic heritage even in the context of life in Israel.

The tales were collected and recorded mainly in the 1950s and 1960s, when Zionist ideology still predominated in the newly established state. According to this ideology, the State of Israel, which had been fighting for its existence since the War of Independence, was the homeland of the Jewish people and was an alternative for the east European Jewish centres that had been destroyed during the Holocaust.

I propose reading the tales chosen for discussion here, 'The beadle and Elijah the prophet' and 'The Golem has not disappeared', in the context of the Zionist discourse and its responses to questions of ethnic and national identity. While 'Kiddush Wine' shares the motif of the blood libel with the IFA tales, it is in the latter that we see the first suggestion of self-defence—a prominent element of Israeli discourse in the years the tales were reported and recorded, and a central component of the national identity they sought to fashion. This identity stands in contrast to the ethnic identity that is the product of the cultural heritage of the diaspora, and creates a tension with which the informant contends in telling the story. My focus here is only on two of the tales in the selection about the Prague ghetto that I have examined, but they implicitly represent all the tensions and problems found in the other tales—both those whose explicit context is the birth of the State of Israel, the settling in the land, and the absorption of the new immigrants (Bar-Itzhak 2005: 3–28, 53–69) as well as the personal narratives that address social codes embedded in the Israeli-Zionist discourse (as implied in Rosen 2009: 106–12).

The background to the dominance of the Zionist discourse in our context was the fundamental traumatic experiences that sustained the collective memory in the early decades of the state (and are still relevant today to representative parts of the population in Israel). As the historian Anita Shapira says regarding the views of the writer Aharon Megged as a representative of the generation that lived through these constitutive experiences,

Meged's memories reflect the traumatic experiences that influenced the world-view of the Palmach generation: growing up in Israel under British rule, which was viewed as hostile and imperialist; the Arab revolt, which made the youth aware of the conflict in the country between Arabs and Jews as a life-or-death struggle; the Second World War, in which the world was divided into good and evil, without any shades of grey; the experience of Jewish weakness and the helpless rage at the Holocaust; the War of Independence as a tragic and heroic culmination of everything that preceded it. The fear and terror that were part of at least the early days of fighting led to the fact that the ultimate victory was accompanied by a feeling of release, which gave it in the eyes of the members of that generation the status of an act of historic justice unexplainable in conventional terms. (Shapira 1997: 23)

It was this sense of shared fate that produced the *dor ba'arets* literature, that of the Palmach generation in the 1950s, which was fully committed to the nationalist ideology of the State of Israel.

What is especially important for the discussion at hand is, as noted, the Zionist ideology of self-defence: the Israel Defence Forces and the value of self-defence it represents were glorified in contrast with the submissiveness and passivity considered to be characteristic of the diaspora. In the context of national ceremonies, the Warsaw ghetto uprising was extolled, whereas the daily tasks of survival and maintaining one's human dignity in that reality were virtually ignored. The Holocaust refugees, the 'ghetto Jews', were perceived as having been led to their fate like sheep to the slaughter. This approach integrated well into the broader position of 'negation of the diaspora' as the state strove to gather the scattered Jewish people into a territorial unit of its own (Shapira 1997: 23).

The impact of the Zionist myth in the early years of the state, which persisted during the period when the IFA tales below were reported and recorded, is clearly illustrated by the post-Zionist position (with a certain affinity to postmodernism) of the New Historians in the 1980s. These scholars claimed an entirely different historiography, one that relinquished the Zionist-ideological component of the State of Israel, that is, its character as a Jewish state. More than being merely a question of academic dispute among historians, the new approach represented a veritable battle over Israel's collective memory. According to the New Historians, who had not undergone the constitutive experience of the Palmach generation, the Zionist agenda and negation of the diaspora were a narrative that had been forced on Israeli society in its early years as opposed to other narratives—those of the Palestinians who had been driven out of their homes and of Jews who lived in a good and creative diaspora. Although this approach brought a new awareness of aspects of Jewish existence in Israel, the historical context of the fragile nascent state was not taken into account and the past was judged as a mirror image of the present, divorced from history as it occurred (Shapira 1997: 19–45).

New History's critique had not yet developed in the 1960s, when the Prague folk narratives were documented as part of the extensive fieldwork carried out by the IFA. Even the avant-garde literature of the 1960s, as seen, for example, in the works of Amos Oz and A. B. Yehoshua, which offered an agenda that identified with universal themes and displaced the *dor ba'arets* literature, was still Zionist in nature (Gertz 1983: 87–95). The pluralism and post-Zionist agenda of the 1980s were not to gain ascendancy and most of Israeli society continued to view the State of Israel as the state of the Jews, committed to defending and protecting its citizens and providing them with shelter and security.

'The Golem from Prague saves Jews from a blood libel' was related by Czech Holocaust survivor Pinchas Gutterman and recorded in 1961 by Ephraim Shechter.[8] The thematic association between the Prague blood libel and Gutterman's identity as a Holocaust survivor representing the refugee gives him credibility as an informant who has personally experienced persecution and antisemitism. The tale opens *in medias res*, describing the blood libel and the pogrom that followed it. A few weeks before the festival of Passover a child's body is found in a deserted ruin on the outskirts of Prague.[9] In response, Jewish shops in the city centre are broken into and Jewish residents, old and young, are murdered. The turning point comes when a 'strange Jew begins hitting the attackers left and right', and 'All the killers were so frightened that they ran away. They all disappeared from Prague's streets.' The tale proceeds with the following narrative elements: the arrest of Jewish leaders; fasting and prayer; a verdict that finds the Jews guilty; the discovery of the real murderer, a poor farmer who pleads guilty and names the local priest as the person who had hired him. The hero of the tale is clearly the strange Jew who succeeds in driving away the rioters. It is only in the epilogue that his identity is revealed as the Maharal's golem—a man of clay whom the rabbi created and brought to life with the power of the Tetragrammaton that he inserted in its mouth (Pascheles 1976: 51–2).

The postponement of the revelation of the identity of the golem to the epilogue is of great importance as it deviates from the conventions of the golem stories, especially as they were determined by Yehuda Rosenberg in his anthology of stories *The Wonders of the Maharal* (Yassif 1991: 57) and as they became known in Jewish and Israeli society. Rosenberg's book was very widely disseminated and was what imparted to the motif of the golem its popularity in both Jewish and non-Jewish society. The audience's expectations of the golem stories, all golem stories, are largely dictated by the image of the golem in Rosenberg's narratives. In these stories the golem enters the scene at the most critical moment and saves the Jewish community from a blood libel by virtue of the Tetragrammaton in its mouth and the combination of letters with which the Maharal created it.[10] I propose viewing the deviation from this model as a rhetorical strategy shaped by the socio-political circumstances in the State of Israel during the period when the story was related.

Thus the tale, similarly to Zionist ideology, alludes to the option of proactive defence as a way to undermine the Jew's image as the Other. The narrator uses a twofold strategy to convince his Israeli audience of the truth of his tale (*logos*): on the one hand, he leaves the golem motif, as noted, until the epilogue, thereby emphasizing the rational and Zionist option of self-defence. The connection between the golem and the blood libel is thereby weakened and this in turn weakens the magical aspect of the story as embodied in the image of the golem with the Tetragrammaton in its mouth. On the other hand, he does not dispose of the golem motif altogether, despite the dominance of the rationalist voice.

This twofold perspective, rational throughout the story and magical in the epilogue, enhances immigrants' affinity, on the one hand, to their identity as Zionists in the safe harbour of the State of Israel, and, on the other hand, to their Czech ethnic and family heritage. Through the mediation of the story the informant embraces his or her new identity as an Israeli, without losing the diaspora ethnic identity. The ability to contain a double identity—both ethnic and national —in the story is what establishes the Prague ghetto as a vibrant and relevant *lieu de mémoire*. The resolution of the twist in the plot, the rescue of the Jews from the blood libel, meets the expectations of the audience and creates empathy, making the story credible and forceful. The priest's admission of guilt as the person who conceived the blood libel gives listeners or readers a sense of satisfaction with the reversal of fortunes in the local court, which bore out the Jewish claims of innocence. Rather than functioning as an anachronistic narrative, the IFA tale becomes a narrative that constitutes a collective identity. By means of the story of the Prague ghetto, the informant contends with the duality arising in the image of a particular ethnic group, which is not entirely consistent with the dominant Zionist ideology. The tale, then, adapts the legend of the golem as magical protector of the Jews in the Prague ghetto to the Zionist rationalism of the State of Israel, without completely relinquishing it.

'The Golem has not disappeared'

The integration of the Zionist discourse into the IFA tales of the Prague ghetto is also implied in 'The Golem has not disappeared',[11] although in a more complex manner. The informant is a Holocaust survivor from Prague. The collector was an Israeli soldier, Shlomo Laba of Jerusalem, who wrote the tale down from memory in 1977, about thirty years after he had heard it while in a displaced persons' camp in Italy after the war (1945). The Holocaust takes the place of the blood libel:

The golem did not disappear and even during the war he came out of his hiding place to protect his synagogue. The Nazis decided to tear down the Altneushul. They came to destroy it and suddenly, from within the silence of the synagogue, they could hear giant footsteps coming from the roof, where the golem was walking, and they saw the shadow of a huge hand fall from the window to the floor. The Germans were terrified. They threw down their tools and ran away as fast as they could.

It was from the standpoint of a reliable informant (Oring 2008: 135–8) that the Holocaust survivor who originally related the tale questioned the credibility of the golem motif. He provided a rational explanation for the Germans' flight: settling noises in the old building may sound like giant footsteps and shadows seen through broken glass in distorted shapes may resemble a giant hand. At the same time, he was willing to believe his tale, which was spread among the Holocaust survivors from Prague and received as truth. The existence of the sanctified Altneushul, which, against all odds, remained standing and survived the war, challenged the reality of the German occupation of Prague. Belief in the tale's truth implies the victory of the Holocaust survivor himself over the Nazis.

In the prologue the soldier Shlomo Laba makes a remark about the secular outlook of the refugee Holocaust survivor, which may well explain the latter's doubts concerning the veracity of his own story. The subtle irony and ambiguity detectable in the tale are generated by the dissonance between the man's nostalgic position, which has its origins in the Prague ghetto's heritage, and his scepticism. The somewhat ironic conclusion, implied by the disparity between the two positions of the informant, is to preserve both the ethnic-traditional ethos and the Zionist-secular one, and to accept the tension between them.

The tale should also be read from the perspective of the Israeli soldier, who transcribes it from memory after three decades (cf. Yassif 2008: 82–4). The description of the Germans' hasty retreat from the Altneushul in terror of the golem while leaving their tools behind embodies a discourse familiar from descriptions of battles during Israel's War of Independence: Arabs attack Israeli soldiers, who fight with old and not very effective weapons, when suddenly there is an unexplained mass retreat by the attackers. The Davidka memorial on Jerusalem's Jaffa Road, for example, commemorates the folklore that developed around the Davidka among Jewish fighters in the battles for Jaffa, Haifa, Safed, and Jerusalem. The Davidka was the nickname for a cannon used by the Israel Defence Forces in the War of Independence. There were only a few such cannons and consequently they had to be transported from place to place in accordance with the army's needs. Due to its inaccuracy, the Davidka was considered an unreliable weapon. And yet its deterrent power was immense: the horrific noise it made terrified the Arab attackers, causing them to abandon their positions in panic (Meivar-Meiberg 1989: 329).

If the Prague tale can indeed be read in this way, as a sublimated form of Zionist discourse as documented by the Israeli soldier, then it anticipates the attitudes of survivor immigrants in Israel. Similarly to the IFA tale discussed above, the sense of vindication for the Holocaust or any anti-Jewish atrocities in the diaspora lies in the possibility of active defence exemplified by the State of Israel, which, by its very existence, radically impacts the immigrant survivors' definitions of ethnic and national identity.

To sum up, the image of the Prague ghetto in the two IFA tales is shaped by a duality of reference, both to the non-Jewish Prague residents outside the ghetto and to the State of Israel. In the mind of the immigrant informants, the ghetto in the hostile non-Jewish space and the State of Israel in the Middle East parallel one another, while the responses to the similarly hostile situations are strikingly different.

The magical solution embodied by the golem persists as an expression of the ethnic identity of the informant, who is a member of the Czech community. However, at the same time, an option of self-defence embodied in the Zionist ideology emerges and shapes the national identity of the narrator-informant in the State of Israel. The ghetto, as a *lieu de mémoire*, evokes mixed feelings of identification and empathy with the traditional, somewhat naïve, experience of the ghetto, alongside a realistic and rational perspective rooted in the secular reality of the State of Israel in the present. In this manner the ghetto becomes a 'site of memory', instilled in the consciousness of the narrator-informant as part of his or her cultural—national and ethnic—identity as an immigrant in Israel.

In comparison to the Pascheles tales discussed above, the Prague ghetto in the IFA tales has become a means of coping with identity conflicts evoked by a new historical-cultural factor—the existence of the State of Israel.

Conclusion

This essay has outlined the process of how narratives from different periods frame the Prague ghetto in the time and place of their narrators, thus establishing it as a site of memory that remains continually relevant, vivid, and meaningful for the narrating community. I have examined the different narratives against the historical background and identity conflicts of their narrators/informants. *Sippurim* was scrutinized in the context of the Jewish quarter in Prague during the second half of the nineteenth century, the period of emancipation and of secularization and Romanticism. The IFA tales were read in light of the Zionist ideology of the State of Israel, which remained dominant up until the 1980s. The various narratives were thus related in a variety of changing socio-historical and personal circumstances, shaping, and giving rise to, collective attitudes through their narrators' choice of rhetorical devices, as well as through the ways in which they were circulated and received by their audiences. They thus became components of ethnic, cultural, and national identity. In the narratives of Pascheles and Brandeis the ghetto is a site of romantic yearning that was destroyed, never to return, but can be reconstructed as a 'site of memory' and nostalgia for the heritage of the past. In the narratives of the IFA the ghetto is linked to both the ethnic heritage of the narrators and the national ideology of the State of Israel, specifically, the ethos of self-defence. It is by containing the option of a dialectical/dual identity in Israel's changing reality that the ghetto has remained a relevant site of memory, even after its real function has ceased to exist.

The cultural images of the ghetto as 'different', while still maintaining continuity, are common to both the Pascheles and Brandeis narratives and the IFA tales. In the Pascheles stories the ghetto's Otherness stems from its comparison with its non-Jewish surroundings. The IFA tales have added a new dimension of Otherness in the contrast between the State of Israel and its hostile neighbours. The common image of the ghetto as a component of Otherness in Jewish identity throughout history is also part of its meaning as a 'site of memory' in the narratives about Prague.

Notes

1   See *Encyclopaedia Judaica*, s.v. 'Ghetto'.

2   *Encyclopaedia Judaica*, s.v. 'Prague'.

3   I am grateful to Professor Haya Bar-Itzhak, head of the IFA, and Dr Idit Pintel-Ginsberg, its academic secretary, for the IFA versions and permission to cite them. My special thanks go to Idit Pintel-Ginsberg for her help in locating them.

4   See The Jews of Czechoslovakia 1968: 533; *Encyclopaedia Judaica*, s.v. 'Pascheles'.

5   See *Encyclopaedia Judaica*, s.v. 'Prague'; Kieval 1992, esp. pp. 246–8.

6   The story was catalogued as oicotype AT*730G, reported by Simha Rabbi of Afghanistan and collected by Pinhas Gutterman, Czechoslovakia.

7   The thirteen IFA tales are 1640, 2627, 2653, 3168, 3171, 3173, 6544, 6555, 6556, 3170, 10837, 11383, and 11450.

8   IFA 3171.

9   The Passover period often saw the spread of blood libels accusing Jews of murdering Christian children to use their blood in the baking of the matzot consumed during the festival.

10   See e.g. 'Blood Libel' and 'The Last Blood Libel in Prague' in Rosenberg 1991: 111, 137.

11   IFA 11383.

References

ALEXANDER-FRIZER, TAMAR. 1999. *The Beloved Friend-and-a-Half: Studies in Sephardi Folk Literature* [Ma'aseh ahuv vahetsi: hasipur ha'amamah shel yehudei sefarad]. Jerusalem and Beer Sheva.

BAR-ITZHAK, HAYA. 2001. *Jewish Poland—Legends of Origin: Ethnopoetics and Legendary Chronicles*. Detroit.

—— 2005. *Israeli Folk Narratives, Settlement, Immigration, Ethnicity*. Raphael Patai Series in Folklore and Anthropology. Detroit.

BAR-ITZHAK, HAYA. 2008. 'Poland: A Materialized Settlement and a Metaphysical Landscape in Legends of Origin of Polish Jews'. In Julia Brauch, Anna Lipphardt, and Alexandera Nocke, eds., *Jewish Topographies: Visions of Space, Traditions of Place*. Farnham, Surrey.

BEN-AMOS, DAN, and LILIANE WEISSBERG. 1999. *Cultural Memory and Construction of Identity*. Detroit.

BRANDEIS, JACOB, ed. 1909. *Sippurim: Ghettosagen, Jüdische Mythen und Legenden*. Prague and Breslau.

DÉGH, LINDA. 2001. *Legend and Belief: Dialectics of a Folklore Genre*. Bloomington, Ind.

Encyclopaedia Judaica. 1971. 22 vols. Jerusalem.

GERTZ, NURITH. 1983. *Hebrew Narrative Fiction in the Sixties* [Hasiporet hayisra'elit bishenot hashishim]. Ramat Aviv.

Jewish Encyclopedia. 1901–6. 12 vols. New York.

KATZ, DAVID. 1993. 'The Motif of the Dance of Death in the Tradition of Jewish Literature' [Der motiv fun toitentanz in der tradizie fun literatur bei yidden], Ph.D. diss., 2 vols. Bar Ilan University.

KESTENBERG-GLADSTEIN, RUTH. 1968. 'The Jews between Czechs and Germans in the Historic Land (1848–1918)'. In *The Jews of Czechoslovkia*, i. 21–71.

KIEVAL, HILLEL J. 1992. 'The Social Vision of Bohemian Jews: Intellectuals and Community in the 1840s'. In Jonathan Frankel and Steven J. Zipperstein, eds., *Assimilation and Community: The Jews in Nineteenth-Century Europe*, 246–83. Cambridge.

——and DANIEL POLAKOVIC. 2008. 'Weisel, Leopold'. *YIVO Encyclopedia of Jews in Eastern Europe*, ii. New Haven. <http://www.yivoencyclopedia.org/>.

KOCHAVI-NEHAB, RONI. 2006. *Sites in the Realm of Memory: Kibbutz Jubilee Books* [Atarim bimeḥozot hazikaron: sifrei yovel shel hakibutsim]. Jerusalem.

KURTZ, LEONARD. 1975. *The Dance of Death and the Macabre Spirit in European Literature*. New York.

MEIVAR-MEIBERG, MEIR. 1989. *In the Shadow of the Fortress: The Story of the Haganah Commander in Safed* [Betsel hametsudah: sipuro shel mefaked hahaganah bitsefat], ed. Gershon Rivlin. Tel Aviv.

NORA, PIERRE. 1989. 'Between Memory and History: Les Lieux de Mémoire'. *Representations*, 26: 7–24.

ORING, ELLIOTT. 2008. 'Legendary and the Rhetoric of Truth'. *Journal of American Folklore*, 121: 127–66.

PASCHELES, WOLF. 1976. *Sippurim*, pt. 1, vol. i. Hildesheim.

ROSEN, ILANA. 2008. 'Hasidism versus Zionism as Remembered by Carpatho-Russian Jews between the Two World Wars'. In Simon J. Bronner, ed., *Jewishness: Expression, Identity, and Representation*. Jewish Cultural Studies 1. Oxford.

——2009. 'Personal Historical Narrative Shaping the Past and the Present'. *European Journal of Jewish Studies*, 3(1): 103–33.

ROSENBERG, YEHUDAH YUDEL. 1991. *The Golem of Prague and Other Tales of Wonder* [Hagolem miprag uma'asim nifla'im aḥerim], ed. Eli Yassif. Jerusalem.

SHAPIRA, ANITA. 1997. 'Politics and Collective Memory: The Debate over the "New Historians" in Israel' (Heb.). In *New Jews, Old Jews* [Yehudim ḥadashim, yehudim yeshanim]. Tel Aviv.

SCHMITZ, SIEGFRIED, and MAIR WIENER. 1926. *Prager Sammlung Jüdischer Legenden*. Vienna and Leipzig.

TENDLAU, ABRAHAM MOSES. 1842. *Das Buch der Sagen und Legenden Jüdischer Vorzeit*. Stuttgart.

The Jews of Czechoslovakia. 1968. Historical Studies and Surveys 1. New York.

THIEBERGER, FREDERIC. 1955. *The Great Rabbi Loew of Prague*. London.

TUAN, YI-FU. 1977. *Space and the Place: The Perspective of Experience*. Minneapolis.

YASSIF, ELI. 1991. Introduction (Heb.) to *The Golem of Prague and Other Tales of Wonder* [Hagolem miprag uma'asim nifla'im aherim], 7–72. Jerusalem.

——2008. 'The Dance of the Ari'. In Haya Bar-Itzhak and Idit Pintel-Ginsberg, eds., *The Power of a Tale: The Jubilee Book of IFA* [Koho shel sipur. Sefer hayovel le'asai], 82–4. Haifa.

Wearing Many Hats: Hair-Covering among Orthodox Jewish Women in Amish Country

AMY K. MILLIGAN

OUR INTERVIEW had just concluded, and Vicki and I parted ways. Nearly four hours had passed in a local coffee shop as we got to know one another and chatted about hair-covering. Deciding to get one last refill before I drove home, I approached the counter alone. As I waited for my coffee, another customer rested her hand on my arm. 'It's such a great thing that you are supporting your friend as she goes through this difficult time. I'm sure it means a lot to her', she nodded reassuringly. The blank look on my face elicited an attempt at clarification. 'When I had my cancer, it was friends like you that kept me going', she explained. I smiled, responding, 'She doesn't have cancer. She's an Orthodox Jew.'

This type of mistaken identity is not unheard of for Orthodox women. Although hair-covering is a concrete expression of observance that serves to differentiate levels of religiosity and mark group allegiance to those within Orthodoxy, it is more often than not a misunderstood or misassigned marker in society at large. This is especially true for Orthodox women in Lancaster, Pennsylvania, known internationally as Amish country because of its agrarian settlements of plain-dressing, horse-and-buggy Amish and Old Order Mennonites that draw over ten million tourists annually. Women in this milieu who cover their hair are often mistaken for Mennonites or questioned about hair loss. In a locale where most tourists as well as residents assume there are few, if any, Jews, many observers are surprised to discover a small, religiously observant Orthodox community tucked away in the heart of Amish country. Residents are familiar with the head coverings (*Kapp* or *Kopp* in Pennsylvania German dialect) worn by 'plain' Amish and Mennonite women, usually consisting of bonnets, scarves, or sheer or organdie fabric worn over the hair (Hostetler 2005: 206–8; Kraybill 2001: 57–63; Scott 1986: 96–103). Most onlookers are, however, less au fait with the hair-covering practices of Orthodox Jewish women. Orthodox women's hair-covering after marriage is a *siman nisuin* (sign of marriage), and although the majority of Jews have abandoned this practice, it is still the expected norm within Orthodoxy. However, removed from larger urban settings where communities are familiar with their Orthodox neighbours, observant women in places like

Lancaster often find themselves misunderstood. Likewise, their role has gone largely unrecognized by the academy. There are relatively few studies of Orthodox Jews living outside urban and suburban areas (see Diamond 2000; Gordon 1959; Levinger 1952; Rose 1977; Showstack 1988; Sklare 1967; Weissbach 2005), and those that have been published frequently focus on the male experience as centrally important to the maintenance of the community.

This essay begins by offering a brief introduction to the Orthodox community at Degel Israel Synagogue, where I have participated regularly as an ethnographic observer. Following this overview, I offer an introduction to the women who were interviewed to help contextualize their hair-covering choices. I hypothesized that, among the cultural practices typically associated with Orthodox identity (for example, observance of *kashrut* and the sabbath), hair-covering is important to women as a way of publicly identifying themselves as Orthodox. In addition to considering the women's explanations of their personal motivations, this contextualized approach also takes into account motivations of which they may not be conscious. On this basis I argue that the diversity of hair-covering practices helps to create boundaries that enable the women, through self-identification, to negotiate the challenges of living in a small religious community.

Orthodox Jewry in Amish Country

The women whom I interviewed are all members of the Degel Israel Synagogue, an Orthodox congregation in Lancaster, Pennsylvania. Situated in the heart of Amish country, the synagogue is distinctive. Lancaster was home to the first Jewish community in central Pennsylvania, as one of the few cities in the United States that could boast a pre-Revolutionary War Jewish settlement established as early as 1747 (see Brener 1979). However, unlike Harrisburg and York, this area of Pennsylvania is no longer associated with a Jewish, especially Orthodox, population. With approximately 508,000 residents, Lancaster County is home to about 6 per cent of the state's population. The area is predominantly white (93.2 per cent) and American-born (96.8 per cent) (US Census Bureau 2011a). The city of Lancaster is more racially diverse, with only 61.6 per cent of residents identifying as white but with most other demographics remaining quite similar (US Census Bureau 2011b). The most recent Lancaster County statistics on religious organizations identify 470,658 individuals who are affiliated to a particular religion—about 93 per cent of the total population. Of these, approximately 5,000 residents are considered religiously 'Other', including those who identify as Baha'i, Church of Jesus Christ of Latter-day Saints, Hindu, Jewish, Muslim, and Unitarian Universalist (ARD 2010a).

Lancaster County is not only predominantly white—it is also overwhelmingly Christian. With almost 90,000 evangelical Protestants and an equal number of mainline Protestants, coupled with nearly 50,000 Catholics and over 240,000 other self-identifying Christians, 92 per cent of the local population are Christian, which is about 10 per cent above the national average (ARD 2010b). Members of the three local synagogues are certainly in the minority.

Unlike other conservative religious groups in the area—for example, the Amish, Conservative Brethren, or Old Order Mennonites—Orthodox Jews are not typically a rurally based group. Although they share with the plain groups some sense of living counter-culturally, their lifestyles are significantly more modern. In distinction to most members of the plain communities, Orthodox Jews are employed by and interact with the local community, have attended secular colleges and graduate schools, and are fully versed in technology. The dress for most Jews at Degel is not noticeably different from that of their non-plain neighbours. Even Orthodox Jews who wear more traditional dress embody a paradox of modernity with their cell phones holstered at their hips. While they defy typical patterns of acculturation, they have created and maintained a careful balance of assimilation and counter-culturalism.

Out of the more than 6 million Jews living in the United States (about 1.7 per cent of the total population), approximately 295,000 Jews are in Pennsylvania (Sheskin and Dashefsky 2010: 20), making up 2.3 per cent of the state's population (ARD 2010b: 43). There are an estimated 3,000 Jews living in the Lancaster area, constituting only 0.59 per cent of the local population (ARD 2010b: 66). There is reason to believe, however, that this number is significantly inflated. In reply to my telephone enquiries on 10 January 2011, the local Reform congregation reported a membership of 353, and the local Conservative synagogue identified 158 current members, significantly less than the 3,000 Jews reported in national statistics. This discrepancy could be explained by the presence of a large non-observant constituency of Jews who still identified themselves as Jewish on the survey or by the inclusion of non-local college students.

It is difficult to calculate an exact membership for Degel Israel. Around eighty families are paying members at the synagogue. In this system, an individual as well as a family of four are counted as a single unit. Further complicating this count is that some of these families do not attend the synagogue and hold membership elsewhere. They maintain membership to honour a historic family affiliation, as a means of supporting a struggling congregation, or as a sign of solidarity. Some local Conservative Jews hold dual membership in order to be able to send their children to Degel Israel's Hebrew school, as the Conservative Hebrew school is extremely small. Sabbath morning services typically garner between ten to twenty men and five to ten women, about 1 per cent of local Jewry and 0.005 per cent of the general local population.

There are roughly 324,000 Orthodox adults and 205,000 Orthodox children in the United States, yielding a total of approximately 529,000 practising American Orthodox individuals (United Jewish Communities 2004: 9). Hence, the Orthodox population of the United States comprises only 10 per cent of the

American ethnic Jewish population (ARD 2010b: 6). The north-east is home to a disproportionate number of Orthodox Jews: 41 per cent of American Jews live in the north-east, but 68 per cent of Orthodox Jews reside there (ARD 2010b: 16). It is no surprise, then, that Degel Israel finds itself in this region—but it fails to conform to the general trend of Jewish urbanization. Contemporary American Jews, as a whole, are city dwellers. This is especially true of the Orthodox (Diamond 2000: 5). Those living in suburbia or in isolated communities are forced to contend with the difficult dynamic of balancing community integration, traditionalism, and spiritual cohesion. Those Jews living in suburbia generally live in rather homogeneous religious communities where, as Etan Diamond describes it, they share 'backgrounds, attitudes, and lifestyles [which] create a sense of community among congregational members, who look out for one another, offering help in times of need and a smile in times of happiness' (ARD 2010b: 6; see Sklare 1967; Weissbach 2005). This homogeneity is, however, not true of Degel Israel.

Located an hour north of metropolitan Baltimore and two hours west of Philadelphia, Degel Israel has become home to what can only be described as a mixed group of Orthodoxy. Were the same individuals to live in a different location, they surely would have subdivided into separate synagogues based on levels of observance and religious belief. Geographical isolation has, however, brought them together under one roof. Although other small and struggling Orthodox synagogues might compromise and merge with Conservative congregations, Degel Israel's members have resisted such change. Their self-identification as Orthodox is strongly associated with their traditional worship style. Although levels of home observance vary, services have a commonly accepted structure—gender-segregated seating, only men at the *bimah* (altar), modest dress, a fully Hebrew liturgy, and traditional interpretations of the text. Their levels of observance may vary, but their shared identity is decidedly more traditional than that of the local Conservative synagogue. Despite their differences, they are wholly dependent on each other if they wish to have a local Orthodox community.

Unlike the Jews of nearby Harrisburg, Pennsylvania, and other suburban Orthodox populations who maintain a distinct Jewish neighbourhood, Lancaster's Orthodoxy is spread out not only around the city but also in the county. Only the most observant—about ten families—live within walking distance of the synagogue. It is due to this, and to the lack of a distinct Orthodox neighbourhood, that most of Degel Israel's members are the only Orthodox Jews—and sometimes the only Jews—in their neighbourhoods. Their Jewish community experience, then, must entirely revolve around the synagogue.

Ranging from Belz hasidim to Modern Orthodox families who are not strictly observant of sabbath laws, the congregation could not be more diverse. One only needs to take a quick glance into the sanctuary on Saturday mornings to be made aware of the striking diversity. Rather than similarly clad individuals praying together, dress in the men's section ranges from *shtreimls* (fur hats worn by hasidic men) and caftans with knee socks to baseball caps and jeans. Likewise, the appearance of the women ranges from *frum* (religiously devout) with completely covered hair and a long dress covering the ankles to short-sleeved dresses with free-flowing locks. It is, however, only through the acceptance of such a diverse membership that Degel Israel is able to persist—forcing members to deal with these tensions in light of the need to maintain a shared community identity.

Hair-Covering Practices at Degel Israel Synagogue

This study focuses on six out of the eight women at Degel Israel Synagogue who cover their hair: Debbie, Chaya, Haddasah, Kathy, Naomi, and Vicki (there were two women who did not participate in the study[1]). In addition to these eight women, there are at least three who cover their hair only at religious services, and one woman who wears a wig to cover thinning hair but does not do so for religious reasons. The women were asked a set list of thirty questions in order to establish a basis for comparison, but they were also encouraged to share personal anecdotes and opinions. Interviews generally lasted about an hour and a half, with the longest running into a fourth hour. Four women chose to meet me in their home, while two elected to meet in a local coffee shop.

The women range in age from 49 to 58. Married, they each have between one and five children. Although Chaya is the only one whose mother covers her hair, the women's married daughters and daughters-in-law all follow this practice. All of the women are high school graduates; Chaya and Vicki attended college, and Kathy and Debbie hold graduate degrees. With the exception of Naomi, they are all employed outside the home. Their professions include owning and operating a well-known local business, writing a newspaper column, working as a prominent attorney, serving as president of a telecommunications business, and overseeing Jewish educational programming. For most of the women, their location in Lancaster is directly related to their jobs or the employment of their spouse. None of the women is a Lancaster County native.

Although all six are affiliated to Orthodoxy, the women classify themselves differently. Chaya prefers the term 'Observant' to Orthodox because of the variety of ways that the word can be interpreted. Likewise, Debbie prefers to be called 'Torah-observant'. Kathy and Naomi self-identify solely as 'Orthodox'; Vicki considers herself 'Modern Orthodox', and Haddasah specifies that she is a member of the Belz hasidim. All six women keep kosher kitchens and are sabbath observant.

Not all of the women were raised in observant families. Only Chaya and Haddasah grew up Orthodox. Vicki and Debbie both come from Conservative families and consider themselves *ba'alot teshuvah* (Jews who recommit themselves to Judaism and begin to live a religiously observant lifestyle). Naomi has a

Figure 1 Wig with hair stopping short of the shoulders in a style typically chosen by older Orthodox women, who generally prefer shorter styles. Younger women will often choose longer wigs that can be pulled back into a bun or ponytail. This wig is made of human hair, but synthetic hair is often used because it is cheaper. *Photograph by Amy K. Milligan*

hard time classifying her past. Although she was raised in a family where it was acceptable for women to wear trousers, her upbringing was somewhat observant. From her description, her family seems to fall somewhere between the hybrid label of 'Conservadox' and Modern Orthodox. Kathy, raised a United Methodist, had a Conservative conversion when she got married. Later, as she and her husband became more observant, she underwent a second, Orthodox, conversion. Similarly, not all of the women began covering their hair immediately after they married. Only Chaya and Haddasah, not coincidentally the only two raised Orthodox, did so from the outset. Kathy, Vicki, Debbie, and Naomi only began to cover their hair as they became more religiously observant.

The women use a variety of methods to cover their hair. Unlike in other communities, where hair-covering choices are more standardized, the women at Degel Israel are not restricted in choosing the type of hair covering that best suits them and meets their needs. Chaya wears a wig outside the synagogue. On the sabbath or when teaching at the Hebrew school, she wears a hat or a snood (a close-fitting hood that encases the hair in a small sack). She does this to ensure that it is clear that her hair is covered, as a good wig can often be mistaken for real hair. Although Vicki, Kathy, Haddasah, and Naomi own wigs, they rarely wear them, generally saving them only for weddings or other special events. Naomi favours pre-tied scarves and wears them almost exclusively. Vicki, on the other hand, wears a variety of scarves, hats, and snoods. Kathy is known as 'the hat lady'

TABLE 1 Head-covering types worn by women members of the Degel Israel Synagogue in different social situations

Name	In the synagogue	In public	At home with guests	At home with family	Special events	At night
Chaya	hat snood	wig	wig	wig	wig	scarf
Naomi	scarf	scarf	scarf		wig	
Kathy	hat	hat	hat		wig	
Debbie	scarf	scarf	scarf	scarf	scarf	
Haddasah	wig with hat	scarf	scarf	scarf	wig	scarf
Vicki	hat snood scarf	hat snood scarf	hat snood scarf	hat snood scarf	wig	

by her colleagues. She has a large collection of hats, ranging from understated to eye-catching. She has made hats her fashion trademark, which she believes helps to keep others focused on her professional role rather than on her religious observance. Haddasah greatly dislikes her wig and rarely wears it, unless she feels that a social situation necessitates it. She wears snoods and pre-tied scarves, but sadly laments that she does not live in a community where *shpitzls* (a head covering worn by some hasidic women that has a braid of hair across the front and is covered by a scarf) are the norm. Debbie is the only woman who never wears a wig. She feels strongly that they defeat the purpose of hair-covering. She ties her own scarves and even had a custom-made scarf created to match the dress she recently wore to her son's wedding.

Of the six women interviewed, only Naomi dyes and professionally styles her hair. Kathy will occasionally have a professional haircut, but also trims her own hair. Vicki, Debbie, and Chaya all cut their own hair and do not colour it. It is only in recent years that Haddasah has allowed her hair to grow out. Previously, like some other hasidic women, she had kept her head shaved, but now she trims the ends as needed.

Another significant variation is whether or not the women keep their hair covered at all times. Both Chaya and Haddasah cover their hair all the time, even when sleeping.[2] Vicki and Debbie cover their hair at all times while awake, but do not cover their hair when asleep. Kathy and Naomi both keep their hair covered when they are outside the house or when guests are visiting. However, in the home and in the presence of immediate family or select close female friends they do not always keep their hair covered.

The final striking difference between the women is their attendance at religious services. Although all of them are sabbath observant, only Chaya and Naomi regularly attend the sabbath morning services at Degel Israel. Debbie is equally active, but almost always chooses to stay with friends in order to go to the larger Orthodox synagogue in Harrisburg, Pennsylvania. Kathy attends about half the sabbath services; however, Vicki and Haddasah never attend services or other events at Degel Israel. Both participated in Saturday morning services for many years, but after some social tensions arose between their families and the rabbi's family, only their husbands continued to attend.

Hair and *Yiddishkeit*

The women of Degel Israel exist as a minority on four levels: as Jews they are already within an American minority group. Within Judaism, Orthodoxy is the minority, and within their local secular community they are the extreme minority. In addition, they represent the few among Degel Israel who have chosen to cover their hair. They are geographically situated in an area unfamiliar with Judaism, especially Orthodoxy. Their beliefs and lifestyle are both unusual and foreign to their neighbours. Even those within their community do not always understand and support their religious choices. Haddasah describes her experience saying, 'Most of the people in this community don't think like me at all. I have loads of friends online, other *hasidishe* women. I need that. I didn't think I was going to need it [when I moved to Lancaster], but I do.' Vicki quips, 'I mean, really, a Jewish woman's worst enemy is, well, another Jewish woman. I honestly feel that way. If you don't go along with the crowd, they try to make you an outcast. That's sometimes what I feel, but it's mostly in small communities. If we were in a larger community, certain people wouldn't even be here. They would have moved out [of Degel Israel] a long time ago. They wouldn't have been tolerated.'

If the same group of women was located in an area with a higher Orthodox population, in addition to subdividing into separate religious communities they would also find themselves subject to greater social pressure to conform. Rather than having social norms imposed upon them by their neighbours and religious community, the women at Degel Israel elect to uphold religious laws. Their Christian neighbours would not know the difference if they drove on the sabbath or if they did not cover their hair.[3] Likewise, the Lancaster Orthodox community would continue to accept them regardless of their choices. Why, then, do these women embrace hair-covering? There seem to be three primary motivations— the externalization of their religious commitment, the wish to mark their level of observance, and their children.

With the exception of Haddasah and Chaya, the women have all had a turning point in their religious lives where they recommitted themselves to Judaism.

Debra Renee Kaufman's analysis in *Rachel's Daughters: Newly Orthodox Jewish Women* is helpful when considering the motivations of the women of Degel Israel (Kaufman 1991). Kaufman only briefly addresses hair and hair-covering in her work, but she clearly considers hair an expressive marker of religious devotion. In the case of newly Orthodox women, covered hair functions as a demonstrable sign of Orthodoxy to both the wearer and the viewer. This is especially true because of the prominent place of covering on the head, demonstrating both an individual choice and the acceptance of a group-established collective appearance.

Both the women in Kaufman's case study and those at Degel Israel use their hair as an expression of their *yiddishkeit* (traditional Judaism). They move away from the secular world in which they were raised and use their hair to mark themselves as newly and decidedly Orthodox. Although the women in Kaufman's study frequently stated their distaste and distrust regarding what they perceived as a hypersexualized society, the women of Degel Israel rarely speak of the secular world in terms of sex. Rather, they focus on the emptiness that they felt before they increased their level of observance. Indeed, it is through this spiritual quest for truth that they have turned to Orthodoxy. Through the reappropriation of their hair, turning it from a fashion accessory to an expression of the sacred, they mark themselves as part of a religious community that is decidedly different from the secular culture they knew earlier. It is their way of distinguishing and 'othering' themselves from their neighbours, families, and previous lifestyle, as well as aligning themselves with their new community.

In their Lancaster County context, this idea of living as religiously other is familiar to their secular neighbours. The women may not theologically agree with the local Amish and Mennonite residents—Anabaptists compose almost 12 per cent of the local population (ARD 2010a)—but they express a certain degree of empathy for the counter-cultural lifestyle choices of plain groups, and appear bolstered by their persistence. Haddasah explains, 'I'm always being asked what I am . . . I have a lot of Amish friends. They kind of understand the whole thing. But they ask me, "Do you cover your hair for the same reason that we are [sic]?" Maybe not exactly, but I'm not going to get into a whole big thing about it. I just say, "Yes, that's it." You know, for religious reasons.' Debbie also finds the area to be fairly tolerant of religious clothing choices because of the local Anabaptist population. She recounts, 'When my son was younger, I never had a problem letting him go into the movie theater bathroom or anything with his *yarmulke*. 'Cause most people in Lancaster wouldn't know a *yarmulke* from a hat. There's so many people walking around here with different stuff on their heads, no one notices any more.'

In their move towards Orthodoxy, these women took on several other important Jewish practices: they uphold the laws of *nidah* (sexual purity), keep kosher homes, and are sabbath observant. None of these, however, is easily demonstrable publicly. Whether it is for their extended families, their local community, or even themselves, hair-covering serves as an external marker of their observance of these other traditions. This externalization also helps to frame and reclaim distinct gender roles, which they believe the secular world to have blurred. Their hair-covering indicates observance within the Orthodox community and, perhaps even more importantly in the Lancaster context, marks them as Jewish women to their secular neighbours. Just as their husbands and sons wear *kipot* (skullcaps) and *tsitsit* (knotted ritual fringes), these women use hair-covering as a public expression of belief. They are Jews not only privately in the home, but also publicly in the street.

Hair-covering could easily be forgone in such a small and diverse community. Indeed, when I made initial enquiries concerning which women covered their hair outside synagogue services, community members struggled to reach a consensus. Living in relative isolation from one another, Degel Israel members do not always have full knowledge of their religious community. The social pressure that one might experience in a more homogeneous environment is much less noticeable here. Women must then choose to regulate for themselves their hair-covering practices. For the most part, other synagogue members would have no way of knowing if these women chose to forgo head-covering during the working week, which is a major difference compared to the realities of predominantly Jewish neighbourhoods.

Several of the women I interviewed mentioned Azriela Jaffe's book, *What Do You Mean, You Can't Eat in My Home? A Guide to How Newly Observant Jews and Their Less Observant Relatives Can Still Get Along* (2005). Jaffe, a former Lancaster resident, is a prominent writer, professional speaker, and Jewish educator. Writing extensively on Jewish topics, she specializes in the role of Orthodox women in the family, especially in terms of negotiating traditionalism with modernity. Several of the Lancaster women pointed to Jaffe as an example of the importance of hair-covering. Although Jaffe had been a popular hostess in the Lancaster community, after she relocated to New Jersey members of her new synagogue were not receptive to her invitations. Finally, after several months, she directly questioned another synagogue member. She was told that it was because of her hair-covering choices that others chose not to dine in her home. They were unsure if she kept an adequately kosher kitchen because of her uncovered hair.[4]

This often told anecdote clearly expresses the anxieties of the women of Degel Israel. Even those who adhere to the most meticulous of private observances could be thought non-observant if they failed to cover their hair. When recommitting themselves to Judaism, all four women identified their first step as keeping a kosher kitchen—including the prohibition of non-kosher products, having separate utensils, plates, and cookware for dairy and meat foods, the *kashering* (rendering something kosher) of sinks, glassware, and dishwashers, and the removal of all non-kosher items. As they increased their level of observance, the women struggled with the idea of hair-covering. As Debbie describes it, 'It's usually the last thing people do [when they become observant]. It's the most noticeable for people to question you about. You're doing something that everyone sees. Keeping a kosher home, no one has to see.' Raised in synagogues where hair-covering was not normative and living in a community where most Orthodox women did not follow this practice required the newly religious women of Degel Israel to exhibit a significant commitment to Orthodox Judaism. Beginning to publicly cover their hair 'othered' them from their secular environment and was, in all cases, the final step in the recommitment process.

The women at Degel Israel, in line with much of contemporary Orthodoxy, distinguish between FFB and BT—shorthand for '*frum* from birth', which refers to those who were raised Orthodox and '*ba'alot teshuvah*', women who have recommitted themselves to Judaism. Hair-covering as a means of distinguishing themselves as religiously observant is not only important to those who have increased their religious observance over time. Haddasah and Chaya, the only two in the group who are considered FFB, use hair-covering as a marker of their own long-standing commitment to the religious lifestyle. Chaya describes the importance she attributes to covering her hair with the following words: 'You feel like you are observing another commandment, even though it is a more implicit than explicit commandment. You feel like, you know, it is another thing you are doing to be observant. And also, you feel like this gives me the status that I know that I cover my hair.'

None of the women I interviewed is a native of Lancaster County. Except for Naomi, all of the women who identify as BT had relocated to the area prior to recommitting themselves to Judaism.[5] Haddasah and Chaya, on the other hand, already covered their hair when they moved to Lancaster. Entering a community where there was such a vast diversity within Orthodoxy, hair-covering was an expressive way to mark themselves as religiously observant. For both women, it was unthinkable that they would cease to cover their hair after relocating. They were both fully committed to the practice, as it was an integral part of their self-identity as Orthodox Jewish women.[6] Haddasah reminisces, 'Before [in Brooklyn], there were women who covered their hair everywhere. Very *frum*. Very *tznius* [modest]. But now, you know, I'm more alone. By myself.'

Several women articulated the difficulty of moving to a small community. Naomi muses, 'From going to a big city to going to this, well it's a change. Yes, a big change from Baltimore. Usually it's the other way around. You move from here to the city.' Haddasah agrees, noting, 'This is a challenge sometimes. It is really hard. There are a lot more politics involved here. There are much more than there are in Brooklyn, 'cause everybody is, well, there are just so few [Orthodox] here.' Unlike the others, Chaya, Naomi, and Haddasah know what it is like living in a larger Orthodox community. Although all of the women expressed the great difficulty experienced when living in an area with such a small Orthodox population, these three, in particular, mused over how much easier it is to live in an Orthodox neighbourhood.[7] Haddasah explained, 'It's everything. The food, the people, neighbourhood, community. Now the only other modestly dressed women I see are Mennonites.'

Chaya and Haddasah's decision to continue to cover their hair, even when the community around them does not, seems to indicate a desire to maintain a connection to the communities that they left. Particularly in the case of Haddasah, who strongly identifies herself as a member of the Belz hasidim—of which she and her husband are the only members in Lancaster County—her hair-covering choices indicate her continued self-identification with the larger Belz community. Although Belz hasidim can be found throughout the world, they are particularly concentrated in Israel and Brooklyn, New York—specifically in the neighbourhood of Borough Park. After near-obliteration during the Holocaust, they have rebounded to become the largest hasidic group in Borough Park. In Samuel Heilman's description, Belz hasidim are 'associated with extreme counter-acculturationist views, rejecting all compromises with secularity' (Heilman 1999: 49; see also pp. 47–69). Haddasah and her husband are living in a cultural diaspora, separated from the rest of their religious community. Haddasah's hair-covering is one way that they can forge a connection between the group that they desire to be a part of and their reality.

For all of the women, their choice to cover their hair is perhaps most important in terms of the greater—rather than the local—Orthodox community. All six women are mothers and consider their hair-covering to have a crucial impact on their children. They perceive this as occurring on two levels. First, the women consider their decision to cover their hair a critical demonstration to their children of the importance of religious observance. As Chaya explains, 'Mothers mould their kids. Moms make a Jewish home Jewish, you know, showing their kids what's important. When she covers her hair, she shows them that, well, she's not afraid to be a Jew when she's not in *shul* (synagogue) or at home. You know, like saying to her kids that she's a Jew 24/7.' In other words, these women believe that through choosing to cover their hair they can influence their children to commit to an Orthodox lifestyle. Although they all indicate that this is the case with children of both genders, they seem particularly concerned with their daughters' future spirituality and practice. Collectively, the women—through their educational choices for their children and their own role-modelling—have attempted to instil in their children the importance and benefits of religious observance.

The second level that the women see as having an impact on their children is in the matchmaking process. As they look for partners for their children, they are highly aware of the role that their hair-covering plays in the process. Some will use a professional Orthodox matchmaker, in this case from Baltimore, who will take into account whether or not potential mates' mothers cover their hair, as well as whether or not the unmarried female intends to cover her hair after marriage. It serves as a strong indicator of the level of religious observance adhered to by the individuals and their families. Lack of hair covering could potentially have a detrimental impact on the matchmaking process. As Kathy explains, 'If it were just me, I might not ever wear a *sheitl* [wig; i.e. instead of a hat]. This may sound crass, but I do it for the sake of my children, for their *shidukhim* [matches].'

A further reason that hair-covering plays such a crucial role in the matchmaking process is that, unlike in other communities where families are familiar with each other and live locally, the children of my interviewees are forced to seek matches outside the Lancaster community. There simply are not enough young Orthodox singles at Degel Israel, nor are they all seeking the same level of observance in potential mates. To prospective partners who are unfamiliar with them, both the interested youth and their parents have to make clear their position on the scale of observance. Hair-covering, in this regard, functions as a form of matchmaking currency. Chaya explains, 'You cover your hair—that means you have a certain level of observancy . . . It's a barometer. Fair or not fair, it's a barometer.' It is an evaluative tool that individuals and families use to assess the level of religious observance of their possible partners.

With no Orthodox Jewish day schools in the locality and because they are tied to Lancaster County by employment, Kathy, Chaya, Debbie, and Naomi all chose to send their children to Orthodox schools in Baltimore, requiring a daily commute of over an hour each way. This choice has helped to ensure that their children would build up a social network in Baltimore, which has a sizable Orthodox population. Of the women I interviewed, only Debbie and Chaya have married children; their matches were all made through their Baltimore connections. Both feel that choosing to cover their hair influenced their match-making process. Chaya elaborates,

In fact, [my daughters] looked for a spouse who would want their wife to cover their hair, because that shows a level of commitment, and they want someone who is at that same level of commitment that they are. Just makes it so much easier. If you hook up with a guy who it doesn't matter [to], that already shows that you aren't on the same wavelength. So, the more you have in common, the better it is. You know, you start on an even plateau as you embark on marriage.

Kathy feels additional pressure to cover her hair in order to enhance her children's matchmaking potential. When in Baltimore, she abandons her hat for a wig, considered the norm in certain circles. This is especially important to her when she visits her children's schools. She explains, 'I do have a *sheitl* [wig], but I have to say that's mostly for the benefit of my children. Like if we go to Baltimore, a wedding, or some social function where I'll be around my children's friends and their families, I'll wear a *sheitl* so that I fit in better.' Although she does not directly acknowledge this, as a convert she probably also feels a certain amount of pressure to prove herself. Hair-covering is the easiest way to publicly demonstrate her commitment to observance.

For Vicki the initial decision to cover her hair was also linked to her children, but in a different way. She explains, 'My daughter had gone to Israel, and she wasn't having a very good year. So, I decided to take [hair-covering] on as a *mitzvah*. I figured it would be kind of for good luck.' After some time, Vicki saw other benefits for her children deriving from her choice. She is the only one of the six women who sent her children through the local public school system. They were often the only Jewish students in their grade and were certainly the only Orthodox Jews in their school. They had no social network in Baltimore to draw on in trying to find potential spouses. Therefore, it became even more important to Vicki that she demonstrate her family's heightened observance through her hair-covering. In a way, her actions helped compensate for the fact that her children had not gone through the Orthodox Jewish day school system.

Haddasah's children had all completed their education before she relocated to Lancaster. Still, in her children's matchmaking processes, her hair-covering played a crucial role; it retained her family's social ties to the Belz hasidim. She expressed a strong desire for her children to marry other hasidic Jews and believes that her personal level of observance helped encourage this endogamy. In the case of her youngest son, who was having difficulty finding a match, Haddasah prayed while lighting sabbath candles, saying, 'I don't know if this is important to you or not, but if something comes up for [my son], I will cover my *sheitl* [with a second head-covering] on Shabbos [the sabbath] and cover my head at night.' She considered briefly rescinding this offer to God, wondering if it was really necessary to cover her hair at night. Encouraged by her son and husband, who told her, 'You made a promise to Hashem [God]! Now you know! No [rescinding] promises to God!' Haddasah realized the power that her promise of hair-covering had exerted over her family.

For the most part, the women interviewed had consciously reflected on their hair-covering choices. There are, however, several factors that appear to motivate them subconsciously: a desire to set themselves apart and identify with other observant women in response to the challenges of living in a small community; a desire to take part, as women, in Jewish practice, and the impact of living in a small community on their personal selection of hair coverings.

Although none of the women directly addressed the idea that hair-covering served as a way of distinguishing themselves from the rest of local Orthodoxy, it does appear to serve such a function. If these women lived in larger, homogeneous communities, their concerns regarding perception of their observance would be likely to decrease. Instead, they find themselves constantly negotiating the stresses of living in an undefined community. The importance of this lack of definition is paramount. Unlike other communities—for example, Williamsburg and Monsey, New York, or even Baltimore—that expect strict observance, one's

Jewish practice, as a member of the Lancaster Orthodox community, could fall anywhere along the spectrum. With so many rituals observed privately, hair-covering is the only public way for the women of Degel Israel to distinguish themselves from other, less observant, local Jews. It also marks them as belonging to the stricter Orthodox Jews within Degel Israel's membership.

The decision to cover their hair, then, creates a cultural link between the Lancaster women and other Orthodox women. Much like Haddasah uses her hair to represent her Belz identity, the other women also perceive hair-covering as a means of identifying with Orthodoxy at large. Unlike their children—who have almost all moved away from Lancaster to settle in areas with higher Orthodox populations—the women of Degel Israel walk a lonely road of observance. With no general cohesion in community ideology, including hair-covering, they represent, through their individual choices, the groups that they would associate with if their geographical situation were altered.

This self-identification process is intrinsically linked to my interviewees' understanding of Jewish law. Although women in larger communities base much of their decision-making process on group cohesion and social pressure, the women at Degel Israel are, in essence, left to their own devices. Although Chaya's choice as the rabbi's wife could serve as a model for hair-covering techniques, none of the women follow her methods. Haddasah's choices are probably influenced by Belzer rabbinic decisions, but there has been no local rabbinic guidance officially provided at Degel Israel. For those who are newly observant, hair-covering is an entry point into an expression of their newly found religious identity. As their world-view evolved, so did their external appearance. All highly educated, these women have elected, in their search for spiritual truth, to add an external dimension to their internal transformation. In an environment that did not necessitate such a decision, social pressure cannot be seen as the source of their choice to cover their hair. Rather, through their own careful consideration, these women have used hair-covering to reaffirm separate gender roles at the same time as offering a uniquely feminine expression of spirituality.

For those women raised within Orthodoxy, hair-covering represents a continued personal relationship to ritual. Although it is not commonly practised as a form of Jewish ritual observance, it has become more than just religious costuming. Through their daily choice to uphold hair-covering, these women have sacralized the act. Much in the same way that their husbands ritually put on tefillin, they cover their hair in a spiritual act that embodies their continued commitment to observance. This is particularly important in the framework of Degel Israel, as the women there struggle to negotiate traditionalism in a more liberal setting. Their choice to adhere to the standards established by Orthodox communities elsewhere rather than adopt the less stringent norm of Lancaster demonstrates the special importance of hair-covering as a ritualized behaviour given the women's geographical context.

When the synagogue fails to create the community that the women aspire to, they take matters into their own hands. Forced to always host social meals if they wish to eat at them—not all families at Degel Israel adhere to the same levels of *kashrut*—and working to create the type of community in which they wish their children to grow up, these women are bulwarks against assimilation. They consciously think about and engage in Jewish ritual on a daily basis. In such a small community there is always work to be done, and they often find themselves as the voice of Lancaster Orthodoxy. Indeed, it is frequently their interpretation and application of Jewish law and ritual that defines the community's practice. In this way their identity has become closely linked to ritual. Even if non-observant Jews and secular neighbours do not recognize it, these women's acts serve as a constant reminder of their nonconformist identity as 'other', as well as of their boundaries within both the religious and local community.

This freedom of interpretation flourishes in a small society that struggles constantly to define itself. Female hair-covering is the clearest external example of shifting boundaries. When considering this, it is helpful to turn to Barbara Goldman Carrell's analysis of female head coverings presented in her article, 'Hasidic Women's Head Coverings' (Carrell 1999). Although her investigation centres on hasidic women, the hierarchy of hair-covering that she outlines seems applicable to the women of Degel Israel. Ranging from women who cover their hair with only scarves to women who exclusively wear human hair wigs, Carrell argues that hair-covering practices are concrete expressions of religious piety. In her hierarchy, the more obvious a woman's head covering—for example, a scarf —the more religiously observant she is. Carrell asserts that only more liberal hasidic women cover their heads with the less obtrusive human hair wigs. She explains, 'the different and ranked modes of Hasidic women's head coverings express, assert, or defend a woman's social position or level of cultural competence' (Carrell 1999: 174). The women's behaviour at Degel Israel mirrors those profiled in Carrell's study, demonstrating that head coverings are an essential part of religious costuming and clearly represent group adherence within a hierarchical model.

The women in Carrell's study are significantly influenced by the hasidic court with which they identify. In other words, there is relatively little autonomy involved in their choice of hair covering. This is, however, not the case at Degel Israel. With no standard community norm, the women are free to choose their own hair-covering methods. The curious phenomenon is, despite a comparatively liberal Orthodox environment with relatively limited social control, these women have elected, for the most part, to forgo wigs in favour of much more conservative scarves. Why would women like Kathy and Debbie, who have prominent positions in the secular community, opt not to wear a less conspicuous wig? And why do the other women wear more conservative head coverings than their situation necessitates?

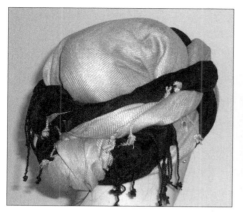 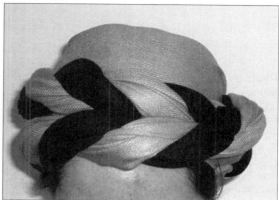

Figure 2 This scarf combines two scarves of different colours. The darker one serves as an accent to the lighter one, which actually covers the hair. The braided crown visible in the image on the right extends around the entire head to create an elaborate hair-covering. *Photograph by Amy K. Milligan*

Figure 3 A pre-tied scarf with a short tail. The short tails are knotted and used to help secure the scarf to the head. The tails are then tucked up under the knot at the nape of the neck. Orthodox women refer to this popular style as 'tikhl-bling' because of the design on the front. *Photograph by Amy K. Milligan*

The answer to these questions is embedded in both the lack of community definition and the women's self-perception. Interestingly, it is only Chaya who frequently dons a wig. This is likely to stem from two reasons—she was raised in an Orthodox community where wigs were the norm and, as the rebbetzin, her level of observance is not open to the same speculation as that of the others. She nevertheless feels it is important to wear more obvious head coverings when at synagogue events, suggesting that she understands the importance of her position as a role model for the community's women.

Haddasah expresses a desire to wear an even more conservative covering than she currently does. Her daughters and daughters-in-law, however, all wear wigs, despite identifying with the same hasidic court. Her aspiration to wear a *shpitzl*

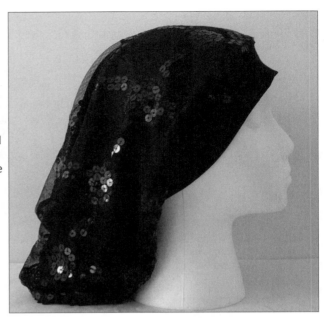

Figure 4 Snood worn by Orthodox women. This model has two layers: the inside shell is black and provides full hair coverage; the outer layer is sheer, and is sequinned. The two are attached to a cotton headband that is worn low over the forehead. Hair flows free in the snood, in contrast to the scarf, which typically conceals hair that has been secured in either a bun or a ponytail. *Photograph by Amy K. Milligan*

may stem from a need to distinguish herself as different from the scarf-wearing women at Degel Israel. She describes her wish to look like other more conservative hasidic women as follows:

With the very *hasidishe* women, I like the look. It's a very spiritual look. Now, it may not always be true, but when you look at them, you say to yourself, 'Wow, she's really got it all together.' Maybe you would be wrong, but a lot of women who cover that way are very very very very *tsniusdik* [modest]. I admire that. I can't help it. It communicates who you are, where you are.

As one of only two hasidic women at the synagogue,[8] Haddasah sees her identification with the local community as secondary to her affiliation with the Belz hasidim. Were she to live in a hasidic area, this detachment would not be necessary, as she would not have to negotiate a dual identity. Through wearing the most conservative hair covering among all Lancaster Orthodox women, she publicly marks herself as the most religiously observant. In essence, with her hair covering Haddasah establishes a boundary between herself and the rest of the women at Degel Israel.

Kathy's choice to wear hats is an individual compromise. One might expect a woman with such a highly public and high-powered job to opt for a wig. This would enable her to avoid questions and, if it were a top-quality wig, it would most probably go completely undetected by most colleagues. Hats, on the other hand, are a more prominent reminder of difference. General American fashion no longer has a hat culture, inviting others to wonder why Kathy always wears one.

Figure 5 Hats such as this black felt hat, worn during winter months or at formal occasions, represent the type of head covering worn by Orthodox women who do not cover their hair daily. *Photograph by Amy K. Milligan*

Hats are, however, significantly less obtrusive than scarves and can be more easily integrated into her professional wardrobe. They maintain a secular professional appearance, while serving as a public marker of religiosity. Unlike scarves, which would undercut Kathy's authority through the potential false interpretation of indicating female submission, her hats empower her to bring her Jewish sensibilities with her to work each day.

Debbie prefers to cover her head with a scarf. She never wears a wig, pointing out that 'It's hypocritical! Why would I cover my hair with hair that is probably more attractive than my real hair?' For her, '*Tikhls* [scarves] are a statement!' They represent her unapologetic commitment to living an observant lifestyle and, lest headscarves be criticized as old-fashioned, Debbie proves that they can be fashion-forward. Unlike the other women, who favour pre-tied scarves, Debbie ties her own and accessorizes them with headbands and accent scarves. She notes, 'Hair covering doesn't have to be frumpy—we can still look good, just without showing our hair, you know?' She goes on to explain that by covering her hair, she is 'saying to the world, "Yes, I am an observant Jew. I'm proud of it. I don't really care what you think. Here it is!"'

Vicki's and Naomi's choices appear to be equally individualized. For Naomi, it is the ease of wearing a scarf and its low cost that are appealing. Vicki finds it unsettling to see herself not looking natural and struggles, like several of the other women, with the idea of human hair wigs as she feels they may be immodest. She recounts, 'The first time I wore my *sheitl* was to my daughter's wedding, and no one recognized me!'

As I have explained above, for all of the women, their hair-covering choices serve to differentiate them from other women at Degel Israel. Although their hair-covering patterns do not fit into Carrell's hierarchy, they have established their own based on both actual and perceived levels of observance. By wearing a prominent head covering, they differentiate and distance themselves from the less observant members of Lancaster Orthodoxy, as well as from their non-Jewish neighbours. Chaya describes this variation in choices and practices eloquently, saying, 'That's the beauty of *yiddishkeit*—that we're not all one mould. Within the framework of halakhah, you find where you are most comfortable. And the bottom line is that we can't judge each other. You know, that's the bottom line.'

Conclusion: Hair and the Creation of Boundaries

It would be difficult to find an Orthodox community so diverse and yet so cohesive as Degel Israel. Recognizing that they must embrace their lack of uniformity in order to create the social support they desire, the members of the synagogue approach ritual with an open mind, allowing for Jews from a range of backgrounds to worship together. That said, there are external reminders of the divisions.

Like many other small synagogues, Degel Israel faces a daily struggle to survive. Members are in constant negotiation within synagogue leadership and communal practice to ensure that all of their voices are heard. Although their lack of community definition causes some strain, it should not be misconstrued as an indication of apathy. On the contrary, to be a participating member of Degel Israel requires constant active engagement with the others and the formation of a social boundary towards the outside world.

Living in a cultural diaspora, one of the ways that some of the women at Degel Israel articulate their distance from other Orthodox Jews is through their head-covering choices. Especially for women like Haddasah and Vicki, who no longer attend services or events at the synagogue, the sense of isolation can be overwhelming. Although they have been able to create some social support online, for the most part they travel whenever possible to be with other similarly minded Jews. The women are, at the same time, more or less fully integrated into the general Lancaster community, which forces them to build their social networks mainly of non-Jews. Their hair coverings serve as a way to distinguish themselves from the other women with whom they work and socialize. Likewise, as we have seen earlier, these same choices clearly represent differences in levels of observance within the synagogue.

Whether out of a conscious or subconscious decision, the women of Degel Israel who cover their hair do not make their choice lightly. It is not something that was forced on them, nor do they consider it patriarchal or oppressive. They perceive the practice as a crucial part of their self-identity and an embodiment of their spirituality. As Haddasah explains, 'I find [hair-covering] liberating! Going out with a covering on, except with a *sheitl* of course, does tell people, "This is what I am!" And I, yes, I like that.' Their daughters, for the most part, seem to be following their mothers' lead and are covering their hair after marriage, albeit almost exclusively with wigs.

With most of the members' children having relocated to areas with larger Orthodox populations, Degel Israel continues actively to seek new transplants to the area through hosting events, creating the Lancaster Yeshiva Center, and fundraising campaigns. Although this outreach suggests that hair-covering will continue among synagogue members due to sustained congregational membership, unless the community attracts a more homogeneous group of new residents, the variety of hair-covering techniques will persist. This diversity serves as an effective coping mechanism: it allows the women to wear three figurative hats wherein they identify as members of their local secular community, of Degel Israel, and of their own strain of Orthodoxy. With their hair-covering choices they construct the necessary boundaries and distinctions between themselves and those around them, creating definition and categories in a religious community that is largely undefined. Their path is sometimes lonely and they often feel isolated, but their adherence to hair-covering demonstrates their defiant attitude towards assimilation. Indeed, it is through these women's intense commitment to religious ritual and observance that Lancaster Orthodoxy continues to thrive.

Notes

1   One of the women, who identified as modern Orthodox, was unable to participate in this study because of scheduling conflicts, and another, a member of the Chabad Lubavitch hasidim, did not respond to my enquiries.

2   Chaya recalls that the only time she has intentionally left her hair uncovered was during childbirth. She had difficulty keeping a covering on during the end phase of labour and went without it. However, immediately after her children were born, she re-covered her hair. Haddasah began covering her hair at night during the matchmaking process for her one son. As she prayed for a match to be made, she offered to cover her hair even while sleeping if a good match could be found.

3   There is, however, a shared commitment between the Plain Anabaptist (e.g. Amish and Old Order Mennonite) and Orthodox Jewish communities to exhibiting and maintaining boundaries with the 'world' and its morally suspect popular culture.

4   According to several of the women, Jaffe has now decided to cover her hair. As an epilogue to the narrative of her social exclusion, the verifying comment expresses the significance of head-covering in response to social pressure in her new community.

5   Naomi's recommitment to Judaism occurred in conjunction with her moving to a different part of Baltimore and transferring synagogues.

6   Indeed, not all women who define themselves as Orthodox consider hair-covering to be part of their religious identity. This is part of the reason that the women in this study feel strongly about identifying themselves as Orthodox not only nominally but also in practice.

7   Even the smallest of tasks becomes more difficult in such a small community. With no local kosher restaurants, if observant people want to eat out they are limited to either the kosher section of Franklin and Marshall College's cafeteria or, during the summer months, the imbiss-style food at the kosher stand at Dutch Wonderland. Likewise, the bulk of their grocery shopping has to be done in Baltimore.

8   The only other hasidic woman, a member of Chabad Lubavitch, has always been seen wearing a wig.

References

ARD (Association of Religion Data) Archives. 2010a. 'County Membership Report: Lancaster County, Pennsylvania'. <http://www.thearda.com/mapsReports/reports/counties/42071_2000.asp>, accessed 28 Dec. 2010.

——— 2010b. 'National Profiles: The United States, General'. <http://www.thearda.com/internationalData/countries/Country_234_1.asp>, accessed 28 Dec. 2010.

BRENER, DAVID. 1979. The Jews of Lancaster, Pennsylvania: A Story with Two Beginnings. Lancaster, Pa.

CARRELL, BARBARA GOLDMAN. 1999. 'Hasidic Women's Head Coverings'. In Linda B. Arthur, ed., Religion, Dress and the Body, 163–80. Oxford.

DIAMOND, ETAN. 2000. And I Will Dwell in their Midst: Orthodox Jews in Suburbia. Chapel Hill, NC.

GORDON, ALBERT. 1959. Jews in Suburbia. Boston.

HEILMAN, SAMUEL. 1999. Defenders of the Faith: Inside Ultra-Orthodox Jewry. Berkeley, Calif.

HOSTETLER, JOHN A. 2005. 'The Amish Use of Symbols and their Function in Bounding the Community'. In David Weaver-Zercher, ed., Writing the Amish: The Worlds of John A. Hostetler, 197–214. University Park, Pa.

JAFFE, AZRIELA. 2005. What Do You Mean, You Can't Eat in My Home? A Guide to How Newly Observant Jews and their Less Observant Relatives Can Still Get Along. New York.

KAUFMAN, RENEE. 1991. Rachel's Daughters: Newly Orthodox Jewish Women. New Brunswick, NJ.

KRAYBILL, DONALD B. 2001. The Riddle of Amish Culture, rev. edn. Baltimore.

LEVINGER, LEE J. 1952. 'The Disappearing Small-Town Jew', Commentary, 14 (July–Dec.): 1961–2.

ROSE, PETER. 1977. Strangers in their Midst: Small-Town Jews and their Neighbors. New York.

SACKETT, SHAYA. 2010. Personal email communication with the author. 27 October.

SCOTT, STEPHEN. 1986. Why Do They Dress That Way? Intercourse, Pa.

SHESKIN, IRA, and ARNOLD DASHEFSKY. 2010. Jewish Population in the United States, 2010. Storrs, Conn.

SHOWSTACK, GERALD LEE. 1988. Suburban Communities: The Jewishness of American Reform Jews. New York.

SKLARE, MARSHALL. 1967. *Jewish Identity on the Suburban Frontier: A Study of Group Survival in the Open Society*. Chicago.

United Jewish Communities. 2004. *National Jewish Population Survey 2000–01—Orthodox Jews: A United Jewish Communities Presentation of Findings*. <http://www. jewish databank.org/Archive/NJPS2000_Orthodox_Jews.pdf>, accessed 21 June 2004.

US Census Bureau. 2011a. 'Lancaster (city), Pennsylvania'. <http://quickfacts. census.gov/qfd/states/42/4241216.html>, accessed 26 Jan. 2011.

——2011b. 'Lancaster County, Pennsylvania'. <http://quickfacts.census.gov/qfd/states/42/42071.html>, accessed 6 Jan. 2011.

WEISSBACH, LEE SHAI. 2005. *Jewish Life in Small-Town America: A History*. New Haven, Conn.

EIGHT

Negative Interfaith Romances and the Reassertion of Jewish Difference in Popular Film

HOLLY A. PEARSE

DISCOURSE ON JEWISH INTEGRATION into modern American life often involves congratulatory observations of how seamlessly Jews have coalesced traditional values with those of American public culture and how successful Jews have been as a minority in the West. In general, Hollywood's depictions of Jewish American life seem to support this image of the Jewish American as part of the mainstream, if not a foundational pillar of American culture. Educated, urbane, and cosmopolitan, the Jews of contemporary American cinema outwardly have little in common with the early flickering, black and white scenes of ragged Jewish greenhorns struggling to gain access to the American Dream. Jews play a disproportionately prominent role in romantic comedies, where the attraction between Jews and non-Jews may symbolize boundary-crossing. The sheer volume of Jewish characters falling in love with non-Jews seems to suggest that Jews have finally 'made it' in America, by way of having made the bedroom fully democratic. But is this so? What do film conventions in romantic comedies tell us about the boundaries, real or imagined, between Jewish and non-Jewish cultures?

When film first started as an American pastime, it was considered a low-class medium, and mostly appealed to immigrants and the working class (Cook 1996), so it often warned of the dangers of wandering outside one's ethnic group. Punishment usually came in the form of death by a mysterious fever, or ruination in general, for example, in 1915's *The Barrier of Faith* (Friedman 1982). Not surprisingly, this was particularly prevalent in American Yiddish cinema, where it outlived the trope in Hollywood cinema, as seen by the 'anti-*Jazz Singer*' *The Cantor's Son* (1937). Others depicted the daily struggles of immigrants to attain Americanness, occasionally ending in failure, such as the 1922 film *Hungry Hearts*, which featured a Jewish mother longing for a white kitchen only to be thwarted by an unkind system.

However, the American Dream was too tempting, and American cinema was soon drawn to the promise rather than the threats of integration, along with the hope of assimilation. By the late 1920s and into the 1930s, the medium had saturated all class levels, marking the period known as Hollywood's 'classical age'. This was the time during which the most significant myths, archetypes, and tropes had settled, and the era that defines what I consider to be the classical liberal Hollywood ideology, the constructions of which are still employed in movies today. In the 1930s Hollywood promoted a vision of America in which one can (and must) rise to one's own personal levels of success and romance, and that romance and self-transformation are more important than any responsibilities of birth or loyalties to ethnicity. America was taking on a new, multicultural face, particularly as the home front mentality of the Second World War took prominence (Friedman 1982). Films promoting intercultural relations seemed to argue that it was progressive to mix across ethno-religious lines, and intermarriage was shown as being more 'American' than traditional endogamy. From the 1928 love story *Abie's Irish Rose* to the 1947 liberal, anti-bigotry classic *Gentleman's Agreement*, democratic associations as being 'modern' and the glossing of (white) ethnic difference were the tone of Hollywood, if these subjects were mentioned at all. *The Jazz Singer* (1927) went so far as to kill off the traditional parent so that the more tolerant, adaptable family members could be liberated and rewarded.

This 'progressive' development is significant in light of the history of Jewish identity, because the majority of Jewish filmmakers and audiences of the 1930s and 1940s were second- or third-generation Americans. Hollywood seemed to provide an ideological structure supporting assimilation, thereby pacifying their possible guilt over their increasing homogenization. By the 1930s Hollywood films focused on the possibilities America offered rather than on the hazards of Americanization, a trend which has since flourished.

However, since the ethnic resurgence of the 1960s and 1970s the course of love between Jews and non-Jews has run less smoothly in Hollywood cinema. At a time when American Jews were starting to marry non-Jews more often than fellow Jews, a survey of American romantic comedy and melodrama shows an inordinate number of relationships on screen between Jews and non-Jews not making it to the final act, and preoccupation with not just the Jewish–gentile romance but also the break-up casts a pall over the 'happy ever after' of Hollywood's romantic cinema. Modern, liberal society continues to maintain an individualistic prioritization of self over hereditary identity in romantic choice, a form of personalism claiming that romance is a tool for creating a new and independent identity that is free from antiquated notions of category. Yet well after the iconoclastic 1960s the commercial film industry continues to address the question of ethnic difference, and suggests that this personalization of intimate action is far from sufficient to create lasting bonds between Jews and the non-Jewish objects of their attraction.

In this essay I interpret the pattern of failed Jewish–gentile romances on the big screen in the late twentieth and early twenty-first centuries. The coded questioning of these romances in films is apparent in a noticeable increase in the number of movies that portray Jews as inherently different.[1] This trend is epitomized by, but not confined to, the work of Woody Allen. The premise of the inter-ethnic relationship has been illustrated, emphasized, and rendered symbolic through the portrayal of romantic failure or dissatisfaction between Jews and non-Jewish lovers. In many cases individualism is still gratified in that it is the Jewish lover who enacts his or her agency in resisting universalism by rejecting the non-Jewish lover, in contrast to earlier portrayals in which the Jewish or non-Jewish community, or nature itself, ruptures the romances. Thus, since the late twentieth century, the cinematic portrayal of romances between Jews and non-Jews has been marked by a self-imposed allosemitic outlook rather than an external labelling convention. This reflects a narrative shift suggesting that, since the 1960s, Jews on the big screen have resisted the universalist whitewashing of their ethnic and cultural difference in America. Perhaps this position is best expressed by the proud Israeli Ari (Paul Newman) in Otto Preminger's *Exodus* (1960): 'Don't you believe it: people *are* different; people *like* to be different; they *have a right to be different.*'

In my analysis I identify obstacles used in the narrative to explain the failure of relationships between Jewish and non-Jewish romantic partners in films that illustrate the ambivalence of Jewish integration into American society. I describe five main blocks to Jewish–non-Jewish marital bliss. While only a few films explore the religious issues involved in exogamy, many more now acknowledge the validity of family objections to interfaith unions. Some root the negative outcome in the failure of liberal society to adequately obliterate social barriers (despite encouraging intermarriage on a theoretical level), in the emotional and mental traps posed by historical rivalries and inequality, or in the existential differences, stereotypical or not, that arise between Jewish and non-Jewish lovers.

In light of these examples, one is justified in wondering whether interfaith romance is promoted in Hollywood as much as a surface glance might suggest, and whether 'love conquers all' still applies to the ambiguous relationship between Jew and non-Jew, even in modern democratic society.

Choosing Chosenness: Religious Obstacles

Ironically, despite the modern position that religion is the main distinguishing factor between Jews and non-Jews, religious difference may be one of the most rarely explored obstacles to Jewish–gentile relationships in American film. It is true, of course, that Hollywood in general has had a long-standing reluctance to focus on a particular religion, as opposed to more generalizable 'values'. Since the 1990s, however, this trend has seen some reversal (Norden 1992). Nevertheless, the fact remains that for the majority of American Jews, shared historical events such as the creation of the State of Israel and the Holocaust might be much more meaningful aspects of their identity as Jews than is Judaism (Friedman and

Desser 1993). While Jewish identity is bolstered in America by religious rituals, such as circumcisions and bar/bat mitzvahs, and by festivals, such as Passover, contemporary Jewish identities are not determined by such formal religious expressions alone. Jacob Neusner put it best when he wryly observed that 'American Judaism has persisted although the Jews have largely ignored it' (1981: 34).

Therefore, specifically religious objections to intermarriage have diminished, and, although Judaism's authorities still have much to say about the challenges of interfaith romance and marriage, popular American film does not offer a great deal on the subject of Judaism. In fact, only a handful of narrative films have been released in North America in the past few decades that actually deal with Judaism openly, as opposed to those which deal with the Jews themselves. Those films that do address this issue often address religious difference in two ways. They either present a post-Enlightenment idea that all religions are fundamentally the same (e.g. *Brooklyn Babylon*, 2001) and particularities are mere window dressings on the 'true' faith of the soul (e.g. *Mrs. Delafield Wants to Marry*, 1986), or suggest that accommodation is as simple as making the token gesture of a superficial conversion.[2]

One film, however, has openly staked a claim for the validity of religious devotion within Hollywood's romantic cinema, and it comes from a most unlikely source—an otherwise formulaic crime drama starring Melanie Griffith and Eric Thal, *A Stranger Among Us* (1992). Some film critics will point out that this was Buena Vista's attempt at retreading the far superior *Witness* (1985), except with hasidic Jews instead of the Amish (Kauffmann 1992), but there is much about this film that is not entirely without value. In particular, it has at its helm one of the finest mainstream Jewish American directors, Sidney Lumet,[3] and a cinematographer, the Polish-born Andrzej Bartkowiak, who so lovingly films the hasidic scenes that the *tableaux* alone make the film a worthwhile experience.

A Stranger Among Us is one of the few commercial film explorations of hasidism in America, and the director uses the non-hasidic police officers, who know next to nothing about the isolated community, as a stand-in for the audience who can be assumed to be equally uneducated about ultra-Orthodox culture. While the hasidim are tenderly captured in an anachronistic, yet timeless, home life, they are also shown in their role as the life-blood of the 47th Street New York diamond industry. The very first lines in the film are in Hebrew, establishing the dominance of religion and Jewish tradition in the film, but we also see the Jews participating, as proud and visible Jews, in modernity rather than hiding from it. In *A Stranger Among Us* the Jews are treated with sensitivity and respect and are shown as 'real people', insofar as any character is realistic in a crime thriller. In fact, Lumet seems to hold their commitment in high regard—while life outside is seen as rootless and violent, this is in contrast to the warmth and fellowship offered within the hasidic group. The urban setting itself brings out the contrast—graffiti-tagged brick walls and dirty streets appear grim compared with clean, luminous, book-lined Jewish homes. The Jewish communal group is imagined as an oasis of health and civilization compared to the depravity of the drifting modern world outside it (Friedman and Desser 1993). Community, which the hasidim understand intimately, has been lost on the outside world, and the non-Jewish interlopers cannot help but appreciate what the hasidim gain in exchange for the relative loss of freedoms. Secular life holds the threats of betrayal, depression, and addiction, while the hasidim suffer only slightly, and willingly, for their Law—their sacrifices, such as having to decline offers of non-kosher dessert treats, are slight compared to what they enjoy. The film, which seems unwilling to address possible problems within closed sectarian life, is not lax in showing us why the hasidim do not regret their boundary choices.

The story features a hard-boiled female detective in New York City who has to find out what happened to the missing sweet-natured adult son of two hasidic diamond merchants. Suspecting that the crime was an 'inside job', Detective Emily Eden (Griffith) decides it is imperative to go under cover and live among this closed group. She is hosted by the rebbe (played by Lee Richardson) and, of course, his handsome, young son and heir, Ariel (Eric Thal). The crime thread is relatively unimportant; it is the love story that is the main vehicle for the drama here. The film's title, while alluding to the deadly secret carried by one of the members of the community, also signifies that it is Eden and her relationship with Ariel and his father that is to be our prime concern.[4] While Ariel is physically beautiful, the real romance stems from the way in which his intelligence and quiet perceptiveness draw Eden to him, as his manner is the complete opposite of the vulgar come-ons of the secular men around her, particularly from a non-religious assimilated Jew, Levine (Jon Pankow). Why Ariel is attracted to Eden is much less clear, despite Melanie Griffith's obvious physical qualities. Yet Ariel's sister might point out one factor in Eden's allure when she compares the modern detective to the female warriors of the Hebrew Scriptures. It is seemingly the attractive power of a capable woman that lies at the root of his desire, especially compounded with the exoticism of a woman from the outside, with all the erotic implications of that status. Thus, in a form of gender inversion, it is Ariel's gentle spirit and deep soul that attract Eden to him while it is her strength and animal roughness that draw Ariel to her.

Friedman and Desser (1993) point out a major contradiction in the film. By holding the peaceful and thoughtful Ariel up as an object of romantic desire, Lumet is promoting mental and emotional acuity as more sexy than the lusty hyper-masculinity of the men outside the community. Yet in the end the fact that this is a mainstream crime drama requires that this gender twist be offset for the viewer. Pacifism and wit must take a backseat to the need for a man in America to be able to use violence when it is required, and the film's formulaic climax has Ariel use a firearm with unrealistic skill to save Eden's life (Friedman and Desser

1993). Still, this violent climax does have a significance other than fulfilling the obligation for male gunplay. Ariel, being a devoted Jew and the next rebbe of the community, simply cannot walk away from his obligations for the lust of a non-Jewish woman. Like the eclair she offers him that he cannot eat, Eden is tempting, perhaps, but she is an empty pleasure compared to the deeper partnership he will find with his arranged bride, the daughter of a French rebbe who he believes is his *beshert* (soulmate). Ariel's belief in the *beshert*, or other half, stands opposed to the idea of the attraction of opposites—one's partner in life should be the missing part of you, not your antithesis. His contact with Eden brings out his violence, and, even though it is permitted in Judaism to kill to protect innocent human life (BT *Sanhedrin 74a*), she has harmed him in his soul by inspiring this act. Her world has intruded on his contemplation far too much, and the shooting is the cathartic eruption of this collision. While he can admire her and have warm memories of her, he cannot ever bond with her or become one with her. In this way, the act of shooting the aggressor to save Eden is a violent substitution for the sexual climax the two can never share, as well as a warning that, while two opposites can attract, that fact alone does not mean they should merge. It is this acceptance of the realities of attraction, but the reminder that we are not obligated to follow through on attraction, and that communal responsibility comes with great rewards, that makes this film resonate with many communitarian critiques of personalist aims. There is something greater than lust, or even love, and that is the connections between members of this religious community based on mutual support and shared values, and one which is highly distinctive and irreducible to universalized ethics.

'I Haff No Son!' The Reality of Family Objections

Part of Hollywood tradition in the twentieth century with regard to intermarriage was to contend that parents with an objection to the relationship were either racist antisemites or Jewish chauvinists who refused to modernize. In these films, dissenting family members are held up as examples of ignorance, prejudice, and irrationality—three deadly sins in post-Enlightenment culture. In more recent years, there has either been a continuation of this image, or, even more common, we have seen the decline of familial objections altogether in American film (*Along Came Polly* (2004), for example). The 1980 remake of *The Jazz Singer* is, primarily, the story of a man grappling with the traditions of his father, as was the 1927 version. The later version does, however, give more voice to the elderly cantor who longs to see his son follow in his footsteps, and it also dares to show the fatherly love that lies behind the concern, something glossed over in the original film. Still, the newer version follows the original by asserting the liberal ideal of romance over tradition, and the father, instead of dying in the end, is still forced to accept his son's interfaith remarriage along with his choice of a pop career over his religious one. Such films once showed the older generation as backward and unable to see the wonders that America has to offer, but allowing the parent to see the light is the new Hollywood way of dispelling their objections.

Nevertheless, there have been more films recently that take the family's concerns over interfaith romance seriously. Some even show the grave consequences of intermarriage for multiple generations of Jews in America, such as *The Angel Levine* (1970) based on a Bernard Malamud short story (1955), in which an old Jewish man (played by Zero Mostel) lives in despair and poverty due, in part, to his estrangement from his intermarried daughter. While the film suggests that it is the father's irrational, prejudiced views that keep him from making peace with his daughter, and encourages the liberal values of tolerance and personal growth, these facts do not sugar-coat the misery of the older generation left behind by the younger Jews who have left the community for the sake of a non-Jewish lover or spouse.

The short film *Oedipus Wrecks*, Woody Allen's contribution to the tripartite *New York Stories* (1989), is particularly illuminating of the theme of Jewish family as well as inter-ethnic romantic relationships played out in the framed fantasy of movies. The short starts out with Sheldon Mills, a pitiful lawyer, who has become distraught over the destructive role his mother plays in his life. His mother's regular efforts to embarrass him have sent him to an analyst, but to no avail. Desperately, he longs for her to disappear, even having secret hopes for her death. The audience gets some indication of why he would have such dreadful ideas when we meet his mother, a diminutive wrecking ball of a woman, who seems to be as disappointed in, and critical of, her son as she is pathologically boastful of him. According to his mother, Sheldon was a beautiful child, and is a sensitive, successful man, who also happens to be a lousy son who is ashamed of her, and changed his name from Millstein for no good reason. Finally, Sheldon cannot wait any longer—he must bring his non-Jewish fiancée Lisa (Mia Farrow) home to meet his mother, even though he knows it will end in disaster. Upon meeting Lisa, his mother produces the family photo album and begins to systematically humiliate him. As soon as Lisa, who has children from a previous relationship, leaves the room, his mother starts in on him about his impending marriage: 'What do you need with a blonde with three children? What are you, an astronaut?'

Dismissing his mother's distress over his loss of Jewishness, now culminating in a mixed marriage, Sheldon and Lisa take his mother and Lisa's three children to a magic show in order to jumpstart the family bonding, at which Mrs Millstein is chosen as the volunteer for a sword trick, and is placed in the Chinese Box. Suddenly, Sheldon gets his wish—his mother disappears, for real! At first he is filled with concern and dismay, and goes through a mournful period trying everything to find his lost mother, until one day he discovers he is a better person without her hovering over him. Finally, he is the man he had always wished to be—relaxed, happy, and sexual without any inhibitions. 'I feel like a new man', he crows to his therapist. 'It's like a weight has been lifted off my shoulders' (the allusion of Millstein/millstone becomes clear). Guiltily, he calls off the private investigators he had searching for his mysteriously missing mother, and he attempts to move on with his life with Lisa.

Then, suddenly, the impossible and fantastic strikes, and his mother not only turns up, but is, somehow, one hundred feet tall and plastered across the New York sky above him, becoming a media sensation as she criticizes him loudly and discusses his life with strangers. Where she was once just wrecking his emotional life, her famous presence in the New York landscape starts to destroy his personal and professional life as well. Finally, Lisa has had enough of Mrs Millstein calling her 'strange foreign names' (in Yiddish) to the news crews and refuses to be humiliated like Sheldon, complaining that it is fine for him but that she is 'not used to this sort of thing'. Finally, at the end of his rope, Sheldon contemplates suicide and his therapist, seeing that it is time for desperate measures, sends him to a friend, Treva (Julie Kavner), who is trained in the occult as a 'spiritualist'. For three weeks, the incredulous Sheldon tries every *faux* foreign ritual Treva can produce from her charlatan's repertoire. Finally, Treva admits that she has never made an occult ritual work despite very much wanting to believe in it—she stayed in business, she explains, because 'people flock to it—their lives are just so empty'. To save him from showing his humiliated face in a public restaurant, Treva cooks Sheldon a chicken dinner to apologize for not being able to get his hundred-foot mother out of the New York sky. While they eat, Sheldon feels more and more relaxed with Treva, a demonstrative Jewish woman who loves to feed him and obsess over how thin he looks. Eventually, both of them realizing their growing attraction is inappropriate, Sheldon returns home to Lisa, weighed down with plates full of leftovers courtesy of Treva. Instead of Lisa, however, he finds only a note from her, explaining how his mother's humiliation has finally made the relationship impossible for her to continue, and that she has simply fallen out of love with him. Dejected, Sheldon picks up a drumstick from the leftovers, unattractive and homely, and a look of recognition comes over his face—Treva, while not as romantic as Lisa, would care for him and accept him, despite his mother.

Rushing out to his mother with his new fiancée, Sheldon proudly introduces his Jewish bride-to-be, and his mother finally smiles in relaxed happiness. 'Fine', she says, 'now I will come down.' She disappears and shows up a minute later, normal sized, walking out onto the balcony to join Sheldon and Treva. The family is reconciled and all are happy, until, to Sheldon's horror, Treva asks his mother if she has any baby photos of her son. The smile falls from Sheldon's face as he realizes what he has done. This is where the short film ends, leaving the audience understanding the joke of the vignette's title. We are not led to believe, though, that his choice of Treva is any worse than his marriage to Lisa would have been.

Now that the secret of his real name has been revealed to the world, Sheldon has a new position of authenticity. Now that he, who was ashamed of everything Jewish, has embraced a Jewish wife and made some peace with his Jewish mother, it is likely that this marriage will last, even if it may not be as exciting as marriage to a pretty, polite non-Jewish woman (who abandoned him when things got rough) might have been. In this short, food is seen as a form of love, and Treva had sent him home with his arms full of it. In contrast, Lisa 'fell out of love' with Sheldon, showing that while romantic love has limits and fades, the bonds of traditional matrimony, as simple and homey as that chicken dinner, may promote a more lasting union, justifying his mother's warnings from the beginning.

Prime (2006) also appears to explore the ways in which the objections of family might appear incongruous in liberal America, but may actually be rooted in a reasonable concern about the welfare of both the Jewish and the non-Jewish partner. The film focuses on the ill-advised yet passionate love affair between a 23-year-old Jewish would-be painter, David Bloomberg (Bryan Greenberg), and 37-year-old Rafi Gardet, played by Uma Thurman. Unbeknownst to either of them, the young man's mother, Lisa (Meryl Streep, as an unlikely yet oddly likeable Jewish mother), is also Rafi's therapist. The psychiatrist, whom we see encouraging Rafi to embrace a temporary romance with a younger man as a way to rejuvenate after a bitter divorce, does not seem as tolerant when advising her son against becoming involved with an older, non-Jewish woman. Speaking from a position of emotion in her role as a mother, yet also as an enlightened therapist, she advises her son that relationships outside one's faith are more of a challenge than he should take on at such a young age.

Although the audience may be prone to seeing her position as hypocritical given her conflicting advice to her patient, one cannot help but be sympathetic to her situation—her patient is a grown woman, while the young man is her son. Further making her a likeable character are her own rational attempts to address the awkward situation—humorously visiting her own therapist to try to deal with it all—with an earnest desire to do the right thing. She is also shown as distinctly lacking the clichéd 'those people' or 'the other kind' attitudes towards non-Jews so often placed in the mouth of Jewish mothers in intermarriage films. She is actually seen as slightly, though affectionately, derisive of the attitudes her own grandparents had of such couplings. In the end, she does attempt to swallow her own misgivings and gives the couple the benefit of the doubt, even though the relationship does ultimately fail, though partially due to the age difference.

While prejudice is not embraced, this film and others like it acknowledge that the familial support of endogamy might actually be born out of wisdom and rational observation. It suggests that not all parental objection is to be brushed aside as the ravings of pre-modern bigots. In *Prime*, Streep's character is both educated and liberal—in fact, her ways of reasoning, in their reliance on academic evidence and logical argument, are fundamentally post-Enlightenment modes of discourse. She opens up a space for parents who are both liberal as well as passionately community-oriented, which previously had been shown as seemingly impossible in interfaith romance films.

Imperfect Tolerance: Hidden Social Barriers

There are several films which point to intolerance as a major stumbling block to Jewish and non-Jewish romance, despite the generally held belief that antisemitism is no longer a problem in the West. On the surface liberalism promotes tolerance and diversity, but these films show that this is not an ideal that Jews will experience with the people around them. Often, this intolerance stems from family objections, either Jewish or non-Jewish, but it also speaks less about family unity and more to the basic axiom that people support 'their own kind' while harbouring suspicions about the other.

An example of a film in which Jews and non-Jews cannot manage to maintain a relationship due to lingering antisemitism in the surrounding culture is *School Ties* (1992). In this movie we see the young, handsome, and Jewish David Green (Brendan Fraser) riding a football scholarship in the 1950s to an upscale prep school in New England, a 'gateway to Harvard', and the *alma mater* of several US presidents, St Matthew's, where the facade of civility and justice masks an unjust core of prejudice. David is from a working-class, single-parent family in Scranton, Pennsylvania, where he grew up with his sister and his father among working-class friends. That he is skilled in football seems to his struggling friends and family a ticket to a better life, so he is encouraged by those around him (including St Matthew's coach, who hails from a similar working-class background) to make the best of things when this opportunity knocks. Yet we get the impression that things might not be so easy for David when his coach drops him off at his new dorm. 'Play your cards close to your vest', the coach tells him, 'Don't tell people any more than they need to know.'

David is, of course, concerned that the upper-class kids and he might not have much in common, but one does not yet get the sense that he is too worried about fitting in. Being from the tough town of Scranton, he does not lack confidence, even in the face of open antisemitism. He is used to the overt antisemitism of his home town, where when a tough guy calls you a 'sheeny bastard' you best him in a physical fight and you feel better. He is unprepared for the more genteel forms of antisemitism he is about to face, which start on his first night in the dorm: he hears a new friend explain how he got his new hi-fi stereo at such a good price because he 'Jewed down' the dealer. Ironically, the Jewish boy from a poor family must hear slurs about the presumed Jewish flair with money from a room full of wealthy Protestant schoolboys. Understanding the atmosphere at the school, David has two choices—fight, and blow his chance at Harvard, or keep silent and 'pass'.[5] Having been told that these young men represent the best of America, and wishing to escape the poverty of his roots and please his father, David complies, and this is communicated as he removes his Star of David necklace before his shower and hides it in his Cur-Aid bandage box. The symbolism is unsubtle—David is 'curing' the thing that appears to be standing in his way on the path to success. Here, he can play pretend, and fit in even if there must always be a part of him that remains hidden away. For a time, this scheme works. His charm, brains, athletic skill, and good looks make him popular among the students, and afford him a reasonable level of success in school. His strength of character and sense of justice establish him as a leader among the boys.

The crisis point, which has been foreshadowed all along, comes when he becomes the object of jealousy of one of the young men, Dillon (Matt Damon), who is driven to extremes by the pressure of living up to his high-bred family legacy, and who is in a non-reciprocated infatuation with a friend of his family, Sally (Amy Locane). Sally, a lovely, demure, and appropriately blonde teenaged beauty who attends St Matthew's sister school, is immediately drawn to David. She sees in him the qualities that one finds in teen film idols of the time: toughness, passion, and independence, but which she finds lacking in the pampered boys who have surrounded her all her life, namely in Dillon. From the beginning of their romance it is David's very difference, his almost exotic foreignness, which attracts Sally. Sally's appeal for David is considerably less esoteric, as she appears to be what every boy in the 1950s was trained to consider perfection, and the two begin to fall in love. The problem is that Sally chalks up David's difference to his lower-class roots, but is horrified when she learns, through the jealous Dillon (who has heard it from an adult alumnus), that the school's star quarterback and her new suitor is really Jewish. So insular is her world that she never expected to see a Jewish boy in the exclusive school, though she protests against David's claim that she is ignorant by listing the Jewish boys she has seen from a distance. Her shock, ultimately, is that she has fallen in love with a Jew without being able to tell he was Jewish, which goes against the ideals of breeding-will-out by which her social set live. Still, it is evident that Sally's dismay does not destroy all of her attraction to David. Rather, it is the jeers and taunts from the other girls of her class that ultimately drive her and David apart—'What's it like to kiss a Jew? Does his nose get in the way?' Her friends have pinpointed the sexual insecurity in Sally, and this is a cruel barb she cannot bring herself to ignore. Even while longing for David, she defends her prejudiced friends by placing the guilt on David, accusing him of hiding this traumatic secret from her on purpose. Sally can only see the damage done to her social standing and reputation, angrily berating David for what he has put her through. David, ultimately, is too different for Sally to embrace in her social situation, and this is the end of their relationship. One can say this break-up is partially by choice, as Sally is not strong enough to resist public opinion, but the film shows us that the cultural climate of the time is fundamentally unfriendly to Jewish–gentile love, and the romance is doomed from the moment David feels obligated to pass as non-Jewish. Even as Sally can only see what she has suffered, David reclaims his pride and rightly points out to her that the lie had not been to her, but to himself, and to his ancestors. Trying to pass for the sake of popularity and a girlfriend he had damaged only himself.

Because *School Ties* is set in the 1950s, the audience may get the impression that it is disconnected from the 1990s, when it was made.[6] The placement of the film in the recent past may give the impression that the Jews may have had issues in pre-contemporary America, while allowing audiences to believe that contemporary Jews do not have such problems, but this disconnect is simply an illusion. All films, no matter what era they portray, speak to their own time—otherwise there would be little value in them for the audiences who patronize them (Bartov 2005). By placing this story of antisemitism in the not-so-distant past the film-makers may critique the culture of exclusion which continues to abound while using the time setting as a subterfuge to disarm the audience and allow it to embrace the message. Current audiences can watch the film and congratulate themselves on living in more enlightened, liberal times, but they may also pick up lessons about empathy for currently excluded minorities in the process. The broader reality of Jewish life in America remains that passing is still an attractive and possible option, and that genteel forms of antisemitism still exist, especially when antisemites feel safe from 'judgemental' Jewish ears.

A more complex filmic exploration of liberalism's failure to defeat intolerance can be found in the controversial film *The Believer* (2001). This film presents a very different way in which cultural antisemitism can destroy a relationship between a Jew and a non-Jew. The anti-hero of the story, Danny Balint (Ryan Gosling), is not initially revealed to be a Jew, as he is first seen as a racist skinhead plaguing the streets. It is not until we have become thoroughly disgusted by his hateful ideas that we are let into Danny's darkest secret—he is Jewish. Danny is filled with antisemitic self-hatred. He claims that Jews' weakness and destructive tendencies make the world hate them, and yet their perverse nature also makes them crave this hatred, as their embracing of antisemitism is the only thing that keeps them Jewish and alive. While other skinheads denounce the Holocaust as rumour, Danny angrily points out that if one truly hates Jews, should one not celebrate the millions killed, for is not Holocaust denial actually denying Nazi efficacy? Instead, Danny blames not the killers but the victims, who did nothing, in his eyes, to save themselves. He is obsessed with the horrors of antisemitism and the violence directed at the Jews over centuries, which force him into a crisis of masculinity. How does a young man live up to the ideals of strength and virility in America while carrying the baggage of the effeminate victim? Danny's solution is to identify with the murderer, not the murdered.

In the midst of this mental and emotional crisis, Danny's passion attracts Carla, the young mistress of the racist ideologue with whom Danny's group affiliates. Lost and clinging to the racist group not out of intellectual affinity but out of loneliness and confusion, Carla (Summer Phoenix) is fragile and without foundations, and she recognizes in Danny the fire and strength she herself lacks. She seeks to be whatever he is, to believe whatever he believes. Slowly, Danny begins to teach her about Judaism and Jews, without telling her he is Jewish. 'Know your enemy', he explains to anyone who wonders how a skinhead is so knowledgeable in Hebrew and in Jewish law. Yet the pull towards Judaism is strong for Carla, who sees it as the antithesis of what she is—communitarian and ancient—and she becomes a force for Judaism in Danny's life, which he ultimately must reject. Neither Nazis nor Jews can satisfy Danny, as he comes to believe both sides are just playing, and no one can be as serious about anything as he is. Eventually, he sets a bomb at a local synagogue only to save the Jews from it, destroying himself in the process, and, in the end, he becomes both the murderer and the murdered—which is where he was always heading. Killed by his own explosive device on Yom Kippur, Danny sacrifices his own young male vitality to atone for the sins he felt the community was guilty of—the sin of weakness, perhaps, and the sin of being hated, certainly. While Yosefa Loshitzky claims that the Jewish ambivalence in what she calls a post-Holocaust film is caused by the fact that 'the diasporic post-Holocaust Jew is unable to redeem the shame inflicted on the Holocaust Jew by the possessors of absolute power' (2005: 142), Danny desires to find redemption or die trying in order to put an end to his pain.

In this story it is not external antisemitic opinions which tear Danny and Carla apart, but, more tragically, the way cultural antisemitism and antisemitic events have penetrated the Jewish self-image. Danny is an extreme character, but beneath his outrageous behaviour, which was inspired by a true story, lies the turmoil of Jewish life in America. Assimilation has made the Jew long for full entry into the American mainstream, but the failure of liberalism to stamp out antisemitism makes some Jews feel unwanted, even as official policy tells them barriers no longer exist for them. As a consequence, while covert Jewish stereo-typing sinks into the Jewish self-image, the Jewish–gentile couple will be forever buffeted by antisemitism, even if this evil is a mere echo that the Jewish partner carries within him- or herself. While other, less privileged, minorities have seem-ingly taken the place of the Jews as oppressed peoples and now draw liberal sympathy, Jews are left remembering more overt forms of antisemitism while at the same time feeling that they are not quite as accepted and welcomed as the politically correct liberal facade would have them believe (Boyarin 1992). In films like *The Believer*, the Jewish belief that antisemitism persists and that Jews will forever be tainted by the image of the victim is often sufficient to strangle any romance between a Jew and a non-Jew before it can ever find its own existence.

Cossacks and Swap Meets: The Problem of History

ALVY   I love what you're wearing.

ANNIE   Aw, yeah? Well, this [tie] was a present from my Grammy Hall.

ALVY   Grammy? You call your grandmother 'grammy'?

ANNIE Yeah.

ALVY   What did you do, grow up in a Norman Rockwell painting?

ANNIE Well, you know . . . What about your grandmother?

ALVY   Well, my grandmother didn't give gifts. She was too busy being raped by Cossacks.

This dialogue from Woody Allen's masterpiece *Annie Hall* (1977), aside from employing his essential Jewish wit by juxtaposing the horrors of history with the comedy of the mundane (Friedman and Desser 1993), encapsulates the issue of history that has risen as an obstacle between Jewish and non-Jewish partners in recent film, of which Allen is one of the masters. His *Annie Hall* has set the standard for, and often defined, the trend of interfaith romance between Jews and non-Jews in American cinema since the 1970s—there are not many films which do not owe at least some of their structure to this classic, as some directly make reference to it and others slyly borrow from it. In it, Alvy Singer, a comedian and 'real New York Jew' according to Annie, falls in love with the perfect *shikse*, his Gentile Dream Girl, and this movie is the jumbled retelling of their love story and its eventual decline and fading out.

What happened? Why did the romance fail? These are the framing questions Alvy asks, even though the scenes we witness from his memory make the failure of the relationship seem fairly inevitable. One of these reasons is the complete disconnect between Alvy's historically informed world-view and Annie's simplistic nature. Where Annie is trapped in a 1950s-style universe in which everything is 'neat' and where life consists of limitless amusement, tennis lessons, and swap meets, Alvy does not allow himself such relaxation. Aside from his personal experience of overt family dysfunction, Alvy is preoccupied with history—sometimes with the great biographies and events, such as the Kennedy assassination, but also with what history does to people along the way, and he is tormented by questions such as how he and the people he knows would stand up to torture by the Gestapo. With a nervousness stemming from his internalization of the Cossack and Nazi menaces, Alvy continues to see antisemitism around every corner, a paranoia which probably lies behind his problem with authority as well as many of the traits in him that Annie hates, such as his desire to avoid adventure and to surround himself with familiar people and things. Certainly, his obsession with death and with movies exploring the Holocaust is rooted in his 'people's' collective trauma, of which he has made himself heir and keeper despite the distance in time. Meanwhile, Annie can have bouts of giggles while telling the story of how relatives she's actually met have died. The differences in family history and community experiences are therefore not just conversation points for Alvy and Annie, but form a fault line in their relationship and play a significant role in their break-up.

This idea that Jewish suffering in history has led to Jewish neurosis is certainly not unique to Woody Allen (cf. Konner 2009), but it is one of the central concerns that characterize his films. Another film in which this generational post-traumatic nervousness is made explicit is his *Anything Else* (2003), in which Allen plays the off-kilter mentor to a protagonist who is a cinematic version of the young Woody Allen, and who is involved in a dysfunctional relationship with a highly strung non-Jewish woman. Drama develops and tragedy strikes out of Allen's obsession with firearms and home protection in response to people in the world who want 'to make us into a lampshade'. In another example, his Kafka-esque *Shadows and Fog* (1991) shows Allen alone and confused in the darkened streets of some fanciful, mythic town filled with allegorical figures and devoid of realism. He starts out trying to help catch a killer, somewhat involuntarily, but ends up being accused of the murders himself, which seems to be a metaphor for the hazy and labyrinthine struggle for justice by Jews in the diaspora—they do not know of what they have now been accused, even as they attempt to be good citizens despite their instinct to stay out of view. Around and around Allen wanders the strange streets, running into his Gentile Dream Girl, whom he helps and encourages, only to lose her in the end. Allen's character is simply unable to free himself from the fog of being an outsider in the streets of a town he did not design. There are numerous other examples in the Allen opus that one could refer to, so strong is the trend.

A more serious illustration of how historical scars and concerns can destroy a love affair between a Jew and a Christian is the harrowing romantic drama *Sophie's Choice* (1983). This rather long character study, based on the novel by William Styron (1979), tells of a naive young Southern man witnessing the post-war interfaith romance/obsession between a Polish Catholic Auschwitz survivor, Sophie (Meryl Streep), and an American Jewish man, Nathan (Kevin Kline), who saves her from starvation and illness as a new refugee in New York City after liberation. Since the Second World War, film seems to have had an increased fascination with the interfaith couple during the Holocaust (Baron 2005), but this is one of the very few well-known examinations of the lives of such couples shortly after the war ended, and offers the interesting switch of non-Jew as victim and survivor. Disturbingly, while Sophie is understandably damaged by her experiences, Nathan becomes a 'vengeful, Old Testament [God]' (Simon 1983: 61), and, driven by his paranoid schizophrenia, he immerses himself in the details emerging about the camps, oscillating between waves of guilt for not having suffered and died in Europe himself and being a perpetrator of further cruelty to one real survivor, Sophie. Nathan is infuriated by the fact that Sophie is not Jewish. While he led a relatively secure life in America and 'missed out' on the pain of Jews in Europe, this gentile woman has somehow been sanctified by the crucible of Auschwitz. He was even, presumably for mental health reasons, barred from serving in the US Army and fighting against the Nazis. As a reaction, Nathan demonizes and brutalizes Sophie for the choices she had to make to survive, such as forging a relationship with Nazi Rudolf Höss, the commandant of Auschwitz

(1940–3), in order to save her last remaining child. He also will never let her forgive herself for having been born to an antisemitic father, and demands to know how much antisemitism within herself helped preserve her life while millions of Jews perished. She did not deserve the 'privilege' of the suffering that she endured and he was denied, according to his twisted perspective; and it is clear that he has no true understanding of what she went through. His psychosis takes on a single goal: to destroy them both as offerings to the enormity of the Holocaust—Sophie for being the 'wrong' victim, and himself for 'escaping' victimization altogether, out of an emasculated and deranged anger over not having the ability 'to reverse history, undo the atrocity, or transport oneself into a time or a place not even accessible to the wildest imagination' (Bartov 2005: 75).

At the crux of this story is a particular understanding of post-war Jewish identity that says that part of being Jewish is being a victim (Bartov 2005). Without this victimization, the psychopathic Nathan feels that he has lost his place in the community and sees Sophie's experience as usurping his position. Sophie accepts his abuse out of her depressive need to be punished for the loss of her children, to feel something (even pain), and to duplicate some contact with her domineering father. Perhaps she is sacrificing herself not only because of what she feels she committed against her children, but also as an atonement for the Jews her father had sentenced to death. By having a relationship with Sophie, by living with her, beating her, and copulating with her, the mad Nathan is attempting to master her and to assume her identity and experience. The sadomasochistic violence gets worse, leading to their eventual suicide pact, because Nathan cannot, no matter how much he demands, steal that history from her. Nathan is a singular zone of contradiction—he desires a non-Jewish woman, who is both blonde and simple, and yet her history belies the old myths about the purity and uncomplicated pleasure of gentile femininity. He presents himself to her as a caring rescuer only to prove himself a brutal victimizer as he lives through his professed horror and obsession over the sufferings of the Holocaust's victims. He ends the life of the only survivor with whom he has ever connected (Bartov 2005).

While one hesitates to use the mentally ill Nathan as an example of Jewish manhood, this film presents a particular vision of historical conflict between the Jewish and non-Jewish lovers. The two are never alone, naked—they always bring their history with them. While this can be said for all couples, when the lovers are a Jew and a non-Jew the history goes beyond the personal and enters the realm of the global. The Jews, as repositories for an ancient story, can never be represented as only themselves, with a recent beginning, as they are forever defined as a deeply historical people who carry the scars of their people's past into interfaith couplings, so much so that when Jews fail to be victimized appropriately their identity dissolves and they cannot function.

The further humiliation of this film is that the story is not simply one of a mentally ill Jew and his Polish Catholic lover, but of how their dysfunctions and passions are trotted out as if on stage for the personal growth of an immature American Protestant boy (Peter MacNicol), for this is also a story about diaspora and shifting places. The Polish refugee and the migrant young Southern writer, Stingo, are there to heal or grow, while the Jew, the only one native to the area of New York, is not allowed to feel at rest there because he has been robbed of any healthy sense of his own place and self. This displacement is at the heart of his obsession with Sophie, who represents a place and a time to which he desires entrance, and causes his eventual suicide. He was not victimized enough to feel his Jewish identity, so he must victimize himself. The self-satisfied 'real American', Stingo, can only watch and marvel at the foreign couple's dramatics which he, in turn, can never really understand.

Never the Twain Shall Meet: Internal Differences

Tied to the historical differences between Jews and non-Jews is the perceived ineffable 'something' that holds the two groups apart. Their conceptual and internal contrasts are much more nebulous than the obstacles outlined above, and can often be a far less comfortable thing to discuss. While not being antisemitic, films illustrating an irrevocable difference between Jews and non-Jews are often guilty of essentializing the Jewish experience and character in America, and often tap into, or reappropriate, old stereotypes about Jews. Blending ideas of historical and religious (or ethical) differences, these films appear to agree with allosemitic ideas according to which Jews are neither specifically inferior nor superior to non-Jews, but, rather, are inherently different or alien, and, for various reasons, will never completely mesh with the mainstream world around them (Bauman 1998). They may even be defined by this separateness (Schiff 1982).

One of the common ways that Jews are shown to be essentially different from their non-Jewish lovers is by highlighting their hypersensitivity to danger and receptivity to historical lessons of persecution, as reflected in the works of Woody Allen. While in *Annie Hall* Alvy sees antisemitism in everyone he meets, in *Stardust Memories* (1980) the lead character gives in to a pathological gloom stemming from a constant preoccupation with the fact that, every second of every day, someone is tortured, starves, or suffers in some dreadful way. This oft-represented and suffocating sensitivity to the potential dangers of the outside world is poignantly described by the youngest son of Julius and Ethel Rosenberg in his memoir:

Although at six I was too young to comprehend the world beyond the Bachs' house, my neighborhood, and school, I knew that there was something dangerous 'out there,' lurking near enough to strike again, that was somehow involved in taking my parents away. A dark cloud of generalized anxiety hovered at the edge of my consciousness—a sense that something about my family was terribly wrong and that my circumstances might get even worse. Most of the time, when I ignored or forgot about the upheavals of my life, I felt reasonably safe with the Bachs, and not too bad. But 'we' (whoever that was) were under attack from whatever was out there, and I wanted to keep a low profile, beneath the notice of any enemies. (Meeropol 2003: 2)

While Robert Meeropol (born Rosenberg) is of course speaking specifically about the arrest, trial, and execution of his Jewish American communist parents as saboteurs and spies for the former Soviet Union, his description is consistent with the representations of the acute sense of otherness and anxiety expressed by Jews in many films. As we have seen, Jewish males in particular are often shown as having heightened sensitivity, making them more desirable to Christian women than their non-Jewish counterparts (Friedman 1982). At the same time, this Jewish hypersensitivity and humanity born of ancestral sufferings is often brought into awkward conflict with the carefree or determinedly sunny disposition of their golden non-Jewish lovers. This is particularly salient in *Annie Hall*, where Alvy tries to instil in Annie a darker understanding of life by forcing books about death on her and taking her to Holocaust documentaries, while she would much rather smoke marijuana and hang out with friendly people and chat. Alvy's grim outlook plays a part in their eventual break-up.

Likewise, in the popular romance *The Way We Were* (1973), Katie (Barbra Streisand), the young Jewish communist campus demonstrator, eventually pushes her lover, Hubble Gardiner (Robert Redford), away with her passionate desire to reform the world when all he wants is to enjoy himself and find a comfortable place in which to make a living. Hubble, who in his carefree blond vigour is essentially a male Annie Hall, is the complete antithesis to Katie, who is uptight, passionately committed, and, to say the least, a bit odd-looking. Katie and Hubble meet in the late 1930s on their upstate New York college campus, where he is intrigued by her strident opposition to Franco and her criticism of nearly everything he and his friends stand for, while she masks her physical attraction for him by a deep bitterness over how easily the world falls at the feet of him and his caste. Bright and ambitious, Katie must work for everything she gains, while, blessed and lazy, Hubble is served the makings of a perfect life without even asking. The film jumps ahead to the 1940s: Hubble is a navy public relations man and Katie a writer on a radio show when the two meet again in a club. Always the ambitious worker, Katie sets her sights on Hubble and steadily wears him down, illustrating the worst stereotypes of Jewish female pushiness and grasping. In the 1950s they move to Los Angeles, where Hubble has sold out his writing talent for a cushy job cranking out scripts for Hollywood, and Katie's ire is continually raised by the decadence and political vapidity she sees around her. At an emotional low point for Katie, another communist Jewish woman from New York points out the palm trees to her as their kin, explaining how they were not native to California, either, and are just as out of place. Eventually, spurred by Katie's protests against the McCarthy House Un-American Activities Committee investigations, Hubble finally makes good on his decade-old threat to leave her in favour of a less complicated life elsewhere. They part, in sadness for what might have been, the day she gives birth to their daughter, whom he sees only once. The film ends in a brief scene in the 1960s as Hubble, who is now successful and happily married to the sort of woman for whom he was always meant, runs into Katie, who is pestering strangers with 'Ban the Bomb' flyers in front of New York Plaza, back where she belongs. She informs him that their daughter is well, but Hubble refuses to visit her. He seems to prefer to leave the past as purely past. Katie, who no longer falsely irons the Jewish curl from her hair, is now married to a Jewish man, who is evidently more of a match for her than Hubble ever was, as she now radiates a satisfaction and maturity she never showed with Hubble. As they catch up, they both drip with sadness over the failure of their marriage, even though they recognize that, while it was a learning experience, the relationship had always been doomed. They part, likely never to run into each other again, and we are left with the strains of Streisand's pop hit mourning the 'memories of the way we were'.

The reason she and Hubble were doomed as a couple is largely because Katie's hypersensitivity spilled over into their personal life. She was so desperate to make Hubble want her, pursuing him with a goal-oriented mindset, that her ambitious and anxious approach to romance was unnerving for Hubble. The very things they desire in each other—her 'integrity and passion and commitment' and his 'grace and charm and vivacity'—constitute the reasons they were ultimately incompatible (Gelmis 1973–4: 108). In both *Annie Hall* and *The Way We Were*, the intense tendencies of the Jewish lovers eventually drive away their more casual Christian partners.[7]

These obstacles to Jewish–gentile love reflect a new view that Jews and non-Jews might be too incompatible, either by nature, by experience, or by choice, to triumph over adversity as a couple. In this reassertion of Jewish difference the foundational beliefs of liberalism are challenged and the implication of these negative outcomes is that Jews may be better off remaining within their own community rather than chasing modern dreams of romantic opposites in the faulty hope that love will be able to conquer all difference.

Conclusion

The films I have explored challenge old ideas that assimilation leads to either safety or happiness for the Jews, and that intermarriage is the one road to romantic bliss. These films, representative of a host of others, exhibit screened obstacles placed in the path of Jews and non-Jews, pointing out that interfaith couples still face challenges in modern culture. Movies such as *Crossing Delancey* (1988), *Annie Hall* (1977), *The Heartbreak Kid* (1972), *Goodfellas* (1990), *A Star is Born* (1972), and others overturn misconceptions about the liberal emphasis placed on individual desires over communal identity. Whereas the Jews were once seen as

rootless promoters of abstraction and deconstruction, it appears that their representation may be opening towards the concrete. The trend away from assimilation and towards group affinity is gaining ground in Hollywood, leading to the
conclusion that the Jews of America are no longer seen as a rootless people, but as
one with significant group ties to places, ideals, and behaviours they wish to preserve. By criticizing liberal myths of tolerance and multicultural acceptance, they
are not necessarily denouncing intermarriage, but they are counterbalancing the
Hollywood glamorization of exogamy by tempering the myth that love conquers
all through showing issues facing romantic partners of different ethno-religious
backgrounds, often denied or outside the awareness of the idealistic couple early
in their romance.

Because the romantic genre typically implies a 'happy ever after' ending, the
number of failed Jewish–gentile relationships seems significant. That they have
increased since the 1960s suggests a resurgence of the sense of difference within
Jewish audiences and filmmakers. While cinema is made for more than Jewish
audiences and by filmmakers of a variety of backgrounds, and so the alienation
of the individual and rejection of the 'happy ever after' must appeal to a wider
group, the question remains as to why Jews are often chosen as protagonists in
unhappy endings. In early cinema first-generation Jewish immigrants feared
assimilation and their experience of America's temptations was seemingly reflected in the products of the silent era. Second and third generations embraced narratives that praised the democratic virtues of intermarriage as an American goal,
reflecting their relative success as well as the home front desire to label antisemitism un-American. By the third, fourth, and fifth generations of the 1960s
and beyond, however, the romance of Hollywood's democratic ideal had worn off.
Jewish dreams of seamless integration had perhaps tarnished in wake of the
McCarthy witch hunts, which publicly and repeatedly denied the Jews' ability to
become 'real Americans' simply by changing their names or adopting suburban
lifestyles. In light of the Red Scare and the civil rights unrest of the 1960s,
commercial film was ready to explore the ways in which the ideal of democratic
romance had failed. Woody Allen's 'chronic dissatisfaction' was more than a good
gag—it described the anxiety and slippage in the Americanization of the Jews as
symbolized through romantic pursuits in movies. The merge with America had
been flirted with, nearly achieved, and occasionally accomplished, but still did not
assuage the discomfort or dissatisfaction Jews experienced within their integrated 'roles'. There remained a difference, which has come out in a rejection
of uncomplicated, individualized love with a gentile object of Jewish desire,
as well as of the notion that such affairs can remain untouched by history. The
collective Jewish experience in America was formerly regarded as positive until
that frame lost its representational charm. Since the reassertion of ethnic difference in the 1960s, Jewish experience has increasingly been framed within
a pattern of assimilation–anxiety/rejection–difference, perhaps reflecting the

nearly forgotten 'not quite white', twilight nature Jews had in the beginning of their Americanization, as dredged up during the 'hidden foreigners' discourse throughout the Red Scare.

As to whether or not cinema still promotes intermarriage, we can say that, judging by these films, Hollywood does still assume a Jewish desire for non-Jews and seemingly supports the legitimacy of exploring interfaith relationships, but, more than ever before, filmic romances are questioning the possibility that these relationships can last beyond the initial excitement of the unknown, and cast doubt on the viability of exogamous marriage in ways that were unknown in the classical Hollywood era.

Notes

1   To describe this phenomenon, the term 'allosemitism' was coined by Polish literary historian Artur Sandauer (2005) and sociologist Zygmunt Bauman (1998) for the perpetual othering of Jews regardless of whether they are loved or hated by a majority group.

2   One film that addresses religious difference is the popular romantic comedy *Keeping the Faith* (2000), starring Ben Stiller and Jenna Elfman, which holds the view that religious objections can be overcome through the simple conversion of the non-Jewish lover to Judaism. When their romance begins, Anna, the non-Jewish businesswoman, has no clue why Jake, a rabbi, would consider her religious affiliation important, even though the reasons should be clear to anyone, and she seems to treat it as something he should 'get over', as if it were a perverse fetish rather than a deeply felt conviction. Her eventual conversion, which she has planned as a surprise for him and which she sees more as a birthday cake than a life-altering decision, fails to have any meaning as it is clear that she is going through the motions to make Jake assent to marrying her. Her liberal ideals, à la Hollywood, tell her that if he will be silly enough to cling to this prerequisite for love's triumph, then she will give up her own beliefs, as if to say one ideal is as good as any other.

3   While he also triumphed with the brilliant *Dog Day Afternoon* (1975) and the alluringly offbeat *The Wiz* (1978), Sidney Lumet is the unabashedly Jewish director of such important and controversial films with Jewish content as *The Pawnbroker* (1964) and *Daniel* (1983).

4   The title also recalls the Jewish obligation to be kind to strangers (Lev. 19: 33–4), which underlies the rebbe's interactions with Eden as well as being the means by which the killer gains access to the charitable community; this makes the portrayal of hasidim quite unusual for the level of friendliness with which they are imbued.

5   Passing involves a complex process of performance and secretiveness, in this case of a member of a socially disadvantaged group who attempts to shift his outward appearance and status to that of a socially advantaged group to avoid detection and promote success. This process is not as internalized or seamless as actual assimilation, as the performer is aware of the performance and suffers anxiety and guilt over the deceptive quality and the fear of 'slippage' or flaws in the performance and its acceptance by the privileged group.

6   The fact that the film is set in the 1950s is interesting, as it continues the nostalgic idea of the Jew as an inherently historical mythic figure (see Friedman 1982).

7   The laid-back attitude of the non-Jewish partner may prevent the conscientious Jewish

partner from understanding the gentile lover and his or her social circle, as, for example, in the youth-oriented film *Reality Bites* (1994), in which a Jewish man (Ben Stiller) fails in his attempt to woo a slacker non-Jewish filmmaker (Winona Ryder) because he cannot live up to her level of disengagement from all of the things he stands for—ambition, work, physical symbols of success—things his first- and second-generation American forebears would have seen as essential aspects of chasing the American Dream. His Jewish quest for security, accomplishment, and respect lead to a complete disconnect from her alienated and spoiled lifestyle of non-striving.

References

BARON, LAWRENCE. 2005. 'Condemned Couples: Lovers and Liquidation'. In Lawrence Baron, *Projecting the Holocaust into the Present: The Changing Focus of Contemporary Holocaust Cinema*, 103–34. Lanham, Md.

BARTOV, OMER. 2005. *The 'Jew' in Cinema: From The Golem to Don't Touch My Holocaust*. Bloomington, Ind.

BAUMAN, ZYGMUNT. 1998. 'Allosemitism: Premodern, Modern, and Postmodern'. In Bryan Cheyette and Laura Marcus, eds., *Modernity, Culture, and 'The Jew'*, 143–56. Stanford, Calif.

BOYARIN, JONATHAN. 1992. *Storm from Paradise: The Politics of Jewish Memory*. Minneapolis.

COOK, DAVID A. 1996. *A History of Narrative Film*, 3rd edn. New York.

FRIEDMAN, LESTER D. 1982. *Hollywood's Image of the Jew*. New York.

——and DAVID DESSER. 1993. *American-Jewish Filmmakers: Traditions and Trends*. Urbana, Ill.

GELMIS, JOSEPH. 1973–4. 'Review of *The Way We Were*'. *Film*, 73–4: 107–9.

KAUFFMANN, STANLEY. 1992. 'Hasidim and Hokum'. *The New Republic*, 17–24 Aug.: 34–5.

KONNER, MELVIN. 2009. *The Jewish Body*. New York.

LOSHITZKY, YOSEFA. 2005. 'The Post-Holocaust Jew in the Age of Postcolonialism: *La Haine* Revisited'. *Studies in French Cinema*, 5: 137–47.

MALAMUD, BERNARD. 1955. 'The Angel Levine: A Story'. *Commentary*, 20 (Dec.): 534–40.

MEEROPOL, ROBERT. 2003. *An Execution in the Family: One Son's Journey*. New York.

NEUSNER, JACOB. 1981. *Stranger at Home: 'The Holocaust,' Zionism, and American Judaism*. Chicago.

NORDEN, EDWARD. 1992. 'Holy Hollywood!' *Commentary*, 94 (Nov.): 51–2.

SANDAUER, ARTUR. 2005. *Studies on Polish Jewry: On the Situation of the Polish Writer of Jewish Descent in the Twentieth Century*. Jerusalem.

SCHIFF, ELLEN. 1982. *From Stereotype to Metaphor: The Jew in Contemporary Drama*. Albany, NY.

SIMON, JOHN. 1983. 'Harrowed Heroine; Harassed Audience'. *National Review* (21 Jan.): 60—4.

STYRON, WILLIAM. 1979. *Sophie's Choice*. New York.

PART III

Exhibitions and Performances of Jewish Culture

NINE

'The Night of the Orvietani' and the Mediation of Jewish and Italian Identities

STEVE SIPORIN

PITIGLIANO is a small, well-preserved Italian hill town built on top of an ancient Etruscan settlement and perched on an outcrop of volcanic tufa in the rugged agricultural region of southern Tuscany. Even though Pitigliano is located about halfway between Florence and Rome, it is difficult to reach by public transportation and is relatively isolated from major tourism routes. Two small rivers run through the steep gorges along the sides of the ridge on which the town rests, and deep, ravine-like paths dating to Etruscan times connect Pitigliano with the surrounding countryside.

One of the town's most striking characteristics, besides its rugged beauty, is the fact that not long ago it was home to proportionately the largest Jewish population of any Italian town or city. The Jews of Pitigliano, who have lived there since at least the sixteenth century, once accounted for as much as 15 per cent of a local

Figure 1 View of Pitigliano. *Photograph by Steve Siporin*

population that varied from 2,000 to more than 4,000 (Salvadori 1991). Today one Jewish family remains.

Several factors besides remarkable beauty combine to make Pitigliano a nostalgic site (particularly, but not exclusively, for Jews): its smallness, its remoteness, its nickname ('the Little Jerusalem'), its un-modern feel—no trains, more people walking than driving cars (which is nearly impossible to do in the narrow streets of the historic centre)—and its relatively philosemitic history. The name of the place, pronounced 'Pi-til-YAH-no', even follows the same rhythm (by coincidence) as 'A-na-TEV-ka', the evocative name of the romanticized shtetl of *Fiddler on the Roof*, musically and aurally imprinted in our memories as the very sound of longing by one of the popular songs from the musical.[1] If we were to seek a Jewish site in Italy capable of evoking similar emotions, we might find it in relatively remote and isolated Pitigliano.

Nostalgia—in this case, for idealized Jewish communities (whether a fictional Russian shtetl or a historic Italian town)—may not earn the respect of intellectuals and academics, but it cannot be ignored either. It is indisputably a powerful force in the modern and contemporary world. Later in this essay I will return to Pitigliano to analyse a series of cultural expressions, particularly in the areas of food and narrative, that partially depend upon the nostalgia that Pitigliano evokes. These expressions may have something to tell us not only about nostalgia but also about Jewish identity in Italy from post-emancipation times (that is, after 1848) down to the present.

First, however, I want to lay the groundwork for that analysis in a discussion about what it has meant to be a Jew in Italy in modern times.

Identity

I have often puzzled over whether to write 'Italian Jewish _____' (fill in the blank with a noun such as 'customs' or 'history') or 'Jewish Italian _____' in any particular context. It seems that in both cases the second term sets the boundaries of the frame, and is primary, while the first term modifies the second by designating a portion of the field within the frame. Or, to use the frame concept in another way, the phrase, depending on its word order, frames a secondary identity within a primary one. In other words, am I writing about Jews who are secondarily Italians or Italians who are secondarily Jews? Grammar seems to insist that the identities cannot be equal.

There are other possibilities to consider. From the viewpoint of the social actors, could the primary identity be purely situational, changing in different circumstances?[2] Maybe there are writing contexts—writing, for instance, about Italians, some of whom are also Jewish—in which 'Jewish Italians' is appropriate, and other writing contexts—writing about Jews, some of whom are also Italian—in which 'Italian Jews' is appropriate. And although we have been warned so often that we have become wary of 'essentializing', is it not reasonable to expect that Jews in Italy ultimately think of themselves (and are thought of) as fundamentally one or the other, Jewish Italians or Italian Jews? Or does my own recurrent uncertainty in choosing the best term reflect an ambivalence felt by many of those who bore this dual identity in the nineteenth and twentieth centuries?[3] Is the distinction clear for a population that has lived in a place—often a relatively accommodating place—for over two thousand years?

Indeed, one of the reasons Italian Jewry is so fascinating and rewarding to study is its persistence as a distinguishable group living in the same place from antiquity to the present day despite its minority status.[4] Ultimately I think my hesitancy and need to constantly think through the meaning of the combined terms 'Jewish' and 'Italian' is not due entirely to my own slowness of thought but rather to the profound, multifaceted integration of Jewish and Italian cultures— the result of two millennia of daily interaction, a length of time and a continuity unmatched elsewhere in western Europe. A great deal has happened over the course of this long, dynamic history, including internal Jewish migrations triggered by local expulsions from particular cities and regions and the reverse, the invitation for them to settle in other areas of Italy, as well as significant influxes of Jews into Italy from elsewhere in Europe, Asia, and Africa. Although the Jewish population in Italy has always remained small, involvement in Italian life in general—across, and in spite of, boundaries—appears to have been constant and continues today, even in new expressive modes. As Elizabeth Schächter has noted, even before emancipation,

Jews were taught to read and write Italian in Jewish schools as part of an educational programme to assist active participation in the host society, in contrast to schools in central and eastern Europe where instruction was in Hebrew and Yiddish. A positive evaluation was placed on Italy's cultural heritage, which was studied alongside Jewish culture, whereas in central Europe, Jews and secular studies were separate. (2011: 13)

Setting aside my own confusion over the terms, is it possible to learn something of how the Jews of Italy have seen themselves? As Italian Jews, or Jewish Italians? Clearly there must be individual variation in self-perception, but we can still ask how groups of individuals have used culture to frame, express, and project an identity with two parts. We can ask how the cultural expression of Jewish identity in Italy has changed over time. There is, furthermore, a perhaps surprising new question I would like to ask of this world of profoundly interpenetrating identities: do non-Jewish Italians play a part in mediating the identity of their Jewish fellow Italians today? If so, what does this mediation mean for their own identity as Italians?

In the Past

It is likely that Italian Jews have felt the need to frame their Jewish identity publicly only recently. Until the nineteenth century, religious/ethnic boundary markers in the form of clothing and social segregation were unambiguous and were forced on Jews by law. During the era in which Jews lived in ghettos (1516–1870),[5] the boundaries were physical: both the non-porous ghetto itself, which Jews could not leave from sundown to sunrise every day, and the yellow or red badge, red hat, blue threads, or other required sign on one's clothing that reminded everyone that the person he or she faced was a Jew.[6] The majority society—or at least its authorities—felt the need to make Jews and Jewish space readily identifiable in order to protect Christians from the 'leaven of disbelief' (Roth 1946: 289) as well as from other supposed threats.[7] Synagogues, even though they could only be located within the ghettos, were not allowed to display Jewish symbols on the exterior of their walls and thus were not obviously identifiable from the ghetto streets. Their very existence was regarded as offensive by Christians. But being *inside* the ghettos (which Christians could enter during daylight hours to pawn objects in order to borrow money as well as buy second-hand goods), synagogues were already on the other side of a religious/ethnic divide translated into the language of space. The Christian dilemma must have been in finding a balance between the requirement that everything Jewish be readily identifiable (to avoid 'contamination') and the offensiveness of seeing Jewish symbols. Since synagogues were already marked as Jewish simply by being located inside the ghetto, their usually visible exterior Jewish symbols could be suppressed without risk that they be mistaken for churches or other buildings. As a result of the coded clothing and the ghetto walls, there was little uncertainty about the boundary between Jews and other 'Italians' and thus little need for the subtler social mechanisms of boundary maintenance, at least in relations between Jews and non-Jews.

I have placed the word 'Italians' in quotation marks because Italian national identity was not invented until the nineteenth century (at the same time Jews were being emancipated, not coincidentally). Those other 'Italians' during the ghetto era probably thought of themselves first as Venetians, Neapolitans, Romans, Pitiglianesi, Florentines, and so on;[8] the *polis* meant more than the *patria*, which had no institutional foundation. Although Jews may have been religiously (and, due to legal restrictions, often occupationally) distinct from their neighbours, they shared most elements of everyday local culture with the others among whom they lived—their material culture, their food, and their language. In these areas Italian Jews had much in common with their Italian neighbours that was not shared with their Jewish co-religionists from Germany and eastern Europe.[9] Certainly there were many cultural differences between Jews and other Italians: Hebrew words in the Jewish versions of local dialects, kashrut applied to local dishes and meals, and the material culture specific to Jewish ritual (*mezuzot, ḥanukiyot*, synagogue ornaments, for example). Nevertheless, the commonalities were great, too. But due to the presence of the ghetto walls and the badge, Jewish identity was clear—sometimes too clear for safety. Because the distinctive sign they were required to display made them into targets for robbery and molestation, Jews who travelled on business often requested (and received) exemption from wearing it during their travels, especially when travelling in remote places like Pitigliano (Salvadori 1991: 39–40).

In the late nineteenth and early twentieth centuries, when the badge was long gone and Italy's former ghettos were on the way to becoming merely historical reference points in their cityscapes,[10] there was a strong impulse among many recently emancipated Italian Jews to re-frame themselves as Italians first, especially as loyal, patriotic Italian nationalists. Jews participated as soldiers in the Risorgimento (the movement for the unification of Italy) and in the First World War in disproportionately high numbers, demonstrating their *italianità*, often at the cost of their own lives (Roth 1946: 488; Stille 1991: 30). Rabbis and Jewish journalists led the charge.[11] For many, Italianness trumped Jewishness, as the following passage from a Jewish memoir makes clear.[12] The time is the First World War and the setting is the synagogue in the Piedmontese city of Casale Monferrato. Austrian prisoners of war are allowed to attend the synagogue, but they are not welcome:

War-time, the temple and sitting in the last rows of benches—silent, disoriented, and maybe even somewhat emotional—were Austrian Jewish soldiers in uniform, prisoners of war, each one packed in next to the other almost as if they wanted to take up the smallest amount of space possible, not to cause trouble. Their fellow Jews—and they were the majority—ignored them. It was clear that they continued to consider them enemies of the homeland; there wasn't a word, not a sign of greeting. (Segre 2008: 38)

One could argue that Jews, living mainly in the cities and large towns of central and northern Italy (the centre of the Risorgimento), often 'became Italians' even before many non-Jews (especially those living in the south) claimed Italian national identity for themselves.[13] Few Italian Jews expressed hesitancy about the unification of Italy and their accompanying emancipation.[14] On the contrary, they were active, enthusiastic, patriotic participants. Dan Vittorio Segre goes so far as to say that 'during the Risorgimento the Jews were the most active group in favor of Italian unification' (Segre 2010). According to Schächter, 'Emancipation [of the Jews] was an inherent feature of emerging nation states such as Germany and Italy' (2011: 3), and liberation from the ghetto and its severe economic restrictions was certainly a dream for poverty-stricken ghetto dwellers (Segre 1986: 13–18). But 'the creation and stability [of emerging nation-states] necessitated integration, homogeneity and uniformity; the construction of a national identity was predicated on inclusive similarity and the rejection of diversity' (Schächter 2011: 3).

Thus emancipation came at the price of difference.[15] As Andrew Canepa argues, 'admission to citizenship required that Jews renounce [not formally, but to themselves] . . . any separate national identity or distinctiveness . . . [It was] expected that they would cease to be Jews' (1986: 403).[16] In order to be Italians, Jews were even willing to modify traditional synagogue ceremonies—in fact, the very customs that made Jewish worship distinctive—in order to conform to what were viewed as 'universally practised customs', that is, middle-class Italian ideals of religious propriety (Sacerdoti 1843: 7, as quoted in Canepa 1986: 420).[17] The extremes to which they were willing to go to show that Judaism did not interfere with patriotism were demonstrated in 1848, the year of the first Italian War of Independence (1848–9), during an emblematic moment in the Risorgimento when Rabbi Salomone Olper publicly kissed a crucifix in Piazza San Marco in Venice 'as a token of good will' (Roth 1946: 493) and 'in the name of Italian unity' (Segre 2008: 61).

In another telling episode during the turmoil of 1848, Rabbi Elia Benamozegh, later to become one of the most prominent rabbis of nineteenth-century Italy, in a speech to his congregation in Livorno urged them to 'swear [*giurate*], O Israelites, swear that you will always love Italy . . . with all your heart and soul, with all your might . . . with an immense and insuperable love' (quoted in Schächter 2011: 16). This speech is remarkable because it unambiguously uses the phraseology of the Shema, the most important of all Jewish prayers, and substitutes 'Italy' for 'the Lord your G-d'. And the context in which this takes place is a rabbi speaking to his congregation.

Nevertheless, the ideal for many Italian Jews of the post-ghetto era was not necessarily a rejection of Jewish identity (indeed, even Benamozegh's nearly blasphemous exhortation to love Italy was stated in Jewish terms), but the creation of a Jewish identity different from the old one, which many saw as backward, narrow, and self-defeating. In this respect Italian Jews were not so different from Jews elsewhere in western Europe. As Amos Elon wrote in his history of German Jewry in modern times, 'the Jews of Germany never ceased in their effort to merge German and Jewish identity' (2002: 8).

In Italy the new identity, it was hoped, would be seamless with Italian identity, fitting snugly within the same frame.[18] Jewishness was to be both visible and invisible, but in precisely the reverse of the way it had been visible and invisible before: Jews had once worn a distinguishing sign as part of their clothing; now they would dress no differently than other Italians. A scene in Primo Levi's *If Not Now, When?* shows how Italian Jews in 1945 appeared to Jewish members of the Palestine Brigade of the British Army and how these proto-Israelis communicated their impressions to a group of death camp survivors from eastern Europe. Chaim, who has fought his way up the Italian peninsula 'from Brindisi to the Alps' (1986: 325), tries informally to orient these Jewish refugees, who are about to enter Italy with Primo Levi: 'They only speak Italian; or rather, the Jews of

Rome speak Roman, the Jews of Venice speak Venetian, and so on. *They dress like everybody else, they have the same face as everybody else'* (Levi 1986: 325; emphasis added).

Synagogues, on the other hand, had once been practically hidden in the contours of the urban physical structure (inside the ghetto), with little to distinguish them from other buildings (of which they were usually a part), so as not to offend the sensibilities of Christians who came to the ghetto to do business. The new synagogues of the 1860s and later—in Florence, Rome, Trieste, Milan, Turin, and elsewhere—were, in contrast, prominent, even monumental, buildings, usually standing alone, publicly proclaiming Judaism as part of the Italian heritage. In other words, Jews themselves were not to be individually distinguishable as Jews (by clothing), but their corporate place in society—a respectable place projected through the language of stately architecture (a particularly cherished expressive genre in Italy, of course)—would be ensured, bringing honour and beauty to every city with a Jewish community.

Ironically, but not surprisingly, this burst of new synagogue architecture owed a great deal to Christian religious architecture. It is said, for instance, that the Great Synagogue of Rome was unwittingly built in the form of a crucifix, the normal pattern of a Catholic church or cathedral (Aboaff 1978). And indeed, the crucifix floor plan is readily perceptible. In the most Jewish of spaces—the synagogue—the frame (the architecture itself) is, then, Italian Catholic while the content that literally fills the frame (ritual) is Jewish. But this particular expression of dual identity was unintentional and a cause of embarrassment for those who realized it (Aboaff 1978).

Although the crucifix floor plan in the Rome synagogue may have been unwitting, the more general attempt to harmonize identities was not. There are other ways in which Jews in Italy used (and continue to use) expressive dimensions of culture to project congruent, dual identities. Foodways, with their special resonance in both Italian and Jewish cultures, offer a salient example. Meals in particular are suited to carrying multi-layered meanings, and since meals take place regularly, they provide recurrent opportunities for symbolic communication, articulating important social ideas through their structure and content (Douglas 1997). The Italian meal, for instance, has specific syntagmatic slots (antipasto, first course, second course, and so on) which Italian Jews fill with appropriate Jewish dishes on Jewish holidays. Structurally the meal is Italian, but its content is Jewish. Both identities are expressed simultaneously, in a successful model of harmony. Apparent oppositions are resolved, and the message is that there is no inherent incompatibility or contradiction. *Italianità*, as structure, can be fulfilled through *ebraicità*, as content. This model is highlighted in festival menus that feature traditional, holiday-appropriate Italian Jewish dishes framed within the Italian meal structure (Siporin 1994).

The experience of Augusto Segre, a Jewish student who was detained and questioned by fascist authorities in Rome in the mid-1930s, shows that this abstract-sounding phenomenon of dual identity could actually become an immediate, concrete, and even desperate problem. A scene in his memoir dramatizes the need to resolve the apparent contradiction not only of identity but of loyalty (which often lies behind the issue of identity): 'I am made to enter a large room with a horseshoe table at the center and two lamps at the sides, pointed toward the seat that awaits me. The two rays of light affect my eyes and prevent me from seeing who my examiners are. There must be six or seven.' (Segre 2008: 194) Segre is interrogated for a while and then,

At this point the question, evidently held in reserve, appears. It is addressed to me in an inquisitorial tone, syllable by syllable: 'Do you feel Jewish or Italian?'
    I hazard a 'What does that mean?'
    I hear shouting, some swear words, and then evidently the one who is presiding, in a Mussolini-like tone: 'Now, let's finish it. You have understood quite well—you can't put one foot in two stirrups. You're either with us or against us. Fascism is clear, transparent, and precise; it's not pharisaical or Masonic.'
    I feel like my tongue is stuck to my palate. Then after a short silence I *hear* my voice responding. And out of distraction, or not to provoke them, I use the formal 'you'. I remember the dilemma posed by Levi at the Continental Hotel, on love toward the father and the mother. I repeat it word for word. ['What would I say to someone who asked me which was greater—the love and affection of a child toward his father or toward his mother? These feelings can coexist—neither one is destined to negate the other.']19 'I'm very proud of being born in Italy and of having an Italian heritage, but I don't see why I should be blamed for also having another heritage.' (2008: 194–5)

In a moment of terror, Segre found the 'right' answer that allowed him to be accepted, even by fascists, as both an Italian and a Jew.20 Some Jews resolved the issue for themselves, individually, by choosing one term to the exclusion of the other—emigrating to Israel, for example, or trying to opt out of being Jewish by converting.21 But for those Jews who remained in Italy and claimed Jewish and Italian identity, expressive culture may have become a way to affirm their cherished belief and fundamental formative experience that being simultaneously Jewish and Italian was not (and is not) contradictory. Their existential problem was similar to what Amos Elon called 'the duality of German and Jew—two souls within a single body—[which] would preoccupy and torment German Jews throughout the nineteenth century and the first decades of the twentieth' (2002: 5).
    Tragically, Italian Jews were betrayed by the country they had supported so fully.22 In the aftermath of the Second World War and the Holocaust,23 Italian Jewry struggled through a low point in its history. A great deal of the magnificent artistic heritage of Italy's synagogues was sent permanently to Israel to be displayed in museums or used in synagogues (or both in some instances) (Nahon 1970). Most of this inheritance came from Jewish communities that had become

so depopulated that they had ceased to function as organized entities with religious services and other communal activities. From the late 1940s small Jewish communities have been disappearing, and the few remaining medium-sized communities continue to shrink (DellaPergola 1976).

Revival

Paradoxically, in contrast to the population decline in most Jewish communities in Italy, the visibility of Jewish culture has increased dramatically since the 1990s (Siporin 2002) thanks to new museums, the restoration of historic synagogues, public concerts, and other events, such as Jewish film festivals or the annual European Day of Jewish Culture, which is supported more enthusiastically in Italy than anywhere else in Europe (Gruber 2010). This cultural revival involves many more non-Jews than Jews, especially as audiences and visitors. The 2009 European Day of Jewish Culture, for instance, 'attracted 62,000 people . . . about twice the number of Jews in Italy' (Gruber 2010). Does this revival parallel the phenomenon of Americans being attracted to Native American culture once Indians were no longer considered threatening? Or is it the unintended realization of something akin to the Nazis' projected 'Museum of an Extinct Race' in Prague (Altshuler 1983)? Do visitors come to Jewish museums and do audiences attend Jewish events out of shame and guilt or is there something more to it? Does the revival of interest in Jewish culture in Italy intersect in any way with the earnest quest that I have described above—the quest to cease being 'strangers at home' (Gunzberg 1992) and to become seamlessly Jewish and Italian and accepted as such?

What is happening in Italy (and specifically Pitigliano, which I will describe shortly) is not happening in isolation and is related to other Europe-wide currents beyond those discussed here. Ruth Ellen Gruber, for instance, in her book *Virtually Jewish: Reinventing Jewish Culture in Europe*, has written about the renewal of former Jewish quarters in eastern Europe, klezmer concerts in Italy, a popular market for books on Jewish subjects, a tourist market for hasidic figurines made of Murano glass or carved out of wood, and countless other examples of seemingly unpredictable and unexpected cultural production. Gruber has written, 'It is easy to dismiss much of the phenomenon as opportunistic "Shoah business" or a debased form of folklore, and some of it obviously *is* exploitative kitsch . . . fashion [and] commercialism . . . But the phenomenon is much more complex' (2002: 8).

The revival in Pitigliano today is part of the same phenomenon, with a similar mix of commercial, aesthetic, and educational motives, as well as something 'much more complex'—which, I suggest, in Italy, is the mediation of Jewish and Italian identities. There are examples of this phenomenon both nationally and internationally, but its richness in Pitigliano derives from the thickness of local Jewish history and culture.

The Revival in Pitigliano

I have described Pitigliano ('the Little Jerusalem'—'La Piccola Gerusalemme') briefly at the beginning of this essay. In 2011 its population was 4,000, including two Jews. The decline in the Jewish population had begun with the political unification of Italy (effectively completed by 1870), when legal barriers (such as the old borders between the separate Italian states) fell, and Italian Jews (indeed all Italians) were able to seek opportunities throughout the entire peninsula, resulting in an internal emigration, particularly to the larger, industrializing cities (see Bacchi 1937–8). The peak Jewish population of 360 in 1864 had dropped to 250 by 1900 and to 70 by 1938 (Bedarida 1950: 293, as cited in Salvadori 1991: 113). With the fascist racial laws of 1938, the Second World War, the German occupation, and the Holocaust, the Jewish population of Pitigliano was reduced to a point below the critical mass needed to sustain itself (Salvadori 1991: 91–104). The synagogue, dedicated in 1598, collapsed in the early 1960s because of damage sustained from bombing during the war. The immediate post-war years marked a low point of interest in Jewish matters in all of Italy, including Pitigliano. Nevertheless, according to oral testimony, discussion of the synagogue's restoration began soon after its collapse (Servi 2000).

Figure 2 Tourists entering the synagogue in Pitigliano. *Photograph by Steve Siporin*

Figure 3 Interior of the synagogue in Pitigliano, opposite the ark. *Photograph by Steve Siporin*

It was another thirty years before the restoration was completed in 1995, and it was then that the synagogue re-emerged, now as a public monument owned by the city rather than as a functioning synagogue owned by the Jewish Community of Pitigliano (which no longer existed as a separate corporate institution).

If the city government restored the synagogue out of a growing sense of the value of Jewish tradition to Pitigliano at large, then once the restoration was complete the synagogue itself strengthened and validated this awareness and opened further possibilities. It became perhaps *the* major tourist attraction of Pitigliano, and soon the number of Jewish cultural activities increased. It was to be expected that economic benefits, especially for enterprises involved in tourism, would

Figure 4 Sign for the Ghetto Wine Bar and Café. *Photograph by Steve Siporin*

provide significant motivation for the revival of interest in Jewish heritage in Pitigliano; but economic self-interest alone does not necessarily provide all the answers. Even the conundrum that I posed earlier regarding Jews in Italy (Italian Jews or Jewish Italians?) may have a part in a Jewish revival witnessed and shared mainly by Italians who are not Jewish.

Jarring cultural expressions, similar to those that Gruber described in eastern Europe, can be witnessed in Pitigliano today. Since all the following examples are from non-Jewish businesses, one might think that today non-Jews are deciding how to present Jewishness publicly. This is partly true. None of these enterprises, however, has met with objections from the Little Jerusalem Association (l'Associazione 'La Piccola Gerusalemme') an organization dedicated to protecting and preserving Pitigliano's Jewish heritage, made up of Jews originally from Pitigliano wherever they might live today, non-Jewish Pitiglianesi (many of whom reside locally), Jews from Israel, Europe, and North America, and anyone who wants to support the group's activities. In fact, the most important products (such as the locally produced kosher wine and olive oil) depend on the initiatives, co-operation, and encouragement of the Little Jerusalem Association as well as the approval and certification of Orthodox rabbis.

The Ghetto Wine Bar and Café, one example of virtual Jewish culture in Pitigliano, opened in the year 2000. To name a place of leisure and pleasure with the word 'ghetto' may seem to be in poor taste to Americans (and historians), but

Figure 5 *Sfratto* on a table. *Photograph by Steve Siporin*

'ghetto' identifies the shop as Jewish or pseudo-Jewish to tourists seeking something Jewish.[24] Note that the sign (Figure 4) is in English, indicating the locale is tourist-oriented. If the shtetl can be romanticized, perhaps the ghetto can too. Handmade matzah is available at the Panificio del Ghetto (Ghetto Bakery) all year round. It is not kosher matzah, but it is modelled after the traditional unleavened bread of Pitigliano that was produced in the community oven (which still exists nearby but is no longer functioning).

What is discordant here is that matzah has been divorced from its calendrical religious and cultural context and has been made into a consumer item based on a local expression of Jewishness that has actually been drained from the matzah by separating it from Passover. Ironically, true 'kosher for Passover' matzah is not available in Pitigliano, not even during Passover.

Sfratto is a pastry perceived to be Jewish and local. It has recently become ubiquitous in local bakeries and is sold with a printed origin legend attached, which claims that *sfratto* was invented by Pitiglianesi Jews in the early 1700s to commemorate the creation of the ghetto a hundred years earlier. According to the legend, the club-shaped *sfratti* refer to the beating on the doors of Jewish homes with a club to notify the Jews that they were being evicted and had to move to the newly designated ghetto (*sfratto* literally means 'eviction'). 'Thus the *sfratto* took on its name and form, in memory of that sad event.'[25] This narrative sounds suspiciously like a story 'cooked up' for tourists. Why would a bad memory be immortalized in a good-tasting dish?[26] Perhaps more to the point, why would the ghetto be memorialized a hundred years after its establishment by Jews who were still forced to live in it? In fact, recipes for *sfratti* as a Rosh Hashanah dish (it contains honey, an important Rosh Hashanah ingredient) are given in several Italian Jewish cookbooks (and now websites), without mention of the supposed origin legend or even of Pitigliano (Goldstein 1998: 198; Vitali-Norsa 1970: 238). Edda Servi Machlin possibly sheds some light on *sfratti* and reconciles the seeming contradictions in her cookbook and memoir:

Sfratti, the honey and nut dessert in the form of sticks, representing the rods with which the Jews were evicted from their homes during the persecutions. The Christian Pitiglianesi adopted them. But whereas the Jews traditionally served them on *Rosh Hashanà* to ward off the possibility of future evictions and as a wish for a good, sweet year, the Gentiles made them for weddings to ward off any marital battles. (1981: 30)

An older Catholic woman from Pitigliano in fact told me that she had always made *sfratti* herself, although she did not connect them to any particular belief or occasion. It seems that the printed legend attached to each purchase of *sfratti* in Pitigliano is based on an oral tradition, but this now standardized version leaves out Servi Machlin's important explanation of how and why *sfratti* are connected to Rosh Hashanah, just as the traditional Pitigliano matzah has been detached from Passover. In both cases what is involved in the conversion of a food custom that is meaningful only to insiders into a commodity is nothing less than the conversion of cyclical (sacred) to linear (profane) time, and the conversion of custom to consumerism.

The Ghetto Wine Bar and Café, non-kosher non-Passover matzah, the *sfratti* and their accompanying legend—these examples of pseudo-Judaism exist for touristic, commercial reasons, and they exploit Jewish heritage in Pitigliano. It is also true that the publicly funded restoration of the synagogue, followed by the restoration of the ghetto, including the *mikveh*, wine cellar, and matzah oven, as well as the production of kosher wine made Pitigliano into a more compelling tourist site (Figure 2) than it had been and thus was in the interests of local businesses and the local economy generally.

Yet, as I have suggested earlier, it does not seem to me that the motivation for local non-Jews paying attention to Pitigliano's Jewish heritage can be reduced solely to economic exploitation, nor can Italian tourism to Jewish sites in Pitigliano be reduced solely to guilt. Do the examples above (and others to come) open up the theoretical possibility that today non-Jewish Italians are bringing Jewishness—consciously or unconsciously—into the frame of Italianness (by valuing Jewish foodways, for instance[27])? Are Italians in a sense carrying out the project of mediating Jewish and Italian identities begun earlier by Jews, but this time from the Italian side of the equation? Have background and foreground reversed, frame and framed supplanted each other as in a sudden shift of magnetic poles? From an early time the Jews of Italy brought the host (Italian) culture into their own Jewish frame to a degree probably unsurpassed elsewhere in western Europe. To what extent might non-Jewish Italians today be incorporating Jewish culture into their understanding of Italianness?

Before attempting to answer this question, it is important to acknowledge that the soul of the revival in Pitigliano is not a non-Jew but rather Elena Servi, the only remaining Jewish woman from Pitigliano living in Pitigliano, and her motivation is clearly not financial, but educational, cultural, and spiritual (see Brockman 2003: 35). It was Signora Servi who set up the Little Jerusalem Association in 1997 'to conserve and enhance the artistic and cultural patrimony of the Jewish Community of Pitigliano' (La Piccola Gerusalemme di Maremma 2011). The association cares for the Jewish cemetery, the museum, the synagogue, and the former ghetto area, and promotes Jewish religious and cultural activities such as the annual European Day of Jewish Culture, an annual Jewish film festival, and occasional weddings and barmitzvahs (of Israelis and Jews from elsewhere in Italy). Again, just as is the case everywhere else in Italy, the majority of participants at these events and activities are typically not Jewish. The local winegrowers' co-operative works closely with the Little Jerusalem Association to produce kosher wine and kosher olive oil. Elena Servi and her small staff of two part-time assistants provide lectures and guided tours for the schoolchildren who come on field trips and to tourists who request information. These services are especially valuable since the majority of tourists are other Italians, who generally lack knowledge and experience of Jews and Judaism.

The synagogue remains the cornerstone of the revival, making all the other Jewish activities possible. Its renovation appears to have been the first step that committed Pitiglianesi to conserving the local Jewish heritage and perhaps to thinking of it as *their* Jewish heritage, since by the time the restoration became a local project, there were only a handful of Jews left in the town. The restored synagogue was part of what made Pitigliano into a Jewish site to be reckoned with, unlike the many Italian towns that display the barest traces of their once thriving Jewish communities, and which contain only the shells of synagogues emptied of their ornaments, recycled for other uses, or no longer accessible—towns that boast no Jewish delicacies, pseudo or real, and that offer no enlightenment whatsoever about their Jewish past.

'The Night of the Orvietani'

The physical monuments and the ephemeral items of material culture are important, but what defines Jewish heritage in Pitigliano, for both Jews and Catholics, may be something less tangible yet perhaps even more fundamental: a shared narrative of Pitigliano's Jewish history. This narrative is a 'story of history' (Glassie 1982), what might be called a 'master narrative', although not in the negative sense sometimes employed by literary critics. It carries forward the post-emancipation task of mediating Jewish and Italian identities, but in Pitigliano, with one Jewish family remaining, the narrative's vitality suggests that the mediation of Jewish and Italian identities is no longer the concern of Jews alone.

The gist of this story of history, a genre closely aligned with the folk genre of legend, is the proposition that Pitigliano escaped the antisemitism characteristic of European and, to a lesser extent, Italian history.[28] The narrative asserts that the relationship between Catholics and Jews in Pitigliano has been exceptionally good.[29] One traditional explanation for Pitigliano's nickname, in fact, is that it is called 'the little Jerusalem' because good personal interfaith relationships made it a symbol of peace, like its namesake. Although various anecdotes could be cited to demonstrate the Pitiglianese belief in the town's exceptionality, there are two major episodes to the narrative, and they echo each other. The first episode took place in 1799, and is referred to as 'the night of the Orvietani', and the second— the rescue of Jews living in Pitigliano during the Holocaust—took place in 1943–4. Here is a summary version of the 1799 incident recounted in a recent popular publication from Pitigliano:

In 1799, during the . . . reaction to the French revolutionaries, a group of dragoons [from Orvieto, thus 'Orvietani'] arrived in Pitigliano; they began to harass the Jews roughly, considering them French sympathizers, and they committed abuses and violence. Unexpectedly, the Christian population of Pitigliano rose up in arms in defense of the Jews, to the point of killing several dragoons and imprisoning the others. This episode remains unique in Italy, where, during the same period, in contrast to Pitigliano, the Jews of other cities underwent grievous violence, and entire Jewish communities, like that of Monte San Savino, were erased. What happened in 1799 definitively cemented the already healthy coexistence in Pitigliano between Christians and Jews, with the latter instituting an appropriate ceremony of thanksgiving, celebrated in their synagogue until recently. (Biondi 2009: 8)

The events of 'the night of the Orvietani' are fully confirmed, and in great detail, by court records of a trial in which the Pitiglianesi who killed the dragoons in defence of the Jews were exonerated (Salvadori 1999; Mano 2007). This remarkable incident also contains the key elements of the master narrative:

1. An attack on Pitiglianesi Jews by outsiders.

2. Defence of Pitiglianesi Jews by Pitiglianesi Christians (at risk to themselves).

3. Contrast with the treatment of Jews elsewhere at the same historical moment.

4. Reference to 'healthy coexistence' between Christians and Jews as the normal state of relations in Pitigliano.[30]

To borrow a phrase from a study of stories told in a border community in Northern Ireland, an area of sectarian conflict, it is the 'local rather than the denominational affiliation that is significant' in this narrative (Cashman 2008: 130). In other words, in this story of history, Pitigliano vs. Orvieto (local affiliation) is significant and stressed, while Jewish v. Christian (sectarian affiliation) is not and is downplayed. The citizens of Pitigliano see an attack on Pitiglianesi Jews as an attack on all Pitiglianesi by outsiders, the Orvietani.[31] For once, the Jews are not the outsiders; they live within the frame of local identity. The Orvietani misread Pitigliano, thinking their denominational affiliation (as Christians, whether from Orvieto or Pitigliano) far outweighs local affiliation (Pitiglianesi, whether Christians or Jews).

What puts this narrative within the realm of folklore is neither the truth nor the falseness of its content, but its repetition and transmission over the course of time through informal media such as popular publications and websites, and especially in conversations in Pitigliano. Pitiglianesi Jews also memorialized the incident, as Biondi mentions above, by celebrating the anniversary of the 'night of the Orvietani' in the synagogue as a local Purim until the late 1930s, when the fascist racial laws were decreed (see Spagnoletto 1999).[32] (Pitiglianesi Catholics also celebrated the event shortly after it happened (Salvadori 1991: 47–8)). The 'night of the Orvietani' is described with pride locally as 'the first time that a population rose to the defence of an ethnic minority against the unwarranted and bullying abuses of troublemakers who wanted to take possession of the property of the Jews, and against the iniquitous and sacrilegious ways in which those shady characters acted' (Celata 1999: 5).

The other major example of this narrative pattern is the rescue of the Jews of Pitigliano in 1943–4. Remarkably, almost all of the Jews remaining in the area at the time survived (Salvadori 1991: 104). As in 1799, it was ordinary peasants and townspeople who defended the Jews, this time by warning and then hiding them, at mortal risk to themselves. Elena Servi, for instance, was 13 years old when her family fled Pitigliano for the countryside. Catholic friends had warned her family of the imminent arrest of all Jews, and their escape was covered up by neighbours. The Servis spent the next eight months (November 1943–June 1944) fleeing from house to house to escape detection. Elena's father owned a fabric store in town and thus knew many country people who came to his store to buy cloth. However, his family was sheltered not only by people he knew but also by others they met for the first time when they arrived at their homes seeking shelter. Twelve different families helped them in all (Servi 2000). Several families from Pitigliano were recognized as Righteous Among the Nations by Yad Vashem, the Holocaust memorial in Israel, in 2002, for helping Pitiglianesi Jews hide from the Nazis (Greco: 2009: 99–100).[33]

These Second World War narratives, of which Elena Servi's experience is a prime example, follow the same pattern as 'the night of the Orvietani':

1. An attack on Pitiglianesi Jews by outsiders.

2. Defence of Pitiglianesi Jews by Pitiglianesi Christians (at risk to themselves).

3. Contrast with the treatment of Jews elsewhere at the same historical moment.

4. Reference to 'healthy coexistence' between Christians and Jews as the normal state of relations in Pitigliano.

Again, it was the 'local rather than the denominational [or perhaps 'racial'] affiliation that [was] . . . significant', to reiterate Cashman's observation (2008: 130).

However, this redemptive narrative is not the only way Pitiglianesi Jews recall the Second World War era. In contrast to Elena Servi's experiences, Edda Servi Machlin,[34] in her *Child of the Ghetto*, a memoir about growing up in Pitigliano between 1926 and 1946, writes, 'I don't know precisely at what age I first became aware of the anti-Jewish sentiments that most of our Christian peers harbored against us . . . the majority of the Pitiglianesi did increase their harassment of us from the onset of the racial laws' (1995: 67, 212). Although she also survived 1943–4 by being hidden in the countryside by Christians, Servi Machlin recounts episodes of near-betrayal. Even today her unnerving experience of returning to Pitigliano after the war and seeing one of her neighbours wearing her clothes is sometimes recalled in Pitigliano, even by non-Jewish locals.[35] She moved to Florence after the war, in 1952, and then to New York in 1958 (1981: 14, 38). In 1970, as she prepared to visit Pitigliano for the first time since she had left, disturbing thoughts about 1944 returned to her: 'even more than the physical condition of our home, which had been ransacked . . . it was the difficult readjustment and reinsertion into the *society which for the most part had rejected us and had wounded our egos perhaps beyond repair* that was troubling me' (1995: 16; emphasis added).

The different emphases in Elena Servi's and Edda Servi Machlin's stories may be due to different experiences, different personalities, the different ages of the two (one still a girl, one a young woman) at the time of the events, and the fact that one continued to live in Pitigliano while the other moved to New York City. They frame the non-Jewish Pitiglianesi in radically different ways, reflecting to some degree how they themselves felt framed—as Jewish co-citizens for Elena Servi, as Jewish others ('rejected') for Edda Servi Machlin. Part of the significance of Servi Machlin's memoir is that it is *not* the story told today in Pitigliano. It does not conform to the master narrative, the story of history that has been embraced.

Like German Jews in Germany, Italian Jews strove to be accepted as Italians. They sought confirmation and in Pitigliano found it not only in the experiences of everyday life, like the times local peasants would join them in the synagogue to pray for rain,[36] but also in a master narrative in which their co-citizens came to their defence when they were threatened by outsiders. At the same time, a counter-narrative expressed the bitter sense of having been rejected and wounded beyond repair.

I do not mean either to discount Servi Machlin's account or to deny the master narrative of Jewish Pitigliano, but only to suggest that Pitigliano has made a collective choice in the way its Jewish history is remembered and the way Jewish identity is framed, constructing a particular vision of itself formed from true but selected and edited historical events and experiences. In this, oral history is no different than written history: editing and selecting are essential to composing a narrative, whether done by professional historians or ordinary people.

Historical events have also given Pitiglianesi Christians questions to ponder about their identity, questions that they may try to answer through the stories they tell. Are they the immediate descendants of persecutors, of indifferent by-standers, of the apathetic, the frightened, or of rescuers? All types surely existed in Pitigliano, but it is the rescuers that dominate the master narratives of 1799 and 1943–4, while persecutors and bystanders dominate Servi Machlin's 'minority opinion'. Questions of local Jewish history turn out to be not only about the place of Jews in Italian society but about what kind of people the non-Jewish Italians (or, in this case, the Pitiglianesi) were and are. The affectionate nickname of their small city is, after all, 'The Little Jerusalem'. Their most important tourist attraction is a synagogue. They produce kosher wine and olive oil and Jewish delicacies. They have restored the architecture of a synagogue and a ghetto, built a Jewish conference centre, initiated a Jewish film festival, held conferences, and more. Hebrew words have even entered their Italian dialect (Salvadori 1991: 131–2; Servi Machlin 1981: 29–30). Yet there are only two Jews left in Pitigliano.

Beginning with a question of Jewish identity, we have arrived at a question of Italian identity. To what extent is Pitiglianese identity framed and defined by an 'other' who is no longer there? To what extent is that 'other' a vacuum some Pitiglianesi feel compelled to try to fill with objects and stories? When I asked the mayor of Pitigliano, Augusto Brozzi—who, along with Elena Servi, was largely responsible for getting the revival of interest in Jewish culture in Pitigliano under way—why he thought it mattered and why he had chosen to undertake the restoration project, he answered, 'to pass on the memory' and 'it's our culture' (Brozzi 2000). What I understood him to be saying was that Jewish history and culture in Pitigliano were not something separate for Jews but part of the whole, part of every resident's identity.

In Mayor Brozzi's view—and in that of many other local people—Jews were and are as much a part of Pitigliano as anyone else. The master narrative, exemplified by stories of the night of the Orvietani and of the German occupation, expresses the ideals and the beliefs of post-emancipation Italian Jewry—that Jewishness fits seamlessly within the frame of *italianità*, that to love Italy 'with all your heart and soul, with all your might' is to be Jewish while being Italian and to be Italian while being Jewish, and that good Italians accept their Jewish neighbours as equally Italian. But the fact that these particular stories persist in a Pitigliano almost devoid of Jews might suggest that they are no longer about Jews claiming their identity as Italians but perhaps about Italians claiming Jewish culture as part of Italianness. Paralleling the Jewish urge to believe that Jews belonged in modern Italy is a contemporary Pitiglianese urge not merely to jus-tify themselves but to do so by affirming that Jews did and do belong.

There exists a substantial and growing body of work on the political and juri-dical emancipation of Italian Jewry and the debate surrounding emancipation during the latter half of the eighteenth and especially the first part of the nine-teenth century (see esp. Voghera 1998; see also Canepa 1977, 1986; Capuzzo 1999; Mano 2013; Milano 1992: 338–82; Schächter 2010). The cultural dimen-sions of emancipation have not received as much treatment. Culture, especially folk culture (oral narratives, customary behaviour, and informal material culture such as foodways) is also significant and gives us a feel for the actual experiences of Italian Jews during this period of dynamic transition. Many who write about Italian Jewry in the post-emancipation era have lamented the rapidity and thor-oughness of assimilation and the betrayal that followed. Certainly, there is much to lament and regret, and the loss can never be compensated for. I think, however, that it is worth considering that many 'assimilating' Italian Jews saw what they were doing not as assimilation but as trying to find ways, through culture, to mediate two deeply felt identities, and to meld them together within one frame.

This tendency did not begin with emancipation—even during the ghetto era and before, Jews had often participated in Italian life as fully as they were allowed. (And they were generally allowed more in Italy than elsewhere in Europe.[37]) Nor did the attempt to participate end, it seems, with the Holocaust. In fact, in an unforeseen reversal, non-Jewish Italians may have recently become interested in the revival of Jewish culture as a way to salvage *their* identity. Jewish history and culture in Italy have become a kind of mirror in which Italians can see themselves more clearly. The pity is that the mirror was always there.

Notes

1 The original Broadway production, based upon Yiddish writer Sholem Aleichem's *Tevye's Daughters* written between 1895 and 1915 (with music composed by Jerry Bock, lyrics by Sheldon Harnick, and book by Joseph Stein), opened in 1964, and the film adaptation was released in 1971. For a discussion of *Fiddler on the Roof* in relation to tradition and nostal-gia, see Bronner 1998: 33–7.

2 Oring (1986: 28) gives the example of Sigmund Freud, who seems to have chosen his identity (German or Jewish) strategically according to the context: 'During a conversation, when a French guest predicted a ferocious war between France and Germany, Freud promptly explained that he was a Jew, adhering neither to Germany nor Austria [see Freud 1975: 203] . . . Yet it is also known that on many occasions, Freud considered himself thor-oughly German . . . and was attached to the idea of a greater Germany.' But these instances only describe outward behaviour; we don't know how Freud regarded himself—primarily German, primarily Jewish, equally both, neither, or to be determined according to the situ-ation, as Oring seems to suggest. There could even be other possibilities, such as Mora-vian, since Freud was born in Moravia. Furthermore, we could ask if his sense of his own identity changed over the course of his life.

3   Some use the different phrases to delineate historical change: '"From Italian Jews to Jewish Italians" ("da ebrei italiani a italiani ebrei") is the expression used by three Italian writers to illustrate the emergence of a new kind of Jew: the emancipated, liberal Jew for whom affiliation to traditional mores was altered' (Schächter 2011: 25). The three historians Schächter cites are Molinari 1991: 31, Salvadori 2000: 64, and Tas 1987: 105.

4   Hughes (1983: 2) used the phrase 'the most ancient of minorities' to describe Italian Jewry. Pugliese (2002) borrowed the same phrase as the title for his collection of essays.

5   *Ghetto* is originally an Italian word, referring to a specific area in Venice, site of the first area of restricted Jewish residence in Italy in 1516; see Ravid 1992: 373–85 for the evolution of the term. The dates I give for the ghetto period mark the outer limits, with the last ghetto being abolished in Rome in 1870. Ghettos were established in some towns in Piedmont as late as 1723 (Canepa 2011) and were abolished in some places, like Venice, as early as 1797.

6   The requirement to wear the distinguishing hat or badge preceded the establishment of ghettos by centuries. Remarkably, there was a case in which an abandoned newborn, found in the Venetian ghetto, was determined by the authorities to be Jewish, not Christian. There was accompanying evidence found with the child indicating Jewish parentage (a *mezuzah*, among other things), and the parents were ultimately located. Nevertheless, the ruling is noteworthy, coming at a time when every effort was made, and every excuse used, to convert Jews to Christianity, including forced or even secret baptism of Jewish infants. See Boccato 1978.

7   According to Roth (1975: 203), 'The disproportionate success of the Jews in their amours was one of the pretexts for the maintenance of the Ghetto system in all its rigor.' It is common for the perceived threat of the Other to be formulated folkloristically in sexual terms (Abrahams and Dundes 1969; Dundes 1997: 106; Ridley 1967).

8   Italian Jewish dialects were versions of local Italian dialects, as their names indicate: Giudeo-Veneziano (Jewish Venetian), Giudeo-Piemontese (Jewish Piedmontese), and so on.

9   As cookbook author and native of Pitigliano Edda Servi Machlin writes, 'Since the Italian Jews are either *Italkim* (from Italy) or *Sephardim* . . . their dishes do not resemble the traditional Central and Eastern European (*Ashkenazic*) ones to which American Jews are accustomed' (1981: 13). Augusto Segre recalls his original dismay at first encountering east European Jewish cooking when he was 18 years old: 'It's certainly not Mother's cooking' (2008: 139).

10   The ghettos in Florence and Rome (chronologically the second and third capitals of the new Italy, after Turin, the first) were torn down in the late 19th century. They were an embarrassment to the new Italy, but the Jews also felt the need to obliterate the memory of what had become an embarrassment to them, too, as if they were somehow responsible for their own degradation. The engraved text above the Piazza della Repubblica in Florence, in the place where the ghetto once stood, makes only indirect reference to the area as a place where Jews were confined and avoids the words 'ghetto' and 'Jew': 'L'antico centro della città / da secolare squallore / a vita nuova restituito' ('The ancient centre of the city, restored from age-old squalor to new life').

11   The following passage from the Jewish newspaper *Il vessillo israelitico* typifies their rhetoric as Italy entered the First World War in 1915:

At this moment every debate is, to us, a crime—just as every request for compensation is a disgrace. We should give without asking for anything because now we want nothing for ourselves. The only thing we want is for the Italian flag to fly above the unredeemed lands so that destiny will finally be fulfilled. We want civilization to spread its beneficent light upon nearby lands—so that our gentle language, and with it the immortal principles of liberty and fraternity, may spread among foreign regions. We want the Sabauda dynasty [Italy's royal house]—magnificent exemplar of every virtue —to be crowned with another wreath of glory. We want to win; we must win. We must show that the feeling of gratitude is deeply rooted in us and that we are taking our place, with flags flying and with unshakable resolution, in this admirable demonstration of harmony that all Italian parties are giving. 'To work, everyone—to war!' (quoted in Segre 2008: 41)

12 Giuseppe Foà, chief rabbi of Turin, actually declared, in a public ceremony commemorating the assassination of Umberto I, 'We feel ourselves to be Italians first and foremost, rather than Jews' (Canepa 1975: 196, quoting Lattes 1900–1: 105).

13 Arnaldo Momigliano spoke of 'parallel nationalization' of regional Italians and Jews. (Cited in Schächter 2010: 18.) Two often cited quotations express the then incomplete work of Italian unification in the late 19th century. The Risorgimento political figure Massimo D'Azeglio observed, after the military and political successes in unifying Italy, that 'though Italy was made, it was now necessary to make the Italians' (Smith 1959: 67). The French writer Maxime du Camp 'in Naples in 1860 heard people in the streets shout "long live Italy" and then ask their neighbour what the word "Italy" meant' (Smith 1959: 55).

14 Although Rabbi Samuel David Luzzatto, a leading 19th-century rabbinical scholar and part of the Wissenschaft des Judentums movement, 'endorsed [his] co-religionists' love of Italy' (Schächter 2011: 16), he also wrote: 'The prosperity of our nation does not depend on emancipation, but rather on love for one's own brother and on our bond of fraternity as children of one family; this is our happiness, which diminishes and is lost in the shadow of emancipation' (quoted in Klausner 1966: 95).

15 For the debate in Italy over Jewish emancipation during the end of the 18th and the first half of the 19th century, see Voghera 1998.

16 Canepa also argues that 'not all Italian Jews were assimilationists in the years after unification' (1986: 423).

17 Here, for example, are instances of such changes as introduced in 1889 in the Jewish Community of Asti (in Piedmont) in a document circulated within the community, entitled 'Modifications Introduced to the Exercise of Public Worship with the Unified Code That Will Go into Effect with the Opening of the New Oratory'. The new rules contravene some of the most cherished customs conserved by the non-bourgeois sector of the community and are even condescending:

    1) All prayers and recitations must be made by the Cantor, in conformity with the rules recommended by the Council and by the Signor Chief Rabbi.

    2) The responses that were in common use until now are absolutely forbidden to the public. It is equally prohibited, absolutely, to accompany the recitation of the prayers by the Cantor aloud.

    3) Putting on the *Tefillin* (Phylacteries) is prohibited in the Oratory. The faithful, in order to fulfill this precept, must put them on in the adjoining room, which is set

aside as a changing room, and when the service is over they must again go to the same room to take them off. . . .

5) The use of the *Taled* is permitted, on condition that it is clean and respectable and such as decorum requires. . . .

7) The ceremonial honors will cease being done by private individuals. The taking out of the Bible will always be done by the person who is officiating. . . .

9) The customary congratulations after the reading of each qerjà (reading of a passage of the Torah) are abolished.

10) The Blessing, which, following ancient custom was bestowed upon the children by the Chief Rabbi, is also abolished. . . .

12) The ceremony of the beating of the *'aravòth* (willows; a small bunch of branches are beaten or stripped of leaves as a symbol of God's forgiveness) on the day of *Hosha'anà Rabbà* (corresponding to the seventh day of *Sukkòth*) is absolutely forbidden. . . .

18) The *Birkàth Kohanìm*, performed until now by the *Kohèn*, is abolished, reserving the customary recitation to the Cantor. (As quoted in Segre 2008: 269)

18   One researcher notes the 19th-century 'adoption of a "dual identity" in the register of births, a Jewish name combined with a non-Jewish one: Tedida alias Ida, Mardocheo [i.e. Mordecai] alias Attilio, Mosè [i.e. Moses] alias Marco' (Shachter 2011: 20, citing Sori 1993: 214). Although having both a secular name and a religious name was a common custom among American Jews, it was an innovation for Italian Jews in the 19th-century period of dramatic transition. Both names apparently had equal legal status since they were both registered with the civil authorities.

19   See Segre 2008: 167. Although Augusto Levi, then president of the Italian Zionist Federation, was defending Zionism among Italian Jews in the speech Segre recalls, and one parent meant Italy and the other Zion, the analogy, as Segre used it at this difficult moment, applies equally well to the situation of Italian Jews.

20   This incident took place before the declaration of the racial laws in 1938, which took Italian citizenship away from Jews.

21   Ultimately this strategy failed since conversion was not regarded as valid for purposes of citizenship once the racial laws had come into effect. The criteria for Italian identity and citizenship then became racial and were applied retroactively. For the tormented twists and turns of Jewish identity in a mixed marriage in fascist Italy, see Lia Levi, *The Jewish Husband* (2009).

22   For treatment of this period in English see De Felice 2001, Stille 1991, and Zuccotti 1987. For personal experiences see Della Seta 1991, Lia Levi 2009, Primo Levi 1961, Loy 2000, Augusto Segre 2008, Dan Vittorio Segre 1987, and Sonnino 2006, among others. Picciotto's *Il libro della memoria: Gli Ebrei deportati dall'Italia (1943–1945)* (2002) is an encyclopaedic work that attempts to identify every Jew who was deported from Italy during the Nazi occupation.

23   My opening question about 'Italian Jewish' vs. 'Jewish Italian' is answered in a unique way in the title of a Holocaust memoir that had remained private for many years but was ultimately published in the original Italian (Sonnino 2004) as *Questo è stato: Una famiglia italiana nei Lager* and then in English (2006) as *This Has Happened: An Italian Family in*

Auschwitz. The title refers simply to an *Italian* family, not an Italian Jewish or Jewish Italian family. Perhaps the word 'Auschwitz' in the title is an adequate reference to Jewishness (and thus there is no need for the qualifier), even though many Auschwitz victims were not Jews. (The original Italian title, however, does not contain the word 'Auschwitz' but rather *Lager*—concentration camps.) Or perhaps the editors, in choosing the unqualified *Italian* in their title, wished to stress that these victims of Italy were Italians? Yet they were sent to Auschwitz not because they were Italians but because they were Jews.

24   In the opinion of an Italian woman attending the 'Modern Jewish Culture: Unities and Diversities' conference held in Wrocław, Poland, in June 2008, where I presented an earlier version of this essay, the word *ghetto* does not have the negative connotation in Italian today that it does in English and only identifies part of a city or town as historically Jewish. It is true that in several Italian cities, including Venice, 'ghetto' is currently understood simply to refer to an area of the city, and many residents apparently use the term without any awareness of its historical meaning. The sign for the Ghetto Wine Bar and Café, however, makes a selling point of an explicitly Jewish association—the image of the *ḥanukiyah*.

25   Here is my translation of the legend attached in printed form to the packaging of each *sfratto*:

> The *sfratto* is a typical Jewish sweet, produced exclusively in Pitigliano, with origins that date back to the middle of the seventeenth century. In the early years of the 1600s, the Jews who lived in the territory of Pitigliano were forced by an edict of the Grand Duke of Tuscany, Cosimo Medici II, to leave their own homes and concentrate themselves in a ghetto area, close to the synagogue. The eviction order [*sfratto*] was served by the bailiff and the notifying messenger by means of the ritual gesture of beating on the doors of Jewish homes with a club. The Jews of Pitigliano, a hundred years later, wanted to remember the order they had suffered under by means of the creation of a sweet. Thus the *sfratto* took on its name and form, in memory of that sad event.

26   Actually, there is at least one other outstanding example in Jewish custom (and probably more) of a tasty dish commemorating a painful experience: *ḥaroset*, the sweet mixture of nuts, apples, honey, and wine chopped or ground together and eaten at the Passover seder, which is said to recall the mortar Jewish slaves used with bricks when they laboured in Egypt. (The ingredients in the *sfratti* filling—coincidentally?—are similar.) But even in the case of *ḥaroset* it is possible that the dish had existed, perhaps as an appetizer, before it was connected to the Passover narrative, just as the legend connecting *sfratti* to the establishment of the ghetto probably comes after the creation of the pastry itself. Another dish, variously called *ruota di faraone* (wheel of Pharaoh), *frizinsàl*, or *hamin*, is eaten on the sabbath of 'Beshalaḥ', also known as Shabat Shirah—the sabbath, usually in late January or early February, on which the passage describing the crossing of the Red Sea is read. The dish is said to depict the overturned chariots and drowning Egyptians. Although the cookbook author Giuliana Vitali-Norsa (1970: 15) calls it 'a bit macabre', the dish commemorates a triumph, not a painful experience, in Jewish history (see Siporin 1984: 361–4). Interestingly, although both of these dishes—*ḥaroset* and *ruota di faraone*—are connected with distant biblical history, *sfratti* commemorate relatively recent local history (the mid-17th century).

27   Elsewhere I have written that 'Italian Jewish cookbooks . . . are no longer intended for Jewish audiences only. They also serve to secure a place for "Jewish cuisine" in the pantheon of "regional" Italian cuisine . . . Tradition-based foodways without religious sanction are

an important and prestigious way in food-conscious Italy to project Jewish identity into the future and into the society at large' (Siporin 1994: 278).

28   It can also be said that one master narrative of Jewish history in Italy is that antisemitism rarely took on the virulence and magnitude typical elsewhere in Europe. For example: 'In Italy there's never been a pogrom, not even when the Roman Church told the Christians to despise the Jews and accused them all of being usurers, not even when Mussolini decreed the racial laws, not even when northern Italy was occupied by the Germans: nobody in Italy knows what a pogrom is, they don't even know what the word means' (Primo Levi 1986: 325). Of course, there have been 'pogroms' (even if the term, being Russian in origin, sounds inappropriate) in Italy. Prominent examples of riots against Jews resulting in deaths include events in Sicily in the late 15th century (Roth 1946: 251–2) and in Siena in 1799 (Roth 1946: 437; Salvadori 1991: 77). There were many more instances in which ghettos and synagogues were sacked without loss of life. The historical record clearly shows that over the centuries there was less persecution in Italy than in most other places in Europe, but my point is not whether the master narrative is historically true or false. My point is that the narrative exists and expresses a historical judgement held by Italian Jews and non-Jews.

29   Roberto Salvadori's scholarly history of Pitigliano (1991) confirms the narrative. Jews in Pitigliano, for instance—unlike Jews almost everywhere else in Italy—had extensive property rights even in the 16th century (1991: 17–18). Elsewhere Salvadori writes that, besides having property rights, Jews in Pitigliano were artisans and that together these privileges 'imply the necessity or inevitability of a daily contact with the Catholic population that was unknown elsewhere' (1999: 16). In his proposal for a dissertation now (2013) in progress at Tel Aviv University, Davide Mano says that 'the judicial records of 1799 disclose new evidence that may indicate the existence of a unique relationship between Christians and Jews in Pitigliano' (Mano 2007; see also Mano 2013).

30   'During that era [the late 1800s and early 1900s] the relations between the Jews and the rest of the population were good. In fact, except for particular or difficult moments, they were always good.' This is the comment of Aldo G. Servi, a Jew who was born in Pitigliano in 1881. His notes were edited by Roberto Salvadori and placed in an appendix to his history of Pitigliano (Salvadori 1991: 130).

31   Orvieto was in the territory of the Papal State while Pitigliano was across the border in Tuscany. The towns were virtually in two different 'countries' although only about 25 miles apart. Tuscany was known for its liberalism while the Papal State was known for its reactionary politics.

32   A local Purim is a day set aside according to Jewish custom in order to celebrate local deliverance from a catastrophe (either human-caused—a riot, for instance—or natural). The celebration is modelled after the festival of Purim, based on the events recounted in the biblical book of Esther. Local Purims were especially common in Italy.

33   Those honoured by Yad Vashem were Fortunato Sonno; Luciano, Vincenzo, and Adele Dainelli; Stefano, Adele, and Sem Perugini; Agostino and Annunziata Nucciarelli; Domenico and Letizia Signorelli; and Martino and Maria Bisogni (Greco 2009: 99–100).

34   Not related to Elena Servi. 'Servi' is a common Jewish name in Italy.

35   Personal communication, R.N., January 2010.

36   For example, Aldo G. Servi recalls, 'Sometimes the farmers, all of whom were Catholics,

would gather at the temple to take part in a special prayer so that God would grant rain' (quoted in Salvadori 1991: 130).

37   One might object that Italy set up a widespread ghetto system and was the first country to do so. But the ghetto system must be understood in the context of a Europe in which Jews had been completely expelled from England, France, Portugal, and Spain and were allowed only in certain areas of the German states. At least the ghetto gave Jews a place to live.

References

ABOAFF, EMILIANO. 1978. Tape-recorded interview conducted by Steve Siporin. Venice, 14 Oct.

ABRAHAMS, ROGER, and ALAN DUNDES. 1969. 'On Elephantasy and Elephanticide'. *The Psychoanalytic Review*, 56: 225–41.

ALTSHULER, DAVID, ed. 1983. *The Precious Legacy: Judaic Treasures from the Czechoslovak State Collections*. New York.

BACCHI, ROBERTO. 1937–8. 'Le migrazioni interne degli ebrei dopo l'emancipazione'. *La rassegna mensile di Israel*, 12: 318–62.

BEDARIDA, GUIDO. 1950. *Ebrei d'Italia*. Livorno.

BIONDI, ANGELO. 2009. 'Gli ebrei a Pitigliano: La Piccola Gerusalemme'. In Carlo Fè and Angelo Biondi, eds., *Gli ebrei a Pitigliano: La Piccola Gerusalemme*, 3–23. Grotte di Castro, Italy.

BOCCATO, CARLA. 1978. 'Il caso di un neonato esposto nel ghetto di Venezia alla fine del '600'. *La rassegna mensile di Israel*, 44: 179–202.

BROCKMAN, ELIN SCHOEN. 2003. 'Pitigliano'. *Hadassah Magazine*, 85(4): 34–41.

BRONNER, SIMON J. 1998. *Following Tradition: Folklore in the Discourse of American Culture*. Logan, Utah.

BROZZI, AUGUSTO. 2000. Tape-recorded interview conducted by Steve Siporin. Pitigliano, 13 May.

CANEPA, ANDREW M. 1975. 'Emancipazione, integrazione e antisemitismo liberale: Il caso Pasqualigo'. *Comunità*, 29(174): 166–201.

——1977. 'L'atteggiamento degli ebrei italiani davanti alla loro seconda emancipazione: Premesse e analisi. *La rassegna mensile di Israel*, 43: 419–36.

——1986. 'Emancipation and Jewish Response in Mid-Nineteenth-Century Italy'. *European History Quarterly*, 16: 403–39.

——2011. 'The Uniqueness of Piemontese Jewry'. Public lecture, Museo Italo Americano, San Francisco, 20 Jan.

CAPUZZO, ESTER. 1999. *Gli ebrei nella società italiana: Comunità e istituzioni tra Ottocento e Novecento*. Rome.

CASHMAN, RAY. 2008. *Storytelling on the Northern Irish Border: Characters and Community*. Bloomington, Ind.

CELATA, ERNESTO. 1999. 'Presentazione'. In Salvadori, *La Notte della rivoluzione e la notte degli orvietani: Gli ebrei di Pitigliano e i moti del 'Viva Maria' (1799)*, 5. Pitigliano.

DE FELICE, RENZO. 2001 [1961]. *The Jews in Fascist Italy: A History*, trans Robert L. Miller. New York.

DELLAPERGOLA, SERGIO. 1976. *Anatomia dell'ebraismo italiano: Caratteristiche demografiche economiche, sociali, religiose, e politiche di una minoranza*. Assisi.

DELLA SETA, FABIO. 1991 [1969]. *The Tiber Afire*, trans. Frances Frenaye. Marlboro, Vt.

DOUGLAS, MARY. 1997 [1975]. 'Deciphering a Meal'. In Carole Counihan and Penny Van Esterik, eds., *Food and Culture: A Reader*, 36–54. New York.

DUNDES, ALAN. 1997. 'Why is the Jew "Dirty"? A Psychoanalytic Study of Anti-Semitic Folklore'. In Alan Dundes, *From Game to War and Other Psychoanalytic Essays on Folklore*, 92–119. Lexington, Ky.

ELON, AMOS. 2002. *The Pity of It All: A Portrait of the German-Jewish Epoch, 1743–1933*. New York.

FREUD, SIGMUND, 1975. *The Letters of Sigmund Freud*, ed. Ernst L. Freud, trans. Tania and James Stern. New York.

GLASSIE, HENRY. 1982. *Passing the Time in Ballymenone: Culture and History of an Ulster Community*. Philadelphia.

GOLDSTEIN, JOYCE. 1998. *Cucina Ebraica: Flavors of the Italian Jewish Kitchen*. San Francisco.

GRECO, GIOVANNI. 2009. 'Gli ebrei di Pitigliano, città rifugio, città dell'ospitalità'. In Roberto Giusti and Giovanni Greco, eds., *Pitigliano 'La Piccola Gerusalemme' terra della libertà e dell'accoglienza*, 95–101. San Giovanni in Persiceto.

GRUBER, RUTH ELLEN. 2002. *Virtually Jewish: Reinventing Jewish Culture in Europe*. Berkeley, Calif.

——2010. 'Introducing Non-Jewish Europeans to Jewish life', *JTA: The Global News Service of the Jewish People*. <http://www.jta.org/news/article/2010/08/31/2740732/introducing-non-jewish-europeans-to-jewish-life>, accessed 16 Sept. 2010.

GUNZBERG, LYNNE M. 1992. *Strangers at Home: Jews in the Italian Literary Imagination*. Berkeley, Calif.

HUGHES, H. STUART. 1983. *Prisoners of Hope: The Silver Age of the Italian Jews 1924–1974*. Cambridge, Mass.

KLAUSNER, JOSEF. 1966 [1910]. 'Il carattere, le credenze, le idee [di Samuel David Luzzatto]'. In Yoseph Colombo, ed., *Nel primo centenario della scomparsa di Samuel David Luzzatto*, 64–102. Milan.

La Piccola Gerusalemme Di Maremma. 2011. Website. <http://www.lapiccolagerusalemme.it>, accessed 11 Dec. 2011.

LATTES, DANTE. 1900–1. 'Rabbini e patriottismo'. *Corriere Israelitico*, 39(5): 105–7.

LEVI, LIA. 2009 [2001]. *The Jewish Husband*, trans. Antony Shugaar. New York.

LEVI, PRIMO. 1961 [1958]. *Survival in Auschwitz [If This is a Man]*, trans. Stuart Woolf. New York.

——1986 [1982]. *If Not Now, When?*, trans. William Weaver. New York.

LOY, ROSETTA. 2000 [1998]. *First Words: A Childhood in Fascist Italy*, trans. Gregory Conti. New York.

MACHLIN, EDDA SERVI. 1981. *The Classic Cuisine of the Italian Jews: Traditional Recipes and Menus and a Memoir of a Vanished Way of Life*. Croton-on-Hudson, NY.

——1995. *Child of the Ghetto. Coming of Age in Fascist Italy: A Memoir, 1926–1946*. Croton-on-Hudson, NY.

MANO, DAVIDE. 2007. 'The "Trial of the Revolution" of Pitigliano: Christians and Jews in the Anti-French Uprisings of 1799', dissertation proposal, School of Historical Studies, Tel Aviv University.

——2013. 'Towards Jewish Emancipation in the Grand-Duchy of Tuscany: The Case of Pitigliano through the Emblematic Figure of David Consiglio'. In Shlomo Simonsohn and Joseph Shatzmiller, eds., *Italia Judaica: Proceedings of the Jubilee Conference*, 107–25. Leiden.

MILANO, ATTILIO. 1992 [1963]. *Storia degli ebrei in Italia*. Turin.

MOLINARI, MAURIZIO. 1991. *Ebrei in Italia: Un problema di identità (1870–1938)*. Florence.

MOMIGLIANO, ARNALDO. 1994. *Essays on Ancient and Modern Judaism*, ed. Silvia Berti, trans. Maura Masella-Gayley. Chicago.

NAHON, UMBERTO. 1970. *Holy Arks and Ritual Appurtenances from Italy in Israel* [Aronot kodesh vetashmishei kedushah me'italyah beyisra'el]. Tel Aviv.

ORING, ELLIOTT. 1986. 'Ethnic Groups and Ethnic Folklore'. In Elliott Oring, ed., *Folk Groups and Folklore Genres: An Introduction*, 23–44. Logan, Utah.

PICCIOTTO, LILIANA. 2002 [1991]. *Il libro della memoria: Gli ebrei deportati dall'Italia (1943–1945)*. Milan.

PUGLIESE, STANISLAO, ed. 2002. *The Most Ancient of Minorities: The Jews of Italy*. Westport, Conn.

RAVID, BENJAMIN C. I. 1992. 'From Geographical Realia to Historiographical Symbol: The Odyssey of the Word *Ghetto*'. In David B. Ruderman, ed., *Essential Papers on Jewish Culture in Renaissance and Baroque Italy*, 373–85. New York.

RIDLEY, FLORENCE H. 1967. 'A Tale Told Too Often'. *Western Folklore*, 26: 153–6.

ROTH, CECIL. 1946. *The History of the Jews of Italy*. Philadelphia.

——1975 [1930]. *History of the Jews in Venice*. New York.

RUDERMAN, DAVID B., ed. 1992. *Essential Papers on Jewish Culture in Renaissance and Baroque Italy*. New York.

SACERDOTI, SABATINO. 1843. *Al dottor Samuele Liuzzi di Reggio: Lettera riguardante gli israeliti italiani*. Parma.

SALVADORI, ROBERTO G. 1991. *La comunità ebraica di Pitigliano dal XVI al XX secolo*. Florence.

——1999. *La notte della rivoluzione e la notte degli orvietani: Gli ebrei di Pitigliano e i moti del 'Viva Maria' (1799)*. Pitigliano.

——2000. *Gli ebrei di Firenze: Dalle origini ai giorni nostri*. Florence.

SCHÄCHTER, ELIZABETH. 2011. *The Jews of Italy, 1848–1915: Between Tradition and Transformation*. London.

SEGRE, AUGUSTO. 1986. *Racconti di vita ebraica: Casale Monferrato—Roma—Gerusalemme, 1875–1985*. Rome.

——2008 [1979]. *Memories of Jewish Life: From Italy to Jerusalem, 1918– 1960*, trans. Steve Siporin. Lincoln, Nebr.

SEGRE, DAN VITTORIO. 1987 [1985]. *Memoirs of a Fortunate Jew: An Italian Story*. Bethesda, Md.

——2010. 'The Roles of the Jews in Italian Society: Interview with Dan Segre'. *Jerusalem Center for Public Affairs Projects and On-Line Publications*, no. 53 (15 Feb.). <http:

//www.jcpa.org/JCPA/Templates/ShowPage.asp?DBID=1&TMID=111&LNGID=1& FID=385&PID=0&IID=3281>, accessed 11 Dec. 2011.

SERVI, ELENA. 2000. Tape-recorded interview conducted by Steve Siporin. Pitigliano, 29 Feb.

SIPORIN, STEVE. 1984. 'The "Table of the Angel" and Two Other Jewish-Venetian Food Customs'. *Lares*, 50: 357–65.

——1994. 'From *Kashrut* to *Cucina Ebraica*: The Recasting of Italian Jewish Foodways'. *Journal of American Folklore*, 107: 268–81.

——2002. 'The Survival of "the Most Ancient of Minorities"'. In Stanislao Pugliese, ed., *The Most Ancient of Minorities: The Jews of Italy*, 361–8. Westport, Conn.

SMITH, DENIS MACK. 1959. *Italy*. Ann Arbor, Mich.

SONNINO, PIERA. 2006 [2004]. *This Has Happened: An Italian Family in Auschwitz*, trans. Ann Goldstein. New York.

SORI, ERCOLE. 1993. 'Una "communità crepuscolare": Ancona tra Otto e Novecento'. In Sergio Anselmi and Viviana Bonazzoli, eds., *La presenza ebraica nelle Marche*, 189–278. Ancona.

SPAGNOLETTO, AMEDEO. 1999. 'La notte degli Orvietani o Purim Sheni di Pitigliano: Ricordi di un rituale a 200 anni dagli avvenimenti'. *La rassegna mensile di Israel*, 65: 141–78.

STILLE, ALEXANDER. 1991. *Benevolence and Betrayal: Five Italian Jewish Families under Fascism*. New York.

TAS, LUCIANO. 1987. *Storia degli ebrei in Italia*. Rome.

VITALI-NORSA, GIULIANA ASCOLI. 1970. *La cucina nella tradizione ebraica: Ricette di cucina ebraica, italiana, askenazita e sefardita raccolte da Giuliana Ascoli Vitali-Norsa*. Padua.

VOGHERA, GADI LUZZATTO. 1998. *Il prezzo dell'egualianza: Il dibattito sull'emancipazione degli ebrei in Italia (1781–1848)*. Milan.

ZUCCOTTI, SUSAN. 1987. *The Italians and the Holocaust: Persecution, Rescue, Survival*. New York.

Jewish Museums: Performing the Present through Narrating the Past

DAVID CLARK

MANY POSTMODERNIST theorists have stressed the importance of spectacle and performance in contemporary societies (Baudrillard 1997), and most commentators have focused on the increasing reliance on hyper-reality and simulation, such as the use of theme parks like Disney World, themed shopping malls, restaurants, and parties, with period or ethnic costumes and stage sets. In some cases the visitor is transported to an imaginary world; in other cases, as in model villages set up for tourists in Africa or Asia, one is offered a glimpse of native life, with costume, dance, and song (Baudrillard 1994; Eco 1987; Stanley 1998). In this essay, however, I shall be focusing on the manner in which actual 'community', and Jewish communities in Italy in particular, are being performed, placed on show, displayed, and made visible in the present through manipulating aspects of the past. In the process objects, spaces, buildings, and people are pressed into service in order to convey a particular narrative.

In her book *Destination Culture* Barbara Kirshenblatt-Gimblett (1998) focuses on museum displays and comments that 'ethnographic' objects in a museum have been collected, appropriated, and removed from their original sites only to be transferred to a new context in the museum. Such fragments then acquire and take on new meanings and new roles. The same object on display can be drafted in to represent any number of different narratives or perspectives. Yet such objects do more than tell a story. Kirshenblatt-Gimblett argues that 'display not only shows and speaks, it also *does*' (1998: 6). By this she means that the display of objects, or indeed the display of people, involves embodying, performing, and enacting the very concepts they are meant to illustrate.

The primary focus of this essay is on inanimate objects or buildings that do not move or speak, dance or sing. Such a focus owes a great deal to Kirshenblatt-Gimblett's seminal article 'Objects of Ethnography', first published in 1991. Her 1992 'From Cult to Culture: Jews on Display at World Fairs' was a further inspiration for my research. I seek here to illustrate how inanimate objects, buildings, and spaces within the built environment can perform community for an audience of real people in the present. While the emphasis is on performing Jewish community to a contemporary audience, each performance is multifaceted, commenting on the past as well as on the present, and indeed being a marker for the future as well. As we shall see in turn, such objects and spaces comment on and present a narrative that tells a story concerning Jewish life in Italy, more especially Venice, Florence, Bologna, and Ferrara, where this research was conducted as part of my Ph.D. dissertation (Clark 2004).

In particular, what is being performed is a certain kind of narrative concerning the manner in which Jews were an integral part of the history and culture of these cities in the past and are still now, both at the local neighbourhood and city level as well as the national level.

In order to perform such a narrative, objects, plaques, and texts are carefully stage-managed for the audience. Such a dramaturgical approach to everyday life has most notably been expounded by Erving Goffman (1959). Goffman's distinction between front region and back region was further discussed by Dean Mac-Cannell (1976), who refers to the importance of stage management in tourist attractions and displays. In the cases outlined below the scene is set and objects are placed on the stage, whether this stage is a glass cabinet in a museum, a plaque on a museum or synagogue wall, or a memorial plaque or stone outside the synagogue entrance. The stage is set and the visitors come to view the spectacle set before them.

In my use of the notion of narrative performance I also partly rely on Richard Schechner's exposition on performance theory (Schechner 2003). In his account of tribal ritual in the Highlands of Papua New Guinea he describes how, through dance and elaborate feasting and speechmaking, each village community is placed on show, reaffirming social and economic ties with neighbouring groups. Some of these rituals involve the bringing together of allies and the reaffirmation of such ties; other rituals entail the bringing together of former warring groups. Each aspect of the proceedings, the arrival and welcoming of guests, the giving and sharing of food, the exchange of gifts, the dancing and singing, took place in real time but simultaneously reflected and mirrored ongoing social relationships, and, at the same, the doing thereof, the feasting and the dancing, the speech-making, sealed these relationships much in the same way as John Austin describes in terms of performative utterances (1962). Austin suggests that certain utterances or forms of speech actually perform or create the state of affairs to which the words refer, such as the naming of a ship or the pronouncement of being legally married by a person formally charged to undertake such a pronouncement, thus creating a legal union by the very act of the pronouncement.

While examples from Papua New Guinea might seem a little far-fetched, what is crucial here is to note the manner in which various elements come together to create a whole, and in the process help to construct community. In my discussion I shall be referring to objects and spaces that do not have their own voice. Sometimes explanatory labels or texts are placed next to the object, building, or memorial. Even such texts need interpretation and can only be heard or made sense of through the understanding of, and connections made by, the audience. Yet the audience is never monolithic, and its members vary considerably in the manner in which they see what is set out in front of them.

The audience that comes to view a Jewish museum, quarter, ghetto, or even synagogue is a very mixed audience indeed, comprising young and old, Jews and non-Jews, locals and tourists, scholars and schoolchildren. Individuals will come with their own expectations and levels of knowledge, and will experience the 'performance' in their own particular way. Here I have found the notion of 'interpretative communities' developed by Eilean Hooper-Greenhill (2000) particularly useful, and I discuss it further below.

My study focuses on four Jewish museums in Venice, Florence, Ferrara, and Bologna, and the immediate spaces surrounding and encompassing the museums themselves. Within these cities the Jewish quarter or ghetto provides the backdrop for the stage; the buildings and spaces in between the buildings are as much part of the stage set as they are part of the story. The visitors wander onto the stage, mingle with objects and buildings from the past, and seek to make sense of both the past and the present, and of the relationship of past and present Jewish communities to their social surroundings.

Below I examine the manner in which Jewish museums and the spaces immediately adjacent to them can be seen to be performing community in the present. My analysis focuses on five key aspects of performing community: space, objects, labels, plaques, and inhabiting space in a visible manner. In each case, I also draw attention to the extent to which such performance addresses an internal Jewish audience or an external one, whether co-citizens or tourists.

A note of caution should be introduced here. I will be describing the manner in which Jewish Italian communities are being 'performed' for an audience. Yet the very existence of a community or what such a community might entail, or indeed, who is part of such a community, is by no means self-evident. Many authors, such as Hillery (1955) and Cohen (1985), have sought to define community. Initial formulations focused on common territory, history, and shared values. More recent studies have underscored institutional arrangements, social interactions, and shared norms and expectations, as well as the importance of community in generating a sense of belonging (Crow and Allan 1994). In the perspective represented in this essay, community is not a fixed given but is, rather, constantly in the process of being constructed, reworked, and reconstructed. Hence, who is perceived to be part of various Italian Jewish communities and whose voice should be heard as representing a community is not always uncontested or without controversy (Clark 2007, 2011). Such issues are especially likely to arise and be aired in the context of museums and exhibitions that seek to display community. Jewish museums are not unique in this, as representing any kind of community is likely to be contentious. Andrea Witcomb (2003) makes the same point; writing about the Australian experience, she notes that 'the representations that result in community galleries are those of particular *sections* of the community' (2003: 101); hence her advocacy for multi-vocality in the museum sphere, with the curator seeking to ensure some kind of balance and fair play.

What I am suggesting is that certain objects, labels, plaques, and spaces are pressed into service to tell a story and make community visible, and yet they do more than this, since in the process of the telling they also help to construct the community. It is in this sense that such items not only show and tell, but also 'do', as Kirshenblatt-Gimblett would claim. I am not suggesting here that this is the only method by which community is constructed, but that it is certainly part of the building blocks with which community is constructed, assembled, and reassembled.

The Development of Jewish Museums in Italy

While Jewish museums were already being set up in Germany, Austria, and Czechoslovakia towards the end of the nineteenth and in the early twentieth centuries, and one was set up in Britain in 1932, such museums did not appear in Italy until after the Second World War. The first Jewish museum in Italy was inaugurated in 1955 in Venice, as the American Joint Distribution Committee sought to lend support to devastated Jewish communities in Europe and aided in the reconstruction of communal infrastructure in the city. The museum was housed in one of the synagogues in the ghetto area, in close proximity to other communal institutions such as the chief rabbi's office, the communal library, and the old people's home.

The next wave of Jewish museums owes much to the changing demographic distribution of Italian Jewry and the dwindling of smaller Jewish communities in provincial towns, already badly affected by deportations to death camps during the Holocaust. In the post-war era the younger generation was drawn increasingly to the urban centres of Rome and Milan. In Casale Monteferrato, in Piemonte, the synagogue had already been declared a national monument in the 1950s but it was not renovated until 1968. Its museum is housed in the ladies' gallery and focuses mainly on the history of Jewish settlement in the area (Cohen-Grossman 2003). Asti synagogue in the same region was restored in 1999 and Soragna, near Padua, saw its synagogue turned into a museum in the 1990s. Such restorations and initiatives were often undertaken with local and regional authority funding but with the active collaboration of members of the local Jewish community. This was greatly facilitated in 1987 when an agreement was signed by the Italian government and the Unione delle Comunità Ebraiche Italiane (the umbrella organization for all Jewish communities in Italy), assigning joint responsibility for the preservation of Jewish cultural heritage to the Italian state and to the local Jewish communities most directly affected. This was enshrined in law in 1989. The Jewish museum in Bologna is another example of such collaboration, in this case initiated by the regional institute for cultural heritage (Istituto per i beni culturali), which retains a statutory responsibility to oversee the preservation of all cultural heritage in the region of Emilia Romagna. The museum is designed as a resource and documentation centre, with relatively few objects on display, but with a great number of text panels, CD-ROMs, and multimedia facilities (Clark 2011).

Another wave of museum initiatives emerged from within the Jewish communities themselves, for example, in Rome in 1977, in Livorno and Florence in 1981, and in Ferrara in 1997. Such museums have quite splendid exhibits of Jewish ritual objects—some of them actually still used by the communities in religious services on festivals, others donated by members of the community or well-wishers. Increasingly—for example, in Florence and Ferrara—museums have displayed photographs and memorabilia associated with the social history of the local Jewish community.

Museums and Exhibitions as Text

Roger Silverstone, a leading pioneer of media and communication who has drawn upon literary and anthropological theory to analyse the story-telling power of modern media, writes: 'Museums are in many respects like other contemporary media. They entertain and inform; they tell stories and construct arguments; they aim to please and to educate' (1994: 162). Yet as Kevin Moore, a major exponent of the role and importance of popular culture, points out, such narratives are all the more appealing, interesting, and exciting to an audience if they entail 'real' objects, places, and people (1997: 135–8). By using the term 'real', Moore wishes to indicate the link between objects, spaces, and people, on the one hand, and historical events clearly associated with those objects and spaces on the other. As an example of the power of the real place combined with the power of real things, Moore suggests a historic house with an outstanding collection of period objects, furniture, and paintings in their original setting, as could be found in a location such as Buckingham Palace, for instance (1997: 138). Another example would be a display of Keppoch's sword in the museum on the site of the battle of Culloden; the sword was actually worn at the battle of Culloden and its owner died there (Pearce 1992: 24–30). The same sword, exhibited in a room at the Museum of Scotland in Edinburgh, for instance, would still elicit some interest, but some of its emotive and evocative power would be lost in the process. Susan Pearce goes to some lengths to dissect the various layers of meaning pertaining to such 'real' objects. In her article 'Objects as Meaning; or Narrating the Past', for example, she examines the layers of meaning attached to a jacket worn at the battle of Waterloo (Pearce 1994).

This process of interpreting the past is perceived and received differently by different audiences (Hooper-Greenhill, 2000). In the context of Jewish museums in Italy we can observe at least four interpretative communities: an internal, Jewish audience subdivided into a local and a visiting audience, and an external, non-Jewish audience, likewise subdivided into a local and a visiting audience. Thus, when it comes to 'performing' Jewish community, different audiences and interpretative communities will respond differently to such performances.

Below I examine in some depth the textual nature of Jewish museums in Italy and the spaces immediately surrounding such museums, often ghetto areas. This entails an examination of the various narrative discourses being presented and displayed, whether through objects, labels, buildings, or spaces. The manner in which these various elements interact with each other constitutes the performance that visitors are invited to watch and in some ways respond to and interpret in their own way.

Making Claims for Belonging

A number of authors have commented on the use of displays, objects, and texts as a means to bolster claims. First and foremost are institutional claims made by museums. Traditionally, what has defined museums, and given them a *raison d'être*, are its collections. Silverstone writes:

the particular biography it constructs for these objects as justification for their inclusion in the collection or display—results in an abstraction. The ensuing meanings are of necessity partial but, more importantly, they are an essential part of the particular claims for authority and legitimacy on which the museum's whole status depends. (1994: 164)

What is being promoted and asserted by museum curatorial staff is the institutional expertise and authority in a particular field of knowledge, to collect and display suitable objects and to identify, label, and place such objects and labels in a suitable narrative framework. Thus, for instance, in connection with an exhibition on change and continuity in the New Guinea Highlands, Henrietta Lidchi comments on the use of photographic displays alongside real objects collected in the field:

it tends to legitimate the photographer/curator voice since the image denotes and guarantees O'Hanlon's having been there in the Highlands. It connotes *authentic* anthropological knowledge which means being appropriately familiar with the Wahgi. By association it authenticates the objects: they were collected while *he-was-there*. (1997: 171)

Hence what is being asserted at the same time are both the expertise of the curator and the authenticity of the objects on display, by displaying photographs of these objects in their original settings, before they were acquired by the museum.

Much of my discussion here revolves around the notion of making claims— not so much claims for authority and expertise, though undoubtedly claims are being made for authenticity, but perhaps even more crucially claims for belonging: belonging to the local Jewish community, belonging to the city, and belonging to the nation. Indeed, in the process of making such claims space, objects, labels, and plaques are all brought into play, to varying degrees and in different combinations, and it is this dynamic process that I illustrate below.

Using Space to Construct Community

Space can be used to perform community both to an internal and an external audience. Ghetto spaces in Italy, for example, have a historical reality and denotation, having been clearly marked out in the past as quarters where Jews were required to reside. But such areas can also be reclaimed as markers to connote a Jewish presence in the city today. Thus, for instance, the ghetto in Bologna operated only for a very short period of time, from 1556 to 1593, when Jews were expelled from the city. Yet in the 1980s the designation of ghetto was being revived to identify the neighbourhood as a distinct part of the city centre.

In Bologna there is a strong cult of memory surrounding the resistance against German occupation and the Italian fascist regime. Sites associated with the resistance are marked by plaques. Commemorations reach a climax annually on 25 April, the day of liberation from German occupation, with marches, speeches, and the placing of wreaths.

There is also a Jewish dimension to this cult of memory. Two plaques now commemorate Jewish deportees, who were rounded up in 1943 and sent to death camps. One plaque is placed on the exterior wall of the synagogue, well outside the former ghetto area, while the other is placed within the ghetto area, on the exterior wall of a former synagogue, now a private residence. Both plaques were erected by the Jewish community in 1988, fifty years after the enactment of racial legislation in Italy.

It is significant that these plaques were put up in the 1980s, at a time when collective memory concerning Jewish sites was being revived throughout Europe. In a previous paper I have noted the relative amnesia exhibited by most European countries concerning Holocaust sites, with few notable exceptions, such as the Ghetto Fighters Monument in Warsaw (Clark 1999). Only in the 1980s did the fact that Jews had been amongst the victims of such atrocities come to be more widely acknowledged. A number of factors contributed to this wave of interest in commemorating the Holocaust from the 1980s onwards (Clark 2007).

Yet there is more to these two plaques than just the politics of memory. I would argue that the erection of the plaque in the Bologna ghetto was the first step in a deliberate attempt to mark out the area and reclaim it as a Jewish space, even though Jews no longer live there. Indeed, there is added poignancy in setting up these two plaques, one in the area of the ghetto, where the Jews used to live in the past, and the other on the wall of the present synagogue. Such physical markers would remind Bologna residents not only of a Jewish past in the city, but also of a Jewish presence in the here and now.

Feldman writes: 'in 1988, as a way of marking the fiftieth anniversary of the ratification of the fascist laws, the Jewish community worked with the city of Bologna, the regional cultural heritage board, and the chamber of commerce on an exhibition tracing the history of the ghetto in the city' (Feldman 2002: 183). The resultant exhibition of large colour photographs of the ghetto not only laid claim to the area as a Jewish residential quarter in the past, but also sought to highlight the continued presence of a Jewish community in Bologna and their right to be considered as full members of the city's social and political fabric. The case of Bologna, then, is a fine example of the narrative emphasizing that Jews were and are part of the city and the nation, and have been for a considerable period of time. This discourse needs to be set in the wider context of Italian Jewry.

There are currently around 30,000 Jews in Italy; this relatively small number has contributed to the low profile accorded to official ties between the state and Italian Jewry. However, this was all to change in the 1980s. I have already indicated the general trend, in the 1980s, in Europe and America, of increased awareness and willingness to acknowledge the Jewish presence, especially in relation to the events of the Holocaust. In Italy there have been two further factors giving impetus to such acknowledgement. Firstly, there were the initial steps taken at reconciliation between the Catholic Church and the Jewish people. This was enshrined in the Vatican encyclical in 1965, rejecting previous charges against the Jewish people of deicide. Such rapprochement was given a further boost by the visit of Pope John Paul II to the Great Synagogue in Rome in 1986 and to Israel in the year 2000. Secondly, there were moves to place relationships between the Italian state and Italian Jewry on a more formal basis. This led to an agreement for active collaboration on a number of issues. Section 1 of article 17 of Law 101, March 1989, made specific reference to cultural heritage. It specified that the state (at central, regional, and local level), the Union of Italian Jewish Communities, and the individual Jewish communities should collaborate in the stewardship and maintenance of all the historical, artistic, architectural, archaeological, archival, and cultural heritage of Italian Jewry. There are currently twenty-one such formally constituted Jewish communities, with Rome and Milan having the largest membership of well over 10,000 each, Florence 1,000 or so members, Venice around 500, Bologna 200, and Ferrara fewer than 100 members.

Within Bologna the impact of the exhibition and of the erection of the plaque went further, marking a sense of new beginning for the city's Jewish community in terms of its self-image and self-representation. To give but one example, the exhibition inspired the creation of a new logo for the Jewish community of Bologna. Incorporating a drawing of the former synagogue in the ghetto and a Hebrew inscription found on a sixteenth-century ghetto building, the logo is used on all official letterheads, leaflets, and pamphlets published by the Bologna Jewish community. The photographic exhibition is now permanently displayed on the walls of the synagogue's social hall.

In the 1980s the ghetto began to assume a new-found significance for the Jewish community in Bologna as a means of marking internally the community's own corporate identity as well as of outwardly asserting the Jews' long-standing presence in the city and their continued involvement in its affairs

The very launch of the Jewish museum in May 1999, in premises provided by the municipality in the ghetto area itself, proved to be a wonderful opportunity for Jewish residents to be on show. Half the Jewish community in Bologna, together with other Jewish dignitaries from neighbouring towns in the region, turned up to the civic ceremony of laying a wreath in front of the ghetto plaque commemorating the deportation of Jews from Bologna in 1943. The presence of Jews in the ghetto streets that day was clearly visible to all who participated in the event. The ceremony was led by the deputy mayor and representatives of central government. The historic space of the ghetto was thus once more turned into a living Jewish space, albeit for the purposes of commemorating the dead. By remembering the past the contemporary Jewish community was also making a visible statement about its continued presence in the city at the turn of the twentieth century, thereby performing community to both an internal Jewish and an external non-Jewish audience. I discuss this event in greater detail below, in the section on inhabiting space.

Using Objects: Performing Community to an Internal Audience

Museums with a collection on display can perform community to an internal audience, as they do in Florence, Ferrara, and Venice, and objects have an important part to play in this performance and in the narration of a particular story. As Kirshenblatt-Gimblett argues, 'display not only shows and speaks, it also does' (Kirshenblatt-Gimblett 1998: 6). Indeed, objects 'perform' stories in a number of different ways—for example, through being handled and manipulated, much in the way puppets tell stories, whether a voice is heard or not. Sometimes the voice is provided by the addition of the written word, through the device of a text panel or a label, as I shall explore in a subsequent section. Yet the object is able to tell a story even without the aid of words. Ritual objects on display in Jewish museums can, for instance, create a sense of continuity with the past in a very real way: they may belong to the local community and may be taken out of their display cabinets and used on ceremonial or festive occasions, thereby linking past and present generations of the same community. Silver Torah crowns, textile mantles, and breastplates, mostly from the eighteenth century, normally displayed in the museum, are in use in the synagogue on festive occasions in Florence and Venice. Other items may be used at weddings or circumcisions. The objects and the life of the community are thus inextricably intertwined.

Many a moving ceremony, for example, has been undertaken in synagogues in recent years in former communist countries with the return of Torah scrolls to their former communities; most of the members of those communities perished in the Holocaust, but a few of their Torah scrolls miraculously survived and were eventually given back to them. To read *in situ* from such Torah scrolls is both a commemoration of the past and a celebration of Jewish survival, whatever shape or form it takes. Indeed what is precisely at stake here is an assertion of Jewish presence here and now, and a hope for its continuation in the future.

Museum objects should therefore not be admired simply for their aesthetic qualities. As Rabbi Della Rocca, the chief rabbi of Venice at the time of my study, was at pains to explain to me, their museum is not a museum in the usual sense of the word. The items on display, as well as the synagogue buildings, all have a use, a function, in religious ritual in the present. He would not wish people to regard either the objects or the buildings as being obsolete, as pertaining only to the past.

This phenomenon of buildings and objects being used for ongoing communal ceremony, rather than simply being gazed upon and admired, reminds me of Hooper-Greenhill's discussion of the importance of performative acts in relation to Maori meeting houses and treasures (Hooper-Greenhill 2000). Both place (meeting house) and objects (*taonga*) assume added meaning in the course of ceremony and speechmaking. Not only are the specific histories of place and objects kept alive by such performative acts, but, even more crucially, the Maori identity of the participants is reinforced and a vital link established between the past and the present, the dead and the living (Hooper-Greenhill 2000).

The use of 'treasured' objects imbued with special ritual meanings, together with the uttering of specific formulations of words appropriate for the occasion, as outlined by Hooper-Greenhill above, is closely related to Austin's notions of performative utterances (Austin 1962) or speech acts (Austin 1976). In both cases, whether contemporary Maori ritual invoking the ancestors or the use of 'treasured' religious artefacts in the contemporary ritual life of Italian Jewish communities, no new legal status is being created, but rather, we may witness the reinforcement of community identity and, crucially, an identity that is very clearly linked to past generations. The objects are part of the narrative, but there need to be people to perform the ritual at appropriate times and in appropriate places. The whole, together, constitutes narrative performance.

Thus, Jewish ritual objects and synagogues which have survived from the past and are still in use by the Jewish community maintain a vital link between past and present generations. But in addition they also reaffirm the community's long-standing history in the locality; its continuity depends partly on maintaining its traditions, customs, and rituals. These rituals may not necessarily be religious ones; as I will illustrate later, the laying of wreaths at plaques, or the institution of cultural festivals, may also provide opportunities for narrative performance and, just as crucially, for placing the community on show.

Using Labels: Performing Community through Intertextuality

Kirshenblatt-Gimblett notes that the second half of the nineteenth century saw greater importance being placed on labels and textual explanations. She describes George Brown Goode, director of the US National Museum, as operating on the principle that the most important thing about an exhibition was the label. Kirshenblatt-Gimblett neatly refers to the manner in which museum objects and the labels attached to such objects become inextricably intertwined and intertextual, referring to each other. She depicts such an interrelationship as 'textualizing objects/objectifying texts' (Kirshenblatt-Gimblett 1998: 30).

While Kirshenblatt-Gimblett focuses on how labels help to structure and order the museum or exhibition narrative, I examine the manner in which such texts can be used to further claims for authority, legitimacy, status, prestige, or simply belonging to the community. Carol Duncan (1995) notes the importance of philanthropists in the development of American museums and art galleries in the nineteenth century. City leaders and officials seeking to promote civic pride and enhance the prestige of their cities welcomed the contribution of wealthy supporters. Donations to museums and art galleries were an important means of validating, legitimating, and reinforcing the prestige and status of donors. In the case of Jewish museums, however, there is another dimension altogether which needs to be taken into account: it is the special blend of family history, communal history, and attachment to the locality that comes to the fore. Moreover, Jewish museums would readily accept all kinds of donated objects, especially if they had a ritual connection.

Narrative performance is often reinforced through the device of attaching explanatory labels to objects on display. Virtually all the items on display in the Jewish museums in Venice, Florence, and Ferrara have brief explanatory labels. Besides providing information on the objects, a significant number of these labels also indicate the name of the donors and sometimes even mention parents or relatives in whose memory the items were donated. In this manner personal family histories become intimately linked with communal history, which reinforces a sense of belonging and attachment to the local Jewish community.

In a way, these late twentieth-century donors were carrying on a tradition that had been long established, in terms of community members making substantial donations to local synagogues by way of gifts of ritual objects. Richard Cohen (1998) points to the donation by the Marx family of a Torah shield in the early nineteenth century to their synagogue in Munich, thereby asserting the family's claim to be considered among the pillars of the synagogue. Cohen further notes

Figure 1 Torah finials on display at the Jewish museum in Venice. *Photograph by David Clark*

the extent of self-representation of members of the Jewish burial society in Prague, who, in 1870, commissioned a series of paintings of the work undertaken by the society, including a group portrait of its leading members. Here there was both visual and textual self-referencing.

The displays of the Jewish museum in Venice provide numerous examples of the unique combination of family, community, and local history described above. There are silver spice boxes donated by Paolo Alazrachi, Adolfo Ottolenghi, and Regina Tedeschi Ottolenghi; Hanukah candelabra donated by Gino Cesana in memory of his wife; amulets donated by Emilio Vitali; a set of finials donated by the Artom-Sullam family, and so forth. Some of the items were clearly family heirlooms with special meanings attached to them. Thus, in one of the display cabinets there is a silver book-binder from the nineteenth century which was used to contain a prayer book, with a dedication to Nella Vivanti. It was donated by Marina Marinoni, in memory of Luisa Vivanti Marinoni. Here we have an object on display that was handed down within the family, along the female line—which is of note in itself—involving at least three generations: from mother to daughter to granddaughter.

Another intriguing set of donations is to be found in the second exhibition room, where, among the textile displays, one of the cabinets is devoted to circumcision (Figure 2). What makes some of the items here particularly fascinating is their link to a family's history. The cabinet contains an assortment of dresses, vestments, shoes, and other items worn at circumcision by various members of the same family, over several generations. The display starts with the dress worn by Laudadio Gentilomo (born in Pesaro in 1779, died in Venice in 1854) and includes items worn by his grandson Amedeo Laudadio Grassini (who lived in

Figure 2 Display cabinet of circumcision clothing at the Jewish museum in Venice. *Photograph by David Clark*

Venice from 1848 to 1908). The items were donated in memory of Amedeo Sarfatti (1902–87), who was in turn a grandson of Amedeo Laudadio Grassini. There is also a brief family tree outlining the relationships between all of these people, involving five generations of Venetian Jews.

Laudadio Gentilomo, according to the family tree, was married to Sara Fior Vivante, from another well-known Venetian Jewish family. The Vivante family had their own coat of arms, and one of the items displayed in the museum is a nineteenth-century silver bookbinder decorated with the Vivante coat of arms. Helen Leneman (1987) notes that when she visited the Venice ghetto in 1986 she was shown around by Cesare Vivante, an office holder within the Venice Jewish community at the time, and probably a member of the same family whose coats of arms are displayed in the museum. Hence many of the items on display provide self-referential cues, especially to Jews born and brought up in the city, concerning well-known Venetian Jewish families.

Roger Fowler (1981) suggests that literary texts make use of certain frames of reference and referential codes. This is achieved through the insertion into the text of generalizations, attitudes, or values generally shared by certain groups within society. 'The purpose of the rhetoric is to create an in-group, an audience . . . who are "in the know"' (1981: 101). The point here is that certain frames of reference may indeed be shared by sections of the audience or readership, in this case members of the Jewish community in Venice, but not by others, thereby promoting a sense of inclusion and belonging for some, or a sense of exclusion for others.

The donation of items to a local Jewish museum goes far beyond the mere act of giving: it may well indicate a desire to be included in the narrative discourse concerning the history (as well as present and future) of the local community. Such a discourse appeals particularly to an internal audience, whose members are keenly aware of the local family histories and their connections with the local community.

Thus objects, and the stories they carry, can perform and construct community either through their interaction with people making use of them in ritual, as described in the previous section, or through their interaction with labels and the use of intertextuality, as outlined in this section.

Using Plaques and Making Claims of Belonging to City and Nation

James Young writes: 'Depending on where the museums are built, and by whom, they remember the past according to a variety of national myths and political needs. All reflect both the past experiences and current lives of the communities, as well as the state's memory of itself' (2004: 42). He goes on to discuss issues arising at Jewish museums in Germany, Israel, and the United States, and the manner in which these museums have helped to incorporate and integrate Jewish memory and the memory of the Holocaust into the state's civic culture. Young is keen to demonstrate how some of the architectural features of the museums and monuments reinforce or challenge certain narratives. Examples could be taken from the monumental glorification by the German Democratic Republic of communist resistance against the Nazi regime at Buchenwald, or from the more subtle narrative of the sharp and brutal break with Berlin's past during the Holocaust as represented in the fragmented Star of David contours of Daniel Libeskind's Jewish Museum in Berlin. Staircases leading nowhere, and the construction of voids that run throughout the building, help to illustrate feelings of absence and invisibility, whilst a fragile thread of continuity and narrative flow is maintained in the museum itself.

While the architectural features of a building may themselves reflect a grand narrative, here I focus more narrowly on one particular aspect, namely, the use of plaques, both inside and outside a building, as a means of telling a certain narrative. In a sense plaques perform a role similar to museum labels and text panels, and yet there is more depth of meaning attached to them. The space where the plaque is placed is often significant in itself; what is being denoted here and marked are 'real' places and 'real' people with historical depth. Thus, for example, the plaque placed in the former ghetto area in Bologna serves both as a reminder of the deportation of eighty-four local Jews in 1943 and as a marker for the former ghetto area.

Such plaques do not appear by accident but are carefully chosen, in terms of their specific location and specific inscription, to convey a particular narrative. Thus, for example, plaques were placed in the 1960s by the left-wing Bologna municipality in prominent squares, commemorating all victims of Nazi atrocities and in some cases listing the names of fallen partisans, sometimes at the actual sites where they fell; there was no mention that any of the victims were Jews. The 1988 plaques in the ghetto and on the outside wall of the synagogue were the first to mention Jewish deportees as such, and the plaque at the synagogue also lists all deportees by name.

Moreover, the spatial conjunction of a museum and a functioning synagogue, as in the case of Florence and Ferrara, can provide further opportunities for narrating and constructing community. In Florence, as one leaves the synagogue building, on the right hand side there is a plaque with the names of all those Florentine Jews who perished in the Holocaust. Listed separately are also the names of partisans shot dead or fallen in battle. Another plaque commemorates those local Jews who died in the First World War. These plaques not only memorialize the dead but also emphasize the fact that Jews fought alongside other Italians—whether in the First World War or as partisans in the Second World War—reinforcing the notion that Italian Jews are also Italian citizens, thus deploying the rhetoric of equivalence.

Laclau and Mouffe (1985) suggest that social antagonism can be diffused by the use of certain kinds of rhetoric, such as the 'logic of equivalence', or softened by the use of the 'logic of difference'. Initial museological representations of Jews focused on the 'logic of equivalence'. Such narratives stressed the manner in which Jews should be considered to be part of the nation, because in some ways they shared similar values with other groups that made up the nation. Various ideational constructs were deployed in order to justify such claims for 'sameness', relying on one of three main discourse formations at the time: the role of the arts and aesthetics in the promotion of civilization, the role of world religions, and the role of elites in setting the right example. Kirshenblatt-Gimblett (1998) in particular focuses attention on the collection of ritual objects belonging to Isaac Strauss, exhibited in the 1878 Paris exposition as part of universal themes within arts and crafts rather than according to their particularistic religious use. They were to be seen as *objets d'art* rather than ritual objects—and if particularistic notions of religion were displayed, as in the case of the Smithsonian exhibits prepared by Cyrus Adler, then these were to be seen in the wider context of the development of world religions (Kirshenblatt-Gimblett 1998: 88–90).

To return to Jewish museums in Italy: the intended message of equivalence on the plaques is that Italian Jews, like other Italians, are first and foremost citizens of that country and proud of it. Napoleon was the first to grant Jews the same rights as the rest of the Italian population under his occupation, and this was further emphasized by deliberately knocking down ghetto walls and gates in those cities he had occupied. Later on it was King Carlo Alberto of the House of Savoy who gave equal citizenship to all Jews in his kingdom in 1848. The same rights were not extended to the rest of Italian Jewry until the unification of Italy in 1861, incorporating Venice in 1866 and Rome in 1870. Jews were then able to participate in all aspects of the nation's life and were fully integrated into the life of the community, making a notable contribution to the arts, mathematics, medicine, law, and economics. In the political sphere Jews were particularly active at the level of local politics, elected to mayor in a number of towns, including Rome in 1907. They also distinguished themselves in central government—Wollenborg as minister of finance in 1900, Ottolenghi as minister of war in 1902—and by 1920 there were nineteen Jewish senators in the Senate (Roth 1946: 479).

The link between the Jewish community and the newly emerging Italian nation-state is given visual expression through various plaques on display. One such plaque can be found in the entrance lobby to the synagogue in Florence, commemorating the visit to the synagogue made by Umberto I of Italy and Margherita of Savoy in May 1887. The theme of the contribution of the local Jewish community to the building of the nation is also prominent in the museum/synagogue in Ferrara. The tour of the museum begins in the courtyard; upon leaving the courtyard via a stone staircase, one passes a plaque on the left-hand side listing the names of members of the congregation who died fighting in the First World War. Another plaque mentions Felice di Leone Ravenna (1869–1937), president of the Jewish community in Ferrara and for a while mayor of the city. One of the exhibition cabinets displays two letters from the 1860s requesting one Leone Ravenna to present himself for duty at the local headquarters for the National Guard. There is also a register of all Ferrara Jews belonging to the National Guard from 1745 to 1820, further emphasizing that Jews were considered full citizens at the time and so expected to do their military duty just like any other male citizens, though a separate document dated 1826, signed by the archbishop, notes the renewal of restrictions on the freedom of Ferrara Jews, presumably on the return of papal rule to the area. Finally, a plaque in the main exhibition hall, dated 1863, praises King Vittorio Emanuele II for ending centuries of harsh enslavement of the Jews through unjust regulations.

What is noteworthy here is the manner in which the spatial juxtaposition binding museum and synagogue together reinforces certain narratives of inclusion. Addressing an internal audience, donors seek to include themselves in the narrative of the local community, while various plaques in the wider synagogue space reaffirm the 'logic of equivalence' to the wider public and make claims for inclusion in the historical discourse of city and nation.

Inhabited Spaces: Making Community Visible

Where museum, synagogue, and ghetto are intimately linked together they acquire special symbolic meaning. Shields states that any given site acquires its own space myths, history, and symbolic meanings (1991). All neighbourhoods in a city have such space myths: towards the end of the nineteenth century, for example, London's East End was regarded as inhabited solely by the poor and by criminals, whilst the West End had a more salubrious connotation. Some neighbourhoods were to be avoided or considered no-go areas, while others were sought-after residential areas. To be on the wrong side of the railway tracks reflects another kind of space myth. Of course, such myths change over time, as the space is occupied by different people or is used for a different purpose, transformed from run-down warehousing to upmarket waterfront areas, for instance.

The ghetto area in Venice has acquired many levels of meaning, both historical, with reference to the times when it was indeed a closed ghetto inhabited only by Jews, and current in the context of a much more fluid, shared space. Today's ghetto is a residential, communal, and touristic neighbourhood in which non-Jewish residents predominate, with their own local institutions, schools, cafés, and way of life, closely integrated with the rest of Venetian life (Clark 2002). Yet there is also this other, symbolic association with a Jewish presence that has been retained in the area. Jewish communal life still pervades the quarter, albeit on a much smaller but still very significant scale, contributing to making it pronouncedly Jewish. The museum is located on the premises of a former synagogue in the main square of the ghetto. But the ghetto itself remains a lively Jewish space with fully functioning synagogues, a community centre, the office of the chief rabbi of Venice, a hasidic seminary, and an old people's home. The Jewish aspect is amplified and extended by a number of shops catering to tourists, selling Jewish curios and items, and a kosher restaurant.

Indeed, it is precisely because the ghetto in Venice is so 'evocative', fusing past and present, that it provides such a wonderful setting for the Jewish cultural festivals occasionally organized by the Jewish museum (Campos Calimani 1998). The historical associations of the Jewish quarter of Kazimierz in Kraków have similarly been successfully exploited in order to institute a highly popular annual Jewish cultural festival, attracting large crowds since the late 1980s (Gruber 2002). The Kazimierz festival takes place against the backdrop of the Holocaust, with only a tiny Jewish population remaining in Poland today, most of whom live in Warsaw, rather than in Kraków.

In Venice performative narration, especially on the occasion of a cultural festival, presents and portrays a slice of Jewish life to an external audience. At the same time it helps to generate tourist income and interest, further strengthening the local economy and the image of Venice as a place of culture. Thus, such narratives combine a number of elements, being aimed at a variety of audiences, both internal and external, both local and tourist. As well as being a tourist spectacle, Jewish cultural festivals provide an internal Jewish audience with the opportunity for making claims for 'inclusion' in the local state while also reaffirming a sense of identity and a sense of belonging to community, city, and nation.

In Bologna spatial narrative based on historical associations and current usage is more restricted, since the former ghetto is no longer a lived-in Jewish space, although until recently there was a Jewish-owned antiques shop in the area. However, the occasion of the launch of the Jewish museum, in May 1999, gave local Jews the opportunity to perform community by literally inhabiting the ghetto for the day. The day was meant to start with an official laying of wreaths in front of the plaque that had been placed there in 1988, marking the fiftieth anniversary of the enactment of racial laws in 1938, as well as the deportation of Bologna Jews in 1943. Although official dignitaries were specifically invited, with the deputy mayor and the president of the chamber of deputies in Rome placing the wreaths, it was meant to be a public occasion and accordingly took place in the street. As mentioned earlier, half the Jewish community attended the laying of wreaths in the morning, but then, as the brief ceremony came to a close, they proceeded to follow the invited dignitaries down the street and into the forecourt of the Jewish museum. The rest of the morning was meant to be a guided tour and reception for invited guests only, with an open day for the public later on in the afternoon. Instead, the Jewish community had turned out in force and could not simply be turned away. They had made themselves visible in a way that was seldom possible for them and were taking what they considered to be their rightful place in the city, inhabiting the ghetto and the Jewish museum, at least during the opening launch of the museum.

As we have seen, some spaces are lived, albeit shared, Jewish spaces, for example the Venice ghetto, and lend themselves readily to performing community all year round. Other spaces are no longer inhabited by Jews in the same way but can be reclaimed on the occasion of cultural or music festivals or other civic occasions, with various groups or interested individuals performing Jewish community, or what is left of it, or what might become of it. On such occasions the Jewish community, or what stands for the Jewish community, becomes visible to the external audience, and indeed to the internal audience as well. Yet cultural festivals have much wider implications: thus both Gruber (2002) and Schischa and Berenstein (2002) note the rapid growth of Jewish cultural festivals in recent decades, even in places where very few Jews now live, and it could be argued that such festivals contribute to the incorporation and integration of Jewish memory into the state's civic culture just as effectively as Jewish museums and monuments do.

It is also interesting to speculate on the extent to which the promotion of cultural festivals, and most notably of Jewish cultural festivals, in areas of former Jewish settlement, actually contributes, often unintentionally, to the further construction and reconstruction of Jewish community in those areas. Following the tremendous success of the Kraków Jewish Culture Festival, Jewish institutions have supported infrastructural developments in the city, with the establishment of a new community centre with well over 400 users coming to education classes for adults as well as children, family programmes, activities for senior citizens, educational programmes for Polish schoolchildren, and so forth. Synagogues have been restored and are now used for communal worship or as cultural centres, whilst others have been refurbished, as in the case of the Isaac Synagogue, for use by incoming or 'returning' hasidic groups and seminaries. The Galicia Jewish Museum offers cultural and educational programming all year round, as well as hosting the burgeoning Jewish Progressive community. Kraków is now an attractive place to live for Jews of all sorts of denominations, and various Jewish philanthropic and communal organizations have invested in community infrastructural development there.

Even the survival of the Jewish community in Venice owes its continued existence, at least in some small part, to the infrastructural assistance given by the American Joint Distribution Committee in the 1950s, determined to help in the reconstruction of European communities after the ravages and horrors of the war, including the renovation of synagogues and the community centre and the establishment of Italy's first Jewish museum.

It seems to me to be an open question: does narrative performance simply reflect ongoing community life or does it actively help in the construction and reconstruction of such community? Do objects, labels, and spaces merely show and tell, or do they actually construct the very reality of community life they tell about?

Conclusion

Writing about contemporary museums, Edward van Voolen notes:

The Jewish museum, once a modest receptacle for the religious and historical remains of an almost extinct people, became a major tourist attraction and a Jewish pilgrimage destination . . . parallel to the immense popularity of Jewish museums as a point of reference to which secularized Jews return in order to connect with their roots and at which non-Jews can discover a common if often dramatic past. (2004: 17–18)

I hope that this essay has illuminated to some degree the manner in which Jewish museums have indeed been able to be a point of reference for both Jewish and non-Jewish audiences. I have explored the manner in which Jewish museums, and probably any historical or cultural museum, do far more than merely display objects and collections. Each museum has its own story or stories to tell, yet each museum is also a space, a venue, an opportunity for 'performing' community. The performative act is one that entails embodying or physically representing something that is essentially symbolic: being part of a community.

Much of the time belonging to a community is either taken for granted or else is not immediately apparent. And yet at certain moments it is brought to the fore and made visible, or at least claims are brought forward for legitimately belonging to the community. In this process of staking a claim various strategies are used to highlight connections that might otherwise remain invisible. Spaces associated with past settlements or historic events are 'reclaimed', as in the ghetto area in Bologna; ritual objects associated with previous generations are used on special occasions in Venice and in Florence; labels are used in displays to denote long-standing connections of people and place; plaques become reminders of shared citizenship; spaces are inhabited in a visible manner, either on a daily and weekly basis, as in the Venice ghetto, or at occasional events, for example, in Bologna or Kraków.

Sometimes claims of belonging are addressed to an internal Jewish audience, as in the case of the display of a family tree in the Jewish museum in Venice, recording five generations of belonging to the local Jewish community, with references to linkages to a number of other notable families in the area. Sometimes, when reclaiming symbolic space, as, for example, in the ghetto of Bologna, or visibly inhabiting space, as we have seen in Venice, connections and linkages are sought with the city as a whole, and claims are made for belonging to the civic community and the local city-state. At other times such claims are made with reference to the wider civic community and the nation-state, as the plaques remind us.

Performing community, then, seems to be the art of taking links and connections that are often hidden or ignored and bringing them to the fore, thereby making them visible once again. Such connections may be self-referential for an internal audience and intertextual for a wider audience, making use of space, objects, labels, and plaques in a dynamic and interactive manner.

Notes

This essay was originally presented in July 2005 at the conference entitled 'Tourism and Performance: Scripts, Stages and Stories', held at Sheffield Hallam University, and was itself partly based on ideas developed in a paper in 2003, but has been considerably altered since.

References

AUSTIN, J. L. 1962. *How to Do Things with Words*. Oxford. 2nd edn. 1976.

BAUDRILLARD, JEAN. 1994. *Simulacra and Simulation: The Body in Theory*. Ann Arbor, Mich.

——1997. *Consumer Society: Myths and Structure*. London.

CAMPOS CALIMANI, ANNA. 1998. 'Il museo della comunità ebraica di Venezia: Problemi e prospettive'. In F. Bonilauri and V. Maugeri, eds., *Musei ebraici in Europa: Jewish Museums in Europe*, 24–7. Milan.

CLARK, DAVID. 1999. 'Creating Jewish Spaces in European Cities: Amnesia and Collective Memory'. In Judith Targarona Borras and Angel Sáenz-Badillos, eds., *Jewish Studies at the Turn of the Twentieth Century*, ii. 274–81. Leiden.

—— 2002. 'A Day in the Ghetto'. *Jewish Renaissance*, 1(2; Winter): 19.

—— 2003. 'Jewish Museums: From Jewish Icons to Jewish Narratives'. *European Judaism, A Journal for the New Europe*, 3(2): 4–17.

—— 2004. 'Jewish Museums in the Diaspora: Constructing Community and Nation'. Ph.D. diss., London Metropolitan University.

—— 2007. 'Sites of Memory or Aids to Multiculturalism? Conflicting Uses of Jewish Heritage Sites'. *Sociological Research Online*, 12/2. <http://www.socresonline.org.uk/12/2/clark.html>, accessed 23 Jan. 2013.

—— 2011. 'Governance, Alliance and Resistance: Jewish Museums in Italy'. In Maria Kousis, Tom Selwyn, and David Clark, eds., *Contested Spaces in the Mediterranean: Ethnographic Essays in Honour of Charles Tilly*, 240–59. New York and Oxford.

COHEN, ANTHONY P. 1985. *The Symbolic Construction of Community*. London.

COHEN, RICHARD I. 1998. *Jewish Icons: Art and Society in Modern Europe*. Berkeley, Calif.

COHEN-GROSSMAN, GRACE. 2003. *Jewish Museums of the World*. Westport, Conn.

CROW, GRAHAM, and GRAHAM ALLAN. 1994. *Community Life: An Introduction to Local Social Relations*. Hemel Hempstead.

DUNCAN, CAROL. 1995. *Civilizing Rituals: Inside Public Art Museums*. London.

ECO, UMBERTO. 1987. *Travels in Hyperreality*. London.

FELDMAN, JEFFREY D. 2002. 'Museum without a Collection: Jewish Culture in the New Italian Multiculturalism'. Ph.D. diss., University of Virginia.

FOWLER, ROGER. 1981. *Literature as Social Discourse: The Practice of Linguistic Criticism*. London.

GOFFMAN, ERVING. 1959. *The Presentation of Self in Everyday Life*. New York.

GRUBER, RUTH ELLEN. 2002. *Virtually Jewish: Reinventing Jewish Culture in Europe*. Berkeley, Calif.

HILLERY, GEORGE A. JR. 1955. 'Definitions of Community; Areas of Agreement'. *Rural Sociology*, 20: 111–23.

HOOPER-GREENHILL, EILEAN. 2000. *Museums and the Interpretation of Visual Culture*. London.

KIRSHENBLATT-GIMBLETT, BARBARA. 1991. 'Objects of Ethnography'. In Ivan Karp and Steven D. Lavine, eds., *Exhibiting Cultures: The Poetics and Politics of Museum Display*. Washington, DC.

—— 1992. 'From Cult to Culture: Jews on Display at World Fairs'. In Reimund Kvideland, ed., *Tradition and Modernisation: Plenary Papers Read at the Société Internationale d'Ethnologie et de Folklore*. Turku.

—— 1998. *Destination Culture: Tourism, Museums and Heritage*. Berkeley, Calif.

LACLAU, ERNESTO, and CHANTAL MOUFFE. 1985. *Hegemony and Socialist Strategy*. London.

LENEMAN, HELEN. 1987. 'In the Venice Ghetto, 1986'. *Response Magazine*, 15(3): 3–11.

LIDCHI, HENRIETTA. 1997. 'The Poetics and Politics of Exhibiting Other Cultures'. In Stuart Hall, ed., *Representation: Cultural Representations and Signifying Practices*, 151–222. London.

MACCANNELL, DEAN. 1976. *The Tourist: A New Theory of the Leisure Class*. London.

MOORE, KEVIN. 1997. *Museums and Popular Culture*. London.

PEARCE, SUSAN M. 1992. *Museums, Objects and Collections: A Cultural Study*. Leicester.

——1994 [1990]. 'Objects as Meaning; or Narrating the Past'. In S. Pearce, ed., *Interpreting Objects and Collections*, 19–29. London.

ROTH, CECIL. 1946. *The History of the Jews in Italy*. Philadelphia.

SCHECHNER, RICHARD. 2003. *Performance Theory*. London.

SCHISCHA, REBECCA, and DINA BERENSTEIN. 2002. *Mapping Jewish Culture in Europe Today: A Pilot Project*. Institute for Jewish Policy Research, Research Report 3. London.

SHIELDS, ROB. 1991. *Places on the Margin: Alternative Geographies of Modernity*, London.

SILVERSTONE, ROGER. 1994. 'The Medium is the Museum: On Objects and Logics in Times and Spaces'. In Roger Miles and Lauro Zavala, eds., *Towards the Museum of the Future: New European Perspectives*, 161–76. London.

STANLEY, NICK. 1998. *Being Ourselves for You: The Global Display of Cultures*. London.

VAN VOOLEN, EDWARD. 2004. 'From Time to Place: Shaping Memory in Judaism'. In Edward van Voolen and Angeli Sachs, eds., *Jewish Identity in Contemporary Architecture*, 12–20. Munich.

WITCOMB, ANDREA. 2003. *Re-Imagining the Museum: Beyond the Mausoleum*. London.

YOUNG, JAMES E. 2004. 'Jewish Museums, Holocaust Museums, and Questions of National Identity'. In E. van Voolen and A. Sachs, eds., *Jewish Identity in Contemporary Architecture*, 42–57. Munich.

Framing Jewish Identity in the Museum of Moroccan Judaism in Casablanca

SOPHIE WAGENHOFER

JEWISH MUSEUMS within predominantly non-Jewish environments are often places of differentiation and separation, as they present the Jewish community as distinct from the non-Jewish population. Jewishness is typically defined, framed, and explained mostly by its singular characteristics, whereas shared traditions with the non-Jewish majority or the daily life routine of secular Jews are often marginalized or even ignored altogether (Laursen 2008). Focusing on the Museum of Moroccan Judaism in Casablanca, I want to draw attention to a museum that tries to go in exactly the opposite direction. Instead of framing a particular Jewish space and stressing the differences between Moroccan Jewry and the Muslim majority, the sameness of Jews and Muslims is emphasized. The ethnographic Museum of Moroccan Judaism (Musée du judaïsme marocain) was founded by the Council of Jewish Communities in Morocco in order to preserve Moroccan Jewish culture and to make it accessible to a broader audience (S. Levy 2007). It opened its doors to the public in autumn 1997 as the first and until now the only Jewish museum in an Arab country.[1] Simon Levy, Professor Emeritus of Spanish Language and Literature and political activist, ran the museum in an honorary capacity, supported by the curator Zhor Rehihil, until his death in December 2011. As a private initiative the museum is financed mainly by the Jewish community. However, it was recognized as an association with public benefit by the government in 2001 and receives some state support, as the curator is employed by the Ministry of Culture.

By looking at the exhibition of the Museum of Moroccan Judaism I want to examine how the Jews are positioned within Moroccan society and culture and through what representations—narratives, symbols, or practices—their Moroccan identity is highlighted. I explore how points of identification with the 'Moroccan nation' are defined and expressed. By doing so, I also consider aspects that are marginalized or even neglected in the exhibition, as they, too, are constitutive of the museum's narrative.

Identity and the Museum

Museums are widely perceived as 'key players in identity politics' (Kirshenblatt-Gimblett 2006: 375). However, scholars of new museology stress the fact that museums are no longer to be understood only as tools for the strengthening of national identity; rather, hitherto marginalized groups have been granted more and more space in the field. Museums are seen as places of negotiation—a process in which the curator as well as the audience are involved. Different perceptions and images of identity, society, or power are presented, challenged, questioned, accepted, or rejected in this space. It is an arena 'for the performance and the contestation of cultural citizenship' (Kirshenblatt-Gimblett 2006: 376). Identity refers, in this context, to the sense of belonging to one or more communities. This sense of belonging is not determined in time and space with a clear beginning or end; rather, it is 'a construction, a process never completed —always in process' (Hall 1996: 2). Stuart Hall emphasizes the constructed character of identities and points to the influence of public discourses on the process of creating a certain identity: 'We need to understand them [identities] as produced in specific historical and institutional sites within specific discursive formations and practices, by specific enunciative strategies' (1996: 4). Groups are not essential entities; collective identity does not exist per se, as something given or natural, but only in the hands of the members of a certain group. Thus drawing lines between groups in order to create a sense of belonging is crucial for the formation and implementation of collective identity. In the following I want to trace how, in the frame of the Museum of Moroccan Judaism, these lines are drawn and how they serve to reinforce the *marocanité* of the Jewish community.

The aim of the museum's management, besides the preservation of artefacts, is to provide information about Moroccan Judaism and to prevent the disappearance of Moroccan Jewish traditions (S. Levy 2007). The exhibition and the museum's supporting programme, such as cultural events, tours, and panel discussions, send a clear political message: Jews are an integral part of Moroccan society. Director Simon Levy wanted to promote Jewish history and culture as one facet of a national patrimony. In an interview with the Moroccan daily *Le Matin du Sahara* he stated that presenting Morocco only as a Muslim Arab country would give an incomplete picture (Ziane 2005). Levy's aim was to highlight the Arab–Jewish dimension of Moroccan culture and to present the attributes 'Jewish' and 'Moroccan' as coherent and interlinked rather then antithetical.

When asked whom he seeks to address with the museum, Levy mentioned two main target groups: Moroccan Jews living abroad and Moroccan Muslims who want to know more about their fellow citizens. His aim is to break down negative images and prejudices, resulting mainly from media reports on the Middle East conflict (S. Levy 1999). At the same time, the museum is also understood as a platform for the Jews still living in Morocco. It is intended as a manifestation of their past, and also of their present; a 'vivid museum for a vivid community', as stated in the brochure of the museum. The majority of visitors, however, are American or European tourists usually on organized tours (Wagenhofer 2013).

Levy's attempt to promote the Jewish community as an integral part of the Moroccan nation was a response to the decline of the Jewish community, the disappearance of Jewish traditions from everyday life and practice, and the growing distance between Muslims and their Jewish co-citizens. Jews are often regarded as not really Moroccan. They are associated with Israel, France, and the United States, or with a sort of 'global Jewry'. The distancing and the gradual disappearance of Jews and Jewish culture from the predominantly Muslim society began with the growing European influence in the nineteenth century and increased due to the mass emigration of Moroccan Jews in the second half of the twentieth century. While up until the 1940s the Jewish community in Morocco was the largest in the Arab world with more than 250,000 members, it numbers approximately 4,000 today (Boum 2010: 56). Direct contact with Jewish co-citizens has become the exception for the majority of Moroccan Muslims. Due to the media reports on the Middle East conflict Jews are often perceived as the enemy, as those who kill Arabs. Even though the king, the authorities, and Jewish official representatives continually stress that Moroccan Jews are not Israelis and that Judaism is not the same as Zionism, the images from the Middle East conflict are still affecting the perception of Jews within Moroccan society (S. Levy 2001). Thus the emphasis on the long presence of Jews in Morocco and on their contribution to history and culture reflects the wish to fight against current prejudices and antisemitic tendencies.

The Museum of Moroccan Judaism is located rather remotely in Oasis, a prosperous suburb of Casablanca. Even though the villa looks unimposing from the street, it was nominated for the Aga Khan award and the grand prix of Moroccan architecture in 2000 (Zerhouani 2002). The building was used as an orphanage until the 1960s and hosted a rabbinical school until 1991. In the mid-1990s it was handed over to the Jewish community to be converted into the projected museum. The Moroccan Jewish architect Aimé Kakon was commissioned to transform the building into a museum space. The inconspicuous villa is marked only by a small sign, with the word 'museum' written in Arabic and French. Asked by a journalist why he avoided the attribute 'Jewish', Levy answered that at the time of its opening it was the only museum in Casablanca, thus a specification was not necessary (Daïf 2004). Even though his observation was true, one might assume that the director rather tended not to emphasize the Jewish character of the institution in order to avoid being attacked. Unlike similar institutions in some European countries, the museum in Casablanca was initially not guarded. However, since the number of threatening calls increased in the course of the Gaza war in winter 2008–9, two policemen now guard the museum twenty-four hours a day. Suicide bomb attacks in May 2003 at five different places in Casablanca, among them the Jewish community centre, a Jewish cemetery, and a restaurant run by a Jew, made it clear that Jewish institutions are vulnerable and potential targets of anti-Jewish violence. Thus a certain caution is necessary to avoid provoking resentment or attacks.

The exhibition space extends over 700 square metres. Three rooms are dedicated to religious practice, displaying the interior of synagogues as well as religious items and books. In two other rooms, objects from everyday life, such as working equipment, costumes, and jewellery, are presented. Beyond that, the museum offers space for temporary exhibitions and events: readings, film screenings, or the celebration of religious festivals. Most of the objects presented in the exhibition originate from the nineteenth and twentieth centuries. They are donations or bequests from Moroccan Jewish families and communities; some artefacts have been bought in the market by Simon Levy and Zhor Rehihil. However, the budget is limited and objects are increasingly difficult to come by as many items have been sold abroad. One example is the library of Rabbi Youssef Benaim from Fes that has been handed to the Jewish Theological Seminary in New York (S. Levy 2007). The presentation of the objects does not follow a chronological order or a given story line. The artefacts are displayed rather loosely without much contextual information. In some cases even explanations referring to the origin, usage, or symbolic meaning of the artefacts are missing. The curator and the director attribute this lack of background information to the limited financial means of the museum. However, most of the visitors ask for a guided tour or at least further information from either the director or the curator. In addition a brochure, written by Simon Levy, is available in Arabic, French, and English, providing visitors with detailed historical information.

Motifs and Symbols in the Museum

A theme that is very prominent throughout the whole exhibition and cuts across the divisions of religious and profane, private and public, and rural and urban is metalwork, which includes the production of jewellery, coins, religious artefacts, and ornaments. Even though nowadays most of the gold- and silversmiths in Morocco are Muslims, the production of jewellery is still associated with the Jews, who had a monopoly in this manufacturing sector up to the early twentieth century. Thus, it is not surprising that metalwork is represented by very different objects and in various contexts in the frame of the exhibition. Beside the display of working tools there is a workshop with the original interior and the equipment of the goldsmith Saul Cohen (1928–2007), which has been brought from Fes and reconstructed in the museum. The museum has a vast collection of jewellery and coins and also displays artefacts that belong to the sphere of religious practice, such as ritual objects or ornaments used in synagogues. Despite the dominance of Jewish producers, no differentiation between 'Jewish' and 'Muslim' jewellery is made. Jewellery produced by Jews is considered Moroccan and a part of the national handicraft tradition. Whereas a differentiation exists between rural and urban and Amazigh (Berber) and Arab jewellery, that of Jews and Muslims is seen as virtually identical (Rabaté 1996).

The identification of jewellery as an important part of Moroccan culture is established by a complex language of symbols with roots in pre-Islamic time and shaped by various cultural and religious influences. As Geertz has noted, these symbols are important as 'a system of inherited conceptions expressed in symbolic forms by means of which we communicate, perpetuate, and develop . . . knowledge about attitudes toward life' (1973: 89). This symbolism invests jewellery with various meanings, such as protection, fertility, health, or wealth. The use of strong symbolic language is a sign of cultural coherence, as Muslims and Jews attribute the same meaning to certain symbols.

The most prominent symbol to be found in the museum is the hamsa, in the Islamic context 'Fatima's hand', and known as 'Miriam's hand' in Jewish culture. It has been a widespread symbol among Jews in North Africa since ancient times, and since the expansion of Islam also among Muslims (Canaan 1914; Sabar 2010). The term hamsa derives from the Arabic term for 'five', a number that is considered a protection against the evil eye. In the exhibition the hamsa is displayed in various forms and functions: as decoration, as pendant, as earrings, or as a doorknocker and, in the religious field, as a hanger for oil lamps, used traditionally in Moroccan synagogues. Moreover, it decorates the website and the brochure of the museum. The choice of the hamsa and its frequent representation in the exhibition reinforces the *marocanité* of Jewish culture. Moroccans, Muslims, and Jews alike are familiar with this symbol as it is still omnipresent in everyday life. The hamsa is fully accepted as typically Moroccan, and is common as jewellery or as a house decoration. It is used by a Moroccan insurance company as well as by the government, which chose the hamsa for a poster campaign for tolerance after the bombings of Casablanca.[2]

Another symbol that is omnipresent as a decorative motif, be it on jewellery or coins or in architecture, is the star with five, six, or eight points. Whereas the five-pointed star is today considered *the* Moroccan symbol, used on the national flag and in the royal emblem, the six-pointed star is nowadays referred to as exclusively Jewish. In the past, however, the different forms of the stars were not clearly attributed to one religion or nation, as is the case today. The star was a universal decorative element in the Hellenistic Roman tradition. The triangle as a symbol of femininity and fertility can be dated as far back as pre-antiquity. The two triangles forming the hexagram represented femininity and masculinity but also referred to the categories of sacred and profane (Soltes 2005). In contrast to present connotations, the hexagram was, for a long time, not considered a Jewish symbol. Six-pointed stars can therefore be found in a Muslim environment and five- or eight-pointed stars in predominantly Jewish contexts.

The shift of meaning that the stars have undergone is further reflected by the objects on display. The museum presents many examples of the hexagram being used in a non-Jewish context: for example on coins and as seals on edicts signed by the Moroccan sultan and on all official documents certificated in Spanish Morocco.[3] Until the beginning of the twentieth century the six-pointed star was even used as the emblem on the Moroccan flag, a fact that the director Simon Levy liked to stress and that is documented in the exhibition by additional graphic material: an excerpt from *Le Protocole et les usages au Maroc* by Mohamed El Alaoui hangs on the wall, showing the national flag with the hexagram in an old photograph. The star was changed to a pentagram on the initiative of the French Marshall Hubert Lyautey by a decree in September 1915. The Star of David as an exclusive reference to Judaism appeared only in the nineteenth century, when it became the symbol of the Zionist movement, whereas previously the menorah had been the ubiquitous symbol in Judaism (Soltes 2005). Consequently, the hexagram as a specifically Jewish image appears predominantly on objects from the end of the nineteenth or from the twentieth century, such as the curtain covering the ark of the Pariente synagogue in Larache from 1930 or donation boxes from the middle of the twentieth century. The diffusion of various kinds of stars is a surprise for most of the visitors. To see the six-pointed star on a Moroccan flag, on Moroccan coins, or on a decree is as surprising as to see the five-pointed star being used as an ornament in a Jewish context, for example on a hanger for oil lamps in the synagogue. This challenges the categorization that defines our current notions of 'Jewish' and 'Muslim' and highlights the fact that this strong division has not always existed. Moreover, the use of different stars in various contexts reflects a common symbolic language, shaped and shared by Muslims and Jews alike.

Since representations of humans and animals are forbidden in normative Judaism and Islam,[4] non-figurative motifs dominate in all kinds of decoration in both traditions. Animals are nevertheless often used as ornamental features—one respect in which normative religion differs from actual practice. A central symbol that is widely used is the bird, especially the dove, decorating all kinds of jewellery and *objets d'art*. Often the thumb of the hamsa is shaped like a small bird or Hanukah lamps are decorated with the bird motif.[5] The dove, also called the spirit of God in Arabic, is considered to be divine (Lausberg 2007). It can be found in Jewish and Islamic tradition alike and thus serves, like the hamsa, as a connective symbol (Qur'an, II, 262, and S. of S. 2: 14).

Language as an Expression of National Belonging

As Arabic is an important marker of national identity and unity in Morocco, the issue of language is also a concern for the Jewish community and thus for the museum. Levy has stated that Jews are often considered 'a kind of European to whom one replies in French even if they spoke in Arabic first' (S. Levy 2001: 19). As the education system of the Moroccan Jewish communities was organized by the French Alliance Israélite Universelle from 1860, Moroccan Jews have often been considered as exclusively francophone by their Muslim fellow citizens.[6] However, the museum's management tries to stress that Moroccan Jews also spoke and still speak the local Arabic dialect. Their language, which differs only slightly from the vernacular language of Moroccan Muslims, is known as Judaeo-Arabic: Arabic written in Hebrew script. Local Jews refer to it as *l-arabiyya dyalna*, meaning 'our Arabic', in contrast to *l-arabiyya dl-mslimīn*, the Arabic of the Muslims (Stillman 1988: 9).

Different objects in the exhibition refer to the use of Arabic among Moroccan Jews, be it the vernacular dialect or modern standard Arabic, the language of politics, literature, and education. One example is a placard entitled *Appel pour la population Israélite au Maroc*, written by Azouz Cohen in French and Judaeo-Arabic. The placard was printed in 1930 as an appeal for the use of modern standard Arabic as the language of instruction in Jewish schools. Cohen speaks of 'true Arabic', which he considers 'not only the official language' but 'also the language of your fathers and the lingua franca of your co-citizens'. This appeal to favour Arabic over French has to be seen in the context of the activities of a nationalist movement within the Jewish community that supported neither affiliation with France nor with Zionist groups, but rather the fight for a democratic and independent Moroccan state. The strategic use of Arabic by Jewish political activists during the struggle for independence was aimed at emphasizing, to both the Muslim Moroccans and the Jewish community, the sense of belonging to the Moroccan nation.

The importance of Arabic is also highlighted in the context of religious and scientific literature. The museum possesses a vast collection of books, most of them donations by families who left the country or from abandoned synagogues and community centres.[7] A special emphasis is placed on the books written in Judaeo-Arabic. The display includes a history book bearing the Judaeo-Arabic title *hist-oriah dl-yahŭd dl-marok bl-arabiyya* (*History of the Jews of Morocco in Arabic*). The fact that it had been translated in 1953 from French to Judaeo-Arabic indicates that there was a preference, at least among some Jews, for reading in the local language rather than in French. An example from the field of religion is a collection of Passover haggadot in Judaeo-Arabic translation displayed in the exhibition.

A notice on the wall of the Sla l-Khadra synagogue in Meknes, dating from the eighteenth century, testifies to the fact that Judaeo-Arabic was also the language of community matters. The sign asks community members not to spit on the synagogue floor and not to accompany the cantor's recitation in a loud voice. The above examples clearly demonstrate the *marocanité* of local Jewry, even in the field of religion. What might look foreign and different at first glance—the Hebrew script—turns out to be the local Arabic dialect—a surprising effect that highlights the strong ties between Jewish tradition and indigenous culture in Morocco.

Gaps in the Museum Narrative

While the objects and symbols presented in the exhibition highlight the similarities between Jews and Muslims and stress the *marocanité* of the Jews, issues that might disturb the image of peaceful coexistence are carefully omitted. Even though Morocco is considered one of the most liberal countries in the Arab world, censorship still exists, especially when it comes to political issues, religion, or criticism of the royal family. To avoid restrictions, Moroccan media often resort to self-censorship and avoid certain topics. This is also true for museums, even if they are run by a private foundation. With regard to the Museum of Moroccan Judaism, the Moroccan anthropologist Aomar Boum comes to the conclusion that 'the curators of the museum consciously ignore topics that are publicly controversial' (Boum 2010: 71). However, it is not sufficient to understand the exclusion of these topics as merely stemming from a wish to avoid problems with the authorities. In the following I point out three topics that are not addressed in the exhibition narrative, even though they suggest themselves: the situation of Moroccan Jews during the Second World War and the Holocaust, the mass emigration of Moroccan Jews, and, finally, antisemitism in Morocco.

The period of the Second World War and the Holocaust is not totally absent from the exhibition; rather, this issue is marginalized. With the Megilat Hitler, a scroll that was written in 1943 based on the biblical Megilat Ester and describing Hitler's defeat by the Allies, the museum displays an object mirroring the situation of Moroccan Jews in the time of the Second World War. In the exhibition, however, this scroll does not have a prominent place. It is presented without detailed information or contextualization, together with various religious objects, such as charity boxes or bags for prayer shawls, and is not given special attention during guided tours.

When asked why the Second World War and the Holocaust are marginalized in the exhibition, Simon Levy gave a straightforward answer: he considered the Holocaust to be a European story. The Second World War and the extermination of the Jews have not been central or identity-sustaining issues for Moroccan Jewry. Although antisemitic laws existed in Morocco, implemented by the Nazi-friendly Vichy regime, the Moroccan Jews did not suffer from persecution in the same way that their European co-religionists did. 'Israel is making a new history of the Jews: it begins with Hitler and nothing comes after', Levy said in an interview with Matthew Klayman, a student from Harvard University.[8] This point of view is difficult for Europeans or Americans to comprehend and is often met with disapproval, as Raphael El Maleh, a Moroccan tour guide specializing in Jewish heritage, has told me in an interview. However, Levy's attitude is shared by other Jews, mostly of Arab origin, as, for example, the cultural scientist Ella Shohat or the filmmaker Sami Shalom Chetrit, who try to challenge the Ashkenazi hegemony in regard to knowledge production, power of interpretation, and struggle for meaning within Israeli society. They emphasize the existence of alternative memories and call for a historiography that is related to the experience of Arab Jews as part of a collective Jewish memory (Shohat 1999). The reason the period of the Holocaust is excluded from the exhibition is not that it is marginal or of less importance to Moroccan Jewry, who were not affected to the same extent as their European co-religionists. Rather it can be understood as a struggle for the acceptance of a particular Moroccan Jewish historical memory and for the right of interpretation. A self-confessed anti-Zionist, Levy wanted to present the specifics of the North African Jews as a counter-narrative to the dominant historiography of Ashkenazi Jewry.

Another issue omitted from the frame of the exhibition is the mass emigration of Moroccan Jews. In the second half of the twentieth century about 250,000 Jews left Morocco for a variety of reasons, economic, political, or personal. The majority of Jewish emigrants settled in Israel, France, and North America. In a subtle way this departure is omnipresent in the museum, as we see objects left behind and not in use any more. The closing down of the orphanage and the rabbinical school also reflects the dwindling of the community. Nevertheless, the mass emigration is not explicitly addressed in the exhibition, a fact that is quite astonishing as it is the central turning point for the Moroccan Jewish community and also for the relation between Muslims and Jews in the kingdom. The issue of emigration is marginalized not only in the Museum of Moroccan Judaism but also in Moroccan society as a whole. The journalist Loubna Bernichi wrote in 2006 in the weekly *Maroc Hebdo International*: 'To this day it is rare for Moroccan Muslim intellectuals to bring up this subject [mass emigration]. Even worse is the fact that no curriculum in the public schools makes mention of the mass emigration of Moroccan Jews.'

It is the question of the reasons for the departure of Moroccan Jews that turns this issue into a taboo. Answers include the explanation that they were afraid, that they felt excluded, and that Jewish–Muslim relations were not always as harmonious as the official narrative claims. Jews possibly also left out of a fear of discrimination caused by the Arab–Israeli conflict and a growing Arabization as well as the increasing emphasis on Islam as *the* religion of the state. Public discussion of these reasons from various perspectives would challenge the image of perfect coexistence. This would be in the interests of neither those Muslims who tend to shift the responsibility exclusively to Zionist organizations, nor the Jews, who do not want to jeopardize the fairly stable relation between the two groups by 'accusing' their Muslim fellow citizens of being, at least partly, responsible for the departure of the Jews (Trevisan Semi 2010). Avoidance of this issue is a means of self-reassurance for the Moroccan Jews: by holding on to the narrative that the relationship has never been problematic, the Jewish community is comforting itself in the face of the Muslim majority. This idea is also illustrated in my third example, the exclusion of antisemitism from the exhibition.

Even though antisemitism did, and still does, exist in Morocco, it is not discussed in the frame of the exhibition. Anti-Jewish sentiments and actions can be observed on different levels and at different levels of intensity within Moroccan society. They range from prejudices and verbal aggression to physical attacks, such as the suicide bombings in Casablanca in May 2003. From time to time the museum and the staff become targets of threats and defamation, mostly in phone calls or, as in winter 2010, in insulting inscriptions on the garden wall. However, dealing in a direct way with the issue of antisemitism makes one an easy target for criticism, as the following example shows. In spring 2009 the Jewish merchant Joseph Amar was killed in Casablanca. This incident caused fear and uncertainty among Moroccan Jews. However, the reactions of the Muslim Moroccans were ambivalent. In an internet forum one could read sentences such as: 'Really, here you can see the Jewish paranoia in its purest form', or 'Jews are always afraid and they consistently try to frighten the whole world'.[9] These statements demonstrate that talking about antisemitism or expressing uncertainty as a Jew can easily provoke incomprehension or even disaffirmation among one's Muslim fellow-citizens. Moreover, Muslims addressing antisemitism also face problems, as the case of the human rights activist Mohamed Mouha illustrates. In February 2008 he founded an organization to fight racism, intolerance, and antisemitism. As a consequence he was socially excluded in his home town, Al-Hoceima, was called a Zionist, and even received death threats.

Discussing antisemitism within Moroccan society is a difficult and sensitive undertaking, for Muslims and Jews alike. Raising the issue is often interpreted as 'complaining' and may provoke the question why Jews are staying in the country at all, whereby the Jewish presence in Morocco as a whole may be called into question. This can easily damage the fragile Muslim–Jewish relationship built on the image of an age-long and peaceful coexistence. Simon Levy wanted to promote the image of a tolerant society where Jewish culture is included. The open problematization of antisemitism may cause tensions, not only with Muslim visitors, who might feel personally offended, but also with the authorities, who try carefully to maintain the narrative of tolerance.

Jewish Space and Place within Moroccan Society

The exhibition in the Museum of Moroccan Judaism corresponds to the dominant official narrative about Moroccan Jewry, which is built on two central images: the age-long presence of Jews as an integral part of Moroccan society and the peaceful coexistence of Muslims and Jews. In recent decades the king, as well as the Moroccan government, have tried to reinforce the image of an open, pluralistic, and tolerant country. In this discourse the Jewish community plays a prominent role, especially when it comes to matters of religious pluralism and tolerance, as Jews are the only indigenous religious minority in the country. The emphasis on peaceful coexistence is not only a means to promote a positive image in Europe and the United States; it is also a signal to radical religious streams within Morocco (Ben-Layashi and Maddy-Weitzman 2010; Zisenwine 2007). However, against the background of the Middle East conflict the issue of Moroccan Jews becomes a sensitive subject and therefore the museum does not receive the same attention from the authorities or the royal family as other private institutions (Boum 2010).

Even though the exhibition fits perfectly into the official narrative, as I have pointed out above, the focus on peaceful coexistence and the avoidance of sensitive issues are more than mere attempts to please the authorities. Rather, they are a response to the present concerns and difficulties of the dwindling Jewish community within a predominantly Muslim society. Since the end of the nineteenth century Moroccan Jewry has undergone profound demographic, social, and political changes that also influenced its relation to the Muslim majority. The narrative of the exhibition is a reaction to these changes and addresses the growing uncertainty of Moroccan Jews. The exhibition takes up the issue of social boundaries between Muslims and Jews, which have become more complicated since clear frames of social and political regulation such as the *mellah* or the *dhimma* fell away and since the Middle East conflict and a growing antisemitism began to inform Jewish–Muslim relations.

Since the fifteenth century *mellah* has been the term used to refer to Jewish space within the Moroccan context. The Jewish quarter, which is often compared to the European ghetto, has become the central symbol for the boundaries between Jews and Muslims and for the inferior status of Moroccan Jewry. The first separate Jewish quarter was founded in 1438 in Fes under Marinide rule. It was located next to the sultan's palace in a quarter called Mellah. The name derived from the Arabic word *mallah* (salt) and referred to the salt marsh located in the immediate vicinity of the newly founded Jewish quarter. This name became the generic term for all Jewish quarters that were subsequently established in Morocco. Examples include Marrakech in the sixteenth, Meknes at the end of the seventeenth, and Essaouira, Rabat, and Salé in the nineteenth century.

However, the existence of a *mellah* must not be understood as creating an insurmountable barrier between Jews and Muslims. As Emily Gottreich has demonstrated with regard to the example of the *mellah* in Marrakech, the boundaries were not impermeable and the contact between the two groups was part of everyday life. Moreover, it should be noted that Jewish quarters were not established in every Moroccan town or village; in many places Jews and Muslims continued to live together in the same quarter (Giller 2008; Gottreich 2007).

Whereas the *mellah* signified the physical boundaries between Jews and Muslims, the concept of *dhimma* (lit. protection) defined legal and social differences. From the beginning of the Islamic expansion Muslim rulers tried to regulate relations with the non-Muslim population by a set of rules that were outlined in the Pact of Umar, whose origin is still controversial and debated in academia (Stillman 1979). These regulations clearly defined the status of non-Muslims, notably Christians and Jews, known also as the people of the book, and in some other regions that of Zoroastrians and Hindus too. In general the *dhimma* guaranteed to non-Muslims religious freedom and the ruler's protection. As *dhimmi* the Jews were able to maintain their own institutions and to organize community life autonomously. In return they had to pay a special tax, the *jizya*, and accept certain restrictions. Opinions differ as to whether the *dhimma* should be understood as a sign of tolerance or rather as a means of oppression (Cohen 1994; Noth 1987). Even though Jews in an Islamic context had more legal security than Jews in Christian Europe, their situation, according to Norman Stillman, was 'marked by tremendous polarities of tolerance and intolerance, assimilation and isolation, and security and insecurity' (1979: 76).

With the growing influence of the European powers in Morocco in the middle of the nineteenth century, this system lost its importance, and Muslim–Jewish relations changed, especially in the urban milieu. Many Jews came as so-called *protégés* under the direct authority of European powers, which invalidated the regulations laid down in the *dhimma* (Lewis 1984). Jewish organizations and philanthropists from Europe, such as Moses Montefiore, came to the Middle East and North Africa to improve the social and economic situation of their co-religionists. From the 1860s the Jewish Moroccan school system was dominated by the French Alliance Israélite Universelle. Due to their language skills and European education, Jews were often favoured for administrative positions, as tradesmen, or in the diplomatic service. Whereas this development has been described by some researchers as an improvement of the political, social, and economic situation of the Moroccan Jews (Fenton and Littman 2010; Ye'or 1999), others have argued that it destabilized their position in Moroccan society. The privileges granted by European powers as well as the adoption by Moroccan Jews of a European way of life, expressed through language, lifestyle, and fashion, led to tensions with the Muslim majority and to cultural discrepancies (Laskier 2003; A. Levy 2003; Stillman 1996).

In present-day Morocco Jews no longer live in the *mellah* and their status is not defined by the *dhimma* any more. Even though all Moroccans have been equal before the law since independence in 1956, social boundaries do still exist. As they lack any legal affirmation they are redefined in new ways. It seems that distinctions are stressed even more today because they are no longer clear (A. Levy 1997; Rosen 1984). The anthropologist André Levy observes that Moroccan Jews tend to withdraw in socio-cultural enclaves, such as specific sports clubs or cultural circles (1999; 2003). As mentioned above, the political climate, the foundation of Israel, and the Arab–Israeli wars have changed the perception of the Jews in Morocco and their relation to the Muslims dramatically. The State of Israel has provided a new frame of reference and a 'real alternative to continued residence in Morocco' (A. Levy 1999: 632). At the same time the foundation of the Israeli state and the resulting tensions in the region started to dominate the image of the Jews in Morocco. This, together with the strengthening of Arab identity in Morocco, gradually alienated Jews from Muslims and reshaped the relationship between the two groups.

The Museum: A Mediator of Muslim–Jewish Relations?

The museum in Casablanca gives the Jewish community its own space within the field of museology and heritage, which means the acknowledgement not only of its past but also of its present existence. It attracts the interest of the media and is widely discussed within Morocco and abroad. Seen as a product and agent of social and political change, the museum not only reflects ideas of Jewish identity but is also a means of negotiating and shaping social relations (Macdonald 1998; Kaplan 1994). Even though the number of museums in Morocco has doubled in the last fifteen years, the country cannot keep up with the global museum boom, and so this institution does not as yet have the significance it would have in Europe or in the United States. Until the 1990s most Moroccan museums were state-run and focused on archaeology or ethnography with an emphasis on Arab Muslim history, culture, and tradition, while minorities were excluded from the narratives presented. However, interest in museums has been growing, and marginalized groups are demanding their own museum as a platform and means to discuss, shape, affirm, or question certain perceptions of identity. An example is the initiative of political prisoners from the 1970s—victims of the so-called 'years of lead' under the reign of Hassan II (1961–99)—to transform the former commissariat Derb Moulay Chérif, a place where many prisoners were kept and tortured, into a museum (Slyomovics 2001; Stora 2000). This illustrates the fact that in Morocco, as elsewhere, museums have become sites of remembrance demonstrating the recognition of one's history or specific culture. The Jewish community was the first minority in Morocco to create its own museum, which was followed by museums of the culture and history of the Sahraoui in Laayoune in 2001 and of the Imazighen (Berber) in Agadir in 2005.

As in other Moroccan museums, visitor numbers are not high in the Museum of Moroccan Judaism. Consequently one may ask how representative and influential this museum is. I would argue that, regardless of the low visitor numbers, it is an important voice in the process of negotiating identity. Similarly to other museum projects, its central message is not only conveyed to those who actually go there but it spreads, through media, cultural discourse, and publications, beyond the museum walls. The museum is visited mainly by foreign tourists, most of them from a Jewish or Moroccan Jewish background. As we can conclude from the entries in the guestbook, most of these visitors come with a strong feeling of nostalgia to see objects related to their own past and family history. 'What a discovery! It needs a stranger to make me discover my most beautiful heritage', a visitor from London wrote in March 2005. Some visitors also highlight the fact that they have learned something new in the museum; this is especially true for Jews with an Ashkenazi background. 'Your collection is inspiring and tells an unknown story to us American Jews. Thank you, Thank you!', reads an entry from December 2005. Similar is the comment of a couple from the US who visited the museum in July 2004: 'We thoroughly enjoyed our Moroccan Jewish experience! We learned about our Sephardic cousins!'

Moroccan Muslims also visit the museum, most of them in the frame of school excursions, but some are individual visitors, often expatriates. Their reactions, as is clear from the informal interviews I conducted between 2006 and 2011, and again from the guestbook entries, are predominantly positive. They stress the importance of such a museum for mutual understanding and as a model for tolerance and acceptance. In May 2005 a Moroccan Muslim woman wrote: 'Many thanks to the museum for presenting to us this part of our identity.' Another Moroccan Muslim visitor describes the museum as 'wonderful work that helps to rediscover a part of ourselves, of our history'. In some cases the political dimension of having a Jewish museum in an Arab country is also referred to. A Moroccan Muslim living in France has noted: 'We need to know and to preserve our Moroccan Jewish patrimony and history. This is our ambassador in the fight for the Palestinian cause . . . Let's stand up together for peace in our world.' Moroccan Jews also point out the importance of the museum. 'I hope this museum will be there as a witness for our future generations', states a Moroccan Jewish woman from France in June 2005.

Even though visitor reactions can be traced by the means of interviews, questionnaires, or guestbook comments, it remains difficult to gauge the actual impact of a museum project or an exhibition on the self-image or the perception of a particular group. However, it is important to reiterate that museums do not only influence their visitors but can contribute to broader discussions. In the case of the Museum of Moroccan Judaism the director and the curator strive to make their message known to a wider audience by participating in colloquia and workshops as well as in exhibition projects outside Casablanca, for example, at the

University of Al-Akhawayn in Ifrane or in the framework of the Art Culinaire festival in Fes. The museum also serves as a major source of information for scholars and journalists researching the history or culture of Moroccan Jews. Moreover, it provides a platform for cultural and political events, where Muslims and Jews, Moroccans as well as foreigners, come together to discuss issues of mutual interest. Thus, the museum has become a space for exchange between the two faiths, a space for information and contact between Muslims and Jews. Even though only a minority is making concrete use of this space by attending events or visiting the exhibition, the museum is widely perceived as a positive symbol for Jewish–Muslim dialogue, as media reports as well as Moroccans' reactions indicate.

Even though it is impossible to fully answer the question to what extent the promotion of tolerance and the emphasis on the proximity of Jews and Muslims can influence mutual perception and help overcome boundaries between the two groups, we have seen that the exhibition narrative reinforces a rather positive image that stands in contrast to the negative picture of Jews within Moroccan society, which is based on the association of Jews with Zionism and Israel. A survey conducted by Moroccan historians and social scientists in 2006 concluded that 'Muslim identity is the dominant identity' in Morocco and that 'the majority of Moroccans define themselves as Muslims rather than as Moroccans' (El Ayadi et al. 2006: 131). However, the survey also noted the trend among the younger generation to define themselves first of all as Moroccans and only second as Muslims. Likewise, while most people declared a stronger affiliation with non-Arab Muslims, among younger people this point of view has been shifting towards a feeling of closeness to Jewish co-citizens (2006: 131). Even though the community is vanishing, it has not disappeared but rather has found a new dynamic in recent decades. Judaism remains a popular theme in present-day Morocco: films and books are released, conferences and cultural events organized, and heritage tours offered. It is an issue that fits well into the new images of a diverse and plural society—a narrative that is favoured by state representatives and, as the quoted survey suggests, also by the younger Muslim population.

Notes

This essay was written as part of the joint research project SFB 640 'Representation of Changing Social Order' at the Humboldt University and the Zentrum Moderner Orient in Berlin, financed by the German Research Foundation. Parts of it were presented at the conference 'Representations of Jews in Contemporary European Popular Culture' at the European University Institute in Florence and published in the EUI Working Paper Series 2010/01. All translations from French or Arabic to English are mine.

1   While the Museum in Casablanca is the only officially recognized Jewish museum in an Arab country, there are private initiatives such as the small Musée Em Habanim located at the Jewish Cemetery in Fes presenting Judaica or the Cheikh Omar Museum in Akka, a

small town in the south of Morocco. Nor is it the only Jewish museum in a Muslim setting as there is the Quincentennial Foundation Museum of Turkish Jews in Istanbul, which opened its doors in 2001.

2   Shalom Sabar (2010) describes a very similar scenario for Israel, where the hamsa is also widely used, not only as a protective symbol in private households or as a pendant or key ring, but also as a company logo, advertising carrier, or a motif on stamps or phone cards.

3   With the Treaty of Fes in 1912 sovereignty over Morocco was divided between France and Spain. Until 1956 the north of Morocco and the territory of West Sahara was a Spanish Protectorate.

4   In Judaism aniconism appears in the Bible: 'Do not represent [such] gods by any carved statue or picture of anything in the heaven above, on the earth below, or in the water below the land' (Exod. 20: 3–6). The Qur'an does not explicitly command aniconism, but references can be found in the *hadith*, oral traditions of the Prophet's sayings and actions that were collected and written down.

5   See <http://www.thejewishmuseum.org>.

6   Only in the north of Morocco, which was under Spanish rule from 1912 until 1956, did Spanish become the dominant language among Jews.

7   The use of Hebrew for prayers in the Moroccan context was always rare and reserved for men, as women traditionally did not learn Hebrew in talmudic schools, and so Judaeo-Arabic translations of prayers and biblical texts were commonly used.

8   In 2009 Matthew Klayman was a student at the Center for Cross-Cultural Learning (CCCL) in Rabat. He wrote his thesis on 'Historical Memory, Identity, and the Holocaust in the Moroccan Jewish Community'. His research was supervised by the historian Mohammed Kenbib and can be accessed at the library of the CCCL. I was present at the interview he conducted with Simon Levy in April 2009 in Casablanca.

9   Quoted from a discussion on the Moroccan website <http://www.yabiladi.com/forum/juifs-maroc-peur-2-3081032.html>, accessed 30 Apr.–3 May 2009.

References

Websites

Homepage of the Jewish Museum in New York: <http://www.thejewishmuseum.org/CollectionOverview/Ceremonial-Art>, accessed 20 July 2009.

Homepage of the Foundation of Moroccan Jewish cultural patrimony and the Jewish Museum: <http://www.casajewishmuseum.com/index.php?page=fondation>, accessed 15 January 2010.

US Department of State, ed., 'Report on Human Rights Practices, released by the Bureau of Democracy, Human Rights and Labor', available at: <http://www.state.gov/g/drl/rls/hrrpt/2003/27934.htm>, accessed 1 May 2009.

Printed Sources

ANDERSON, BENEDICT. 2006. *Imagined Communities: Reflections on the Origin and Spread of Nationalism*. London and New York.

BEN-LAYASHI, SAMIR, and BRUCE MADDY-WEITZMAN. 2010. 'Myth, History and Realpolitik: Morocco and its Jewish Community'. *Journal of Modern Jewish Studies*, 9: 89–106.

BENSIMON, AGNES. 1991. *Hassan II et les Juifs: L'Histoire d'une émigration secrète*. Paris.

BERNICHI, LOUBNA. 2006. 'Pourquoi les juifs ont quitté le Maroc'. *Maroc Hebdo International*, 719: 26–8.

BILU, YORAM, and ANDRÉ LEVY. 1996. 'Nostalgia and Ambivalence: The Reconstruction of Jewish–Muslim Relations in Oulad Mansour'. In Harvey E. Goldberg, ed., *Sephardi and Middle Eastern Jewries*, 288–311. Bloomington, Ind.

BIN-NUN, YIGAL. 2009. 'La Négociation de l'évacuation'. In Shmuel Trigano, ed., *La Fin du Judaïsme en terres d'Islam*, 303–58. Paris.

BOUM, AOMAR. 2010. 'The Plastic Eye: The Politics of Jewish Representations in Moroccan Museums'. *Ethnos*, 75: 49–77.

BURKE, PETER. 1989. 'History as Social Memory'. In Thomas Butler, ed., *Memory: History, Culture and the Mind*, 97–113. London.

CANAAN, TAWFIK. 1914. *Aberglaube und Volksmedizin im Land der Bibel*. Hamburg.

COHEN, MARC. 1994. *Under Crescent and Cross: The Jews in the Middle Ages*. Princeton.

DAÏF, MARIA. 2004. 'Un musée très discret'. *Telquel*, 119: 18–21.

EL AYADI, MOHAMMED, et al. 2006. *L'Islam au quotidien: Enquête sur les valeurs et les pratiques religieuses au Maroc*. Casablanca.

FENTON, PAUL, and DAVID LITTMAN. 2010. *L'Exil au Maghreb: La Condition juive sous l'Islam, 1148–1912*. Paris.

Fondation Du Patrimoine Judéo-Marocain. 2006a. *Bulletin d'information*, 1 (Sept.).

——2006b. *Le Musée du Judaïsme Marocain*. Brochure of the Jewish Museum. Casablanca.

GEERTZ, CLIFFORD. 1973. *The Interpretation of Cultures*. New York.

GILLER, SUSAN. 2008. 'The Mellah of Fez: Reflections of the Spatial Turn in Moroccan Jewish History'. In Julia Brauch et al., eds., *Jewish Topographies: Visions of Space and Traditions of Place*, 101–18. Aldershot.

GOTTREICH, EMILY. 2007. *The Mellah of Marrakesh: Jewish and Muslim Space in Morocco's Red City*. Bloomington, Ind.

GOTZMANN, ANDREAS. 1989. *Gold- und Silberschmuck der Juden in Marokko. Kunsthandwerk als ein Aspekt kultureller Zusammenhänge*. Heidelberg.

HALL, STUART. 1996. 'Who Needs Identity?' In Stuart Hall and Paul Du Gay, eds., *Questions of Cultural Identity*, 1–17. London.

HIRSCHBERG, HAIM ZWI. 1974. *A History of the Jews in North Africa: From Antiquity to the Sixteenth Century*. Leiden.

HOWE, MARVINE. 2005. *Morocco: The Islamist Awakening and Other Challenges*. Oxford.

KAPLAN, FLORA. 1994. *Museums and the Making of 'Ourselves': The Role of Object in National Identity*. London.

——2006. 'Making and Remaking National Identity'. In Sharon Macdonald, ed., *A Companion to Museum Studies*, 152–69. London.

KIRSHENBLATT-GIMBLETT, BARBARA. 2006. 'Reconfiguring Museums: An Afterword'. In Cordula Grewe, ed., *Die Schau des Fremden*, 361–76. Stuttgart.

KLAYMAN, MATTHEW. 2009. *Historical Memory, Identity, and the Holocaust in the Moroccan Jewish Community*. Center for Cross-Cultural Learning, SIT Working Papers. Rabat.

LASKIER, MICHEL. 2003. 'Morocco'. In Michel Laskier et al., eds., *The Jews of the Middle East and North Africa in Modern Times*, 471–504. New York.

LAURSEN, JANNE. 2008. 'The Danish Jewish Museum: A New Museum Asserts its Character'. In Katherine J. Goodnow and Haci Akman, eds., *Scandinavian Museums and Cultural Diversity*, 42–53. Oxford.

LAUSBERG, SYLVIE. 2007. *Maroc: Deux passions, une mémoire*. Paris.

LEVY, ANDRÉ. 1999. 'Playing for Control of Distance: Card Games between Jews and Muslims on a Casablancan Beach'. *American Ethnologist*, 26: 632–53.

——2003. 'Notes on Jewish–Muslim Relationships: Revisiting the Vanishing Moroccan Jewish Community'. *Cultural Anthropology*, 18: 365–97.

LEVY, SIMON. 1997. 'Pour répondre à l'urgence: La Fondation du patrimoine culturel judéo-marocain'. Unpublished manuscript. Casablanca.

——2001. *Essais d'histoire et de civilisation judéo-marocain*. Rabat.

——2007. 'Dix ans après sa naissance, la Fondation du Patrimoine Culturel Judéo-Marocain dresse un premier bilan'. In International Council of Museums, ed., *Hommage à Niamat Allah El Khatib Boujibar*, 219–29. Casablanca.

LEWIS, BERNARD. 1984. *The Jews of Islam*. Princeton

MACDONALD, SHARON. 1998. Introduction. In Sharon Macdonald, ed., *Theorizing Museums: Representing Identity and Diversity in a Changing World*. Oxford.

MARLEY, DAWN. 2002. 'Diversity and Uniformity: Linguistic Fact and Fiction in Morocco'. In Kamal Salhi, ed., *French in and out of France*, 335–76. Bern.

NOTH, ALBRECHT. 1987. 'Abgrenzungsprobleme zwischen Muslimen und Nicht-Muslimen. Die "Bedingungen Umars (as-surut al-Umariyya)" unter einem anderen Aspekt gelesen'. *Jerusalem Studies in Arabic and Islam*, 9: 290–315.

OUAFAE, MOUHSSINE. 1995. 'Ambivalence du discourse sur l'arabisation'. *International Journal of the Sociology of Language: Sociolinguistics in Morocco*, 112: 45–61.

RABATÉ, JACQUES, and ROSE RABATÉ. 1996. *Bijoux au Maroc*. Aix-en-Provence.

ROSEN, LAWRENCE. 1972. 'Muslim–Jewish Relations in a Moroccan City'. *International Journal of Middle East Studies*, 3: 435–49.

——1984. *Bargaining for Reality*. Chicago.

SABAR, SHALOM. 2010. 'From Sacred Symbols to Key Ring: The Ḥamsa in Jewish and Israeli Societies'. In Simon Bronner, ed., *Jews at Home: The Domestication of Identity*, 140–62. Jewish Cultural Studies 2. Oxford.

SCHARF, MICHAL. 1988. *The Hitler Scroll in North Africa* [Megilat hitler bitsefon afrikah]. Lod.

SCHROETER, DANIEL J. 2008. 'The Shifting Boundaries of Moroccan Jewish Identities'. *Jewish Social Studies: History, Culture, Society*, 15: 145–64.

SENKYR, JAN. 2003. 'Marokko lanciert Kampagne gegen Islamismus'. *Länderbericht der Konrad Adenauer Stiftung Rabat*. <http://www.kas.de/proj/home/pub/25/1/year-2003/dokument_id-1984/index.html>, accessed 8 Apr. 2009.

SHOHAT, ELLA. 1999. 'The Invention of the Mizrahim'. *Journal of Palestinian Studies*, 29: 5–20.

SLYOMOVICS, SUSAN. 2001. 'A Truth Commission for Morocco'. *The Middle East Report: Morocco in Transition*, 218: 18–21.

SOLTES, ORI. 2005. *Our Sacred Signs: How Jewish, Christian and Muslim Art Draw from the Same Source*. New York.

STERN, KAREN. 2003. *Inscribing Devotion and Death: Archaeological Evidence for Jewish Populations of North Africa*. Leiden.

STILLMAN, NORMAN. 1979. *The Jews of Arab Lands: A History and Source Book*. Oxford.

——1988. *The Language and Culture of the Jews of Sefrou, Morocco*. Manchester.

——1996. 'Middle Eastern and North African Jewries Confront Modernity: Orientation, Disorientation, Reorientation'. In Harvey Goldberg, ed., *Sephardi and Middle Eastern Jewries: History and Culture in the Modern Era*, 59–72. Bloomington, Ind.

STORA, BENJAMIN. 2000. 'Maroc, le traitement des histoires proches'. *Esprit. Les Historiens et le travail de mémoire*, 8: 88–101.

TESSLER, MARK. 1978. 'The Identity of Religious Minorities in Non-Secular States: Jews in Tunisia and Morocco and Arabs in Israel'. *Comparative Studies in Society and History*, 20: 359–73.

TREVISAN SEMI, EMANUELA. 2010. 'Double Trauma and Manifold Narratives: Jews' and Muslims' Representations of the Departure of Moroccan Jews in the 1950s and 1960s'. *Journal of Modern Jewish Studies*, 9: 107–25.

WAGENHOFER, SOPHIE. 2013. *Ausstellen, verorten, partizipieren. Das Jüdische Museum in Casablanca*. Berlin.

YE'OR, BAT. 1999. 'The Dhimmi Factor in the Exodus of Jews from Arab Countries'. In Malka Hillel Shulevitz, ed., *The Forgotten Millions: The Modern Jewish Exodus from Arab Lands*, 33–51. London.

ZERHOUANI, KHADDOUJI. 2002. 'Le Musée judéo-marocain'. *Architecture du Maroc*, 8: 39–42.

ZIANE, NADIA. 2005. 'Simon Lévy, directeur du Musée du judaisme marocain: Le Vrai Maroc, pluriel et tolérant doit être reflété dans notre système éducatif'. *Le Matin*, 6 Feb.

ZISENWINE, DANIEL. 2007. 'From Hassan II to Muhammed VI: Plus ça change?'. In Bruce Maddy-Weitzman and Daniel Zisenwine, eds., *The Maghrib in the New Century*, 132–49. Gainesville, Fla.

TWELVE

The Framing of the Jew: Paradigms of Incorporation and Difference in the Jewish Heritage Revival in Poland

MAGDALENA WALIGÓRSKA

'WE WANT TO COME BACK', announced large red posters scattered in the streets of Berlin in the spring of 2012. Adorned with a fusion of the Star of David and the white eagle, the Polish national emblem, the posters displayed the Manifesto of the Jewish Renaissance Movement in Poland. The bold appeal articulated at the 7th Berlin Biennale formed part of the First Congress of the Jewish Renaissance Movement in Poland, staged by the Israeli multimedia artist Yael Bartana, known in Poland for her provocative works *Mary koszmary* (*Nightmares*, 2007), *Mur i wieża* (*Wall and Tower*, 2009), and *Zamach* (*Assassination*, 2011). Bartana's films, in which she proposes that three million Jews should return to Poland, have provoked controversy both in Poland and in Israel. The artist, whose utopian vision employs Zionist rhetoric to call for new Jewish settlements in Poland, is not only critical of the politics of Israel but of nationalism in general, arguing for a new Jewish Poland beyond ethnic divides:

We want to come back.

Not to Uganda, Argentina, Syria, or Madagascar. Not even to Palestine. It is Europe we are interested in. The land of our fathers and forefathers. Awake or asleep, we continue to dream of Poland.

The squares in Warsaw, Łódź, and Kraków shall be filled with new settlements. Like many decades ago, we wish to once again settle in a land where no one expects us. We believe we are fated to live here, to establish families here, die here, and bury the remains of our dead here.

We want to heal the trauma—ours and yours. Once and for all.

We direct our appeal not just to Jews. We accept into our ranks all those for whom there is no place in their homeland—the expelled and the persecuted. There will be no discrimination in our movement. We will not dig into your life stories, or check your residence cards or refugee status. We shall be strong in our weakness.[1]

The above manifesto not only pictures Poland as the ultimate homeland of Jews, but also presents Poles and Jews as complementary, almost symbiotic in their relationship. One of the most powerful passages in that text speaks of the elementary need for the other in order to be fully able both to experience the outside world and to construct one's own identity:

> With one religion, we cannot listen.
> With one colour, we cannot see.
> With one culture, we cannot feel.
> Without you, we cannot even remember.

The Manifesto of the Jewish Renaissance Movement in Poland, although formulated by an Israeli artist, is symptomatic of the way many contemporary Polish artists, writers, and even politicians come to conceptualize and interpret the relationship of Jews and non-Jews in Poland. Incorporating Jews and Jewish heritage into the category of Polish culture has been to a degree a natural corollary of the unprecedented rise of interest in the Jewish past which has been taking place in post-1989 Poland. As literary, historiographical, and artistic projects dealing with Jews started proliferating in the last two decades, accompanied by festivals of Jewish culture and the revitalization of Jewish sites across Poland, it has become evident for many local cultural organizers as well as municipal and even state authorities that Jewish heritage belongs in the realm of the national culture. This symbiotic vision coexists, however, with the opposite frame, that picturing the Jew as marked and essentially different from the ethnic Pole. The recent resurgence of memory about Jews in Poland has produced not only a multitude of cultural products relating to Jewish themes, but also a discursive space around them, including articles, reviews, public speeches, and the like. This essay, drawing on examples from literary works, performance art, and musical productions on the one hand, and public discourse on the other, analyses incorporation and exclusion as two dominant themes in the narratives of Jewishness, examining them as rhetorical frames which organize the collective perception of Poland's 'significant others'.

In his *Marvelous Possessions* Stephen Greenblatt investigates the modes of representing the other and the alien culture, looking at the most extreme conditions of encounter in the history of civilization: the discovery and colonization of America. To name 'the decisive emotional and intellectual experience in the presence of radical difference' he uses the concept of wonder (2003: 14). The state of wonder, subsuming both excitement and ambivalence, admiration and uncertainty, accompanies the 'first encounter' with the other, Greenblatt claims. '[T]hrilling, potentially dangerous, momentarily immobilizing, charged at once with desire, ignorance, and fear', wonder is the paradigmatic human response in the face of the unknown (2003: 20). And although Greenblatt relates wonder to the European discovery of the New World, the concept also captures some of the tensions behind the recent revival of Jewish heritage in Poland.

In the wake of the systemic changes of 1989, when Poland slowly began regaining its memory about Jews after decades of silence and an apparent amnesia, the blank spots in Polish historiography seemed indeed like an unknown land awaiting its explorers. The generation of Poles who had had virtually no direct contact with Jewish culture or with Polish Jews set out to discover what Janusz Makuch and Krzysztof Gierat, creators of the first Jewish Culture Festival in Poland, called Atlantis—the lost continent of Jewish heritage. This process, which began with the intellectual effort of addressing the difficult Polish Jewish past, soon also inspired the wider popular culture. The beginnings of the Jewish revival were marked not only by the opening of the first Jewish studies department at the Jagiellonian University in 1986, or path-breaking publications such as Jan Błoński's critical essay on the Polish guilt towards Jews, 'The Poor Poles Look at the Ghetto', but also by the appearance of a plethora of books, records, films, guided tours, and theme restaurants inspired by Jewish motifs. Poles who might have forgotten Jews, or had never known them, wondered about the other they unexpectedly encountered.

To be sure, Jews did not appear to the Polish mind *ex nihilo* only with the Jewish heritage boom. Polish popular culture abounds with representations of the other which have inhabited the Polish lands and the Polish imagination for centuries. At the same time, however, the way Poles came to conceptualize Jews decades after the Holocaust resembled to an extent the experience of facing the New World. The discovery of the culture of the other, notes Greenblatt, is always mediated by the powerful concepts and representations of our own culture. What is more, we tend to take fragments of the culture we encounter as its entirety. Imagining the rest that we do not know, we commit an act of appropriation, ascribing our own understanding of the world to the cultural system we have not yet penetrated (Greenblatt 2003: 122). The recent Polish 'discovery' of Jewishness is doubly mediated. Not only are Poles likely to imagine Jewish culture through a prism of their own, but they are also largely deprived of direct contact with living Jews. In 1988 Alexander Hertz wrote that, for the coming generation of Poles, the image of the Jew was going to be nothing more than a 'vague memory more and more transformed into a legend' (1988: 197). As it turned out, it was this very generation, for whom mere representations or re-enactments of Jewish life were a substitute for face-to-face interactions with Jewish neighbours, that called into being the Jewish heritage revival.

Greenblatt identifies two opposing reactions triggered by wonder. One of them is a progression from perceiving the other as essentially different to a form of subsuming the other in the definition of the self. It entails 'articulations of the hidden links between the radically opposed ways of being and hence . . . some form of acceptance of the other in the self and the self in the other'. The other reaction to wonder, however, is based on 'articulations of . . . radical differences'. In this case we proceed from some kind of identification with the other to total estrangement. '[F]or a moment', writes Greenblatt, 'you see yourself confounded with the other, but then you make the other become an alien object, a thing, that you can destroy or incorporate at will.' It is the recognition of the other as the essential alien here that allows 'renaming, transformation, and appropriation' (2003: 135). These two contrasting patterns of wonder lead to two different outcomes. Articulating 'hidden links' between the self and the other, we put the emphasis on shared values and on the similarities between 'us' and 'them'. We frame the other as the member of a higher-level category which embraces both groups, referring to the idea of brotherhood. Articulating 'radical differences', by contrast, implies that we reject the value system of others, consider them inferior, and force them to adapt to our standards, values, and frameworks. Conceptual- izing the other as an object results in considering the other not only as a malleable thing that can be transformed, but also, as Greenblatt emphasizes, as something that can be possessed. Wonder is a 'prelude to appropriation'. A prelude which in the Americas ended in the 'greatest experiment in political, economic, and cul- tural cannibalism in the history of the Western world' (2003: 136).

The Polish fascination with Jewish heritage oscillates between the same two extremes of incorporation and appropriation. Jews exist in the Polish collective imagination either as part of Poland's multicultural past, where they are pictured in harmonious coexistence with ethnic Poles, or as essentially different others, whose distinctiveness defines the outer boundaries of the category of Polishness. Although the two paradigms, that of 'hidden links' and that of 'radical differ- ences', have resurged with particular force within the contemporary Jewish herit- age boom, both of them are powered by older tropes existing in Polish culture.

Incorporation

The Jewish Culture Festival in Kraków is the central venue where the links between Polish and Jewish culture are articulated and celebrated. Initiated in 1988 by Janusz Makuch and Krzysztof Gierat, the festival grew over time to accommodate over two hundred events, including not only concerts but also a variety of workshops, film shows, lectures, and walking tours. In 2012 nearly 25,000 people attended the festival. The final open-air concert in Szeroka Street gathered around 15,000 spectators, and over a million Poles watched the tele- vised broadcast. More than two decades after its inception, the Jewish Culture Festival, which takes place in the wonderfully preserved historic Jewish quarter of Kraków, Kazimierz, extends well beyond the ten-day-long summer event. Since 2009, the foundation organizing the festival has also run the Cheder Café, which houses a small library and hosts numerous cultural events during the year. The festival, which ranks among the most important events of this kind worldwide, has become not only one of the major attractions in Kraków but also a popular mass media icon of Jewish culture. Its significance is also recognized at state level. Almost a third of its budget comes from the Polish Ministry of Culture and Heritage and the president of Poland is the honorary patron of the event.

Links between Jewish and Polish heritage are given special emphasis at the festival. 'I cordially welcome you to Kazimierz, the Jewish town whose history and culture are inextricably linked with the history and culture of Kraków and Poland', wrote Tadeusz Jakubowicz, the president of the Jewish religious community in Kraków, in his letter of welcome to the festival participants in 2004. Speaking of the central importance of Kazimierz he stated:

The vestiges of our culture, the signs of living memory, are evident here. Whoever can decipher the signs of the past will easily read from them the history of our harmonious coexistence with Polish society. Jews, Poles—Poles, Jews—WE all come from here, from Kazimierz, from Kraków . . . I hope that being in Kazimierz, in Kraków, at the festival, you can feel at home, as if in our shared house. (Jakubowicz 2004: 6)

Jakubowicz not only interprets Kazimierz as a space shared by Poles and Jews, and the festival as an integral part of Polish culture, but also refers to the inclusive 'we', a superordinate category which refers to both Jews and Poles. Interestingly, the boundary that this new category is to dissolve runs between 'Jews' and 'Poles', not 'Jews' and 'non-Jews'. It is Poland that provides the 'shared house', Polish culture that serves as the common denominator. On a similar note the minister of culture, Andrzej Zakrzewski, stated in his welcome address of 1999: 'The Kraków Jewish Culture Festival is a great celebration—also a celebration of Polish culture' (Zakrzewski: 1999: 2). 'Polish' appears here clearly not as a category distinct from 'Jewish', but one which subsumes it. This is also pictured in the policy of the Polish Ministry of Culture and National Heritage which, in 2009, subsidized not only the Jewish Culture Festival in Kraków, but also its counterpart in Warsaw, as well as the Warsaw Jewish Film Festival, the Simcha Jewish festival in Wrocław, the Łódź of Four Cultures festival, and the Meeting of Three Cultures in Leżajsk, all of which were centred around Jewish heritage.

In 2010 the Jewish festival in Kraków celebrated its twentieth anniversary. The jubilee volume published on the occasion, *The Second Soul* (*Druga dusza*), presented the event as part of Poland's multi-ethnic heritage. As the head of the festival, Janusz Makuch, emphasized, the festival should be seen in the context of cultural overlaps and cross-fertilizations that used to take place in the historic region of Galicia:

Everything used to be interconnected here into an extremely rich and colourful pluralist web, especially in Kraków. Thank God, we're not ethnically clean here, very dirty rather, ethnically and culturally mixed with each other. This Polish-Jewish-Ukrainian-Gypsy-and-whatever-else borderland interests me, obviously, and inspires me. Everything that is a ferment, a chaos, all of these junctions and interpenetrations. It used to be a whole world—the multicultural, multilayered, multidimensional Galicia. (Dodziuk 2010: 85–6)

Makuch not only incorporates Jewish heritage into the more universal category of the multi-ethnic Galician legacy but challenges the very concept of clear-cut boundaries in culture. He sees the Jewish heritage of Kraków as part of the Galician melting pot, as a hybrid, and interconnected with other cultures. The history of the region is also interesting here: Galicia, originally a southern province of Poland that was annexed by Austro-Hungary during the partitions of Poland, no longer exists as an independent entity. The area was part of the Austro-Hungarian empire until 1918, and then belonged to the independent interwar Polish Republic. Today its territory is divided between Poland and Ukraine. The multi-ethnicity, prosperity, and liberal spirit of the region inspire many myths, with Galicia becoming a successful 'brand' in Kraków: it is featured in the names of restaurants and klezmer bands, and there is even a Galicia Jewish Museum, whose permanent exhibition is devoted to the traces of Jewish civilization in the area, and whose bookstore offers a variety of maps, albums, and guidebooks related to the region. Galicia is, however, not only a nostalgic destination but also a space which has come to symbolize the coexistence of Jews and non-Jews.

To be sure, the Jewish/Polish dichotomy is still central to the discourse on the Jewish heritage revival in Poland (see Gruber 2002: 10 ff.; Orla-Bukowska 2008). Only the two elements are increasingly seen in an interplay rather than as mutually exclusive. The Polish Jewish intellectual Konstanty Gebert writes that Polish culture has been the environment which nourished the festival of Jewish culture and made it possible. The non-Jewish Polish audience responds so enthusiastically to anything Jewish because Polish culture 'absorbed and assimilated the contents of Jewish culture' to a degree that allows Poles to embrace it. The Jewish festival, according to Gebert, 'Judaizes' Polish culture and, at the same time, 'goyifies' Jewish culture. Gebert's *bon mot* has a further twist. The Polish neologism 'to goyify' (*zagoić*) is a homonym of the verb 'to heal', which gives his vision of mutual influence a new dimension. Healing, he suggests, is possible only by diffusion (Gebert 2010: 262).

Gebert's 'Judaizing' and 'goyifying' correspond to two processes that are referred to as 'foreignization' and 'domestication' in translation studies. Domesticating consists in filtering a given text through the sensitivity of the reader, inserting it in the world of the new addressee, and adapting it to the needs of the target audience. It might involve rewriting, simplification, and cultural assimilation, helping readers to understand the foreign text by substituting the unknown with references to their own culture. It often provokes, however, 'absolute loss', as that which does not have an equivalent in the target culture is likely to be left out altogether: lost in translation. A domesticated text is easy to read, smoothed out, and devoid of alien-sounding idioms and incomprehensible metaphors. By the same token, the elements of Jewish heritage or Jewish history that are 'goyified', or undergo domestication, become compatible with Polish national myths and popular clichés. Foreignizing, in contrast, relies on bringing the codes of the translated text into the target language. The cultural product thus translated remains to a certain extent alien but may retain more of its original meaning (Eco 2003; Rubel and Rosman 2003). The 'Judaization' of Polish culture taking place during the Jewish festival would consist in exposing the Polish 'reader', or consumer of culture, to Jewish symbols, myths, and traditions which remain unabridged. Reading a 'foreignized' text requires more effort on the part of the reader but allows one to come closer to the Jewish vernacular. And it is probably this effort invested in understanding the other that constitutes for Gebert the healing function of initiatives like the Jewish festival in Kraków.

It is not only in Kraków, however, that Jewish culture is framed in terms of incorporation. The mayor of Wrocław, Rafał Dutkiewicz, speaking at the opening of the renovated White Stork Synagogue in 2010, said: 'We are meeting in the renovated White Stork Synagogue to return to our city once and for all its Jewish heart . . . the 850-year-long Jewish history of this city is not over. We open its new chapter, treating the Jewish heritage of Wrocław as part of our collective identity and culture, common to all Wrocławians'.[2] Wrocław, which promotes itself as the 'city of dialogue' and has a designated area around the synagogue called the District of Mutual Respect, has long employed the language of multi-ethnicity to create its new image. As the founding myth of post-1945 Wrocław as historically Slavic lost currency with the fall of communism, the city authorities set out to acknowledge its other ethnic groups (Thum 2005). The attention devoted to Jewish heritage constituted an important element of this new policy. The list of institutions dealing with Jewish heritage in Wrocław includes the Centre for the Culture and Languages of the Jews, which opened in 1993 at Wrocław University, the Centre of Jewish Culture and Education (since 2005), and the Jewish Information Centre (since 2008). Moreover, the renovated White Stork Synagogue hosts many cultural events, among others the annual Jewish festival and Israeli Independence Day. There are also plans to open a Museum of Silesian Jewry in the synagogue's basement (Zabłocka-Kos 2009).

Jewish heritage has been included in the vision of the new, post-1989 Poland not only at the level of official policies and political declarations but also in contemporary popular culture. Sława Przybylska, who was among the first Polish singers to perform Jewish songs before 1989, wrote in the sleeve notes to her 1993 record *Alef Bejs* that Yiddish songs represent to her 'the extraordinary synthesis of biblical profundity and Slavic nostalgia' (Przybylska 1993). The Kraków-based klezmer band Di Galitzyaner Klezmorim put the idea of this 'synthesis' into practice, recording 'Chopin's Freilach', an adaptation of a piece by Frédéric Chopin in 'klezmer style'. This extraordinary piece won the 1999 'Chopin Open' competition in Kraków, which has convinced the artists that just as pre-Second World War klezmer music drew from Polish folklore, the new klezmer pieces can successfully incorporate Polish music too.[3]

Apart from emphasizing the commonalities and mutual inspiration in Polish and Jewish music, some Polish artists use the medium of traditional Jewish folk music to put across the message of a more universal brotherhood of the two groups. Popular pop singer Justyna Steczkowska recorded in 2002 a Polish version of the traditional Yiddish song 'Ale brider' ('Wszyscy braćmi być powinni') with slightly changed lyrics. While the Yiddish original conveys a universal message: 'We are all brothers . . . and are singing joyful songs' (*Un mir zaynen ale brider / Oy, oy, ale brider / Un mir zingn freylekhe lider / Oy, oy, oy!*), the Polish lyrics by Roman Kołakowski are somewhat more specific and prescriptive: 'All should be brothers . . . because they were born innocent, the Jew and the goy' (*Wszyscy braćmi być powinni! / Oj, oj!—prawda święta! / Bo rodzili się niewinni / Żyd i goj!*).[4]

Some Polish musicians take the idea of brotherhood even further, not only advocating warmer relations between Jews and non-Jews, but also suggesting that the boundary between the two groups is rather fuzzy. The authors of *Pan Kazimierz* (2007), a popular musical about the Jewish district of Kraków, introduce one of their songs on the musical's CD with the note: 'We are all a bit antisemitic, just as we are all a bit Jewish. In a country where several million Jews lived for 700 years, it would be hard to find even a handful of people who could in all certainty state that none of their ancestors was Jewish.' The seemingly reconciliatory message that 'we are all a bit Jewish' has two disturbing implications. First, it suggests that the opposite of Jewish is antisemitic, and secondly that being antisemitic is a universal defect, and just as harmless as being Jewish. Blurring the Jewish/non-Jewish boundary does not serve here to establish commonalities between the two groups, but rather masks problem areas in their relations.

The incorporation of Jewishness into the category of Polishness of course has its historical precedents. The Romantic period, which was also the time of the national struggle for independence, produced the idea of the spiritual coalition of Poles and Jews against the occupying powers, which, to a certain extent, outlived the epoch of partitions. Adam Mickiewicz, celebrated poet and a representative of Slavic messianism, believed not only that Poland was predestined to redeem Europe through its singular suffering as a partitioned country, but also in the particular relationship of Jews and Poles. Considering Jewry as the 'elder brother' of Catholic Poles, Mickiewicz, at the time of the Crimean War, even dreamt of organizing a Jewish legion which could fight alongside Poles in an uprising against the Russians (see Janion 2000, 2009). In fact, Polish Jewish patriots such as Colonel Berek Joselewicz (1764–1809), who fought in the Kościuszko Uprising of 1794, or Warsaw rabbi Dov Ber Meisels (1798–1870), who openly supported the Polish national movement, remained for a long time icons of Polish–Jewish brotherhood. The deeply symbolic image of Rabbi Meisels taking part, together with Catholic and Protestant clergy, in the funeral of the victims of an anti-Russian demonstration in Warsaw in 1861, immortalized by Aleksander Lesser in one of his paintings, became a powerful statement of Jewish solidarity with the Poles (Szapiro 2007). Just how important the image has remained is attested by the fact that Stanisław Krajewski's *Żydzi, Judaizm, Polska* (1997), which was among the first publications on the Polish–Jewish dialogue after 1989, used this very painting as its cover image. Therefore the narrative of Jews as exemplary Poles, although by no means mainstream, was definitely present in the Polish imagination and inspired many of the Jewish heritage revivalists.

But if this inclusive frame, celebrating the brotherhood of Poles and Jews, has such a long tradition, has the function that it performs remained the same? Frame theory assumes that every situation or issue can be approached from a number of viewpoints. However, it is the particular interpretations, or frames, which are generated in interpersonal communication and in public discourse that organize our thinking, providing definitions and interpretations (Chong and Druckman 2007: 104–6). The process of framing consists in the 'sender' of a given message offering one interpretation rather than another. 'Framing', according to Entman, 'essentially involves selection and salience. To frame is to select some aspects of a perceived reality and make them more salient in a communicating text, in such a way as to promote a particular problem definition, causal interpretation, moral evaluation, and/or treatment recommendation for the item described.' A rhetorical frame, therefore, concentrates on a certain aspect of the perceived reality and ignores others. By this means framing not only highlights a chosen perspective on a given problem but also offers a remedy (Entman 1993: 52). A frame is effective, however, only if the symbols, endorsements, and links on which it builds are culturally familiar to the audiences they address (Chong and Druckman 2007: 110–11). In other words, the more a frame makes use of stereotyped images and keywords, the more it is likely to be resonant.

If we consider incorporation as one of the ways of framing Jewish culture in today's Poland, what moral stance does it represent, and what does it remedy? No doubt, presenting Jewish culture as part of Poland's multicultural heritage is a way of countering the ethno-nationalist narrative, which equates Poles with Catholics. Opening up the category of Poles to include ethnic and religious minorities offers, on the one hand, an alternative to the radical right-wing discourse promoting Catholicism as the common denominator of all Poles. On the other hand, it provides an opportunity to voice protest against antisemitism, or to counter the image of Poland as an antisemitic country. By doing so it helps to present Poland as a democratic, inclusive state, attentive to the needs of its minorities—an image that post-communist Poland, aspiring to join, and then to play an active role within, the European Union, wishes to cultivate.

Referring to a superordinate category subsuming both Poles and Jews, such as that of 'Poland's heritage', or interconfessional brotherhood, has, however, one more implication. Celebrating common values is ultimately also a way of celebrating one's own group. Michał Bilewicz, in his study of the encounters between young Poles and Jews in the context of youth meetings and the March of the

Living, taking place annually on Yom Hashoah (Holocaust Remembrance Day) in the Auschwitz-Birkenau concentration camp, identifies the use of superordinate, inclusive categories as one of the strategies used by members of groups which have had a conflicted past. Confronted with the dark pages of one's group history, writes Bilewicz, one may choose a higher level of identification, for example, the category of 'European' rather than 'German'. This strategy may have a direct influence on intergroup contact: 'superordinate or inclusive social categories', as Bilewicz argues, 'can reduce the effects of a conflicted past on contemporary intergroup relations and may potentially enable successful intergroup contact' (2007: 553). By creating a category of Cracovians, Wrocławians, or Galicians which subsumes both Poles and Jews, it is possible for Poles to give salience to the narratives of Polish–Jewish symbiosis, or Poland as the Promised Land for Jews, de-emphasizing the ambiguous role of Poles as victims but also as bystanders and co-perpetrators in the Holocaust. Framing the Polish–Jewish relationship in terms of commonalities and overlaps, Poles are able to ascribe a positive value to these shared qualities and thus project a favourable image of their group. Inclusion of Jews in the vision of Polishness might therefore, just as much as a gesture of apology, be an identity-saving strategy (see Waligórska 2005).

Difference

Lisa Appignanesi, reporting on her travel to Poland in *Losing the Dead* (2000), comments with anger about a feature film on shtetl Jews she watched in Łódź. 'I saw it as an exercise in mythography', she writes:

Jews in Poland, it occurred to me, were fine as long as they could be framed in the exoticism of utter difference and had nothing to do with the complexity of recent history or common everyday encounters. Poles couldn't deal with Jews whose identity wasn't primarily bound up with a visible Jewishness. They couldn't deal with ordinary people who happened to have been born Jewish. (Appignanesi 2000: 77)

Although Appignanesi's experience in Poland was rather fleeting, her observation might not have been totally ungrounded. Despite the fact that the language of political correctness may be dominated by inclusionary categories in Poland, the representations of Jews in popular culture still often play on the articulation of difference and a 'visible Jewishness'.

Aj, waj! Czyli historie z cynamonem (*Ay, Vay! or Stories with Cinnamon*) was a particularly successful theatre production in 2005. The conservative daily *Rzeczpospolita* listed it as the fourth best theatre production of the year and the Comedy Festival Talia rewarded it as the best stage production. Directed by Rafał Kmita, the show, which consists of short, cabaret-like musical episodes populated by shtetl Jews and peppered with unsophisticated humour, has been running continuously since the premiere. Kmita's Jews: haggling merchants, housewives, but also a prostitute, all involved in comical everyday situations, are in fact archetypical. With their unmistakable costumes: black hats, *tsitsit*, caftans, *shtreimls* and sidelocks, their exaggerated gestures, and marked speech they look and sound Jewish. Indeed, they even seem to smell Jewish. In a market scene a female market trader, who has just palmed off a jar of bathing soap to an elderly Jew, concludes, maliciously: 'Now you're going to be a good-smelling, old, ugly Jew!' Although the Jewish monthly *Midrasz* critically reviewed the show as spreading 'Stürmer-like stereotypes' (Szwarcman 2006: 20–1), the audiences seem to be unwaveringly fascinated by the performance, rating it on YouTube as 'ingenious', 'incredible', and 'fantastic'.

The musical productions of the Warsaw Jewish festival Warszawa Singera (Singer's Warsaw) also frequently refer to the aesthetics of difference. *Tradition*, the open-air closing show of the 2007 festival, was a case in point. Its protagonists, clad in an Orthodox Jewish garb, were perfectly well distinguishable from their non-Jewish neighbours in their picturesque and nostalgic figuration of the life of an archetypal Jewish small town. Apart from long coats and artificial beards for men, and headscarves, shawls, or turbans for women, the identity of the Jewish characters was punctuated by large props they were holding: a rooster, a fish, a basket of *beyglekh*. The Jews, who constantly interacted with their non-Jewish neighbours and even celebrated with them a Jewish wedding, were thus visually identifiable, displaying a whole range of markers which made them unmistakable among likewise distinctly costumed Poles, Ukrainians, and Roma parading through the carnival-like shtetl.

The attributes which are supposed to accentuate the special, marked status of Jews also appear in their contemporary literary portrayals. One of the key characters in Paweł Jaszczuk's crime novel *Foresta Umbra* (2004), which takes place in pre-Second World War Lviv, is a Jewish lawyer, Samuel Hillel. Hillel is helping his friend, an investigative journalist, to solve a recent murder case by reading 'kabbalah cards' for him. In the scene of the kabbalah session, which consists in nothing other than reading Tarot cards, Hillel, an educated and assimilated Polish Jew, speaks the language of a fortune-teller. Using his paranormal abilities, presented here as a Jewish skill (the so-called kabbalah cards are old and venerated and have been in his family's possession for a long time), he is able to warn the protagonist about impending danger and hint at the identity of the serial killer. Hillel the Jew is a figure possessing secret knowledge apparently inherited from his ancestors (Jaszczuk 2004: 30–1). Jaszczuk's novel, named the best Polish crime novel of 2004, is just one example of fiction which presents the Jew as the essential other defined, if not by distinguished looks, then by uncanny abilities.

Another frequent 'Jewish' attribute, appearing not only in literature but also in the performing arts, is the so-called *żydłaczenie*, a markedly Jewish type of speech. A favourite device of the cabaret and theatre, it remains one of the most successful ways to give a character an unmistakably Jewish air. The effect of *żydłaczenie*, defined by the *Dictionary of Polish Language* as 'speaking Polish with a Jewish intonation', can be achieved by using a phonetically distorted pronunciation or ungrammatical structures. In his highly acclaimed debut novel *Lala* (2006), the young Polish writer Jacek Dehnel pictures the world of pre-war Polish nobility. In one of the episodes, set in the Jewish commercial centre of Warsaw, Nalewki Street, a resolute Jewish hat seller is trying to persuade a young girl to purchase an expensive hat she cannot afford. Finally, the Jew, charmed by the girl's appearance, decides to sell it far below the initial price. All through the negotiations the hat seller speaks in a very distinctive way. By means of unorthodox spelling (*pietnaszcze* instead of *piętnaście* (fifteen), *pieniące* instead of *pieniądze* (money), *panienkha* instead of *panienka* (miss)), Dehnel conveys a speech that is still recognizable as Polish, but which is lame, caricatural, and comical. Since the narrator observes that '[m]ost Jews in Warsaw were the poor of Nalewki Street, [who] were trading in whatever they could get hold of in hundreds of tiny stores, inhabiting the basements of dilapidated houses, quarrelling in the streets, and elbowing their way on the pavements' (Dehnel 2006: 163–4), the reader can easily assume that most Jews of Warsaw spoke with the Jewish inflection. It is not only the frantic movement, confusion, and disorderliness but also the 'Jewish' sound that defines Jewish space in *Lala*—the sound which, although purportedly originating from pre-Second World War Warsaw, is still unmistakable to the contemporary Polish ear.

Representations of the Jew as visually and aurally distinct from the ethnic Pole have a rich tradition in Polish popular and high culture. The Jew, recognizable by his or her marked behaviour, costume, and manner of speech, appeared, for example, in countless Polish-language vaudeville shows and theatre productions of the nineteenth century. Typically, these popular genres would hardly ever picture assimilated and educated Jewish physicians, lawyers, or journalists, but rather bankers and innkeepers with names such as Szwindelman, which were supposed to betray the 'true character' of the personages (Taborski 2004: 91–2). The old visual codes that used to portray the Jew as the other have survived not only in contemporary stage productions but also in folk art. The paradigmatic Jew has 'distinctive, dark eyes, a relatively large nose, clearly marked, large, sometimes protruding, ears . . . a beard . . . and noticeable *peyes*', writes Olga Goldberg-Mulkiewicz in her analysis of post-1945 figurines of Jews created by Polish folk artists. The Jew is also usually male, and portrayed with a dark palette of colours (2003: 168).

The frame of difference may lead to that of exclusion. As the ethnographer Joanna Tokarska-Bakir argues, the Polish rural population perceived their Jewish neighbours as externally different and staged them in various folk traditions, such as costumed processions at Christmas, with exaggerated markers of physical difference (for example, a hawk-like nose). These repeated performances of otherness contributed to the establishing of Jews within the rural community as essentially alien. Analysing the representations of Jews in the writings of the Polish ethnographer Oskar Kolberg (1814–90), Tokarska-Bakir states that in Polish folk belief, as captured in the nineteenth century, the Jew, accused of deicide, ritual murder, and affiliation with the devil, was the radical other, indeed, barely human. From the perspective of pre-modern, religious antisemitism, the boundary between what was non-Jewish and Jewish not only marked difference and distance, but was a boundary 'between the world and the anti-world' (2004: 67).

The conceptualization of the Jew as the antonym of the Pole influenced both the realm of folk culture and the political discourse of the late nineteenth century. The ethno-nationalist National Democracy movement, with its main ideologist Roman Dmowski (1864–1939), intensively employed anti-Jewish tropes in the process of nation-building. As Joanna Michlic notes, 'in the National Democracy's worldview the Jew signified the archetype of everything defined as "not-Polish" or "anti-Polish"' (2007: 131). The legacy of Dmowski, whose political descendants, the League of Polish Families, entered the Polish parliament in 2001 and co-created the government in the years 2006–7, still circulates on the Polish political scene and finds adherents.

The post-1989 revival of Jewish heritage in Poland might not directly evoke antisemitic paradigms of the Jew as anti-Pole, but it does recycle certain ways of picturing the Jew which date from the nineteenth century and earlier. We find the familiar stereotype of the caftan-clad Jew with a crooked nose, often counting money, reproduced in countless Jewish souvenirs such as wooden figurines, paintings, fridge magnets, or kosher vodka bottles, and sometimes even in more well-meaning attempts at commemorating Jews or preserving Jewish heritage (see Gruber 2009; Murzyn-Kupisz, forthcoming; Waligórska 2010).

The discourse of radical difference, according to Greenblatt, is one of the patterns of wonder, fascination with, and incomprehension of, the other. Conceptualizing the other as diametrically different from the self, he believes, allowed the discoverers of the New World 'renaming, transformation, and appropriation'. The recognition of difference, Greenblatt notes, 'excites a desire to cross the threshold, break through the barrier, enter the space of the alien' (2003: 135). One of the ways of crossing this boundary is translation. Europeans, observing the natives of Mexico before any translators were available to them, described the world of the other using concepts from their own cultural background. They compared personages conducting religious rituals to priests, sites of worship to churches, and elevated constructions to altars, attempting to understand what was happening in front of their eyes in terms of the categories they knew (Greenblatt 2003: 130–2). Making hypotheses about a reality radically different from their own, they were domesticating the image of the other. Domestication, which involves rewriting, simplification, and a loss of meaning, is associated in particular with the colonial context and the approach of the Western nations to the subaltern others (Rubel and Rosman 2003: 15). In the dynamics of 'wonder' described by Greenblatt, domestication, based on equivalences and similarities, easily transforms into 'absolute possession', with the conquistadors destroying the natives' temples and idols and replacing them with Catholic icons. The failure at translation leads to effacement and supersession.

The discourse of difference within the Jewish heritage revival in Poland does involve domestication too. Samuel Hillel of Jaszczuk's novel is performing a kabbalistic rite which has nothing to do with Jewish theology, but which features an element easily recognizable to non-Jewish readers: a deck of Tarot cards. Adding a 'Jewish flavour' to his novel, Jaszczuk relies on an imagined vision of 'Qabbala' popular among nineteenth-century non-Jewish esotericists. The Jew in this image has magical features, and represents the uncanny and the mysterious. Jewish characters clad in hasidic garb—a commonplace in popular theatre and musical productions—play a similar function. Their presence is a form of cultural translation: the vividly recognizable is here offered as the Jewish standard, and the particular becomes generalized to match the expectations of 'readers'.

The emphasis on radical difference between the self and the other usually serves the maintenance of the boundary between two groups. '[I]dentities can function as points of identification and attachment only *because* of their capacity to exclude, to leave out, to render "outside", abjected', notes Stuart Hall. 'Every identity has at its "margin", an excess, something more' (1996: 4–5). The Jew framed in terms of difference might therefore function as the 'margin' of Polish identity—the 'outside' that limns the 'inside'. However, this boundary-maintaining function, perfectly comprehensible while Jews constituted a sizeable minority in Poland, is intriguing today, when Jews compose less than 0.1 per cent of the population. Is the discourse of radical difference between Poles and Jews a fossil of the pre-Second World War intergroup identity negotiations, or does it play a new role?

Othering, according to Greenblatt, is a prelude to appropriation, to 'renaming' the other. Employing Jewish themes in Polish literature, music, and stage productions, performed mostly by non-Jews and for non-Jews, is a form of translating Jewishness according to the cultural script in which the Jew is a figure that belongs to the past and is an object of fascination or ridicule. The Jew as radically different is confined to pre-Holocaust reality, be it the shtetl or the metropolitan ghetto, and is a trigger of nostalgia. The Jew's exotic look and language coexist in these representations with domesticated elements (for example, Tarot cards stand for the kabbalah, *żydłaczenie* replaces Yiddish) which give Polish spectators the illusion that Jewish culture is fully familiar, accessible, and transparent to them. Jewishness remains attractively alien, but is at the same time simplified. This combination of external distinctiveness and internal domestication opens the door to 'absolute possession', something that Eric Lott, in his analysis of blackface minstrel shows, terms a 'ventriloquial self-expression through the art forms of someone else' (Lott 1993: 92), where fascination blends with commodi-fication resulting in an 'erotic economy of celebration and exploitation' (1993: 6).

Incorporation and othering are two simultaneous frames which, however, are not fully independent of each other, but are rather in a dynamic relationship. The discourse of incorporation, emphasizing superordinate categories of Poland's multi-ethnic heritage and insisting that Poles and Jews 'should be brothers', implies an essential difference, a rift that the inclusive frame seeks to bridge. On the other hand, the representation of the exotic, essentially different Jew is usually accompanied by domestication and an attempt to filter otherness through the Polish lens. Alexander Hertz, in his seminal analysis of the image of Jews in Polish culture, speaks of a 'kindred–alien' relationship between Poles and Jews. In his view Poles perceived Jews as alien or kindred depending on the social context of the interaction between them. The kindred–alien dichotomy was 'hist-orically conditioned' and 'constantly undergoing change', with the two categories coexisting simultaneously and applicable 'depending on the level of our en-counters with others' (1988: 50–1). Hertz's kindred–alien model was, however, based on the scenario of direct intergroup contact and assumed that members of the two groups could interact face to face.

In the post-Holocaust context the frames of incorporation and difference have a fundamentally different function to Hertz's kindred–alien categories. The inclusive and exclusive frames do coexist and are in a dynamic interplay, but they represent an absent other that the average Pole is hardly likely to encounter. The kindred–alien dyad no longer serves to categorize another person we physically face; rather, it plays a role in our self-definition. The Holocaust constitutes here a 'founding event' whose memory defines the peoples who witnessed it, and whose centrality makes Jews indispensable 'in the historical self-interpretation of the post-modern period' (Motzkin 1996: 274–5). After the Holocaust we, Europeans, cannot define ourselves if not in relation to what Carl Jung has called the 'magical impurity' hanging over the whole of Europe after the Holocaust (Jung 1986: 223–4). At the same time, however, the Holocaust represented a radical destabil-ization of the cultural system in Poland, in which the Jew had constituted a crucial reference point for the ethnic Pole. The resurgence of memories about Jews might therefore be motivated by the need to handle this double identity crisis.

The repressed and the forgotten, or 'the unconscious of culture', as Renate Lachmann puts it, become verbalized in a unique way in the genre of fantasy. 'The fantastic confronts culture with its oblivion' and is a space where we define our relationship to the other (1996: 289). The genre, which is characterized by visual extravagance and the aura of the marvellous (enigma, adventure, murder, return of the dead, esoteric knowledge), unveils the 'covered memory' in that it pictures all the different forms of otherness that haunt us (the stranger and the otherworldly). It is a 'literature of desire, which seeks that which is experienced as absence and loss' (Jackson in Lachmann 1996: 287). At the same time as exploring the margin, fantastic literature sheds light on the core and is a 'return of the own in the guise of the foreign and strange' (1996: 292). Remarkably, many of the contemporary Polish representations of Jews, particularly in popular culture, make use of the fantastic mode. The visual extravagance of performances such as Kmita's *Ay, Vay! or Stories with Cinnamon* or Szymon Szurmiej's *Tradition*, the presence of esoteric Jewish characters, and the wider popularity of Jewish topoi in the Polish novel (see Bator 2010; Huelle 1987; Krajewski 2009; Lewandowski 2009) suggest that the Jew occupies an important position in the unconscious of Polish culture. The medium of the fantastic accommodates both the frame of incorporation and that of difference. 'The "other", which the fantastic conceptualizes', notes Lachmann, 'has an ambivalent status: it appears to be extracultural/cultural; repressed/returning. It reports an absence and simultaneously insists on its presence' (Lachmann 1996: 289). The Jews in contemporary Poland are considered as both belonging and not belonging to the realm of 'Polish culture'; constituting a tiny minority, they are both absent from the social landscape of Poles and vividly present in their imagination. Indeed, they seem to haunt them.

Yael Bartana's *Nightmares* visualizes a response to this haunting. The first film of her *Polish Trilogy* addresses the Jewish absence/presence in the Polish conscience, and formulates a bold manifesto for a Jewish return to Poland. The protagonist, played by young left-wing activist Sławomir Sierakowski, gives a speech on behalf of all Poles, addressing the Jewish ghosts who populate Polish nightmares.

Jews! Fellow countrymen! People! People! You think the old woman who still sleeps under Rifke's quilt doesn't want to see you? Has forgotten about you? You're wrong. She dreams about you every night. Dreams and trembles with fear. Since the night you were gone, and her mother reached for your quilt, she has had nightmares. Bad dreams. Only you can chase them away. Let the three million Jews that Poland has missed stand by her bed and finally chase away the demons. Return to Poland! To your country! (Bartana 2007)

On the one hand, Poles in Bartana's *Nightmares* call for an exorcism, and long for a return of the Jews who could absolve them and ease their trauma of witnessing, and profiting from, the Holocaust. At the same time, they also seem to need Jews as their perpetual 'others'. 'Today we look with boredom at our faces so like one another', states the speaker in Bartana's film, 'In the streets of big cities we seek out strangers and listen intently to their speech. Yes, today we know we cannot live alone. We need others, and there are no others dearer to us than you! Come back!' (Bartana 2007) The return of the Jews would not only break the ethnic homogeneity of Poland's population but also save Poles from the anxiety of not being able to connect to one another without the background against which they could define themselves.

On the cover of *Kolorowanka: A Colouring Book for Ages 4–9*, a blond-haired boy and a dark-haired girl in pioneer shirts are holding a red flag with the white eagle and the Star of David. The colouring book of the Jewish Renaissance Movement in Poland, published by Yael Bartana in co-operation with the Museum of Modern Art in Warsaw, pictures the Polish Jewish kibbutz in Muranów, erected for a few days in the summer of 2009 (Bartana and Landsberg 2010). The temporary kibbutz, featuring in Bartana's *Mur i wieża* (*Wall and Tower*, 2009), was to be a foretaste of the new Polish Jewish kibbutzim that the Jewish Renaissance Manifesto is postulating. Bartana's kibbutz, meant as a part of 'group psychotherapy during which national demons are conjured up and brought to the light of the day',[5] did indeed raise controversies among the local inhabitants in Warsaw. For many disoriented bystanders the settlement on Anielewicz Square, simulating the arrival of colonizing Jews, embodied the threat of Jewish return.

'We are facing one of many potential futures we may experience', states the Manifesto of the Jewish Renaissance Movement, 'leaving behind our safe, familiar, and one-dimensional world.' A significant Jewish immigration to Poland, visualized in Bartana's interventions, would for many Poles be the end of the safe and familiar boundaries. Although the paradigms of Polish–Jewish brotherhood and of Jewish difference stand for two contrasting frames, they both assume Jewish absence and focus on the Jewish past. Jewish presence and the Jewish present, as materialized in Bartana's manifesto, would inevitably shake old frames and challenge the assumptions behind them. But would they also inspire new cultural paradigms beyond incorporation and othering?

Notes

1   The Manifesto of the Jewish Renaissance Movement in Poland (poster); the full text is also available online: <http://www.jrmip.org/?page_id=5>.

2   Rafał Dutkiewicz's speech at the opening of the White Stork Synagogue on 6 May 2010. <http://www.youtube.com/watch?v=-P4kqwJGNdM>, accessed 23 Sept. 2010.

3   Di Galitzyaner Klezmorim. Personal interview, 24 Apr. 2004.

4   'Wszyscy braćmi być powinni', appeared on Steczkowska's CD *Alkimja* (lyrics by Roman Kołakowski).

5   'Berlin: Polski Express III'. <http://www.krytykapolityczna.pl/Zaproszenia/Polski-Express-III/menu-id-34.html>, accessed 5 Oct. 2010.

References

APPIGNANESI, LISA. 2000. *Losing the Dead: A Family Memoir*. London.

BARTANA, YAEL. 2007. *Mary koszmary/ Nightmares*. HD video, 10'27", available at: <http://www.artmuseum.pl/filmoteka/?l=0&id=200>.

——and HADAR LANDSBERG. 2010. 'Kolorowanka Mur i Wieża'. *Krytyka Polityczna*, 20–1(105): 22.

BATOR, JOANNA. 2010. *Chmurdalia*. Warsaw.

BILEWICZ, MICHAŁ. 2007. 'History as an Obstacle: Impact of Temporal-Based Social Categorisations on Polish–Jewish Intergroup Contact'. *Intergroup Processes and Intergroup Relations*, 10(4): 551–63.

CHONG, DENNIS, and JAMES N. DRUCKMAN. 2007. 'Framing Theory'. *Annual Review of Political Science*, 10: 103–26.

DEHNEL, JACEK. 2006. *Lala*. Warsaw.

DODZIUK, ANNA. 2010. *Druga dusza: O dwudziestu Festiwalach Kultury Żydowskiej w Krakowie*. Warsaw.

ECO, UMBERTO. 2003. *Dire quasi la stessa cosa: Esperienze di traduzione*. Milan.

ENTMAN, ROBERT M. 1993. 'Framing: Toward Clarification of a Fractured Paradigm'. *Journal of Communication*, 43(4): 51–8.

European Commission Against Racism and Intolerance. 2005. 'The Third Report on Poland', 14 June. <http://www.hfhrpol.waw.pl/pliki/Raport2005.pdf>, accessed 13 Jan. 2013.

GEBERT, KONSTANTY. 2010. 'Posłowie: Do kogo należy kultura żydowska?'. In Anna Dodziuk, *Druga dusza: O dwudziestu Festiwalach Kultury Żydowskiej w Krakowie*, 257–62. Warsaw.

GOLDBERG-MULKIEWICZ, OLGA. 2003. *Stara i nowa ojczyzna: Ślady kultury Żydów polskich*. Łódzkie Studia Etnograficzne 42. Łódź.

GREENBLATT, STEPHEN. 2003. *Marvelous Possessions: The Wonder of the New World*. Oxford.

GRUBER, RUTH ELLEN. 2002. *Virtually Jewish: Reinventing Jewish Culture in Europe*. Berkeley, Calif.

——2009. 'Beyond Virtually Jewish . . . Balancing the Real, the Surreal and Real Imaginary Places'. In Monika Murzyn-Kupisz and Jacek Purchla, eds., *Reclaiming Memory: Urban Regeneration in the Historic Jewish Quarters of Central European Cities*, 63–79. Kraków.

HALL, STUART. 1996. 'Introduction: Who Needs Identity?'. In Stuart Hall and Paul du Gay, eds., *Questions of Cultural Identity*. London.

HERTZ, ALEKSANDER. 1988. *The Jews in Polish Culture*. Evaston, Ill.

HUELLE, PAWEŁ. 1987. *Weiser Dawidek*. Gdańsk.

ISER, WOLFGANG. 1996. 'The Emergence of a Cross-Cultural Discourse: Thomas Carlyle's *Sartor Resartus*'. In Sanford Budick and Wolfgang Iser, eds., *The Translatability of Cultures: Figurations of the Space Between*, 245–64. Stanford, Calif.

JAKUBOWICZ, TADEUSZ. 2004. Letter of Address. *Festiwal Kultury Żydowskiej 26.06.–4.07.2004*, p. 6. Kraków.

JANION, MARIA. 2000. *Do Europy tak, ale razem z naszymi umarłymi*. Warsaw.

——2009. *Bohater, spisek, śmierć: Wykłady żydowskie*. Warsaw.

JASZCZUK, PAWEŁ. 2004. *Foresta Umbra*. Poznań.

JUNG, CARL. 1986. 'Nach der Katastrophe'. In *Gesammelte Werke*, x: *Zivilisation im Übergang*, 223–4. Olten.

KRAJEWSKI, MAREK. 2009. *Głowa Minotaura*. Warsaw.

KRAJEWSKI, STANISŁAW. 1997. *Żydzi Judaizm Polska*. Warsaw.

LACHMANN, RENATE. 1996. 'Remarks on the Foreign (Strange) as a Figure of Cultural

Ambivalence'. In Sanford Budick and Wolfgang Iser, eds., *The Translatability of Cultures: Figurations of the Space Between*, 282–93. Stanford, Calif.

LEWANDOWSKI, KONRAD T. 2009. *Perkalowy Dybuk*. Wrocław.

LOTT, ERIC. 1993. *Love and Theft: Blackface Minstrelsy and the American Working Class*. New York.

MICHLIC, JOANNA B. 2007. 'The Jews and the Formation of Modern National Identity in Poland'. In Athena S. Leoussi and Steven Grosby, eds., *Nationalism and Ethno-symbolism: History, Culture and Ethnicity in the Formation of Nations*. Edinburgh.

MOTZKIN, GABRIEL. 1996. 'Memory and Cultural Translation'. In Sanford Budick and Wolfgang Iser, eds., *The Translatability of Cultures: Figurations of the Space Between*, 265–81. Stanford, Calif.

MURZYN-KUPISZ, MONIKA. Forthcoming. 'The Socio-Economics of Nostalgia: Redis-covering the Jewish Past in the Polish Provinces'. In Erica Lehrer and Michael Meng, eds., *Constructing Pluralism: Space, Nostalgia, and the Transnational Future of the Jew-ish Past in Poland*. Bloomington, Ind.

ORLA-BUKOWSKA, ANNAMARIA. 2008. 'Goje w żydowskim interesie: Wkład etnicz-nych Polaków w życie polskich Żydów'. In Robert Cherry and Annamaria Orla-Bukowska, eds., *Polacy i Żydzi: Kwestia Otwarta*, 223–41. Warsaw.

PRZYBYLSKA, SŁAWA. 1993. *Alef Bejs: Pieśni i piosenki żydowskie*. Tonpress.

RUBEL, PAULA, and ABRAHAM ROSMAN. 2003. 'Introduction: Translation and Anthro-pology'. In Paula Rubel and Abraham Rosman, eds., *Translating Cultures: Perspectives on Translation and Anthropology*. Oxford.

SZAPIRO, PAWEŁ. 2007. *Żyd niemalowany*. Warsaw.

SZWARCMAN, DOROTA. 2006. 'Czy muzyka żydowska musi być kiczowata?' *Midrasz*, 3: 20–1.

TABORSKI, ROMAN. 2004. 'Stereotypy Żydów w dramacie polskim drugiej połowy XIX wieku'. In Eleonora Udalska and Anna Tytkowska, eds., *Żydzi w lustrze dramatu, teatru i krytyki teatralnej*, 84–93. Katowice.

THUM, GREGOR. 2005. 'Wrocław and the Myth of the Multicultural Border City'. *European Review*, 13(2): 227–35.

TOKARSKA-BAKIR, JOANNA. 2004. 'Żydzi u Kolberga'. In *Rzeczy mgliste*, 49–72. Sejny.

WALIGÓRSKA, MAGDALENA. 2005. 'A Goy Fiddler on the Roof: How the Non-Jewish Participants of the Klezmer Revival in Kraków Negotiate their Polish Identity in a Confrontation with Jewishness'. *Polish Sociological Review*, 4(152): 367–82.

——2010. 'The Magical Versus The Political Jew: Representations of Jews on the Polish and German Klezmer Scene'. In Magdalena Waligórska and Sophie Wagenhofer, eds., *Cultural Representations of Jewishness at the Turn of the 21st Century*, 117–34. EUI Working Paper 2010/01. Florence.

ZABŁOCKA-KOS, AGNIESZKA. 2009. 'In Search of New Ideas: Wrocław's "Jewish District"—Yesterday and Today'. In Monika Murzyn-Kupisz and Jacek Purchla, eds., *Reclaiming Memory: Urban Regeneration in the Historic Jewish Quarters of Central Euro-pean Cities*, 325–42. Kraków.

ZAKRZEWSKI, ANDRZEJ. 1999. Letter of Address. In *IX Festiwal Kultury Żydowskiej w Krakowie. 27 VI–4 VII 1999*, 2. Kraków.

PART IV

How Real is the European Jewish Revival?

THIRTEEN

Beyond Virtually Jewish: Monuments to Jewish Experience in Eastern Europe

RUTH ELLEN GRUBER

EN ROUTE FROM ROME to Lviv in December 2010, I got caught in wintry air-travel chaos and was stranded for a night at Vienna's airport. Along with hundreds of other frustrated travellers, I stood in line for a good (or bad) five hours, inching forward to the airline desk to rebook my missed flight. Waiting, I got to talking with two young men from Lviv standing behind me; they were students at a pontifical institute in Rome heading home for the holidays and had missed the same connection as I had. They asked me why I was going to Lviv, and I explained that I was on the international jury for a design competition to mark three key sites of Jewish history in the city. One of the students asked if I was Jewish myself, and when I answered in the affirmative, his response made it clear that he probably had never before knowingly met a Jew. But, he told me, he had enjoyed his visits, more than once, to a great Jewish restaurant he knew in Lviv—it was called At the Golden Rose. 'The food and atmosphere are really good', he told me—but what he particularly enjoyed was the restaurant's signature gimmick: patrons were supposed to 'haggle' over what they eventually paid for their meal.

I knew the Golden Rose restaurant. It is located in the rundown former Jewish quarter forming part of the ensemble of historic buildings centred on the main market square that is listed by UNESCO on its roster of World Heritage Sites. The restaurant overlooks the gaping ruins of the sixteenth-century Golden Rose, or Turei Zahav, synagogue, which, like most physical traces of Jewish life in the city, was destroyed in the Second World War and woefully neglected afterwards. The restaurant had opened in 2008, and I had visited it shortly thereafter with a group of colleagues who, like myself, were attending a conference in Lviv that October on Jewish heritage and history in east-central Europe, organized by the Lviv Center for Urban History of East Central Europe.[1] I gave the keynote presentation for the conference, a talk I called 'Touching and Retouching: Balancing Real, Surreal and Real Imaginary Jewish Spaces'. The title made reference to the actual physical restoration and reconstruction of Jewish heritage sites, but also to the way that we reconstruct (or construct) things, in our minds and on the ground, to

Figure 1 Interior of the Golden Rose Café, Lviv. *Photograph by Ruth Ellen Gruber*

create new realities rather than 're-create' past models. In the talk I drew from my previous work on the 'virtually Jewish' phenomenon—an intense, visible, vivid Jewish presence in places where few Jews actually live today. And I reflected on its more recent evolution: how open Jewish or 'Jewish-style' expression— religious, cultural, pop-cultural, or otherwise—was becoming now part of the mainstream, but also how, over the past ten or fifteen years, the proliferation of post-communist tropes such as nostalgic (or pseudo-nostalgic) Jewish-style cafés had served in some places to brand 'Jewishness' as a recognized and recognizable commercial commodity that increasingly formed an off-the-shelf ethnic decor- ative and catering category alongside 'Chinese', 'Japanese', 'Indian', 'Middle Eastern', and even 'Wild West'.

Discussion at the conference echoed the continuing debate over models for development of Jewish town quarters and heritage sites in places where, as in Lviv, large pre-Second World War Jewish populations had been wiped out and few if any Jews live today: issues included the legitimacy of commercial and tourist exploitation of Jewish heritage; the danger of promoting stereotypes; the blurry

Figure 2 Exterior of the Ariel Café, Kraków. *Photograph by Ruth Ellen Gruber*

lines between expressions that deal with Jews and Jewish culture as living entities and those that treat, and sometimes separate, them as an isolated, exotic, or even codified category. As ever, there were passionate exchanges over the goods and ills of how Kraków's Kazimierz district, the city's historic Jewish quarter, has evolved since the early 1990s from a desolate slum where the first Jewish-style cafés stood out like odd but welcome oases on the district's main square, Szeroka, to one of Europe's premier Jewish tourist attractions, whose commercial and cultural infrastructure made it the emblematic example of commodification and 'Jewish' branding. It was in Kazimierz that I had watched a Japanese tour group, led by a guide, troop into the Ariel 'Jewish' café and then exit again, about two minutes later. 'Now we go on to the Royal Palace', the guide told the group, which included a monk in a saffron robe. The café, with its name written in Hebrew-style letters, its prominent signage featuring a towering menorah flanked by lions, and its interior walls covered by painted portraits of rabbis (or, at least, of old-fashioned, rabbinical-looking bearded men) clearly was on the itinerary as an attraction in itself, on a par with other city sights. I wondered what the tourists had thought about (or whether they had even noticed) the collection of kitschy souvenirs on

Figure 3 A tourist takes a photograph inside the Ariel Café. *Photograph by Ruth Ellen Gruber*

sale at the cash desk: the carved wooden figurines of Jews, many of them clutching coins—'good luck' tokens harking back to the old stereotype of Jewish affinity with money—and the souvenir refrigerator magnets showing 'Jewish heads' that resembled the crudest of Nazi-era stereotypes and bore the legend 'Kazimierz'. I had asked an attendant once why objects like these were on offer. He had shrugged: 'They're Jewish.'

Along these lines, the Golden Rose restaurant, the new and only 'Jewish-style' restaurant in Lviv, stole the show, or at least part of the show, during our 2008 conference, as five or six of us conference participants went off (in field-trip fashion) to see how this latest manifestation of a 'Jewish' café interpreted the brand. Physically there was little to set it off from many of the other 'Jewish-style' restaurants and cafés that have sprung up in eastern Europe, consciously or not drawing their inspiration from those in Kraków. In fact, I found the décor of the Golden Rose not too bad at all—rather subdued, actually, compared to some of the other examples I have seen. There was the usual dark wood, lacy tablecloths, candlesticks, and old (or faux-old) pictures on the wall that have come to symbolize 'Jewish' in the same way that dragons and tasselled lanterns symbolize

Figure 4 A chess set in a Venice gift shop, with figures representing Ashkenazim and Sephardim. *Photograph by Ruth Ellen Gruber*

Chinese, a Chianti flask on a red-checked tablecloth means Italian, and swinging doors, rough planking, and even wooden Indians symbolize the Wild West (in local theme chain restaurants such as 'Sioux' in Poland, 'Old Wild West' in Italy, and 'Buffalo Grill' in France).[2] But—at least on that first visit—at the Golden Rose there were no refrigerator magnets bearing stereotype 'Jewish' profiles for sale as at the Ariel, no carved wooden figures of Jews clutching money, as at the Tsimmes restaurant in Kiev, and no fiddler playing Yiddish tunes from a perch set up on the wall next to a mocked-up thatched roof, as at the Anatewka in Łódź (where, when I visited the first time, the waiters were dressed as hasids, ritual fringes and all).[3]

What set the Golden Rose apart was the uniquely hands-on interactive entry into the 'Jewish' experience it afforded patrons. To some extent performativity plays a role in all the new, consciously Jewish-themed venues: guests are invited to engage with the simulation wrought by the décor, menus, background music, and scattered talisman objects, all aural and visual prompts for a literary image of the pre-war Jewish past: sepia-toned and slightly exotic, representing what people wish (or have decided to wish) that the Jewish world had really been once upon a time. '[W]e have frozen time by furnishing our suites with antiques and avoid-ing the introduction of modern accessories', the Alef café/restaurant/hotel in Kraków once advertised. 'When dining in our restaurant you will step back in time and immerse yourself in pre-war Kazimierz while listening to live concerts of traditional Gypsy and Jewish music.'

Real pre-war Jewish-run taverns, and eateries and cafés where Jews were wont to congregate, did not, to be sure, fit this cosy, reconstituted image. This is how the novelist Alfred Döblin described a 'Yiddish tavern' in the Polish town of Góra Kalwaria (in Yiddish, Ger, or Gur) that he visited in 1924: 'An old tavern keeper lets us in. Inside, we are inspected by his stooped wife and his daughter—in her thirties, with a squinting, obviously blind eye. There is no cognac, no beer. Cold roast goose, jars of pickles, jars of herring and onions are gathered on the table. At the next table [are] two young fish vendors, loudly smacking their lips on a piece of sausage' (Döblin 1991: 78).

Much more upscale, the historian Lucy Dawidowicz was taken by a Jewish man friend to a sophisticated restaurant in Vilnius in 1939. There '[a] string trio played waltzes and tangos while couples spun around the small dance floor. We feasted on tea and pastries—Polish pastries were rich and luscious. I imagined that Paris must be like this' (Dawidowicz 1989: 56). And even in the infamous Second World War Warsaw ghetto, the musician Władysław Szpilman, whose story of Holocaust survival is recounted in the book and the award-winning film *The Pianist*, played in several posh cafés, achieving 'great success' performing piano duets at the Sztuka (Art) café, the biggest in the ghetto. 'Besides the con-cert room there was a bar where those who liked food and drink better than the arts could get fine wines and deliciously prepared *cotelettes de volaille* or *boeuf Stroganoff*', he wrote. 'Both the concert room and the bar were nearly always full' (Szpilman 1999: 16).

Today, however, few people have any direct memory of Kraków, Warsaw, Lviv, Vilnius, Ger, and so on, from the time when large Jewish populations actually lived there.[4] Moreover, in Kraków the tourism-driven Jewish regeneration of the Kazimierz district began two decades and more ago, sparked in part by the Jewish Culture Festival, which was founded in 1988, when Poland was still under communist rule, and by Steven Spielberg's 1993 movie *Schindler's List*, which was filmed in Kraków. This means that few of today's tourists—and fewer if any of the student-aged young Poles who now congregate in the district's many new cafés, Jewish or not—have any direct memories of Kazimierz before the festival began drawing crowds, or of when there were no modern Jewish museums and culture centres offering their programmes, and no Jewish (or Jewish-style) commercial venues plying their trade. The new Jewish constructs, including the cafés, the coded visuals, and even the souvenirs, by now form part of the Jewish (or 'Jewish') reality of the post-Holocaust, post-communist world, in Kraków and elsewhere: integral parts of the texture of living cities, with, layer by layer, their own models, perspectives, and shorthand stereotypes that add to the palimpsest. They are 'new authenticities' that can form what I have called 'real imaginary' spaces: places that are in themselves real, with all the trappings of reality, but at the same time are quite different from the 'realities' on which they are modelled or are attempting to evoke—along the lines, perhaps, of Jean Baudrillard's 'simulacra', where the simulation can become the thing in itself, or, as Umberto Eco put it, where 'imagination demands the real thing and, to attain it, must fabricate the absolute fake; where the boundaries between game and illusion are blurred . . . and falsehood is enjoyed in a situation of "fullness"' (Eco 1986: 8). Indeed, some of the romanticized 'new-old' Jewish-style cafés that were opened in the 1990s have by now acquired a sort of 'real' patina of age.[5]

So what does it mean in these contexts to say something is 'Jewish' or has a 'Jewish character'? For synagogues and Jewish cemeteries, the definition is usually obvious. But function and religion, even historical designation, are just part of the equation. As noted, stereotyped visions and even toxic clichés also come into play. Particularly in urban settings, 'Jewish' has much broader connotations that span a wide spectrum. Does 'Jewish' mean intellectual? commercial? dynamic? educated? artistic? creative? multicultural? rich? poor? foreign? assimilated? excluded? exclusive? quaint? money-grubbing? Israeli? sad-eyed? big-nosed? old-fashioned? pre-war? religious? secular? Yiddish? victim? communist? bourgeois? dead and gone? 'Other'? Indeed, back in the 1930s the Polish Jewish literary critic Artur Sandauer coined the useful (but strangely little-known) term 'allosemitism' to describe the idea of Jews as the perpetual 'Other'. Allosemitism can embrace both positive and negative feelings towards Jews—everything, as the sociologist Zygmunt Bauman put it, from love and respect to outright condemnation and genocidal hatred. At root is the idea that, good or bad, Jews are different from the non-Jewish mainstream and thus can't be dealt with in the same way or measured by the same yardstick (see e.g. Bauman 1998).

When my colleagues and I visited the Golden Rose restaurant in 2008, we were confronted at the door by a rack holding a collection of wide-rimmed black hats complete with long, fake sidelocks. Patrons were encouraged to try them on and 'play the Jew': we did, too, some of us a bit guiltily—though the one Israeli in the group said he was quite comfortable with the clowning. And then there was the haggling ('like a Jew') over what to pay. No prices were listed on the menus— the waitress was supposed to quote you an amount and you had to 'bargain her down' to the actual price the management had (secretly) set. It was all a deliberately provocative sort of 'Jewish-style' self-irony:[6] in Budapest, Chabad Lubavitch had perpetrated a similar form of clowning at the big 'Sziget' summer music festival with a life-size figure of a hasid with a hole cut where visitors could insert their own faces and be photographed in full hasidic regalia, that is, as a 'Jew'.

But can there be Jewish self-irony without the Jews and without the self? In the airport line, I spoke a bit more about Jews and Lviv with the student standing behind me. In his frame of reference—probably the frame of reference of most people in Lviv today—the Golden Rose restaurant was 'Jewish'. Aside from the ruins it overlooked of the synagogue, blown up by the Nazis in 1943, some scattered commemorative plaques and a few faded (but preserved) Yiddish wall advertisements, it was probably the most easily visible (and publicly accessible) 'Jewish' site in town. I think I observed to the young man (though not in these words) that many Jews would be uncomfortable with the image created by the café's deracinated agglomeration of stereotypes in a city whose large Jewish population had been annihilated in the Holocaust, and where the heavy hand of the Soviet regime had suppressed Jewish expression in the post-war period. I only remember one of his remarks: 'Well, you know', he said, 'a lot of people don't like Jews.'

Back in 2002, in my book *Virtually Jewish: Reinventing Jewish Culture in Europe*, I noted that there was 'a growing sense of urgency among Jews':

unless they themselves take positive action, the 'Jewish thing' may be hijacked, if not watered down to a homeopathic degree: Jewish cultural products displacing Jewish culture. An affirmation that Jews and Jewish culture are not simply dusty or sanctified museum relics is essential. Without a living Jewish dimension, the virtual Jewish world may become a sterile desert—or a haunted Jewish never-never land. (Gruber 2002: 238)

Jewish culture, I quoted the Polish sociologist Paweł Spiewak as saying, runs the risk of being 'reduced to symbols and food'. In isolation, he said, 'it may lose its meaning and become "just a type of folklore" that people recognize or label as "Jewish" without any deeper understanding or association' (Gruber 2002: 236). And I quoted the British scholar Jonathan Webber: 'There is a problem of representation', he said. 'There is a difference between official, established Judaism and how Jews actually live. And there is an imagined Judaism, created *ex nihilo*. How do we Jews represent Jewish culture in relation to ourselves, to non-Jews, in the media? Should we participate or stand by?' Not only that, he warned. 'Representation is a moving target. Jewish culture is undergoing such changes that to pin it down to one representation is an illusion' (quoted in Gruber 2002: 238–9).

More than a decade later these questions are still quite relevant, and still unresolved. The situation is in flux, and, I imagine, will remain so for the foreseeable future, as new trends and evolving inputs and approaches also now determine the ways in which Jewish heritage is preserved and presented and former Jewish quarters are restored and 'come alive'.

In much of my own work I have used the definition of the term 'Jewish space' that was articulated in the 1990s by the historian Diana Pinto. That is, the Jewish space in Europe meaning the place, real or imagined, occupied by Jews, Jewish culture, and Jewish memory within mainstream European society, regardless of the size or activity of the local Jewish population (see, among others, Pinto 1996).

But there are other definitions of Jewish space—and Jewish place—that make more explicit reference to the living Jews and Jewish communities now existing or struggling to exist; and 'Jewish space' and its varied manifestations have become the focus of much recent scholarship, including conferences and publications. Some of this new thinking was elaborated in *Jewish Topographies: Visions of Space, Traditions of Place* (Brauch et al. 2008), a collection of essays that investigate 'Jewish space' from within the Jewish world, rather than from the 'virtually Jewish' perspective of interaction with the surrounding society. The essays are the product of a six-year research project at the University of Potsdam, Germany, called Makom, or 'place' in Hebrew, whose aim was to explore the relevance of space and place in Jewish life and culture—Jewish spaces as actual environments that are shaped by Jews, where Jewish life may be rooted, where Jewish activities go on, and where 'Jewish things' happen and often, in turn, define the identity of the physical places where they are happening. The essays describe a variety of circumstances where Jewish experience is or has been strongly linked, physically or emotionally, to specific environments. Most deal with concrete settings: Jews defiantly (and astonishingly) cultivating gardens in the midst of Second World War ghettos. Jews hiking and kayaking through the pre-war Polish countryside to gain connection with the land in which they lived. The architectural and spatial symbolism of the *eruv* in today's Germany. A 'map' of the new alternative Jewish subcultures that have recently emerged in present-day Budapest, a reality whose development I myself have also followed at first hand for some years.[7] There is even a look at 'Jewish space' on the internet, called 'Virtual Jewish Topography'.[8]

But borderlines blur, and the different definitions of Jewish space can, and do, converge and overlap. Jews—and Jewish products, ideas, creations, and creativity —travel and are shared, in person and, importantly now, online through websites, email, and social media: I myself receive regular Jewish Facebook updates from groups and individuals in Hungary, Poland, Serbia, the Czech Republic, Romania, Lithuania, Ukraine, Bulgaria, Italy, and elsewhere. Offline, Paweł Spiewak's concerns about the reduction of Jewish experience to 'symbols and food' are borne out in a certain way by the trend towards 'Jewish' branding.[9] But Jewish input, in fact, plays an increasingly important role in many of the new 'real imaginary' constructs I have described, whether it comes from the mere—and growing—presence of Jewish tourists and other visitors, or from local Jewish individuals or entrepreneurs, or from the emerging local Jewish communities that, in a number of places, now actively (and indeed loudly) assert their rightful position as stakeholders. One of my Facebook friends is a young woman from Budapest, who both raps in a klezmer/hip-hop/fusion group and chants the service as the cantorial soloist for a small reform congregation in the Hungarian capital. She now lives in Berlin and is studying at the cantorial school of the Abraham Geiger Kolleg in Potsdam.

Memory, the impact of memory, and, in particular, the various uses to which memory is put and how memory varies in the minds of different people considering the same past are issues that have suffused much of my work over the past two decades. How are Jews and Jewish heritage remembered? Which Jewish places, practices, and personalities are incorporated into the local consciousness? How do local people choose to portray an important part of the population that was savagely removed, almost overnight? Where do the realities of today's rebuilding Jewish communities fit in? How are Jews seen, and interacted with, now? Examples range from indifferent disregard to kitschy commercialization to an earnest attempt to acknowledge and build on the past (and/or present) Jewish experience.

It can be hard to explain these varied trajectories, and I sometimes find myself engaged in surprisingly passionate discussions, even arguments, with interlocutors who are shocked by things that I have long taken for granted. Some still see any and all manifestations of these phenomena as little short of blasphemous. One man with whom I had a recent heated discussion seemed convinced that the only thing that klezmer music means when heard today in Poland is a tune played to accompany distasteful (or exploitative) dancing on a grave. Some American or Israeli Jewish observers are metaphorically 'surprised' to find that a country like Poland 'is in colour' (see e.g. Eshman 2010). Some—even now, more than twenty years since the fall of communism—are still shocked to find active Jewish communities. 'American Jews don't tend to think about European Jewry often, and when we do, it is to lament its imminent demise, the victim of an aging, diminishing population, and a sharply disturbing increase in anti-Semitism', Gary Rosenblatt, the editor of the *New York Jewish Week*, wrote in the summer of 2010.

In fact, after more than two decades of chronicling the closely entwined trends that are creating east-central Europe's new Jewish and 'Jewish' authenticities, I'm still not totally sure what I think about all this. Sometimes, in fact, I get tired of trying to 'make sense' of the many different and often contradictory facets of what goes on: sometimes I just want to say 'Enough!' Some things I like, some things I do not. There are 'Jewish-style' cafés, like Kraków's Klezmer Hois, where I spend long, pleasant hours and feel perfectly at ease, and there are those, like the Ariel a few hundred metres away, that make me cringe. Yes, I told the man I mentioned above with whom I argued over klezmer music: you are right, there is ugly commercial exploitation, and some of the people involved are only out to make a buck. But that is—and has been—only part of the story.

If we look again at Kraków's Kazimierz district, to use the best-known and best-documented (and perhaps the most debated) example, the process of rediscovery, re-creation, and exploitation of Jewish heritage has generated criticism, to be sure: as we have seen, some of what goes on is in highly questionable taste. But these days one of the things I find most interesting there is how the rediscovery and even exploitation of the Jewish quotient has jump-started a general rehabilitation. The emblematic boom zone of Jewish cafés, Jewish culture festivals, kitschy souvenirs, and nostalgic shtetl chic has now become one of the city's most vibrant neighbourhoods for youth-oriented nightlife: people who once complained that Kazimierz was empty now complain about the noise. And while venues drawing on the Jewish associations of Kazimierz were the first to open up for business, today things are different. District-wide, explicitly Jewish venues are now in the minority. Most are still located on or near Szeroka, but even Szeroka now boasts an Indian restaurant and an Italian place, as well as chic new bars blaring hip-hop. Just a couple of hundred metres away, the trendy venues on plac Nowy, the old Jewish market square, eschew any overt Jewish character. That square, rather, forms the pulsating centre of pubs, bars, and music clubs aimed at the youth market. Kupa Street, which runs outside the Izaak Synagogue, serves as an invisible but almost tangible border between the diverse pop-cultural enclaves.

Moreover, the Jewish development of Kazimierz goes far beyond surface kitsch. It has also encompassed a serious embrace (even a bear hug) of Jewish memory, Jewish culture, and, increasingly, of the Jewish present. Synagogue buildings and other sites have been restored, with both public and private funding, and a comprehensive system of signage identifies Jewish heritage sites. Linked with other heritage routes in the city, this network of strategically placed maps and information panels frames a narrative of Jewish history in the local physical context. Jewish books are being published and sold here too, and Jewish teachings are being taught on a variety of levels in a variety of cultural centres and other institutions. Living Jews, meanwhile, are also a much more evident part of the mix now: as tourists, as pilgrims, as students, as teachers, as performers, as café-goers, as seekers of family roots, as commemorators of the Holocaust—and also as members of a tiny Jewish resident population that has begun to stake its own, much more confident, public claim in delineating the parameters of the Kraków Jewish universe. This is significant. Depending on whom you talk to, there may be fewer than 200 Jews living in the city, or, perhaps, more than 500: in either case a drop in the bucket in a city of more than 750,000. According to one joke that made the rounds a couple of summers ago, 'There are now five rabbis in Kraków—for three Jews and twenty opinions.' A couple of those rabbis were Chabad emissaries who deal mainly with foreign visitors. But one was rabbi of the local Orthodox congregation, and another, a woman, anchored a new Reform Jewish group that meets for services at the Galicia Jewish Museum, a privately established focal point for Jewish learning that opened in 2004. More important is the full-service new Jewish Community Centre that opened in 2008 and serves now as a sort of 'neutral space' open to all Jewish streams and segments; non-Jews, too, can become members. 'People talk about Kazimierz as being the "former" Jewish quarter of Kraków, but I say, why former?' the JCC's New York-born director Jonathan Ornstein told me:

I think that it is the *present* Jewish quarter of Kraków. You can't measure it in numbers, but in feeling. Here, we have an intact Jewish quarter. Jews live freely; people know things about Judaism and Jewish traditions; there's a Jewish studies program at the university; there's the Festival. And now the JCC is a magnet. People are finding their way back.

I tend to agree with Ornstein, even though I am far from sanguine about the long-term survival of a local Jewish community in Kraków. It is indicative, nevertheless, that Ornstein, a dark-haired hipster with a stud in his tongue, prefers the lively pub scene on plac Nowy to the nostalgic, tourist-oriented Jewish cafés on Szeroka: contemporary life over sepia-toned nostalgia. 'Nobody alive today has a good memory of Kazimierz when it was better than it is now', he continued. 'There was the war, and then after the war it was derelict for decades. Now it's the hippest place in the city. The whole "former" thing is based on history, not living memory.' Since this conversation, Ornstein has gone even further. It has never been better, he says, to be a Jew in Kraków. 'When we say "Never better" it's not in terms of numbers, or the amount of things in Jewish life, or the synagogues that are functioning and all that', he told me in June 2011. However, he went on, 'in terms of the way the Jewish community interacts with the non-Jewish community and the direction that things are going, I think that there's never been a more optimistic time to be Jewish in Kraków than there is now.'[10]

Lviv, a legendary centre of Jewish life and learning—so close to Kraków as the crow flies, so reminiscent in atmosphere and architecture, and so linked in history—is only just now beginning to confront many of the issues related to Jewish history, heritage, and memory that emerged in Poland and other countries twenty years and more ago. The lingering impact of Soviet repression explains part of this lag. But other elements are in play. Lviv was left an orphan of history by a century of upheaval, as war and conquest radically shifted both borders and populations. Indeed, Lviv's changing geographical status was the root of famously apocryphal anecdotes about how identity is framed and defined: an elderly person literally could have remained in the city all his or her life, but have been born in Habsburg Austria (when, as the historic capital of Galicia, the city was known as Lemberg), gone to school in Poland (when it was called Lwów), spent adulthood in the Soviet Union (when it was known as Lvov), and retired in Ukraine.

Before the Second World War more than half of Lviv's population were ethnic Poles, about 15 per cent were Ukrainians, and about one-third were Jewish—the city's more than 100,000 Jews formed the third-largest Jewish community in Poland. The Jewish community was annihilated in the Holocaust. And then, after the Soviet Union took power in 1944, most of the local Polish population was expelled westwards and replaced by Russians and Ukrainians, and also some Jews moved in from the east. These newcomers occupied the city's historic architectural space but had few if any bonds to local history. Sovietization meant the quashing of Ukrainian ethnic aspirations as well as of open Jewish expression. Since Ukraine gained independence two decades ago Lviv has become a stronghold of Ukrainian national fervour. The importance (even the fact) of its historic Polish and Jewish components has been largely minimized, suppressed, or forgotten—as has the active complicity of local Ukrainians in the Nazi genocide against the Jews. A widespread and even wilful amnesia about the city's multi-ethnic history was imposed—and then entrenched—as the dominant mindset.

In his pessimistic book about vanishing memory and vanishing physical traces of Jews in Ukrainian Galicia, the Brown University historian Omer Bartov describes today's western Ukraine as 'a region suspended in time, just a little while longer, before it too will be swept with the tide of modernization and globalization, commemoration and apology'. Sooner or later, he writes,

the people of Western Ukraine's Galicia too will become aware of what they had lost and forgotten, but by then they will have destroyed these last material traces of the past in their rush to catch up with the present and will have to recreate another past, one capable of more conveniently accommodating the spirit of tolerance and nostalgia in the incineration of difference and memory. (Bartov 2007: 9)

According to the Ukrainian Holocaust scholar Anatoly Podolsky (2008), 'Ukrainian society seems incapable or unwilling to perceive its national history as a history of various cultures. The "other" tends to be excluded and viewed as something alien.'

It was against this background that the design competition to mark sites of Jewish history in Lviv took place. Maybe Bartov is right and it is too late to counter the ingrained collective amnesia in a meaningful way. Still, against this background, I believe—or I believed at the time—that the competition represented a signal milestone: an unprecedented co-operative public–private initiative specifically conceived as part of a nascent process of reframing the way Jews and the Jewish experience in Lviv are and will be viewed and understood. Its official brief spelled this out, stating its aim as follows:

to respond to the emerging awareness of Lviv's multi-ethnic past by contributing to the rediscovery of the city's Jewish heritage and to enhance and promote this emerging awareness . . . through the visualization and creation of spaces that commemorate the heritage of the city's almost completely vanished Jewish community. The competition seeks ideas that underline Lviv's unique history, and calls for visions that go beyond the narrow and sometimes controversial historical debate: a multi-disciplined approach with wide public outreach is therefore required. These ideas are to reflect the history of the site (or sites) through architectural, landscape or other design proposals and help Lviv inhabitants to discover the history of people who lived here before. Submissions should also show how the site (or sites) can be integrated into the contemporary urban context to benefit the life of the city.[11]

Organized by Lviv city authorities in association with the Center for Urban History of East Central Europe and the Deutsche Gesellschaft für Technische Zusammenarbeit (GTZ), the competition grew directly out of the 2008 conference on Jewish urban history I had attended. In particular, it stemmed from the extensive discussions some of the participants had had with a variety of city officials on how to 'reimagine' Jewish Lviv. Among other things, out of those talks came a commitment to a broad-concept competition to this end. But rather than focus on devising a 'master plan' for Jewish heritage it was decided to single out for redesign and development three emblematic sites related to Lviv's Jewish history. These were located in three different parts of town and spanned centuries of Jewish presence there, from medieval times to the Holocaust. They were: the desolate 'Valley of Death' that was linked to the notorious Janivski (Yanovsky) camp set up by the German occupiers in the Second World War, where more than 100,000 Jews (and others) were tortured and killed; the 'synagogue square' site of two totally destroyed synagogues next to the visible ruins of the Golden Rose in the city's former downtown Jewish quarter; and the so-called 'Besojlem', the small piece of open ground that is the only part of the destroyed old Jewish cemetery that has not been built over—all the rest is now covered by a big and bustling market bazaar, the Krakovsky Market. This is a particularly sensitive site as pre-war burial sites still exist here, though they are no longer marked, and there has been a long and contentious history of unsuccessful attempts by the remnant Jewish community to regain the cemetery—or at least have the market removed.

This was the biggest such design competition ever held in post-war Lviv: architects from the United States, Israel, and twelve other countries submitted a total of seventy projects for the three sites. In fact, I can think of few other Jewish-themed design competitions in Europe with a similar scope. There have been major international competitions, to be sure, but while some—such as those for the Jewish Museum and the National Memorial to the Murdered Jews in Europe in Berlin, the Judenplatz Holocaust Memorial in Vienna, the Museum of the History of Polish Jews in Warsaw, and the Memorial at the Bełżec death camp in Poland—grabbed headlines or engendered controversy, they all generally focused on one site, one museum, or one monument alone, rather than a coordinated complex of sites that were to be publicly usable, designated Jewish spaces as well as memorials. Moreover, the competition coincided with the implementation of a new system of tourist signage in the city that included at least some Jewish sites among the general attractions.

Our nine-member jury was an international mix of architects, urban planners, and other experts, each of whom looked at the proposals from a different viewpoint and experience, and some of whom had scant acquaintance with specific Jewish issues. For two days, in the draughty, Soviet-era Palace of Arts, where the designs were all displayed, we debated each proposal not simply on its

Figure 5 Jury members examine proposals for memorial designs, Lviv. *Photograph by Ruth Ellen Gruber*

appearance but on its feasibility, on its sensitivity to place, and, importantly, on its sensitivity to Jewish concerns, including halakhah, or Jewish law. While no one from the local Lviv Jewish community was on the jury (in part, I was told, because the factionalism within the community would have made it difficult to select a representative), three of us, including myself, were Jewish: one of our roles was seen as that of protecting Jewish interests in the judging process. Indeed, jury member Sergey Kravtsov, from the Center for Jewish Art in Jerusalem, was born in Lviv and is one of the foremost experts on the city's Jewish history and architecture. Moreover, Josef Zissels, the long-time head of one of Ukraine's national umbrella Jewish organizations, made it clear from the start of deliberations that designs had to fulfil several basic conditions in order for them to be accepted by the Jewish authorities. These included guarantees of rabbinical consultation where halakhic matters were concerned; minimum intrusion at the Besojlem cemetery site, and surveys to determine the boundaries of the burials there. He urged that the Jews who had lived and died in Lviv should not be treated as an abstract collective mass, and he stressed that the local Jewish community needed to agree to the projects before implementation.

Figure 6 The synagogue square, Lviv. *Reproduced by courtesy of the Center for Urban History of East Central Europe*

All of the submissions were anonymous, so we had no idea where they came from. In the end, we were almost totally unanimous in our choices for first prize in each category. A team from Irvine, California, won first prize for the Janivski concentration camp site with a project that would turn the site into a form of land art—a raised walkway curving around a slope covered with slabs representing symbolic tombstones. A Berlin-based team won first prize for the synagogue square site, with a design that incorporated the archaeological excavations of one destroyed synagogue and traced the form of another on the pavement of an envisaged plaza. And Ronit Lombrozo, from Jerusalem, won first prize for Besojlem with a design that paid particular heed to the fact that the space was a cemetery, where bodies are still buried. It envisaged a raised walkway and also the use of unearthed tombstones as part of a memorial site. Other prizes and honourable mentions went to designs from Italy, Poland, Germany, Austria, and Ukraine.

I am writing this only a few weeks after the competition, and it remains to be seen, of course, when—and whether—the winning projects will be carried through. Kinks in the designs need to be worked out, funding needs to be raised, and input from the Jewish community needs to be considered. Politics, too, can always intervene. But the entire process bodes well for the future—at least so I hope. 'These are not finished projects, and they will not be executed in the exact way that is on the plans', the Swiss architect Karl Fingerhut, who headed our jury, said at the public event presenting the winning designs. 'A lot of work is still needed to adapt them to the specific needs and goals of place. But the projects develop a specific identity, atmosphere, and character of how to deal with these places.'

It remains to be seen whether this initiative will have a broader impact or spur other attempts to reclaim historic memory. I was particularly impressed, though, that the winners included several young architects from Lviv who were only in their early twenties. I found their approaches to reintegrating a component of local history that has been suppressed, ignored, forgotten, and/or distorted for far too long to be thoughtful and sensitive—even though the world whose memory they were attempting to recover must seem to them like ancient history. The competition had made them think—and think very much outside the local box. I asked one young man, who won third prize for the Besojlem site, how he had come up with his design, which I found close in concept to a Holocaust memorial in the Czech Republic: a huge Star of David sunk into the earth. (A Holocaust memorial in Pirot, Serbia also employs this design.) 'I wasn't sure if this was appropriate', he told me. 'So I went online: when I saw that there already was a Holocaust monument using a similar idea, I figured it would be all right.'

Postscript

After the prizes were announced and most of the other jurors had left for home I remained in Lviv for another day, in part because I wanted to revisit the Golden Rose restaurant. It was a few days before Christmas—the PA system, in fact, was playing 'Deck the Halls with Boughs of Holly' as we walked in. Most of the little tables were filled with a very youthful clientele. My friend and I ordered honey brandy and what turned out to be a delicious onion cake. The waiter brought us a plate of matzo with our drinks: 'Here, Jewish bread', he said as he laid the plate on the table. We spent a pleasant half-hour in the restaurant. I did not notice any rack with hats and *peyes*, and I wasn't asked to haggle: I paid what the waiter told me to pay. A video screen on the wall played a silent loop that showed grainy, pre-war scenes of Jewish life in the city.

The Golden Rose is by no means the only quaintly decorated venue in the old Jewish quarter that harks back to cosier pre-war days. But it is still the only overtly 'Jewish' venue—and 'Jewish' there seems to be an increasingly questionable commodity. A friend who went to the café in December 2011 took pictures showing 'Jewish coffee' now served in mugs bearing crude stereotype caricatures of big-nosed Jews clutching money under the name of the restaurant; souvenirs with similar ugly images, apparently now the café's logo, were on sale.[12] And this is what the 'In Your Pocket' guide to Lviv says about the place:

Here are a few things to know before you go. 1. There are no prices listed on the menu as you are expected to barter. Being a foreigner, they're likely to just quote you a reasonable price. 2. For the right price you can secretly arrange to have your waiter smuggle in some pork dishes. How kosher is this place? 3. They offer a fantastic selection of salads, vegetable dishes, Galician desserts and traditional Jewish breads. 4. For a taste of Lviv you'll never forget, try the homemade vodka.[13]

The review includes the photo of a man standing outside the entrance, his head cocked to one side, gesticulating with his hands, and wearing one of those big black hats with the long black *peyes*.

Post-Postscript, February 2013

I haven't been back to Lviv since we judged the competition more than two years ago. If I were writing this essay today, it certainly would be somewhat different. I admit that in January 2011 I was still on something of a high from my cultural jury duty experienced but a few weeks earlier. But as I have pointed out (hedging my bets as I knew I must), it was too soon to tell what eventually would come of our efforts. By now, however, I more than suspect that even my cautious optimism over the impact of the competition to mark the three sites of Jewish heritage in Lviv may have been too optimistic, at least in the short term. But who knows? Archaeological excavations in the 'Synagogue Square' took place in September 2012, and there seems to be some slow progress in at least beginning to implement a memorial there, despite contention from some quarters. There also may be some glimmerings of movement towards implementing the Besojlem memorial—though little has been registered regarding the Janivski site, and construction of a big shopping centre threatens the integrity of one of the city's only two intact synagogues, the nineteenth-century Glanzer shul. The impact of big recent electoral gains by the ultra-nationalist Svoboda party also remains to be seen. Still, new efforts to mark Holocaust mass graves, a media outcry over construction of a hotel in Lviv's downtown Jewish quarter next to the ruins of the Golden Rose synagogue, and the desire to show a democratic face in light of the 2012 soccer World Cup may yet have a bearing on how the city engages with its complex and problematic history.

Notes

In preparing this essay I have drawn on, and incorporated, some of my earlier writing, including several of my 'Ruthless Cosmopolitan' columns for the Jewish Telegraphic Agency (JTA), and also 'Jüdische und "Jüdische" Cafés' (Gruber 2009a), 'Beyond Virtually Jewish . . . Balancing the Real, the Surreal and Real Imaginary Places' (Gruber 2009b), and 'Scenes from a Krakow Café' (Gruber 2010). I would also like to mention the website of the Lviv Center for Urban History of East Central Europe, with its growing interactive resources, <http://www.lvivcenter.org/en/>.

1 The centre, established in 2004 by the Swiss Austrian historian Harald Binder, aims to be not only a centre for research and projects but also a facilitator, providing a 'neutral space' where the sometimes conflictual elements of Lviv's political and cultural society and policy-makers can come together for discussions. The conference coincided with the opening of an exhibition on Lviv's multi-ethnic history, 'Wo Ist Lemberg?/Lviv A World A Way'.

2 '"Jewishness" has become an attractive quality, that is supposed not only to attract the eye, the imagination, but also to open the wallets of potential customers', the young Kraków scholar Agata Dutkowska has stated. 'The question of authenticity of the relation with the Jewish community is secondary. The disheritaged space has no owners and everyone can feel free to use Jewish symbols for marketing strategies' (Dutkowska 2008).

3 This has changed, it seems (see the Postscript to this essay).

4 A remarkable project that recognizes the diversity and sophistication of pre-war Gur/Ger came to fruition in 2011, after I had completed this essay. It is the Ger Mandolin Orchestra, which memorializes the (Jewish) Mandolin Orchestra active in Góra Kalwaria in the 1920s and 1930s. It was devised by Avner Yonai, the grandson of one of the few members to have survived the Holocaust. The group Yonai put together includes an international set of Jewish and non-Jewish mandolinists who play a repertoire that includes mainstream secular pieces of the era as well as Jewish tunes.

5 In Poland, most big cities other than Kraków were largely destroyed during the Second World War. The Old Town in Warsaw, for example, was famously rebuilt stone by stone in the immediate post-war years. It is an 'absolute fake', but most visitors by now probably see it as 'really' old.

6 The Golden Rose in fact forms part of a chain of 'provocative' theme restaurants that includes, for example, one dedicated to Ludwig Masoch, the Lviv-born 'inventor' of masochism, and one to the Ukrainian Insurgent Army, or UPA, the brutal, ultra-nationalist partisan force that operated in western Ukraine in the 1940s.

7 See e.g. my article 'Night and Day in Jewish Time' (Gruber 2009–10). In the present essay I am focusing not on a city like Budapest, where there are a substantial number of Jews (as many as 90,000 by some estimates) and where there is a visible and viable Jewish community, but in cities and countries where few Jews live. I find it interesting that a Jewish café in Budapest called Mazel Tov uses some of the Kraków café tropes—with a difference: the host of pictures covering its walls are all of what can be described as modern Jewish heroes and celebrities, from Woody Allen and Barbra Streisand to philosopher Agnes Heller and Facebook's Mark Zuckerberg. There is no 'shtetl nostalgia' and no attempt to keep even kosher-style.

8 As another example, the papers from a conference in Vilnius in 2006 were published in Šiaučiūnaitė-Verbickienė and Lempertienė 2007. The German scholar Joachim Schloer has been prominent in this line of study.

9 In October 2011 Spiewak was named director of the Jewish Historical Institute in Warsaw.

10 Ornstein and I were speaking on the occasion of the remarkable '7@Nite' or 'Night of the Synagogues' in Kraków, 4–5 June 2011. Annamaria Orla-Bukowska describes this excep-

tional event in her essay below. Further 'Nights' took place in 2012 and 2013, and it is likely that it will become an annual event.

11   For quote see <http://archilviv.city-adm.lviv.ua/en/content/view/56/9/>.

12   Francesco Spagnolo describes an advertisement for the restaurant in his essay below.

13   <http://www.inyourpocket.com/ukraine/lviv/Where-to-eat/Jewish/Pid-Zolotoiu-Rozoyu_48141v>, accessed 11 Dec. 2011.

References

BARTOV, OMER. 2007. *Erased: Vanishing Traces of Jewish Galicia in Present-Day Ukraine*. Princeton, NJ.

BAUMAN, ZYGMUNT. 1998. 'Allosemitism: Pre-Modern, Modern, Post-Modern'. In Bryan Cheyette and Laura Marcus, eds., *Modernity, Culture, and 'the Jew'*. Stanford, Calif.

BRAUCH, JULIA, ANNA LIPPHARDT, and ALEXANDRA NOCKE, eds. 2008. *Jewish Topographies: Visions of Space, Traditions of Place*. Farnham, Surrey.

DAWIDOWICZ, LUCY. 1989. *From That Place and Time: A Memoir, 1938–1947*. New York.

DÖBLIN, ALFRED. 1991. *Journey to Poland: A German Novelist Seeks his Jewish Roots on the Eve of the Nazis' Rise to Power*, trans. Joachim Neugroschel. New York.

DUTKÓWSKA, AGATA. 2008. 'Visual Semiotics of Kazimierz, Krakow'. Paper presented at the conference 'Representations of Jews in the European Popular Culture', Florence, 24–26 Nov.

ECO, UMBERTO. 1986. *Travels in Hyperreality*, trans. William Weaver. New York.

ESHMAN, ROB. 2010. 'The New Life'. *Los Angeles Jewish Journal*, 20 Oct. <http://www.jewishjournal.com/rob_eshman/article/the_new_life_20101020/>, accessed 30 Jan. 2013.

GRUBER, RUTH ELLEN. 2002. *Virtually Jewish: Reinventing Jewish Culture in Europe*. Berkeley, Calif.

——2009a. 'Jüdische und "Jüdische" Cafés'. In Michal Friedlander and Cilly Kugelmann, eds., *Koscher & Co.: Über Essen und Religion*, 222–7. Berlin.

——2009b. 'Beyond Virtually Jewish . . . Balancing the Real, the Surreal and Real Imaginary Places'. In Monika Murzyn-Kupisz and Jacek Puchla, eds., *Reclaiming Memory: Urban Regeneration in the Historic Jewish Quarters of Central European Cities*, 63–80. Kraków.

——2009–10. 'Night and Day in Jewish Time'. *Hadassah Magazine*, 91(3). Viewed online at <http://www.hadassahmagazine.org/site/apps/nlnet/content2.aspx?c=twI6LmN7IzF&b=5724115&ct=7809845>.

——2010. 'Scenes from a Krakow Café'. *Moment*, Jan.–Feb. Viewed online at <http://www.oldsite.momentmag.net/moment/issues/currentyear/02/201002-Poland.html>.

GRUBER, SAMUEL D. 2008. 'Can Lviv Be Developed as a Jewish Heritage Center?' Paper presented at Center for Urban History, Lviv, October. See also blog postings at <http://samgrubersjewishartmonuments.blogspot.com/>.

MURZYN, MONIKA A. 2006. *Kazimierz: The Central European Experience of Urban Regeneration*. Kraków.

PINTO, DIANA. 1996. *A New Jewish Identity for Post-1989 Europe*. JPR Policy Paper No. 1. London.

PODOLSKY, ANATOLY. 2008. 'A Reluctant Look Back: Jews and the Holocaust in Ukraine'. *Osteuropa* 8–10. <http://www.osteuropa.dgo-online.org/issues/issue.2008. 1217541600000>, accessed 28 Nov. 2012.

ŠIAUČIŪNAITĖ-VERBICKIENĖ, JURGITA, and LARISA LEMPERTIENĖ, eds. 2007. *Jewish Space in Central and Eastern Europe: Day-to-Day History*. Newcastle upon Tyne.

SZPILMAN, WŁADYSŁAW. 1999. *The Pianist*, trans. Anthea Bell. London.

FOURTEEN

Unsettling Encounters: Missing Links of European Jewish Experience and Discourse

FRANCESCO SPAGNOLO

IN THE AUTUMN OF 2010, more or less while Ruth Ellen Gruber was serving on a jury for a design competition to mark the sites of the Jewish past in the city of Lviv, I travelled to Israel. My trip had two main purposes. I was to speak at a conference on the Jews in Italy, held at Tel Aviv University, and at the same time conduct research in the sound archives of the National Library of Israel into the music of the Jews in the island of Corfu, Greece. While in Jerusalem, unexpectedly, I found myself attending a fascinating conference on Jewish–Ukrainian relations, held at the recently reopened Israel Museum, involving scholars, intellectuals, writers, artists, community activists, and political figures from Ukraine, Poland, Israel, Canada, and the United States.[1] Given my schedule I could only attend this conference in the evenings. But I soon realized that I knew many of the participants, and that some were close friends I had not expected to see in Israel at that time. Ukraine is not the subject of my own research, and I have never been there. However, the topic fascinated me for a number of reasons, including the fact that the political overtones of the conversation—which focused on the question whether Ukrainians and Jews *can* actually have a conversation—were overtly part of the programme and in a way the true underlying topic of the conference. The programme focused on 'cross-cultural influences in music, art, architecture, language, as well as mutual stereotypes embedded in the respective cultures'. There were many awkward moments in the discussion, and embarrassments experienced on all sides. Yet the event, and the select group of participants, suggested that successful communication was not an unattainable goal and that it might rest on a new understanding of the shared past.

I have not been to Ukraine for a very specific reason. My mother's family came from Lviv, and almost all of our relatives were murdered there during the war. I was brought up (in Italy) with the dictum, often repeated by my mother and the few other remaining relatives, that 'there is nothing left there for us'. Even though I have been able to identify this as a mantra that fails to clarify where there would ever be anything 'for us' at all, my own travels across eastern Europe have never brought me close enough to Ukraine. In my experience, Ukraine, Galicia, and the city of Lviv have remained an 'imaginary land', as virtual as most of my European Jewish life.

All of us who have lived as Jews in post-war Europe are in a position to share a number of disturbing stories that highlight prejudice, ignorance about the Holocaust, or, put differently, the fact that, while Jews are a true minority, most people —even in major cities with a significant Jewish population—are not aware of them as a living component of their world. In Europe Jews are all too aware of their own virtuality: they know that they exist as reminders, and perhaps as ghosts—witnesses to the birth of Christianity (its 'elder brothers'),[2] ghosts of the victims of the Holocaust, or emblems of the idea of a yet to be ethnically emancipated Europe where different cultures and religions can actually coexist rather than constantly negotiating how to acknowledge, let alone respect, one another.

My own inventory of unsettling encounters, which draws on personal (and overall rather mild) experiences in Italy and France, includes directors of national radio programmes using 'Zionist' only as a derogatory term, countless anti-semitic dinner-party jokes, a friendly neighbour compulsively telling stories featuring greedy Jews to show me that she enjoyed 'Jewish humour', a PR agent trying to obtain reproduction rights of a photograph of Albert Einstein from the rabbinical office of Milan (on the assumption, I presume, that the 'Jews' would own the copyright for images of their own kind), and—more troublingly—a famous Roma musician and cultural activist proudly sharing with me that he often concluded his band's performances with a version of 'Havah nagilah', 'you know, the song that Jews sang on their way to the gas chambers'.[3] (These are only a few of my memories. I used to keep a file on such awkward occurrences, but, having moved across the globe several times over the last decade, I luckily managed to mislay it.)

Ruth Ellen Gruber begins her exploration of the 'real imaginary Jewish spaces' of today's eastern Europe with one such anecdote, in which a Ukrainian student at one of Rome's pontifical institutes shares how prejudice can be enjoyable, or at least freely enjoyed, by some. Her descriptions of the encounter with the young man and of her initial and subsequent visits to the Golden Rose restaurant in Lviv are haunting in several ways. 'What he particularly enjoyed'—she reports—'was the restaurant's signature gimmick: patrons were supposed to "haggle" over what they eventually paid for their meal.' One way to read the story is: the young man has never met a 'real' Jew and he greatly enjoys 'Jewish food' without questioning the tradition of prejudice that comes with the marketing style of the Ukrainian restaurant he frequents. You can have your prejudices and eat them, too.

As I was reading Gruber's essay, a photograph reached me via a distant relative who was conducting research in Lviv. The coincidence is too marked not to be mentioned, and the information coming from the image complements Gruber's description. The photograph reproduces a quadrilingual ad—in Yiddish (in Hebrew characters), Polish, Ukrainian, and English (all printed in Latin characters)—

for the same restaurant, which is described as 'one of L'viv bestloved dining out venues'.[4] The flyer is, in itself, a haunting artefact. The use of Hebrew characters confers a touch of exoticism, otherwise demolished by a marketing strategy clearly aimed at tourists (and by the spelling errors). It reads:

Halytcian-Jewish caff 'Under Golden Rose' 2, Staroevreiska str., Lviv (*near old synagogue*) Tel.: (032) 236-75-53 Hours: 10:00-02:00 Menu: engl./ukr., Wi-Fi. Cuisine: Halytcian/ Jewish. The ONLY restaurant in Ukraine with NO prices in menu—You should bargain over bill, to come to reasonable solutions.

This 'artefact', and Gruber's story complementing it, cannot but generate questions, as they encompass several levels of interaction (or transaction) between Jews and non-Jews living in Europe. Gruber's initial point is that this is but one example of countless similar restaurants, cultural venues, gadgets, puppets, and the like found across eastern Europe, and that all of these examples reflect the collective need to define what is 'Jewish' in the same way that other 'ethnic' identities (Italian, Chinese, etc.) are defined by marketing paradigms. However, the 'Under Golden Rose' flyer and its likes raise a whole set of questions at an even broader level. First, we encounter the paradigm of the use of time and space to assign to Jews the notion of antiquity. The name and location of the restaurant, as well as its description in multiple languages mark both the ancient, and culturally mixed, ethnic origins of the food served there, and its connectedness with the place and its history (the 'old synagogue'). At the same time, the nature of the flyer also suggests that interactions between Jews and non-Jews, including visitors' perception of the place fostered by how the restaurant is presented (i.e. marketed) to them, are aspects of a financial transaction (food consumption, in this particular case), and that all history is always marketable. Not only customers and waiters but also Jews and non-Jews will, in the end, find a 'reasonable solution'. Antiquity and marketability are two very important categories associated with Jewish life in Europe, and especially with the realm of 'cultural production'.

As a student of Jewish cultural history what I find particularly thought-provoking in Gruber's anecdote isn't so much what it adds to the inventory of misguided Jewish–non-Jewish interactions echoing the Holocaust. On the contrary—and this is the point of my response to her article—I find that Gruber's ensuing analysis clearly tries to direct us (the collective community of those who study, and think about, 'things Jewish') beyond such an inventory, and explores the 'missing links' that mark the discontinuity of the European Jewish experience and discourse. Gruber is capable of moving beyond the anecdotal, and in this case turns the 'Golden Rose' story into an opportunity to introduce us to contemporary fieldwork on the vestiges of the past. What is really haunting, then, in her accounts are not just the unsettling encounters, the awkward artefacts, the kitschy locations she so poignantly describes. It is the ensuing intellectual realization of the gap that still exists in our understanding of the history of cultural interactions between Jews and non-Jews before the Holocaust, and of the great extent to which our collective understanding remains Holocaust-directed—to the point that it informs our collective interpretation of Jewish history *tout court*. By focusing on the performative dimension of today's 'virtually Jewish' culture, Gruber's account of the Jewish ways of eastern Europe moves beyond fear and prejudice (without ever erasing, or debasing, them), and helps us embrace a wide-ranging experience that includes memory, hope, and awareness. It is this path-breaking approach that has characterized her writing over the last two decades.

Gruber's work includes several books—among them a seminal guidebook, *Jewish Heritage Travel* (1992 and 2007), a travelogue, *Upon the Doorposts of Thy House* (1994), and *Virtually Jewish* (2002)—countless articles in the international press, and blog posts, resulting from decades of reporting from Europe to North America and Israel. During this time her investigations have turned into a veritable body of fieldwork, leading to continued cultural activism aimed at bridging people, communities, institutions, and countries across the European and Jewish divides. Already in *Virtually Jewish*, and even more so in her more recent articles, she has extended this practice by connecting communities with their past, especially when and where the connections have been willingly suppressed. It is true that her work is very much in the present, that her phenomenology is all contemporary. Yet her real focus is the past and its power to affect 'the way we reconstruct things, in our minds and on the ground, to create new realities rather than "re-create" past models'.

By underscoring Gruber's focus on the past, it becomes possible to see contemporary culture festivals, restaurants and cafés, architectural competitions, the ways in which old cemeteries or synagogues are either hidden from the public eye or forgotten, or instead renovated even in the absence of Jewish life (or perhaps precisely because of that absence), the sprawling celebrations of the annual 'European Day of Jewish Culture', as actual vestiges and continuations of a European cultural past, and not solely new events in which the past is re-enacted and performed. And this past is not 'only' the Holocaust but also the history of Jewish–non-Jewish relations that preceded it, which the Holocaust destroyed along with the lives of its victims, and which our collective historiography has not yet fully succeeded in embracing. It is a centuries-old reality of shared cultural production within Jewish spaces.

Throwing light on this is no small feat. Since I first met Ruth Gruber in the mid-1990s, I've kept wondering whether what she has accomplished would have been possible without her North American background. Even though I am not entirely happy with my own response to this question in the negative, I tend to think that this may be precisely the case. Europeans, Jews and non-Jews alike, probably needed such a participant observer to unveil the reality, and the persistence, of their own past, beyond the realm of the imaginary.

Cultural production plays a pivotal role in the relationship between the past, the present, and the imaginary. As Gruber aptly observes, performativity is its key element, as it enables a relationship with the past that is played out at several levels. Restaurant venues, theatrical and musical performances, and collective 'days of remembrance' and of cultural celebration all seem to be informally designed to allow both individuals and groups to perform what they perceive their lives would have been like either *before* the Holocaust, or *without* the Holocaust. This collectively created imaginary reality is not only directed at historical reconstruction but also enables a veritable 'archaeology of feelings', the possibility of exploring what, along with countless human lives, was truly lost: human interactions.[5] This archaeology can only count on one, very effective, device: the evocative power of fragments. And fragments of the past come to us in many shapes and forms: as quotations, but also as ruins, or vestiges, as well as leftovers, detritus, even garbage, or keepsakes, including the kitschy decor of Jewish-style cafés. It is primarily through such fragments that the collective strategy of remembering what was lost and has not been written down by anyone can be deployed.

My own research—which for the last decade has been devoted to the history of Italy's synagogue life and liturgical music—prompts me to read Gruber's east Europe-centric essay in a comparative, and chronologically broader, light. If my assumption that today's 'real imaginary' spaces of cultural production are part of an unspoken collective strategy used by Jewish and non-Jewish Europeans to continue the history of their shared lives and feelings is correct, then we can expand the scope of this observation beyond eastern Europe. By observing the mechanisms of cultural production in early modern Europe one cannot help but notice that it invariably involved interaction between Jews and non-Jews. Not only between Jewish and non-Jewish *cultures*, but between actual individuals, and groups.

This real space of cultural interaction is rarely observed beyond the realm of intellectual history, and thus outside the lives of the cultural elites. However, it is particularly visible in the production of material culture, including (synagogue) music. One striking observation that comes from my research into synagogue music is that virtually all 'new' Italian Jewish liturgical music since the composer Salamone Rossi (active in Mantua and Venice between 1570 and 1630, who wrote polyphonic settings for Hebrew texts) involved the interaction of Jewish and non-Jewish musicians at all levels of production: composition (and printing/publication), performance, and reception. In other words, most of the 'Jewish musical culture' produced at the dawn of the modern era was the result of Jewish and non-Jewish composers (and music scholars) working closely together, of Jewish and non-Jewish performers presenting together these compositions within the walls of a synagogue (which was often located behind the gates of a ghetto), and of Jewish and non-Jewish synagogue-goers attending their performances together. Non-Jews, in this context, were indeed 'synagogue-goers', like their Jewish neighbours: they attended services, listened to music and prayers, looked at illustrated manuscripts of liturgical texts (like the book of Esther), on special occasions read Italian translations of the Hebrew texts sung as part of the liturgy, received specially prepared Hebrew publications as mementos of their visit (if their social status required it), and listened to sermons delivered in Italian by rabbis and other Jewish preachers.

From this perspective, it may become possible to argue that there never was a 'Jewish culture without the non-Jews', and that such a notion is as odd—albeit certainly not as tainted by centuries of discrimination and power struggles—as that of a 'Jewish culture without the Jews', or a 'Jewish self-irony without the Jews and without the self'. Because the 'self', in the context of Jewish cultural production, seems to have always included the 'other'.

I find it particularly telling that Gruber's essay focuses on the 'monuments' to Jewish experience, since the presence and the role of the 'other' (the non-Jews) was already taken into consideration when some of the most important European Jewish monuments, such as the large synagogues of the time of the Emancipation, were being erected.[6] The Emancipation was a time in which European Jews not only built their first architectural monuments, but also built them in a 'monumental' style, with exceedingly large dimensions. The Italian rabbi Lelio Della Torre (1805–71), one of the most authoritative promoters of liturgical reforms in the nineteenth century, warned against the monumental frenzy, specifically criticizing both the dimensions and the intent of the new architectural endeavours that characterized his era, and argued that it was directed more towards non-Jewish visitors than to the actual ritual needs of the Jewish communities. In 1870, over a decade before the majestic new synagogue of Florence was inaugurated (1882), the rabbi complained:

I will only say that such large proportions are nowadays needed [only] in the large European capitals, were the Jewish population is counted by the tens of thousands . . . but not in our towns, where, exception made for two or three communities, the most populated ones count a little more than two thousand souls. Thus, today's way of thinking makes one fear that the grandiose monuments that are being built or planned here for the rituals will be attended [in the future] more by curious visitors than by the pious ones. (Della Torre 1870)

The shared experience of synagogue life continued in Italy well into the twentieth century, ending with the proclamation of the Fascist antisemitic laws in 1938. This experience never resumed in the same way after 1945, and non-Jews rarely attend today's synagogue services. (Incidentally, the composition of new liturgical music has also been discontinued.) There are, however, two yearly occasions on which Jews and non-Jews, almost ritually, come back together once again in Italy's synagogues, finding one another and creating a new reality from the suppressed memory of a shared past. These are the Giorno della Memoria (Italy's own version of International Holocaust Remembrance Day) and, even more poignantly, the European Day of Jewish Culture, two institutionally sanctioned annual events that are the epitome of the real imaginary Jewish space that Ruth Ellen Gruber has so vividly chronicled for us and helped us to embrace.

Notes

I am grateful to Simon Bronner for soliciting this response, which takes into account not only Ruth Ellen Gruber's essay published in the present volume but an ongoing intellectual conversation with the author, dating back over fifteen years.

1   'Ukrainian Jewish Encounter: Cultural Interaction, Representation and Memory,' Jerusalem, 18–20 Oct. 2010. I could only find a description of the initiative online at <http://ujeicontent.squarespace.com/about/>, as well as a summary of the programme at <http://muzejew. org.ua/New-Vstrecha-En.html> (accessed 24 June 2011).

2   For a deconstruction of the famous definition by Pope John Paul II, *fratelli maggiori* (1986), see Bonfil 2000.

3   On the role of inventory in modern Jewish intellectual practice, see Shandler 2010.

4   Quotes from the flyer reproduce the original spelling exactly.

5   I first explored the notion of an 'archaeology of feelings' regarding Jewish attitudes towards contemporary eastern Europe in '(Ri-)Annodare: Da Milano alla Moldova' (Spagnolo 2002).

6   See esp. Lerner 2000 and Davidson 2001.

References

BONFIL, ROBERT. 2000. 'The History of the Jews in Italy: Memory and Identity'. In Bernard D. Cooperman and Barbara Garvin, eds., *The Jews of Italy: Memory and Identity*, 35–9. Bethesda, Md.

DAVIDSON, IVAN KALMAR. 2001. 'Moorish Style: Orientalism, the Jews, and Synagogue Architecture'. *Jewish Social Studies*, 7(3): 68–100.

DELLA TORRE, LELIO. 1870. 'Modesti appunti'. *L'Educatore Israelita*, 18 (19 June): 202–3.

LERNER, L. SCOTT. 2000. 'The Narrating Architecture of Emancipation'. *Jewish Social Studies*, 6(3): 1–30.

SHANDLER, JEFFREY. 2010. *Keepers of Accounts: The Practice of Inventory in Modern Jewish Life*. David W. Belin Lecture in American Jewish Affairs, at the Jean and Samuel Frankel Center for Judaic Studies. Ann Arbor, Mich.

SPAGNOLO, FRANCESCO. 2002. '(Ri-)Annodare. Da Milano alla Moldova'. *Rassegna Mensile di Israel*, 68/1 (Jan.–Apr.): 297–306.

FIFTEEN

Virtual Transitioning into Real: Jewishness in Central Eastern Europe

ANNAMARIA ORLA-BUKOWSKA

Socialistically Real Jewishness

In the spring of 1986 a Polish American classmate and I finally undertook to locate the Stara Synagoga and investigate the Kraków historical museum exhibition listed in the newspaper. Having lived and studied in the city for several months, we thought we knew it very well. Still, a map was needed to pinpoint ulica Szeroka, and to determine which tram to take and at which stop to disembark. Expecting a long ride to some distant and dark corner of the metropolis, we were quite surprised to arrive at our destination a mere two stops from the city centre. Looking back up Starowiślna Street, the clear view of the Mariacki Church roof confounded us; it was obvious we could have easily walked.

Truth be told, what registered during that first outing on Szeroka Street was a police station, abandoned buildings, and crumbling facades. Although depressingly grey disintegration dominated nearly all communist-era cityscapes, what we saw here surpassed the usual level of decay. After going through the museum, but not noting anything else of interest in the vicinity, we returned directly to the Old City, which was physically close yet mentally distant.

There was a lived Jewishness to Kraków at the time, giving lie to the often—and even recently—repeated slogan, 'For 50 years the area saw very little activity, and not one Jewish person' (Teich 2011). The Socio-Cultural Society of Jews (known as TSKŻ) officially carried on its activities in Sławkowska Street in the city centre; the Jewish Religious Community was functioning in Skawińska located on the traditionally Christian side of Kazimierz; funerals were occasionally conducted at the Miodowa cemetery just beyond the district, and services were held weekly at the Rema Synagogue. Nevertheless, only the last of these was situated in today's tourist target area. Certainly all of this was undetectable to uninitiated inhabitants or any vacationers—then as scarce a commodity as goods in the shops.

Communist Evolving into Post-Communist

The above notwithstanding, various impetuses laid the foundations in the 1980s for a perceptible non-Jewish Jewishness. Diverse initiatives by Polish Christians generated an increasing number of articles and books (above and underground) about Judaism, Polish Jewish history, and the Holocaust; lectures and film screenings were held (which would eventually evolve into the Jewish Culture Festival); the Jagiellonian University established a Research Centre on the History and Culture of Jews in Poland (today's Jewish Studies Department), and work was begun to transform a former *beit midrash* into the Center for Jewish Culture. However, here again, only the last of these was actually taking place in the former Jewish quarter.

Nonetheless, by the early 1990s the Jewish Culture Festival was in full swing with the hub of activity now shifted to Kazimierz. The Center for Jewish Culture on Meiselsa was housing a packed calendar of events, and the first businesses—including Noah's Ark, Jarden, and what would later be branded the 'good' (favoured by locals) and 'bad' (ensnaring tourists) Ariels—were opening on Szeroka Street (see Kugelmass and Orla-Bukowska 1998). It was at this point that the earliest outside observers—among them Ruth Ellen Gruber (see esp. Gruber 1994)—began to report on a new form of Jewishness emerging in Kraków, in Poland, and in central eastern Europe. It was also then that questions first arose concerning its 'reality' or 'virtuality'—a dilemma unresolved to date, and the topic at hand.

Virtual or Real Jewishness in Central Eastern Europe?

The first issue one needs to place under the microscope is an attempted definition of the virtual and the real. Naturally, the question arises as to whether a boundary can be demarcated between them at all. Certainly the lines between enactment, performance, deception, and masquerade are always smudged (see Kugelmass and Orla-Bukowska 1998). A capacious matter up for discussion is what constitutes the difference between a nostalgic return to, for instance, bell-bottom jeans and sitars—considered natural—and a return to, for instance, Yiddish and klezmer music—considered artificial. Does one of these contribute something qualitatively 'better'? Is one more substantively 'real' than the other?

Then again, how authentically 'Jewish' are sundry economic and cultural market offerings anywhere, and how many bona fide Jews are consumers thereof? Among other things popping up in Poland in the 1980s was the Nissenbaum Foundation—a by-product of a highly profitable, early capitalist joint venture, the Pol-Niss liquor company. On the one hand, this company and foundation—which have not survived the transition from communism to capitalism—were seen by both outsiders and insiders as 'really' Jewish by virtue of the founding owner being a Polish Jewish Holocaust survivor who had settled in Germany after the war. Yet its vodkas and water, bearing rabbinic certificates, were, in fact, no more kosher than a run-of-the-mill, home-distilled version. On the other hand, the highly successful Jewish Culture Festival—which has survived through thick and thin—is often seen as 'virtual' because its founder and the great majority of its participants are not Jewish. This detail keeps hiccuping in discourse— sensed as an oddity, if not a 'problem'—and contributes to the assessment of Jewish culture in Poland as not genuine.

Here one might ask if a bagel shop in New York City is more verifiably Jewish because there are more Jewish residents (a correlation between Jewish-associated products and the number of local self-identifying Jews), or because more Jews are eating the bagels (a correlation between the number of self-identifying Jews consuming the Jewish-associated product)? But then, is the New York bagel shop still 'real' if the customers are mostly not Jews, or if the owner is Armenian, or if it is not in a Jewish neighbourhood? Along these lines, is the 'intense, visible, vivid Jewish presence' to which Ruth Ellen Gruber attests less real because the Jews actually living in Poland are few? And hence is Kraków's Klezmer-Hois restaurant and hotel more real than the rest because its owners are Jewish, and/or because Polish and non-Polish Jews do hang out there?

With reference to Poland, as well as other central eastern European states, oft-cited commentators label this trend—either as a whole or elements thereof— as kitsch or Disneyland. Tongue firmly planted in cheek, Jonathan Ornstein of the Kraków Jewish Community Center (JCC) dubs it 'Jew-ra-ssic Park' (Teich 2011). Even some Cracovians are wont to describe the Jewish Culture Festival as Cepelia, referring to the communist-era monopoly which produced and sold folklore goods. Again probing the boundaries, if an ethnologist in the United States studies old-time music in the hills of Kentucky and brings recordings back to 'civilization', triggering a craze for banjos and dulcimers, is this virtual or real? Or if a vinyl record aficionado discovers this same music and starts the fad, is that more virtual?

Does reality decrease if something initiated by devoted and sincere elites is subsequently consumed by 'common folk', who then prompt the business-minded to mass-produce, distribute, and sell it? Thus the next query about the branding of Jewishness, in Gruber's words, 'as a recognized and recognizable' commodity (p. 336 above) is whether it is a less legitimate phenomenon when it pertains to commercial ventures and more so when it pertains to cultural ones. On the one hand, initial results from an ongoing research project reveal that the number one reason for non-Poles to attend Kraków's Jewish Culture Festival is the unplanned discovery of the event, while for Poles it is to revisit something they have previously enjoyed (Orla-Bukowska and Tomanek 2012). On the other hand, running a very close second for Poles and non-Poles alike is a specific interest in Jewish culture. Whatever the case, one cannot help but notice that, as

Teich states, 'Whether real or just a simulated reality, Jewish culture is in high demand in Krakow' (Teich 2011).

Cultural or Commercial?

In truth, financial profit is always involved as 'money makes the world go round'. If you build it, they will come; if they buy it, you will offer it—including caricatures bordering on or undeniably crossing the line of good taste. While in London for a conference, a Sephardim-versus-Ashkenazim chess set making the most of physiognomic traits and clichéd garb drew a colleague's gaze to a Golders Green shop display.[1] Correspondingly, the stalls in Kraków offer carved wooden souvenirs, an undying component of Polish folk art: Górale with sheep, sleepy peasants holding a jug, plump housewives gripping a rolling pin, and Jewish traders with a sack or a grosz.

The 'Jews are good with money' stereotype is actually not negative per se: many people would be flattered to be seen as having a *kepele* for business. In truth, the role of Jews in middle-class socio-economic strata has been extensively documented; in comparison to their percentage in the general population, they were over-represented therein. Something about the stereotype, however, made a Jewish friend in western Europe flinch when he had to fight for his early retirement compensation. At the same time, as a social anthropologist stepping back to capture the big picture, I also consider the Italian restaurant in Kraków with Godfather-like figures standing outside and passers-by posing for photographs with the life-size Marlon Brando and son mannequins.

The goal of the first businesses in the former Jewish districts of central eastern Europe naturally had to be the opening of wallets, but this is a two-way street. These businesses were not only making a buck, but also making a connection with—as well as drawing attention to—the local Jewish artefacts and architecture. The enterprises (even the tackiest) have not merely 'taken advantage' but have also rendered the culture and history more attractive, more engrossing. A recent article bears witness to this balancing between maladroit virtuality and graceful reality:

Jewishness has been adopted as a selling point, almost a badge of cool, in a way that is sometimes tasteless . . . Ornstein says: 'You have some fake Jewish-style restaurants, and I would love those to be restaurants run by Jews, kosher restaurants and actually be realistic . . . [but] we're moving in that direction. These days in Poland, the fact that you can call a restaurant a Jewish restaurant and that brings people in, is in itself a positive thing.' (Vasagar and Borger 2011)

In a similar vein, are Roma music, an Irish pub, an Oktoberfest tent, a French bistro, and Fourth of July fireworks not an added value in Poland? Do such phenomena become culturally counterfeit outside their 'native' lands? Should lines be drawn (and if so, where) in the globalization of cultural offerings as commodities?

Although 'the boundaries between game and illusion are blurred', as Eco reminds us (cited by Gruber in her essay above), some of what is taking place rings very true. Even if simulacra led them in, most of the participants are engaged for reasons leaning towards noble. It is the visibly virtual that draws drunken Englishmen to a stag party pub crawl on plac Nowy. Yet it also drew another Englishman, Prince Charles, to create the financial backing which built the Jewish Community Center on Miodowa Street in record time. Yes, there is clumsy cultural reproduction that is utterly superficial, literally mimicking layers of flaking history. But beneath the surface, on a day-to-ordinary-day level, cultural practice is much deeper and there is certainly much real cultural production.

Albeit everything is in the eye of the beholder, in his or her interpretation of what is happening: the interpretation of the business entrepreneur, of the trekking tourist, of the researching scholar, and of the Jewish and non-Jewish observers. Whatever the packaging, for over a generation the phenomenon has been leading a number of average Poles (Jews but primarily non-Jews) to an increased interest in Polish Jewish history and culture, in Polish Jews, and in Polish Jewish identity. This still being quite noticeable and intriguing, an Israeli journalist was effusive: 'I am moved anew by the authentic meetings with young Catholics, full of curiosity about Jewish culture, language, food and music' (Hurvitz 2011). Moreover, a complementary interest in Jewishness has also been motivating an ever-growing number of non-Polish visitors—including members of Jewish 'pilgrimages' (on the earliest of these, see Kugelmass 1993)—to set foot in Poland.

Spatially the changes are evident. In the 1990s (to the naked eye) all seemed centred exclusively on Szeroka Street with the single 'outlying' venue being on Meiselsa. Today, however, Jewishness has seeped back and spilt throughout Kazimierz. Szeroka is no longer the only street in town: day-tripping down Miodowa today, one passes the Tempel Synagogue, the JCC, the Kupa Synagogue, and Klezmer-Hois, and finishes past the viaduct at the cemetery.

In fact, the geographical realm of Jewishness—virtual and real—is expanding. Visitors are setting foot not only in Kazimierz or the Old City, but progressively more often in Podgórze, with its Second World War ghetto sites including the Schindler Factory Museum and the site of Płaszów camp, also brought to the fore by Spielberg's film. Real is the Podgórze branch of the Kraków History Museum, officially named Fabryka Schindlera, but whose exhibition (to the surprise of many a visitor) constitutes a general presentation of the city under German occupation. Virtual is that created by Steven Spielberg: apart from the fact that Amon Göth could not shoot into the camp from his villa, the film set is disintegrating not at Płaszów but over 2 kilometres away from the historic site. Moved by the disappointment of early post-premiere tourists who wanted to experience Spielberg's 'reality', Zdzisław Leś, founder of the Jarden Bookshop, produced the

Retracing Schindler's List guidebook (Teich 2011). Some consumers seem to prefer the virtual, and concessions to this demand must be allowed as well.

All of the aforementioned taken into account, the Jewishness of Kraków and Poland today includes ever broader circles, which in turn inspires more enriched tour guide narratives. The non-Jewish tourist learns about Jewish history and culture, like the middle-aged resident of Będzin who excitedly recounted discovering the Jewishness of her own backyard, as it were, when the 2010 Jewish Culture Festival included a walking tour there. For the first time in her life, she saw how much Jews were a part of her home town's history.[2] Likewise, the Jewish tourist learns about Polish Jewishness and Judaism in its contemporary forms as lived by his or her Polish Jewish peers.

Phantom Pain

More than money is stimulating this package. One spur is that, as Antoni Sułek points out, 'Paradoxically, "Jews" do occupy much space in the social consciousness' (Sułek 2011: 1). More to the point, 'Jews' as a symbolic concept in the contemporary Polish collective imagination comprise a far broader entity than those living there presently, also signifying 'those who lived in Poland once upon a time—after the war, before the war, or even further into the past' (Sułek 2011: 1). Furthermore, this phenomenon is more broadly spread across this part of the continent. In Austria, for instance, 'the colloquial visions regarding the ratios are similarly false. In 1991, only 14 percent of the Austrians surveyed by the AJC knew how few Jews there really are in their country: less than 1 percent. Yet some 22 percent of the respondents thought that this percentage was higher than 10' (Sułek 2011: 3–4).

As Gruber asks here, 'How do local people choose to portray an important part of the population that was savagely removed, almost overnight?' (p. 344). And just as she (among others) has noted earlier (see Gruber 2002: 40–1), Sułek also reaffirms that, in central eastern Europe, 'Jews constitute a "phantom pain," like an amputated limb which continues to ache. Jews remain present in the social consciousness belying their almost complete disappearance in the region' (Sułek 2011: 4). The need to interact even with an apparition is a strong aching all across central eastern Europe—precisely the region in which Jews were once the most numerously and most densely settled.

Antisemitism or Anti-Antisemitism?

The reality of Jewishness in central eastern Europe is further questioned by Westerners due to their perceptions of above-average antisemitism in this region. Such an accusation reared its ugly head in the 2011 spat between Poland and Israel over football player Maor Melikson, whose dual citizenship gave him the option of representing either state. Harsh Israeli comments described his tentative choice of Poland as a traitorous affinity for an antisemitic country. In a similar vein, American Jews habitually remark that antisemitism could never be found 'at home', ignoring (among others) the formalized discrimination of Jews in US clubs, hotels, and universities well after the Second World War.

Volumes have been written regarding the issue—and much has also been written about the problems in testing for it in any society.[3] Yet equal attention should be on the other side of the coin. As Rabbi Michael Schudrich (chief rabbi of Warsaw and of Poland) elaborates: '"The flaw in all these surveys is that—let's say they show that 20% of Poles have antisemitic attitudes—everyone misses what the other 80% is thinking"' (Vasagar and Borger 2011). Among that remaining 'other 80%' are the activists—non-Jewish and some even strongly Christian —who continue to play a key role in the renaissance of Polish Jewish life. Most of them maintain close bonds to the living culture and community (see Cherry and Orla-Bukowska 2007). In fact, this author is proud to be among the cardholding non-Jewish members of the JCC Kraków.

Of greater validity is the question of the after-effects for societies traversing the virtual–real tightrope: what the participants in this phenomenon perceive, what this makes them feel, what it does to their attitudes, and, finally, what it directs them to actually do. Indubitably, as Gruber says, 'the rediscovery and even exploitation of the Jewish quotient has jump-started a general rehabilitation' (p. 345 above). In fact, there has been a 'decline in antisemitism among all age groups over the decade' (Vasagar and Borger 2011) and a survey illustrates that adult Polish Roman Catholic attendees of the Jewish Culture Festival are decidedly leaning towards religious and cultural openness in general, as well as towards anti-antisemitism and a social proximity with Jews in particular (Orla-Bukowska and Tomanek 2012). Interestingly, a recent study among younger Poles (aged 15–49) has shown 20 per cent to be decidedly or rather in favour of a synagogue being built in their neighbourhood (IIBR 2011).

Undeniably this is 'allosemitism': an awareness of the Jews as Others (keeping in mind that Christians have been as much the Other for Jews), but arousing as many positive as negative feelings these days. Poles' participation in (or being carried upon) the present wave of activity may well have contributed to the decrease in the number of antisemites in society, as well as a corresponding increase in anti-antisemites (see Orla-Bukowska 2007). Although a direct cause-effect relationship cannot be scientifically proven, it makes sense that 20-year-olds—who grew up on the Jewish Culture Festival and whose teachers (having undertaken continuing education on the Holocaust) took them to clean up the local Jewish cemetery or had them cook cholent—are the ones now enrolling in Jewish subjects at university and volunteering Saturday nights to sit down and talk to Israeli teenagers during the latter's Holocaust pilgrimages here. Such committed anti-antisemitism must correlate with strong antisemitism not rising.

Deeds do speak louder than words. One case in point is the civic engagement which makes the Jewish Culture Festival possible:

The festival founders, its growing contingent of volunteers, most of the tour guides, many of the course instructors, and, of course, the overwhelming and awe-inspiring crowds of those in attendance are Polish non-Jews. Apart from this broadening grass-roots support, [its] honorary patron is the president of the Republic of Poland; apart from the financial backing of various foundations, it is granted funds from the national, provincial, and city governments. (Orla-Bukowska 2007: 276)

Another example is Kraków's March of Memory from Podgórze to Płaszów, retracing the route of the 1943 ghetto liquidation. Initiated by the same dedicated activists who started up the local Polish–Israeli Friendship Society and the cultural festival, it originally drew a mere handful of people; in recent years the marchers have numbered several hundred to a thousand. On an individual level of involvement, close to 200 non-Jewish Polish citizens have already been publicly recognized by the Israeli embassy—under the auspices of the Traison Foundation and with a formal ceremony included in the Jewish Culture Festival programme—for their local preservation of Jewishness (often with their own monetary contributions yet nary a reward). Representing every possible region of the country, and many of them from small villages, they restore physical land-marks or invent less tangible ways to connect with their missing cohabitants. Moving still further in this constructive direction, schoolchildren hear the testi-monials of Polish Jewish Holocaust survivors and Polish non-Jewish recipients of the Yad Vashem Righteous Among the Nations honour; once forgotten Jewish cemeteries as well as synagogues are reconsecrated from Brzostek to Oświęcim, and new plaques announce where Mordechai Gebirtig, Natan Gross, and other Polish Jews lived.

Performativity?

For some people the aforementioned phenomena constitute 'performativity', what Gruber sees as engagement with simulation via auditory and visual prompts of Jewish life before the Holocaust. Here a certain elucidation is re-quired: the dark wood, crocheted tablecloths, often mismatched porcelain, over-stuffed furniture, candlesticks, and the faux-old (or not) artwork on the wall—all sensed as synonymous with 'Jewishness'—actually more generally evoke the Habsburg culture of Prague, Bratislava, Budapest, Lviv, and Kraków (see e.g. Kugelmass and Orla-Bukowska 1998: 332). On the one hand, it is intriguing that nostalgia for the Austro-Hungarian empire is linked to Jewishness. Yet on the other, these cafés—and many are found in city centres, with nary a link made to any ethnicity—hark back to the romantic 'glory days' of semi-autonomous Galicia. Perchance this simply reflects a longing for the look and feel of pre-war central eastern Europe in all its multireligiosity, multiethnicity, and multiculturalism—of which Jewishness was indubitably a vibrant part. Kazimierz (at a time when it was far from attractive) was submitted by Poland, along with Kraków's city centre, to the UNESCO list of World Heritage Sites; now Lviv seems to have followed suit with its Jewish district. This seems to imply that (to some extent) 'Jewishness' has been and is seen as part and parcel of the urban heritage complex. It would be interesting if Prague, Budapest, and other central European metropolises have acted in a similar manner.

Gruber describes the clowning of Chabad Lubavitch in Hungary and tackily dressed waiters in Ukraine. Of course, masquerading is not unknown on the streets of France, England, or Belgium, though judgements seem more lenient there. That said, from a Jewish perspective, there is no room for forgiveness. *Regards*, a periodical for the francophone Jewish community in Belgium, did a cover story in April 2009 on carnival revellers in Aalst posing as Jews in repugnant masks and ersatz hasidic get-up. Then again, even if it all starts as makebelieve, the interactivity of the crowds dancing to, singing, and playing klezmer music during the Jewish Culture Festival fuels their discovery of workshops on cantorial singing, Hebrew, and Yiddish, as well as lectures on Tishah Be'av and kashrut. Ben Zion Miller's 2010 lecture on the former filled the Kupa Synagogue; the workshops on the latter by a female *mashgiaḥ* always overflow. More meaningfully, this performativity has spread from Kraków to Warsaw and Łódź, but also to Włodawa, Chmielnik, Będzin, Bobowa, and Oświęcim. Further, going beyond the quaintness of restaurants and chanteuses luring customers off the streets, the movement encompasses musicians fusing personal styles with those of their past and present Jewish peers, as well as history tours, book fairs, film festivals, and so on.

In the 1970s and 1980s there was certainly no model for this kind of work in the Soviet bloc; undertaking grassroots efforts under- or aboveground under communism was a perilous endeavour. In the twenty-first century, doing this under capitalism—with, or oft-times without, government, private foundation, foreign, or national assistance—has entailed a rapid learning process. Some initiatives are carefully planned from within, but others come from 'bull in a china shop' outsiders, oblivious to the needs and desires of the local Jews and non-Jews. Passers-by are hard pressed to discern the difference.

However, looking at this from the perspective not of the tourists but of average (or perhaps above-average) Poles, the eateries, bookshops, festivals, and museum exhibitions—introduced at various levels and in various localities over the past three decades—all provide 'an opportunity for mediated and imagined interactions with [other groups], so the perceived boundaries between them could be, at least virtually and in a mediated fashion, transcended and yet maintained' (Gazit 2010: 403). This is true whether the Other is a phantom pain or is physically present.

Being

Gal Hurvitz (2011) recapitulates the previously noted assessment: in Poland, 'Judaism is cool'. And being cool has led to it becoming real. Assuaging qualms felt early in this process (see Gruber 2002), Jewishness has neither been hijacked nor reduced solely to symbols and food. Clearly neither a two-dimensional facade nor a fossilized archaeological specimen, it is very much a living culture with as many configurations in representation as there are Jews.

Yes, it is a small—yet certainly not extinct and, indeed, multiplying—Jewish population. Moreover, it is a community quite naturally diversifying religiously, with five rabbis (including a Lubavitcher and a female Reform rabbi) at ease with not only living in Kraków, but also walking its streets in *kipah* and *tsitsit*. As a matter of fact, in the initial post-communist decade, young Poles of minority status (not only Jews but Ukrainians, homosexuals, and others too) were highly into outing themselves—brandishing symbols and performing identity. Today members of the Jewish community are quite comfortable with their identity, feeling no need to flaunt it. They participate in services if they are religious; they do not if they are not. They keep kosher if this is important to them; they eat Polish ham if its taste reminds them of home. They wear the Magen David if branding is their style; they do not if 'no logo' is their choice. They are true to themselves. This pluralism among Polish Jewry is as good a sign as any that the fortress is not besieged; the community is safe and secure enough for each person to be able to go in his or her own direction—Orthodox, Reform, humanist, or whatever. 'Never better'—the slogan coined by Jonathan Ornstein (Gruber 2011)—is likely to apply to many Jewish communities across the region. A young woman in Budapest rapping in klezmer/hip-hop/fusion (see p. 343 above) is no doubt as real as the mix of musical styles and religiosity represented by Matisyahu in Brooklyn.

Belying the 'Jewish-style' boasts on businesses catering to tourists, most important is that Kazimierz does constitute an intact Jewish neighbourhood within which spatial *eruv* the local Jew can move on a Friday evening from the JCC to the synagogue, and back again for sabbath dinner, finishing off at the very postmodern pub, where payment for consumed food and beverages can nonetheless be made the next evening. The sense of a Jewish space and place is very obviously felt.

So is it more important what we experts see in analysis or is it more important what people feel and—most significantly—what that experience motivates them to do? The reasons for wearing a Magen David pendant, an Israeli flag pin, or a *kipah* by both Polish non-Jews and Jews are certainly non-commercial. If something between virtual and real Jewishness makes Polish Jews feel proud, inspires interest among local non-Jews in Jewish history and culture, and slowly but surely wears down intolerance, then, even if an abominable faux pas like the Golden Rose in Lviv—or the 'bad' Ariel in Kraków, or the less gauche Mandroga in Lublin (see Hurvitz 2011)—occasionally comes into sight, perhaps it would be throwing the baby out with the bathwater to wholly discount this phenomenon. Once more: is the Jewish brand in central eastern Europe any different from the Jewish brand in San Francisco or Miami? Is kosher pizza in Toronto more real?

Postmodern Virtual into Real

Late on the night of Saturday, 4 June 2011 (coincidentally, the twenty-second anniversary of Poland's 1989 elections, which had whisked the country into democracy), starting with Havdalah led by a local rabbi, hundreds of Poles (Jews and, above all, non-Jews) embarked on a pioneering journey that would take them through all seven of Kraków's synagogues between 10.30 p.m. and 2 a.m. The aim of the now annual 7@Nite—co-organized by the local Jewish community centre, the Jewish religious community, and the Polish Joint Distribution Committee—is 'to educate non-Jewish Poles about contemporary Jewish life and culture' (Gruber 2011). The programme peregrinated from one synagogue to the next with concerts (including a DJ), prayers, lectures and talks, photography and multimedia exhibits, dance and art workshops, films, games, and family activities. Again, an idea was 'built' and—despite competition with other scheduled attractions as well as the late hour—the consumers of this cultural product came in droves: thousands of them, young and old, singles and families, priests and nuns and atheists, from Kraków itself or coming to town especially for this event. As Ornstein described the audience: '[H]ow many people came? 10,000. We were thinking 2,000 . . . maybe. But 10,000?!' (Teich 2011). If this had only been virtual wrapping paper, would they have come from farther away, from other cities and smaller villages?

Several days earlier, local newspapers had begun promoting 7@Nite in listings as well as articles (Żurawik 2011: 6). More significantly, regional news reports devoted more in-depth coverage to this event than to the annual Dragon Parade (Parada Smoków) with its fire-breathing monsters and fireworks on the river below Wawel Castle that very same night. On-air comments included the university student declaring that 'I'm studying Hebrew and about the Near East and so I'm interested' to a middle-aged couple announcing that 'We're going to Israel this year and wanted to get a taste of the atmosphere' (TVP3 2011). Tadeusz Jakubowicz, president of the religious community (and originally hesitant about the idea), summarized the goal: 'That the synagogues should live, that they should not be lifeless' (TVP3 2011). Clearly alive, all were full for all of the events. Of course, as Gruber points out above (p. 342), enactment—the most positive sort as well—is centred around 'the most easily visible (and publicly accessible)' sites.

An interview with one of the organizers reconfirmed what everyone already knows here: such events would not be arranged and certainly such crowds would not attend if not for the foundation laid precisely by the Jewish Culture Festival and other forms of more or less virtual Jewishness. As Jonathan Ornstein admitted in one article, thanks to the festival, 'the residents of Kraków know quite a lot about Jewish culture' (Żurawik 2011: 6). The modus operandi initially involved some non-Jews, who facilitated a transition to central eastern European Jews promoting their real versions of themselves. The current, second, stage of Jews getting involved has been 'totally made possible by this first stage', as Ornstein emphasizes (Vasagar and Borger 2011). Journalist Margaret Teich elaborates: 'In other words, it wasn't just the movie [Schindler's List] that brought about a new openness towards Jews in Krakow . . . And it's not the movie that will keep people engaged' (Teich 2011).

Not long ago, the Jewish Studies Department moved from the city centre to Kazimierz and is now kitty-corner to the offices of the Jewish Culture Festival. Moreover, the festival itself has opened the Cheder Café, offering a space in which to drink coffee, to peruse a volume pulled from the shelves, and to attend events of the year-round programme promoting multicultural tolerance (not only of Jews). Perhaps it is not a coincidence that the starting or end-point of the annual March of Equality (formerly March of Tolerance and organized as part of the Queer May program) has more recently been in Kazimierz. Up in the city centre guides point out where the Jewish community first settled in the Middle Ages on St Anne's Street, and point to the plaques on Jagiellońska Street, where Żegota (the Polish non-Jewish partisan unit formed to save Jews from the Holocaust) had a local base, and on Szpitalna Street, where the Jewish Fighting Organization (Żydowska Organizacja Bojowa) bombed a German officers' club in 1942.

Increasingly, the Jewishness of Poland is luring not only the elderly, who are nostalgic, but above all the young, who are curious. It draws people who want to learn about Judaism, who want to study Jewish history, and who want to enjoy Jewish culture. More importantly, it is inspiring Poles—young and old—to explore their country's multicultural heritage and their own personal ancestry. This, in turn, can develop into increasingly real Jewishness—or Romaniness, Armenianness, Germanness, Ukrainianness, and so on. Pluralism is also clearly promoted by various institutions in Kazimierz—from Romani representatives speaking at the Cheder Café to Japanese being taught at the JCC.

In the long run—as Gruber and several others have duly noted over the last decade—the initially virtual draws the attention not only of tourists but of governments, philanthropists, and activists. In the long run it pulls in the political, financial, social, and ethical support which, in turn, pilots the 'realization' of at least some elements. Looking back at the past quarter of a century, it is clear that many benefits have been reaped from what was initially likened to sordid exploitation. Currently nostalgia plays a smaller, if any, role. Central east European presidents, clergy, and university rectors are here and now participating in various Jewish religious ceremonies organized by the thriving Jewish communities.

Would this be possible today if not for the first-stage Jewishness, which paved the way to this deeper level of enactment, this different type of performativity?

The Twenty-First-Century Virtually Real

Reading the first paragraph of this article, anyone who has come to Kraków in the more recent past will undoubtedly chuckle. A visitor can hardly overlook the Kazimierz district these days and, in fact, quite the contrary can occur: with attractions, lodging, and eateries in abundance in this neighbourhood, many groups disregard or dispense with the Old City. This is especially true of Jewish groups on pilgrimages to the Holocaust sites. As a case in point, a few years ago an Australian March of the Living delegation, though staying in a hotel which literally faced the Planty commons encircling the Old City, never managed to cross the street to enter the main market square. Likewise, these delegations usually see exclusively 'Jewish' Warsaw, Lublin, and Łódź.

In fact, the fundamental reason for my remaining in Poland since 1985 has been precisely this incrementally yet incessantly burgeoning interest in and access to 'things Jewish'. That said, Jewish branding in Poland actually preceded my relocation by centuries. It has historically included not only the pretzels sold on the streets of Kraków which the oldest residents still call *bajgle* (bagels), but also Polish words such as *cymes* (tzimmes), or *koszer* (kosher). Whatever one thinks about the bad taste of commercialization, the highly positive connotations in Polish society of something being *cymes* (Polish slang for 'the cat's pyjamas'), or *koszer* (connoting purity or fairness), or quite simply Jewish, doubtless convey an affirmative message.

It is a reinvention, but something has been built to which people come, and transformations have ensued. When describing and analysing the dialogue between the real and the virtual in Kazimierz a decade ago, Jack Kugelmass and I were taken aback by the appearance of the first non-Jewish-themed locale on Szeroka—a techno-disco whose advertising 'flaunt[ed] a fleshy, middle-aged woman wearing nothing but her violin' (Kugelmass and Orla-Bukowska 1998: 339). Even as social anthropologists, we, too, were not immune to the overriding idea that Kazimierz was and should be 'Jewish'. And yet such natural, organic development—the tangible and intangible—is precisely what has guaranteed that Kazimierz remains real and evidences its non-Disneylandization.

True, still playing a Jewish note, the 'good Ariel' has relocated up the street to the old *mikveh* and renamed itself Klezmer-Hois; the 'bad Ariel' has contagiously overtaken half of one side of Szeroka; there is the illegally built and disputed Rubinstein Hotel, and the legitimate Hotel Ester. However, as Gruber notes, this is now an integrated street: there is Bombay, which offers Indian cuisine; the former Nissenbaum Restaurant is now the upscale Szara na Szerokiej; and Ulica

Krokodyla—although referring to a work by the Polish Jewish writer, Bruno Szulc—does not pretend to be anything other than a pleasant hangout.

The 1980s interest in replanting some Jewishness in the most Jewish of Kraków districts, subsequently augmented by the 1990s capitalist investments (such as the Ariel) and activist undertakings (the Jewish Culture Festival), did originally appear to be leading in the direction of artificiality (not to mention virtuality). Yet illustrating that such festivals are not playing a broken klezmer record were the performances of Matisyahu at the 2010 Jewish Culture Festival in Kraków and at the 2011 Oświęcim Life Festival. Abraham Inc., Yemen Blues, and Sway Machinery, who performed at the 2011 Jewish Culture Festival, are also far from a time-frozen harking back to the past. Beyond a doubt, Jewish culture and communities found in central eastern Europe will never be qualitatively the same as they were before the war, and the consumers of contemporary Jewishness in this corner of the world will always be predominantly non-Jews. That said, as Ornstein reiterates, the current phase is one in which 'people with Jewish roots [are] getting involved in the Jewish community' (Vasagar and Borger 2011).

Along the way something real has happened. This is true in Kraków, but also in Lublin, Warsaw, and Łódź; it is true in Budapest, Prague, and Lviv. This reality is reflected in the Jewish Festival in Chmielnik (Poland), the renovated synagogue —a museum-cum-art gallery—in Trnava (Slovakia), and the Northern Transylvania Holocaust Memorial Museum in Șimleu Silvaniei (Romania). The Jewishness of the above examples is a postmodern fusion of nostalgic restoration and innovative creation, celebrations of the earlier local Jewish communities and commemorations of their demise in the Holocaust, as well as the return of former residents of these quarters (or, increasingly, their descendants) and the everyday life of contemporary 'home-grown' Jews. Indeed, boding well for the future, the virtual Jewishness, whose avant-garde was once non-Jewish, has been transformed into a real Jewishness led by demythologized and quite real Jews. Most significantly, the narrative continues in its natural physical context; Jewry here provides a 'living dimension' that is integrated, not isolated—an indigenous variety healthily embedded in its native soil.

Yes, popping in for a weekend, the typical sightseer will be limited in his or her field of vision to the electric cart drivers hawking tours, the historical sites described in a guidebook, and the quaint photo-opportunity settings of some kiosks, shops, and cafés, and will thereafter speak of the expected and delivered Disneyland. The locals, however, see a neighbourhood through which they pub-crawl from Szeroka to plac Nowy to Bożego Ciała and even down to Mostowa, where intriguing art and handicrafts can be found, where a bite of most anything edible can be had, where concerts and performances of every genre are held, and, simply, in which friends live. While activity has not really bled over to the other half of Kazimierz—to the opposite side of Krakowska Street, which was traditionally 'Christian'—still, contemporary Cracovians do cross paths on a daily basis with Israeli groups, with one of the rabbis traversing the route between the Rema, the Izaak, and the Kupa synagogues, or with local Polish Jews headed for the JCC. Similarly, in Podgórze, anyone going to the so-dubbed Schindler's Factory museum passes by the equally new Museum of Contemporary Art Kraków (MOCAK), which shares the original factory space, and vice versa: whoever heads for MOCAK must notice the historical museum. As Jonathan Ornstein consistently underscores, it has never been better 'in terms of the way the Jewish community interacts with the non-Jewish community' (Gruber 2011) and so many of these interactions are anchored to the extant, physically Jewish neighbourhood of seven synagogues.

The state of affairs has been, is, and will most certainly be in flux: after all, both the non-Jewish and Jewish cultures have been organically changing, mutating, and adapting to each other for ages. More to the point, all the layers of the palimpsest are constantly and concurrently being negotiated. There is so much more here than meets the eye:

On a bright afternoon recently in Kazimierz a boy in a *kippah* (skullcap) walked along the street where a few hours earlier a golf cart filled with tourists had trundled past. Poland was once home to the second largest Jewish community in the world, and any revival is the faintest echo of what was destroyed—but it is a source of great pride to a city with 700 years of Jewish history. (Vasagar and Borger 2011)

These are truly 'closely entwined trends that are creating east-central Europe's new Jewish and "Jewish" authenticities' which Gruber has discerned (p. 344 above).

The historical and the postmodern, the Jewish and non-Jewish experiences, and the virtual and the real have become tightly interlaced. The twenty-first-century rebranding of Kraków (and not only of that city) now includes real Polishness, real Jewishness, and, most significantly, real Polish Jewishness. In other towns large and small across central eastern Europe, no doubt a deeper investigation of the consequences in everyday life and for average people would reveal more of this 'lacklustre' form of Jewishness than of the kitschy Golden Rose type so adept at attracting the limelight.

Whatever shape or form it takes, the Jewishness of central eastern Europe leads a young Ukrainian to taste central European Jewish cuisine, tourists to step into a synagogue (which they would never do at home), tour guides to enrich their commentary with annotations regarding Jewish life in other districts and localities, local governments to sponsor festivals (see Gruber 2013 for an expanding list), scholars of all generations to write and confer, and ordinary citizens to satisfy a deepening curiosity about Jewish history and culture—from medieval times, through the Holocaust, to today.

Even better, this Jewishness is leading the inhabitants of this part of the European continent to expand horizons and explore past and present multiculturalism in general. Delving into the first footnote in Gruber's essay, one sees that, in 2008, Lviv was concurrently housing the Jewish Heritage and History conference as well as an exhibition celebrating the city's historical multiculturalism, 'Wo Ist Lemberg?/Lviv A World A Way'. This is the other wondrous miracle taking place: superficial attraction is often followed by a deeper interest in demythologized Romanis, Tatars, Karaites, and all the other cultures of the multifarious groups whose past (and, increasingly, present) is so embedded in this terrain. Diversity was already evident in the early period of Kazimierz rediscovery, in the 1990s confluence of various ethnic musical genres, cafés and galleries, diplomatic missions, tourist groups, and the like (see Kugelmass and Orla-Bukowska 1998). The contemporary landscape is reflecting history and facilitating rediscovery by today's inhabitants of the people who lived here before. Despite their initial gawky and ungainly blundering and stumbling, the societies of central eastern Europe (and of the world) are better, not worse, off for this—so long live virtual Jewishness and what lies beyond it!

Notes

This essay was written in the course of the 2009–13 grant awarded to the author by Poland's Ministry of Research and Higher Education to study the Jewish Culture Festival and its audience.

1   Erica Lehrer, also featuring in this volume, captured this expensive (over £1,000) Venetian glass item with her camera just before store closing (12 Dec. 2010). Ruth Ellen Gruber has also documented these in Venice.

2   Personal conversation, 4 July 2010.

3   Antisemitism not being the topic of this essay, I refer interested readers to the comprehensive and thorough analysis of trends in Poland and Europe over the past three decades found in Sułek 2011. Particularly intriguing is his comparison of disparate responses elicited by differently phrased questions.

References

CHERRY, ROBERT, and ANNAMARIA ORLA-BUKOWSKA, eds. 2007. *Rethinking Poles and Jews: Troubled Past, Brighter Future*. Lanham, Md.

GAZIT, NIR. 2010. 'Boundaries in Interaction: The Cultural Fabrication of Social Boundaries in West Jerusalem'. *City & Community*, 9(4): 390–413.

GRUBER, RUTH ELLEN. 1994. *Upon the Doorposts of Thy House: Jewish Life in East-Central Europe Yesterday and Today*. New York.

——2002. *Virtually Jewish: Reinventing Jewish Culture in Europe*. Berkeley, Calif.

——2011. '"Never Better" in Krakow?' *JTA* (15 June), <http://www.jta.org>, accessed 16 June 2011.

——2013. 'Jewish Culture, etc. Festivals in Europe 2013' (4 Jan.). <http://jewish-heritage-travel.blogspot.fr/2013/01/jewish-culture-etc-festivals-in-europe.html>, accessed 9 Feb. 2013.

HURVITZ, GAL. 2011. 'Poland, once the cradle of anti-Semitism, has fallen in love with Judaism'. *Israel Hayom* (22 July), <http://www.israelhayom.com>, accessed 23 July 2011.

IIBR (Interaktywny Instytut Badań Rynkowych). 2011. 'Opinie na temat bieżących wydarzeń' (10 May), unpublished survey results commissioned by *Newsweek Polska*.

KUGELMASS, JACK. 1993. 'The Rites of the Tribe: The Meaning of Poland for American Jewish Tourists'. In Jack Kugelmass, ed., *Going Home: How Jews Invent their Old Countries*, YIVO Annual 21, 395–453.

——and ANNAMARIA ORLA-BUKOWSKA. 1998. '"If You Build It They Will Come": Kraków's Kazimierz in Post-Communist Poland'. *City & Society*, Annual Review, 315–53.

ORLA-BUKOWSKA, ANNAMARIA. 2007. 'Gentiles Doing Jewish Stuff: The Role of Polish Non-Jews in Polish Jewish Life'. In Robert Cherry and Annamaria Orla-Bukowska, eds., *Rethinking Poles and Jews: Troubled Past, Brighter Future*, 197–214. Lanham, Md.

——and KRZYSZTOF TOMANEK. 2012. 'Festiwal Kultury Żydowskiej Kraków 2010–2011: Raport z badań przeprowadzonych wśród uczestników Festiwali w roku 2010 i 2011'. Unpublished report of study conducted under the auspices of a Polish Ministry of Research and Higher Education grant (2009–13). Kraków.

SUŁEK, ANTONI. 2011. 'Ordinary Poles Look at the Jews'. *East European Politics and Societies*, <http://eeps.sagepub.com>, accessed 30 Aug. 2011.

TEICH, MARGARET. 2011. 'Schindler's Town: How Krakow Got a Tourism Boost from Spielberg's Movie', <http://www.faspe.info/journalism2011/2011/07/schindlers-town-how-krakow-got-a-tourism-boom-from-spielbergs-movie/>, accessed 17 Sept. 2011.

TVP3 news broadcast, 5 June 2011, 18.30 news.

VASAGAR, JEEVAN, and JULIAN BORGER. 2011. 'A Jewish Renaissance in Poland'. *Guardian* (7 Apr.), <http://guardian.co.uk>, accessed 7 Apr. 2011.

ŻURAWIK, MATEUSZ. 2011. 'Lepiej nie było nigdy' (an interview with Jonathan Ornstein). *Gazeta Wyborcza—Kraków* (1 June): 6.

Virtual, Virtuous, Vicarious, Vacuous? Towards a Vigilant Use of Labels

ERICA LEHRER

'Seeing is forgetting the name of the thing one sees.'
LAWRENCE WECHSLER

SINCE THE PUBLICATION of her widely cited book *Virtually Jewish* in 2002, Ruth Ellen Gruber has become a kind of spokesperson in relation to the recent European phenomenon of non-Jewish interest and participation in Jewish-themed activities—a trend that includes the emergence of new kinds of Jewish festivals, cafés, commemorations, monuments, museums, educational programmes, and even new kinds of Jews.[1] Eastern Europe, and particularly Poland, has been a focus of interest in this new development. This is both because the country has been the most energetic generator of the kind of events that comprise the phenomenon, and also because against the backdrop of recent history—Poland is today home to all of the former Nazi extermination camps—it is perhaps here that one can sense most clearly the moral significance (or ambivalence) of the sudden celebration of Jewishness in post-Holocaust Europe.

Despite ten years having passed since the publication of Gruber's book, the topic is still ripe for research. After the early emergence of a few remarkable non-Jewish engagements with Jewishness out of the silence of communism, catalysed by a wave of Western Jews making first contact with their 'old country' after the fall of the Iron Curtain, the phenomenon has continued to proliferate, shifting from an avant-garde to an increasingly normalized occurrence. A recent workshop at the United States Holocaust Memorial Museum focused on a range of these manifestations—from the north-western city of Szczecin to the south-eastern provincial town of Chmielnik—in the form of provocative art actions, new strategies of material heritage preservation, and local economic development initiatives.[2]

Virtually Jewish framed the discussion of non-Jewish engagements in Jewishness in terms of key tensions—between sincerity and self-congratulation, appreciation and appropriation, and whether it is all 'good for the Jews'—that echo the experiential frames of Jewish visitors encountering these unconventional manifestations. As the title of her contribution to the present volume ('Beyond Virtually Jewish') attests, Gruber has evolved in her thinking on the subject, even as the subject matter itself has developed. Her new take (expressed here and in other recent essays) suggests that what had been largely inauthentic engagements with Jewishness are, with time, becoming 'newly authentic', as once foreign themes have become familiar and real Jews have emerged as stakeholders, exercising their influence in these formerly non-Jewish Jewish spaces.

I have been a visitor to, and later a researcher of, the phenomena in question since the spring of 1990, when I was surprised by a banner advertising the second annual Jewish Culture Festival, and heard a cantor from Washington DC singing in the Old Synagogue in Kraków's then-dingy Kazimierz neighbourhood. I have since examined the development of a web of public and private practices around Jewish culture and memory in the quarter, as well as engaging more directly in a series of creative interventions there.[3] I have appreciated Gruber's continued attention to, and observations about, this fascinating subject. Even more do I applaud the shift in perspective suggested by her new terminology, which seems to reflect her engagement with discussions of her work that have taken place in academic settings.

But because I also have an intimate sense of the terrain, and bring to it anthropological angles of view, I see a need to broaden the discussion. My thoughts here build on the critique of *Virtually Jewish* I elaborated in a review written shortly after the book first appeared (Lehrer 2005), and point towards issues I expand on in my book *Jewish Poland Revisited*, an ethnography of Jewish heritage tourism in Kraków's much-discussed Kazimierz district. In essence, I take issue with the notion—sometimes explicit and sometimes implicit in Gruber's discussions— that there is an essential Jewishness, a 'real thing' that can be held up as a unitary standard. Based on my observations, Poland's Jewish revival emerged out of intercultural dialogue and the phenomenon is fundamentally a hybrid one. 'Virtual' and 'authentic', I suggest, are a false dichotomy that as an analytical tool do more to obscure than to illuminate. I also argue—with a bit of the protectiveness that ethnographers typically grow to feel for their subjects—that in Poland, at least, the purveyors of what Gruber calls 'virtual Jewishness' include the individuals most active in, sympathetic to, and educated about Jewishness today.

Given how a cottage industry of Jewish youth tours continues to present Poland through an outdated and often highly ideological lens, I have a sense of urgency about what is needed to make headway in our—and the broader public's —understanding of current developments. This involves increasing our vigilance regarding the labels we use and how we use them. Labels predispose us to seeing certain things and not noticing others, they carry values that subtly praise or belittle, they render evolving phenomena static, and they homogenize varied fields of activity. In short, any move to get 'beyond virtually Jewish' must make sure to dispense with a complex of *etic* terms—such as 'kitsch', 'tasteful', 'authentic', and even 'real'—that do similar evaluative work and hamper our understanding.[4] Jewish cultural production is a key arena of Polish–Jewish relations, constituted by subjective impressions often based on fear and fantasy rather than face-to-face communication. In this domain such labels keep us confined in our own points of view.

Vanquishing 'Virtual'

'Virtually Jewish' is a catchy, timely phrase. It is in the spirit of our cyber-age and touches on the anxieties that have accompanied information globalization and the increasing digital mediation of the social world. It is so catchy, in fact, that—despite the richness of the book whose cover it adorns—the term has had a flattening effect on discussions of the subject that it jump-started. Contemporary concerns that authentic experiences have been replaced by simulacra dovetail with and exacerbate the worries about assimilation circulating in the North American Jewish community at the same moment it has re-encountered its mythologized pre-Holocaust heartland. In this climate, 'virtually Jewish' has been taken to mean, in effect, *not* Jewish, or not *authentically* Jewish. It has become polite intellectual shorthand for the more popular slur, 'Jewish Disneyland'. Perhaps most problematic for scholarship, the label 'virtually Jewish' trains us to regard a range of phenomena as lesser or lacking versions of something else, rather than unique things in themselves.

The circumstances of non-Jewish interest in Jewishness raise profound questions and trouble long-standing assumptions. Social and cultural analysts must scrutinize the complex conditions of 'various Jewish "epistemologies" or ways of knowing who and what is Jewish', rather than trying to judge which ones are authentic (Glenn and Sokoloff 2010). Moreover, we need to ask: who claims the right and who has the resources to propagate their perspective regarding what is 'really' Jewish and what is not? What influences do Jews and Jewish themes have on majority cultures, and, conversely, how do other cultural trends influence configurations of Jewishness? How are ethnic groups and cultures formed and sustained, and how are they re-established in the wake of decimation? What kinds of engagement with Jewishness perpetuate dominant cultural and political agendas, and what modes encourage alternative projects? What does Jewishness mean to various Jews and non-Jews?

While Gruber is descriptively expansive, illustrating a great deal more complexity than many other observers have managed, what she reveals is underserved by her own framework. In order to grasp local meanings and lived experiences surrounding Jewishness in eastern Europe, we need to first acknowledge the predetermined, normative, lachrymose views of Jewishness that are both widespread in current Western descriptions of this region and also represent a force exerted directly on it by foreign Jews and Jewish institutions that have the power to define, label, and fund. The disambiguation of terminology is particularly important because of Gruber's own success; the half-life of appealing labels can be very long. That is to say, while Gruber's analytical categories may have evolved, the notion of 'virtually Jewish'—and the ingrained habits of looking that gave rise to and are reinforced by the term—still pervade the discussion.[5] While her work opened an important conversation, the vagaries of 'virtual Jewishness' in the marketplace of ideas have diminished discussion and focused attention on the failure of one thing to be something else, rather than to try to understand a new phenomenon in its own right.

Actually Jewish (and Other Transvaluing Terms)[6]

I have spent a long time over the years sitting in the Jewish cafés, klezmer cabarets, and, mostly, the Jarden Jewish Bookshop in Kraków's Kazimierz neighbourhood, a quarter Gruber calls the 'emblematic example of commodification and "Jewish" branding'. When Gruber describes these venues as 'an off-the-shelf ethnic decorative and catering category', my heart sinks. Such descriptions play on readers' pre-existing sensitivities. They treat such places as static representations that tell us nothing about their evolving character and function, their multivalent meanings to those who patronize them, the amalgam of shifting motivations of their creators, nor the larger forces to which they are responding. They close off a consideration of context, audience, intention, and process. In short, they fail to capture what I think is most interesting and important about these sites.

I think of all the people I have seen pass through Kazimierz's venues, finding in them a haven to explore Jewishness, or a touchstone for deeply felt personal quests surrounding it: Radek, who described the significance of these places in his path towards practising Judaism and constructing a Jewish identity, saying, 'I found my real [Jewish] self for the first time. I met the most important people in my life there'; a journey that continued with *aliyah* (emigration) to Israel. And Janina, who began as a 'Schindler's List' tour guide in one shop and is now Professor of Jewish History at a major US research university. On a different trajectory, there was the visiting Israeli Neta, who mused on the couch in the Jarden Jewish Bookshop that she was shocked to realize through her interactions here 'how Polish my parents really were' in their culture and mannerisms; a Jewish American graduate student who said she and her mother 'found it stunning that a young woman like their non-Jewish tour guide would be so interested' in Jewish culture; and a British Jewish man who told me, sitting in Noah's Ark café, that 'this atmosphere . . . feels like it exactly fills the holes I feel in myself'.

These are actual experiences of Jewishness for those who have them. As anthropologist Richard Kurin has succinctly put it, 'a semiotic analysis that says people are becoming signs of themselves tells us about the categories of semiotics; it does not tell us anything about the thoughts, feelings, or actions of those people' (Kurin 1991: 340). Terms like 'virtual' risk belittling the delicate emotional journeys undertaken by people to whom these new Jewish spaces, events, and experiences have been important sites of identification, self-discovery, historical reckoning, or cultural activism—people who feel their identification with Jewishness to be very real. Indeed, a clear claim for such recognition (no doubt expressed with a touch of protest against dismissal by Western Jews) comes from prominent Polish Jewish community leader Stanisław Krajewski, who stated amidst the hubbub of Kazimierz's twentieth annual Jewish Culture Festival in 2008, 'This place, at this moment . . . is the only place in Poland where being a Jew I feel like a host. This is a Jewish place more authentic than any other in Poland.'

Given the scepticism with which the 'Jewish phenomenon' is looked on by outsiders, I have tried in my own work to find terms that describe what the people participating in Jewish phenomena think they are doing, rather than focus on the ways others may see them as failing at being something else. At times these are terms that have emerged locally, inevitably articulated in dialogue with foreign Jewish criticisms, of which Poles engaging with Jewish themes are highly aware. Thus I have written of participants in the Jewish revival phenomenon who call themselves *shabbos goyim*, filling needs as caretakers and adopters of orphaned Jewish spaces and traditions; I have highlighted the unexpected ways in which a Jewish café or bookshop can be a site or form of Jewish community, of memorial practice, of reconciliation, or of identity activism (Lehrer 2010a, 2010b, 2013).

Of course these are also labels. But given that we cannot avoid them entirely, I propose using ones that defamiliarize and surprise, that force people to see beyond surfaces, to break their habitual frames, and to imagine new possibilities. My plea for fresh eyes is in no way meant to belittle the need for mourning the Holocaust and understanding the world that it destroyed, nor to surrender a critical approach to optimistic cultural production. But it seems essential to ask not only about what is absent, but to engage deeply with the possibility of new fruit growing in the spaces that were emptied. Not re-creation (which is, of course, impossible), but efforts to go forward from here, with all that has been broken.

Revisiting 'Jewish Space'

An alternative conceptualization that has not received nearly the popular attention it deserves—although Gruber mentions her own appreciation of it—is Diana Pinto's notion of 'Jewish space', described as 'an open cultural and even political agora where Jews intermingle with others qua Jews, and not just as citizens. It is a virtual space, present anywhere Jews and non-Jews interact on Jewish themes or where a Jewish voice can make itself felt' (Pinto 2002: 251). As we see, Pinto also invokes virtuality, but she embraces it as a feature of culture-sharing.[7] Jewish space does not rely on notions of real and fake, or of Gruber's 'parallel universes' that indicate separate 'inside' and 'outside' realms or standpoints in treatments of Jewish themes. Rather, Jewish space helps us discern a domain of actions and reactions, cultural project cross-fertilizations, inter-ethnic collaborations, and identity blurrings among variously defined Jews and non-Jews who share this field of interest.

Jewish communal revival in Poland was constituted by the intertwining of Jewish and non-Jewish impulses even before the end of communism. The re-emergence of Jewishness in communist Poland after its almost total demise in the wake of the antisemitic campaign of 1968 was a highly dialogic project. During an era when Jewish Poland was dead to the West, Catholic activists grappling with the moral burdens of Polish history staged Jewish culture weeks that encouraged a reawakening among many assimilated Jews, and the figure of the traditional Jew 'first emerged as the intriguing representative of a lost Polish past' within 'the pluralist worldview of Solidarity' (Irwin-Zarecka 1989; Steinlauf 2001).

Today's leisure- and tourism-based manifestations of Jewishness thus should not be viewed as solely commercial. Rather, they reflect socioeconomic trans-formation intertwined with cultural politics and the return of history. Not incidentally, the phenomenon has taken this new shape in the same period during which Western Jews have been flooding into eastern Europe—a revisiting of the past catalysed in part by Steven Spielberg's use in 1993 of Krakow's Kazimierz as the stage set for *Schindler's List*. So the question of new engagements in this region's Jewish heritage—tasteful and tasteless, superficial and deep—is not just what 'they' are doing, but what we *all* are doing.

As analysts and visitors, we have to include ourselves in the frame and consider our own relationships to the phenomena we observe. As anthropologist of tourism Edward Bruner argues, tourists change the culture of the places they visit, 'find[ing] in the local society the cultural enhancements that their tourist ancestors had fashioned', and catalysing local cultural re-examination (Bruner 2005). In Poland, local culture brokers have engaged with the flows of Jewish-ness, in its social, cultural, political, and even religious aspects, in an inter-subjective process that refines and reshapes understandings of what Jewishness and Polishness are for all involved. But Kazimierz's Jewish-themed venues are frequented not only by tourists. They also attract scholars, members of the rabbinate and clergy, and visiting Israeli diplomats, as well as all manner of artists, students, educators, researchers, returning refugees, and other seekers.

Wojciech Ornat's Café Ariel/Klezmer Hois began in Kazimierz's then empty Szeroka Street, but '[a]s soon as it opened, [it] became the centre of all non-ceremonial Jewish activity' in the city, serving as the venue for key ritual events as well, including a foreign Jewish wedding, sabbath dinners, and a party for Israel's independence day (Jochnowitz 1998: 226). Ornat began designing the Jewish dishes on the menu based on the family recipes of Róża Jakubowicz, the mother of the president of Kraków's Jewish community (Jochnowitz 1998: 227), which have been subsequently critiqued by 'Jewish grandmothers' from abroad in a transnational Jewish culinary dialogue. These venues have acquired not only what Gruber calls the 'real' patina of age in the last fifteen years, but loyal followings, as well as ties to the local Jewish community and to Jews visiting from across the globe, who have used them as jumping-off points for their own new cultural initiatives. Poland's commercial Jewish spaces have served as gateways and scaffolds for a variety of Jewish quests. Café Ariel and the Jarden Jewish Bookshop paved the way for—and sometimes were handmaidens in helping to create—subsequent foreign Jewish initiatives that emerged later, such as Hotel Eden or the Galicia Jewish Museum.

Kazimierz is exceptional. A hub of foreign Jewish travel (due, more than anything, to its proximity to Auschwitz), it has been animated by a range of cosmopolitan issues at least since its rediscovery in the late 1980s by local and foreign heritage seekers. Yet new research on the blossoming of similar initiatives deep in the Polish provinces, in places like Chmielnik, suggests that these are also the product of dialogues (including jointly funded initiatives) involving visiting Jewish teachers, returning local Holocaust survivors and their families, tourists, and a range of media commentators (see e.g. Murzyn-Kupisz, forthcoming). That the dialogue is spreading is attested by the multigenerational local audience listening to an Israeli pop star (the grandson of local Holocaust survivors) performing a Hebrew song on the stage of the Jewish festival in rural Szczekociny, or by the annual Czulent-Ciulim festival that has been taking place since 2003 in the tiny hasidic pilgrimage centre of Lelów, celebrating the local Polish dish *ciulim* that developed out of cholent (Polish *czulent*), the traditional Jewish sabbath dish—with the participation of some hasidim who frequent Lelów to enact their religious obligations.[8] Such manifestations may be the cutting edge of vernacular, popular Jewish memory work in Poland today.

Pondering Pluralism

Foreign Jewish observers of Polish engagement with Jewish heritage have tended, unsurprisingly, to focus on the implications for the Polish–Jewish relationship, with its unresolved moral questions of historical revelation, redress, and reconciliation. But seen from the Polish side, the shifting meanings and boundaries of 'Jewishness' emerging from these engagements are centrally about shifting meanings of Polishness. Jewish spaces, then, must be viewed not only in relation to a (foreign or locally emerging) 'Jewish community core', but as barometers of the potential for cultural pluralism in Poland (and Europe) more broadly.

Even if a celebratory focus on Jewishness is deemed 'good for the Jews', what of the whole spectrum of Poland's past and future others? What of Roma, Ukrainian, or German heritage, let alone the cultures of a growing Asian immigrant population or a gay community? Poland's Jewish space—perhaps the first robust public space of cultural difference to emerge after communism—has been, in its first twenty years of existence, a space to imagine forms of identity beyond the dominant 'Polish Catholic'. It has been something of a draw for *other* others, such as Protestant Poles who do charity work for Kraków's housebound Jewish Holocaust survivors, German youth fulfilling their civil service duties in the city's Center for Jewish Culture, or the African Polish girl or Vietnamese Polish boy who volunteer for the Jewish Culture Festival. Gays, in particular, have been a noteworthy presence at Jewish events and undertakings, and during my research with young Poles exploring their multiple identities, I saw more yarmulkes worn in Kraków's gay bars than on the street in Kazimierz.

While there is much that feels triumphant in the re-establishment of institutions for 'core' Jewish communal life, culture, and practice, the 'more confident, public claim' noted by Gruber that Kraków's tiny local Jewish community has begun to stake 'in delineating the parameters of the Kraków Jewish universe' also comes with certain potential losses. This is in part because the parameters being established are not all that local. The 'meant-for-real-Jews' Jewish spaces, such as the new Jewish Community Center or Chabad, are constituted by fancy Western-funded facades, foreign leaders, and imported conceptions of Jewishness. One wonders whether some individuals with significant—if non-normative—connections to Jewishness will be told (or will feel) they don't belong, and whether the 'real Jews' who are told they do will less frequently enrich the larger, pluralist cultural spaces with their presence. The emergence of a more modular landscape of pluralism, where each 'culture' gets its own separate space, might diminish the space where each person's internal plurality—along with significant inter-group encounters, reckonings, and reconciliations—can be explored.

Power, Play, and Possibility

Terms such as 'kitsch' and 'tasteful' are not only personal judgements, but they trap us in a system of value that privileges particular upper-middle-class American and Israeli Jewish concerns, obscuring the range of realities. Such labels also efface their own power—to validate or delegitimize—presenting the most subjective of impressions as neutral, objective, common sense.

Power in these heritage spaces is varied in its forms and sources. In the local symbolic economies that have grown up with and around such sites, cash and capital compete with intangible assets such as sincerity, loyalty, commitment, generosity, memory, and ethnic, linguistic, or cultural competence. And there are competing American and Israeli Jewish politics—both dominant and subaltern activisms—being enacted in and through Poland's Jewish spaces.

There is the unforgiving gaze of the Jewish youth missions, such as March of the Living and its Israeli equivalents, that occupy these spaces once a year for their own predetermined memorial purposes, and there are Israeli and American Jewish artists, for example Yael Bartana and Shimon Attie, who exploit the openings these spaces provide to highlight challenging cultural issues. The San Francisco-based Taube Foundation is something of a renegade among American Jewish organizations for its embrace of present-day Poland as a vital site of Jewish life, funding and putting its imprimatur on what it deems the best endeavours, many of which are educational or relate to the Jewish communal revival but include some of Poland's Jewish cultural festivals and Kraków's Cheder Café, projects that many Jews reject as kitsch, appropriation, or even desecration.

What makes the new Jewish phenomenon so compelling, I would venture, is the way it partakes in a kind of 'play', the product of what Mary Louise Pratt has called a 'contact zone', or a social space where cultures meet, clash, and grapple with each other, complete with parody, denunciation, imaginary dialogue, and a proliferation of vernacular expression (Pratt 1991). Gruber notes how a group of Lubavitch hasidim in Hungary encouraged passers-by to try on hasidic garb, and the Polish Jewish student group Żoom used a popular music festival to set up a booth called 'Get to know the Jew!', in which they stood by a life-size figure of a Jew (with a long beard and traditional dress) with a sign reading 'Hug me'. Intended to prompt conversation about long-standing stereotypes, their act created a space for their own Jewish voices to be heard, in a critique of how even 'part of the Jewish Polish community promotes this [folkloric] image'.

The problem, then, is not really about the symbols, about the selling of 'stuff', or even about the stereotypes that pervade this phenomenon.[9] If it were, there would be as much consternation about the chess sets sold in London's Jewish enclave of Golders Green, made up of little figurines of Jews (Ashkenazim vs. Sephardim), almost indistinguishable in garb and facial features from the counterpart Polish figurines that are so often decried. One can see similar figurines in Italy, Israel, and America—as well as the Ukraine, where they are specially configured as nested matrushka dolls, to the specifications of hasidim who visit the city of Uman on pilgrimage.[10]

Indeed, there would be as much concern about Hollywood's *Fiddler on the Roof*, coffee-table photo albums of hasidim, Marc Chagall posters, or *Heeb* magazine, all of which help American Jews maintain their sense of distinction as a group, despite (or because) of the fact that most of them are far more similar to their non-Jewish neighbours than they are to the Jews of their domestic memorabilia. Stereotypes are everywhere. We live among them and with them, and we use them—sometimes unthinkingly, and sometimes in edgy ways—to negotiate and explore our changing social worlds.

To be sure, the difficult question is this: do we draw no lines in the (however shifting) sand? There are extremes: restaurants that encourage 'Jewish' haggling, lucky charm refrigerator magnets with Jewish caricatures indistinguishable from Nazi propaganda, and Jewish figurines holding gold coins. These images carry with them the traces of ugly, violent histories that are more visible, consequential, and much more painful to some of us than to others. I cannot think of a good defence for stereotypes, beyond the fact that we all employ them. But neither does it seem possible to delineate precisely which representations are acceptable or 'real', given the range of differently situated interpreters. Rather, we might ask (for the purposes of analysis) how stereotypes work and (for the aims of activism) what work they can be made to do.

I share Gruber's weariness in the face of the incessant questioning of (mostly) American Jews about whether the Jewish phenomena are 'real' or 'fake'. My hope is that we can resist straightforward answers in favour of provoking new questions. While the first part of Gruber's new essay title points, importantly, 'beyond' the scope of 'virtuality' she set out in her book, the subtitle—'monuments to Jewish experience'—tugs it subtly back again. While important new monuments are being created, we limit our view of this region to seeing it as only a monument if our pain over unimaginable loss keeps us from acknowledging either the vibrancy of the present or possible futures. Eastern Europe is a land of Jewish fragments. But these fragments are increasingly being taken up as sites of pluralistic engagement. Jewish spaces here are as much cultural meeting places and sites of overlap and blurring as they are places for the reinforcement of boundaries or the practice of 'othering'. They present opportunities for healing and new culture-building for both Jews and their former neighbours. The risk is that these spaces will be divorced from the needs and concerns of living Jews, whose existence has given rise to them. But rather than evidence of Jewishness being 'hijacked', the Jewish phenomenon can be seen as an opportunity to re-engage with the possibility of both Jewish life and cultural pluralism. By dismissing these spaces, Jews simply leave it to others to appreciate—in their own ways—aspects of cultural richness most of us have left behind. We might instead consider how such spaces might draw Jews and others together, to forge a link between remembering the past and the ongoing drama of living with difference.

Notes

My thanks go to Barbara Kirshenblatt-Gimblett, Michael Meng, Patty Mullally, and Monica Patterson for their very helpful comments on an earlier draft of this essay.

1   Gruber's book was published in Polish as *Odrodzenie kultury żydowskiej w Europie* [Revival of Jewish Culture in Europe] by Pogranicze in 2004.

2   The papers will be published in Lehrer and Meng (forthcoming).

3   Participant observation is cultural anthropology's methodology. It traditionally involves

intensive involvement with a group of people in their everyday environment, usually over an extended period of time. My evolving impressions were recorded in Lehrer 1994 and 2001, and in a photographic exhibition entitled *The Motives of Memory* (Lehrer 1995–6) shown first at Grinnell College and in 1996 at the University of Michigan. A first attempt at more direct 'cultural activism' around the issue is described in Lehrer 2007, a second one can be seen at <http://www.conversationmaps.org/odpowiedz/>, and a third is planned for 2013 (see <www.jewishfigs.org>).

4   Etic (as opposed to emic) categories are those that are pre-established and used by an analyst to organize and interpret data, rather than categories generated by participants in a phenomenon. I would also include here the expanded vocabulary Gruber uses in an effort to come to terms with new developments, categorizing Jewish spaces as 'real, surreal, or imaginary' and distinguishing the 'creation' from the 're-creation' of Jewish reality.

5   A *New York Times* article dated 5 June 2012 ('Reasserting and Redefining Jewish Culture in Poland') uses the term 'pseudonostalgia' to describe Gruber's take on Poland's new Jewish phenomena, suggesting an even less authentic relationship to the past than the common accusations against straightforward nostalgia. <http://www.nytimes.com/2012/06/06/arts/06iht-poleculture06.html?_r=1&pagewanted=all>, accessed 12 Dec. 2012.

6   I thank Barbara Kirshenblatt-Gimblett for her use of the phrase '*actually* Jewish' in a discussion at the 2010 Association for Jewish Studies meeting. She called for returning the conversation about Poland's Jewish phenomenon from one about 'virtuality' to one about 'actuality', the latter dealing with the 'things in themselves', and not things as lesser versions of other things.

7   A survey of dictionary definitions of the words 'virtual' and 'virtually' helps remind us of the terms' other possible meanings. Among those useful to consider are 'being something in effect even if not . . . conforming to the generally accepted definition of the term'; 'having the essence or effect but not the appearance or form of'; 'being such in essence or effect though not formally recognized or admitted'; 'almost entirely; for all practical purposes'. There are also the ways in which the more straightforwardly technological meaning of 'virtual' has intersected with Jewish memorial and cultural revival efforts, including the Museum of the History of Polish Jews' 'Virtual Shtetl' portal (<www.sztetl.org.pl>), Polin: Polish Jewish Heritage (<http://polin.org.pl/start/>), and the site <www.kirkuty.xip.pl>, which links to about 500 Jewish cemeteries across Poland, and many other individual Polish Jewish memorial websites.

8   Photographs of the event can be seen at <http://www.lelow.pl/cliulimfoto/ciulim.html>, accessed 3 July 2011.

9   In capitalist economies the commodification of culture permeates the most intimate, spiritual realms, and the proliferation of distinctions and choices it enables is part and parcel of how we define ourselves. Commodification also enables things and ideas that are otherwise not broadly accessible, or have not previously been valued, to travel and spread. Entrepreneurs attend to market forces in order to uncover (as well as create) social needs that less responsive, or more exclusive, institutions do not. For a discussion of how 'evolving technologies, material forms, and styles of mediated communication contribute to new patterns of religious identification, practice, and power' vis-à-vis Orthodox Judaism, see Stolow 2010.

10   For a consideration of Poland's Jewish figurines, see Lehrer 2003.

References

BRUNER, EDWARD. 2005. 'The Role of Narrative in Tourism'. Unpublished manuscript (Oct.). University of Illinois at Urbana-Champaign Anthropology Department workshop series.

GLENN, SUSAN, and NAOMI SOKOLOFF, eds. 2010. *Boundaries of Jewish Identity*. Seattle.

GRUBER, RUTH ELLEN. 2002. *Virtually Jewish: Reinventing Jewish Culture in Europe*. Berkeley, Calif.

IRWIN-ZARECKA, IWONA. 1989. *Neutralizing Memory: The Jew in Contemporary Poland*. New Brunswick, NJ.

JOCHNOWITZ, EVE. 1998. 'Flavors of Memory: Jewish Food as Culinary Tourism in Poland'. *Southern Folklore*, 55(3): 224–37.

KURIN, RICHARD. 1991. 'Cultural Conservation Through Representation: Festival of India Folklife Exhibitions at the Smithsonian Institution'. In Ivan Karp and Stephen D. Levine, eds., *Exhibiting Cultures: The Poetics and Politics of Museum Display*, 315–43. Washington, DC.

LEHRER, ERICA. 1994. 'Memory for Sale'. *Grinnell Magazine* (Spring).

——1995–6. *The Motives of Memory: Commercializing the Jewish Past in Poland*. Photo exhibition shown at Grinnell College, Grinnell, Ia.

——2001. 'The Only Jewish Bookshop in Poland'. *Pakn Treger*, 36 (Summer): 34–7.

——2003. 'Repopulating Jewish Poland—in Wood'. In Michael C. Steinlauf and Antony Polonsky, eds., *Polin: Studies in Polish Jewry* 16, 335–55. Oxford.

——2005. Review of Gruber, *Virtually Jewish*. In *Cultural Analysis: An Interdisciplinary Forum on Folklore and Popular Culture*, 4. <http://socrates.berkeley.edu/~caforum/volume4/vol4_toc.html>.

——2007. 'Jewish? Heritage? In Poland? A Brief Manifesto and an Ethnographic-Design Intervention into Jewish Tourism in Poland'. *Bridges: A Jewish Feminist Journal*, 12(1) (Fall): 36–41.

——2010a. 'Can There Be a Conciliatory Heritage?' *International Journal of Heritage Studies*, 16(4–5): 269–88.

——2010b. '"Jewish Like an Adjective": Confronting Jewish Identities in Contemporary Poland'. In Susan Glenn and Naomi Sokoloff, eds., *Boundaries of Jewish Identity*, 161–87. Seattle.

——2013. *Jewish Poland Revisited: Heritage Tourism in Unquiet Places*. Bloomington, Ind.

——and MICHAEL MENG, eds. Forthcoming. *Constructing Pluralism: Space, Nostalgia, and the Transnational Future of the Jewish Past in Poland*. Bloomington, Ind.

MURZYN-KUPISZ, MONIKA. Forthcoming. 'Rediscovering the Jewish Past in the Polish Provinces: The Socio-Economics of Nostalgia'. In Erica Lehrer and Michael Meng, eds., *Constructing Pluralism: Space, Nostalgia, and the Transnational Future of the Jewish Past in Poland*. Bloomington, Ind.

PINTO, DIANA. 2002. 'The Jewish Challenges in the New Europe'. In Daniel Levy and Yfaat Weiss, eds., *Challenging Ethnic Citizenship: Germany and Israel Perspectives on Immigration*, 239–52. New York.

PRATT, MARY LOUISE. 1991. 'Arts of the Contact Zone'. *Profession*, 91: 33–40.

STEINLAUF, MICHAEL. 2001. '"Dreyfus" and "Jedwabne"'. In *Jedwabne and Beyond: A Roundtable*. Conference of the Association for Jewish Studies (Dec.), Washington, DC.

STOLOW, JEREMY. 2010. *Orthodox by Design: Judaism, Print Politics, and the ArtScroll Revolution.* Berkeley, Calif.

WECHSLER, LAWRENCE. 1982. *Seeing is Forgetting the Name of the Thing One Sees: A Life of the Contemporary Artist Robert Irwin.* Berkeley, Calif.

The Last Word

R U T H   E L L E N   G R U B E R

I AM WRITING this postscript more than a year after I completed the essay at the start of this section. In that space of time, as one would expect of a phenomenon in constant flux, the situation on which I was reflecting has evolved in many ways. I have found none of these changes really surprising, and none, I think, drastically alters the progression of my thinking: if anything, they confirm the various movements and directions—up, down, sideways, and around—that I have been observing for years as the 'Jewish space' continues to be filled by a growing variety of real, surreal, 'real-imaginary', and (yes) virtual actors and enactors.

I have been amused and bemused, at times uneasy, at times dismayed, and on occasion tremendously excited by some of the developments: the Night of the Synagogues in Kraków in June 2011, which Annamaria Orla-Bukowska describes in her richly panoramic essay, was thrilling.[1] Some months later, in November 2011, I took part in another telling manifestation of the ways in which a variety of inputs combine and create. This was a week-long festival of Polish Jewish culture held in the heart of the old Jewish ghetto in Venice, organized by the Polish Institute in Rome on the occasion of Poland's presidency of the European Union. Its programme (put together in collaboration with a number of Italian and Polish organizations and institutions) was a revealing mix of diverse inputs and interests, Polish and Italian, Jewish and not. It was the fruit of the sort of interaction 'not only between Jewish and non-Jewish *cultures*, but between actual individuals, and groups' about which Francesco Spagnolo writes in his essay above. Spagnolo, in fact, underscores what many who comment on my 'virtually Jewish' work often forget or choose to ignore: my book *Virtually Jewish* was not about Poland; in that book, my exploration of Kazimierz and its Jewish café, culture, and tourist scene formed only part of a much broader look at the relationship between Jews, Jewish space, and the non-Jewish mainstream in Italy, Germany, the Czech Republic, and other parts of Europe, as well as in Poland. One of the key inspirations for *Virtually Jewish* was the ground-breaking concept of 'Jewish space' coined by Diana Pinto in the mid-1990s to describe the place occupied by Jews, Jewish culture, and Jewish memory within mainstream European society, regardless of the size or activity of the local Jewish population: 'Indeed', she wrote, 'it is possible that the larger the "Jewish space", the smaller the number of actual Jews.'[2] I still remember how strongly I was struck by this notion when I heard her elaborate it, possibly for the first time, at the conference 'Planning for the Future of European

Jewry' held in Prague in 1995. It was the impetus for my own first writing on this topic, a 1996 monograph for the American Jewish Committee titled *Filling the Jewish Space in Europe*, out of which *Virtually Jewish* grew.[3] By now, as I noted in my main essay, the various and evolving notions of 'Jewish space' and 'Jewish spaces' have become the focus of much debate, scholarship, and interest in Europe, with a number of recent books, seminars, conferences, courses, and other work on various aspects of the topic.[4]

At the Polish Jewish Culture Festival in Venice I spoke about the evolution of Kazimierz and new ways of being and defining 'Jewish': those that veer towards a caricaturish branding, but also those that reflect new individual and communal self-awareness, not to mention those that meet in the middle. In fact, though it was billed as a festival of *Polish* Jewish culture, much of the programme focused on the history, culture, and Jewish personalities of Kraków, rather than, say, on Warsaw—which, of course, had a far bigger Jewish population before the Second World War and even today is the primary centre of reviving Polish Jewish communal life.[5] The Venice setting made this particularly significant. This is because Kraków's Kazimierz and the Venice ghetto today share many similarities. For one thing, they are the two largest and best-preserved old Jewish quarters in Europe, recognized and delineated enclaves with many synagogues and other historical infrastructure intact. This visible physicality excites the popular imagination; it makes both districts a concrete focus—a destination—for visitors and the scene of tourist development. Both are Jewish places (and spaces) where the number of tourists, including the number of Jewish tourists, utterly dwarfs the very small local Jewish population. And both, too, are places where a number of different interests, Jewish and not, compete and coalesce in the definition of Jewish space and identity.[6]

'There is a paradox here', the Venetian (and Jewish) scholar Shaul Bassi told me in 2010. Bassi heads the Venice Center for International Jewish Studies, an institution that aims to foster intellectual and cultural interaction with Jewish Venice, particularly in light of the upcoming 500th anniversary of the creation of the Venice ghetto in 1516. The centre was one of the several local partners that collaborated with the Polish Institute in putting together the Polish Jewish Culture Festival programme. 'The Jewish community as such is eroding and many are unaffiliated or disaffected', Bassi said, 'but at the same time the ghetto has never been so famous. There has never been such a profound interest in the ghetto as a site of memory.'[7]

I do not think Spagnolo, who has long been one of my most constant and insightful sounding boards on 'virtual' and other Jewish issues, and Orla-Bukowska, an anthropologist who lives and works in Kraków and has an intimate knowledge of the Kazimierz scene, know each other. But their essays here are welcome contributions to the dynamic and ongoing discussions I have had with both of them for many years. We do not always agree with each other by any means, and we come to our ways of thinking from very different backgrounds, directions, and sets of experience. But that is the point. As their essays demonstrate, our divergences provide a constant stimulus to our discussions: they build on each other, opening new and exciting directions for debate, understanding, and analysis.

The thrust of Erica Lehrer's detailed essay is somewhat different; in part, perhaps, because I have never really had with her the type of open-ended exchanges that I have enjoyed over the years with Spagnolo and Orla-Bukowska. I truly appreciate that Lehrer raises many questions and, yes, takes me to task. This critique is thought-provoking. Yet I somehow feel that, rather than truly open the way to discussion, her challenges seem caught in their own methodological framework. Moreover, unlike Spagnolo and Orla-Bukowska, she seems at times not really to 'get' what I am getting at. This is particularly apparent in how she approaches my very notion of the concept 'virtual', an expression that has caught on in far more (and more far-reaching) ways than I ever anticipated.[8] Lehrer narrows the scope of this term in my work, missing, it seems, not only the pun it contains, but also the carefully shaded nuances I have sought to include in my elaborations of a concept that, if anything, is characterized by ambiguity.[9] At the same time, while chiding me for employing 'labels' and coining a 'catchy' phrase that—like it or not—has resonated with both the public and the academic world, she herself reaches for counterpart catchphrases to define her own ideas. She seeks, as she puts it, labels 'that defamiliarize and surprise, that force people to see beyond surfaces, to break their habitual frames, and to imagine new possibilities'—which is, I believe, just what 'virtually Jewish' has succeeded in doing.

Lehrer's attempt to bring a consolidated anthropological approach to the observation of these phenomena is welcome. But, at least in this exposition, it causes her to delve at times into the merits of her own processes—and what these experiences mean to *her*—rather than to acknowledge the need for (or validity of) a multi-dimensional view in approaching a multi-faceted subject, a subject that is constantly evolving in so many ways, with so many questions still unresolved—or even not yet asked. Anthropology is one approach to interpretation. But other approaches, including my own—that of 'interpretative journalism' if a label must be attached to it—equally use critical observations of cultural scenes to draw out their meanings.

In a revealing admission, Lehrer confesses to 'a bit of the protectiveness that ethnographers typically grow to feel for their subjects'. Perhaps that is part of the problem. Indeed, I would have relished having had with her the sort of lively give and take over these issues that I have long enjoyed with Orla-Bukowska and other anthropologists, as well as with a range of cultural critics, 'heritage brokers', artists, 'participant-observers', tourists, Jewish activists, and others! (After all, my own experience with post-Holocaust Polish Jewry dates back to 1980, when, during a makeshift gathering on Erev Yom Kippur, Stanisław Krajewski, whom Lehrer quotes in her essay, appealed to me as a 'real Jew' to come home with him, his wife, and a friend and tell them what they should do to keep the holiday. When I protested that I was not observant, did not speak Hebrew, keep kosher, or even go much to synagogue, his response was 'No, but you have known all your life that you are Jewish, and we are just finding out.' In 2011, more than thirty years later, a Polish diplomat who is interested in 'things Jewish' and feels drawn to Jewish culture and experience, willingly described herself to me as a 'virtual Jew'.[10])

The fact is, I feel, that any approach to making sense of living, breathing, evolving phenomena such as the Jewish and 'Jewish' development of Kazimierz —or Lviv or Prague or Berlin or Venice—must entail broadening the discursive landscape and expanding the time frame of any analysis. Only a flexible, fluid, ongoing, and open dialogic relationship among a range of different viewpoints, inputs, and perspectives can help convey the complexity of a contemporary reality that is—and will, I'm sure, remain—in a continuing state of change.

Notes

1   Further 'Nights' took place in 2012 and 2013, and it will likely become an annual event.

2   Pinto formulated these ideas in print in 1996, in the monograph *A New Jewish Identity for Post-1989 Europe*:

> It is important to stress that a rich 'Jewish space', containing a multitude of 'things Jewish', is not dependent on the size or even presence of a living Jewish community in any particular country. Indeed, it is possible that the larger the 'Jewish space', the smaller the number of actual Jews. In countries with sizeable Jewish communities, such as Britain and France, there is a lively and active Jewish community but perhaps less of that 'Jewish space' that is distinct from the community itself. Conversely, Germany— where the Jewish community is small by pre-war standards, and is not composed of descendants of the old German Jewish community—has without doubt the most impressive 'Jewish space' in Europe. That space appears to be limitless; non-Jews can embark on university degrees in Judaic studies confident of entering an expanding professional field. Other countries which are practically devoid of Jews, such as Poland or Spain (where important communities once thrived), have created vibrant 'Jewish spaces' in recent years.

Similarly, in the early 1990s, sociologist Y. Michal Bodemann described the emergence in Germany of a 'Judaizing terrain' made up of 'converts to Judaism, of members of joint Jewish-German or Israeli-German associations, and of many "professional almost-Jews" outside or even inside the apparatuses of the Jewish organizations and [Jewish communities].' Jewish culture, he wrote,

> is being manufactured, Jewish history reconstructed, by these Judaizing milieux—by German experts of Jewish culture and religion [who] enact Jewish culture from within German biographies and from within German history; this has an important bearing on the type of Jewish culture that is actually being produced: a culture that is not lived, that draws heavily from the museum, and that is still no less genuine for that. (see Bodeman 1994)

3   In her essay above Erica Lehrer quotes an elaboration of 'Jewish space' made by Pinto some years later, in 2002: 'an open cultural and even political agora where Jews intermingle with others qua Jews, and not just as citizens. It is a virtual space, present anywhere Jews and non-Jews interact on Jewish themes or where a Jewish voice can make itself felt' (Pinto 2002: 251).

4   Scholars such as the German Joachim Schloer and the Hungarian Eszter Gantner have devoted much attention to the topic. See, for example, the website of a project in which Gantner has been involved: <http://jewish-spaces.com/de>. See also Brauch et al. 2008 and Šiaučiūnaitė-Verbickienė et al. 2007.

5   For an illuminating look at the recent Jewish revival in Poland, particularly that of the third post-Holocaust generation, see Reszke 2013.

6   I found it interesting that both Annamaria Orla-Bukowska and Erica Lehrer, both of whose focus is Kraków, comment in their essays here on a 'Sephardi versus Ashkenazi' glass chess set from Venice, which they saw in London. I have written about this very chess set, most recently in 'Non-Jewish, Non-Kosher, Yet Also Recommended' (Gruber 2011—it is also pictured as Figure 4 in my main essay here), describing the ambiguous role played by such stereotype glass figurines in demarcating local, 'authentic', and projected Jewish realities in Venice, where the imported traditional 'Ashkenazi' look of the very visible Chabad presence is in many ways the new public face of Judaism, and where the chess set itself is sold in David's Shop, a Jewish-run souvenir shop in the ghetto that specializes in Murano glass Judaica for a mainly Jewish tourist market. The proprietor, David Curiel, told me (Nov. 2011) that almost all of his sales of such figurines are to Jewish purchasers. In November 2011 the shop's website also offered a 'Jews versus Catholics' chess set. See <http://www.davidshop.com/c/63/murano_glass_chessgame_Asknazi Sephardity. html>.

7   Bassi has written about some of these themes: see Bassi 2011.

8   In November 2011, when formally presenting to me Poland's Knight's Cross of the Order of Merit, the Polish consul general to Los Angeles, Joanna Kozinska-Frybes, specifically cited my book *Virtually Jewish* and its exploration of how Jewish space is filled with non-Jews. She described *herself* as 'virtually Jewish'—a non-Jewish Pole drawn to and interested in Jewish culture, heritage, history, and traditions.

9   Among other things, my use of the term 'virtual' deliberately, and punningly, played on the cyberspace concept of virtual worlds and virtual communities existing on the internet. Even a decade ago these included many, many Jewish websites. As I wrote in *Virtually Jewish*:

> People can enter, move around and engage in cyberspace virtual worlds without physically leaving their desks or quitting their 'real world' identities. Online, however, they can assume other identities, play other roles and be, or act as if they are, whoever they want. Like virtual worlds on the Internet, the various aspects of 'virtual Jewry' are linked together and overlapping. One can approach them either passively, as a mere consumer, or 'interactively,' as a participant, through, for example, performance and interpretation. They may be enriched by input from contemporary Jewish communal, intellectual, institutional, or religious sources, or they may be self-contained within totally non-Jewish contexts. (2002: 21)

10   See note 8 above.

References

BASSI, SHAUL. 2011. '"Scusi, e' qui la pagoda?"': Il Ghetto di Venezia come spazio del malinteso'. In Shaul Bassi, *Essere qualcun altro: Ebrei postmoderni e postcoloniali*. Venice.

BODEMANN, Y. MICHAL. 1994. 'A Reemergence of German Jewry?' In Sander L. Gilman and Karen Remmler, eds., *Reemerging Jewish Culture in Germany: Life and Literature since 1989*. 57–8. New York.

BRAUCH, JULIA, ANA LIPPHARDT, and ALEXANDRA NOCKE, eds. 2008. *Jewish Topographies: Visions of Space, Traditions of Place*. Farnham, Surrey.

GRUBER, RUTH ELLEN. 1996. *Filling the Jewish Space in Europe*. International Perspectives. New York.

——2002. *Virtually Jewish: Reinventing Jewish Culture in Europe*. Berkeley, Calif.

——2011. 'Non-Jewish, Non-Kosher, Yet Also Recommended'. In Jonathan Karp and Adam Sutcliffe, eds., *Philosemitism in History*. Cambridge.

PINTO, DIANA. 2002. 'The Jewish Challenges in the New Europe'. In Daniel Levy and Yfaat Weiss, eds., *Challenging Ethnic Citizenship: Germany and Israel Perspectives on Immigration*, 239–52. New York.

PINTO, DIANA. 1996. *A New Jewish Identity for Post-1989 Europe*. JPR Policy Paper 1/1996. London.

RESZKE, KATKA. 2013. *The Return of the Jew: Identity Narratives of the Third Post-Holocaust Generation of Jews in Poland*.

ŠIAUČIŪNAITĖ-VERBICKIENĖ, JURGITA, and LARISA LEMPERTIENĖ, eds. 2007. *Jewish Space in Central and Eastern Europe: Day-to-Day History*. Newcastle upon Tyne.

Contributors

Jonathan Boyarin is the Mann Professor of Modern Jewish Studies in the Department of Anthropology, Cornell University. He has also taught at the University of North Carolina, the University of Kansas, Dartmouth College, and at Wesleyan University. He holds degrees in law (J.D., Yale, 1998) and anthropology (Ph.D., New School for Social Research, 1984). His work focuses on topics such as modern Yiddish culture; the Jewish community on the Lower East Side; the politics of territorial and anamnestic identity; the interplay of orality and literacy; and comparative diasporas. Among his most recent books are *Jewish Families* (2013), *Mornings at the Stanton Street Shul: A Lower East Side Summer* (2011), and *The Unconverted Self: Jews, Indians and the Identity of Christian Europe* (2009). Other major titles in Jewish cultural studies include *Jewishness and the Human Dimension* (2008), *Powers of Diaspora: Two Essays on the Relevance of Jewish Culture* (with Daniel Boyarin, 2002), *Jews and Other Differences: The New Jewish Cultural Studies* (with Daniel Boyarin, 1997), *Thinking in Jewish* (1996), *Storm from Paradise: The Politics of Jewish Memory* (1992), and *Polish Jews in Paris: The Ethnography of Memory* (1991).

Simon J. Bronner is Distinguished University Professor of American Studies and Folklore at the Pennsylvania State University, Harrisburg, where he is lead scholar of the campus's Holocaust and Jewish Studies Center. He has also taught at Harvard, Leiden, and Osaka universities. He is the author and editor of over thirty books, including *Greater Harrisburg's Jewish Community* (2011), *Explaining Traditions: Folk Behavior in Modern Culture* (2011), and *Encyclopedia of American Folklife* (2006). He edits the Material Worlds series for the University Press of Kentucky and has published in Jewish cultural studies in the *Journal of Modern Jewish Studies*, *Jewish History*, *Yiddish*, *Markers*, and *Chuliyot: Journal of Yiddish Literature*. As well as editing the Littman Library's Jewish Cultural Studies series, he leads the Jewish Folklore and Ethnology section of the American Folklore Society and is president of the Fellows of the American Folklore Society. He has received the Mary Turpie Prize from the American Studies Association and the Wayland D. Hand Prize and the Peter and Iona Opie Prize from the American Folklore Society for his scholarship and educational leadership.

David Clark has studied anthropology in Canada, Uganda, the United States, and Britain. He completed his doctoral work at London Metropolitan University on Jewish museums in Italy. He has taught tourism and arts, and heritage management at Thames Valley University, London, and at London Metropolitan University from

1985 to 2011. His current research focuses on European expatriates in Crete and he remains an active member of Etz Hayyim Synagogue, the sole remaining synagogue in Crete. He is also on the editorial committees of the Jewish cultural magazine *Jewish Renaissance* and of *Exiled Ink*, a magazine devoted to the works of refugee writers currently living in Britain and elsewhere in Europe. He has contributed book chapters and articles to *Contested Mediterranean Spaces* (2011), the *Journal of Mediterranean Studies* (2005), the *Journal of Management, Spirituality and Religion* (2004), *European Judaism* (2003), *Jewish Studies at the Turn of the 20th Century* (1999), and *Tourism and Tourist Attractions* (1998).

Ruth Ellen Gruber is an American writer and independent scholar living in Europe. She is the co-ordinator of the website <www.jewish-heritage-europe.eu>—a project of the Rothschild Foundation (Hanadiv) Europe. With her 2002 book *Virtually Jewish: Reinventing Jewish Culture in Europe* she coined the term 'virtually Jewish' to describe the way the so-called 'Jewish space' in Europe is often filled by non-Jews. Among her other books are *National Geographic Jewish Heritage Travel: A Guide to Eastern Europe* (2007); *Letters from Europe (and Elsewhere)* (2008), and *Upon the Doorposts of Thy House: Jewish Life in East-Central Europe, Yesterday and Today* (1994). Her current and ongoing projects are 'Sauerkraut Cowboys, Indian Dreams: Imaginary Wild Wests in Contemporary Europe', an exploration of the American frontier in the European imagination, and '(Candle)sticks on Stone: Representing the Woman in Jewish Tombstone Art'. Her honours and awards include a Guggenheim Fellowship, National Endowment for the Humanities summer stipend grant, and other research grants from the Littauer Foundation, the Memorial Foundation for Jewish Culture, and the Hadassah-Brandeis Institute (HBI). In 2011 she was decorated with the Knight's Cross of the Order of Merit, one of Poland's highest honours awarded to foreign citizens. She also serves on the editorial board of Jewish Cultural Studies.

Samuel D. Gruber is Lecturer in Judaic Studies at Syracuse University. He received his BA in medieval studies from Princeton University, and his Ph.D. in architectural history from Columbia University with a dissertation on medieval Todi, Italy. Gruber is a fellow of the American Academy of Rome. He served as founding director of the Jewish Heritage Program of World Monuments Fund and Research Director of the US Commission for the Preservation of America's Heritage Abroad, has consulted on cultural heritage projects for numerous organizations and institutions, and is the author of *American Synagogues: A Century of Architecture and Jewish Community* (2003) and *Synagogues* (1999) and numerous reports and articles.

Rella Kushelevsky teaches in the Department of the Literature of the Jewish People at Bar-Ilan University, Israel. She is the author of *Moses and the Angel of Death* (1995) and *Penalty and Temptation: Hebrew Tales in Ashkenaz* (2010). Her current research focuses on medieval Jewish story compilations in Germany and northern France (Ashkenaz), for which she has received two grants from the Israeli Science Foundation. She holds the Sznajderman Chair in the Study of Hasidism and is a member of the IFA scientific board. She is co-editor of Thema—A Series of Thematological Studies in the Literature of the Jewish People at Bar-Ilan University, as well as of *Criticism and Interpretation—Journal of Interdisciplinary Studies in Literature and Culture*, Bar-Ilan.

Erica Lehrer is associate professor in the Departments of History and Sociology/ Anthropology at Concordia University in Montreal, where she also holds the Canada Research Chair in Post-Conflict Memory, Ethnography and Museology and directs the Centre for Ethnographic Research and Exhibition in the Aftermath of Violence (CEREV). Her book *Jewish Poland Revisited: Heritage Tourism in Unquiet Places* (2013) explores the intersection of Polish and Jewish 'memory projects' in the historical Jewish neighbourhood of Kraków. She has also co-edited *Curating Difficult Knowledge: Violent Pasts in Public Places* (2011) and carried out experimental curatorial projects based on her research.

Magdalena Luszczynska is a doctoral student at the Hebrew University of Jerusalem, where she was awarded a Presidential Scholarship for Excellent Students. She holds undergraduate and MA degrees in cultural anthropology from the University of Warsaw; a BA in Hebrew and Jewish studies, and an MA in digital humanities, for which she was awarded a University College London Alumni Scholarship. Her writing on Jewish culture has received a British Association for Jewish Studies Student Essay Prize and the Raphael Patai Prize from the American Folklore Society.

Amy K. Milligan teaches at Elizabethtown College in the Departments of Religious Studies and Women and Gender Studies. She is the recipient of the American Folklore Society's 2011 Raphael Patai Prize in Jewish Folklore and Ethnology as well as Penn State University's 2012 Sue Samuelson Award for Academic Excellence in American Studies. She has contributed essays to the *Encyclopedia of American Women's History*, the *Encyclopedia of American Studies*, and the *Encyclopedia of Greater Philadelphia*, as well as a chapter on 'The Shulchan Arukh' in *Milestone Documents in World Religions* (2011). She currently serves as the Global Religions section chair for the Mid-Atlantic American Academy of Religion.

Annamaria Orla-Bukowska is a social anthropologist at the Jagiellonian University in Kraków. Her general field of research is majority–minority relations, with a specialization in Polish Christian–Polish Jewish relations. She lectures not only at the Jagiellonian but also for the State Museum Auschwitz-Birkenau and the Centre for Social Studies in Warsaw. Dr Orla-Bukowska was a Koerner Holocaust Fellow in 1999 at the Oxford Centre for Hebrew and Jewish Studies; a Yad Vashem Fellow in 2004; and in 2009 a Skalny Center Fellow at the University of

Rochester. Her publications include *Rethinking Poles and Jews: Troubled Past, Brighter Future* (co-edited with Robert Cherry, 2007). With Krzysztof Tomanek, she is currently analysing the results of their three-year research project on the audience of Kraków's Jewish Culture Festival.

Holly A. Pearse holds a Ph.D. in religion and culture from Wilfrid Laurier University, Ontario, and currently teaches religion, gender, and culture there. In 2008 she won a Hadassah-Brandeis fellowship for her research into the gendered portrayal of Jewish–gentile romance in American film. She contributed to the first volume of the Jewish Cultural Studies series and has written articles on various topics concerning Jewishness and pop culture for publications such as *Jewish Quarterly*. Her areas of interest include religion and art, paradigms of romance and individual identity, religious violence and criminality, the culture of comedy, ethnoreligious constructions of gender, and Holocaust cinema.

Steve Siporin is a folklorist who holds a joint appointment in English and history at Utah State University, where he teaches a wide variety of folklore classes and is director of the Folklore Program. He is the author *American Folk Masters: The National Heritage Fellows* (1992), co-editor of *Worldviews and the American West: The Life of the Place Itself* (2000), and translator of Augusto Segre's lyrical memoir, *Memories of Jewish Life: Italy to Jerusalem, 1918–1960* (2008). He has received fellowships and grants from the Memorial Foundation for Jewish Culture, the Lady Davis Foundation, the Hebrew University of Jerusalem, and the Fulbright Program. He serves on the editorial board Jewish Cultural Studies.

Francesco Spagnolo is the curator of the Magnes Collection of Jewish Art and Life and a lecturer in the Department of Music at the University of California, Berkeley, as well as a host for the cultural programs of RAI Radio 3 (Italian National Radio) in Rome. He received his Ph.D. from the Hebrew University of Jerusalem and has taught philosophy, musicology, and Jewish and Italian studies at the University of Milan and the University of California, Santa Cruz. His publications include *Il ballo del camaleonte* (1999) and *Estetica delle situazioni estreme* (2000), the Italian edition of Imre Toth's *Palimpsest* (2003), the audio-anthology *Italian Jewish Musical Traditions* (2006), and articles on philosophy, music, film, and literature in academic journals and encyclopedias.

Sophie Wagenhofer is research fellow at Humboldt University Berlin. She studied history, Jewish studies, and Islamic studies in Vienna and Berlin and wrote her Ph.D. dissertation on the Jewish Museum in Casablanca. Her research interests centre on modern transnational history, museology, and the politics of memory. She is the author of two monographs—*Ausstellen, verorten, partizipieren. Das Jüdische Museum in Casablanca* (2013) and *Zur Inszenierung und Instrumentalisierung des Araberbildes im Nationalsozialismus* (2010)—and has edited *Cultural*

Representations of Jewishness at the Turn of the 21st Century (2010). Besides academic research she works at the Jewish Museum in Berlin.

Magdalena Waligórska is Alexander von Humboldt Fellow in the Department of German Philology at the Free University in Berlin. She has written on different aspects of Jewish heritage revival in Poland and Germany, in particular the klezmer revival, and representations of Jews in Polish and German popular culture in the journals *Polish Sociological Review*, *Osteuropa*, and *Ethnomusicology*. She is co-editor of *Cultural Representations of Jewishness at the Turn of the 21st Century* (2010) for the European University Institute, and author of *Klezmer's Afterlife: An Ethnography of the Jewish Music Revival in Poland and Germany*, to be published by Oxford University Press.

Jonathan Webber is a British social anthropologist now living in Kraków, where he is a professor at the Institute of European Studies at the Jagiellonian University, having taught for twenty-eight years at the universities of Oxford and Birmingham. His publications have focused on modern Jewish society, Holocaust studies, and Polish Jewish studies; he has held visiting fellowships in Australia, France, Germany, Hungary, and the USA, and has given lectures at forty academic institutions worldwide. In 1999 he was awarded the Gold Cross of the Order of Merit by the President of the Republic of Poland for services to Polish–Jewish dialogue. He also serves on the editorial board of Jewish Cultural Studies.

Marcin Wodziński is Professor of Jewish History and Literature at the University of Wrocław. His special fields of interest include the regional history of the Jews in Silesia, Jewish sepulchral art, and the social history of Jews in nineteenth-century Poland, especially the history of hasidism and Haskalah. His books include *Hebrew Inscriptions in Silesia 13th–18th c.* (in Polish; 1996), *Bibliography on the History of Silesian Jewry II* (2004), *Haskalah and Hasidism in the Kingdom of Poland: A History of Conflict* (Littman Library, 2005), and *Hasidism and Politics: The Kingdom of Poland, 1815–1864* (Littman Library, 2013). He serves on the editorial board of Jewish Cultural Studies.

Index